Seventh Edition

Media | Impact

An Introduction to Mass Media

Shirley Biagi

California State University, Sacramento

THOMSON

WADSWORTH

AUSTRALIA · CANADA · MEXICO · SINGAPORE · SPAIN · UNITED KINGDOM · UNITED STATES

THOMSON
WADSWORTH

Publisher: Holly J. Allen
Senior Development Editor: Renée Deljon
Assistant Editor: Shona Burke
Editorial Assistant: Laryssa Polika
Senior Technology Project Manager: Jeanette Wiseman
Senior Marketing Manager: Kimberly Russell
Marketing Assistant: Andrew Keay
Advertising Project Manager: Shemika Britt
Project Manager, Editorial Production: Mary Noel
Art Director: Robert Hugel
Print/Media Buyer: Barbara Britton
Permissions Editor: Sommy Ko
Production Service: Thompson Steele
Text Designer: Cuttriss & Hambleton
Photo Researcher: Sarah Evertson/Image Quest
Copy Editor: Yonie Overton
Illustrator: Thompson Steele

Cover Designer: Denise Davidson
Cover Image: © Getty Images
Compositor: Thompson Steele
Printer: Transcontinental Printing/Interglobe
Chapter Opener Photo Credits: *Chapter 1* Getty Images; *Chapter 2* © Mark Mainz/Getty Images; *Chapter 3* Glenn A. Kaupert/ © *The Chicago Tribune*; *Chapter 4* Scott Goodwin Photography, Inc.; *Chapter 5* Electronic Publishing Services Inc., N.Y.C.; *Chapter 6* © Mark Richards/Photo Edit; *Chapter 7* © Getty Images; *Chapter 8* © Joe Fornabaio; *Chapter 9* © Tony Savino/The Image Works; *Chapter 10* Jonathan Farey/Getty Images; *Chapter 11* Ken James/Getty Images; *Chapter 12* Getty Images; *Chapter 13* HECTOR MATA/AFP/ Getty Images; *Chapter 14* © Mark E. Gibson/CORBIS; *Chapter 15* © 2003 *Newsweek, Inc.* All rights reserved. Reprinted with permission. Photo by Edward Keating; *Chapter 16* ROMEO GACAD/AFP/Getty Images

For more information about our products,
contact us at: **Thomson Learning Academic
Resource Center 1-800-423-0563**

For permission to use material from this text or product,
submit a request online at
http://www.thomsonrights.com

Any additional questions about permissions can be
submitted by email to thomsonrights@thomson.com

Library of Congress Control Number: 2004102714
   Student Edition ISBN: 0-534-63054-5
   Instructor's Edition ISBN: 0-534-63061-8

Thomson Wadsworth
10 Davis Drive
Belmont, CA 94002-3098
USA

Asia
Thomson Learning
5 Shenton Way #01-01
UIC Building
Singapore 068808

Australia/New Zealand
Thomson Learning
102 Dodds Street
Southbank, Victoria 3006
Australia

Canada
Nelson Thomson Learning
1120 Birchmount Road
Toronto, Ontario M1K 5G4
Canada

Europe/Middle East/Africa
Thomson Learning
High Holborn House
50/51 Bedford Row
London WC1R 4LR
United Kingdom

Latin America
Thomson Learning
Seneca, 53
Colonia Polanco
11560 Mexico D.F.
Mexico

Spain/Portugal
Paraninfo
Calle Magallanes, 25
28015 Madrid, Spain

Brief Contents

Detailed Contents

PART ONE
The Mass Media Industries

Chapter 1

Chapter 2
Books   32

Chapter 9

Digital Communications and the Web   178

PART TWO
Mass Media Support Industries

▶ Chapter 10

Advertising 204

PART THREE
Media Issues and Global Outlook

Chapter 15

Ethical Practices and Policies   324

Quick View Guide to the Impact Boxes and Illustrations

Impact | Timeframe

Impact | Audience

Impact | Business

Preface

The journey for students and scholars who follow the mass communications industries can be exhausting. Changes seem to happen faster than we can chronicle them. While it's challenging to keep up with these changes, thanks to the new technologies, this edition of *Media/Impact* is more current than ever. Published in July, this book was being updated as late as June. New publishing technology makes this exceptional timeliness possible, and the result is an edition that includes even more up-to-the-minute information than ever. Here are some of the recent media developments that you'll find inside:

- Janet Jackson's Super Bowl performance and the FCC's response

- Clear Channel's suspension and then cancellation of Howard Stern's radio show; and

- Up-to-date statistics and study findings, such as how U.S. advertising dollars are currently spent.

Responding to our reviewers' requests not just for continued timeliness, we have further updated and improved this edition of *Media/Impact* by incorporating the following changes and new features.

▶ New to This Edition

- New **Chapter One** and **streamlined organization**. With this edition, *Media/Impact* has returned to a traditional 16-chapter organization. The new Chapter One, Understanding Mass Media Today, provides an introduction to both the field of mass communication and today's media environment. With Chapter Two (Books) the industry-specific chapters begin. Digital Media are now presented in detail in Chapter 9, so this chapter appears in historical order, following the other media industries. The new chapter introduced in the last edition—News and Information (Chapter Twelve)—has proven very popular and continues in this edition.

- Increased attention to **media literacy**. In this edition, a "Critical Question" accompanies a selected Impact box in every chapter to help students absorb, evaluate and respond to the information they're reading. Also, the Media/Impact CD-ROM now includes 16 CNN® Today video clips that correspond with each chapter topic, and are paired with critical thinking questions (see details below under Resources for Students).

- Updated coverage of **new technologies**. These discussions address recent developments, such as the rapid penetration of wireless fidelity (wi-fi), recordable DVDs, new cellular technologies and new convergence technologies as well as expanded and clarified discussions of what digital media are and how they work.

- Updated coverage of **media issues**. New discussions cover topics such as war and terrorism, recent court decisions involving FCC deregulation and embedded journalists. Additionally, Chapter 15, Ethical Practices and

Policies, now includes a discussion of the Jayson Blair controversy at *The New York Times*.

- New **visuals**. This edition offers more than 100 new photos, cartoons and updated graphics.

▶ Proven Features that Continue in This Edition

Students and instructors have consistently praised *Media/Impact* for its media-as-business perspective as well as the following features:

- **Impact boxes.** Four types of Impact boxes are distributed throughout the chapters—**Impact/People, Impact/Culture, Impact/Business and Impact/Audience**—to provide brief readings on various media topics, and to highlight important media profiles, the effects of media on culture and society, and the ramifications of the latest media ownership and income data. New and updated graphics in the boxes pinpoint critical information and illustrate important concepts to help students make sense of the numbers. Where possible, industry projections have been included to give students a look at how the experts see the media's future.

- **Impact/TimeFrame.** These boxed timelines appear in Chapter One and continue through all the industry chapters to give students a visual guide to key recent and historical developments. The narrative of each industry chapter also adds historical context.

- **Media/Review** chapter summaries. Appearing at the end of each chapter, these quick chapter reviews are divided into four thematic categories—**History, Business, Culture** and **Technology**—to help students better understand and retain the chapters' information, as well as further engage their critical thinking.

- **Running glossary.** All key terms appear in the margins of each chapter with concise definitions right where students need them.

- **Graphically illustrated statistics.** The Impact boxes present statistics in graphical format. The statistics are also accompanied by captions to further help students understand critical media studies and their findings.

- **Impact/Interactive.** Concluding each chapter, these sections direct students to the various interactive resources that accompany the text, list relevant Web resources (Working the Web) and present **InfoTrac® College Edition exercises** to help students extend their study of critical media topics with free full-text articles available online through Thomson's InfoTrac College Edition database. Please see detailed descriptions below under "Resources for Students."

- **Glossary of Media Terms.** This comprehensive glossary appears at the end of the book to provide all of the key terms defined within the chapters' running glossary in one handy reference.

- **Media Information Guide.** This additional reference tool at the end of the book provides hundreds of resources for students who want to expand their knowledge of media topics. It includes an alphabetical listing of more than 150 Web sites referenced throughout the text. (This guide also appears on the Media/Impact Web site with live links to all listed URLs.)

▶ Resources for Students

Media/Impact's seventh edition offers a full complement of print and media resources, all integrated with the text to maximize their usefulness for students:

- **Impact/Interactive**, the Media/Impact **CD-ROM.** For each of the 16 chapter topics covered in **Media/Impact,** this CD-ROM features a two- to three-minute CNN® Today video clip with corresponding critical thinking questions and a list of suggested articles available on InfoTrac College Edition, along with a link to the database. The clips are organized by chapter and address current media topics such as female war correspondents, cameras in the courtroom, music and movies on the Internet and Wi-Fi technology. The CD-ROM also provides direct access to the **Media/Impact** Web site.

- **Media/Impact Web site.** The book's companion Web site offers interactive chapter outlines and study guides, chapter-by-chapter activities and learning resources such as quizzes, concept animations, and key term flash cards. Crossword puzzles also are available and give students a fun way to test their knowledge. The text's Media Resource Guide also appears in electronic format with live links to all URLs given in the text. The book's Web site is available online at http://communication .wadsworth.com/biagi7, but its premium content is only available when accessed through the book's CD-ROM.

- **InfoTrac® College Edition.** Every new copy of the text is accompanied by four months of free access to InfoTrac College Edition, our online library. The new and improved InfoTrac College Edition database is fully searchable and puts cutting-edge research and the latest headlines at your students' fingertips, offering more than 10 million articles from nearly 5,000 diverse sources, such as academic journals, newsletters, and up-to-the-minute periodicals. The range of content includes *The New York Times, Newsweek, Time, USA Today, American Journalism Review, Advertising Age, Broadcasting & Cable, Multimedia Week, PR Week, Variety* and thousands more (see a complete list of publications available at http://www.infotrac-college.com). InfoTrac College Edition activities appear at the end of each chapter. Additional InfoTrac College Edition activities are available on the book's Web site (and in the Instructor's Resource Manual). Plus, students now also gain instant access to critical thinking and paper writing tools through *InfoWrite.*

- **Media Literacy Workbook, Second Edition.** This workbook by Kimb Massey, San Jose University, available for bundling with the text, is an invaluable resource for students in an introductory course. Covering 16 core mass communication topics and offering two to three activities for each, the workbook helps students develop the skills they need to be active and critical consumers of media. Students are asked to complete activities such as reflecting on and evaluating their own media consumption, trying new models of interpretation, and investigating the impact of media on culture and society.

- **InfoTrac College Edition Student Activities Workbook for Mass Communication 2.0.** Available for bundling with the text, this workbook features extensive individual and group activities focusing on specific course topics to help instructors and students get the most from InfoTrac College Edition.

▶ Resources for Instructors

- *The Media/Impact Instructor's Resource Manual.* Thoroughly revised by William Swain, University of Louisiana, Lafayette, this manual includes chapter outlines, lecture ideas, suggested student assignments, Web links, InfoTrac College Edition exercises (to supplement those in the book and on the book companion Web site), worksheets for in-class discussion, test bank questions, sample syllabi and a list of CNN Today videos (available through Wadsworth) with a video correlation guide for classroom use (see additional details below).

- The instructor's password-protected **Media/Impact Web site.** Accessible directly through the book's CD-ROM or online at http://communication.wadsworth.com/biagi7, this site presents the *Instructor's Resource Manual* in electronic format, as well as additional resources such as PowerPoint slides, practice quizzes, and other activities and teaching tools. *NewsEdge* provides daily news feeds to the site.

- **ExamView® Computerized Testing.** Create, deliver, and customize tests and study guides (both print and online) in minutes with this easy-to-use assessment and tutorial system. You can build tests of up to 250 questions using up to 12 question types. Using ExamView's complete word processing capabilities, you can enter an unlimited number of new questions or edit existing questions.

- *Multimedia Manager for Media/Impact.* Thoroughly revised by Matthew Melton, Lee University, this text's Multimedia Manager will invigorate your lectures with pre-designed Microsoft® *PowerPoint®* presentations containing numerous images, text, and cued CNN videos. Multimedia Manager is fully customizable—you can modify the slides or add your own content in minutes to get a powerful, personalized presentation!

- **CNN Today Videos for Mass Communication and Electronic Media.** Thomson/Wadsworth exclusives, the six-volume mass communication and two-volume electronic media video series will help you launch your lectures with riveting footage from CNN, the world's leading 24-hour global news network. Our CNN Today Videos allow you to integrate the newsgathering and programming power of CNN into the classroom to show students the relevance of course material to their everyday lives. Organized by topics covered in a typical course, these videos are divided into short segments that are perfect for introducing key concepts. High-interest clips are followed by questions designed to spark class discussion.

- **WebTutor™ Advantage for Web CT and Blackboard.** Ready to use as soon as you log in, WebTutor Advantage is a complete course management system and communication tool that is conveniently pre-loaded with content specific to and organized like your text. You can customize the content any way you choose—from uploading images and text to adding Web links and your own activities. Whether you customize or not, WebTutor helps you manage your course and stay connected with your students by providing virtual office hours, posted syllabi and other course materials, threaded discussions, and quizzes for tracking student progress. Communication tools include a course calendar, asynchronous discussion and real-time chat, a whiteboard, and an integrated e-mail system.

Contact your Wadsworth/Thomson Learning representative for details, examination copies, or a demonstration of any of these teaching and learning resources, which are available to qualified adopters.

▶ Acknowledgments

As always, the extraordinarily professional team at Wadsworth has given *Media/Impact* their very best attention, and it shows in the quality of this book. It seems impossible, but each edition is better than the last, and the Wadsworth editorial and production teams are the reason. Their names appear on the copyright page. It's also my pleasure to acknowledge William Swain of the University of Louisiana, Lafayette, who thoroughly updated the *Instructor's Resource Manual* for *Media/Impact*'s seventh edition, and Matthew Melton of Lee University, who updated the text's *Multimedia Manager*.

This seventh edition of *Media/Impact* also reflects the suggestions, contributions and ideas of hundreds of faculty reviewers over the last 17 years, for which I am very grateful. The reviewers who provided the detailed feedback that guided the changes for this edition are:

Margaret L. Bates, City College of New York
Patricia Bradley, Temple University
Richard Craig, San Jose State University
David Donnelly, Quinnipiac University
Neil Goldstein, Montgomery County Community College
John L. Hart, Irvine Valley College
Timothy James, Community College of Southern Nevada
William L. Knowles, University of Montana
Jay Morris, Ohio University, Eastern
Mark C. Timney, Keene State College

▶ People Who Are Centrally Important

Again I must thank Susan Badger, CEO of Thomson Higher Education. She has, from the beginning of her leadership at Wadsworth, contributed greatly to the book's success with her support and enthusiasm. My students, of course, keep me honest by facing me in every class I teach using the book, candidly offering me their opinions and ideas. I also regularly receive e-mails from students around the world who have been introduced to the book, and their comments add an international perspective. As always, I couldn't have finished this project—yet again—without the unyielding support of my favorite media expert, Vic Biondi.

I hope you have a chance to explore all of *Media/Impact*'s valuable features. Please let me know what you think. My e-mail address is sbiagi@saclink .csus.edu.

Shirley Biagi
Sacramento, CA

About the Author

Shirley Biagi is a professor in the Department of Communication Studies at California State University, Sacramento. Her best-selling text, *Media/Impact*, is also published in Canadian, Greek, Spanish and Chinese editions.

Biagi is the author of several other Wadsworth communications texts, including *Media/Reader: Perspectives on Mass Media Industries, Effects and Issues* and *Interviews That Work: A Practical Guide for Journalists*. She is co-author, with Marilyn Kern-Foxworth, of *Facing Difference: Race, Gender and Mass Media*. She also currently is an Internet and publications consultant to the California Chamber of Commerce.

From 1998–2000, she was Editor of *American Journalism*, the national media history quarterly published by the American Journalism Historians Association. She has served as guest faculty for the Center for Digital Government, the Poynter Institute, the American Press Institute, the National Writers Workshop and the Hearst Fellowship Program at the *Houston Chronicle*.

She also was one of eight project interviewers for the award-winning Washington (D.C.) Press Club Foundation's Women in Journalism Oral History Project, sponsored by the National Press Club. Interviewers completed 57 oral histories of female pioneers in journalism, available free on the Press Club's Web site at http://npc.press.org/wpforal

Biagi's international experience includes currently serving on the board of the Arab-United States Association of Communication Educators (AUSACE) and guest lectureships at Al Ahram Press Institute in Cairo, Egypt, and Queensland University in Brisbane, Australia.

CHAPTER 1

What's Ahead

W hen was the last time you spent 24 hours without the media? From the moment you get up in the morning until the time you go to bed at night, the media are waiting to keep you company.

Radio news gives you headlines in the shower and traffic reports on the freeway. Newspapers offer you national and local news and help you keep up with the latest college basketball standings and Garfield's attempts to steal another piece of lasagna. Magazines describe new video games and keep you current with the latest fashion trends. Your homework competes with the newest paperback novel and your favorite television shows and your DVD player, where you can screen the latest movies. And waiting on your computer is e-mail from your overseas college friend, with digital pictures of him with his latest girlfriend.

According to industry estimates, adults spend more than half their waking lives with the media—more time than they spend sleeping. (See **Illustration 1.1**, page 4.) During the day, the average person spends more time with the media than without them. Some form of mass media touches nearly every American every day—economically, socially and culturally. The mass media can affect the way you vote and the way you spend your money. They sometimes influence the way you eat, talk, work, study and relax. This is the **impact** of mass media on American society.

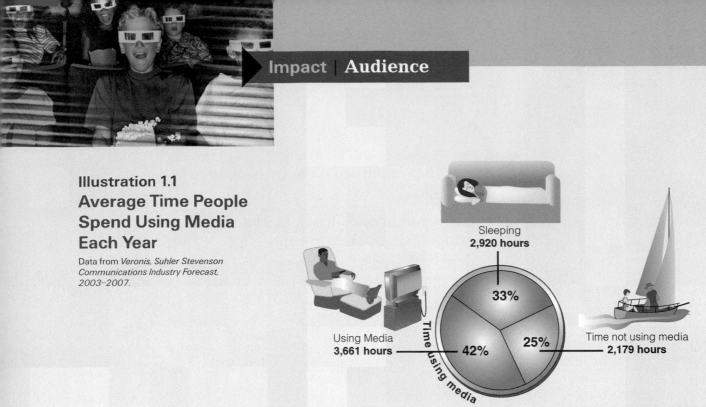

Illustration 1.1
Average Time People Spend Using Media Each Year

Data from *Veronis, Suhler Stevenson Communications Industry Forecast, 2003–2007.*

Sleeping
2,920 hours

Using Media
3,661 hours

Time using media

33%

42%

25%

Time not using media
2,179 hours

Total hours in a year = 8,760

▶ Mass Media's Large Presence in Our Lives

The media's wide-ranging presence distinguishes American mass media from the media in many other countries. In no other country do the mass media capture so much of people's time and attention. In no other country do the media affect so many aspects of the way people live. And in no other country do the media collect so much money for delivering information and entertainment. The American media industries earn about $399 billion a year. (See **Illustration 1.2.**)

Today's American society has inherited the wisdom and mistakes of the people who work in the mass media and the society that regulates and consumes what the mass media produce. Consider these situations:

- You are in a bookstore with $10 to spend. You can't decide whether to buy a romance novel by Nora Roberts, a book of poems by Maya Angelou or a travel guide to Peru. What are the economic consequences of these decisions by book buyers for the book publishing industry? (See Chapter 2.)

- You are a newspaper publisher in a small New England town in the 1700s. You print an article that angers the local public officials and they throw you in jail. Even though you're in jail, you want to continue to publish the newspaper. What do you do? (See James Franklin and the *New England Courant* in Chapter 3.)

- On the Internet, a friend sends you the latest songs from Beyoncé, which you download and publish on your personal Web site. You get the music you want, but her music company sues you because you haven't paid royalties to use the songs. Will you be prosecuted? (See Chapter 5.)

If a friend sends you a copy of the latest song by Beyoncé on the Internet and you use the song on your Web site without permission, you can be prosecuted for copyright violation.

AP/Wide World Photos

Illustration 1.2
U.S. Media Industries Annual Income

The U.S. media industries collect $399 billion a year. Television and newspapers are the top money-makers.

Data from *Veronis, Suhler Stevenson Communications Industry Forecast, 2003–2007.*

32% Television, including Cable & Satellite	17% Movies & Video	16% Newspapers	15% Books	7% Internet	6% Radio	4% Magazines	3% Recordings

- You are a public figure, and you believe you've been misquoted and misrepresented in a major magazine story written by a freelance journalist. You sue the author and the magazine. Eventually the case reaches the U.S. Supreme Court. What implications will the court decision have on the media's liability for the stories they print and broadcast? (See *Masson* v. *The New Yorker* magazine, Chapter 14.)

People who work in the media industries and people who watch, listen to, read and govern what the media offer make decisions like these every day. The future of American mass media will be determined by these choices.

▶ Mass Communication in the Digital Age

Wired This one word often has been used to describe someone who understands all the latest technologies, knows what's going on. In the 1930s, if you were wired, your house had electricity throughout. You put your radio near an electrical outlet, with the furniture positioned so the family could listen to the programs. In the 1950s, if you were wired, you had an antenna on the roof for your new TV set, which was connected at the wall to an electrical outlet and the antenna. To be wired was to be connected.

In the 1990s, if you were wired, you still needed an electrical outlet at home and at work to be connected to your computer, and the furniture in your family room still was arranged to accommodate the cable or satellite and perhaps telephone lines for your interactive TV set.

Wireless In the new world of mass communication, to be connected is to be wireless (often called Wi-Fi, an abbreviation for **wi**reless **fi**delity. New technologies are emerging that will allow you to use any technology in any location without wires. This means you can move the furniture anywhere in the media room, watch movies on your portable computer, listen to radio by satellite, and download music, books and newspapers to a device you carry in your pocket. You and your mass media are totally mobile.

Wi-Fi An abbreviation for Wireless Fidelity.

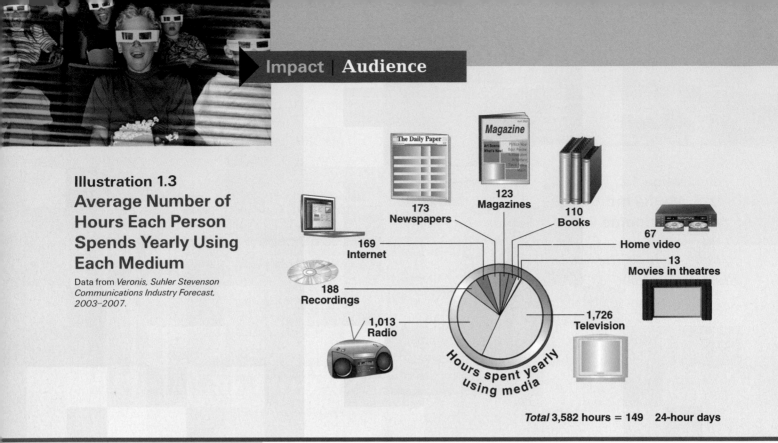

Illustration 1.3
Average Number of Hours Each Person Spends Yearly Using Each Medium

Data from *Veronis, Suhler Stevenson Communications Industry Forecast, 2003–2007.*

173 Newspapers

123 Magazines

110 Books

67 Home video

13 Movies in theatres

169 Internet

188 Recordings

1,013 Radio

1,726 Television

Hours spent yearly using media

Total 3,582 hours = 149   24-hour days

Critical Question

How do your media consumption habits compare with the national averages? If you notice any significant differences, to what do you attribute them? Explain.

A model at a recent Internet trade show demonstrates "wearable technology." These are wireless information appliances designed so people can use media wherever and whenever they want.

AP/Wide World Photos

The new mass media is as easy to use as a telephone, with pictures and sound, offering massive choices of information, entertainment and services whenever and wherever you want them. You can:

- Watch your favorite program whenever you want to see it;

- See a first-run movie and conduct an on-screen dialog with the movie's producer about her latest movie release;

- Play the newest video game online with three people you've never met;

- Download ten new books to a pocket-size device to carry in your backpack on your next camping trip;

- Check your family ancestry and create a family tree, leading you to connect with overseas relatives you didn't know existed;

- Stop on the street corner in a new town and, using a pocket device, call up directions to the closest Italian restaurant, complete with the latest local recommendations about where to find the best pizza.

The new digital environment is an intricate, webbed network of many different types of communications systems that eventually will connect every home, school, library and business in the United States. Most of the systems in this digital environment are invisible. Electronic signals have replaced wires, freeing people up to stay connected no matter where or when they want to communicate.

This global communications system uses broadcast, telephone, satellite, cable and computer technologies to connect everyone in the world to a variety of services. Ideally, this communications system will be accessible and affordable for everyone. As futurist George Gilder phrased it, the issue is, "Who will ride the next avalanche of bits on the information superhighway—and who will be buried under it?"

▶ Understanding the Communication Process

To understand mass communication in the digital age, first it is important to understand the process of communication. Communication is the act of sending ideas and opinions from one person to another. Writing and talking to each other are only two ways human beings communicate. We also communicate when we gesture, move our bodies or roll our eyes.

Three terms scholars use to describe how people communicate are:

- *Intrapersonal communication*
- *Interpersonal communication*
- *Mass communication*

Movies such as *Lord of the Rings*, available to large groups of different kinds of people simultaneously, represent one form of mass communication. Director Peter Jackson (second from right) celebrates winning four Golden Globes in 2004 for *Lord of the Rings: The Return of the King*. Also celebrating (from left) producer Barrie Osborne and actors Donnie Monaghan, John Rhys Davis and Elijah Wood.

Each form of communication involves different numbers of people in specific ways.

If you are in a grocery store and you silently debate with yourself whether to buy a package of double-chunk chocolate chip cookies, you are using what scholars call *intra*personal communication—communication within one person.

To communicate with each other, people rely on many of the five senses—sight, hearing, touch, smell and taste. Scholars call this direct sharing of experience between two people *inter*personal communication.

Mass communication is communication from one person or group of persons through a transmitting device (a medium) to large audiences or markets. **In *Media/Impact* you will study mass communication**.

To describe the process of mass communication, scholars draw charts and diagrams to convey what happens when people send messages to one another using mass communication. This description begins with six easily understood terms: *sender, message, receiver, channel, feedback* and *noise*. (See **Illustration 1.4**, page 8.)

Pretend you're standing directly in front of someone and you say, "I like your Chicago Cubs hat." In this simple communication, you are the sender; the message is "I like your Chicago Cubs hat," and the person in front of you is the receiver (or audience). This example of interpersonal communication involves the sender, the message and the receiver.

In mass communication, the **sender** (or **source**) puts the **message** on what is called a **channel**. The sender (source) could be your local cable company, for example. The channel (or **medium**) delivers the *message*. The channel could be the cable line that hooks into the back of your TV set. A medium is the means by which a message reaches an audience. (The plural of the word *medium* is *media*; when scholars discuss more than one

Mass Communication
Communication from one person or group of persons through a transmitting device (a medium) to large audiences or markets.

Medium   The means by which a message reaches the audience. The singular form of the word *media*.

Illustration 1.4
Elements of Mass Communication

The process of mass communication: A **sender** (source) puts a message on a **channel** (medium) that delivers the **message** to the **receiver**. **Feedback** occurs when the receiver responds, and that response changes subsequent messages from the source. **Noise** (such as static or a dropped connection) can interrupt or change the message during transmission.

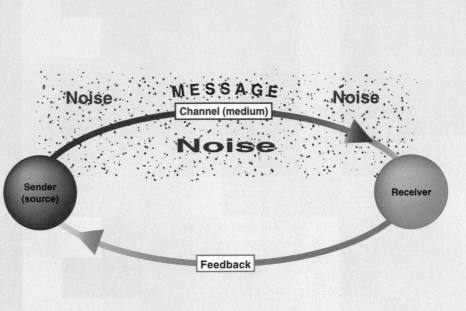

| Media | Plural of the word medium. |

| Noise | Distortion (such as static) that interferes with clear communication. |

| Feedback | A response sent back to the sender from the person who receives the communication. |

medium, they refer to **media**. Your television set is the medium that delivers the message simultaneously to you (and many other people). The **receiver** is the place where the message arrives. **Noise** is the distortion (such as static or a dropped connection) that can interfere with clear communication.

Feedback occurs when the receivers process the message and send a response back to the sender (source). Using a very crude example, say that the cable company (sender/source) sends an advertisement for pizza (the message) over the cable line (channel) into your TV set (medium). If you (the receiver) use the controls on your interactive TV set to order a pizza, the order you place (feedback) ultimately will bring you a pizza. This entire loop between sender and receiver, and the resulting response (feedback) of the receiver to the sender, describes the process of mass communication.

Using a very general definition, mass communication today shares three characteristics:

1. A message is sent out on some form of mass communication system (such as the Internet, print or broadcast).

2. The message is delivered rapidly.

3. The message reaches large groups of different kinds of people simultaneously or within a short period of time.

Thus, a telephone conversation between two people would not qualify as mass communication, but a message from the President of the United States, broadcast simultaneously by all of the television networks, would qualify.

Mass media deliver messages to large numbers of people at once. The businesses that produce the mass media in America—newspapers, magazines, radio, television, movies, recordings and books—are the traditional mass media industries. Today, the Internet is creating new digital delivery systems for information and entertainment.

▶ Understanding the Mass Media Industries

The term **mass media industries** describes eight types of mass media businesses. The Internet is the newest media industry. The other media industries are

- Books
- Newspapers
- Magazines
- Recordings
- Radio
- Movies
- Television

The use of the word *industries* emphasizes the major goal of mass media in America—financial success.

▶ How Do the Media Industries Work?

Books, newspapers and magazines were America's only mass media for 250 years after the first American book was published in 1640. The first half of the 20th century brought four new media—recordings, radio, movies and TV—in less than 50 years. The latest addition to the media mix, of course, is the Internet.

To understand where each medium fits in the mass media industries today, it is important to examine the individual characteristics of each medium.

Book Publishing   Publishers issue about 55,000 titles a year in the United States, although some of these are reprints and new editions of old titles. Retail bookstores in the United States account for one-third of all money earned from book sales.

The rest of book publishing income comes from books that are sold through book clubs, in college stores, to libraries and to school districts for use in elementary and high schools. Book publishing is expected to grow slightly in the next decade, primarily due to new income from audiobooks and electronic books (e-books).

Newspapers   There are about 1,500 daily newspapers in the United States. Newspapers are evenly divided between morning and afternoon delivery, but the number of evening papers is declining. Papers that come out in the morning are growing in circulation, and papers that come out in the afternoon are shrinking.

The number of weekly newspapers also is declining. Advertising makes up about two-thirds of the printed space in daily newspapers. Newspaper income is stable, but not growing.

AP/Wide World Photos

American movies are very popular overseas, representing substantial income for U.S. film companies.

Magazines   According to the Magazine Publishers of America, about 18,000 magazines are published in the United States. This number is declining slowly. The number of magazines going out of business is larger than new magazines being launched.

To maintain and increase profits, magazines are raising their subscription and single-copy prices and fighting to maintain their advertising income. The number of magazine subscriptions people buy is going up, but newsstand sales are down. Magazine income is expected to decline over the next decade.

Recordings   Most recordings are bought by people who are over 30. Compact discs (CDs) account for almost all recording industry income. The rest of the money comes from vinyls and music videos. Industry income has been declining sharply because new technologies mean that many people share music over the Internet rather than buy the recordings.

Radio   About 13,000 radio stations broadcast programming in the United States, evenly divided between AM and FM stations. About 2,100 radio stations are public stations, most of them FM. The average American household owns five radios. Radio revenues are expected to grow slightly in the next decade.

Movies   Nearly 37,000 theater screens exist in the United States. The major and independent studios combined make about 400 pictures a year. The industry is collecting more money because of higher ticket prices, but fewer people go to see movies in theaters, and the number of movie theaters is declining.

The major increase in income to the movie industry in the past decade has been from video and DVD sales. The year 1986 marked the first time the number of videotape rentals was higher than the number of movie ticket purchases. Recently DVDs surpassed videotape as the way most people watch movies. U.S. movie companies also earn a substantial portion of their income from sales overseas. Industry income is expected to increase slightly in the next decade.

Television   About 1,600 television stations are operating in the United States. One out of four stations is a public station. Many stations are affiliated with a network—NBC, CBS, ABC, Fox, UPN, or WB—although a sizable number of stations, called *independents*, are not affiliated with any network. About 90 percent of the homes in the United States are wired for cable, and a growing number of households now receive programming by satellite

The average cable subscriber pays $37 a month. The average monthly charge for satellite customers is $34. TV network income is declining, while income to independents, cable operators and satellite operators is increasing quickly. Total industry revenue is expected to grow in the next decade.

The Internet   The newest media industry also is growing the fastest. Economists predict the number of consumers online will increase 40 percent between 2000 and 2005 and that the amount of money spent for Internet advertising will rise 25 percent—from $8 billion in the year 2000 to $10 billion by the year 2005. Internet media have become a new mass medium as well as an integral part of traditional print, audio and video media.

▶ Three Important Mass Media Concepts to Understand

The media are key institutions in our society. They affect our culture, our buying habits, and our politics. They are affected in turn by changes in our beliefs, tastes, interests and behavior. Three important concepts about the mass media can help organize your thinking about mass media and their impact on American society.

1. The mass media are profit-centered businesses.

2. Technological developments are an integral part of changes in the way mass media are delivered and consumed.

3. Mass media both reflect and affect politics, society and culture.

1. The Media Are Profit-Centered Businesses

▶ Who Owns the Media?

What you see, read and hear in the mass media may tease, entertain, inform, persuade, provoke and even perplex you. But to understand the American mass media, the first concept to grasp is that the central force driving the media business in America is the desire to make money. American media are businesses, vast businesses. The products of these businesses are information and entertainment.

Of course, other motives shape the media in America: the desire to fulfill the public's need for information, to influence the country's governance, to disseminate the country's culture, to offer entertainment and to provide an outlet for artistic expression. But American media are, above all, profit-centered.

▶ Who Controls the Messages?

To understand the mass media industries, it is important to know who owns these important channels of communication. In the United States, all media are privately owned except the Public Broadcasting Service (PBS) and National Public Radio (NPR), which survive on government support and private donations. The annual budget for all of public broadcasting (PBS and NPR combined) is less than 2 percent of the amount advertisers pay every year to support America's commercial media.

In some media industries, ownership is controlled by more companies today than in the 1950s. There are six major movie studios today, for example, compared to the Big Five of the 1940s. The number of companies that own broadcast stations has increased since the 1940s and so has the number of magazine publishers. The number of companies that publish newspapers and the number of companies that produce recordings, however, have declined.

Overall, American media ownership has been contracting rather than expanding. This means that larger companies are buying smaller companies. The trend is for media companies to cluster together in larger groups. Fewer companies own more types of media businesses, and a small number of companies now control more aspects of the media business. This trend is called **concentration of ownership** and takes five different forms.

1. Chains. Benjamin Franklin established America's first newspaper chain in the 1700s, when he was publishing his own newspaper, the *Pennsylvania Gazette*, as well as sponsoring one-third of the cost of publishing the *South Carolina Gazette*. (He also collected one-third of the *South Carolina Gazette*'s profits.) William Randolph Hearst expanded this tradition in the 1930s. At their peak, Hearst newspapers accounted for nearly 14 percent of total national daily newspaper sales and 25 percent of Sunday sales. Today's U.S. newspaper chain giant is Gannett, with 74 daily newspapers, including *USA Today*.

2. Broadcast Networks. A broadcast network is a collection of radio or television stations that offers programs, usually simultaneously throughout the country, during designated program times. Unlike newspaper ownership (which is not regulated by the government), broadcast station ownership and operation are regulated by the **Federal Communications Commission**, a government regulatory body whose members are appointed by the president.

The four major networks are ABC (American Broadcasting Company), NBC (National Broadcasting Company), CBS (Columbia Broadcasting System) and Fox Broadcasting. NBC, the oldest network, was founded in the 1920s. This network and the two other original networks (CBS and ABC) were established to deliver radio programming across the country, and the network concept continued with the invention of television.

Fox is among the youngest networks, founded in 1986, and serves only television. Time Warner and Paramount Communications launched fifth and sixth TV networks in 1996—WB (Warner Brothers) and UPN (United Paramount Network), respectively.

Networks can have as many **affiliates** as they want. Affiliates are stations that use network programming but are owned by companies other than the networks. No network, however, can have two affiliates in the same geographic broadcast area, due to government regulation of network affiliation.

3. Cross-Media Ownership. Many media companies own more than one type of media property: newspapers, magazines, radio and TV stations, for example. Gannett, which owns the largest chain of newspapers, also owns television and radio stations. The merger of Capital Cities/ABC with Disney joined the programming power of Disney with the distribution system of the ABC television network. Rupert Murdoch's News Corporation owns newspapers, TV stations, magazines, 20th Century-Fox Film and Fox Broadcasting.

4. Conglomerates. When you go to the movies to watch a Columbia picture, you might not realize that Sony owns the film company. Sony is a conglomerate—a company that owns media companies as well as businesses that are unrelated to the media business. Media properties are attractive investments, but some conglomerate owners are unfamiliar with the idiosyncrasies of the media industries and struggle to make their companies profitable after acquiring them.

5. Vertical Integration. The most noticeable trend among today's media companies is vertical integration—an attempt by one company to control several related aspects of the media business

Affiliates   Stations that use network programming but are owned by companies other than the networks.

Conglomerates   Companies that own media companies as well as businesses that are unrelated to the media business.

Vertical Integration   An attempt by one company to simultaneously control several related aspects of the media business.

"He's not a bad person, but he wants to own two TV stations in the same market."

at once, with each part of the company helping the others. For example, besides publishing magazines and books and operating America Online, Time Warner owns Home Box Office (HBO), Warner movie studios, various cable TV systems throughout the United States and Cable News Network (CNN).

▶ Competition and Convergence

To describe the financial status of today's media industries also is to talk about acquisitions. The media are buying and selling each other in unprecedented numbers and forming media groups to position themselves in the marketplace to maintain and increase their profits. Since 1986, all three original TV networks—NBC, CBS and ABC—have been sold to new owners, making each of the three original networks smaller parts of different larger media companies.

Today's media companies face heavy pressure to deliver hefty profits to their shareholders. They also are driven by forecasts for media **convergence**, the melding of the communications, computer and electronic industries because of advances in digital technology. These companies want to seek alliances that will help them compete in the future.

Convergence The melding of the communications, computer and electronics industries.

The people who manage U.S. media companies today want to make money. As in all industries, there are people who want to make money quickly and people who take the long-term view about profits, but certainly none of them wants to lose money. One way to expand a company is to acquire an already established company that's successful.

Media acquisitions have skyrocketed for two reasons:

1. Most media companies today are publicly traded, which means their stock is sold on one of the nation's stock exchanges. This makes acquisitions relatively easy. A media company that wants to buy another publicly owned company can buy that company's stock when the stock becomes available.

The open availability of stock in these companies means any company or individual with enough money can invest in the American media industries (which is exactly how Rupert Murdoch, owner of Fox Broadcasting, joined the U.S. media business).

2. Beginning in 1980, the Federal Communications Commission (FCC) gradually deregulated the broadcast media. **Deregulation** means the FCC withdrew many regulatory restrictions on broadcast media ownership. Before 1980, for example, the FCC allowed a broadcast company to own only five TV stations, five AM radio stations and five FM radio stations.

Deregulation The process of ending government monitoring of an industry.

Companies also were required to hold onto a station for three years before the station could be sold. The post-1980 FCC eliminated the three-year rule and raised the number of broadcast holdings allowed for one owner. Today, there are very few FCC restrictions on broadcast media ownership.

▶ Why Media Properties Are Selling

Ownership turnover is highest in the newspaper and broadcast industries. Several factors have affected the market for these properties:

1. Newspaper and broadcast properties are attractive investments. Many companies report profits of 10 percent a year, which is about double the average profit for a U.S. manufacturing company.

2. Newspapers and broadcast stations are scarce commodities. Because the number of newspapers has been declining and the government regulates the number of broadcast stations that are allowed to operate, a limited number of stations is available. As with all limited commodities, this makes them attractive investments.

3. Many newspapers, especially, have gone through a cycle of family ownership. If the heirs to the founders of the business are not interested in joining the company, the only way for them to collect their inheritance is to sell the newspaper.

4. Newspapers and broadcast stations are easier to buy than to create. Because these businesses require huge investments in equipment and people, they are expensive to start up.

5. In broadcasting, the major factor that encouraged ownership changes in the 1980s was deregulation. This allowed people who had never been in the broadcast business before to enter the industry, using bank loans to pay for most of their investment. But deregulation had other effects, too. In the 1990s, the introduction of new technologies, especially the Internet, changed the economics of the industry.

Some new owners of media companies approach broadcast properties as they would any other business—hoping to invest the minimum amount necessary. They hope to hold onto the property until the market is favorable and then sell at a huge profit.

"We have a calendar based on the book, stationery based on the book, an audiotape of the book, and a videotape of the movie based on the book, but we don't have the book."

▶ Advantages of Concentration

Supporters of concentrated ownership say a large company can offer advantages that a small company could never afford—training for the employees, higher wages and better working conditions. According to one Gannett executive, John C. Quinn:

> *A publisher's instinct for good or evil is not determined by the number of newspapers he owns. A group can attract top professional talent, offering training under a variety of editors, advancement through a variety of opportunities. . . . It can invest in research and development and nuts-and-bolts experience necessary to translate the theories of new technology into the practical production of better newspapers.*
>
> *Concentrated ownership can provide great resources; only independent, local judgment can use the resources to produce a responsible and responsive local newspaper. That measure cannot be inflated by competition, nor can it be diluted by monopoly.*

William A. Henry III of *Time* magazine, who won a Pulitzer Prize at the *Boston Globe*, points out that several of the newspapers considered the nation's best—including *The New York Times* and *The Washington Post*—are chain newspapers, although he acknowledges that these two newspapers are still dominated by family owners who hold the majority of the stock. The same arguments that are made against chain ownership can be made against independent ownership, he said.

Most independent owners run papers in ways that comfort them, their friends and their general social class. A great many reporters have gotten into trouble over the years by going after buddies or business associates of the owners. And a great many more have compromised themselves by writing puffy, uncritical pieces about cultural institutions, department stores, restaurants or socialites favored by the owner or his spouse.

▶ Disadvantages of Concentration

The major arguments of people who favor concentration are that a corporation can offer financial support to a small newspaper or broadcast station and that responsible, autonomous local management is the key to successful group ownership. Yet several studies have shown that chain newspapers are more likely to support the candidates the newspapers favor in elections, and in presidential elections, 85 percent or more of the papers in a chain endorse the same candidate.

This is an example of the consequences of corporate control that forms the major argument against group ownership—that concentration limits the diversity of opinion and the quality of culture available to the public and reduces what scholars call **message pluralism**. In an article in the magazine *The New Republic* entitled "Invasion of the Gannettoids," former newspaper reporter Philip Weiss described what he says happens when corporate culture takes over American journalism:

The problem with Gannett isn't simply its formula or its chairman, but the company's corporate culture. The product is the company—cheerful, superficial, self-promoting, suspicious of ideas, conformist, and implicitly authoritarian. But the Gannett story is more, too. For as many as six million daily readers, most of them in one-newspaper towns, Gannett serves as chief interpreter and informer about society—and does so unstained by ideals of independence or thoroughness.

The loss of message pluralism in television angers critics the most, since broadcasting still is licensed to serve the public interest, convenience and need. Broadcasters claim this requirement is out of date because it was adopted when broadcast outlets were scarce. Today, broadcasters say many channels of information are available to the public.

Ben H. Bagdikian, Dean Emeritus, Graduate School of Journalism at the University of California, Berkeley, describes how the loss of message pluralism can affect every aspect of communication:

It has always been assumed that a newspaper article might be expanded to a magazine article which could become the basis for a hardcover book, which, in turn, could be a paperback, and then, perhaps a TV series and finally, a movie. At each step of change an author and other enterprises could compete for entry into the array of channels for reaching the public mind and pocketbook. But today several media giants own these arrays, not only closing off entry points for competition in different media, but influencing the choice of entry at the start.

▶ Advertisers and Consumers Pay the Bills

Most of the $399 billion a year in income the American mass media industries collect comes directly from advertising. Advertising directly supports newspapers, radio and television. (Subscribers actually pay only a small part

Illustration 1.5
How People Spent Their Media Dollars, 2001–2003

Data from *Veronis, Suhler Stevenson Communications Industry Forecast, 2003–2007.*

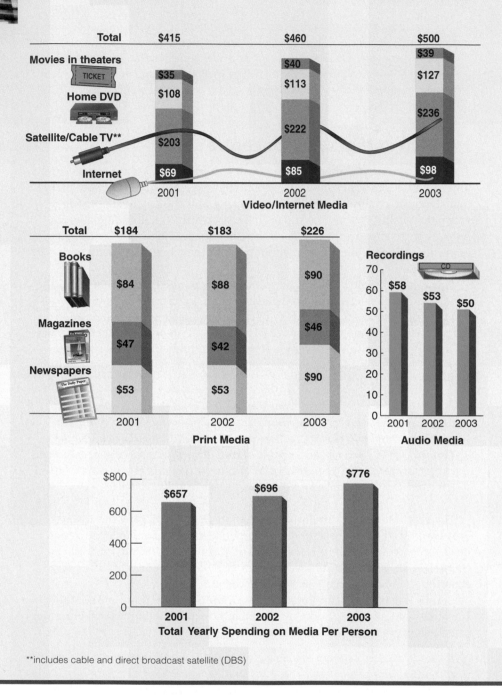

Video/Internet Media

	2001	2002	2003
Total	$415	$460	$500
Movies in theaters	$35	$40	$39
Home DVD	$108	$113	$127
Satellite/Cable TV**	$203	$222	$236
Internet	$69	$85	$98

Print Media

	2001	2002	2003
Total	$184	$183	$226
Books	$84	$88	$90
Magazines	$47	$42	$46
Newspapers	$53	$53	$90

Audio Media

Recordings

2001	2002	2003
$58	$53	$50

Total Yearly Spending on Media Per Person

2001	2002	2003
$657	$696	$776

**includes cable and direct broadcast satellite (DBS)

Pictograph A symbol of an object that is used to convey an idea.

of the cost of producing a newspaper.) Magazines receive more than half their income from advertising and the other portion from subscriptions. Income for movies, recordings and books, of course, comes from direct purchases and ticket sales. (See **Illustration 1.5**.)

This means that most of the information and entertainment you receive from TV, radio, newspapers and magazines in America is paid for by people who want to sell you products. You support the media industries *indirectly* by buying the products that advertisers sell. General Motors spends nearly a billion dollars a year on network TV advertising. Sears spends $300 million a year just on newspaper advertising. Multiply the spending for all this advertising in all media, and you can understand how easily American media industries accumulate $399 billion a year.

You also pay for the media *directly* when you buy a book or a CD or go to a movie. This money buys equipment, underwrites company research and expansion, and pays stock dividends. Advertisers and consumers are the financial foundation for American media industries.

2. Technological Developments Are an Integral Part of Changes in the Way Mass Media Are Delivered and Consumed

▶ Three Information Communications Revolutions

The channels of communication have changed dramatically over the centuries, but the idea that a society will pay to stay informed and entertained is not new. In Imperial Rome, people who wanted to find out what was going on paid professional speakers a coin (a *gazet*) for the privilege of listening to the speaker announce the day's events. Many early newspapers were called *gazettes* to reflect this heritage.

Early attempts at written communication began modestly with **pictographs**. A pictograph is a symbol of an object that is used to convey an idea. If you have ever drawn a heart with an arrow through it, you understand what a pictograph is. The first known pictographs were carved in stone by the Sumerians of Mesopotamia in about 3500 B.C.

The stone in which these early pictographic messages were carved served as a medium—a device to transmit messages. Eventually, messages were imprinted in clay and stored in a primitive version of today's library. These messages weren't very portable, however. Heavy clay tablets don't slip easily into someone's pocket.

In about 2500 B.C., the Egyptians invented papyrus, a type of paper made from a grasslike plant called sedge, which was easier to write on, but people still communicated using pictographs.

The First Information Communications Revolution

Pictographs as a method of communication developed into *phonetic writing* in about 1000 B.C. using symbols to represent sounds. Instead of drawing a representation of a dog to convey the idea of a dog, scholars represented the sounds d-o-g with phonetic writing. The invention of phonetic writing has been called *the first information communications revolution*. "After being stored in written form, **information could now reach a new kind of audience, remote from the source and uncontrolled by it**," writes media scholar Anthony Smith. "Writing transformed knowledge into information."

About 500 years later, the Greek philosopher Socrates anticipated the changes that widespread literacy would bring. He argued that knowledge should remain among the privileged classes. Writing threatened the exclusive use of information, he said. "Once a thing is put in writing, the composition, whatever it may be, drifts all over the place, getting into the hands not only of those who understand it, but equally of those who have no business with it."

The Greeks perfected parchment, made of goat and sheep skins, in about 200 B.C. This was an even better medium on which to write. By about A.D. 100, before the use of parchment spread throughout Europe, the Chinese had invented paper, which was much cheaper to produce than parchment. Europeans didn't start to use paper until more than a thousand years

Today to 3500 B.C. Three information communications revolutions form the basis for today's digital media

TODAY
Digital electronic information delivery is the standard for all media.

▼

A.D. 2000
Internet advertising income reaches $8 billion annually.

▼

A.D. 1980
The Federal Communications Commission begins to deregulate the broadcast media.

▼

A.D. 1951
The Third Information Communications Revolution
Digital computers are developed to process, store and retrieve information.

▼

A.D. 1939
NBC debuts TV at the New York World's Fair.

▼

A.D. 1927
The Jazz Singer, the first feature-length motion picture with sound, premieres in New York.

▼

A.D. 1899
Guglielmo Marconi first uses his wireless radio.

▼

A.D. 1877
Thomas Edison first demonstrates the phonograph.

▼

A.D. 1741
The first American magazine is published.

▼

A.D. 1690
The first American newspaper is published.

continued on next page

Impact | TimeFrame

Today to 3500 B.C. Three information communications revolutions form the basis for today's digital media

continued

▼
A.D. 1640
The first American book is published.

▼
A.D. 1455
The Second Information Communications Revolution
Johannes Gutenberg invents movable type and publishes the Gutenberg Bible.

▼
A.D. 1445
The Chinese invent the copper press.

▼
A.D. 1300
Europeans start to use paper.

▼
A.D. 100
The Chinese invent paper.

▼
200 B.C.
The Greeks perfect parchment.

▼
1000 B.C.
The First Information Communications Revolution
Phonetic writing is developed.

▼
2500 B.C.
The Egyptians invent papyrus.

▼
3500 B.C.
The first known pictographs are carved in stone.

later, in about A.D. 1300. The discovery of parchment and then paper meant that storing information became cheaper and easier.

As Socrates had predicted, when more people learned to write, wider communication became possible because people in many different societies could share information among themselves and with people in other parts of the world. But scholars still had to painstakingly copy the information they wanted to keep or pay a scribe to copy for them. In the 14th century, for example, the library of the Italian poet Petrarch contained more than 100 manuscripts that he himself had copied individually.

In Petrarch's day, literate people were either monks or members of the privileged classes. Wealthy people could afford tutoring, and they also could afford to buy the handwritten manuscripts copied by the monks. Knowledge—and the power it brings—belonged to an elite group of people.

The Second Information Communications Revolution

As societies grew more literate, the demand for manuscripts flourished, but a scribe could produce only one copy at a time. What has been called *the second information communications revolution* began in Germany in 1455, when Johannes Gutenberg printed a Bible on a press that used movable type.

More than 200 years before Gutenberg, the Chinese had invented a printing press that used wood type, and the Chinese also are credited with perfecting a copper press in 1445. But Gutenberg's innovation was to line up individual metal letters that he could ink and then press with paper to produce copies. Unlike the wood or copper presses, the metal letters could be reused to produce new pages of text, which made the process much cheaper. The Gutenberg Bible, a duplicate of the Latin original, is considered the first book printed by movable type (47 copies still survive today, 550 years later).

As other countries adopted Gutenberg's press, the price for Bibles plummeted. In 1470, the cost of a French, mechanically printed Bible was one-fifth the cost of a hand-printed Bible. *The second revolution*—**printing—meant that knowledge, which had belonged to the privileged few, would one day be accessible to everyone**. This key development was one of the essential conditions for the rise of modern governments, as well as an important element of scientific and technological progress.

Before the Gutenberg press, a scholar who wanted special information had to travel to the place where it was kept. But once information could be

"I'll be O.K. It's just some damn virus I picked up from a computer."

duplicated easily, it could travel to people beyond the society that created it. The use of paper instead of the scribes' bulky parchment also meant that books could be stacked end to end. For the first time, knowledge was portable and storable.

Libraries now could store vast amounts of information in a small space. And because these smaller, lighter books could be carried easily, classical works could be read simultaneously in many cities by all different kinds of people. Another benefit of the development of printing was that societies could more easily keep information to share with future generations.

This effort to communicate—first through spoken messages, then through pictographs, then through the written word and finally through printed words—demonstrates people's innate desire to share information with one another. **Storability, portability** and **accessibility** of information are essential to today's concept of **mass communication**. By definition, **mass communication is information that becomes available to a large audience quickly.**

Computers, shown here being used by a carpenter, represent the third information communications revolution, the foundation of today's rapidly changing technology that affects politics, society and culture.

The Third Information Communications Revolution
Today's age of communication has been called the *third information communications revolution* because **computers have become the electronic storehouses and transmitters of vast amounts of information that previously relied on the written word.**

Computer technology, which processes and transmits information much more efficiently than mechanical devices, is driving the majority of changes affecting today's media. This has become possible with the development of digital computers, beginning around 1950. This means that *changes in today's media industries happen much faster than in the past.* Satellite broadcasts, digital recordings and the international computer network called the Internet are just three examples of the third information communications revolution.

Although each medium has its own history and economic structure, today all of the media industries compete for consumers' attention. Satellite and electronic technology will transform the media business more than we can foresee—enabling faster transmission of more information to more people than ever before.

▶ Taking Advantage of Digital Delivery

The economics of the communications industries makes digital delivery very important. All the industries involved in building and maintaining this interconnected network—broadcast, cable, telephone, computer, software, satellite and the consumer electronics industries—want a piece of the estimated $1 trillion that digital delivery represents. Leaders of the media industries in the United States believe the nation is ideally positioned to develop such a network because many Americans already have most of the tools that such a system needs.

Because the United States already leads the world in so many of the digital environment's necessary elements, it has become logical—and very profitable—for the media industries in this country to develop the technology to package and deliver information worldwide.

One-Way Versus Two-Way Communication
The classic model of mass communication (see **Illustration 1.4**, page 8) describes a process that begins with a sender (or source), who puts a message on a

channel (a medium); the channel delivers the message to the receiver. This can be described as the equivalent of a one-way road, sender to receiver. Digital delivery begins in the same way. The channel carries information and entertainment (messages) from many different sources (senders) to many different people (receivers).

The messages that return from the receiver to the sender are called *feedback*. In this new digital environment, messages and feedback can occur instantaneously. The sender and the receiver can communicate with each other simultaneously. This makes the new systems **interactive**.

To accomplish this interactivity, today's delivery system must develop from a communications system that works like an ordinary television (sending messages and programming one-way from the sender to the receiver) to a two-way digital system that can send and receive messages simultaneously and that works more like a combination television and computer.

"Dumb" Versus "Smart" Communication

The television set is a "dumb" appliance; it can only deliver programming. You can change the channel to receive different programs, but you can't talk back to the people who send the programming to your television set to tell them when you'd like to see a particular program. You can't watch something when you want to watch it, unless you remember beforehand to record the program. You also can't add anything to the programs on your TV, such as your personal commentary about sports programs, or replace a bad movie with a good one. This type of mass communication—in which the programs are sent to you on an established schedule and you are a passive receiver (a couch potato) for the program—is *one-way*.

As communications devices, however, telephones are smarter. When you talk on the telephone, the person on the other end of the conversation can listen to you and talk back right away (and, in the case of a teleconference, this can involve several people at the same time). This makes telephone communication interactive, giving you the ability to talk back—to receive as well as to transmit messages. Telephone communications are *two-way*.

To communicate rapidly, telephone communication uses a system of digitized information. When you talk, the telephone system uses electronic signals to transform your voice into a series of digits—ones and zeroes—and then reassembles these digits into an exact reproduction of your voice on the other end of the line. This method of storing and transmitting data is called **digital**.

Digital   In a form that can be transmitted and received electronically.

Like telephone communications, computers also operate using digitized information and they also are interactive. Written words, audio and video are translated and stored as *bits*. These bits can easily be transmitted, using two-way communication. This is the reason that someone can, for instance, dial up the Internet on a computer and receive and send information. To dial up the Internet, a computer typically uses a device called a *modem*, which connects the computer to a telephone line, making two-way communication possible.

And, unlike television and telephones, computers can store digital information for future use. This ability to store information makes the computer different from broadcast, cable, telephone and satellite communications. "In the information economy, the best opportunities stem from the exponential rise in the power of computers and computer networks," says futurist George Gilder.

"It's very important that you try very, very hard to remember where you electronically transferred Mommy and Daddy's assets."

Impact | People

Nathan Myhrvold: The Dawn of Technomania

Nathan Myhrvold, a quantum physicist, is the former Director of Operations at Microsoft.

by Nathan Myhrvold

It is easy to get caught up in technomania. Those who are most deeply involved with technology want to know more, those who fear it want reassurance, and those who see an opportunity—financial or other—don't want to miss out. *It's gonna change everything. It's gonna be here next Thursday. Watch out or you'll be left behind! . . .*

In some ways, every attribute of technomania has a parallel in the industromania of a hundred years ago. By 1897, large factories had sprouted, creating the notion of "going to work" in urban areas. Previously, cities had been centers of commerce which served the primary source of wealth—the agrarian countryside. Now they became the centers of both population and power. This caused other shifts, as organized labor started to take hold, and a political transformation followed.

Inventions emerged from everywhere—the typewriter in 1874, the telephone in 1876, the internal-

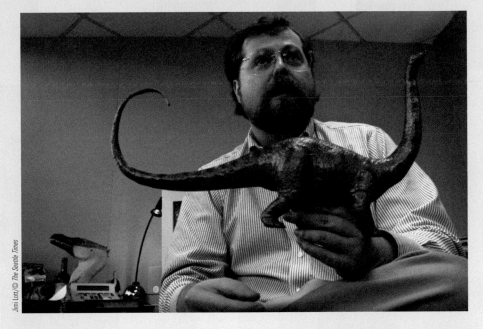

Jimi Lott/© The Seattle Times

combustion engine and the phonograph in 1877, electric lights in 1880, the zipper in 1891, and radio in 1895. . . . Few imagined that the industrial revolution would continue at the same pace for 60 years more. . . .

Still, we may not be able to gauge the real impact of the information revolution for 50 or 60 years more. Consider our cities, which in many cases have been transformed into artifacts of industrialization. Will large numbers of

people begin to telecommute and, in that way, return to a pastoral America? Or will the cities somehow become even more necessary to our lives? Technomania, like its industrial equivalent in 1897, is a reminder that all this lies just beyond our knowing. What has happened already is bound to be very small in comparison to what lies ahead.

The New Yorker, Oct. 20—27, 1997, pp. 236—37. Used by permission.

▶ How the New Communications Network Functions

Today's communications network combines different elements from existing media industries. Today, the broadcast industry produces content and delivers one-way communication by antenna; the cable industry delivers one-way communication and two-way communication by underground (or overhead) cable; the telephone companies efficiently deliver digital two-way communication using fiber optics and wireless technology; and the computer industry offers digital storage capability.

A digital communications network combines all these elements: content, two-way digital communication and digital storage. **Illustration 1.6** (page 22) shows how this communications network works.

Illustration 1.6
How the New Communications Network Functions

The new communications network combines different elements of broadcast, cable, telephone, satellite and computer technology to create an international digital communications network.

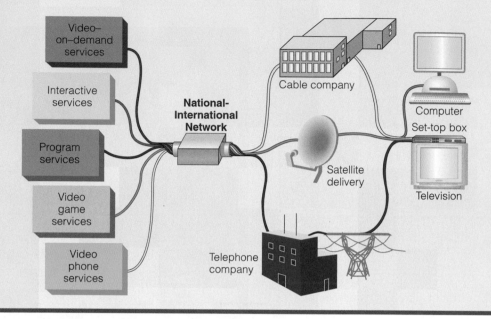

The Receiver (You, the Subscriber)   A digital network begins with you, the receiver/subscriber. You choose which services you want. You turn on your television or your computer. The screen shows you a menu of services. A **set-top box** sitting on top of your television is your electronic link to the new communications network. The computer receives the messages directly by modem or through a wireless signal. The services include:

- An online edition of your local newspaper
- A listing of programs by category (such as comedy, dramas or specials)
- A national video news service
- A worldwide video news service
- A library database research service
- A sports video and information service
- A family and lifestyle video and information service
- A travel video and information service
- A shopping video and information service
- A music video and information service
- An online video game site
- A listing of bulletin board discussion group services and chat rooms by topic
- A video telephone message service, with video messages from the day's callers
- An electronic **e-mail** message service
- A first-run movie service

E-mail   Electronic mail delivered over the Internet.

By clicking items on the menu, you glance through the offerings of each service and then make your choices. Your television/computer will show several screens at once so that you can use several services at the same time, each on a different screen. For example, you might check your bank balance while you watch a basketball game or check your e-mail messages while you watch the news headlines.

The software also tracks your usage, detailing the charges for the services you choose. As there is for today's cable users, there will probably be a basic service fee and then additional charges added as you use premium services.

The Channel (Cable, Telephone and Satellite Companies)

Cable, telephone and satellite companies provide communications delivery. The cable, telephone and satellite companies act as a conduit for all services, gathering them from the national or international network. These companies may offer only specific services; they might package some services together (local, national and international news services, for example); or they may offer an unlimited menu of all services available and let you make the choices.

Cable, telephone and satellite companies will compete for consumers' business. Customers will choose which type of service they want, based on each company's offerings and pricing. Some services will be billed as pay-per-view (there might be a $5 charge to view a first-run movie, for example) or per-minute (to use a library database for research, for example). Billing for these services would arrive monthly or, of course, the company could bill the amount directly to your checking account or your credit card. Cable, telephone and satellite companies will be connected to the program services by a national and international network or by satellite.

This international network and the satellite system already are in place today—the long-distance carrier networks such as AT&T and MCI and satellite services such as USSB and Hughes. Domestic long-distance networks would probably appear as a basic fee on your television/computer bill; international services would be an additional cost. The **Internet**, an international web of computer networks, will become the backbone of the new network, available to anyone with a television/computer and a cable, satellite or telephone hookup.

Internet   An international web of computer networks.

The Sender (Internet Service Providers)

Internet service providers (**ISP**s) offer services, including:

ISP   Internet service provider.

- Video on demand, such as movies
- Interactive services, such as banking, shopping, bulletin boards, Internet newspapers and information research services
- Music services
- Program services (comedies, game shows, soaps and sports)
- Video game services

Today's broadcast networks and cable channels eventually will become program services, so that you could subscribe to NBC and ABC and not CBS, for example. The ISP would offer programming in **bundles** and you could select the bundle you wanted. An ISP, such as America Online (AOL), will provide different programs and services (content) to you in a usable format.

Bundles   A collection of programs and services offered together for a set fee.

Satellite companies such as DirecTV are competing with cable and telephone companies to deliver Internet services to consumers.

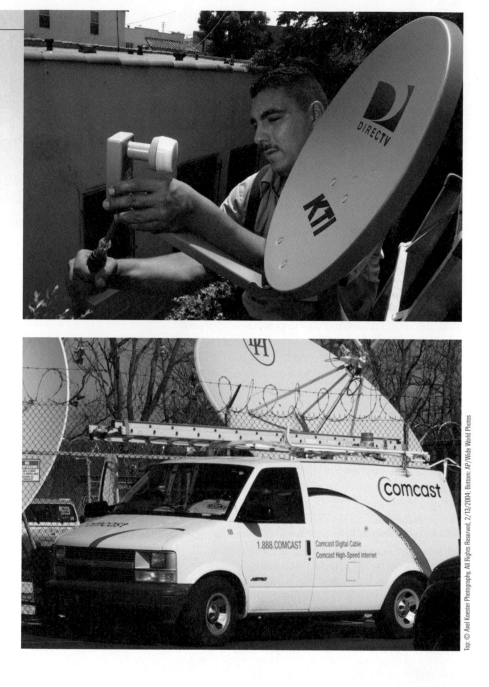

The Message (Content)　All print, audio and video that is digitized into bits becomes content for a digitized communications system. In a world of networked, rapid, digitized communications, *any* digitized textbook, novel, movie, magazine article or news story, for example, qualifies as content.

Information and entertainment that have already been produced, stored and digitized will form the basic content. Companies that hold the copyrights on information and entertainment can quickly and easily market the content they already own as products, because they don't have to buy the rights to digitize the content. Media companies that already produce content, such as newspaper publishers, book publishers, TV program producers and movie producers, are busy creating and buying more "inventory" for the online world. "Movie companies have been increasing production," says *The Wall Street Journal*, "because there is a general feeling that as 'content providers' they will be big winners.

As information and entertainment products are digitized, they become available in many different formats. This is the reason a music video of Disney songs is available online as soon as a new Disney movie is released; a profile of a well-known musician, complete with video and sound, can be made available online during the musician's worldwide concert tour; and a publisher can assemble excerpts and photos from a new book, along with an interview with the author, and make it available on the communications network as the book hits bookstores. The availability of digital content means all the mass media industries will become interdependent and interconnected.

▶ Development of Communications Technology

The development of communications technology directly affects the speed with which a society evolves. An entire country with only one telephone or one radio may be impossible for people in the United States to imagine, but there still are many countries in which ten families share a single telephone and people consider a television set to be a luxury.

In the United States and other countries such as Japan that have encouraged technological advancements, communication changes are moving faster than ever before. For the media industries, this means increasing costs to replace old equipment. For consumers, this means a confusing array of products that need to be replaced soon after you buy them—DVDs replacing VCRs, for example, and CDs replacing cassettes.

By today's standards, the earliest communications obstacles seem unbelievably simple: how to transmit a single message to several people at the same time and how to share information inexpensively. Yet it has taken nearly 5,500 years to achieve the capability for instant communication that we enjoy today.

3. Mass Media Both Reflect and Affect Politics, Society and Culture

The media industries provide information and entertainment. But media also can affect political, social and cultural institutions. Although the media can actively influence society, they also mirror it, and scholars constantly strive to delineate the differences.

When the advertising industry suddenly started using patriotic themes to market products after the U.S. military moved into Iraq in 2003, was the industry pandering to the public, or were advertisers proudly reflecting genuine American sentiment or both? Did the spread of patriotic advertising themes silence those who disagreed with the government? What role did the mass media play in setting the political agenda? If you were a scholar studying the mass media, how would you view these developments?

This is an example of the difficulty scholars face when analyzing the media's political, social and cultural effects. Early media studies analyzed each message in the belief that once a message was sent, everyone would receive and react to the message in the same way. Then studies proved that different people process messages differently—a phenomenon described as **selective perception**. This occurs because everyone brings many variables—family background, interests and education, for example—to each message.

Selective Perception The concept that each person processes messages differently.

Roughing It, but Not Quite Getting Away from It All

by Tom McNichol

Olema, Calif.—Ah, the sounds of the great outdoors: the rustle of ancient oaks, the chirp of a songbird nesting above your campsite, and somewhere, far in the distance, the screech of a modem connecting to the Internet. At the Olema Ranch Campground, 35 miles north of San Francisco at the edge of Point Reyes National Seashore, Internet access is just another campsite amenity, like firewood or a laundry room. Guests with a computer can go online by plugging into a communal phone jack just outside the camp's general store. . . .

Connected campgrounds like Olema Ranch (www.olemaranch.com) have become popular by catering to vacationers who want to get away from it all while still keeping up with e-mail. . . . At Olema Ranch, guests with a wireless-enabled computer can also get online through a Wi-Fi network without leaving their tents or RVs. An antenna for the wireless system sits atop the camp clubhouse. . . .

© Copyright 2003 by Peter DeSilva

Eddy Mulyono of Castro Valley, Calif. uses a Wi-Fi network to go online on his laptop at the Olema Ranch Campground.

"I spent a lot of money completely revamping our computer system and installing the wireless network, but I feel like it's been worth it from the reaction we've gotten," says Noreen Urquart, owner of Olema Ranch. "A lot of people expect a campground to have Internet access now."

The New York Times, July 31, 2003, p. E-4. Copyright © 2003 by the New York Times Co. Reprinted with permission.

▶ Diverse Audiences Mean Differing Effects

Complicating the study of the media's political, social and cultural effects is the recent proliferation of media outlets. The multiplying sources for information and entertainment mean that, today, very few people share identical mass media environments. This makes it much more difficult for scholars to determine the specific or cumulative effects of mass media on the general population.

Still, scholars' attempts to describe media's political, social and cultural roles in society are important because, once identified, the effects can be observed. The questions should be posed so we do not become complacent about media in our lives, so we do not become immune to the possibility that our society may be cumulatively affected by media in ways we cannot yet identify.

▶ The Importance of Understanding Mass Media Today

Once you understand the mass media separately, you can consider their collective effects. After you understand how each type of media business works, you can examine why people who work in the media make the decisions they do. With this information, you can evaluate the *impact* of these decisions on you and on society.

Media | Review

Getty Images

History

▶ The invention of phonetic writing in 1000 B.C. was considered the *first information communications revolution.*

▶ The invention of movable type in 1455 marked the *second information communications revolution.*

▶ The invention of digital computers in 1951 ushered in the *third information communications revolution.*

Technology

▶ The new world of mass media uses wireless communications technology, an intricate webbed network of many different types of communications systems.

▶ The development of communications technology directly affects the speed with which a society evolves.

▶ Storability, portability and accessibility of information are essential to today's concept of mass communication.

▶ Today, communication changes are moving faster than ever before. For the media industries, this means increasing costs to replace old equipment. For consumers this means a confusing array of products.

Business

▶ The new information network uses broadcast, telephone, cable, satellite and computer technology.

▶ The current delivery system for information and entertainment is primarily a one-way system.

▶ The new communications network is a two-way system.

▶ The ability to talk back—to receive as well as transmit messages—makes the telephone interactive.

▶ The new communications network is interactive.

▶ The new communications network needs content, two-way digital communication and digital storage.

▶ Cable companies, satellite services and/or telephone companies will deliver services on the new communications network.

▶ All U.S. media are privately owned except the Public Broadcasting Service (PBS) and National Public Radio (NPR), which survive on government support and private donations.

▶ Overall, American mass media ownership has been contracting rather than expanding, with fewer companies owning more aspects of the media business. This trend is called *concentration of ownership.*

▶ Concentration of ownership takes five forms: chains, broadcast networks, cross-media ownership, conglomerates and vertical integration.

▶ The mass media industries—books, newspapers, magazines, recordings, radio, movies, television and the Internet—earn about $300 billion a year.

▶ Above all, the major goal of the American mass media is to make money. Except for National Public Radio (NPR) and the Public Broadcasting Service (PBS), all U.S. media operate primarily as profit-centered businesses.

▶ Media acquisitions in the United States have skyrocketed because most conglomerates today are publicly traded companies and because, beginning in 1980, the federal government deregulated the broadcast industry.

▶ The trend of mergers and acquisitions is expected to continue as changing technology expands the global market for media products.

▶ U.S. media industries continue to prosper, but the share of profits is shifting among the different types of media industries.

▶ Advertisers and consumers pay most of the cost for the U.S. media.

Culture

▶ Many Americans already have all the tools that such a system needs to get started—television, telephone, cable and satellite services, and computers.

▶ Information and entertainment that already have been produced, stored and digitized have become the first content on the new network.

▶ Communication is the act of sending ideas and attitudes from one person to another.

▶ *Intra*personal communication means communication within one person.

▶ *Inter*personal communication means communication between two people.

▶ Mass communication is communication from one person or group of persons through a transmitting device (a medium) to large audiences or markets.

▶ Many motives shape the American media, including the desire to fulfill the public's need for information, to influence the country's governance, to disseminate the country's culture, to offer entertainment and to provide an outlet for creative expression.

▶ Different media expand and contract in the marketplace to respond to the audience.

▶ The media are political, social and cultural institutions that both reflect and affect the society in which they operate.

▶ By definition, mass communication is information that is made available to a large audience quickly.

▶ Multiplying sources of information and entertainment mean that, today, very few people share identical mass media environments.

The Impact/Interactive CD-ROM that accompanies this text is your gateway to many electronic resources for broadening and testing your critical understanding of the material in Chapter 1. The CD-ROM features the following interactive elements for this and every chapter in the book.

▶ A two- to three-minute timely, high-interest CNN® Today video clip with critical viewing questions and a link to relevant selections available within the InfoTrac® College Edition database

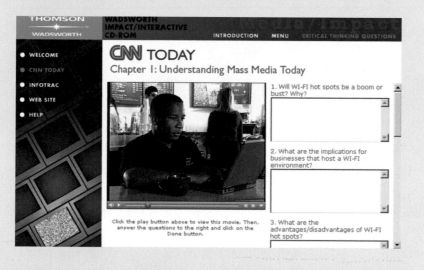

▶ Chapter-specific activities such as personal inventories and media projects

▶ A link to the *Media/Impact* Web site that offers helpful information and many additional electronic learning resources including:

- An interactive chapter outline and study guide

- Interactive glossary term flashcards and crossword puzzles, concept animations, Internet activities and practice quizzes

- Live links for all URLs given in the chapter so you can easily access the additional information each site offers

▶ A link to InfoTrac College Edition—our online database of more than a million articles representing cutting-edge research and the latest headlines. Updated daily, this online library is available 24 hours a day, seven days a week. The InfoTrac College Edition activities provided on pages 30 and 31 are designed to help you use this valuable resource.

▶ Working the Web

Live links for all of the sites listed below are provided on the *Media/Impact* book companion Web site, which can be accessed through your Impact/Interactive CD-ROM.

> ▶ **Time Warner**
> www.timewarner.com
>
> ▶ **Walt Disney (owners of ABC)**
> www.disney.com
>
> ▶ **Gannett Company, Inc. (owners of *USA Today*)**
> www.gannett.com
>
> ▶ **General Electric (owners of NBC)**
> www.ge.com/busindex.htm
>
> ▶ **Media History Project on the Web**
> www.mediahistory.umn.edu
>
> ▶ **Microsoft**
> www.microsoft.com

▶ InfoTrac College Edition Activities

Using InfoTrac College Edition's online database of full-text articles and abstracts, do the following activities as directed by your instructor. The database can be accessed through your Impact/Interactive CD-ROM.

1. Using InfoTrac College Edition, type in the keyword "wireless media" and read at least three articles about the impact of wireless technological developments on society. As you read the articles, decide whether you think wireless media technologies make life simpler or more complex. Do wireless technologies really give you more information, and more freedom, than wired technologies? How? Write a brief paper on your findings and be prepared to discuss the issue in class.

2. Using InfoTrac College Edition, type in the keywords "media conglomerate" or "concentration of media ownership" and read at least three articles that discuss concentration of media ownership and its effect on consumer access to information. Print the articles and either:

   a. write a brief paper on your findings, or

   b. bring the articles to class for a small-group discussion of the pros and cons of concentrated media ownership.

3. Using InfoTrac College Edition, type in the keywords "media convergence" and read at least three articles that discuss issues about developing digital technology and the convergence of the communications, computer and electronic media industries. What do the articles tell you about how your career in communications and your lifestyle will be better, or at least different, as these technologies converge in the next decade?

4. Using InfoTrac College Edition, type in the keywords "media deregulation" and read at least three articles on the impact of media deregulation in the last 20 years. Be sure you understand what changes in media ownership are permitted under recent media deregulation. Consider what those potential changes would mean for the variety of information and viewpoints available in the United States. Write a brief paper on your findings and be prepared to discuss the issue in class.

5. Using InfoTrac College Edition, type in the keyword "interactive" and learn more about the advent of consumer interaction with communications organizations and increasing consumer control of the messages they receive. As you read the articles, think about how satisfied you are with your ability to shop or to find information on the Web. If you could tell your television or radio what you want to see or hear, what types of news, advertising or entertainment would you seek? Write a brief paper on your findings and be prepared to discuss the issue in class.

CHAPTER 2

What's Ahead

> "*There are no intelligent, unhappy people in my books.*
>
> *I want to be known as a writer of good entertaining*
>
> *narrative. I'm not trying to be taken seriously by the*
>
> *East Coast literary establishment. But I'm taken very*
>
> *seriously by the bankers.*"
>
> Judith Krantz, author

"I'm not sure I can explain how to write a book," said essayist and author E. B. White, who wrote 19 of them, including *Charlotte's Web*. "First you have to *want* to write one very much. Then, you have to know of something that you want to write about. Then, you have to begin. And, once you have started, you have to keep going. That's really all I know about how to write a book."

The process of writing a book is a little more complex than White suggests, and every year in the United States, publishers produce about 55,000 individual titles. This number includes revised editions of previously published books, but most of the titles are new.

The publishing industry always has been tugged by what publishing scholars Lewis A. Coser, Charles Kadushin and Walter W. Powell call "the culture and commerce of publishing"—the desire to preserve the country's intellectual ideas versus the desire to make money. But a publisher who doesn't make a profit cannot continue to publish books.

Coser and his colleagues describe the four characteristics of book publishing in America today:

1. The industry sells its products—like any commodity—in a market that, in contrast to that for many other products, is fickle and often uncertain.

Today to 1620: Books retain their central place as a mass medium

TODAY
The majority of books are sold through book chains, and audiobooks are the fastest growing category of book sales. E-books also are starting to attract readers.

▼

1999
Publishers target teens with R-rated themes in an attempt to lure them back to reading.

▼

1960
Publishing houses begin to consolidate, concentrating power in a few large corporations, and decreasing the role of small presses and independent booksellers.

▼

1948
New American Library begins publishing serious fiction by African American authors, including Richard Wright, James Baldwin and Lorraine Hansberry.

▼

1939
Robert de Graff introduces Pocket Books, America's first series of paperback books.

▼

1926
Book-of-the-Month Club is founded, increasing the audience for books.

▼

1900
Elementary education becomes compulsory, which means increased literacy and more demand for textbooks.

▼

1891
Congress passes the International Copyright Law of 1891, which requires publishing houses to pay royalties to foreign authors as well as American authors.

continued on next page

Books

2. The industry is decentralized among a number of sectors whose operations bear little resemblance to each other.

3. These operations are characterized by a mixture of modern mass-production methods and craftlike procedures.

4. The industry remains perilously poised between the requirements and restraints of commerce and the responsibilities and obligations that it must bear as a prime guardian of the symbolic culture of the nation.

Many new owners of publishing houses try to bring some predictability to the market. Says Coser, "Publishers attempt to reduce . . . uncertainty . . . through concentrating on 'sure-fire' blockbusters, through large-scale promotion campaigns or through control over distribution, as in the marketing of paperbacks. In the end, however, publishers rely on sales estimates that may be as unreliable as weather forecasts in Maine."

▶ How American Book Publishing Grew

Today, the book publishing industry divides responsibilities among many people. But when Americans first started publishing books, one person often did all the work. Aboard the *Mayflower* in 1620, there were two dogs and 70 adults and only a few books. The Pilgrims were very practical. They brought a map of Virginia and John Smith's *Description of New England,* but the main books they carried were their Bibles.

The first books in the United States were imports, brought by the new settlers or ordered from England after the settlers arrived. In 1638, the colonists set up a press at Cambridge, Massachusetts, and in 1640 they printed America's first book: *The Bay Psalm Book.* As the only book, it became an instant bestseller. There were only about 3,500 families in the colonies at the time, and the book's first printing of 1,750 sold out.

By 1680, Boston had 17 booksellers, but most of the books still came from England. Between 1682 and 1685, Boston's leading bookseller, John Usher, bought 3,421 books. Among the books he ordered were 162 romance novels.

In 1731, Benjamin Franklin decided that Philadelphia needed a library. So he asked 50 subscribers to pay 40 shillings each to a Library Company. The company imported 84 books, which circulated among the subscribers. This circulating library was America's first.

The year after he established the circulating library, Franklin published *Poor Richard's Almanack.* Unlike most printers, who waited for someone to come to them with a manuscript, Franklin wrote his own books. The typical author sought a patron to pay for the book's printing and then sold the book at the print shop where it was published.

▶ Looking for a Wider Audience

To expand readership, early publishers sold political pamphlets, novels, poetry and humor. In addition, three events of the 19th century ensured that the book publishing industry would prosper in the 20th century: passage of the International Copyright Law, formation of publishing houses, and establishment of compulsory education.

Political Pamphlets   The big seller of the 1700s was Thomas Paine's revolutionary pamphlet *Common Sense,* which argued for independence from Great Britain. From January to March 1776, colonial presses published 100,000 copies of Paine's persuasive political argument—one copy for every 25 people in the colonies—a true bestseller. Throughout the Revolutionary War, Paine was America's best-read author.

Novels and Poetry

Political pamphlets became much less important after the new nation was established, and printers turned their attention to other popular reading, especially fiction. Historians credit Benjamin Franklin with selling *Pamela* by Samuel Richardson in 1744, the first novel published in the United States, although it was a British import that first appeared in England in 1740.

Because there was no International Copyright Law, colonial printers freely reprinted British novels like *Pamela* and sold them. It was cheaper than publishing American authors, who could demand royalties. (See International Copyright Law of 1891, below.)

Like other media industries, book publishing has always faced moral criticism. Novels, for example, didn't start out with a good reputation. One critic said that the novel "pollutes the imaginations." Women wrote one-third of all of the early American novels, and women also bought most of them.

Especially popular after the Civil War and before the turn of the century were dime novels, America's earliest paperbacks. Dime novels often featured serial characters, like many of today's mystery novels. The stories and characters continued from one novel to the next. Eventually most of them cost only a nickel, but some early paperbacks were as expensive as 20 cents.

Poetry generally has been difficult to sell, and it is correspondingly difficult for poets to get published. Literary scholar James D. Hart says that although poetry was never as popular as prose, the mid-1800s was "the great era of poetry . . . . It was more widely read in those years than it has been since."

Humor

Humor has been a durable category in book publishing since the days of humorist Mark Twain. Made famous by his *Celebrated Jumping Frog of Calaveras County*, Twain became a one-man publishing enterprise. One reason his books sold well was that he was the first American author to recognize the importance of advance publicity.

Like most books, Twain's novels were sold door-to-door. Sales agents took advance orders before the books were published so that the publisher could estimate how many to print. More than three-fourths of the popular books sold in America before 1900 were sold door-to-door.

International Copyright Law of 1891

Before 1891, publishers were legally required to pay royalties to American authors, but not to foreign authors. This hurt American authors, because books by American authors cost more to publish.

After the International Copyright Law of 1891, all authors—foreign and American—had to give permission to publish their works. For the first time, American authors cost publishing houses the same amount as foreign authors. This motivated publishers to look for more American writers. In fact, after 1894, American writers published more novels in the United States than foreign writers did.

Publishing Houses

Many publishing houses that began in the late 18th century or at some time during the 19th century continued into the 20th century. Nineteenth-

---

Impact | TimeFrame

Today to 1620: Books retain their central place as a mass medium

continued

▼
1776
Thomas Paine publishes the revolutionary pamphlet *Common Sense.*

▼
1731
Benjamin Franklin creates the first lending library.

▼
1640
America's first book, *The Bay Psalm Book*, is printed at Cambridge, Massachusetts.

▼
1620
Imported books arrive in the colonies on the *Mayflower*.

MODERN-DAY BOOK REPORT

© Dan Piraro. Reprinted with special permission of King Feature syndicate.

century book publishing houses were just that—book publishing houses. They were nothing like today's multimedia corporations. These pioneering companies housed all aspects of publishing under one roof: They sought out authors, reviewed and edited copy, printed and then sold the books.

Compulsory Education   By 1900, 31 states had passed compulsory education laws. This was important to book publishing because schools buy textbooks and education creates more people who can read. Widespread public education meant that schools broadened their choices, and textbook publishing flourished. Expanded public support for education also meant more money for libraries—more good news for the publishing industry.

▶ Creating a Mass Market

The first quarter of the 20th century enabled still more publishing houses, such as Simon & Schuster and McGraw-Hill, to meet the public's needs. Publishers that specialized in paperbacks started in the 1930s and 1940s: Pocket Books (1939), Bantam Books (1946) and New American Library (1948).

If you drop a product's price drastically, sales can explode. That's exactly what happened to book publishing with the introduction of book clubs and paperbacks.

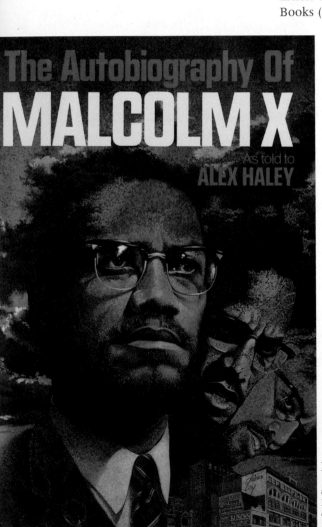

Book Clubs   Book clubs replaced door-to-door sales agents as a way to reach people who otherwise wouldn't buy books. Book-of-the-Month Club was founded in 1926, and Literary Guild in 1927. By 1946, there were 50 book clubs in America, and the Book-of-the-Month Club was selling nearly 12 million copies a year.

Paperbacks   In 1939, Robert de Graff introduced America's first series of paperback bestsellers, called Pocket Books, which issued titles that had already succeeded as hardbound books. They were inexpensive (25 cents), and they fit in a pocket or a purse. Suddenly, a book could reach millions who had never owned a book before. Paperbacks democratized reading in America.

Other publishers joined Pocket Books: New American Library (NAL), Avon, Popular Library, Signet and Dell. NAL distinguished itself by being the first mass market reprinter willing to publish serious books by African American writers—Richard Wright's *Native Son*, Lillian Smith's *Strange Fruit* and Ralph Ellison's *Invisible Man*. Signet's unexpected hit in the 1950s was J. D. Salinger's novel *Catcher in the Rye*, still popular today.

Grove Press Tests Censorship   Book publishers have always resisted any attempts by the government to limit freedom of expression. One of the first publishers to test those limits was Grove Press.

In 1959, Grove published the sexually explicit *Lady Chatterley's Lover* by D. H. Lawrence (originally published in 1928); in 1961, the company published *Tropic of Cancer* by Henry Miller (originally published in Paris in 1934). Both books had been banned as obscene. The legal fees to defend Miller's book against charges of pornography cost Grove more than $250,000, but eventually the U.S. Supreme Court cleared the book in 1964.

Grove Press challenged publishing in 1965 when the company published the controversial book, *The Autobiography of Malcolm X.*

Scott Goodwin Photography, Inc.

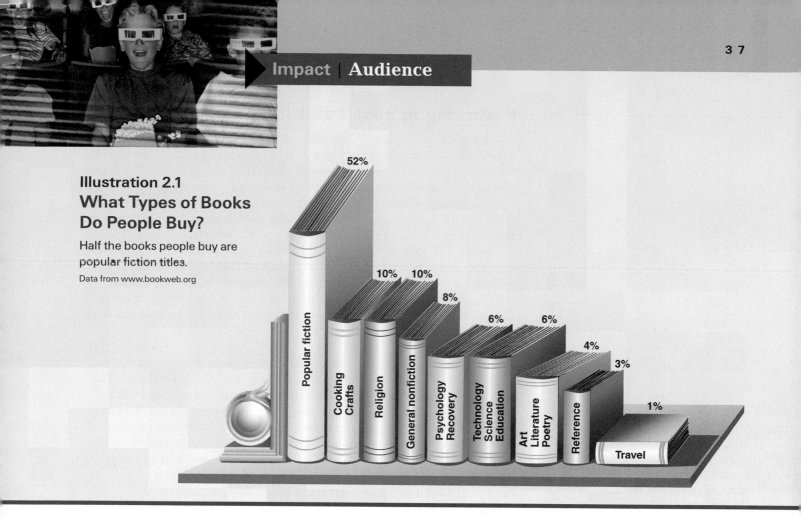

Impact | Audience

Illustration 2.1
What Types of Books Do People Buy?

Half the books people buy are popular fiction titles.

Data from www.bookweb.org

52% Popular fiction
10% Cooking Crafts
10% Religion
8% General nonfiction
6% Psychology Recovery
6% Technology Science Education
4% Art Literature Poetry
3% Reference
1% Travel

The publisher again challenged conventional publishing in 1965, when it issued in hardback the controversial *The Autobiography of Malcolm X*, the story of the leader of the African American nationalist movement.

▶ Book Publishing Consolidates

Forecasts for growing profits in book publishing in the 1960s made the industry attractive to corporations looking for new places to invest. Before the 1960s, the book publishing industry was composed mainly of independent companies whose only business was books. Then, rising school and college attendance from the post-World War II baby boom made some areas of publishing, especially textbooks, lucrative investments for media companies that had not published books before.

Beginning in the 1960s, publishing companies began to consolidate. Publishing expert John P. Dessauer said, "Publishing stocks, particularly those of educational companies, became glamour holdings. And conglomerates began to woo every independent publisher whose future promised to throw off even a modest share of the forecast earnings."

Dessauer acknowledges that the new owners often brought a businesslike approach to an industry that was known for its lack of attention to the bottom line. But, according to Dessauer, another consequence of these large-scale acquisitions was that "in many cases they also placed the power of ultimate decision and policymaking in the hands of people unfamiliar with books, their peculiarities and the markets." The same pace of acquisitions continues today.

▶ Working in Book Publishing

When authors get together, often they tell stories about mistakes publishers have made—about manuscripts that 20 or 30 publishers turned down but that some bright-eyed editor eventually discovered and published. The books, of course, then become bestsellers. Some of the stories are true.

But the best publishing decisions are made deliberately, to deliver an awaited book to an eager market. Successful publishing companies must consistently anticipate both their competitors and the market.

Books must not only be written, they must be printed and they must be sold. This whole process usually takes at least 18 months from the time a project is signed by an editor until the book is published, so publishers are always working ahead. The classic publisher's question is, "Will someone pay $25 (or $5 or $10—whatever the projected price of the book is) for this book 18 months after I sign the author?"

Authors and Agents
Publishers acquire books in many ways. Some authors submit manuscripts "over the transom," which means they send an unsolicited manuscript to a publishing house, hoping the publisher will be interested. However, many of the nation's larger publishers refuse to read unsolicited manuscripts and accept only books that are submitted by agents.

Publishers pay authors a **royalty** for their work. A royalty amount is based on an established percentage of the book's price and may run anywhere from 6 to 15 percent of the cover price of the book. Some authors receive an **advance,** which is an amount the publisher pays the author before the book is published. Royalties earned by the book once it is in print then are charged against the advance payment, so the book first must sell enough copies to pay off the advance before the author receives additional money after the book is published.

Agents who represent authors collect fees from the authors they represent. Typically, an agent's fee is 10 to 15 percent of the author's royalty. If a publisher priced a book at $20, for example, the author would receive from $2 to $3 per book, depending on the author's agreement with the publisher; the agent would then receive 20 to 45 cents of the author's $2 to $3, depending on the agent's agreement with the author.

Today the author is only one part of publishing a book. Departments at the publishing house called *acquisitions, production, design, manufacturing, marketing* and *fulfillment* all participate in the process. At a small publishing house, these jobs are divided among editors who are responsible for all of the steps.

The Publishing Process
The *author* proposes a book to the acquisitions editor, usually with an outline and some sample chapters. Sometimes an agent negotiates the contract for the book, but most authors negotiate their own contracts.

The *acquisitions editor* looks for potential authors and projects and works out an agreement with the author. The acquisitions editor's most important role is to be a liaison among the author, the publishing company and the book's audience. Acquisitions editors also may represent the company at book auctions and negotiate sales of **subsidiary rights,** which are the rights to market a book for other uses—to make a movie, for example, or to print a character from the book on T-shirts.

The *production editor* manages all of the steps that turn a double-spaced typewritten manuscript into a book. After the manuscript comes in, the production editor sets up a schedule and makes sure that all of the work gets done on time.

Royalty   An amount the publisher pays an author, based on an established percentage of the book's price; royalties run anywhere from 6 to 15 percent.

Advance   An amount the publisher pays the author before the book is published.

Subsidiary Rights   The rights to market a book for other uses—to make a movie or to print a character from the book on T-shirts, for example.

Impact | Culture

Luring Today's Teens Back to Books

by Patrick M. Reilly

Books aimed at teenagers, like teen movies and music before them, are increasingly turning R-rated.

Book publishers want to combat the age-old problem they call "the gap." That's the point in their mid-teens when formerly avid readers of series like "Babysitters Club" and "Goosebumps" suddenly drop books for school sports, parties and homework. . . .

That's why publishers are launching risky campaigns to try to get and keep the attention of teens. They're introducing titles that venture into dark areas of drug use and casual sex . . . .

"When you are competing with TV, movies and videos, you have to keep up. And if being slightly provocative is the way to do it, it is probably OK," says Kara Welsh, who oversees the MTV Books line for Pocket Books.

"Teenagers today don't fit neatly into old categories about childhood," adds Marc Aronson, a senior editor at Henry Holt, a unit of Germany's von Holtzbrinck Group . . . .

Holt had a success with *Smack*, an unflinching look at British youth on the dole and lost in a world of drugs. Steve

In an attempt to lure a younger audience, books for teens are taking on edgier themes.

Geck, director of children's books for the Barnes & Noble book chain, says that *Smack*, which won two major fiction awards in the U.K., did "very well," selling roughly what a good hardcover fiction title for adults might.

Amazon.com, Inc., the largest Internet bookseller, plans to unveil a separate teen area with its own bestseller list and featured titles. It will be labeled "teen," not "young adult," a term that publishers have found is a big turnoff for teens.

The Wall Street Journal, March 24, 1999, B1. Reprinted by permission.

The *designer* decides what a book will look like, inside and out. The designer chooses the typefaces for the book and determines how the pictures, boxes, heads and subheads will look and where to use color. The designer also creates a concept—sometimes more than one—for the book's cover.

The *manufacturing supervisor* buys the typesetting, paper and printing for the book. The book usually is sent outside the company to be manufactured.

Marketing, often the most expensive part of creating a book, is handled by several different departments. *Advertising* designs ads for the book. *Promotion* sends the book to reviewers. Sales representatives visit bookstores and college campuses to tell book buyers and potential adopters about the book.

Fulfillment makes sure that the books get to the bookstores on time. This department watches inventory so that if the publisher's stock gets low, more books can be printed.

Book designers use digital technology to help them create a book's interior and exterior appearance.

▶ The Business of Book Publishing

Twenty thousand American companies call themselves book publishers today, but only about 2,000 publishing houses produce more than four titles a year. Most publishing houses are small: 80 percent of all book publishers have fewer than 20 employees.

Today, fiction accounts for about half of all books sold. The rest are nonfiction, such as biography, economics and science. The number of new books and new editions has stabilized, but the per-copy price is going up. Today, paperbacks and hardbacks cost nearly three times what they cost in 1977.

Books fall into six major categories. These classifications once described the publishing houses that produced different types of books. A company that was called a textbook publisher produced only textbooks, for example. Today, many houses publish several different kinds of books, although they may have separate divisions for different types of books and markets.

Trade Books   These are books designed for the general public, usually sold through bookstores and to libraries. Trade books include hardbound books and trade (or "quality") paperbound books for adults and children.

Typical trade books include hardcover fiction, current nonfiction, biography, literary classics, cookbooks, travel books, art books and books on sports, music, poetry and drama. Many college classes use trade books as well as textbooks. Juvenile trade books can be anything from picture books for children who can't read yet to novels for young adults.

Religious Books   Hymnals, Bibles and prayer books fall into this category. Recently, religious publishers have begun to issue books about social issues from a religious point of view, but these books are considered trade books, not religious books.

Professional Books   These are directed to professional people and are specifically related to their work. Professional books fall into three subcategories. *Technical and science books* include the subjects of biological and

Some Best-Seller Old Reliables Have String of Unreliable Sales

by Bill Goldstein

Some of America's most popular authors are finding that being big isn't what it used to be.

Tom Clancy, Stephen King, Mary Higgins Clark and Sue Grafton, usually among the most bankable of best-selling writers, sold far fewer of their books than expected this past year . . . .

"Brand name authors still dominate the best-seller lists. They are still the bread and butter of the industry," said Laurence J. Kirschbaum, chief execu-tive of the AOL Time Warner Book Group . . . . But a change is afoot, he said. "There is no longer a quintessen-tial best seller. The market is diluted to come extent by the incredible number of brand-name authors out at the same time."

And some retailers and publishing industry executives blame publishers for giving readers too much of the same thing by individual authors. Mr. King released two horror books in 2002, and Ms. Clark, the suspense novelist, published three . . .

One retailing executive insisted that the downturn was not because of the economy. "Too many authors are cranking out at least a book a year," the executive said. "Readers can't keep up. It's the bottom-line pressure to be on schedule, to deliver at least a book a year. You have 10 percent of people saying, I can wait for the paperback or wait until I hear more about it. And then they may not buy."

The New York Times, January 1, 2003, C-1. Copy-right © 2003 by The New York Times Co. Reprinted with permission.

Eroding Appeal

The recent books of some-best selling authors have not done as well as their previous titles.

	WEEKS ON THE NEW YORK TIMES BEST SELLER LIST	LAST TIME ON LIST
Steven King		
From a Buick 8	11	1/12/03
Everything's Eventual	11	6/16/02
Black House	15	1/13/02
Dreamcatcher	15	7/15/01
Hearts in Atlantis	16	1/16/01
The Girl Who Loved Tom Gordon	18	8/22/99
Bag of Bones	20	3/17/99
Tom Clancy		
Red Rabbit	17	1/12/03
The Bear and the Dragon	21	1/28/02
Rainbow Six	25	2/14/99
Executive Orders	24	2/9/97
Debt of Honor	25	2/19/95
Mary Higgins Clark		
Daddy's Little Girl	9	6/30/02
On the Street Where You Live	12	7/22/01
Before I Say Goodbye	12	7/30/00
We'll Meet Again	13	8/8/99
You Belong to Me	12	7/19/98

earth sciences as well as technology. They may be designed for engineers or scientists, for example. *Medical books* are designed for doctors and nurses and other medical professionals. *Business and other professional books* are addressed to business people, librarians, lawyers and other professionals not covered in the first two categories.

Mass Market Paperbacks   Here, definitions get tricky. These books are defined not by their subjects but by where they are sold. Although they also can be found in bookstores, **mass market books** are mainly distributed through "mass" channels—newsstands, chain stores, drugstores and supermarkets—and usually are "rack-sized." Many are reprints of hardcover trade books; others are originally published as mass market paperbacks. Generally, they're made from cheaper paper and cost less than trade paperbacks.

Mass Market Books   Books distributed through "mass" channels— newsstands, chain stores, drugstores and supermarkets.

Textbooks   These books are published for elementary and secondary school students (called the "el-hi" market) as well as for college students. Most college texts are paid for by the students but are chosen by their professors.

Very little difference exists between some college texts and some trade books. The only real difference between many textbooks and trade books is that texts include what publishers call *apparatus*—for example, test questions and summaries. The difference may be difficult to discern, so the Association of American Publishers classifies these two types of books (that is, trade books and textbooks) according to where they are sold the most. A book that is sold mainly through college bookstores, for example, is called a textbook.

University Press Books   A small proportion of books are published every year by university presses. These books are defined solely by who publishes them: A university press book is one that is published by a university press. Most university presses are nonprofit and are connected to a university, museum or research institution. These presses produce mainly scholarly materials in hardcover and softcover. Most university press books are sold through direct mail and in college bookstores.

▶ Corporations Demand Higher Profits

The result of consolidation is that the giants in today's publishing industry are demanding increasingly higher profits. The companies look for extra income in three ways: subsidiary rights, blockbuster books and chain bookstore marketing.

Subsidiary Rights   Trade and mass market publishers are especially interested in, and will pay more for, books with the potential for subsidiary-rights sales. The rights to make a CD-ROM version of a book, for example, are subsidiary rights. In the 19th century, a hardcover trade book's profit was determined by the number of copies sold to individual readers. Today, profits come from the sale of subsidiary rights to movie companies, book clubs, foreign publishers and paperback reprint houses. The same rights govern whether a book character becomes a star on the front of a T-shirt. For some publishing houses, subsidiary-rights sales are the difference between making a profit and going out of business.

Blockbusters   Selling a lot of copies of one book is easier and cheaper than selling a few copies of many books. This is the concept behind publishers' eager search for **blockbuster** books. Publishers are attracted to

Blockbuster   A book that achieves enormous financial success.

Impact | **Business**

Illustration 2.3
How Do Book Publishers Make Their Money?

Trade books and mass market paperbacks represent the glamour of the book industry and account for 34 percent of all books sold.

Data from *Veronis, Suhler Stevenson Communications Industry Forecast, 2003–2007.*

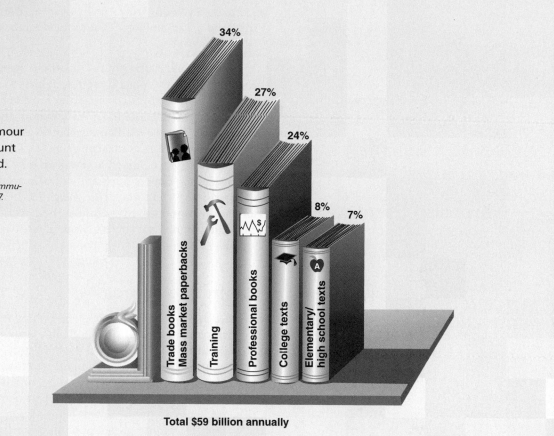

Total $59 billion annually

best-selling authors because they usually are easy to market. There is a "brand loyalty" among many readers that draws them to buy every book by a favorite author, so publishers try to capitalize on an author's readership in the same way movie producers seek out stars who have made successful films.

Judith Krantz, who received $3.2 million for her sex-filled *Princess Daisy,* explained the benefits of being a blockbuster author: "I'm no Joan Didion— there are no intelligent, unhappy people in my books. I want to be known as a writer of good, entertaining narrative. I'm not trying to be taken seriously by the East Coast literary establishment. But I'm taken very seriously by the bankers."

Following are some amounts that publishers and moviemakers paid for blockbusters:

- Hillary Rodham Clinton received an $8 million advance for her memoir, *Living History.*

- Mystery writer Mary Higgins Clark received $35 million in advance from Simon & Schuster for her next six books. Simon & Schuster says that 22 million copies of Clark's books are in print in the United States.

- Random House paid $6.5 million in advance for General Colin Powell's autobiography. Powell served as Chairman of the Joint Chiefs of Staff during the Gulf War and as Secretary of State during the Iraq War and figured prominently in both military actions.

- Michael Crichton, author of *Jurassic Park,* received $2.5 million from Time Warner for the film rights to his next book. This amount tied the record paid for movie rights to John Grisham's *The Client.*

- Tom Clancy, who wrote *The Hunt for Red October* and *Patriot Games,* also received a $2.5 million advance for the film rights to his new novel *Without Remorse.*

Only the big publishing houses can afford such a bidding game. Some publishers have even developed computer models to suggest how high to bid for a book, but these high-priced properties are a very small part of book publishing, perhaps 1 percent. The majority of editors and writers rarely get involved in an argument over seven-figure advances. Many authors would be pleased to see five-figure advances in a contract.

Some critics believe that what has been called a blockbuster complex among publishing houses hurts authors who aren't included in the bidding. One Harper & Row editor told *The Wall Street Journal* that seven-figure advances "divert money away from authors who really need it and center attention on commercial books instead of less commercial books that may nonetheless be better. God help poetry or criticism."

▶ Chain Bookstores

The most significant change in book marketing in the past 30 years has been the growth of book chains. The big chains, such as Borders and Barnes & Noble, account for more than half the bookstore sales of trade books. They have brought mass-marketing techniques to the book industry, offering book buyers an environment that is less like the traditional cozy atmosphere of a one-owner bookstore and more like a department store.

"The large chains are the power behind book publishing today," says Joan M. Ripley, a former president of the American Booksellers Association. "Blockbusters are going to be published anyway, but with a marginal book, like a volume of poetry, a chain's decision about whether to order it can sometimes determine whether the book is published."

Discount chains are another factor in book marketing. Discount chains buy in huge volume, and they buy books only from publishers that grant them big discounts. Books that are published by smaller publishing houses, which usually cannot afford these large discounts, never reach the discount chain buyer. But for the blockbusters, issued by bigger houses, the discount chain is just one more outlet.

Like the resistance to book clubs when they were first introduced, the skepticism among book publishers about chain bookstores has changed into an understanding that chain stores in shopping malls have expanded the book market to people who didn't buy very many books before. But a major unknown factor is what happens when a small number of companies control the distribution of an industry's products.

▶ Small Presses Challenge Corporate Publishing

The nation's large publishing houses (those with 100 or more employees) publish 80 percent of the books sold each year, but many of the nation's publishers are small operations with fewer than ten employees. These publishers are called *small presses,* and they counterbalance the corporate world of large advances and multimedia subsidiary rights.

Small presses do not have the budgets of the large houses, but their size means they can specialize in specific topics, such as the environment or bicy-

Digital Books Down, But Not Out

by Franklin Paul, Reuters on AOL

Readers hungry for a good page-turner will still turn to bookstores and libraries, but cheaper computers and changing consumer habits suggest that electronic books, or e-books, still have a future . . . .

As with digital music, multiple books—say, Shakespeare's collected works—can be stored on a memory card the size of a stick of gum, making them popular with travelers, students and professionals. They are read on handheld devices running operating systems by Palm or Microsoft or on a PC or notebook computer.

E-books may find their niche with tech-savvy youth unfazed by the notion of browsing literature on a screen and the growing legion of retirement-age readers, according to Richard Doherty, research director at Envisioneering Group.

"Two audiences that will benefit best are young people who loathe the

Scott Goodwin Photography, Inc.

Electronic books offer links to databases for delivery of book content on a small screen.

idea of a library . . . and aging people who want the convenience of large type on demand," or freedom from lugging heavy hardcover tomes . . . .

"We think that in the long term, e-book technology has a great future,"

said Adobe's Russell Brady. "Market acceptance has not taken off quite as quickly as was predicted, but we are certainly continuing to invest in this area."

Reuters, September 15, 2003 on AOL. Reprinted with permission.

Critical Question

What are, or might be, some of the disadvantages of electronic books? In which situations do the advantages outweigh the disadvantages? Explain.

cling, for example, or specific types of writing that are unattractive to large publishers, such as poetry.

Small presses are, by definition, alternative. Many of them are clustered together in locations outside of the New York City orbit, such as Santa Fe, New Mexico, and Santa Barbara, California. The book titles they publish probably are not familiar: *Bicycle Technology: Technical Aspects of the Modern Bicycle* by Rob Van der Plas, published by Bicycle Books; *Nine-in-One, Grr! Grr!*, a Hmong folktale by Blia Xiong and Cathy Spagnoli, published by Children's Book Press; *Warning! Dating May Be Hazardous to Your Health* by Claudette McShane, published by Mother Courage Press; or *48 Instant Letters You Can Send to Save the Earth* by Write for Action, published by Conari Press.

Still, some small presses and some small press books are quite successful. One example of a small press success is *The Lemon Book* by Ralph Nader and Clarence Ditlow. This step-by-step guide to buying a car and what to do if you get a bad one grabbed the attention of the *Larry King Show*, *Good Morning America*, and more than 50 other local TV and radio programs. The book sold 42,000 copies in its first year. As *The Lemon Book* demonstrates, specialization and targeted marketing are the most important elements of small press success.

▶ Technology Transforms the Future

Technology is a major factor in most aspects of book publishing. Because books cost so much to publish, any advances in technology that lower production costs benefit the industry. Several changes are happening:

1. Computers already can monitor inventories more closely so that publishers can order a new printing of a book that is running low in stock.

2. Book publishing is an on-screen industry. Publishers now receive manuscripts from authors electronically via the Internet. These manuscripts are edited on a computer and then sent into production by computer, the same process used at newspapers.

3. Electronic graphics make books more interesting to look at, and many book publishers are using CDs and Web sites to produce expanded versions of traditional books and to add materials that enhance a book's content and marketability.

4. Publishers are using Web sites to promote their books and to advertise blockbusters.

5. Although the larger publishers are still buying one another, the number of small publishers that issue fewer than 20 books a year is increasing. New York is still the center of book publishing, but the number of houses based in the East is declining. Seven percent of the country's book publishers are now in California, and that percentage is growing.

6. Always looking for more income from the content they own, book publishers are very successfully producing many books as audiobooks and electronic books (e-book). (See Impact/Culture on page 45.)

E-Books Electronic books.

Audiobooks, first introduced in the 1980s, have been a growing sales category for book publishers. Book publishers produce classics and popular new titles on tapes and CDs for people who are more willing to listen to a book than to read it.

Books on tape and CD are necessarily abridged copies of the originals because it takes too much space to record the entire book. One answer for longer books may be MP3 technology, originally used on the Internet to share music.

In the future, formats such as MP3 may mean consumers can download books, for a fee, from the Internet to be played in a handheld appliance designed to play and record MP3 files. A CD recorded in the MP3 format would hold 48 hours of playback, ten times more than a standard CD.

Because book publishing has been in America's culture so long, the contrast between book publishing's simple beginnings and its complicated corporate life today is especially stark. This may be because Americans maintain a mistaken romantic idea about book publishing's early days, according to the authors of *The Culture and Commerce of Publishing*.

"The myth is widespread that book publishing in the 19th and 20th centuries was a gentlemanly trade in which an editor catered to an author's every whim . . . . There once may have been more gentlemen in publishing than there are now, but there were surely sharp operators, hucksters, and pirates galore. In publishing, as in many other spheres of social life, there is very little that is new."

"What's that book everybody's listening to?"

Media | Review

© Mark Mainz/Getty Images

History

▶ The first *book* printed in America was *The Bay Psalm Book*, printed in 1640.

▶ The first *novel* published in the United States was *Pamela*, printed by Benjamin Franklin.

▶ The International Copyright Law of 1891 expanded royalty protection to foreign writers, which also benefited American authors.

▶ The formation of publishing houses in the 18th and 19th centuries centralized the process of producing books.

▶ Early book clubs, such as Book-of-the-Month, also expanded the market for books and widened the audience.

Technology

▶ Computer technology and desktop publishing are changing the way books are published, lowering the cost, streamlining the process and creating new products, such as CDs, for book publishers.

▶ Electronic books (e-books) offer digital copies of thousands of titles instantly.

▶ Electronic graphics make today's books more interesting to read.

▶ Audiobooks in MP3 format allow consumers to download and purchase book files on the Internet and listen to books on their computers or a specialized MP3 player.

Business

▶ The process of publishing a book usually takes at least 18 months from the time an author is signed until the book is published.

▶ The six departments at a publishing house are: acquisitions, production, design, manufacturing, marketing and fulfillment.

▶ American book publishers produce about 55,000 titles every year. Most of these are nonfiction.

▶ Books can be grouped by six categories: trade books, religious books, professional books, mass market paperbacks, textbooks and university press books.

▶ Before the 1960s, the book publishing industry was composed mainly of independent companies whose only business was books. Publishing company consolidation began in the 1960s, and this pattern of consolidation continues today.

▶ To reduce their risks, many publishers look for blockbuster books (and best-selling authors), that they can sell through large-scale promotion campaigns.

▶ Publishers are especially interested in books with subsidiary rights potential.

▶ Small presses are, by definition, alternative.

Culture

▶ Early publishers widened their audience by publishing political pamphlets, novels, poetry and humor.

▶ The adoption of compulsory education throughout the United States was important for book publishing because schools buy textbooks and education creates more people who can read.

▶ Grove Press challenged book censorship by publishing *Lady Chatterley's Lover* in 1959 and *Tropic of Cancer* in 1961. Both books had been banned in the United States as obscene.

Impact | Interactive

The Impact/Interactive CD-ROM that accompanies this text is your gateway to many electronic resources for broadening and testing your critical understanding of the material in Chapter 2. The CD-ROM features the following interactive elements.

▶ A two- to three-minute timely, high-interest CNN Today video clip with critical viewing questions and a link to relevant selections available within the InfoTrac College Edition database

▶ Chapter-specific activities such as personal inventories and media projects

▶ A link to the *Media/Impact* Web site that offers helpful information and many additional electronic learning resources including:

• An interactive chapter outline and study guide

• Interactive glossary term flashcards and crossword puzzles, concept animations, Internet activities and practice quizzes

• Live links for all URLs given in the chapter so you can easily access the additional information each site offers

▶ A link to InfoTrac College Edition—our online database of more than a million articles representing cutting-edge research and the latest headlines. Updated daily, this online library is available 24 hours a day, seven days a week. The InfoTrac College Edition activities provided below are designed to help you use this valuable resource.

▶ Working the Web

Live links for all of the sites listed below are provided on the *Media/Impact* book companion Web site, which can be accessed through your Impact/Interactive CD-ROM.

▶ **Amazon.com**
www.amazon.com

▶ **American Booksellers Association**
www.bookweb.org/aba

▶ **American Booksellers Foundation for Free Expression**
www.abffe.org

▶ **Association of American Publishers**
www.publishers.org

▶ **Barnes & Noble**
www.barnesandnoble.com

▶ **Bookfinder**
www.bookfinder.com

▶ InfoTrac College Edition Activities

Using InfoTrac College Edition's online database of full-text articles and abstracts, do the following activities as directed by your instructor. The database can be accessed through your Impact/Interactive CD-ROM.

1. Read "Impact/Culture: Luring Today's Teens Back to Books" in Chapter 2. Then using InfoTrac College Edition, look up "young adult literature" or "teen books" and find at least two articles about what publishing companies are doing to attract teenage readers/buyers. As you read, consider why young adult and teenage readers are so important to book publishers. Also consider why young adult and teenage readers, as opposed to older book readers/buyers, require different reading material and different book promotions. Write a brief paper on your findings and be prepared to discuss the issue in class.

2. Chain bookstores have grown tremendously in America. Using InfoTrac College Edition, look up "chain bookstores" or one particular chain ("Barnes & Noble, Inc." or "Borders," for example) and read at least three articles about how chain bookstores operate and the impact they have had on book reading. Do the articles tell you what chain bookstores do for readers (and for books) that other bookstores can't or don't do? What can smaller bookstores do for book readers and customers that chain bookstores can't or don't do? Write a brief paper on your findings and be prepared to discuss the issue in class

3. Using InfoTrac College Edition, use the keywords "small press" to examine publication opportunities for authors and special interest books. Read at least three articles on the topic, and consider the following questions: If you wrote a book as a new author, where would you try to place it first: With a large, established publisher or with a small press? Why? Would the subject or genre of your book make a difference in who you would approach to publish your book? If your first book is successful, where would you try to place your second? Write a brief paper on your decision and the reasons for it and be prepared to discuss the issue in class.

4. Using InfoTrac College Edition, type in the keywords "subsidiary rights" and/or "ancillary rights" to learn more about the profit potential beyond book sales. Read at least three articles, and either:

   a. write a brief paper on your findings, or

   b. bring the articles to class for a small-group discussion.

5. Read "Impact/Culture: Digital Books Down But Not Out" in Chapter 2. Then, using InfoTrac College Edition, look up the keyword "e-book" or "electronic book" and read at least three articles on the emerging e-book industry. As you read the articles, consider whether e-books will make more knowledge available to readers and whether e-books will give readers greater freedom to read when and where we want: Is there a downside to e-books? Write a brief paper on your findings and be prepared to discuss the issue in class.

What's Ahead

In 1882, Harrison Gray Otis bought a 25 percent share of the *Los Angeles Times* for $6,000. In 2000, the Chandler family (Otis' descendants) sold the *Los Angeles Times*, *Newsday*, the *Baltimore Sun* newspapers, the *Hartford Courant* and other newspapers and media properties they owned to the Tribune Company, based in Chicago. The sale was valued at $6 billion.

The success of Times Mirror demonstrates the rapid growth of newspapers since their beginnings in the United States more than three centuries ago. American newspapers began in colonial America as one-page sheets that consisted primarily of announcements of ship arrivals and departures and old news from Europe.

Today's large urban newspapers such as the *Los Angeles Times* rely on satellite-fed information, and these papers often run to 500 pages on Sunday. (*The New York Times* holds the record for the largest single-day's newspaper. On November 13, 1987, the *Times* published a 1,612-page edition that weighed 12 pounds.)

Today to 1690: Newspapers adapt to maintain their audience share

TODAY
Newspapers use color, graphics and creative information design to grab readers' attention, and most newspapers offer Internet editions with interactive news features.

▼

1990S
Newspapers launch special sections to appeal to declining audiences— teens and women.

▼

1982
Gannett creates *USA Today,* using a splashy format and color throughout the paper.

▼

1950
Newspaper readership begins to decline following the introduction of television.

▼

1900
One-third of the nation's newspapers follow the popular trend toward yellow journalism.

▼

1827
John B. Russwurm and the Reverend Samuel Cornish launch *Freedom 's Journal,* the nation's first black newspaper.

▼

1734
John Peter Zenger is charged with sedition. While he is in jail, his wife, Anna Zenger, continues to publish *The New York Weekly Journal,* making her America's first woman publisher.

▼

1721
James Franklin publishes the *New England Courant,* the first newspaper to appear without the Crown's "By Authority" sanction.

▼

1690
Publick Occurrences, America's first newspaper, is published.

Newspapers

▶ What Is Newsworthy?

Technological developments in the 20th century changed the role that newspapers play in the delivery of news. Newspapers were the only mass medium for the timely delivery of news from 1690 until the introduction of radio in 1920. For more than 200 years, newspapers were the only way for large numbers of people to get the same news simultaneously. There was no competition.

The invention of broadcasting in the early 20th century changed newspapers' exclusive access to news. Broadcasting offered instant access to information. Yet, despite increasing competition for its audience, newspapers continue to be a significant source of information and news.

The newspaper industry also historically has played an important role in defining the cultural concept of an independent press, based on the belief that the press must remain independent from government control to fulfill its responsibility to keep the public informed. Concepts about what the public should know, when they should know it, and who should decide what the public needs to know developed in America during a time when newspapers were the main focus of these discussions.

▶ Toward an Independent Press

The issue of government control of newspapers surfaced early in the history of the colonies. At first, newspapers were the mouthpieces of the British government and news was subject to British approval. The British government subsidized many colonial newspapers, and publishers actually printed "Published by Authority" on the first page to demonstrate government approval.

The first colonial newspaper angered the local authorities so much that the newspaper issued only one edition. This newspaper, *Publick Occurrences,* which was published in Boston on September 25, 1690, is often identified as America's first newspaper.

The first and only edition of *Publick Occurrences* was just two pages, each the size of a sheet of today's binder paper (then called a half-sheet), and was printed on three sides. Publisher Benjamin Harris left the fourth side blank so that the people could jot down the latest news before they gave the paper to friends. Harris made the mistake of reporting in his first issue that the French king was "in much trouble" for sleeping with his son's wife. Harris' journalism was too candid for the governor and council of the Massachusetts Bay Colony, who stopped the publication four days after the newspaper appeared.

The nation's first consecutively issued (published more than once) newspaper was the *Boston News-Letter,* which appeared in 1704. It was one half-sheet printed on two sides. In the first issue, editor John Campbell reprinted the queen's latest speech, some maritime news, and one advertisement telling people how to put an ad in his paper. Like many subsequent colonial publishers, Campbell reprinted several items from the London papers.

The next challenge to British control came when James Franklin started his own newspaper in Boston in 1721. His *New England Courant* was the first American newspaper to appear without the crown's "By Authority" sanction. *Thus, James Franklin began the tradition of an independent press in this country.*

Benjamin Franklin Introduces Competition

In 1729, Benjamin Franklin moved to Philadelphia and bought the *Pennsylvania Gazette* to compete with the only other newspaper in town, the *American Weekly Mercury*, published by Andrew Bradford. The *Pennsylvania Gazette* became the most influential and most financially successful of all the colonial newspapers. In the same print shop that printed the *Gazette*, Franklin published *Poor Richard's Almanack* in 1732, an annual book that sold about 10,000 copies a year for the next 25 years. *Benjamin Franklin proved that a printer could make money without government sanctions or support.*

BOSTONIANS READING THE STAMP ACT.

In New York, John Peter Zenger started the *New-York Weekly Journal* in 1733. The *Journal* continually attacked Governor William Cosby for incompetence, and on November 17, 1734, Zenger was arrested and jailed, charged with printing false and seditious writing. (**Seditious language** is writing that authorities believe could incite rebellion against the government.) While Zenger was in jail, his wife Anna, continued to publish the paper.

Truth Versus Libel: The Zenger Trial

Zenger's trial began on August 4, 1735, nine months after his arrest. His defense attorney argued that truth was a defense against libel, and that if Zenger's words were true, they could not be libelous. (A **libelous statement** is one that damages a person by questioning that person's character or reputation.)

The trial established a *landmark precedent for freedom of the press in America—the concept that truth is the best defense for libel*. If what someone publishes is true, the information cannot be considered libelous. (The issue of libel is discussed in Chapter 14.)

Women's Early Role as Publishers

Colonial women were not encouraged to work outside the home at all. Therefore, women who published newspapers during the colonial period are especially notable because they are among the few examples of women who managed businesses early in the nation's history.

Early colonial women printers, such as Anna Zenger, usually belonged to printing families that trained wives and daughters to work in the print shops. By the time the American Revolution began, at least 14 women had been printers in the colonies. One of these family-trained printers was the first woman publisher.

Elizabeth Timothy became editor of the weekly *South Carolina Gazette* in Charleston when her husband, Lewis, died unexpectedly and their son, Peter, was only 13. Elizabeth Timothy published her first edition on January 4, 1737, under her son's name. Her first editorial appealed to the community to continue to support the "poor afflicted Widow and six small Children." Mother and son ran the paper together until 1746, when Peter formally took over the business.

Birth of the Partisan Press

As dissatisfaction with British rule grew in the colonies, newspapers became political tools that fostered the

Furious colonists reacted to the Stamp Act in 1765 by threatening to stop publication and by printing editions that mocked the tax. The Stamp Act was repealed a year later.

Seditious Language Writing that authorities believe could incite rebellion against the government.

Libel A false statement that damages a person by questioning that person's character or reputation.

debate that eventually led to the colonies' independence. By 1750, 14 weekly newspapers were being published in the colonies.

The Stamp Act

Opposition to the British Stamp Act in 1765 signaled the beginning of the revolutionary period. The Stamp Act taxed publishers a halfpenny for each issue that was a half-sheet or smaller and one penny for a full sheet. Each advertisement was taxed two shillings. All the colonial newspapers, even those loyal to the crown, fought the act.

Many newspapers threatened to stop publication, but only a few of them did. Most editors published editions that mocked the tax. William Bradford III issued the famous tombstone edition of the *Pennsylvania Journal* on October 31, 1765. The front page, bordered in black, was printed showing a skull and crossbones where the official stamp should have been.

The Stamp Act Congress met in New York in October 1765, and adopted the now-familiar slogan, "No taxation without representation." Parliament, facing united opposition from all the colonial publishers, repealed the Stamp Act on March 18, 1766.

Journalists learned to improvise. This press operation, assembled to publish New Mexico's first newspaper, was set up under a juniper tree near Kingston, New Mexico.

The Alien and Sedition Laws

During the early part of the country's history, newspapers often were an outlet for journalists who opposed the new government. The Alien and Sedition Laws, passed by Congress in 1798, were the federal government's first attempt to control its critics. Congress said that anyone who "shall write, print, or publish. . .false, scandalous and malicious writing or writings against the government of the United States, or either house of the Congress of the United States, or the President of the United States," could be fined up to $2,000 and jailed for two years.

Several people went to jail. A Boston publisher was jailed for libeling the Massachusetts legislature. A New York editor was fined $100 and jailed for four months. By 1800, the angry rhetoric had dissipated. The Alien and Sedition Laws expired after two years and were not renewed. However, *throughout American press history, the tradition of an independent press, established by James Franklin in 1721, continued to confront the government's desire to restrain criticism.*

© Bettman/CORBIS

▶ Newspapers Take Advantage of 19th Century Technology

Technological advances of the 19th century—such as cheaper newsprint, mechanized printing and the telegraph—meant that newspapers could reach a wider audience faster than before. Confined to eastern cities and highly educated urban audiences during the 1700s, newspaper publishers in the 1800s sought new readers—from the frontier, from among the nation's growing number of immigrants and from within the shrinking Native American population. This expansion resulted in three new developments for American newspapers: frontier journalism, ethnic and cultural newspapers, and the alternative press.

Frontier Journalism   Gold, silver and adventure lured people west, and when the people arrived they needed newspapers. The *Indiana Gazette*, the *Texas Gazette*, the *Oregon Spectator*, the *Weekly Arizonian* and Colorado's *Rocky Mountain News* met that need, aided by the telegraph, which moved news easily from coast to coast.

The wide-open land beckoned many journalists. The most celebrated journalist to chronicle the frontier was Samuel Clemens, who traveled to Nevada in 1861, prospecting for silver. Clemens didn't find any silver, but a year later the Virginia City *Territorial Enterprise*—the area's largest paper—hired him for $25 a week. Clemens first signed his name as Mark Twain on a humorous travel letter written for the *Enterprise*.

Ethnic and Native American Newspapers   English-language newspapers did not satisfy everyone's needs. In the first half of the 19th century, many newspapers sought to succeed by catering to ethnic and cultural interests. In the early 1800s, Spanish-speaking people in Georgia could read *El Misisipi*. Herman Ridder's German newspaper, *New Yorker Staats-Zeitung*, founded in 1845, was the most successful foreign-language newspaper in the United States. It formed the financial basis for today's Knight-Ridder chain. People outside the mainstream of society, such as Spanish and German immigrants, used newspapers to create a sense of community and ethnic identity.

In the 1800s, Native Americans who had been displaced by the settlers also felt a need to express their culture through a newspaper. As a non-mainstream group, they especially wanted to voice their complaints. On February 21, 1828, the nation's first Native American newspaper appeared. The *Cherokee Phoenix* was edited by a Native American who had been educated at a northern seminary, Elias Boudinot.

The Cherokee nation held exclusive control over the four-page paper, which was printed half in English and half in an 86-character alphabet that represented the Cherokee language. (Authorities shut down the press in 1832 because they felt Boudinot was arousing antigovernment sentiment.)

Dissident Voices: The Early Alternative Press   Two strong social movements—emancipation and women's suffrage—brought new voices to the American Press. This **alternative press** movement signaled the beginning of a significant American journalistic tradition. Newspapers became an outlet for the voices of social protest, a tradition that continues today. (The alternative press also is called the **dissident press**.)

Five early advocates of domestic change who used the press to advance their causes—the abolition of slavery and suffrage for women—were John B. Russwurm, the Reverend Samuel Cornish, Frederick Douglass, Jane Grey Swisshelm and Ida B. Wells.

Russwurm and Cornish, who were African American, started *Freedom's Journal* in 1827 in New York City with very little money. They launched their newspaper to respond to racist attacks in several local newspapers. *Freedom's Journal* lasted for two years and reached only a few readers, but it was the beginning of an African American press tradition that eventually created more than 2,700 newspapers, magazines and quarterly journals.

What has often been called the most important African American pre-Civil War newspaper was Frederick Douglass' weekly *North Star*. "Right is of no Sex—Truth is of no Color—God is the Father of us all, and we are all Brethren" read the masthead. Beginning in 1847, Douglass struggled to support the *North Star* by giving lectures. The newspaper eventually reached 3,000 subscribers in the United States and abroad with its emancipation message.

Like Douglass, Ida B. Wells and Jane Grey Swisshelm campaigned for civil rights. Swisshelm's first byline appeared in 1844 in the *Spirit of Liberty*,

Elias Boudinot published the first Native American newspaper, the *Cherokee Phoenix*, from 1828 to 1832.

Dissident Press   Media that present **alternative** viewpoints that challenge the mainstream press.

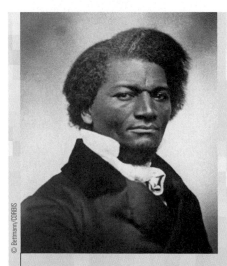

Frederick Douglass, founder of the weekly newspaper *North Star*, is often called the most important African American pre-Civil War newspaper.

Impact | TimeFrame

1889 to 1690: 19th century alternative newspapers evolve to serve a multicultural audience

▼
1889
Ida B. Wells becomes part-owner of the *Memphis Free-Speech and Headlight*, and begins her anti-lynching campaign.

▼
1848
Jane Grey Swisshelm publishes the first issue of the abolitionist newspaper, the *Pittsburgh Saturday Visiter*, which also promoted women's rights.

▼
1847
Frederick Douglass introduces the weekly *North Star*, considered America's most important African American pre-Civil War newspaper.

▼
1827
John B. Russwurm and the Reverend Samuel Cornish launch *Freedom's Journal*, the nation's first black newspaper.

▼
1821
Elias Boudinot launches *The Cherokee Phoenix*.

▼
1808
El Misisipi, America's first Spanish-language newspaper, begins publication in Georgia.

▼
1690
Publick Occurences, America's first newspaper, is published.

Penny Press   A newspaper produced by dropping the price of each copy to a penny and supporting the production cost through advertising.

published in Pittsburgh. Four years later she began her own abolitionist publication, the *Pittsburgh Saturday Visiter*, which also promoted women's rights. (For more information about Ida B. Wells, see Impact/People on page 57.)

As a correspondent for Horace Greeley's *New York Tribune* in Washington, D.C., Swisshelm convinced Vice President Millard Fillmore to let her report from the Senate press gallery. The gallery had been open to male journalists for 55 years, and on May 21, 1850, Swisshelm became the first female journalist to sit in the gallery.

These pioneers—Russwurm, Cornish, Douglass, Wells and Swisshelm—had used newspapers to lobby for social change. These dissident newspapers offered a forum for protest, which is an important cultural role for an independent press.

▶ Making Newspapers Profitable

The voices of social protest reached a limited, committed audience, but most people could not afford to subscribe to a daily newspaper. Newspapers were sold by advance yearly subscription for $6 to $10 at a time when most skilled workers earned less than $750 annually. Then, in 1833, Benjamin Day demonstrated that he could profitably appeal to a mass audience by dropping the price of a newspaper to a penny and selling the paper on the street every day.

Toward Mass Readership: The Penny Press   Day's *New York Sun* published sensational news and feature stories to interest the working class. He was able to lower the price to a penny by filling the paper with advertising and by hiring newsboys to sell the paper on street corners. The first successful **penny paper** reported local gossip, sensationalized police news, and carried a page and a half of advertising in a four-page paper.

Newsboys bought 100 papers for 67 cents and tried to sell them all each day to make a profit. Even *The New York Times*, founded by Henry J. Raymond in 1851, was a penny paper when it began. The legacy of the penny paper continues in today's gossip columns and crime reporting.

▶ Newspapers Dominate the Country

For the first 30 years of the 20th century—before radio and television—newspapers dominated the country. Newspapers were the nation's single source of daily dialogue about political, cultural and social issues. This was also the era of the greatest newspaper competition.

Competition Breeds Sensationalism   In large cities such as New York, as many as ten newspapers competed for readers at once, so the publishers looked for new ways to expand their audience. Two New York publishers—Joseph Pulitzer and William Randolph Hearst—revived and refined the penny press sensationalism that had begun in 1833 with Benjamin Day's *New York Sun*.

Like Benjamin Day, Pulitzer and Hearst proved that newspapers could reap enormous fortunes for their owners. They also demonstrated that credible, serious reporting is not all that people want in a newspaper. Pulitzer and Hearst promoted giveaways and fabricated stories.

An ambitious man who knew how to grab his readers' interest, Joseph Pulitzer published the first newspaper comics and sponsored journalist Nellie Bly on an around-the-world balloon trip to try to beat the fictional record in the popular book, *Around the World in 80 Days*. Bly finished the trip in 72 days, 6 hours and 11 minutes, and the stunt brought Pulitzer the circulation he craved.

Ida B. Wells Uses Her Pen to Fight 19th Century Racism

Ida B. Wells didn't start out to be a journalist, but the cause of emancipation drew her to the profession. Wells, who eventually became co-owner of the *Free Speech and Headlight* in Memphis, Tennessee, documented racism wherever she found it. She is known for her pioneering stand against the unjustified lynching of African Americans in the 1890s.

In 1878, both of Wells' parents and her infant sister died in a yellow fever epidemic, so 16-year-old Wells took responsibility for her six brothers and sisters, attended Rush College and then moved the family to Memphis where she became a teacher.

A Baptist minister, who was editor of the Negro Press Association, hired Wells to write for his paper. She wrote under the pseudonym Iola.

In 1892, Wells wrote a story about three African American men who had been kidnapped from a Memphis jail and killed. "The city of Memphis has demonstrated that neither character nor standing avails the Negro, if he dares to protect himself against the white man or become his rival," she wrote. "We are out-numbered and without arms." While in New York, she read in the local paper that a mob had sacked the *Free Speech* office.

Wells decided not to return to Memphis. She worked in New York and lectured in Europe and then settled in Chicago, where she married a lawyer, Ferdinand Lee Barnett. Ida Wells-Barnett and her husband actively campaigned for African American rights in Chicago, and she continued to write until she died at age 69 in 1931.

The Granger Collection

Ida B. Wells, part-owner of the *Memphis Free Speech* and *Headlight*, wrote under the pseudonym Iola.

In San Francisco, young William Randolph Hearst, the new editor of the *San Francisco Examiner*, sent a reporter to cover Bly's arrival. In 1887, Hearst convinced his father, who owned the *Examiner*, to let him run the paper. Hearst tagged the *Examiner* "The Monarch of the Dailies," added a lovelorn column, and attacked several of his father's influential friends in the newspaper. He spent money wildly, buying talent from competing papers and staging showy promotional events.

Yellow Journalism Is Born: Hearst's Role in the Spanish-American War

In New York, Hearst bought the *New York Journal*, hired Pulitzer's entire Sunday staff and cut the *Journal's* price to a penny, so Pulitzer dropped his price to match it. Hearst bought a color press and printed color comics. Then he stole Pulitzer's popular comic, "Hogan's Alley," which included a character named the Yellow Kid.

Hearst relished the battle, as the *Journal* screamed attention-grabbing headlines such as "Thigh of the Body Found," and the paper offered $1,000 for information that would convict the murderer. Critics named this sensationalism **yellow journalism** after the Yellow Kid, an epithet still bestowed on highly emotional, exaggerated or inaccurate reporting that emphasizes crime, sex and violence. By 1900, about one-third of the metropolitan dailies were following the trend toward yellow journalism.

Beginning in 1898, the Spanish-American War provided the battlefield for Pulitzer and Hearst to act out their newspaper war. For three years, the two newspapers unrelentingly overplayed events in the Cuban struggle for independence from Spain, each trying to beat the other with irresponsible, exaggerated stories, many of them manufactured.

Yellow Journalism News that emphasizes crime, sex and violence; also called **jazz journalism** and **tabloid journalism**.

© Bertmann/CORBIS

© Bertmann/CORBIS

Joseph Pulitzer (top) and William Randolph Hearst (bottom), whose New York newspaper war spawned the term *yellow journalism*.

The overplaying of events that resulted from the sensational competition between Pulitzer and Hearst showed that newspapers could have a significant effect on political attitudes. The Spanish-American War began a few months after the sinking of the U.S. battleship *Maine* in Havana harbor, which killed 266 men. The cause of the explosion that sank the ship was never determined, but Pulitzer's and Hearst's newspapers blamed the Spanish.

Hearst dubbed the event "the *Journal's* War," but in fact Hearst and Pulitzer shared responsibility, because both men had inflamed the public unnecessarily about events in Cuba. *The serious consequences of their yellow journalism vividly demonstrated the importance of press responsibility.*

Tabloid Journalism: Selling Sex and Violence   The journalistic legacy of Day, Pulitzer and Hearst surfaced again in the **tabloid journalism** of the 1920s, also called **jazz journalism**. In 1919, the publishers of the *New York Daily News* sponsored a beauty contest to inaugurate the nation's first tabloid. A **tabloid** is a small-format newspaper, usually 11 inches by 14 inches, featuring illustrations and sensational stories.

The *Daily News* merged pictures and screaming headlines with reports about crime, sex and violence to exceed anything that had appeared before. It ran full-page pictures with short, punchy text. Love affairs soon became big news and so did murders. In the ultimate example of tabloid journalism, a *Daily News* reporter strapped a camera to his ankle in 1928 and took a picture of Ruth Snyder, who had conspired to kill her husband, as she was electrocuted at Sing Sing prison.

Snyder's picture covered the front page, and the caption stated, "This is perhaps the most remarkable exclusive picture in the history of criminology." Photojournalism had taken a sensational turn. Today, yellow journalism's successors are the supermarket tabloids, such as the *National Enquirer*, which feature large photographs and stories about sex, violence and celebrities.

▶ Unionization Encourages Professionalism

The first half of the 20th century brought the widespread unionization of newspaper employees, which standardized wages at many of the nation's largest newspapers.

Labor unions were first established at newspapers in 1800, and the International Typographical Union went national in the mid-1850s. Other unions formed to represent production workers at newspapers, but reporters didn't have a union until 1934, when *New York World-Telegram* reporter Heywood Broun called on his colleagues to organize. Broun became the Newspaper Guild's first president. Today, the Guild continues to cover employees at many of America's urban newspapers. Unions represent roughly one in five newspaper employees.

With the rise of unions, employee contracts, which once had been negotiated in private, became public agreements. In general, salaries for reporters at union newspapers rose, and this eventually led to a sense of professionalism, including codes of ethics.

▶ Newspapers in the Television Era

The invention of television affected the newspaper industry dramatically. Newspaper publishers had learned how to live with only one other 20th century news industry—radio. In the 1920s, when radio first became popular, newspapers refused to carry advertising or time logs for the programs, but eventually newspapers conceded the space to radio.

Right: This 1928 photo of Ruth Snyder's execution exemplifies the screaming headlines and large photographs that still prosper in today's tabloid journalism (left).

In the 1950s, however, television posed a larger threat: television offered moving images of the news, in addition to entertainment. The spread of television demonstrated how interrelated the media were. The newspaper industry relinquished its supremacy as the major news medium and was forced to share the news audience with broadcasting. And over time, television's influence changed both the look and the content of many newspapers.

The Revival of the Alternative Press

The social movements of the 1960s briefly revived one portion of the newspaper industry—the alternative press. Like their 1800s predecessors in the abolitionist and emancipation movements, people who supported the revival of the alternative press in the 1960s felt the mainstream press was avoiding important issues, such as the anti–Vietnam War movement, the civil rights movement and the gay rights movement.

In 1964, as a way to pass along news about the antiwar movement, the *Los Angeles Free Press* became the first underground paper to publish regularly. The *Barb* in Berkeley, California, *Kaleidoscope* in Chicago, and *Quicksilver Times* in Washington, D.C., soon followed. In 1965, Jim Michaels launched the nation's first gay newspaper, the Los Angeles *Advocate*.

What the 1960s underground press proved already had been proven in the 19th century—in America, causes need a voice, and if those voices are not represented in the mainstream press, publications emerge to support alternative views.

Declining Readership

Since the 1970s, the overall number of newspapers has declined. Many afternoon papers died when TV took over the evening news. Other afternoon papers changed to morning papers. Then, newspaper publishers realized television could provide the news headlines, but newspapers could offer the background that television news could not.

Newspaper publishers also began to realize they could play on the popularity of television personalities, who became news items. Eventually, advertisers

Tabloid   a small-format newspaper that features large photographs and illustrations along with sensational stories.

"Actually, I work for a newspaper, but people won't talk to me without it."

realized that viewers cannot clip coupons out of their television sets or retrieve copies of yesterday's TV ads, so advertisers began to use newspapers to complement television advertising campaigns.

Today, the majority of small dailies are part of a chain, and most cities have only one newspaper. And in an attempt to match television's visual displays, newspapers have introduced advanced graphics and vivid color. However, newspapers are still very profitable.

▶ Working for Newspapers

Many colonial publishers handled all of the tasks of putting out a newspaper single-handedly, but today's typical newspaper operation is organized into two separate departments: the editorial side and the business side. The *editorial* side handles everything that you read in the paper—the news and feature stories, editorials, cartoons and photographs. The business side handles everything else—production, advertising, distribution and administration.

On the editorial side at a medium-size daily newspaper, different *editors*—a news editor, a sports editor, a features editor and a business editor, for example—handle different parts of the paper. The managing editor oversees these news departments. A copyeditor checks the reporters' stories before they are set in type, and a layout editor positions the stories. Editorial writers and cartoonists usually work for an editorial page editor. All these people report to the *editor-in-chief* or the *publisher* or both.

A *business manager* and his or her staff run the business side of the paper: getting the paper out to subscribers, selling advertising and making sure the paper gets printed every day. These people also ultimately report to the editor-in-chief or the publisher. Sometimes the publisher is also the owner of the paper. If a corporation owns the paper, the publisher reports to its board of directors.

Almost all newspapers today run Web sites and many newspapers have created New Media departments to introduce strong graphic and video elements to their Internet editions.

▶ The Business of Newspapers

Today, newspapers sell 55 million copies daily, and most adults read a newspaper every day. (See **Illustration 3.1**.) Big-city newspapers are losing readers as people move to the suburbs, and suburban newspapers are growing, as are suburban editions of big-city papers. Newspapers depend primarily on advertising for support. Subscriptions and newsstand sales account for only a small percentage of newspaper income.

Newspaper companies in the 1980s, looking for new ways to make money, rediscovered and expanded on some old ideas. Gannett introduced a new national newspaper with bold graphics and shorter stories in the 1980s, and more newspaper organizations joined the syndication business. Many newspapers introduced Internet editions in the 1990s.

Internet Editions   Most newspaper publishing companies have launched electronic delivery of news and newspapers to capture new audiences for the information they gather. Newspapers arriving on-screen at com-

Impact | Audience

Illustration 3.1
Percentage of Population Who Say They Read a Newspaper Every Day

Who reads newspapers? Although newspaper circulation is holding steady, daily readership is declining—especially among young adults, aged 18 to 24.

Data from the Newspaper Association of America, 2003.

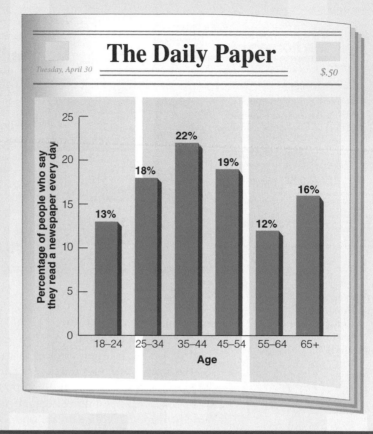

The Daily Paper

Tuesday, April 30 — *$.50*

Percentage of people who say they read a newspaper every day

- 18–24: 13%
- 25–34: 18%
- 35–44: 22%
- 45–54: 19%
- 55–64: 12%
- 65+: 16%

Age

Critical Question

When was the last time you read a printed newspaper? Do you subscribe to any newspapers, either their print or online versions? Why do you subscribe? If you don't read newspapers, how do you get the news?

puters are just part of the reader-friendly future, according to many industry analysts.

Newspapers are trying to generate some income from home and business computer users, and information services, based on the huge archives of newspaper stories, also are becoming easier to use. Many larger newspapers offer the week's news free online, but charge $3 to $5 to retrieve the full text of stories that are older than seven days.

Internet editions publish shorter highlights of the day's news, as well as special features that don't appear in the daily newspaper. Chat rooms offer subscribers the chance to discuss the news, for example, and other interactive features offer Internet links to more information on stories that appear in the Internet edition, archives of past stories plus updated photos and audio and video clips from breaking news events. This is just one way newspapers are trying to retain their audience and advertisers using a new delivery system.

National Newspapers   Of all the nation's group owners, the Gannett newspaper chain has been the biggest gambler. In 1982, Gannett created *USA Today*, which it calls "The Nation's Newspaper," to compete with the country's two other major national newspapers, *The Wall Street Journal* and *The New York Times*. Dubbing it "McPaper" with only "McNuggets" of news,

Newspapers such as the *Chicago Tribune* and the *Honolulu Star-Bulletin* have introduced Internet editions to try to attract advertisers and get more readers.

critics said *USA Today* was the fast-food approach to newspapers. It features expensive color graphics, a detailed national weather report, comprehensive sports coverage and news stories that rarely run longer than 600 words.

USA Today went after a different audience than the *Journal* and the *Times* did—people who don't want to spend a lot of time reading but who like to know the headlines. Someone in an airport or someone who wants something to read on a coffee break, Gannett argued, may not need a paper the size of *The Wall Street Journal* or a large metropolitan daily. Gannett's innovations also have influenced many other newspapers, which have added graphics and color and have shortened the average length of stories.

USA Today, the *Journal* and the *Times* publish regional editions by satellite so that a local bank, for example, can place an ad. Each area's regional edition is distributed in a defined geographic area, so a local advertiser (such as the bank) pays a lower price than someone who advertises nationwide.

USA Today, the *Journal* and the *New York Times* are today's leaders in the competition to become the nation's most successful national newspaper. Each paper has more than 2 million daily readers.

Syndicates News agencies that sell articles for publication to a number of newspapers simultaneously.

Syndicates Newspapers also can add to their content without having to send their own reporters to stories by using **syndicates**, which are news agencies that sell articles for publication to a number of newspapers simultaneously. The first syndicated column was a fashion letter distributed in 1857.

Today, more newspapers are syndicating their columns and features to try to add income. Syndicates mainly provide columnists and comics—Dave Barry, Molly Ivins and Dear Abby, as well as *Dilbert* and *Cathy*, for example. The price of syndicated copy for each newspaper is based on the newspaper's circulation. A large newspaper pays more for syndicated copy than a small newspaper.

▶ Technology Transforms the Future

Since their colonial beginnings, newspapers have shown their ability to appeal to changing audiences, adapt to growing competition and continue to attract advertisers. The Newspaper Association of America and other newspaper analysts describe these advances:

- Reporters and photographers in the field send their stories from laptop computers using wireless technology. Photographers use video and digital cameras, sending their pictures to the newsroom electronically. News photography systems can reproduce still pictures for newspapers from video images and electronic cameras.

- Newspapers are selling more of the information they gather. Once a story is in a digital format, the information can be easily sold to people who want that information: lawyers, researchers and home computer users.

- Satellite publishing is bringing customized national newspapers in regional editions so advertisers will be able to choose their audiences more selectively.

Three other emerging trends that will affect the future of the newspaper industry are the growing challenges by publishers to newspaper unions; the intensifying concentration of chain ownership; and the changing newspaper audience.

Unions Versus Technology

New technology means that machines are doing work formerly done by people. For newspaper unions, this has meant a consistent effort among newspaper owners to challenge union representation.

Before 1970, newspapers needed typographers to hand-set metal type, and labor unions represented most of these typographers. With the introduction of photocomposition, newspaper management slowly moved to eliminate the typographers' jobs. The unions fought the transition, and many newspaper workers went on strike—notably at the *New York Daily News* in 1990, at the *San Francisco Chronicle* and *San Francisco Examiner* in 1994, and at the *Detroit News* in 1996.

With the threat of technology eliminating even more jobs in the future, newspaper unions are understandably worried. Membership in the Newspaper Guild (which covers reporters) has remained steady, but most of the other unions have lost members. Forecasts report that union influence at big-city newspapers will remain strong but that the effort to diffuse union influence at smaller newspapers will continue.

© Reuters

Unionization of newspaper employees began in the 1800s. Unions continue to be a big factor at urban newspapers. Workers at the *Detroit News* walked the picket line in 1996.

Chain Power

Overall newspaper circulation is declining. Instead of editors competing locally within a community, like Hearst battling Pulitzer, national chains now compete with one another (See **Illustration. 3.2**, page 64.)

This doesn't necessarily mean that every newspaper in a chain speaks with the voice of the chain owner. Chains can supply money to improve a newspaper's printing plant and to add more reporters. But critics say the tendency to form chains can consolidate and limit the sources of information for readers. (See Chapter 1 for more discussion of media consolidation.)

Trying to Retain Readers

Although newspapers still hold power for advertisers, recent studies reveal that younger readers are deserting the medium. "It dawned on us that if we don't start luring teenagers into the paper and start them reading us now, they may not subscribe in the future," according to Grant Podelco, arts editor of the Syracuse (New York) *Herald-Journal*.

**Illustration 3.2
Top Ten U.S.
Newspaper Chains**

Data from Paul Kagan Associates, adage.com

The Daily Paper

Tuesday, April 30 $.50

Top 10 U.S. Newspaper Chains

Company

1. Gannett Co., Inc.
2. Tribune Co.
3. Knight-Ridder, Inc.
4. The New York Times
5. Advance Publications, Inc.
6. Dow Jones & Co., Inc.
7. Cox Enterprises
8. Hearst Corp.
9. The McClatchy Co.
10. Medianews Group

To stop the slide among young readers, many newspapers have added inserts directed to, and sometimes written by, teenagers. *The Wall Street Journal* introduced a high school classroom edition. At the *Chicago Tribune*, five teenage film reviewers appear in the newspaper every Friday with their choices, and a "Preps Plus" section covers high school sports. *The Dallas Morning News* runs a half-sheet called "The Mini Page," subtitled "Especially for Kids and Their Families," which carries puzzles, explanatory stories about current issues and a teacher's guide.

Women readers also are abandoning newspapers in unprecedented numbers. Karen Jurgenson, editorial page editor of *USA Today*, says that readership surveys show women today are less likely to be daily newspaper readers than men. "Women across the board are more likely than men to feel that the paper doesn't speak to them," she says.

To attract more female readers, the Charlotte *Observer* created a daycare beat, and some newspapers are attempting to devote more space to women's sports. Newspapers also are experimenting with a section targeted specifically for women. The *Chicago Tribune*, for example, launched a section called "WomaNews." Newspaper executives also blame television and the Internet for the declining audience, but others say people's reading habits reflect the changing uses of family time.

In some cities with large Latino populations, newspapers are expanding the market by publishing Spanish-language editions. In areas like Dallas–Fort Worth, where about a fifth of the population is Latino, newspaper companies see an ever increasing audience with a desire for information.

Dallas-Fort Worth Papers Fight It Out in Spanish

by Simon Romero

A newspaper war is brewing in Texas. Or make that a newspaper per Guerra.

Knight Ridder Inc., the nation's second-largest newspaper publisher after the Gannett Company, said today that it would expand publication of its Spanish-language paper in the Dallas-Fort Worth area, responding to demographic changes in North Texas and increased competition from the Belo Corporation, which owns *The Dallas Morning News* and has announced its own plan for a daily Spanish-language paper. . . .

Both papers will be competing for readers and advertisers in a fast-changing market. Latinos account for 22 percent of the 5.9 million people in the Dallas-Fort Worth metropolitan area, according to Claritas, a demographic market research company in San Diego. Dallas and Fort Worth already have a thriving broadcast market in Spanish. . . .

"The demographics of the market are impossible to ignore," said Gilbert Bailon, president and editor of *Al Dia* and a former executive editor of the *Morning News*. . . .

Both *Al Dia* (loosely translated as "Current" or "Of the Day") and *Diario La Estrella* ("Daily Star") plan to use editorial content from their parent

Left: Courtesy of Diario la Estrella; Right: Reprinted with Permission of Al Dia

organizations as well as from their own editorial staffs. . . "The key is to leverage off the existing English-language product, while preserving the identity of the Spanish-language paper," said Alberto Ibarguen, publisher of *The Herald,* which is providing *La Estrella* with advice and loaning it some if its staff.

The New York Times, August 4, 2003, C-6. Copyright © 2003 by The New York Times Co. Reprinted with permission.

(See Impact/Culture, "Dallas-Fort Worth Papers Fight It Out in Spanish," above.)

Newspapers are competing to maintain their audience because audiences attract advertisers—and profits. The average daily newspaper is about two-thirds advertising, and in some newspapers advertising runs as high as 70 percent.

National advertisers (such as Procter & Gamble) buy television time as much as they buy newspaper space, but for small community businesses nothing works as well as local newspapers. Seventy cents of each local advertising dollar goes to newspapers. There may be fewer newspaper owners in the country, but as long as newspapers can maintain their profitability, the survivors will continue comfortably.

Glenn A. Kaupert/© *The Chicago Tribune*

Media | Review

History

▶ The issue of government control of newspapers surfaced early in colonial America, when the authorities stopped *Publick Occurrences* in 1690, after a single issue, because the paper angered local officials.

▶ The tradition of an independent press in this country began when James Franklin published the first newspaper without the heading "By Authority."

▶ The John Peter Zenger case established an important legal precedent: If what a newspaper reports is true, the paper cannot successfully be sued for libel.

▶ As dissatisfaction grew over British rule, newspapers became essential political tools in the effort to spread revolutionary ideas, including opposition to the British Stamp Act and the Alien and Sedition Laws.

▶ Newspapers spread their reach in the 1800s to include people on the frontier, the growing number of immigrants and the Native American population.

Technology

▶ The technological advances of the 19th century, such as cheaper newsprint, mechanized printing and the telegraph, meant that newspapers could reach a wider audience faster than ever before.

▶ New 19th century technologies also lowered production costs, which made newspaper publishing companies attractive investments.

▶ The introduction of television contributed to a decline in newspaper readership that began in the 1950s.

▶ Most newspaper publishing companies have launched Internet newspapers to capture new audiences for the information they gather.

Business

▶ The penny press made newspapers affordable for virtually every American.

▶ Unionization at newspapers standardized wages for newspaper employees and increased professionalism.

▶ The future financial success of newspapers depends on their ability to appeal to a shifting audience and meet growing competition so they can continue to attract advertisers.

▶ Newspapers still hold power for advertisers, but recent studies reveal that younger readers are deserting the medium faster than any other group. Readership among women also has declined.

Culture

▶ The emancipation and suffrage movements found a voice through the dissident press, which marked the beginning of newspapers as a tool for social protest.

▶ Intense competition bred yellow journalism, which nurtured the sensational coverage of the Spanish-American War in 1889. This underscored the importance of press responsibility.

▶ The social causes of the 1960s briefly revived the alternative press.

▶ To stop the recent slide in readership, many newspapers have introduced features and special sections targeted toward teenagers and women.

Impact | Interactive

The Impact/Interactive CD-ROM that accompanies this text is your gateway to many electronic resources for broadening and testing your critical understanding of the material in Chapter 3. The CD-ROM features the following interactive elements.

▸ A two- to three-minute timely, high-interest CNN Today video clip with critical viewing questions and a link to relevant selections available within the InfoTrac College Edition database

▸ Chapter-specific activities such as personal inventories and media projects

▸ A link to the *Media/Impact* Web site that offers helpful information and many additional electronic learning resources including:

• An interactive chapter outline and study guide

• Interactive glossary term flashcards and crossword puzzles, concept animations, Internet activities and practice quizzes

• Live links for all URLs given in the chapter so you can easily access the additional information each site offers

▸ A link to InfoTrac College Edition—our online database of more than a million articles representing cutting-edge research and the latest headlines. Updated daily, this online library is available 24 hours a day, seven days a week. The InfoTrac College Edition activities provided below are designed to help you use this valuable resource.

▸ Working the Web

Live links for all of the sites listed below are provided on the *Media/Impact* book companion Web site, which can be accessed through your Impact/Interactive CD-ROM.

▸ **American Society of Newspaper Editors**
www.asne.org

▸ **Chicago Tribune**
www.chicagotribune.com

▶ **Dallas Morning News**
www.morningnews.com

▶ **Denver Post**
www.denverpost.com

▶ **Honolulu Star-Bulletin**
http://starbulletin.com

▶ **Los Angeles Times**
www.latimes.com

▶ **Miami Herald**
www.miami.com/herald

▶ **The New York Times**
www.nytimes.com

▶ **Newspaper Association of America**
www.naa.org

▶ **Portland Oregonian**
www.oregonian.com

▶ **Seattle Post-Intelligencer**
http://www.seattlep-i.nwsource.com

▶ **USA Today**
www.usatoday.com

▶ **The Washington Post**
www.washingtonpost.com

▶ InfoTrac College Edition Activities

Using InfoTrac College Edition's online database of full-text articles and abstracts, do the following activities as directed by your instructor. The database can be accessed through your Impact/Interactive CD-ROM.

1. Look up the subject heading "newspaper industry" on InfoTrac College Edition and choose three articles on the industry that interest you. What do the articles tell you about the financial condition of the newspaper industry in the 21st century? Do you believe it will prosper, hold its own or decline in financial strength in the next 10 to 20 years? Why? Write a brief paper on your findings and be prepared to discuss the issue in class.

2. Read Chapter 3 in the textbook and use InfoTrac College Edition to research your choice of the following figures in newspaper history:

   • Benjamin Franklin

   • Ida B. Wells

   • John Peter Zenger

   • Frederick Douglass

   • Mark Twain (Samuel Clemens)

   • William Randolph Hearst

   • Joseph Pulitzer

   Choose two of the historical newspaper figures above. Print at least one article for each about his or her involvement with newspapers and/or journalism. How would newspapers in the United States be different today without the influence of the historic figures that you read about? Bring the articles to class. Be prepared to speak briefly about the people you have selected, and/or find more sources about one of the people and write a detailed paper, as directed by your instructor.

3. Using InfoTrac College Edition, look up articles using the keywords *"Wall Street Journal* and *USA Today,"* or *"Wall Street Journal"* and *"USA Today"* separately. See what you can learn about what makes these two national daily newspapers different and why they appeal to different audiences. Write a brief paper on your findings and be prepared to discuss the issue in class.

4. Look up the subject heading "alternative press" on InfoTrac College Edition and choose three articles that tell you something about how diverse viewpoints can reach the interested public. From your readings, decide whether you think the number and influence of alternative newspapers will increase or decrease in the next 10 to 20 years. Why? Write a brief paper on your conclusions and be prepared to discuss the issue in class.

5. Using the keywords "Internet newspaper" on InfoTrac College Edition, choose three articles that tell you how newspapers are adapting to competition from online news sources. As you read, consider whether newspapers will eventually abandon printing on paper for Internet publishing or whether newspaper print and Internet editions will continue to publish simultaneously. Find some leading newspapers on the World Wide Web and examine how the online content differs from the print versions. Also consider how you think the Internet editions could become profitable. Write a brief paper on your findings and conclusions, and be prepared to discuss the issue in class.

4

> "This is a reflection of advertisers going for more targeted media placement. The people who really have the money are a very small segment of the population so you have to look more carefully at the affluent marketplace."

Valerie Muller, Media Director for DeWitt Media, which places magazine ads for BMW

By the early 1950s, magazine mogul Henry Luce's *Time* and *Fortune* were well-established. He often traveled with his wife, Ambassador Clare Boothe Luce. Many of the people Henry Luce met overseas wanted to talk with him about sports instead of asking him questions of international importance.

"Luce knew nothing about sports," says *Los Angeles Times* sports columnist Jim Murray, who in the early 1950s was writing about sports for *Time* magazine. "But every place he'd go, all over the world, the conversation would veer to the World Cup or the British Open or whatever.

"He got fascinated and irritated, I guess, and finally said, 'Why this all-consuming interest in games?' We said, 'Well, that's the way the world is, Henry.' He said, 'Well, maybe we ought to start a sports magazine.'" The result, of course, was *Sports Illustrated*, which today is ranked among the nation's most profitable magazines and is published by the media giant AOL Time Warner.

Sports Illustrated was one of the earliest magazines to anticipate today's trend in magazines. Today, successful magazines cater to specialized audiences. You probably have seen a copy of *Sports Illustrated* recently, or perhaps you have read *Glamour, PC World* or *Maxim*. All of these publications are ranked among the country's top 200 magazines. They give their readers information they can't find anywhere else, and their vast readership might surprise you.

Impact | TimeFrame

Today to 1741: Magazines grow as a specialized medium that targets readers

TODAY

Magazines are very specialized, targeting narrow groups of readers for advertisers. Today, large media companies publish most magazines and a few magazines are published only on the Internet.

▼

2000

Oprah Winfrey launches the lifestyle magazine *O*.

▼

1999

Time Warner (publishers of *Time* magazine) merges with America Online to form the media giant AOL Time Warner (now Time Warner).

▼

1993

Newsweek launches an Internet edition of the magazine.

▼

1985

Advance Publications buys *The New Yorker* for more than $185 million, beginning the era of magazine industry consolidation.

▼

1945

John Johnson launches *Ebony* and then *Jet*.

▼

1925

Harold Ross launches *The New Yorker*.

▼

1923

Henry Luce creates *Time*, the nation's first news magazine, and then *Fortune* and *Life*.

▼

1910

W. E. B. Du Bois and the National Association for the Advancement of Colored People (NAACP) start *The Crisis*.

continued on next page

▶ Magazines Reflect Trends and Culture

Glamour, published by Condè Nast, reaches more than 2 million readers every month and is ranked among the nation's top ten women's magazines. PC World, the nation's fastest growing computer magazine, caters primarily to small business and home computer users. Nearly a million people read the magazine every month, and the magazine's readership is very attractive to advertisers.

The company that publishes *PC World* also publishes several other computer magazines. *Maxim,* a flashy magazine aimed at college-age men, is one of the most successful magazine launches ever. These examples highlight a significant fact about the history of the magazine industry: *Magazines reflect the surrounding culture and the characteristics of the society.* As readers' needs and lifestyles change, so do magazines. The trend toward specialty and online magazines is the latest chapter in this evolution.

▶ Colonial Magazines Compete with Newspapers

In 1741, more than 50 years after the birth of the colonies' first newspaper, magazines entered the American media marketplace. Newspapers covered daily crises for local readers, but magazines could reach beyond the parochial concerns of small communities to carry their cultural, political and social ideas and foster magazine identity as part of a nation.

The magazine industry began in 1741, in Philadelphia, when Benjamin Franklin and Andrew Bradford raced each other to become America's first magazine publisher. Franklin originated the idea of starting the first American magazine, but Bradford issued his *American Magazine* first, on February 13, 1741. Franklin's first issue of *General Magazine* came out three days later. Neither magazine lasted very long. Bradford published three issues and Franklin published six. But their efforts initiated a rich tradition.

Because they didn't carry advertising, early magazines were expensive and their circulations remained very small, but like colonial newspapers, early magazines provided a means for political expression.

▶ The First National Mass Medium

Newspapers flooded the larger cities by the early 1800s, but they circulated only within each city's boundaries, so national news spread slowly. Colleges were limited to the wealthy, and books were expensive. Magazines became America's only *national* medium, and subscribers depended on them for news, culture and entertainment. The magazine that first reached a large public was *The Saturday Evening Post,* started in 1821.

The early *Posts* cost a nickel each and were only four pages, with no illustrations. One-fourth of the magazine was advertising, and for 40 years it was one of America's most important weeklies.

▶ Reaching New Readers

Magazines like *The Saturday Evening Post* reached a wide readership with their general interest content. But many other audiences were available to 19th century publishers, and they spent the century locating their readership. Four enduring subjects that expanded the magazine audience in the 1800s were women's issues, social crusades, literature and the arts, and politics.

Women's Issues   Because women were a sizable potential audience, magazines were more open to female contributors than were newspapers. Two central figures in the history of women's magazines in America were Sarah Josepha Hale and Edward Bok.

In 1830, Louis A. Godey was the first publisher to capitalize on a female audience. Women, most of whom had not attended school, sought out *Godey's Lady's Book* and its gifted editor, Sarah Josepha Hale, for advice on morals, manners, literature, fashion, diet and taste.

When her husband died in 1822, Hale sought work to support herself and her five children. As the editor of *Godey's* for 40 years beginning in 1837, she fervently supported higher education and property rights for women. By 1860, *Godey's* had 150,000 subscribers. Hale retired from the magazine when she was 89, a year before she died.

Social Crusades   Magazines also became important instruments for social change. *The Ladies' Home Journal* is credited with leading a crusade against dangerous medicines. Many of the ads in women's magazines in the 1800s were for patent medicines like Faber's Golden Female Pills ("successfully used by prominent ladies for female irregularities") and Ben-Yan, which promised to cure "all nervous debilities."

The Ladies' Home Journal was the first magazine to refuse patent medicine ads. Founded in 1887 by Cyrus Curtis, the *Journal* launched several crusades. It offered columns about women's issues, published popular fiction and even printed sheet music.

Editor Edward Bok began his crusade against patent medicines in 1892, after he learned that many of them contained more than 40 percent alcohol. Next, Bok revealed that a medicine sold to soothe noisy babies contained morphine. Other magazines joined the fight against dangerous ads, and partly because of Bok's crusading investigations, Congress passed the Pure Food and Drug Act of 1906.

Fostering the Arts   In the mid-1800s, American magazines began to seek a literary audience by promoting the nation's writers. Two of today's most important literary magazines—*Harper's* and *The Atlantic Monthly*—began more than a century ago. *Harper's New Monthly Magazine*, known today as *Harper's*, first appeared in 1850.

The American literary showcase grew when *The Atlantic Monthly* appeared in 1857, in Boston. The magazine's purpose was "to inoculate the few who influence the many." That formula continues today, with *The Atlantic* still provoking literary and political debate.

Impact | TimeFrame

Today to 1741: Magazines grow as a specialized medium that targets readers

continued

▼
1893
Samuel A. McClure founds *McClure's Magazine*, the nation's first major showcase for investigative magazine journalism, featuring muckrakers Ida Tarbell and Lincoln Steffens.

▼
1887
Cyrus Curtis begins publishing *The Ladies' Home Journal*.

▼
1865
The Nation, featuring political commentary, appears in Boston.

▼
1830
Louis A. Godey hires Sarah Josepha Hale as the first woman editor of a general circulation women's magazine, *Godey's Lady's Book*.

▼
1821
The Saturday Evening Post becomes the first magazine to reach a wide public audience.

▼
1741
Benjamin Franklin and Andrew Bradford publish America's first magazines.

A sample of 1875 fashions displayed in *Godey's Lady's Book,* edited by Sarah Josepha Hale. Women formed an early sizable audience for magazines.

© Bettmann/CORBIS

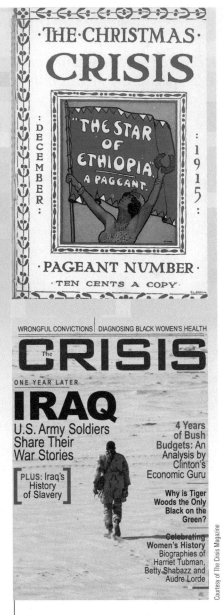

The Crisis, founded by W. E. B. Du Bois in 1910 as the monthly magazine of the National Association for the Advancement of Colored People (NAACP), continues to publish today.

Muckrakers Investigative magazine journalists who targeted abuses by government and big business.

Political Commentary   With more time (usually a month between issues) and space than newspapers had to reflect on the country's problems, political magazines provided a forum for public arguments by scholars and critical observers. Three of the nation's progressive political magazines that began in the 19th and early 20th centuries have endured: *The Nation, The New Republic* and *The Crisis.*

The Nation, founded in 1865, is the oldest continuously published opinion journal in the United States, offering critical literary essays and arguments for progressive change. This weekly magazine has survived a succession of owners and financial hardship.

Another outspoken publication, which began challenging the establishment in the early 1900s, is *The New Republic,* founded in 1914. The weekly's circulation has rarely reached 40,000, but its readers enjoy the role it plays in regularly criticizing political leaders.

An organization that needed a voice at the beginning of the century was the National Association for the Advancement of Colored People (NAACP). For 24 years, beginning in 1910, that voice was W. E. B. Du Bois, who founded and edited the organization's monthly magazine, *The Crisis.*

Du Bois began *The Crisis* as the official monthly magazine of the NAACP. Du Bois attacked discrimination against African American soldiers during World War I, exposed Ku Klux Klan activities and argued for African American voting and housing rights. By 1919, circulation was more than 100,000. *The Crisis* continues today to publish monthly.

The Postal Act Helps Magazines Grow   Passage of the Postal Act of 1879 encouraged the growth of magazines. Before passage of the Act, newspapers traveled through the mail free while magazines had to pay postage.

With the Postal Act of 1879, Congress gave magazines second-class mailing privileges and a cheap mailing rate. This meant quick, reasonably priced distribution for magazines, and today magazines still travel on a preferential postage rate.

Aided by lower mailing costs, the number of monthly magazines grew from 180 in 1860 to over 1,800 by 1900. However, because magazines travel through the mail, they are vulnerable to censorship (see Chapter 14).

▶ Magazines Launch Investigative Journalism

Colorful, campaigning journalists began investigating big business just before the turn of the 20th century. They became known as **muckrakers.** The strongest editor in the first ten years of the 20th century was legendary magazine publisher Samuel S. McClure, who founded *McClure's Magazine* in 1893.

McClure and his magazine were very important to the Progressive era in American politics, which called for an end to the close relationship between government and big business. To reach a large readership, McClure priced his new monthly magazine at 15 cents an issue, while most other magazines sold for 25 or 35 cents.

Ida Tarbell joined *McClure's* in 1894 as associate editor. Her series about President Lincoln boosted the magazine's circulation. Subsequently, Tarbell tackled a series about Standard Oil. (See Impact/People, "Muckraker Ida Tarbell Targets John D. Rockefeller" on page 75.)

Tarbell peeled away the veneer of the country's biggest oil trust. Her 19-part series began running in *McClure's* in 1904. Eventually the series became a two-volume book, *History of the Standard Oil Company,* which established Tarbell's reputation as a muckraker.

The muckrakers' targets were big business and corrupt government. President Theodore Roosevelt coined the term *muckraker* in 1906 when he com-

Impact | People

Ida Tarbell Targets John D. Rockefeller

When John D. Rockefeller refused to talk with her, Ida Tarbell sat at the back of the room and watched him deliver a Sunday-school sermon. In her autobiography, *All in the Day's Work*, written when she was 80, Tarbell described some of her experiences as she investigated the Standard Oil Company:

"The impression of power deepened when Mr. Rockefeller took off his coat and hat, put on a skullcap and took a seat commanding the entire room, his back to the wall. It was the head which riveted attention. It was big, great breadth from back to front, high broad forehead, big bumps behind the ears, not a shiny head but with a wet look. The skin was as fresh

In 1904, muckraker Ida Tarbell targeted oil magnate John D. Rockefeller, who called her "that misguided woman."

as that of any healthy man about us. The thin sharp nose was like a thorn. There were no lips; the mouth looked

as if the teeth were all shut hard. Deep furrows ran down each side of the mouth from the nose. There were puffs under the little colorless eyes with creases running from them.

"Wonder over the head was almost at once diverted to wonder over the man's uneasiness. His eyes were never quiet but darted from face to face, even peering around the jog at the audience close to the wall. . . .

"My two hours' study of Mr. Rockefeller aroused a feeling I had not expected, which time has intensified. I was sorry for him. I know no companion so terrible as fear. Mr. Rockefeller, for all the conscious power written in face and voice and figure, was afraid, I told myself, afraid of his own kind."

---

pared reformers like Tarbell to the "Man with the Muckrake" who busily dredged up the dirt in John Bunyan's book, *Pilgrim's Progress*.

By 1910, many reforms sought by the muckrakers had been adopted, and this particular type of magazine journalism declined. The muckrakers often are cited as America's original investigative journalists.

▶ Targeted versus General Readership: *The New Yorker* and *Time* Magazines

Magazines in the first half of the 20th century matured and adapted to absorb the invention of radio and then television. As with magazines today, magazine publishers had two basic choices:

1. publishers could seek a *definable, targeted loyal audience;* or
2. publishers could seek a *broad, general readership.*

Harold Ross, founding editor of *The New Yorker*, and Henry Luce, who started Time Inc., best exemplify these two different types of American publishers in the first half of the 20th century.

Harold Ross and *The New Yorker* Harold Ross' *The New Yorker* magazine launched the wittiest group of writers that ever gathered around a table at New York's Algonquin Hotel. The "witcrackers," who met there regularly for lunch throughout the 1920s, included Heywood Broun, Robert Benchley, Dorothy Parker, Alexander Woollcott, James Thurber and Harpo Marx. Because they sat at a large round table in the dining room, the group came to be known as the Algonquin Round Table.

Harold Ross persuaded Raoul Fleischmann, whose family money came from the yeast company of the same name, to invest half a million dollars in *The New*

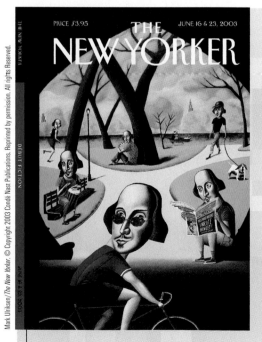

Published since 1925, *The New Yorker* is one of the nation's most successful magazines, and continues today to be the primary showcase for American writers and artists.

Originated by Henry Luce in the 1950s, *Sports Illustrated* and **SI.com** are just two of the many media outlets controlled today by the media giant Time Warner.

Yorker before the magazine began making money in 1928, three years after its launch. Ross published some of the country's great commentary, fiction and humor, sprinkled with cartoons that gave *The New Yorker* its charm. Ross edited the magazine until he died in 1951, and he was succeeded by William Shawn.

After one owner—the Fleischmann family—and only two editors in 60 years, *The New Yorker* was sold in 1985 to Advance Publications, which subsequently sold the magazine to one of the nation's largest magazine groups, Condè Nast. *The New Yorker* continues today to be the primary showcase for contemporary American writers and artists.

Henry Luce's Empire: *Time*

Henry Luce is the singular giant of 20th century magazine publishing. Unlike Harold Ross, who sought a sophisticated, wealthy audience, Luce wanted to reach the largest possible readership.

Luce's first creation was *Time* magazine, which he founded in 1923 with his Yale classmate Briton Hadden. Luce and Hadden paid themselves $30 a week and recruited their friends to write for the magazine.

The first issue of *Time* covered the week's events in 28 pages, minus six pages of advertising—half an hour's reading. "It was of course not for people who really wanted to be informed," wrote Luce's biographer W. A. Swanberg. "It was for people willing to spend a half-hour to avoid being entirely uninformed." The brash news magazine became the foundation of the Luce empire that eventually also launched *Fortune, Life, Sports Illustrated, Money* and *People Weekly*. Today, *Time* is only a small part of the giant company Time Warner, which includes television stations, movie studios, book publishing companies, Home Box Office, CNN and America Online.

Many of Luce's magazines fostered look-alikes such as *Ebony*, an African American magazine introduced in the 1940s by John H. Johnson. The Johnson chain also launched *Jet* magazine. By the year 2000, *Ebony* and *Jet* had a combined readership of three million. Johnson is grooming his daughter, Linda Johnson Rice, to assume management of the company.

Linda Johnson Rice with her father, John H. Johnson, publisher and founder of Johnson Publications. Rice is gradually taking over responsibility for Johnson Publications.

▶ Specialized Magazines Take Over

In the 1950s, television began to offer Americans some of the same type of general interest features that magazines provided. General interest magazines

collapsed. Readers wanted specialized information
they could not get from other sources. These new targeted magazines segmented the market, which meant
each magazine got fewer readers.

Very few general interest magazines survive today.
The trend, since television expanded the media marketplace, is for magazines to find a specific audience interested in the information that magazines can deliver.
This is called *targeting an audience*, which magazines can
do more effectively today than any other media.

"There's an article in here that explains why you're such an idiot."

Three Types of Magazines   Today's
magazines can be categorized into three types:

1. Consumer publications

2. Trade, technical and professional publications

3. Company publications

You probably are most familiar with **consumer magazines**, which are
popularly marketed: *Time, Glamour* and *Maxim*, for example. *Rolling Stone* and
Muscle & Fitness also are considered consumer magazines. In the magazine
business, *consumer* magazines are not just those that give buying advice. This
term refers to all magazines sold by subscription or at newsstands, supermarkets and bookstores. As a group, consumer magazines make the most money
because they have the most readers and carry the most advertising.

People in a particular industry read **trade, technical and professional
magazines** to learn more about their business. *Veterinary Practice Management*,
for example, is a trade magazine, published as "a business guide for small animal practitioners." So are the *Columbia Journalism Review* (published by
Columbia University) and *American Medical News* (published by the American
Medical Association). Media companies issue these magazines for their specific subscribers (*Veterinary Practice Management*, for example); universities or
university-connected organizations for their subscribers (*Columbia Journalism
Review*, for example); or professional associations for their members (*American
Medical News*, for example). Most trade, technical and professional magazines
carry advertising directed at the professions they serve.

Company magazines are produced by businesses for their employees,
customers and stockholders. These magazines usually don't carry advertising.
Their main purpose is to promote the company. Chevron, for instance, publishes a company magazine called *Chevron USA Odyssey*.

Consumer Magazines   All
magazines sold by subscription or at
newsstands, supermarkets and
bookstores.

Trade Magazines   Magazines
read by people in a particular
industry to learn more about their
business.

Company Magazines   Magazines
produced by businesses for their
employees, customers and
stockholders.

▶ Working for Magazines

Magazine employees work in one of five divisions:

1. Editorial

2. Circulation sales

3. Advertising sales

4. Manufacturing and distribution

5. Administration

The *editorial* department handles everything regarding the content of the
magazine, except the advertisements. This is the department for which magazine editors work, and they decide the subjects for each magazine issue, oversee
the people who write the articles and schedule the articles for the magazine.
Designers who determine the "look" of the magazine also are considered part of

Illustration 4.1
Advertising Provides Nearly Half the Revenue for Most Magazines.

Source: Magazine Publishers of America, adage.com

Subscriptions + single copy sales
53¢

Advertising
47¢

ABC   Audit Bureau of Circulations.

The trend toward specialized audience targeting will continue. As the audience becomes more segmented, magazines publishers will seek more specific readership, such as the Latino audience sought by the magazine *Hispanic*.

the editorial department . The *circulation* department manages the subscription information. Workers in this department enter new subscriptions and handle address changes and cancellations, for example.

The *advertising* department is responsible for finding companies that would like to advertise in the magazine. Advertising employees often help the companies design their ads to be consistent with the magazine format. *Manufacturing* and *distribution* departments manage the production of the magazine and get it to readers. This often includes contracting with an outside company to print the magazine. Many magazine companies also contract with an outside distribution company rather than deliver the magazines themselves. *Administration*, as in any media company, takes care of the organizational details—the paperwork of hiring, paying bills and managing the office, for example.

Because advertisers provide nearly half a magazine's income (See **Illustration 4.1**), tension often develops between a magazine's advertising staff and its editorial staff. The advertising staff may lobby the editor for favorable stories about potential advertisers, but the editor is responsible to the audience of the magazine. The advertising department might argue with the editor, for example, that a local restaurant will not want to advertise in a magazine that publishes an unfavorable review of the restaurant. If the restaurant is a big advertiser, the editor must decide how best to maintain the magazine's integrity.

Circulation figures for member magazines are verified and published by the Audit Bureau of Circulations (**ABC**), an agency of print media market research. Advertisers use ABC figures to help them decide which magazines to use to reach their audience.

Putting the magazine together and selling it (circulation, advertising, administration, manufacturing and distribution) cost more than organizing the articles and photographs that appear in the magazine (editorial). Often a managing editor coordinates all five departments.

The magazine editor's job is to keep the content interesting so people will continue to read the magazine. Good magazine editors can create a distinctive, useful product by carefully choosing the best articles for the magazine's audience and ensuring the articles are well-written.

Illustration 4.2
Top Ten Fastest Growing Magazine Categories, 1993–2003

Bridal magazines are the fastest growing magazine category, along with football and dog magazines.

Source: National Directory of Magazines 2003, Oxbridge Communications.

Critical Question

It seems as if there is a magazine for every possible subject or target audience. Is there a subject you're interested in but that no magazine addresses specifically? What is your area of interest? Would it be suitable for a magazine—why or why not?

Full-time magazine staffers write many of the articles, such as a food editor who creates recipes or a columnist who writes commentary. Nearly half the nation's magazines, however, use articles by **freelancers**. Freelancers do not receive a salary from the magazine; instead, they are paid individually for each of their articles published in the magazine. Many freelancers write for several magazines simultaneously. Some freelancers specialize—just writing travel articles, for example. Other freelancers work just as the tradition of their name implies: They have a pen for hire, and they can write about any subject a magazine editor wants.

Freelancers Writers who are not on the staff of a magazine but are paid for each individual article published.

▶ The Business of Magazines

Today, trends in magazine publishing continue to reflect social and demographic changes, but magazines no longer play the cutting-edge social, political and cultural role they played in the past (See **Illustration 4.2**). Instead, most magazines are seeking a specific audience, and many more magazines are competing for the same readers.

Newsweek and *U.S. News & World Report* compete with *Time* to serve the reader who wants a weekly news roundup. *Fortune* is no longer alone; it has been joined by magazines like *Business Week, Forbes* and *Nation's Business.* Some new magazines, such as *Maxim,* have been launched successfully to appeal to a younger audience. However, most magazine audiences have grown older and today read magazines like *PC World, Money* and *Better Homes and Gardens.*

Women continue to be the single, most lucrative audience for magazines. *Family Circle* and *Woman's Day* are called **point-of-purchase magazines** because they are sold mainly at the checkout stands in supermarkets and are one part of the women's market. *Vogue, Glamour* and *Cosmopolitan* cater to the fashion-conscious, and women's magazines have matured to include the

Point-of-Purchase Magazines Sold mainly at checkout stands in supermarkets, magazines that consumers buy directly, not by subscription.

Maxim, a flashy magazine aimed at college-age men, is one of the most successful magazine launches ever.

working women's audience with *Savvy*, *Self* and *Working Woman*, for example. The market is divided still further by magazines like *Essence*, aimed at professional African American women, and the specifically targeted *Today's Chicago Woman* for female executives who live in Chicago.

Segmenting the Audience

The newest segment of the magazine audience to be targeted by special-interest magazines are owners of personal computers. Titles like *PC Magazine*, *PC World* and *PC Week* already are among the nation's top 500 magazines, and so is *Wired*.

The tendency to specialize has not yet reached the level suggested by one magazine publisher, who joked that soon there might be magazines called *Working Grandmother*, *Lefthanded Tennis* and *Colonial Homes in Western Vermont*. But magazine publishers are seeking readers with a targeted interest and then selling those readers to the advertisers who want to reach that specific audience—skiers, condominium owners, motorcyclists and toy collectors.

Besides targeting a special audience, such as gourmets or computer hackers, today magazines also can divide their audience further with regional and special editions that offer articles for specific geographic areas along with regional advertising, or webzines, which are online magazines available on the Internet. The news weeklies, for example, can insert advertising for a local bank or a local TV station next to national ads. This gives the local advertiser the prestige of a national magazine, at a lower cost.

One specialization success is *Modern Maturity*. Unlike most other successful specialized magazines, which are published by commercial publishers, an association publishes *Modern Maturity*. People who join the American Association of Retired Persons (AARP) receive the magazine as part of their association membership. With nearly 21 million readers, this bimonthly magazine provides articles on investments, careers and personal relationships for read-

ers 50 years and older. *Modern Maturity* boasts more readers than any other American magazine (see **Illustration 4.3,** page 82).

Modern Maturity's success story is a comment on the current state of the magazine industry. The audience for magazines, as for newspapers, is growing older. Younger readers are less likely to read magazines than their parents. In 1990, for the first time, the number of magazines published in the United States stopped growing.

Magazine Launches

Most new magazines are small-scale efforts produced on a computer and financed by loyal relatives or friends. Sex is the favorite category for new magazines, followed by lifestyle, sports, media personalities and home subjects. In 2000, television personality Oprah Winfrey launched a lifestyles magazine called *O*.

But only a few new magazines succeed. Today, only one in three new magazines will survive more than five years. The reason most magazines fail is that many new companies do not have the money to keep publishing long enough to be able to refine their editorial content, sell advertisers on the idea and gather subscribers—in other words, until the magazine can make a profit. All magazines are vulnerable to changing economic trends.

The number of magazines people buy each year remains static and revenues are declining. Although magazines once were very inexpensive and advertising paid for most of the cost of production, publishers gradually have been charging more, and subscribers seem willing to pay more for the magazines they want.

With circulation declining, advertising income at magazines has also been going down. The smaller the audience, the less magazines can charge their advertisers. This drop in revenue means several popular magazines have stopped publishing. The most recent example is the *Industry Standard*. Launched in 1997 to take advantage of the dot-com boom, the magazine once carried 300 pages of advertising. In 2001, the magazine unceremoniously folded, a victim of the downturn in the high-tech economy.

A Valuable Audience

The average magazine reader is a high school graduate, married, owns a home and works full-time. This is a very attractive audience for advertisers. Advertisers also like magazines because people often refer to an ad weeks after they first see it.

Many readers say they read a magazine as much for the ads as they do for the articles. This, of course, is also very appealing to advertisers. The

In 2000, Oprah Winfrey launched a lifestyles magazine called *O*, designed to capitalize on her popular TV show.

AP/Wide World Photos

Illustration 4.3
Top Ten U.S. Consumer Magazines

Modern Maturity, a magazine targeted at readers over 55, is America's top-selling magazine. The most successful magazines target a mature readership and women.

Source: Audit Bureau of Circulations

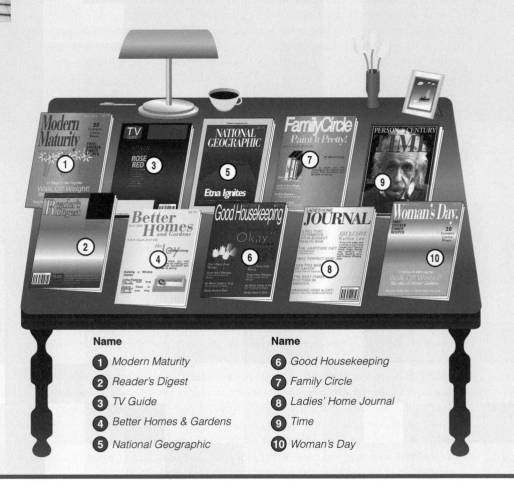

Name		Name	
1	Modern Maturity	6	Good Housekeeping
2	Reader's Digest	7	Family Circle
3	TV Guide	8	Ladies' Home Journal
4	Better Homes & Gardens	9	Time
5	National Geographic	10	Woman's Day

Pass-Along Readership People who share a magazine with the original recipient.

Japanese-speaking readers can find Japanese translations of popular magazines at a specialty bookstore in New York.

AP/Wide World Photos

Magazine Publishers Association reports that people keep a magazine an average of 17 weeks and that each magazine has at least four adult readers. This magazine sharing is called **pass-along readership**.

▶ Technology Transforms the Future

In 1984, for the first time, the price paid for individual magazine companies and groups of magazines bought and sold in one year reached $1 billion. *U.S. News & World Report* sold for $100 million. *Billboard* sold for $40 million. Like other media industries, magazines are being gathered together under large umbrella organizations, and this trend is continuing.

The trend toward more refined audience targeting by magazines also will continue. As the audience becomes more segmented, magazine publishers envision a time when they will deliver to each reader exactly what he or she wants to read. This means an infinitely defined readership, so advertisers will be able to reach only the people they want.

Changes in the way magazines do business in the future will be affected by technology as well as by the shifting economics of the industry. Developments in technology means:

• Magazines are trying to expand readership through Internet editions. In 1993, for example, *Newsweek* launched an Internet edition of its weekly

Gossip Goes Glossy and Loses Its Stigma

by David Carr

The tatty, telling stories about the famous and the celebrated beckon alluringly at the checkout counter, but faced with the grimy tabloid presentation, readers may wish for fake nose and glasses when it's time to buy.

Yet the same themes—romance and scandal—can transform a dirty pleasure into a harmless, tasty confection when rendered in a glossy, upbeat format, as in *Us Weekly* or *In Touch Weekly.* Add a patina of star-infused fashion and beauty coverage—*Instyle* having long ago established the utility of celebrities as mannequins—and suddenly the smart set is leaving the checkout line . . . with an article about Billy Bob still pining for Angelina and Angelina pining for somebody, poking out of the bag above the Roma tomatoes and arugula.

Sensing a shift, American Media, the biggest publisher of traditional tabloids, has moved the editorial staff of *The Star* to New York and will soon try to transform that newsprint checkout comic into a fancy magazine. Perhaps more telling, in less than a month, its smudgy siblings will test whether upgrading to glossy paper from newsprint will also get them invited to the party.

The medium has transformed the message, creating thousands of new readers, some of them pretty upscale. No mass magazine grew faster on the newsstand last year than *Us Weekly*, increasing 53 percent, for a weekly average of 505,000 single-copy sales and a total circulation of 1.1 million.

© Scott Goodwin Photography, Inc.

Tabloid gossip is showing up in new glossy magazines, aimed at a more upscale audience.

magazine. In 1994, *Business Week* began offering its magazine over America Online, including a feature that gives readers access to Internet conferences with editors and newsmakers and forums where readers can post messages related to topics covered in each issue of the magazine. Many major consumer magazines today publish Internet editions.

- Editors review final copy on-screen and transmit the full-color product by satellite directly to remote printing plants located for the quickest distribution to subscribers, newsstands, supermarkets, bookstores and other outlets.

- Advertisers can target their audiences better because magazines can divide their audiences not only by geography, income and interest, but also by zip code.

- Subscribers are paying as much as half the cost of producing each magazine. If subscription prices rise substantially, fewer people will be able to afford to buy magazines, thus decreasing the potential audience.

- Internet publishing is expanding the number of small magazines launched. Using a personal computer, a scanner, desktop publishing software and image-setting equipment, desktop operations can do everything to get a magazine ready for production.

- A few companies have launched magazines, such as *salon.com* and *slate.com* that are published only on the Internet.

Magazines survive because they complement the other media and have their own special benefits. Wayne Warner, president of Judd's, Inc., which prints more than 77 American magazines as diverse as *The New Republic*, *Modern Plastics* and *Newsweek*, best describes the advantages of magazines as a medium: "With magazines, we can read *what* we want, *when* we want, and *where* we want. And we can read them again and again at our pace, fold them, spindle them, mutilate them, tear out coupons, ads, or articles that interest us and, in short, do what we damn well please to them because they are 'our' magazines."

Media | Review

Scott Goodwin Photography, Inc.

History

▶ American magazines began in 1741 when Andrew Bradford published *American Magazine* and Benjamin Franklin published *General Magazine*.

▶ Like colonial newspapers, early magazines provided a means for political expression.

▶ *The Saturday Evening Post*, first published in 1821, was the nation's first general interest magazine.

▶ The Postal Act of 1879 encouraged the growth of magazines because it ensured quick, reasonably priced distribution for magazines. Today's magazines still travel on a preferential postal rate.

▶ *McClure's Magazine* pioneered investigative reporting in the United States early in the 20th century. *McClure's* published the articles of Ida Tarbell, who was critical of American industrialists.

Technology

▶ Many magazines have launched Internet sites to expand their readership.

▶ Some magazines, such as *salon.com* and *slate.com,* are published only on the Internet.

▶ Technology helps magazines target their audiences better because publishers can target their magazines by geography, income and interest group, as well as by zip code.

Business

▶ Magazines in the first half of the 20th century adapted to absorb the invention of radio and television. To adapt, some publishers sought a defined, targeted audience; others tried to attract the widest audience possible. *The New Yorker* and *Time* magazines are media empires that began during this period.

▶ Magazines in the second half of the 20th century survived by targeting readers' special interests. Specialization segments an audience for advertisers, making magazines the most specific buy an advertiser can make.

▶ Magazine prices could rise as subscribers are asked to pay as much as half the cost of producing each magazine. This rise in prices may mean the audience for magazines will become smaller than it is today.

▶ Magazine publishers hope to use Internet magazines (webzines) to expand readership and, perhaps, advertising revenue.

▶ Publishers can capitalize on the success of one publication by spinning off magazines that target subsets of readers.

Culture

▶ Magazines widened their audience in the 1800s by catering to women, tackling social crusades, becoming a literary showcase for American writers and encouraging political debate.

▶ The audience for magazines is growing older and young readers are less likely to read magazines. In 1990, for the first time, the number of magazines published in the country stopped growing.

▶ Women continue to be the single, most lucrative audience for magazines.

▶ Tabloid companies, which once published only newspapers, have moved into the magazine market with celebrity gossip and photos in a glossy format to capture upscale readers at the checkout stand.

▶ Each magazine, according to the Magazine Publishers Association, has at least four adult readers, and people keep a magazine an average of 17 weeks.

Impact | Interactive

The Impact/Interactive CD-ROM that accompanies this text is your gateway to many electronic resources for broadening and testing your critical understanding of the material in Chapter 4. The CD-ROM features the following interactive elements.

▶ A two- to three-minute timely, high-interest CNN Today video clip with critical viewing questions and a link to relevant selections available within the InfoTrac College Edition database

▶ Chapter-specific activities such as personal inventories and media projects

▶ A link to the *Media/Impact* Web site that offers helpful information and many additional electronic learning resources including:

- An interactive chapter outline and study guide

- Interactive glossary term flashcards and crossword puzzles, concept animations, Internet activities and practice quizzes

- Live links for all URLs given in the chapter so you can easily access the additional information each site offers

- A link to InfoTrac College Edition—our online database of more than a million articles representing cutting-edge research and the latest headlines. Updated daily, this online library is available 24 hours a day, seven days a week. The InfoTrac College Edition activities provided below are designed to help you use this valuable resource.

▶ Working the Web

Live links for all of the sites listed below are provided on the *Media/Impact* book companion Web site, which can be accessed through your Impact/Interactive CD-ROM.

▶ **American Society of Journalists and Authors**
www.asja.org

▶ **Folio: The Magazine for Magazine Management**
http://mediacentral.com

▶ **O, the Oprah Magazine**
www.oprah.com

▶ **Salon Magazine**
www.salon.com

▶ **Slate Magazine**
www.slate.com

▶ **Sports Illustrated**
www.sportsillustrated.cnn.com

▶ InfoTrac College Edition Activities

Using InfoTrac College Edition's online database of full-text articles and abstracts, do the following activities as directed by your instructor. The database can be accessed through your Impact/Interactive CD-ROM.

1. Look up a current print magazine ("*Maxim* magazine," "*Cosmopolitan* magazine," or "Oprah magazine") or another one you like and print at least three articles about it. Look for evidence of the magazine's audience, appeal, profitability and ownership. Do the articles indicate that the magazine has its critics? Who, and why? Do you expect the maga-

zine to last for decades? Or will its appeal be short-lived? Why? Write a brief paper on your findings and conclusions and be prepared to discuss the issue in class.

2. Magazines, like most other media, thrive through advertising. Use the keywords "magazine advertising" on InfoTrac College Edition. Read at least three articles on the subject and consider the following questions: What does your research tell you about how magazine advertising is changing? Is the amount of magazine advertising increasing or decreasing? Has the audience for magazine advertising changed? Look at advertising in several different magazine genres (by going to the library or browsing at the magazine stand in most large chain bookstores) and decide whether most ads in each magazine place their emphasis on information, or image. Write a brief paper on your findings and conclusions and be prepared to discuss the issues in class.

3. Look up "online magazines" on InfoTrac College Edition and find at least two articles that interest you about online magazines. Print the articles, then come to class and, in small groups, develop an idea for your own online magazine. Create a title, a focus and a list of articles that might appear in the magazine. Identify the audience for your magazine and discuss how you would market your magazine to the public, as well as who would advertise in the publication. Then share your creation with the rest of the class.

4. Look up the keywords "special interest magazine" on InfoTrac College Edition. Read at least three articles about magazines that are aimed at audiences interested in particular topics. How does the audience for special interest magazines differ from the audience for general interest magazines? Are special interest magazines growing in number and circulation, holding their own, or shrinking? Is it easy for special interest magazines to attract advertising dollars? Why, or why not? Do you think advertising in special interest magazines differs in content or style from advertising in general interest magazines? If so, how and why? Write a brief paper on your findings and conclusions and be prepared to discuss the issue in class.

5. Look up the keywords "new magazines" and "magazine startups" on InfoTrac College Edition. Read at least three articles about new magazine enterprises and what happens to them. As you read, decide whether you would be interested in starting your own magazine. Why, or why not? What kind of financial, technological and human resources do you think you would need to start a magazine? Imagine a focus for a magazine you might start. Identify the audience for your magazine and discuss how you would market your magazine to the public, as well as who would advertise in the publication. Write a brief paper on your findings and conclusions and be prepared to discuss the issue in class.

Recordings

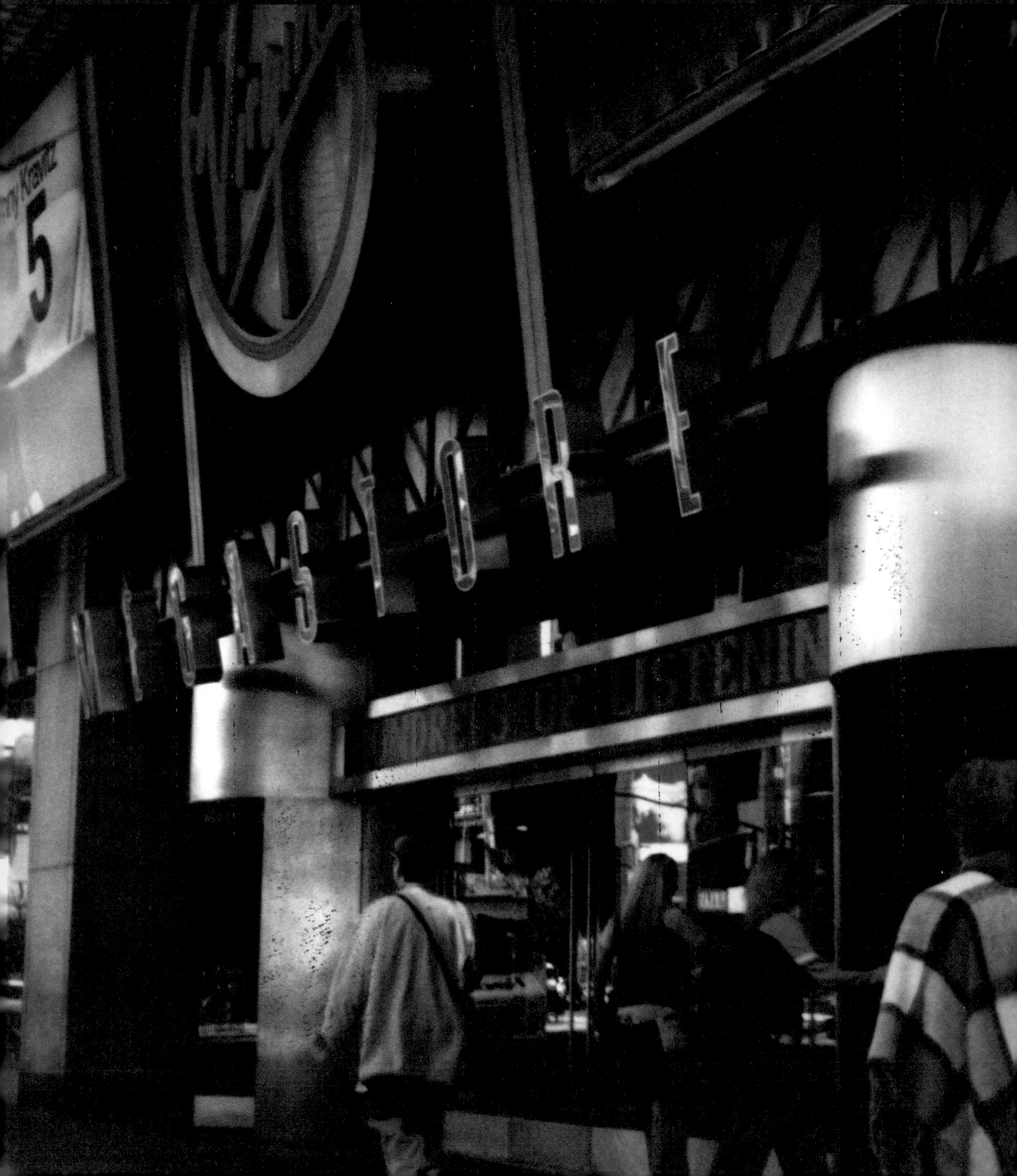

CHAPTER 5

What's Ahead

> "*It's not something you feel guilty about doing. You don't get the feeling it's illegal because it's so easy.*"
>
> College student Dan Langlitz at Pennsylvania State University, talking about downloading free music from the Internet

"Popular music is like a unicorn," writes R. Serge Denisoff in his book *Solid Gold*. "Everyone knows what it is supposed to look like, but no one has ever seen it." More than half the recordings sold every year in the United States are categorized as popular music.

If the average person buys four recordings a year, as the Recording Industry Association reports, popular music is recorded on two of them. Other types of music—country, gospel, classical, show tunes, jazz and children's recordings—make up the other half, but most of the big profits and losses in the recording business result from the mercurial fury of popular music.

Like the radio and television industries, the recording industry is challenged by rapidly changing technology. The recording industry also is at the center of recent debates over the protection of artistic copyright. In 2003, the Recording Industry Association of America sued 261 people for downloading music from the Internet, saying CD shipments were down 15 percent from the year before. Of all the media industries, the recording industry is the most vulnerable to piracy and has suffered the biggest losses as a result of Internet technology. But in 1877, when Thomas Edison first demonstrated his phonograph, who could foresee that the music business would get so complicated?

Today to 1877: The recording industry caters to a young audience

TODAY
The recording industry earns more than half its revenue from people under 34, and the industry is fighting copyright infringement and Internet file-sharing to protect earnings.

▼

2001
Napster, which used file-sharing software designed to download music on the Internet, shuts down after Recording Industry Association of America (RIAA) sues for copyright infringement.

▼

1999
MP3 technology makes it easy for consumers to download music files from the Internet.

▼

1985
The recording industry begins to consolidate into six major international corporations. Only one of these companies is based in the United States.

▼

1979
Sony introduces the Walkman as a personal stereo.

▼

1970
David Geffen starts Asylum Records.

▼

1958
Motown introduces the "Detroit Sound" of African American artists, popularizing rock 'n' roll.

▼

1956
Stereo arrives.

▼

1947
Peter Goldmark develops the long-playing record.

continued on next page

Recordings

▶ From Edison's Amazing Talking Machine to 33⅓ RPM Records

Today's recording industry would not exist without Thomas Edison's invention, more than a century ago, of what he called a phonograph (which means "sound writer"). In 1877, *Scientific American* reported Thomas Edison's first demonstration of his phonograph. Edison's chief mechanic had constructed the machine from an Edison sketch that came with a note reading, "Build this."

In 1887, Emile Berliner developed the gramophone, which replaced Edison's cylinder with flat discs. Berliner and Eldrige Johnson formed the Victor Talking Machine Company (later to become RCA Victor) and sold recordings of opera star Enrico Caruso. Edison and Victor proposed competing technologies as the standard for the industry, and eventually the Victor disc won. Early players required large horns to amplify the sound. Later the horn was housed in a cabinet below the actual player, which made the machine a large piece of furniture.

In 1925, Joseph Maxfield perfected the equipment to eliminate the tinny sound of early recordings. The first jukeboxes were manufactured in 1927 and brought music into restaurants and nightclubs.

By the end of World War II, 78 rpm (**r**evolutions **p**er **m**inute) records were standard. Each song was on a separate recording, and "albums" in today's sense did not exist. An album in the 1940s consisted of a bound set of ten envelopes about the size of a photo album. Each record, with one song recorded on each side, fit in one envelope. (This is how today's collected recordings got the title "album" even though they are no longer assembled in this cumbersome way.) Each shellac hard disc recording ran three minutes. Peter Goldmark, working for Columbia Records (owned by CBS), changed that.

▶ Peter Goldmark Perfects Long-Playing Records

In 1947, Peter Goldmark was listening with friends to Brahms' Second Piano Concerto played by pianist Vladimir Horowitz and led by the world-famous conductor Arturo Toscanini. The lengthy concerto had been recorded on six records, 12 sides.

Goldmark hated the interruptions in the music every time a record had to be turned over. He also winced at the eight sound defects he detected. After several refinements, Peter Goldmark created the long-playing (**LP**) record, which could play for 23 minutes.

▶ William S. Paley Battles Sarnoff for Record Format

CBS's William Paley realized that he was taking a big risk by introducing LP records when most people didn't own a record player that could play the bigger 33⅓ rpm discs. While the LP record was being developed, Paley decided to contact RCA executive David Sarnoff, since RCA made record players, to convince Sarnoff to form a partnership with CBS to manufacture LPs. Sarnoff refused.

Stubbornly, Sarnoff introduced his own 7-inch, 45 rpm records in 1948. Forty-fives had a quarter-size hole in the middle, played one song on a side, and required a different record player, which RCA started to manufacture.

Forty-fives were a perfect size for jukeboxes, but record sales slowed as the public tried to figure out what was happening. Eventually Toscanini convinced Sarnoff to manufacture LPs and to include the 33⅓ speed on RCA record players to accommodate classical-length recordings. CBS, in turn, agreed to use 45s for its popular songs. Later, players were developed that could play all three speeds (33⅓, 45 and 78 rpm).

Hi-Fi and Stereo Rock In

The introduction of rock 'n' roll redefined the concept of popular music in the 1950s. Contributing to the success of popular entertainers like Elvis Presley were the improvements in recorded sound quality that originated with the recording industry.

First came *high fidelity,* developed by London Records, a subsidiary of Decca. Tape recorders grew out of German experiments during World War II. Ampex Corporation built a high-quality tape recorder, and Minnesota Mining and Manufacturing (3M) perfected the plastic tape. Tape meant that recordings could be edited and refined, something that couldn't be done on discs.

Stereo arrived in 1956, and soon afterward came groups like the Supremes with the Motown sound, which featured the music of African American blues and rock 'n' roll artists. At the same time, the FCC approved "multiplex" radio broadcasts so that monaural and stereo could be heard on the same stations. The development of condenser microphones helped bring truer sound.

In the 1960s, miniaturization resulted from the transistor. Eventually the market was overwhelmed with tape players smaller than a deck of playing cards. Quadraphonic (four-track) and eight-track tapes seemed ready to become the standard in the 1970s, but cassette tapes proved more adaptable and less expensive.

In 1979, Sony introduced the Walkman as a personal stereo. (The company is Japanese, but the name Sony comes from the Latin *sonus* for sound and *sunny* for optimism.) Walkmans were an ironic throwback to the early radio crystal sets, which also required earphones.

Today's compact discs (CDs) deliver crystal sound, transforming music into digital code on a 4.7-inch plastic and aluminum disc read by lasers. Discs last longer than records and cassettes, and they can play for as long as 74 minutes. Rewritable CD (**CDR**) players, which allow consumers to copy music as well as play music, gained widespread acceptance quickly after they were launched in the year 2000.

These players make it even harder for the recording industry to police unauthorized use of copyrighted material. Music videos and the music channels MTV and VH1 also expanded the audience and the potential income for featured artists.

Working in the Recording Industry

Recordings, like books, are supported primarily by direct purchases. But a recording company involves five separate levels of responsibility before the public hears a sound: artists and repertoire, operations, marketing and promotion, distribution, and administration.

Artists and repertoire, or A&R, functions like an editorial department in book publishing—to develop and coordinate talent. Employees of this division are the true talent scouts.

Operations manages the technical aspects of the recording, overseeing the sound technicians, musicians, even the people who copy the discs. This work centers on creating the master recording, from which all other recordings are

Impact | TimeFrame

Today to 1877: The recording industry caters to a young audience

continued

1943
Ampex develops tape recorders and Minnesota Mining and Manufacturing perfects plastic recording tape.

1877
Thomas Edison first demonstrates the phonograph.

Rpm Revolutions per minute.

LP Long-playing record.

CDR Compact disks that can record and rerecord data and music.

© Hulton Archives/Getty Images

Improvements in recorded sound quality—hi-fi and stereo—contributed to the success of popular entertainers like Elvis Presley.

Students Shall Not Download. Yeah, Sure.

by Kate Zernike

State College, PA—In the rough and tumble of the student union here at Pennsylvania state university, the moral code is pretty pragmatic.

Thou shall not smoke—it will kill you.

Thou shalt not lift a term paper off the Internet—it will get you kicked out.

Thou shalt not use a fake ID—it will get you arrested.

And when it comes to downloading music or movies off the Internet, students here compare it with underage drinking: illegal but not immoral. Like alcohol and parties, the Internet is easily accessible. Why not download, or drink, when "everyone" does it?

This set of commandments has helped make people between the ages of 18 and 29, and college students in particular, the biggest downloaders of Internet music.

"It's not something you feel guilty about doing," said Dan Langlitz, 20, a junior here. "You don't get the feeling it's illegal because it's so easy." He held an MP3 player in his hand. "They sell these things, the sites are there. Why is it illegal?"

Students say they have had the Internet for as long as they can remember and have grown up thinking of it as theirs for the taking.

The array of services available to them on campus has only encouraged that sense.

Penn State recently made the student center, known as the Hub, entirely wireless, so students do not even have to dial up to get on the Internet. In comfortable armchairs, they sit clicking on Google searches, their ears attached to iPods, cellphones a hand away. . . .

Many courses put all materials—textbook excerpts, articles, syllabuses—online. Residence halls offer fast broadband access—which studies say makes people more likely to download.

"It kind of spoils us, in a sense, because you get used to it," said Jill Wilson, 20, a sophomore.

The New York Times, September 20, 2003. © 2003 by The New York Times Co. Reprinted with permission.

At Penn State, Lucas Deichi, a junior, goes online at the student center, which is wireless so students don't have to dial up to get on the Internet.

The clear sound of today's recording artists, such as Jennifer Lopez, is the direct result of the development of sophisticated technology that began with CBS Records' introduction of long-playing records (LPs) in the 1940s.

made. Before stereophonic recording was developed in 1956, a recording session meant gathering all the musicians in one room, setting up a group of microphones and recording a song in one take. Today, artists on the same song—vocals, drums, bass, horns, guitars—are recorded individually, and then the separate performances are mixed for the best sound.

The producer, who works within the operations group, can be on the staff of a recording company or freelancer. Producers coordinate the artist with the music, the arrangement and the engineers.

Marketing and promotion decides the best way to sell the recording. These employees oversee the cover design and the copy on the cover (jacket or sleeve). They also organize giveaways to retailers and to reviewers to find an audience for their product. Marketing and promotion might decide that the artist should tour or that the recording needs a music video to succeed. Recording companies often use promoters to help guarantee radio play for their artists. This has led to abuses such as payola (see Chapter 6).

Distribution gets the recording into the stores. There are two kinds of distributors: independents and branches. Independents contract separately with different companies to deliver their recordings. But independents, usually responsible for discovering music that is outside of the mainstream, are disappearing as the big studios handle distribution through their own companies, called branches. Because branches are connected with the major companies, they typically can offer the retailer better discounts.

Administration, as in all industries, handles the bills. Accounting tracks sales and royalties. Legal departments handle wrangles over contracts.

All of these steps are important in the creation of a recording, but if no one hears the recording, no one will buy it. This makes promotion particularly important. Live concerts have become the best way for artists to promote its music. Many recording artists say that CD sales alone don't make them any money and that the only way to make a living is to perform before a live audience.

Concerts have become high-profile showcases for technological innovation. In 2003, the group Phish performed before 60,000 people who paid $137.50 each to hear the band perform at a former Air Force base in Limestone, Maine. The concert provided an example of today's complex digital engineering.

"While the recording industry frets about the financial impact of music trading over the Internet, innovative bands like Phish are embracing the latest technologies to create spectacular live concerts and phantasmagoric festival experiences that are more like computer-controlled theme parks than like the rock festivals of yesteryear," reports *The New York Times.*

Photos: © C. Taylor Crothers

The band Phish has become an innovator in the production of high-energy live concerts, using today's complex digital engineering onstage and off, where Chris Kuroda, Phish's lighting director, manipulates one of the new light consoles. If one console fails, the other can take over the job of both. Live concerts are the main way recording artists make income today. Music sales are declining because people are downloading free music from the Internet.

"Before the Phish events, festivals in the U.S. didn't really have much else in terms of ancillary events, and Phish really stepped it up in terms of the décor and the decoration and the other activities," Richard Goodstone, a partner at Superfly Productions, told *The New York Times.* "The real difference between your normal rock festival like Lollapalooza and Ozzfest is that there's a lot of music, but now we're trying to make it a complete experience in terms of the activities that really interact with the patrons out there, so it's not just a one-element kind of event."

People who attended the concert were "all served by advanced technology," reported the *Times,* "whether they were listening to the crystalline sound system, gazing at the intense light shows, exploring the participatory art installations tucked into a forest grove, listening to the Bunny [Phish's temporary radio station, set up just for the concert] or burning custom CDs." Digital technology has become an important element of selling a band to its fans, as well as selling the band's music.

Berry Gordy Jr., Founder of Motown

"Imagine a world without the Supremes, Smokey Robinson, Marvin Gaye, Stevie Wonder, Diana Ross, Michael Jackson, Lionel Richie, the Temptations and the Four Tops," someone once said, "and you've just imagined a world without Berry Gordy."

Gordy, who worked on the Ford assembly line and sold cookware door to door, submitted in the end to his passion for songwriting and transforming no-names into stars.

As a songwriter, Gordy found early success with hits like "Lonely Teardrops," sung by Jackie Wilson. But Gordy soon realized he wanted more control. "To protect my songs, which are my loves, I had to find singers who could sing and record them like I heard them in my head."

At 29, with an $800 loan from his family, Gordy founded Motown. He leased a two-story house at 2648 West Grand Boulevard in Detroit.

"Everything was makeshift," he says. "We used the bathroom as an echo chamber."

Gordy borrowed from his assembly line experience in refining Motown acts. The kids learned harmony from the vocal coach, steps from the choreography coach, and manners from the etiquette coach. Meanwhile, Motown's songwriters pounded out new tunes. When it was time to perform, the kids—Diana, Marvin, Stevie, Smokey and the rest—piled into the Motown Revue bus and headed out on the road, competing to see who could win the most applause.

By 1975, Motown had become the biggest black-owned business in America, with activities spanning several record labels, film and television. "I had no idea that Diana Ross would become an industry or that Michael Jackson would become an industry or that the Temptations would become an industry," Gordy says. "While I say

© Kevin Winter/Getty Images

Berry Gordy Jr., founder of Motown and Tamla Records, was an innovator who popularized Detroit's Mo(tor)town sound in the 1960s and 1970s.

I'm a songwriter and businessman, really, deep down, I think I'm a teacher, like my father."

© Scott Goodwin Photography, Inc.

The main publication that chronicles popular music is *Billboard* magazine.

▶ The Recording Business

About 5,000 companies in the United States produce tapes and CDs. These companies sell over one billion recordings each year. The biggest recording industry profits are divided among four major companies. (See page 95.) The main recording centers in the U.S. are Los Angeles, New York and Nashville, but most large cities have at least one recording studio to handle local productions.

The recording industry, primarily concentrated in large corporations, generally chooses to record what has succeeded before. "Increasingly, the big record companies are concentrating their resources behind fewer acts," reports *The Wall Street Journal*, "believing that it is easier to succeed with a handful of blockbuster hits than with a slew of moderate sellers. One result is that fewer records are produced."

Most radio formats today depend on popular music, and these recordings depend on radio to succeed. The main measurement of what is popular is *Billboard*, the music industry's leading trade magazine. *Billboard* began printing a list of the most popular vaudeville songs and the best-selling sheet music in 1913. In 1940, the magazine began publishing a list of the country's top-selling records.

Impact | Business

**Illustration 5.1
The Music
Industry's Big Four**

Source: IFPI, *The New York Times,* 11/7/03, B-3.

Company
Universal
Sony BMG
EMI
Warner

Today, *Billboard* offers more than two dozen charts that measure, for example, air play and album sales as well as the sale of singles. Elvis Presley has had 149 recordings on the charts, for example, and 20 Beatles hits reached No. 1. Radio, governed by ratings and what the public demands, tends to play proven artists.

▶ Where the Money Is: Sales and Licensing

The industry collects income from direct sales and from music licensing.

Direct Sales The promotional tour was once the only way a company sold recordings. But in the 1980s, music videos became a very visible form of promotion for an artist. This shift changed the industry's economics. Jennifer Lopez and Britney Spears are attractive to record companies because they are recording artists who also can perform well in videos.

Music Licensing: ASCAP versus BMI For the first 30 years of commercial radio, one of the reasons broadcasters used live entertainment was to avoid paying royalties to the recording companies. Today, two licensing agencies handle the rights to play music for broadcast: the American Society of Composers, Authors and Publishers (ASCAP) and Broadcast Music, Inc. (BMI).

ASCAP, founded in 1914, was the first licensing organization. As noted in Chapter 6, ASCAP sued radio stations in the 1920s that were playing recorded music. Eventually some radio stations agreed to pay ASCAP royalties through a blanket licensing agreement, which meant that each station that paid ASCAP's fee could play any music that ASCAP licensed.

"Two Stones tickets, please, senior discount."

ASCAP American Society of Composers, Authors and Publishers.

Illustration 5.2
What Types of Music Do People Buy?

The industry's market for popular music is reflected in the types of music that sell, and rock music sales far outstrip all other kinds of music.

Data from the Recording Industry Association of America, 2002.

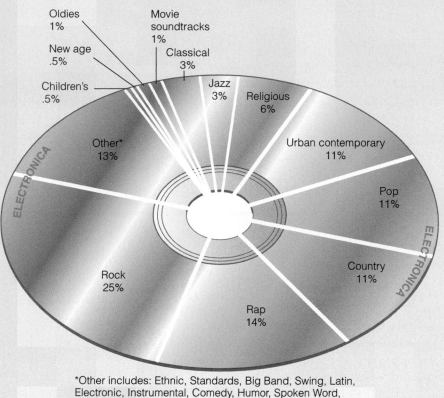

Oldies 1%
Movie soundtracks 1%
New age .5%
Classical 3%
Children's .5%
Jazz 3%
Religious 6%
Other* 13%
Urban contemporary 11%
ELECTRONICA
ELECTRONICA
Pop 11%
Rock 25%
Country 11%
Rap 14%

*Other includes: Ethnic, Standards, Big Band, Swing, Latin, Electronic, Instrumental, Comedy, Humor, Spoken Word, Exercise, Language, Folk and Holiday Music.

Throughout the 1930s, many stations refused to pay ASCAP because they didn't have enough money. These stations agreed to explore the idea of forming a separate organization so they could license the music themselves.

In 1939, broadcasters came together to establish a fund to build their own music collection through **BMI**. ASCAP and BMI became competitors—ASCAP as a privately owned organization and BMI as an industry-approved cooperative. BMI used the same blanket licensing agreement, collecting payments from broadcasters and dividing royalties among its artists. ASCAP licensed the majority of older hits, but rhythm and blues and rock 'n' roll gravitated toward BMI.

Today, most broadcasters subscribe to both BMI and ASCAP. They also agree to play only licensed artists, which makes getting on the air more difficult for new talent. BMI and ASCAP, in turn, pay the authors, recording artists, producers, and sometimes even the recording companies—whoever owns the rights to use the music.

Recording industry income has received a boost from the higher prices that consumers pay for CDs. However, Internet piracy means growth in the actual number of recordings sold is much slower than it once was.

BMI Broadcast Music, Inc.

▶ Challenges to Income and Content

Three issues face today's recording industry: piracy, content labeling and artists' copyright protection from file sharing on the Internet.

Impact | People

David Geffen, Founder of Geffen Records

Between high school and the time he landed a job as an usher at the CBS-TV studios in New York City, David Geffen says, he had about 17 jobs. "They were just jobs," he says. "I had to pay the rent." But when he finally got a job at CBS, "I thought, Oh, God, I love this," Geffen says. "I got to watch them rehearse TV shows with people like Judy Garland and Red Skelton, and I was thinking, 'Well, I'm not talented, what can I do?'"

He got a job on a new CBS TV series, *The Reporters*—as the receptionist. After studying the scripts one day, Geffen made some suggestions to the producer. "He fired me on the spot," Geffen recalls.

The show's casting director offered a sympathetic ear. "I told her I really loved the entertainment business, and was there anything I could do? She said, 'Well, what can you do?' And I

David Geffen, founder of Geffen Records, eventually sold the company for $700 million and then co-founded the movie studio DreamWorks.

said, 'Nothing. I don't know how to do anything.' She considered that for a moment and said, 'You don't know how to do anything. Hmmm. You could be an agent.'"

Missing the joke, Geffen grabbed the Yellow Pages and picked out the

agency with the biggest ad—and that's how he ended up at the mailroom of the William Morris Agency. "In delivering the mail, you get into everyone's office and you hear them talking on the phone," Geffen says. "It was the first time in my life that I had the epiphany—'I can do this!'"

Moving up from the mailroom, he plunged into the still-emerging world of rock 'n' roll, signing and managing artists from Laura Nyro to the Eagles. In 1970 he started Asylum Records, and later, after a turbulent year at Warner Bros. Pictures, he got back on track with Geffen Records. Eventually he sold Geffen for $700 million and went on to co-found the DreamWorks movie studio with Steven Spielberg and Jeffrey Katzenberg.

"Their Wildest Dreams," *Fortune*, Aug. 16, 1999.
Copyright © 1999 Time, Inc. All Rights Reserved.

▶ Pirates Steal Industry Revenue

The recording industry loses substantial income when people make their own tapes and CDs. The Japan Phonograph Record Association estimates that cassette recorder owners make 8 billion illegal copies of tapes and CDs every year. The Recording Industry Association of America (RIAA) has even proposed royalties for music that is digitally transmitted on cable.

Another threatening type of piracy for the industry is overseas copying of prerecorded cassettes and CDs that are then sold in the United States. Pirates control 18 percent of album sales; the recording industry estimates this represents $300 million a year in lost income.

▶ Industry Adopts Content Labels

In 1985, the Parents Music Resource Center (PMRC) called for recording companies to label their recordings for explicit content. The new group was made up primarily of the wives of several national political leaders, notably Susan Baker, wife of then-Treasury Secretary James A. Baker III, and Tipper Gore, wife of then-Senator Al Gore.

Saying that recordings come under the umbrella of consumer protection, the PMRC approached the National Association of Broadcasters and the Federal Communications Commission with their complaints. "After equating rock music with the evils of 'broken homes' and 'abusive parents,' and

Illustration 5.3
Who Pays for Music?

Because many younger listeners download music, the recording industry's average consumer is growing older. People over 30 account for more than half the industry's revenues.

Data from the Recording Industry Association of America, 2002.

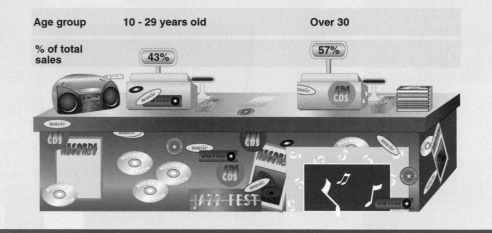

Age group	10 - 29 years old	Over 30
% of total sales	43%	57%

Critical Question

Have you legally or illegally downloaded music from the Internet? What do you like about the option of purchasing music online? Explain.

In 2003, entrepreneur Steve Jobs of Apple introduced I-Tunes, a Web site that offers a way for consumers to legally download music directly from the Internet. Other pay music services soon followed.

CHRIS HARDY/San Francisco Chronicle

labeling it a 'contributing factor' in teen pregnancy and suicide, they single[d] out Madonna, Michael Jackson, Mötley Crüe, Prince, Sheena Easton, Twisted Sister, and Cyndi Lauper for their 'destructive influence' on children," reported Louis P. Sheinfeld, who teaches journalism law at New York University.

The result was that, beginning in January 1986, the Recording Industry Association (whose member companies account for 95 percent of U.S. recording sales) officially urged its members either to provide a warning label or to print lyrics on albums that have potentially offensive content. Like the movie industry when it adopted its own ratings system (see Chapter 7), the recording industry favored self-regulation rather than government intervention.

In 1990, the nation's two largest record retailers ordered all of their outlets to stop stocking and selling sexually explicit recordings by the controversial rap group 2 Live Crew. A Florida judge ruled that the group's album *As Nasty As They Wanna Be* was obscene, even though it carried a warning about explicit lyrics. The Luke Skywalker record label, which produced the album, said the controversy increased sales, but the ban meant that more than 1,000 stores nationwide refused to sell the music. Eventually, the decision was overturned, but sales of the album already had plummeted.

▶ Internet Delivers Free Copyrighted Music

Portable MP3 players, Walkmanlike minicomputer devices about the size of pagers that allow users to download music to a computer chip–based player were introduced in 1999. Because they have no moving parts and use a computer chip, they are easier on batteries than portable tape- and CD-players. "They are the hottest new thing in portable audio players," said Amy Hill, spokesperson for the Consumer Electronics Manufacturing Association. "Every teenager I know wants one of these things."

In 1999, a software-sharing program available on the Web at a place called Napster.com, skyrocketed into popularity. With the program, computer users

Impact | People

Michael Robertson, CEO of mp3.com

by Alice Foege

"Hell's Bells," a raucous anthem by the rock group AC/DC, blared from loudspeakers as Michael Robertson, the chief executive of mp3.com, walked to the podium. It seemed an unlikely introduction at last month's New York Music and Internet Expo for a man who wore a conservative camel hair sports jacket—and who had an evangelical Christian background.

Yet after his keynote speech, Mr. Robertson, a 32-year-old entrepreneur with blond surfer looks, received warm handshakes from teenagers with nose rings and hip-hop artists in baggy jeans. In the 16 months since he started his San Diego-based business, which distributes music over the Internet with a digital compression technology known as MP3, Mr. Robertson has been embraced by struggling musicians as a fellow revolutionary.

© AFP PHOTO/TOM KURTZ/CORBIS

Michael Robertson, chief executive of mp3.com, is hailed by some musicians as a revolutionary because of his distribution of music on the Internet.

Even though he says he really isn't.

"I'm no revolutionary, I'm a pure-bred capitalist," Mr. Robertson said later. "I'm just talking about a new way of delivering music."

The New York Times, 4/11/99. Copyright © 1999 by The New York Times Co. Reprinted by permission.

could download music over the Internet for free, called **file sharing**. Then, using MP3 technology (which provides high-quality sound and requires very little computer storage space), users could keep and use the music. (See Impact/People: Michael Robertson, CEO of MP3.com.) The Recording Industry Association of America (RIAA) immediately sued Napster, claiming copyright infringement.

Then in April 2000, heavy-metal rock group Metallica sued Napster for copyright infringement. Rapper Dr. Dre filed suit two weeks later. In July 2000, an appeals court ordered Napster to shut down the site, but Napster delayed.

Napster finally shut down the site in 2001. In May 2002, Napster aligned with German media giant Bertelsmann AG to develop a membership-based distribution system. The new system, based on a subscription fee, will have to comply with all music copyright agreements.

Still, people continued to download music, aided by new free music services such as kazaa.com and grokster.com. So in 2003, the Recording Industry Association of America (RIAA) personally sued 261 music downloaders across the United States, intensifying its efforts to stop music piracy. On average, every defendant had shared 1,000 songs each.

"A lot of people think they can get away with what they are doing because peer-to-peer file sharing allows them to hide behind made-up screen names," the president of the RIAA told *The New York Times.* "They are not anonymous.

File Sharing Peer-to-peer music swapping over the Internet.

Nancy Davis and her daughter, Kari, were among 261 people named in a Recording Industry Association of America lawsuit in 2003 that alleged Kari shared at least 1,000 songs at Kazaa's file-sharing Web site. A subsequent court ruling stopped prosecution of people who download free music, leaving the legal issues unresolved.

KATY RADDATZ/San Francisco Chronicle

The law is very clear. What they are doing is stealing." Copyright laws allowed the industry to seek from $750 to $150,000 for each violation.

The lawsuits included copies of screen shots of many users' entire online music-sharing accounts, showing the names of each song and how many times the user downloaded music. RIAA offered not to pursue the individual lawsuits for people who are willing to sign a notarized statement saying they will stop sharing music files and delete files they now have. A subsequent court ruling stopped the prosecution of people who download free music, leaving the legal issues unresolved.

▶ Technology Transforms the Future

From the beginning, profits in the recording industry have been tied to technology. Ever since William S. Paley and David Sarnoff decided to produce LPs and 45s, the consumer has followed equipment manufacturers, looking for better, more convenient sound.

Today, recording companies worry that Internet pirates will copy digitized music, which can be sent over the Internet. Online subscribers can now browse through online music catalogs, downloading samples of music they like. But once digitized, the music is available to anyone and can be sent over the Internet around the world.

The challenge for music company executives is to develop a way to protect this new technology with an even newer technology that will make copying impossible. The expansion of MP3 digital technology also signaled a new era for music lovers, making good quality music available on the Internet. MP3 software and file-sharing services such as Kazaa and Grokster allow any computer user with an Internet connection to download the latest music for free. Despite aggressive attempts by the Recording Industry Association of America to stop music file sharing, it is still a widespread practice with vast copyright and income implications for recording artists and recording companies.

Aware of the potential damage to recording company income, officials of the Recording Industry Association of America (RIAA) have cracked down on Internet pirates and people who download copyrighted music on the Internet, but policing the Internet for music sharing is difficult and expensive. The economic implications for the recording industry could be substantial if people are able to easily access the songs they want for free.

When Thomas Edison demonstrated his phonograph for the editors of *Scientific American* in 1877, the magazine reported that

> *Mr. Thomas Edison recently came into this office, placed a little machine on our desk, turned a crank, and the machine inquired as to our health, asked how we liked the phonograph, informed us that it was very well, and bid us a cordial good night. These remarks were not only perfectly audible to ourselves, but to a dozen or more persons gathered around.*

None of the discoveries by Edison's successors has been a new invention, only a refinement. Berliner flattened the cylinder; Goldmark and Sarnoff slowed down the speed; hi-fi, stereo and quadraphonic sound increased the fidelity; and cassettes, compact discs, digital recorders, and MP3 refined the sound further. But the basic discovery of the foundation for today's recording all began in 1877 with Thomas Edison.

Reflecting on the movie version of Edison's life, Robert Metz describes the development of the phonograph: An Edison employee was tinkering with "a makeshift device consisting of a rotating piece of metal with a pointed piece of metal scratching its surface. The device was full of sound and fury—and signified a great deal. . . . And thus, supposedly through idle play, came the first permanent 'record' of ephemeral sound. By any measure, it was an invention of genius."

Media | **Review**

Electronic Publishing Services Inc., N.Y.C.

History

▶ Thomas Edison first demonstrated his phonograph in 1877.

▶ Emile Berliner developed the gramophone in 1887.

▶ Berliner and Eldrige Johnson formed the Victor Talking Machine Company (later RCA Victor) to sell recordings.

▶ Joseph Maxfield perfected recording equipment to eliminate the tinny sound.

Technology

▶ The first standard records were 78 rpm.

▶ Peter Goldmark, working for William S. Paley, developed the long-playing record (33⅓ rpm).

▶ The 45 rpm record was developed by David Sarnoff's staff at RCA.

▶ Eventually record players were sold that could play all record speeds—33⅓ rpm, 45 rpm and 78 rpm.

▶ Digital audiotape (DAT) recorders could replace today's current technologies.

▶ CDRs, compact discs that can record as well as play, are now available to consumers.

▶ Music-sharing company Napster.com, sued in 1999 for copyright infringement by the Recording Industry Association of America (RIAA), shut down in 2001. In May 2002, Napster aligned with German media giant Bertelsmann to offer music by subscription.

▶ MP3 digital technology, perfected in 1999, allows consumers to download and store good-quality music directly from the Internet.

▶ Consumers continue to use music-sharing sites such as Kazaa and Grokster, even though the downloaded songs are covered by copyright.

▶ In 2003, the Recording Industry Association of America sued 261 individual music downloaders, hoping to stop the flow of free music on the Internet, but people still continue to download.

Business

▶ A recording company is divided into artists and repertoire, operations, marketing and promotion, distribution and administration.

▶ About 5,000 labels produce recordings in the United States, but four large corporations dominate the recording industry.

▶ Recording companies sell over one billion recordings a year.

▶ The recording industry collects income from direct sales, music licensing and music videos, but recording income today is declining.

▶ Three issues facing today's recording industry are piracy, attempts to control music content through labeling, and copyright protection for music file sharing.

Culture

▶ Recording industry efforts to improve recorded sound quality contributed to the success of rock 'n' roll entertainers like Elvis Presley and Diana Ross.

▶ The recording industry responded to threats of government regulation of music lyrics by adopting its own standards for music labeling.

Impact | Interactive

The Impact/Interactive CD-ROM that accompanies this text is your gateway to many electronic resources for broadening and testing your critical understanding of the material in Chapter 5. The CD-ROM features the following interactive elements for this and every chapter in the book.

▶ A two- to three-minute timely, high-interest CNN Today video clip with critical viewing questions and a link to relevant selections available within the InfoTrac College Edition database

▶ Chapter-specific activities such as personal inventories and media projects

▶ A link to the *Media/Impact* Web site that offers helpful information and many additional electronic learning resources including:

- An interactive chapter outline and study guide

- Interactive glossary term flashcards and crossword puzzles, concept animations, Internet activities and practice quizzes

- Live links for all URLs given in the chapter so you can easily access the additional information each site offers

▶ A link to InfoTrac College Edition—our online database of more than a million articles representing cutting-edge research and the latest headlines. Updated daily, this online library is available 24 hours a day, seven days a week. The InfoTrac College Edition activities provided below are designed to help you use this valuable resource.

▶ Working the Web

Live links for all of the sites listed below are provided on the *Media/Impact* book companion Web site, which can be accessed through your Impact/Interactive CD-ROM.

- ▶ **ITunes**
  Itunes.com

- ▶ **Kazaa**
  Kazaa.com

- ▶ **Interscope Records–Geffen–A & M Records**
  www.geffen.com

- ▶ **MP3.com**
  www.mp3.com

- ▶ **RealNetworks (audio on the Internet)**
  www.real.com

- ▶ **Recording Industry Association of America**
  www.riaa.com

InfoTrac College Edition Activities

Using InfoTrac College Edition's online database of full-text articles and abstracts, do the following activities as directed by your instructor. The database can be accessed through your Impact/Interactive CD-ROM.

1. Look up "recording industry" or "RIAA" (Recording Industry Association of America) on InfoTrac College Edition and find three articles that interest you about the industry—what the industry is doing to increase sales or create new formats, for example. Be specific and narrow your interest to a specific industry issue. Write a brief paper on your findings and conclusions and be prepared to discuss the issue in class.

2. Using InfoTrac College Edition, look up the keywords "music lyrics" or "music censorship" to learn more about public opinion issues facing the recording industry. Read at least three articles, and decide whether you think some music lyrics constitute a threat to the well-being of some audiences—children, for example—that justifies some form of censorship. If so, what form of censorship or labeling do you think is appropriate? Is there a way to encourage the music recording industry to police itself—to tone down the lyrics, or control distribution of music with explicit lyrics? Write a brief paper on your findings and conclusions and be prepared to discuss the issue in class.

3. Read "Impact/People: Michael Robertson, CEO of mp3.com" in Chapter 5. Then look up "MP3" on InfoTrac College Edition and read at least three articles on this technology. In a 750-word paper, explain what MP3 is and how it's changing the recording industry. Be prepared to discuss your findings in class.

4. Using InfoTrac College Edition, look up the keywords "music sharing" or "file sharing" to learn more about the recording industry's challenges and lawsuits over consumers who share music files over the Internet. After reading several articles on the topic, decide whether you think music sharing or file sharing is wrong. Why, or why not? Do you think the recording industry can stop music file sharing with a selective law-

suit campaign? If not, do you think the recording industry can survive economically? Do you think new laws or Internet regulations are needed to define and control music file sharing? How would you solve the problem? Write a brief paper on your findings and conclusions and be prepared to discuss the issue in class.

5. Using InfoTrac College Edition, look up the keywords "record promotion" or "music promotion" and read at least three articles to learn what the recording industry has done in recent years to boost sales. Is it working? Choose three articles that interest you, print them and either:

a. write a brief paper on your findings, or

b. bring the articles to class for a small-group discussion.

CHAPTER 6

"I think it's an inevitability that radio goes digital."

Gordon Hodge, radio industry analyst

What's Ahead

Today, our memory and impressions about events that happened in the first half of the 20th century are directly tied to radio. Newspapers offered next-day reports and occasional extras, and magazines offered long-term analysis. But radio gave its listeners an immediate record at a time when world events demanded attention.

Radio also gave people entertainment: big bands, Jack Benny, George Burns and Gracie Allen, Abbott and Costello, Bob Hope, and the original radio character, the Shadow ("The weed of crime bears bitter fruit. Crime does not pay! The Shadow knows!").

Radio became America's second national mass medium, after magazines. Radio transformed national politics by transmitting the voices of public debate, as well as the words, to the audience. Radio also expanded Americans' access to popular, as well as classical, culture; opera played on the same dial as slapstick comedy.

▶ Radio's Pervasive Presence

The legacy of news and music remains on radio today, but the medium that was once the center of attention in everyone's front room has moved into the bedroom, the car and the shower. Radio wakes you up and puts you to sleep.

Today to 1899: Radio technology and format programming chase the audience

TODAY

The radio industry is consolidating into large groups of stations using standardized formats, but more than 3,000 stations are webcasting on the Internet.

▼

2001

Sirius Satellite Radio and XM begin offering digital satellite radio service.

▼

1996

Congress passes the Telecommunications Act of 1996, which encourages unprecedented consolidation in the radio industry.

▼

1970

NPR goes on the air.

▼

1960

The Manhattan Grand Jury indicts disc jockey Alan Freed for payola.

▼

1959

Gordon McLendon introduces format radio at station KABL in San Francisco.

▼

1939

Mercury Theater on the Air broadcasts "War of the Worlds," demonstrating how quickly broadcast misinformation can cause a public panic.

▼

1936

Edwin H. Armstrong licenses frequency modulation (FM).

▼

1934

Congress establishes the Federal Communications Commission to regulate broadcasting.

continued on next page

Radio

Radio goes with you when you run on the trail or sit on the beach. Internet radio even follows you to your computer. Consider these industry statistics about radio today:

- 99 percent of America's homes have radios.
- 95 percent of America's cars have radios, and radio reaches four out of five adults in their cars at least once each week.
- 40 percent of Americans listen to the radio sometime between 6 A.M. and midnight.
- 7 percent of America's bathrooms have radios.
- More than 3,000 stations are Webcasting on the Internet.

Although radio is more accessible today, what you hear is not the same as what your parents or grandparents heard. Advertisers, who once sought radio as the only broadcast access to an audience, have many more choices today. For audiences, radio has become an everyday accessory rather than a necessity. No one had envisioned radio's place in today's media mix when radio's pioneers began tinkering just before the turn of the 20th century. All they wanted to do was figure out a way to send sounds along a wire, not through the air.

▶ Radio Takes a Technological Leap

Today, we are so accustomed to sending and receiving messages instantaneously that it is hard to imagine a time when information took more than a week to travel from place to place. In the early 1800s, the pony express took ten and a half days to go from St. Joseph, Missouri, to San Francisco, California. Stage coaches needed 44 hours to bring news from New York to Washington.

Technological advances brought rapid changes in how quickly information could move throughout the country. First came the invention of the telegraph and the telephone, which depended on electrical lines to deliver their messages, and then wireless telegraphy, which delivers radio signals through the air.

In 1835, Samuel F. B. Morse first demonstrated his electromagnetic telegraph system in America. In 1843, Congress gave him $30,000 to string four telegraph lines along the Baltimore & Ohio Railroad right-of-way from Baltimore to Washington. The first official message—"What hath God wrought?"—was sent from Baltimore to Washington, D.C., on May 24, 1844.

Telegraph lines followed the railroads, and for more than 30 years Americans depended on Morse's coded messages printed on tape, sent from one railroad station to another. Then on March 10, 1876, Alexander Graham Bell sent a message by his new invention, the telephone, to his associate Thomas A. Watson in an adjoining room of their Boston laboratory: "Mr. Watson, come here. I want you."

Both Morse's telegraph and Bell's telephone used wires to carry messages. Then in Germany in 1887, the physicist Heinrich Hertz began experimenting with radio waves, which became known as Hertzian waves—the first discovery in a series of refinements that led to the development of radio broadcasting.

Radio's Revolution Broadcasting was truly a revolutionary media development. Imagine a society in which the only way you can hear music or enjoy a comedy is at a live performance or by listening to tinny noises on a record machine. The only way you can hear a speech is to be in the audience. Movies show action but no sound.

Without the inventions of broadcasting's early pioneers such as Heinrich Hertz, you could still be living without the sounds of media that you have come to take for granted. Four pioneers besides Hertz are credited with advancing early radio broadcasting in America: Guglielmo Marconi, Reginald Aubrey Fessenden, Lee de Forest and David Sarnoff.

Wireless Breakthrough: Guglielmo Marconi

Twenty-year-old Guglielmo Marconi, the son of wealthy Italian parents, used the results of three discoveries by Morse, Bell and Hertz to expand his idea that messages should be able to travel across space without a wire. Marconi became obsessed with the idea, refusing food and working at home in his locked upstairs room.

Soon Marconi could ring a bell across the room or downstairs without using a wire. Eventually Marconi was able to broadcast over a distance of nine miles. "The calm of my life ended then," Marconi said later. The *New York Herald* invited Marconi to the United States to report the America's Cup Race in October 1899. Marconi reported "by wireless!" American business people, intrigued by the military potential of Marconi's invention, invested $10 million to form American Marconi.

To experiment with the new discovery, amateur radio operators created clubs. Two experimenters, Reginald Aubrey Fessenden and Lee de Forest, advanced the Marconi discovery to create today's radio.

Experimental Broadcasts: Reginald Aubrey Fessenden

Reginald Aubrey Fessenden, a Canadian, began wireless experiments in the United States in 1900 when he set up his National Electric Signaling Company to attempt sending voices by radio waves. On Christmas Eve 1906, "ship wireless operators over a wide area of the Atlantic . . . were startled to hear a woman singing, then a violin playing, then a man reading passages from Luke. It was considered uncanny; wireless rooms were soon crowded with the curious," wrote broadcast historian Erik Barnouw.

The noises were coming from Fessenden's experimental station at Brant Rock, Massachusetts. Fessenden's 1906 experiment is considered the world's first voice and music broadcast.

Detecting Radio Waves: Lee De Forest

De Forest called himself the father of radio because in 1907 he perfected a glass bulb called the Audion that could detect radio waves. "Unwittingly then," wrote de Forest, "had I discovered an invisible Empire of the Air."

Besides being an inventor, de Forest was a good publicist. He began what he called "broadcasts" from New York and then from the Eiffel Tower. In 1910, he broadcast Enrico Caruso singing at the Metropolitan Opera House. Later his mother broadcast an appeal to give women the vote. Gradually, the Audion became the foundation of modern broadcasting.

Radio for the People: David Sarnoff

In 1912, 21-year-old wireless operator David Sarnoff relayed news from Nantucket Island, Massachusetts, that he had received a distress call from the *Titanic* on his Marconi Wireless. Four years later, when Sarnoff was working for the Marconi Company in New York, he wrote a visionary memo that predicted radio's future, although in 1916 his ideas were widely ignored.

"I have in mind a plan of development which would make radio a household utility. The idea is to bring music into the home by wireless," Sarnoff wrote. Eventually, as commercial manager and then president of RCA, Sarnoff would watch his early vision for radio come true.

Impact | TimeFrame

Today to 1899: Radio technology and format programming chase the audience

continued

▼
1920
Station KDKA in Pittsburgh goes on the air, the nation's first commercial radio station.

▼
1907
Lee de Forest introduces the Audion tube, which improves the clarity of radio signal reception. Reginald Aubrey Fessenden transmits the first voice and music broadcast.

▼
1899
Guglielmo Marconi first uses his wireless radio to report the America's Cup Race.

© Superstock

Radio today has become an every-day accessory rather than a necessity.

▶ Federal Government Polices the Airwaves

The federal government decided to regulate broadcasting almost as soon as it was invented. **This decision to regulate broadcasting separated the broadcast media, which were regulated early, from the print media, which are not regulated directly by any federal government agency.**

As amateurs competed with the military for the airwaves, Congress passed the Radio Act of 1912 to license people who wanted to broadcast or receive messages. The federal government decided to license people to transmit signals because **there were only a certain number of frequencies available to carry broadcast signals.** Many amateurs, trying to send signals on the same frequency, were knocking each other off the air. The government intervened to try to keep the operators out of each other's way.

Then, during World War I, the federal government ordered all amateurs off the air and took control of all privately owned stations, and the military took over radio broadcasting. After the war, with the freeze lifted, the navy argued that it should maintain the monopoly over the airwaves that it had enjoyed during the war.

Faced with strong arguments by the amateurs that they should be able to return to the airwaves, Congress decided against a navy monopoly. Instead, the government sanctioned a private monopoly formed by General Electric, Westinghouse, AT&T, Western Electric Company and United Fruit Company. General Electric bought out American Marconi and its patents, and in 1919, these five sympathetic interests pooled the patents they controlled to form Radio Corporation of America (RCA).

David Sarnoff became RCA's general manager in 1921. Because of this early monopoly, RCA dominated radio development for many years, but eventually smaller operations formed all over the country as radio fever spread from coast to coast.

▶ Experimental Stations Multiply

A plaque in San Jose, California, celebrates the 1909 founding of the experimental station FN: "On this site in 1909, Charles D. Herrold founded a voice radio station which opened the door to electronic mass communication. He conceived the idea of 'broadcasting' to the public, and his station, the world's first, has now served Northern California for half a century." Today, that station is San Francisco's KCBS.

Various other stations claim they were among the earliest radio pioneers. Station 9XM broadcast music and weather reports from Madison, Wisconsin; 6ADZ broadcast concerts from Hollywood; 4XD sent phonograph music from a chicken coop in Charlotte, North Carolina; and 8MK in Detroit, operated by *Detroit News* publisher William E. Scripps, transmitted election returns.

These radio operators broadcast messages to each other and their friends, but not the general public. These amateur radio operators were early examples of broadcast entrepreneurs. They were tinkerers, fascinated with an invention that could carry sounds through the air. One of these tinkerers, Frank Conrad, is credited with creating the beginnings of the nation's first **commercial** radio station.

▶ KDKA Launches Commercial Broadcasting

An ad in the September 29, 1920, *Pittsburgh Sun* changed broadcasting from an exclusive hobby to an easy-to-use medium available to everyone. The ad described a 20-minute evening concert broadcast from the home of Frank Conrad, a "wireless enthusiast" who worked for Westinghouse.

Using perhaps the first version of today's Walkman, a couple on Guglielmo Marconi's yacht, *Electra,* do the fox trot while sailing to Albany, New York, in 1922.

Library of Congress

Conrad often broadcast concerts from his garage on his station 8XK. But his boss at Westinghouse, Harry P. Davis, had an idea: Why not improve the broadcasts so more people would want to buy radios? Davis talked Conrad into setting up a more powerful transmitter at the Westinghouse plant by November 2, so that Conrad could broadcast election returns.

On October 27, 1920, using the powers of the 1912 Radio Act, the U.S. Department of Commerce licensed station KDKA as the nation's first **commercial** station. The broadcast began at 8 P.M. on November 2, 1920, and continued past midnight, reporting that Warren G. Harding was the nation's next president. KDKA immediately began a daily one-hour evening schedule, 8:30 to 9:30 P.M.

▶ The Radio Audience Expands Quickly

The crude KDKA broadcasts proved that regular programming could attract a loyal audience. KDKA was just the beginning of what eventually became radio networks. The radio craze led almost immediately to a period of rapid expansion as entrepreneurs and advertisers began to grasp the potential of the new medium. Almost as quickly, government was compelled to step in to expand its regulation of radio broadcasting.

Radio's potential as a moneymaker for its owners fueled competition for the airwaves. Three important developments for radio's future were the:

1. Blanket licensing agreement

2. Decision that radio would accept commercial sponsors

3. Radio Act of 1927

Blanket Licensing   At first, stations played phonograph records; then they invited artists to perform live in their studios. Some of the nation's best talent sought the publicity that radio could give them, but eventually, the performers asked to be paid.

In 1923, the American Society of Composers, Authors and Publishers (**ASCAP**) sued several stations for payment, claiming that broadcasting ASCAP-licensed music on the radio meant that people would buy less sheet music. Station owners argued that playing the songs on their stations would publicize the sheet music.

Eventually the stations agreed to pay ASCAP royalties through a blanket licensing agreement, which meant the stations paid ASCAP a fee ($250 a year at first). In exchange, the stations could use all ASCAP-licensed music on the air. (ASCAP licenses its music to stations the same way today. Eventually another licensing organization, Broadcast Music, Inc., or BMI, also would collect broadcast royalties. See page 115.)

ASCAP   American Society of Composers, Authors and Publishers.

Blanket Licensing Agreement
An arrangement whereby radio stations become authorized to use recorded music for broadcast by paying a fee.

Commercial Sponsorship   Once station owners agreed to pay for their programs, they had to figure out where they would get the money. AT&T had the answer with an idea they pioneered at their station WEAF in New York. WEAF inaugurated the policy of selling advertising time to sponsors. Its first sponsored program cost $100 for ten minutes.

The success of commercial sponsorship, as a way to support radio, settled the issue of who would pay the cost of airing the programs. Advertisers paid for programs through their advertising; the American public paid for the programs indirectly by supporting the advertisers who supported radio.

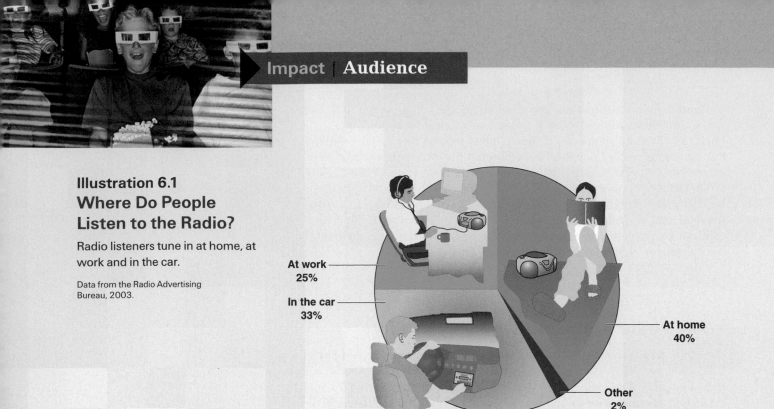

Illustration 6.1
Where Do People Listen to the Radio?

Radio listeners tune in at home, at work and in the car.

Data from the Radio Advertising Bureau, 2003.

At work 25%

In the car 33%

At home 40%

Other 2%

▶ Congress Regulates Radio

As more stations began to crowd the air, their signals interfered with one another. With only so many good frequencies available, the provisions of the Radio Act of 1912 (see page 110) began to seem inadequate. Congress passed the Radio Act of 1927, which formed the Federal Radio Commission under the jurisdiction of the Department of Commerce. The president appointed the commission's five members, with the approval of the Senate.

The limitations on air space required that broadcasting in the United States would operate under a type of government regulation unknown to newspaper and magazine publishers. Stations were licensed for three years and were required by the commission to operate "*as a public convenience, interest or necessity requires.*"

The commission, created to protect the stations by allocating frequencies, also became the license holder. The stations could operate only with the government's approval, and stations could be sold or transferred only if the commission approved. The Radio Act of 1927, including the concept that broadcasters would operate in the "*public convenience, interest or necessity,*" **became the foundation for all broadcast regulation in the United States.**

In 1934, Congress established the **Federal Communications Commission (FCC)** to regulate the expanding wireless medium, making the FCC a separate agency of government and no longer a part of the Department of Commerce. It is important to remember that the commission's original purpose was to allocate the broadcast spectrum so station broadcasts would not interfere with one another. The FCC was not originally envisioned to oversee broadcast content.

The FCC began work on July 11, 1934, with seven commissioners appointed by the president, with Senate approval. This same basic structure and purpose govern the commission's actions today, but now there are only five commissioners. The establishment of the FCC in 1934 also set the precedent for the later regulation of television.

FCC Federal Communications Commission.

▶ Radio Becomes a Powerful Force

Most radio stations mixed entertainment, culture and public service. Radio created a new kind of collective national experience. Radio in the 1930s and 1940s became a powerful cultural and political force. Radio gave multitudes of people a new, inexpensive source of information and entertainment.

The commercialization of American broadcasting also gave advertisers access to this audience at home. Radio's massive audience sat enraptured with sponsored programming of many types: comedy, music, serials, drama and news. Eventually, all these types of programming migrated to television.

▶ "War of the Worlds" Challenges Radio's Credibility

On Halloween Eve, October 30, 1939, the *Mercury Theater on the Air* broadcast a play based on the H. G. Wells story "War of the Worlds." The live 8 P.M. broadcast played opposite the very popular Edgar Bergen program on NBC, and rarely had even 4 percent of the audience. Very few people heard at the beginning of the program the announcement that the Mercury Theater was performing a version of the Wells story.

The program began with the announcer introducing some band music. A second voice then said, "Ladies and gentlemen, we interrupt our program of dance music to bring you a special bulletin. At 20 minutes before 8 o'clock Central Time, Professor Farrell of Mount Jennings Observatory, Chicago, reports observing several explosions of incandescent gas occurring at regular intervals on the planet Mars."

More dance music followed and then more bulletins about the Martians, with the startling news that 1,500 people near Princeton, New Jersey, had died when a meteor hit the town. Then the announcer said it was not a meteor but a spaceship carrying Martians armed with death rays.

Two professors from the Princeton geology department actually set out to locate the "meteors." In Newark, more than 20 families rushed out of their homes, covering their faces with wet handkerchiefs to protect themselves from the "gas." After a burst of horrified calls, CBS began repeating the announcement that the program was just a play.

The episode demonstrated how easily alarming information could be innocently misinterpreted, especially because the listeners had no other source to check the reliability of what they were hearing. Radio listeners truly were a captive audience.

The fear created by Orson Welles' "War of the Worlds" broadcast demonstrated how easily alarming information could be misinterpreted on the radio.

▶ Radio Networks Expand

The formation of the networks as a source of programming and revenue is a crucial development in the history of American radio. A **network** is a collection of stations (radio or television) that offers programs, usually simultaneously, throughout the country, during designated times. As the networks

Network A collection of stations (radio or TV) that offers programs, usually simultaneously, throughout the country.

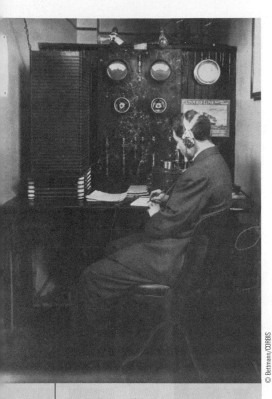

© Bettmann/CORBIS

David Sarnoff, who began his broadcast career as a wireless operator, eventually became president of Radio Corporation of America (RCA).

stretched across the country, they provided a dependable source of programming. Most stations found it easier to affiliate with a network and receive its programming than to develop local programs.

David Sarnoff Launches NBC   NBC grew out of the government's original agreement with RCA. RCA, GE and Westinghouse formed the National Broadcasting Company in 1926. By January 1927, NBC, headed by David Sarnoff, had formed two networks: the Red network (fed from WEAF) and the Blue network (originating from station WJZ in Newark). Station engineers drew the planned hookups of the two networks with red and blue colored pencils—hence their names.

RCA faced criticism about its broad control over the airwaves because RCA continued as the world's largest distributor of radios, which were made by Westinghouse and General Electric.

William S. Paley Starts CBS   Twenty-six-year-old William S. Paley, heir to a tobacco fortune, bought the financially struggling Columbia Phonograph Company in 1929. He changed the name to Columbia Broadcasting System. He put the CBS network on the air with 25 stations. Programming originated from WABC in New York. Paley became the nemesis of NBC, then controlled by David Sarnoff, and this early competition between Sarnoff and Paley shaped the development of American broadcasting.

Edward Noble Buys ABC   In 1941, the FCC ordered RCA to divest itself of one of its networks. In 1943, RCA sold NBC-Blue to Edward J. Noble (who had made his fortune as head of the company that produced LifeSavers candy). Noble paid $8 million for the network that became the American Broadcasting Company, giving the country a three-network radio system.

Radio networks prospered until the 1980s, when NBC sold its radio network, and CBS and ABC (who also own television properties) gave more attention to their television holdings.

▶ Radio in the TV Era

Initially, it seemed that television would cause the death of radio. As soon as television proved itself, advertisers abandoned radio, said comedian Fred Allen, "like the bones at a barbecue." The talent fled, too—Bob Hope, Milton Berle, Jackie Gleason. Public affairs programs like *Meet the Press* made the move to TV, as did Edward R. Murrow's radio news program, *Hear It Now*, which became *See It Now*.

Five developments in the 1940s, 1950s and 1960s changed the medium of radio and guaranteed its survival alongside television:

1. the FCC's licensing of FM
2. a new source of recorded music for broadcast
3. the introduction of radio formats
4. the introduction of reliable clock and car radios
5. Alan Freed and the payola scandals

The FCC Recognizes FM: Edwin H. Armstrong   After working for more than a decade to eliminate static from radio broadcasts, engineer Edwin H. Armstrong applied to the FCC in 1936 to broadcast using his new technique, frequency modulation (FM). Because of the way FM signals travel through the air, FM offered truer transmission with much less static. Armstrong faced difficult opposition from David Sarnoff, who had been an early Armstrong sponsor.

The FCC received 150 applications for FM licenses in 1939, but then froze licensing during World War II. After the war, Armstrong again faced Sarnoff, and this time Armstrong lost. RCA, which was using Armstrong's frequency modulation in its TV and FM sets, refused to pay him royalties. Armstrong sued RCA.

RCA fought Armstrong for four years, saying that RCA had been among the early developers of FM, citing RCA's sponsorship of Armstrong's beginning experiments. In 1953, Armstrong became ill and suffered a stroke, then committed suicide. RCA then quickly settled the suit with Armstrong's widow for $1 million.

FM eventually became the spectrum of choice for music lovers, far surpassing the broadcast quality of AM.

Edwin H. Armstrong's invention of FM made radio signals clearer. For nearly 20 years, Armstrong battled RCA's David Sarnoff for royalties. Disheartened by the legal battle, Armstrong committed suicide, but his widow eventually won the royalty payments.

Licensed Recordings Launch Disc Jockeys

Early radio station owners avoided playing records because they would have had to pay ASCAP royalties. The FCC also required stations that played records to remind their audiences every half-hour that they were listening to recorded music, not a live orchestra. This discouraged record-spinning.

In 1935, newscaster Martin Block at New York's independent station WNEW began playing records in between his newscasts, and then he started a program called *Make Believe Ballroom*. He is generally considered America's first disc jockey. Then, in 1940, the FCC ruled that once stations bought a record, they could play it on the air whenever they liked, without the half-hour announcements.

To counteract ASCAP's insistence on royalties, broadcasters formed a cooperative music licensing organization called Broadcast Music, Inc. Most rhythm and blues, country and rock 'n' roll artists eventually signed with **BMI**, which charged stations less for recording artists than ASCAP. With an inexpensive source of music available, a new media personality was created—the DJ.

BMI Broadcast Music, Inc., a cooperative music licensing organization.

Gordon McLendon Introduces Format Radio

How would the stations know which mix of records to use? The answer came from Gordon McLendon, the father of format radio. At KLIF in Dallas, McLendon combined music and news in a predictable rotation of 20-minute segments, and eventually KLIF grew very popular. Next he refined the music by creating the Top 40 format. Top 40 played the top-selling hits continually, interrupted only by a disc jockey or a newscast.

By 1959, McLendon launched the beautiful-music format at KABL in San Francisco. In 1964, he used a 24-hour news format for Chicago's WNUS, using three news vans with "telesigns" that showed news on the roofs in lights as the vans drove around town.

Formats meant stations could now share standardized programs that stations previously had to produce individually. Eventually, the idea of formatted programming spread, which made network programming and the networks themselves less important to individual stations.

Clock and Car Radios Make Radio Portable

Clock and car radios helped ensure radio's survival by making it an everyday accessory. Transistor radios, first sold in 1948 for $40, were more reliable and cheaper than tube radios. Clock radios, introduced in the 1950s, woke people up and caused them to rely on radio for the first news of the day.

Drive-Time Audience People who listen to the radio in their cars during 6 to 9 A.M. and 4 to 7 P.M.

William Lear, who also designed the Lear jet, invented the car radio in 1928. Early car radios were enormous, with spotty reception, but the technology that was developed during World War II helped refine them. In 1946, 9 million cars had car radios. By 1963, the number was 50 million. **Drive-time audiences** (who listened from 6 to 9 A.M. and 4 to 7 P.M.) were growing at the time that a radio station owner coined the term.

A Columbia University report, commissioned by NBC in 1954, defined radio's new role. "Radio was the one medium that could accompany almost every type of activity. . . . Where radio once had been a leisure-time 'reward' after a day's work, television was now occupying that role. Radio had come to be viewed less as a treat than as a kind of 'companion' to some other activity." Like magazines, radio survived in part because the medium adapted to fill a different need for its audience.

Payola The practice of accepting payment to play specific recordings on the air.

Alan Freed and the Payola Scandals The rise of rock 'n' roll coincided with the development of transistor and portable radios, which meant radio played a central role in the rock revolution. "Rock and radio were made for each other. The relationship between record companies and radio stations became mutually beneficial. By providing the latest hits, record companies kept stations' operating costs low. The stations, in turn, provided the record companies with the equivalent of free advertising," wrote radio historian David MacFarland.

Eventually this relationship would prove too close. On February 8, 1960, Congress began hearings into charges that disc jockeys and program directors had accepted cash to play specific recordings on the air. The term **payola** was coined to describe this practice, combining "pay" and "Victrola" (the name of a popular record player).

In May 1960, the Manhattan grand jury charged eight men with commercial bribery for accepting more than $100,000 in payoffs for playing records. The most prominent among them was Alan Freed, who had worked in Cleveland (where he was credited with coining the term rock 'n' roll) and at New York's WABC.

In February 1962, he pleaded guilty to two counts of accepting payoffs, paid a $300 fine and received six months' probation. Then Freed was found guilty of income tax evasion. He died in 1965 while awaiting trial, at age 43. In September 1960, Congress amended the Federal Communications Act to prohibit the payment of cash or gifts in exchange for air play.

AP/Wide World Photos

Disc jockey Alan Freed admitted in 1962 that he accepted payments (payola) for playing specific recordings on the air.

▶ Working in Radio

About 12,000 radio stations are on the air in the United States. They are about evenly divided between FM and AM.

Today, network programming plays a much smaller role than when radio began. National Public Radio (NPR) is the only major public network. Many commercial stations today use *program services*, which provide satellite as well as formatted programming.

Many stations are part of a *group*, which means a company that owns more than one station in more than one broadcast market. Other stations are part of a *combination AM/FM (a combo)*, which means one company owns both AM and FM stations in the same market. A few stations remain family-owned, single operations that run just like any other small business.

Impact | People

Radio Gets Static on Hill: Senate Panel on Consolidation Cites Dixie Chicks Ban

They may have been thousands of miles away, but the members of the Dixie Chicks were the stars of a Senate Commerce hearing . . . examining the effects of consolidation in the radio industry.

Senators used the band as an example of what can go wrong when a single media company controls hundreds of stations across the United States.

The country group was banned from radio stations owned by Cumulus Media, Inc. and Cox Communications after lead singer Natalie Maines told an audience at a March concert in London that the band was "ashamed the president of the United States is from Texas."

While Sen. John McCain, R-Ariz., said he disagreed with Maines' sentiment, the fact that giant radio groups could ban a group's music because of a political statement was an "incredible, incredible act" that serves as an example of how radio industry consolidation is causing the "erosion of the First Amendment."

What troubled McCain and several of the other senators is not that a decision was made to keep the band off the air, but rather that the decision was made in a corporate headquarters miles away from the station to stop playing the group's music.

"If a local station made a decision not to play a particular band, then that is what localism is all about," McCain said. "But when a corporate decision is made that (a company's radio stations) will not play a group because of a political statement, then that comes back to what we're talking about with media consolidation."

Hollywood Reporter, July 9, 2003, p. 1.

AP/Wide World Photos

In 2003, during the Iraq conflict, lead singer Natalie Maines of the Dixie Chicks (center) told a concert audience that she was "ashamed the president of the United States is from Texas." Cox Communications and Cumulus Media, Inc. banned the group's songs from its stations. Congressional leaders, in hearings about the ban, said consolidation in the radio industry has made station groups too powerful.

The *general manager* runs the radio station. The *program manager* oversees what goes on the air, including the news programs, the station's format and any on-air people. Salespeople, who are called *account executives*, sell the advertising for programs.

Traffic people schedule the commercials, make sure they run correctly and bill the clients. *Production people* help with local programming and produce commercials for the station. *Engineers* keep the station on the air. *Administrative people* pay the bills, answer the phones and order the paper clips. At a small station, as few as five people handle all these jobs.

▶ The Business of Radio

Instead of dying after the spread of television, radio managed to thrive by adapting to an audience that sought the portability and immediacy that radio offers. Nothing can beat radio for quick news bulletins or the latest hits. Radio

Popular singers like Clint Black have made country music one of radio's most popular formats.

Cross-Ownership The practice of one company owning radio and TV stations in the same broadcast market.

"I love it when you use your 'All Things Considered' voice."

also delivers a targeted audience much better than television because the radio station you prefer defines you to an advertiser much better than the television station you watch.

The advertising potential for an intimate medium like radio is attracting entrepreneurs who have never owned a station and group owners who want to expand their holdings, given the FCC's deregulation. When you listen to the radio in your car or through earphones while you jog, for instance, radio is not competing with any other medium for your attention. Advertisers like this exclusive access to an audience. Three important issues for people in radio today are:

1. deregulation
2. ratings
3. formats

▶ Congress Creates National Public Radio (NPR)

The Public Broadcasting Act of 1967 created the Corporation for Public Broadcasting and included funding for public radio and TV stations. National Public Radio (NPR) launched a national program on FM in 1970, but many radios still didn't have an FM dial. Most public stations—owned by colleges and universities and staffed by volunteers—were staffed irregularly.

Then NPR started the program *All Things Considered* for the evening drive-time and in 1979 launched *Morning Edition,* hosted by Bob Edwards. Today, *Morning Edition* and *All Things Considered* have a very loyal audience for their long interviews on topical issues and reports on breaking news by seasoned reporters such as Juan Williams. By design, public radio is an alternative to the commercial networks.

▶ The Telecommunications Act of 1996 Overhauls Radio

The Telecommunications Act of 1996 was the first major overhaul of broadcast regulation since the Federal Communications Commission was established in 1934. The Act continues a deregulation policy of commercial radio that began in the 1980s.

Before the Act was passed, the FCC limited the number of radio stations that one company could own nationwide. The Telecommunications Act removed the limit on the number of radio stations a company can own, and in each local market, the number of stations that one owner can hold depends on the size of the market. (For a complete discussion of the Telecommunications Act, see Chapter 14.)

The Telecommunications Act also allows **cross-ownership,** which means that companies can own radio and TV stations in the same market, and broadcast and cable outlets in the same market. As soon as the Act passed in February 1996, radio station sales began to soar. Today many radio companies own hundreds of stations each. Supporters of the changes say radio will become more competitive because these larger companies will be

Impact | Culture

Internet Radio's Brave New World
The Coolest Stations on the Web

by Jeff Salamon

Nowadays, with media consolidation rampant, the only place you'll find that sort of freedom is on the left end of the dial, where low-watt college and community stations spin everything from Bulgarian folk music to hardcore punk. But if you're out of their modest broadcast range, you're out of luck—unless you're hooked up to the Internet, in which case you have it better than the hippies ever did.

There's already some consolidation going on in Web radio—Broadcast.com and ImagineRadio have grouped together large numbers of stations on their Web sites—but the nature of the medium ensures that alternatives will always be available. . . .

Rapweek Now that even your mom knows who Lauryn Hill is, you might want to start exploring hip-hop's underground, which is every bit as ornery and vital as the punk underground of the Eighties. This weekly show, beamed out of New York, is a good place to start. Hosts Eddie III and DL throw in a few familiar names, but for every act you know . . . they mix in ten you don't . . . . Along with some uncontestable wit ("I don't like Oprah/She's just corny/Medi-okra"), you get fresh beats, déjà vu-inducing samples, and some virtuoso scratching and mixing. **www.rapweek.com**

Photo by Len Irish.

DL (left) and Eddie III spin everything from the Roots to Pumpkinhead on rapweek.com.

Radio Free Kansas Fortysome-thing Steve Taaffe is a bit older than most Webcasters, and it shows—his heartland site is split between his collection of vintage-radio airchecks ("Rockin' Radio WCIF/FM, Carbondale!") and his deep library of grog rock. Among his archival treasures are shows spotlighting Norwegian metal and the late-Sixties Canterbury scene. **www.tafcommedia.net**

Underground Radio 3WK 24/7, this year-old Web site is the FM radio station of your dreams. In one typical set, the popular bumps up against the obscure, moving from the white-boy funk of Fun Lovin' Criminals' "Korean Bodega" to the shoe-gazer revivalism of All Natural Lemon and Lime Flavors' "In Between and After." **www.yuk.com**

able to give the stations better support than small, single owners. Opponents point out that consolidation in the radio industry will lead to less program variety for consumers and too much power for companies that own large numbers of radio stations nationwide. (See Impact/Business, "Radio Gets Static on Hill: Senate Panel on Consolidation Cites Dixie Chicks Ban," page 117).

▶ Are Radio Ratings Accurate?

Radio station owners depend on ratings to set advertising rates, and the stations with the most listeners command the highest ad rates. A company called Arbitron provides the radio business with its ratings. To find out what radio

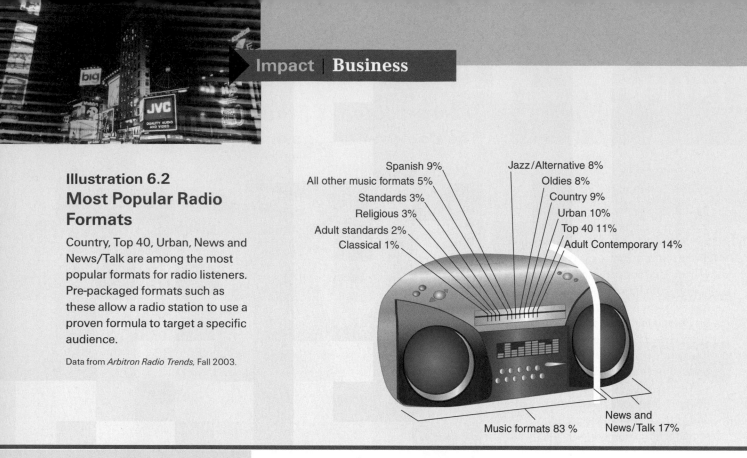

Illustration 6.2
Most Popular Radio Formats

Country, Top 40, Urban, News and News/Talk are among the most popular formats for radio listeners. Pre-packaged formats such as these allow a radio station to use a proven formula to target a specific audience.

Data from *Arbitron Radio Trends,* Fall 2003.

Spanish 9%
All other music formats 5%
Standards 3%
Religious 3%
Adult standards 2%
Classical 1%

Jazz/Alternative 8%
Oldies 8%
Country 9%
Urban 10%
Top 40 11%
Adult Contemporary 14%

Music formats 83 %

News and News/Talk 17%

Critical Question

Which radio format or formats do you listen to most often, and why? How often do you switch between stations, and when and why do you switch? To what extent do you fit the profile of the audience these stations target?

stations people are listening to, Arbitron requests that selected listeners complete and return diaries sent to them by the company.

Arbitron uses four measures of radio listening: average quarter-hour, "cume," ratings and share.

1. *Average quarter-hour* means the average number of people listening to a station in any given 15-minute period.

2. *"Cume"* stands for the cumulative audience—the estimated number of people listening to a station for five minutes or more in any given 15-minute time period.

3. *Ratings* is the percentage of the total population that a station is reaching.

4. *Share* stands for the percentage of people listening to the radio that a station is reaching.

Arbitron often is criticized because minorities, non–English-speaking listeners and people ages 18 to 24, don't return the diaries in the same proportion as the other people who are surveyed. Arbitron acknowledges the problems and has tried filling out diaries for people over the phone and adding bilingual interviewers. Still, questions persist. However, no other major competing radio ratings service exists, and stations are very dependent on ratings to set their rates for advertising. Arbitron critics contend that its ratings hurt the different rock and ethnic formats, while aiding the

AP/Wide World Photos

Today's radio stations are highly automated. Often the on-air talent simultaneously runs the equipment.

Left: Lawrence Lucier/Getty Images; Right: William Thomas Cain/Getty Images

In 2004, comedian and commentator Al Franken (left) launched a radio commentary program to counteract conservative radio talk show host Rush Limbaugh. Franken and Limbaugh are part of one of radio's most popular formats—News/Talk.

middle-of-the-road, news, and talk formats, whose audiences are older and more responsive to the diaries.

▶ Radio Depends on Ready-Made Formats

Today's radio station owners, looking for an audience, can use one of several ready-made formats. By adjusting their formats, radio managers can test the markets until they find a formula that works to deliver their audience to advertisers.

If you were a radio station manager today, and you wanted to program your station, you could choose from several popular formats listed here according to the number of stations currently using them.

1. **News/News/Talk.** A station with this format devotes most of its air time to different types of talk shows, which can include call-in features, where listeners question on-the-air guests. Its typical audience is 35 and older. It is difficult for a radio station to survive on news alone, so most stations are in big cities because of the continuing source of news stories. In 2004, comedian and commentator Al Franken launched a news/talk radio program to challenge conservative news/talk host Rush Limbaugh.

2. **Adult Contemporary.** This program format includes adult rock and light rock music by artists such as Kenny G and Anita Baker. It aims to reach 25- to 40-year-olds in all types of markets.

3. **Contemporary Hit/Top 40.** Playing songs on *Billboard's* current hits list, a Top-40 station closely follows trends among listeners, especially teenagers.

4. **Country.** The Grand Ole Opry first broadcast country music on WSM in Nashville in 1925, and this radio format is among the most popular, aimed at 25- to 45-year-olds in urban as well as rural areas.

5. **Spanish.** Spanish stations are the fastest-growing foreign-language format, as radio owners target the nation's expanding Latino population. Spanish-language radio usually features news, music and talk. Most Spanish-language stations are AMs that recently have been converted from less-profitable formats.

Satellite Digital Radio

Two companies began beaming digital radio broadcasts into cars and homes beginning in 2001. Here is how they do it.

The New York Times, Oct. 19, 2000, D1. Copyright © 2000 by The New York Times Co. Adapted with permission.

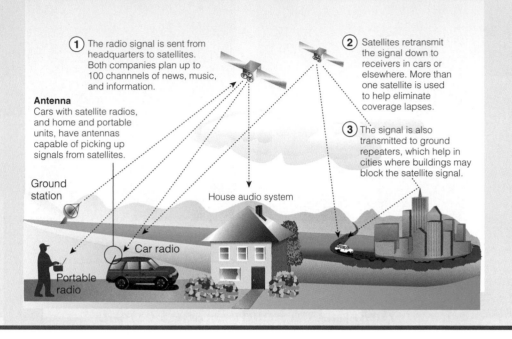

① The radio signal is sent from headquarters to satellites. Both companies plan up to 100 channnels of news, music, and information.

Antenna
Cars with satellite radios, and home and portable units, have antennas capable of picking up signals from satellites.

Ground station

② Satellites retransmit the signal down to receivers in cars or elsewhere. More than one satellite is used to help eliminate coverage lapses.

③ The signal is also transmitted to ground repeaters, which help in cities where buildings may block the satellite signal.

House audio system

Car radio

Portable radio

6. **Album-Oriented Rock (AOR).** Directed toward 18- to 24-year-olds, this format delivers contemporary hits, like Top 40, but with songs from a longer span of time—from within the past two years, for example, instead of the past month.

7. **Middle of the Road (MOR).** "Not too hard, not too soft" is the phrase most often used to describe this format. You could also add "not too loud, not too fast, not too slow, not too lush, not too new." The audience is 25 to 35 years old, and the music may include the Beatles, James Taylor, the Supremes and Stevie Wonder.

8. **Religious.** "Here's the news of today and the promise of tomorrow," begins one station with religious programming. Although some denominations own stations and broadcast their points of view, many stations have adopted religious programming purely as a way to make a profit. These stations offer inspirational music, news, weather, sports and drama.

Two of the fastest-growing formats are News/Talk and Spanish-language radio. The number of stations using a News/Talk format doubled between 1993 and 1998. Larry King, Rush Limbaugh and Howard Stern are the most notable "personalities" who have profited from the expanding audience for News/Talk.

News/Talk radio is very popular in Los Angeles, but the most-listened-to radio station in the Los Angeles area is a Spanish-language station. The popularity of the station in an area with an expanding Spanish-language population shows how cultural changes in urban areas quickly can affect the economics of radio in that area.

Stations can divide these traditional formats into even more subcategories: AOR is splitting into modern rock and oldies; some adult contemporary stations play only love songs. The use of recorded program formats means that a station can specialize its programming simply by changing the tapes or discs.

This makes disc jockeys as personalities much less important than they once were. Many stations operate without disc jockeys altogether or limit personality programming to morning and evening drive-time. The rest of the day and evening these stations can rely on an engineer and an announcer to carry the programming.

Today, networks, which once dominated radio programming, mainly provide national news to their affiliates. Station managers can program their own stations, mixing local news, music and announcements.

Stations also can get programming from syndicated and satellite program services. Syndicates provide pre-packaged program formats. Satellites make program distribution easier; satellite networks, such as Satellite Music Network, promise the broadcaster original, up-to-date programming without a large, local staff.

▶ Technology Transforms the Future

The most significant trend in radio is the move toward more segmentation of the audience, similar to the division of audiences in the magazine industry. Identifying a specific audience segment and programming for it is called **narrowcasting**. "With narrowcasting, advertising efficiency goes way up as overall costs go down . . . . We are approaching the unstated goal of all radio programmers: to create a station aimed so perfectly that the listener will no longer have to wait, ever, for the song that he wants to hear," says radio historian Eric Zorn.

Demand programming is a new term that describes radio's future possibilities. In the ultimate form of narrowcasting, a listener would be able to order up any particular selection at any time—do-it-yourself request radio.

Demand programming may become possible through a new technology known as **digital audio broadcast** (DAB). Digital audio can send music and information in the form of zeroes and ones, as in a computer code. This eliminates all the static and hiss of current broadcast signals and could mean infinite program choices for consumers. Stations also have begun sending their digital signals over the Internet.

The newest technology in the radio business is **satellite digital radio**. Launched in 2001, satellite digital radio offers more than 100 channels of varied music and talk, with limited advertising on some stations and no advertising on others.

For a subscription fee, two companies—Sirius Satellite Radio (based in New York) and XM (based in Washington)—offer the service. They're betting people will pay $9.95 to $12.95 a month to hear uninterrupted programming. The service requires special radios with a small satellite radio receiver.

In 2002, General Motors began offering satellite radios as a factory-installed option on some models. Car buyers can finance the subscription fee with their automobile financing. Ford and DaimlerChrysler began offering the service in 2003.

As radio technology grows more complex and new formats and different program delivery systems are tested, the competition for your ear expands the choices that advertisers can make to reach you. The more stations and digital radio services (such as satellite digital radio and Internet radio) there are competing for customers, the harder every station must compete for each advertising dollar. This means less revenue for each station because each station's potential audience becomes smaller. In the 1950s, radio learned how to compete with television. Now it must learn how to compete with itself.

Veteran New York disk jockey Jim Kerr broadcasts his show nationwide from a Manhattan studio for Sirius Satellite Radio.

Narrowcasting   Segmenting the radio audience.

Demand Programming   Allows the listener to order up any selection at any time.

Digital Audio Broadcast   A new form of audio transmission that eliminates all static and makes more program choices possible.

Satellite Digital Radio   Radio transmission by satellite, with limited or no advertising, available by subscription.

Media | Review

History

▶ Radio was America's second national mass medium, after magazines.

▶ Radio transformed national politics and also expanded Americans' access to popular, as well as classical, culture.

▶ Radio history began with Samuel F. B. Morse's invention of the telegraph, first demonstrated in 1835. Then came Alexander Graham Bell's invention of the telephone, demonstrated in 1876, and Heinrich Hertz's description of radio waves in 1887.

▶ Guglielmo Marconi's promotion of wireless radio wave transmission began in 1897.

▶ Reginald Fessenden advanced wireless technology, but Lee de Forest called himself the father of radio because he invented the Audion tube to detect radio waves.

▶ David Sarnoff made radio broadcasting a visible business in the United States.

▶ National Public Radio (NPR) was funded by the federal government in 1967 and began broadcasting national programming in 1970. Today, NPR programs such as *Morning Edition* and *All Things Considered* still attract a very loyal audience.

Technology

▶ Clock and car radios expanded radio's audience, but the role of radio changed with the advent of TV, which meant radio had to compete with visual entertainment and TV news.

▶ Originally, the three radio networks (NBC, CBS and ABC) provided most radio programming. Today, most stations use a variety of sources to program themselves.

▶ Edwin H. Armstrong is responsible for the invention of FM radio. Today, FM stations are three times as popular as AM stations.

▶ Demand programming, digital audio broadcast, satellite digital radio and Internet radio mean more program choices for listeners, another challenge to the radio industry's growing competition within itself.

Business

▶ Two important developments were blanket licensing and commercial sponsorship.

▶ Blanket licensing means that radio owners can use recorded music inexpensively.

▶ Commercial sponsorship established the practice of advertisers underwriting the cost of American broadcasting.

▶ The Radio Act of 1927 established the concept that the government would regulate broadcasting "as a public convenience, interest or necessity requires."

▶ The Radio Act of 1927 is the foundation for all broadcast regulation in the United States, including the establishment of the Federal Communications Commission (FCC) in 1934.

▶ Arbitron is the primary ratings service for radio.

▶ Stations use ratings to set their rates for advertising.

▶ The most significant trend in radio today is the move toward more segmentation of the audience, similar to the division of audiences in the magazine industry.

▶ The Telecommunications Act of 1996 removed the limit on the number of stations one company can own. Today many radio companies own hundreds of stations each.

▶ In each local market, the number of radio stations one owner can hold depends on the size of the market. The larger the radio market, the more stations one company is allowed to own within it.

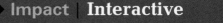

Culture

▶ The federal government intervened to regulate broadcasting almost as soon as it was invented.

▶ Early regulation separated the broadcast media from the print media, which are not regulated directly by the federal government.

▶ Radio in the 1930s and 1940s became a powerful cultural and political force.

▶ In the 1930s, radio programming expanded to include comedy, music, serials, drama and news.

▶ Radio also indirectly created a collective national experience that had not existed before.

▶ A broadcast of "War of the Worlds" by the *Mercury Theater on the Air* demonstrated the vulnerability of a captive audience.

Impact | Interactive

The Impact/Interactive CD-ROM that accompanies this text is your gateway to many electronic resources for broadening and testing your critical understanding of the material in Chapter 6. The CD-ROM features the following interactive elements for this and every chapter in the book.

▶ A two- to three-minute timely, high-interest CNN Today video clip with critical viewing questions and a link to relevant selections available within the InfoTrac College Edition database

▸ Chapter-specific activities such as personal inventories and media projects

▸ A link to the *Media/Impact* Web site that offers helpful information and many additional electronic learning resources including:

  • An interactive chapter outline and study guide

  • Interactive glossary term flashcards and crossword puzzles, concept animations, Internet activities and practice quizzes

  • Live links for all URLs given in the chapter so you can easily access the additional information each site offers

▸ A link to InfoTrac College Edition—our online database of more than a million articles representing cutting-edge research and the latest headlines. Updated daily, this online library is available 24 hours a day, seven days a week. The InfoTrac College Edition activities provided below are designed to help you use this valuable resource.

▸ Working the Web

Live links for all of the sites listed below are provided on the Media/Impact book companion Web site, which can be accessed through your Impact/Interactive CD-ROM.

▸ **Canadian Broadcasting Corporation (CBC) Radio**
www.radio.cbc.ca

▸ **Infinity Broadcasting**
www.infinityradio.com

▸ **Inside Radio**
www.insideradio.com

▸ **National Public Radio**
www.npr.org

▸ **Radio Advertising Bureau**
www.rab.com

▸ **The Radio Archive**
www.oldradio.com

▸ **Sirius Satellite Radio**
www.siriusradio.com

▸ InfoTrac College Edition Activities

Using InfoTrac College Edition's online database of full-text articles and abstracts, do the following activities as directed by your instructor. The data base can be accessed through your Impact/Interactive CD-ROM.

1. Try listening to some current National Public Radio (NPR) news programs to identify which reporters are on the air and how they broadcast news. Using InfoTrac College Edition, look up the keywords "public radio," "NPR" or the name of an NPR journalist who interests you. Read at least three articles on the topic and consider such issues as funding sources, audience levels (expanding, stable or shrinking), criticisms of NPR news and the sources of such criticism, and how story selection and content may differ from other news broadcasts on radio and television.

Write a brief paper on your findings and conclusions and be prepared to discuss the issue in class.

2. Using InfoTrac College Edition, look up the following keywords: "talk radio," "Rush Limbaugh," "Al Franken," "Howard Stern" or another talk radio show or personality. Read at least three articles about talk radio and consider both the economic impact of the talk format on radio, and the social impact of talk radio on listeners. As you read, consider the following questions: Is talk radio information or entertainment? Can it be both? Are leading political talk radio hosts inherently propagandists? Do talk show hosts (or a specific talk show host) usually identify their sources of information? Do you listen to talk radio? Why, or why not? Is the audience for talk radio increasing, stabilizing or shrinking? Who listens to talk radio, and why do they listen? Does talk radio change minds? If you need more information about talk radio, visit the campus library. (Or call in and interview a talk show host.) Write a brief paper on your findings and conclusions and be prepared to discuss the issue in class.

3. Read "Impact/Culture: Radio's Brave New World" in Chapter 6, and then look up "Web radio" or "Internet radio" on InfoTrac College Edition. Read at least three articles about Web radio, make notes, and reach some conclusions about the subject that you can share in class in a small-group discussion. Consider the following questions: Is Web radio effective competition for broadcast or digital radio? Or does it have some other value and purpose? Do your articles contain any information about the costs and profit potential of Web radio broadcasting? What are the social and cultural implications of broadcasting cultural content, such as the music of a particular culture, around the world on the Web? (Try KBON.com. For an example of a collective Web site, try warpradio.com.) Write a brief paper on your findings and conclusions and be prepared to discuss the issue in class.

4. Read "Impact/Culture: Satellite Digital Radio" in Chapter 6. Then look up "satellite digital radio" or "digital audio broadcasting" on InfoTrac College Edition. Print at least two articles and either:

   a. write a brief paper on your findings, or

   b. bring the articles to class for a small-group discussion.

5. Using InfoTrac College Edition, look up the keywords "radio ratings" to learn more about topics related to the measurement of the audience for radio. Read at least three articles on radio ratings. Attempt to learn what Arbitron does, how radio stations use ratings to promote the station and what the relationship of ratings is to radio advertising. Write a brief paper on your findings and be prepared to discuss the information in class.

CHAPTER 7

7

What's Ahead

> *No picture shall be produced which will lower the moral standards of those who see it. Hence the sympathy of the audience shall never be thrown to the side of crime, wrongdoing, evil or sin."*
>
> Motion Picture Production Code, 1930

The movie industry has been called "an industry based on dreams" because it is such an imaginative, creative medium. It also would be easy to assume that the movie industry is one of the biggest media industries because the publicity surrounding movie celebrities captures a great deal of attention. It is often surprising to learn that the movie industry accounts for a smaller amount of media industries' income than newspapers, television or books.

Movies and movie stars need the public's attention because the audience determines whether or not movies succeed. Movies are very costly investments, and most movies lose money. Investors, therefore, often favor "bankable" talent that brings fans to a movie, rather than new talent that is untested. Yet even movies featuring established talent can fail; no one in the movie industry can accurately predict which movies will be hits.

▶ Movies Reflect the Nation's Culture

Perhaps more than any other medium, movies mirror the society that creates them. Some movies offer an underlying political message. Other movies reflect changing social values. Still other movies are just good entertainment. But all movies need an audience to succeed.

Old-Style Sundance versus Starry Premieres

by Rick Lyman

Once a festival where unknowns came to be discovered and hungry agents scoured the field for the next big thing, Sundance has gradually become as much of a launching festival as a film market, the sort of event at which a distributor might unveil a film coming out in the next few months in hopes of attracting attention and publicity . . . .

The second trend is that as Hollywood moves toward making more sequels and franchise pictures oriented toward teenagers, actors who want to do more serious, stretching work—even some of the biggest stars—will have to migrate to independent film. Already in that position, of course, are the stars with fading careers they are hoping to regenerate with an eye-catching role in a Sundance hit.

More troubling to the people who run Sundance—which prides itself as being an egalitarian refuge for people who love film, not a haven for preening stars—is that for the first time (in 2003) some of the visiting big names have begun to act as if they were at the Golden Globes . . . .

"People are always trying to say, 'Oh, Sundance is going Hollywood,'" said Robert Redford, who founded the event. "It's either that or that Sundance is dead . . . ."

These are tough times for independent film, he said. Production money is getting harder to find. Too many movies are competing for too few art-house screens. Maybe sometimes the celebrities do glitz up the works. Not that he has much room to talk, he said, having a foot in that world as well.

"Sure, there is a lot of change happening," he said. "All over the world, it's working way down to Sundance. But I'll tell you one thing is emblematic of independent film. It always finds a way."

The New York Times, January 23, 2003, B-1. Copyright © 2003 by The New York Times Co. Reprinted with permission.

AP/Wide World Photos

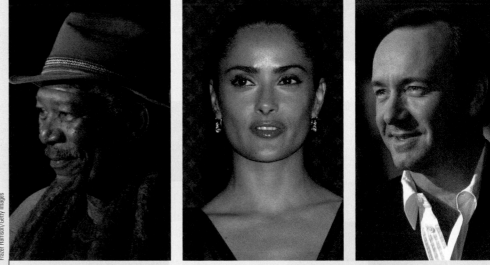

Frazer Harrison/Getty Images

The Sundance Film Festival in Park City, Utah, which was once purely a place where new filmmakers could exhibit their films, now attracts well-established stars like (left to right) Morgan Freeman, Salma Hayek and Kevin Spacey.

Critical Question

Have you seen a movie that was independently produced and distributed—or that started as an independent film before being picked up by a major studio/distributor? In what ways did the independent movie differ from mainstream Hollywood movies? Did your response to the independent movie differ from your response to mainstream movies? How so, and why?

This woman in motion is one of the early images photographed by Eadweard Muybridge, who captured motion on film. Muybridge's experiments led to the development of the first motion picture camera.

Like other media industries, the movie industry has had to adapt to changing technology. Before the invention of television, movies were the nation's primary form of visual entertainment. The current use of special effects—something you seldom get from television—is one way the movie industry competes with television for your attention and dollars. But special effects don't fit every movie, and they are very expensive. Today, as always, the economics of moviemaking is very important.

▶ Moviemakers Learn How to Capture Motion on Film

Movies were invented at a time when American industry welcomed any new gadget, and inventors wildly sought patents on appliances and electrical devices. The motion picture camera and projector were two of the Industrial Revolution's new gadgets.

Early Inventors Nurture the Movie Industry　Movies were not the invention of one person. First, a device to photograph moving objects had to be invented and then a device to project those pictures. This process involved six people: Ètienne Jules Marey, Eadweard Muybridge, Thomas Edison, William K. L. Dickson, and Auguste and Louis Lumière.

Marey and Muybridge　Ètienne Jules Marey, a scientist working in Paris, sought to record an animal's movement by individual actions—one at a time—to compare one animal to another. He charted a horse's movements on graphs and published the information in a book, *Animal Mechanism*.

Unknown to Marey, photographer Eadweard Muybridge was hired by railroad millionaire and horse breeder Leland Stanford to settle a $25,000 bet. Stanford had bet that during a trot, all four of a horse's feet simultaneously leave the ground. In 1877, Muybridge and Stanford built a special track in Palo Alto, Calif., with 12 cameras precisely placed to take pictures of a horse as it moved around the track. The horse tripped a series of equidistant wires as it ran, which in turn tripped the cameras' shutters. Stanford won his $25,000—

Impact | TimeFrame

Today to 1877: Movies mature as a popular medium

TODAY
Movie theaters collect about one billion tickets a year, but more people see movies on video than in movie theaters. Distribution companies plan to send their movies by satellite to satellite dishes on top of theaters and directly to consumers' homes.

▼
2001
The Motion Picture Association of America (MPAA) challenges the availability of recordable DVD technology (DVD-R).

▼
1994
Steven Spielberg, Jeffrey Katzenberg and David Geffen launch DreamWorks SKG, the first new movie studio created in the United States since United Artists.

▼
1966
The Motion Picture Producers Association (MPPA) introduces a voluntary content ratings system for the movies.

▼
1948
The U.S. Supreme Court breaks up the large studios' control of Hollywood by deciding in the case of *United States* v. *Paramount* that the studios are a monopoly.

▼
1947
The Hollywood Ten are called to testify before the House Un-American Activities Committee.

▼
1930
The Motion Picture Producers and Distributors Association (MPPDA) adopts a production code to control movie content.

continued on next page

one photograph showed that all four of the horse's feet did leave the ground—and the photographic series provided an excellent study of motion.

Muybridge expanded to 24 cameras, photographed other animals, and then took pictures of people moving. He traveled throughout Europe showing his photographs. Eventually, Muybridge and Marey met. In 1882, Marey perfected a photographic gun camera that could take 12 photographs on one plate—the first motion picture camera.

Thomas Edison
Thomas Edison bought some of Muybridge's pictures in 1888 and showed them to his assistant, William K. L. Dickson. Edison then met with Marey in Europe, where Marey had invented a projector that showed pictures on a continuous strip of film, but the strip film moved unevenly across the projector lens, so the pictures jumped.

William K. L. Dickson
Back in America, Dickson perforated the edges of the film so that, as the film moved through the camera, sprockets inside the camera grabbed the perforations and locked the film in place, minimizing the jumps. Dickson looped the strip over a lamp and a magnifying lens in a box 2 feet wide and 4 feet tall. The box stood on the floor with a peephole in the top so people could look inside. Edison named this device the kinetoscope.

On April 11, 1894, America's first kinetoscope parlor opened in New York City. For 25 cents, people could see ten different 90-second black-and-white films, including *Trapeze, Horse Shoeing, Wrestlers* and *Roosters.*

Auguste and Louis Lumière
In France, the Lumière brothers, Auguste and Louis, developed an improved camera and a projector that could show film on a large screen. The first public Lumière showing was on December 28, 1895: ten short subjects with such riveting titles as *Lunch Hour at the Lumière Factory*, which showed workers leaving the building, and *Arrival of a Train at a Station*. Admission was 1 franc and the Lumières collected 35 francs.

Edison Launches American Movies
Four months after the Lumière premiere in France, Edison organized the first American motion picture premiere with an improved camera developed by independent inventor Thomas Armat. Edison dubbed the new machine the Vitascope, and America's first public showing of the motion picture was on April 23, 1896, at Koster and Bial's theater in New York. Edison sat in a box seat and Armat ran the projector from the balcony.

At first, movies were a sideshow. Penny arcade owners showed movies behind a black screen at the rear of the arcade for an extra nickel. But soon the movies were more popular than the rest of the attractions, and the arcades were renamed *nickel*odeons.

In 1900, there were more than 600 nickelodeons in New York City, with more than 300,000 daily admissions. Each show lasted about 20 minutes. The programs ran from noon until late evening, and many theaters blared music outside to bring in business.

By 1907, Edison had contracted with most of the nation's movie producers, as well as the Lumière brothers and the innovative French producer Georges Mèliés, to provide movies for the theaters. Licensed Edison theaters used licensed Edison projectors and rented Edison's licensed movies, many of which Edison produced at his own studio.

The important exception to Edison's licensing plan was his rival, the American Biograph and Mutoscope Company, commonly called Biograph. Biograph manufactured a better motion picture camera than Edison's, and

Edison was losing business. In 1908, Biograph signed an agreement with Edison, forming the Motion Picture Patents Company (MPPC).

Novelty Becomes Art   All of the early films were black-and-white silents. Sound was not introduced to the movies until the 1920s, and color experiments did not begin until the 1930s. Two innovative filmmakers are credited with turning the novelty of movies into art: Georges Mèliés and Edwin S. Porter.

Georges Mèliés   French filmmaker Georges Mèliés added fantasy to the movies. Before Mèliés, moviemakers photographed theatrical scenes or events from everyday life. But Mèliés, who was a magician and a caricaturist before he became a filmmaker, used camera tricks to make people disappear and reappear and to make characters grow and then shrink. His 1902 film, *A Trip to the Moon*, was the first outer-space movie adventure, complete with fantasy creatures. When his films, which became known as trick films, were shown in the United States, American moviemakers stole his ideas.

Edwin S. Porter   Edison hired projectionist/electrician Edwin S. Porter in 1899, and in the next decade Porter became America's most important filmmaker. Until Porter, most American films were trick films or short documentary-style movies that showed newsworthy events (although some filmmakers used titillating subjects in movies such as *Pajama Girl* and *Corset Girl* to cater to men, who were the movies' biggest fans). In 1903, Porter produced *The Great Train Robbery*, an action movie with bandits attacking a speeding train.

Instead of using a single location like most other moviemakers, Porter shot 12 different scenes. He also introduced the use of dissolves between shots, instead of abrupt splices. Porter's film techniques—action and changing locations—foreshadowed the classic storytelling tradition of American movies.

▶ The Studio System Flourishes

None of the players in the early movies received screen credit, but then fans began to write letters to Biograph star Florence Lawrence addressed to "The Biograph Girl." In 1909, Carl Laemmle formed an independent production company, stole Florence Lawrence from Biograph and gave her screen credit. She became America's first movie star.

Biograph was the first company to make movies using the studio system. The **studio system** meant that a studio hired a stable of stars and production people who were paid a regular salary. These people were then under contract to that studio and could not work for any other studio without their employer's permission.

In 1910, Laemmle lured Mary Pickford away from Biograph by doubling her salary. He discovered, says film scholar Robert Sklar, "that stars sold pictures as nothing else could. As long as theaters changed their programs daily—and the practice persisted in neighborhood theaters and small towns until the early 1920s—building up audience recognition of star names was almost the only effective form of audience publicity."

The **star system**, which promoted popular movie personalities to lure audiences, was nurtured by the independents. This helped broaden the movies' appeal beyond the working class. Movie houses began to show up in the suburbs. In 1914, President Woodrow Wilson and his family watched a popular movie at the White House. From 1908 to 1914, movie attendance doubled.

Impact | TimeFrame

Today to 1877: Movies mature as a popular medium

continued

▼

1927
The Jazz Singer opens in New York, the first feature-length motion picture with sound.

▼

1916
Brothers Noble and George Johnson launch Lincoln Films, the first company to produce serious narrative movies for African American audiences, which are called race films.

▼

1915
Director D. W. Griffith introduces the concept of the movie spectacular with *The Birth of a Nation*.

▼

1877
Eadweard Muybridge catches motion on film when he uses 12 cameras to photograph a horse's movements for Leland Stanford in Palo Alto, Calif.

Courtesy of the Academy of Motion Picture Arts and Sciences

George Mèliés created these fanciful creatures for his 1902 movie, *A Trip to the Moon*, introducing fantasy to motion pictures.

Studio System   An early method of hiring a stable of salaried stars and production people under exclusive contracts to a specific studio.

Star System   Promoting popular movie personalities to lure audiences.

D. W. Griffith Introduces the Spectacular   In 1915, the first real titan of the silent movies, director D. W. Griffith, introduced the concept of spectacular entertainment. His movies were so ambitious, so immense, that no one could ignore them.

Most early movies were two reels long, 25 minutes. At first Griffith made two-reelers, but then he expanded his movies to four reels and longer, pioneering the feature-length film.

Griffith's best-known epic was as controversial as it was spectacular. In *The Birth of a Nation* (1915), the Southern-born Griffith presented a dramatic view of the Civil War and Reconstruction, portraying racial stereotypes and touching on the subject of sexual intermingling of the races. It was an ambitious film on a bitter, controversial topic, shown to an audience that had not reconciled the war's divisions. The movie's cost—about $110,000—was five times more than that of any American film until that time.

With this and his subsequent epics, Griffith showed the potential that movies had as a mass medium for gathering large audiences. He also proved that people would pay more than a nickel or a dime to see a motion picture. Films had moved from the crowded nickelodeon to respectability.

▶ Movies Become Big Business

The movie business was changing quickly. Five important events in the 1920s transformed the movie industry:

1. the move to California
2. the adoption of block booking
3. the formation of United Artists
4. the efforts at self-regulation
5. the introduction of sound

The Movies Move to Hollywood   During the first decade of the 20th century, the major movie companies were based in New York, the theater capital. Film companies sometimes traveled to Florida or Cuba to chase the sunshine because it was easier to build sets outdoors to take advantage of the light. But this soon changed.

In 1903, Harry Chandler owned the *Los Angeles Times*, but he also invested in Los Angeles real estate. Chandler and his friends courted the movie business, offering cheap land, moderate weather and inexpensive labor. The moviemakers moved to Hollywood.

Block Booking   People who owned theater chains soon decided to make movies, and moviemakers discovered they could make more money if they owned theaters, so production companies began to build theaters to exhibit their own pictures. The connection between production, distribution and exhibition grew, led by Paramount's Adolph Zukor, who devised a system called **block booking**.

Block booking meant a company, such as Paramount, would sign up one of its licensed theaters for as many as 104 pictures at a time. The movie package contained a few "name" pictures with stars, but the majority of the movies in the block were lightweight features with no stars. Because movie bills changed twice a week, the exhibitors were desperate for something to put on the screen. Often, without knowing which movies they were getting in the block, exhibitors accepted the packages and paid the distributors' prices.

Block Booking   The practice of requiring theaters to take a package of movies instead of showing the movies individually.

Left: AP/Wide World Photos; Right: Bettman/CORBIS

(Left) Douglas Fairbanks, Mary Pickford, Charlie Chaplin and D. W. Griffith, who founded United Artists in 1919. (Right) In 1994, Jeffrey Katzenberg (left), Steven Spielberg and David Geffen launched Dream-Works SKG, the first new major studio created in the United States since United Artists in 1919. Dream-Works continues to operate today as the primary independent studio in the United States.

United Artists Champions the Independents

In 1919, the nation's five biggest movie names—cowboy star William S. Hart, Mary Pickford, Charlie Chaplin, Douglas Fairbanks and D. W. Griffith—decided to rebel against the strict studio system of distribution and form their own organization. Eventually Hart withdrew from the agreement, but the remaining partners formed a company called United Artists. They eliminated block booking and became a distributor for independently produced pictures, including their own.

In its first six years, UA delivered many movies that today are still considered classics: *The Mark of Zorro*, *The Three Musketeers*, *Robin Hood* and *The Gold Rush*. These movies succeeded despite the fact that UA worked outside the traditional studio system, proving that it was possible to distribute films to audiences without using a major studio.

Moviemakers Use Self-Regulation to Respond to Scandals

In the 1920s, the movie industry faced two new crises: scandals involving movie stars and criticism that movie content was growing too provocative. As a result, the moviemakers decided to regulate themselves.

The star scandals began when comedian Roscoe "Fatty" Arbuckle hosted a marathon party in San Francisco over Labor Day weekend in 1921. As the party was ending, model Virginia Rappe was rushed to the hospital with stomach pains. She died at the hospital, and Arbuckle was charged with murder. Eventually the cause of death was listed as peritonitis from a ruptured bladder, and the murder charge was reduced to manslaughter. After three trials, two of which resulted in hung juries, Arbuckle was acquitted.

Then director William Desmond Taylor was found murdered in his home. Mabel Normand, a friend of Arbuckle's, was identified as the last person who had seen Taylor alive. Normand eventually was cleared, but then it was revealed that "Taylor" was not the director's real name and there were suggestions that he was involved in the drug business.

Hollywood's moguls and business people were aghast. The Catholic Legion of Decency announced a movie boycott. Quick to protect themselves, Los Angeles business leaders met and decided that Hollywood should police itself.

The *Los Angeles Times'* Harry Chandler worked with movie leaders to bring in ex–Postmaster General and former Republican party chairman Will Hays to respond to these and other scandals in the movie business. Hays' job was to lead a moral refurbishing of the industry. In March 1922, Hays became the first president of the Motion Picture Producers and Distributors Association (MPPDA), at a salary of $100,000 a year. A month later, even though Arbuckle had been acquitted, Hays suspended all of Fatty Arbuckle's films.

Besides overseeing the stars' personal behavior, Hays decided that his office also should oversee movie content. The MPPDA, referred to as the Hays Office, wrote a code of conduct to govern the industry.

In 1930, the MPPDA adopted a production code, which began by stating three general principles:

1. No picture shall be produced which will lower the moral standards of those who see it. Hence the sympathy of the audience shall never be thrown to the side of crime, wrongdoing, evil or sin.

2. Correct standards of life, subject only to the requirements of drama and entertainment, shall be presented.

3. Laws, natural or human, shall not be ridiculed, nor shall sympathy be created for its violation.

The code then divided its rules into 12 categories of wrongdoing, including:

- Murder: "The technique of murder must be presented in a way that will not inspire imitation."

- Sex: "Excessive and lustful kissing, lustful embraces, suggestive postures and gestures are not to be shown."

- Obscenity: "Obscenity in word, gesture, reference, song, joke, or by suggestion (even when likely to be understood only by part of the audience) is forbidden."

- Costumes: "Dancing costumes intended to permit undue exposure or indecent movements in the dance are forbidden."

An acceptable movie displayed a seal of approval in the titles at the beginning of the picture. Producers balked at the interference, but most of them, afraid of censorship from outside the industry, complied with the monitoring. Although standards have relaxed, the self-regulation of content still operates in the motion picture industry today.

New Technology Brings the Talkies

By the mid-1920s, silent movies were an established part of American entertainment, but technology soon pushed the industry into an even more vibrant era—the era of the talkies. MPPDA President Will Hays was the first person to appear on screen in the public premiere of talking pictures on August 6, 1926, in New York City. Warner Bros. and Western Electric had developed the movie sound experiment, which consisted of seven short subjects, called *The Vitaphone Preludes*.

The Warner brothers—Sam, Harry, Jack and Albert—were ambitious, upstart businessmen who beat their competitors to sound movies. On October 6, 1927, *The Jazz Singer*, starring Al Jolson, opened at the Warners' Theater in New York, and was the first feature-length motion picture with sound. The movie was not an all-talkie, but instead contained two sections with synchronized sound.

The success of *The Jazz Singer* convinced Warners' competitors not to wait any longer to adopt sound. By July 1, 1930, 22 percent of theaters still showed silent films. By 1933, fewer than one percent of the movies shown in theaters were silents.

▶ Rise of the Movie Moguls

In the 1930s, The Big Five dominated the movie business: Warner Bros., Metro-Goldwyn-Mayer, Paramount, RKO and 20th Century Fox. The Big Five collected more than two-thirds of the nation's box office receipts. United Artists remained solely a distribution company for independent producers.

The Big Five all were vertically integrated: They produced movies, distributed them worldwide and owned theater chains, which guaranteed their pictures a showing. The studios maintained stables of stars, directors, producers, writers and technical staff. Film scholar Tino Balio calls the studios at this point in their history a "mature oligopoly"—a group of companies with so much control over an industry that any change in one of the companies directly affected the future of the industry.

In the 1930s, Walt Disney became the only major successful Hollywood newcomer. He had released *Steamboat Willie* as "the first animated sound cartoon" in 1928. Disney was 26 years old, and he sold his car to finance the cartoon's sound track.

After some more short-animated-feature successes, Disney announced in 1934 that his studio would produce its first feature-length animated film, *Snow White and the Seven Dwarfs*. The film eventually cost Disney $2.25 million, more than MGM usually spent on a good musical. *Snow White* premiered December 21, 1937, at the Cathay Circle Theater in Hollywood.

Box office receipts sagged in the 1930s as the Depression settled into every aspect of America's economy. Facing bankruptcy, several theaters tried to buoy their profits by adding Bingo games and cut-rate admissions. The one innovation that survived the 1930s was the double feature: two movies for the price of one.

The Depression introduced one more factor into motion picture budgets: labor unions. Before the 1930s, most aspects of the movie business were not governed by union agreements. But in 1937, the National Labor Relations Board held an election that designated the Screen Actors Guild to bargain for wages, working conditions and overtime. The Screen Writers Guild was certified in 1938 and the Screen Directors Guild soon afterward.

Unionization limited the moguls' power over the people who worked for them, but union agreements were approved in the late 1930s. The Depression ended, and the studios once again prospered.

▶ Movies Glitter During the Golden Age

With glamorous stars and exciting screenplays, supported by an eager pool of gifted directors, producers and technical talent, plus an insatiable audience, the movie industry reached its apex in the late 1930s and early 1940s. The most successful studio in Hollywood was MGM, which attracted the best writers, directors and actors.

MGM concentrated on blockbusters, such as *The Great Ziegfeld*, *The Wizard of Oz* and *Gone with the Wind*. Not only did *Gone with the Wind*'s phenomenal success demonstrate the epic character that movies could provide, but also the movie was a technological breakthrough, with its magnificent use of color. The movie business was so rich that even MGM's dominance didn't scare away the competition.

The Kobal Collection

In the late 1930s and early 1940s, spectaculars such as *The Wizard of Oz* helped to make MGM the most successful studio in Hollywood.

Paul Robeson and Josephine Baker Light Up a Black Screen

by Teresa Moore

The halcyon age for African Americans on the big screen was the period between 1910 and 1950, when blacks—and some whites—produced more than 500 "race movies," showcasing all-black casts in a variety of genres, including Westerns, mysteries, romances and melodrama.

Although most of these movies have disintegrated into silver nitrate stardust, a few dozen of these early films—silents and talkies—are available on video. . . .

In the naturally sepia-toned world of race movies, African Americans could—and did—do just about anything.

There were black millionaires and black detectives, black sweethearts and socialites. Black heroines who swooned—tender, wilting ladies who never swept a broom or donned a do-rag. Black heroes who could be gentle and genteel, tough and smart. Black villains of both genders, out to separate black damsels and grandees from their virtue or fortune.

Race movies were so-called because they were made for black

Photos: Bettmann/CORBIS

Paul Robeson and Josephine Baker were important stars who appeared in early "race movies," showcasing African American casts.

Southern audiences barred from white-owned theaters. The films were shown either in the black-owned movie palaces of the urban North and Midwest or in "midnight rambles"—special midnight-to-2-A.M. screenings in rented halls or segregated theaters of the South.

"In some ways these filmmakers were more free because they were making the movies for themselves," said Michael Thompson, a professor of African American history at Stanford.

▶ Challenges from Congress and the Courts

Before television arrived throughout the country in 1948, two other events of the late 1940s helped reverse the prosperous movie bonanza that began in mid-1930:

1. the hearings of the House Un-American Activities Committee (HUAC)
2. the 1948 U.S. Supreme Court decision in *United States* v. *Paramount Pictures, Inc., et al.*

The House Un-American Activities Committee
In October 1947, America was entering the Cold War. This was an era in which many public officials, government employees and private citizens seemed preoccupied with the threat of communism and people identified as "subversives." The House of Representatives Committee on Un-American Activities, chaired by J. Parnell Thomas, summoned ten "unfriendly" witnesses from Hollywood to testify about their communist connections.

(Unfriendly witnesses were people whom the committee classified as having participated at some time in the past in "un-American activities." This usually meant that the witness had been a member of a left-wing organization in the decade before World War II.) These eight screenwriters and two directors came to be known as the Hollywood Ten.

The Ten's strategy was to appear before the committee as a group and to avoid answering the direct question, "Are you now or have you ever been a member of the Communist party?" Instead, the Ten tried to make statements that questioned the committee's authority to challenge their political beliefs.

In a rancorous series of hearings, the committee rejected the Ten's testimony; the witnesses found themselves facing trial for contempt. All of them were sentenced to jail and some were fined. By the end of November 1947, all of the Hollywood Ten had lost their jobs. Many more movie people would follow.

In an article for the *Hollywood Review*, Hollywood Ten member Adrian Scott reported that 214 movie employees eventually were blacklisted, which meant that many studio owners refused to hire people who were suspected of taking part in subversive activities. The movie people who were not hired because of their political beliefs included 106 writers, 36 actors and 11 directors. This effectively gutted Hollywood of some of its best talent.

The Kobal Collection

The Hollywood Ten, targeted in 1947 by the House Un-American Activities Committee, eventually went to jail for refusing to answer questions before the committee about their political beliefs.

United States v. Paramount Pictures

The U.S. Justice Department began another antitrust suit against the studios in 1938. In 1940, the studios came to an agreement with the government, while admitting no guilt. They agreed to:

1. Limit block booking to five films.

2. Stop **blind booking** (the practice of renting films to exhibitors without letting them see the films first).

3. Stop requiring theaters to rent short films as a condition of acquiring features.

4. Stop buying theaters.

After this agreement, the Justice Department dropped its suit with the stipulation that the department could re-institute the suit again at any time.

By 1944, the government was still unhappy with studio control over the theaters, so it reactivated the suit. In 1948, *United States* v. *Paramount Pictures* reached the Supreme Court. Associate Justice William O. Douglas argued that, *although the five major studios*—Paramount, Warner Bros., MGM-Loew's, RKO and 20th Century Fox—*owned only 17 percent of all theaters in the United States, these studios* did *hold a monopoly over first-run exhibition in the large cities.*

As a result of the Supreme Court decision, by 1954 the five major production firms had divested themselves of ownership or control of all of their theaters. Production and exhibition were now split; vertical integration was crumbling.

When the movie companies abandoned the exhibition business, banks grew reluctant to finance film projects because the companies could not guarantee an audience—on paper. Soon the studios decided to leave the production business to the independents and became primarily distributors of other peoples' pictures. The result was the end of the studio system.

Blind Booking The practice of renting films to exhibitors without letting them see the film first.

Movies, which once were available only in theaters, are now available just about anywhere on video, including the backseat of a car.

© Darryl Bush/ San Francisco Chronicle

▶ Movies Compete for the Television Audience

In the 1950 Paramount movie *Sunset Boulevard*, aging silent screen star Norma Desmond (played by Gloria Swanson) romances an ambitious young screenwriter (played by William Holden) by promising him Hollywood connections.

"You're Norma Desmond. You used to be in silent pictures. You used to be big," says the screenwriter.

"I *am* big," says Desmond. "It's the pictures that got small."

Desmond could have been talking about the movie business itself, which got much smaller after 1948, when nationwide television began to offer home-delivered entertainment. The House hearings and the consent decrees in the Paramount case foretold change in the movie business, but television truly transformed Hollywood forever. In the 1950s, the number of television sets grew by 400 percent, while the number of people who went to the movies fell by 45 percent.

Theaters tried to make up for the loss by raising their admission prices, but more than 4,000 theaters closed from 1946 to 1956. Attendance has leveled off or risen briefly a few times since the 1950s, but the trend of declining movie attendance continues today. The movie industry has tried several methods to counteract this downward trend.

Wide-Screen and 3-D Movies   Stunned by television's popularity, the movie business tried technological gimmicks in the 1950s to lure its audience back. First came 3-D movies, using special effects to create the illusion of three-dimensional action. Rocks, for example, seemed to fly off the screen and into the audience. To see the 3-D movies, people wore special plastic glasses. The novelty was fun, but the 3-D movie plots were weak, and most people didn't come back to see a second 3-D movie.

Next came Cinerama, Cinemascope, VistaVision and Panavision—wide-screen color movies with stereophonic sound. All of these techniques tried to give the audience a "you are there" feeling—something they couldn't get from television.

Changes in Censorship   On May 26, 1952, the Supreme Court announced in *Burstyn* v. *Wilson* that motion pictures were "a significant medium for the communication of ideas," which were designed "to entertain as well as to inform." The effect of this decision was to protect movies under the First Amendment. The result was fewer legal restrictions on what a movie could show.

In 1953, Otto Preminger challenged the movies' self-regulating agency, the Production Code Administration. United Artists agreed to release Preminger's movie *The Moon Is Blue*, even though the PCA denied the movie a certificate of approval because it contained such risqué words as *virgin* and *mistress*. Then, in 1956, United Artists released Preminger's *Man with the Golden Arm*, a film about drug addiction, and the PCA restrictions were forever broken.

Buoyed by the *Burstyn* decision and the United Artists test, moviemakers tried sex and violence to attract audiences away from television. In the 1950s, Marilyn Monroe and Jane Russell offered generously proportioned examples of the new trend. Foreign films also became popular because some of them offered explicit dialogue and love scenes.

Spectaculars   One by one the studio moguls retired, and they were replaced by a new generation of moviemakers. "They [the second generation] inherited a situation where fewer and fewer pictures were being made, and fewer still made money," says film historian Robert Sklar, "but those that captured the box office earned enormous sums. It was as if the rules of baseball had been changed so that the only hit that mattered was a home run."

Spectaculars like *The Sound of Music* (1965) and *The Godfather* (1971) and its sequels rewarded the rush for big money. But then a few majestic flops taught the studios that nothing demolishes a studio's profits like one big movie bomb.

Movie Ratings   In 1966, Jack Valenti, former presidential adviser to Lyndon Johnson, became president of the Motion Picture Producers Association and renamed it the Motion Picture Association of America (MPAA). One of Valenti's first acts was to respond to continuing public criticism about shocking movie content. (Valenti ran the MPAA until his retirement in 2004. See Impact/Culture, page 146.)

The MPAA began a rating system modeled on Great Britain's: G for general audiences, M (later changed to PG) for mature audiences, R for restricted (people under 17 admitted only with an adult), and X for no one under 18 admitted. Valenti acted as the MPAA's lobbyist for the nation's major studios. The PG-13 rating—special parental guidance advised for children under 13—has been added, and the X rating has been changed to NC-17X.

Standards for the R rating have eased since the ratings system began, further blurring the effectiveness of the ratings system for the public.

© 2000, The Washington Post Writers Group. Reprinted with permission.

"That was **not** enough sex and violence for a P.G.!"

▶ The Business of Movies

In today's system of moviemaking, each of the major studios (such as Disney, Viacom/Paramount, Dream-Works, 20th Century Fox, Warner Bros. and Sony Pictures Entertainment) usually makes fewer than 20 movies a year. The rest come from independent producers, with production, investment, distribution and exhibition each handled by different companies. Most of these independently produced movies are distributed by one of the seven large studios (see Illustration 7.3, page 145).

Today, the dream merchants aim at a mature audience. Movies are targeted at people of all ages, especially children and people over 30. So the biggest box office successes are movies that appeal to this over-30 audience, such as *Seabiscuit*, and films that appeal to children (who typically bring their parents with them to the show), such as *Lord of the Rings*.

Today's movies are created by one group (the writers and producers), funded by another group (the investors), sold by a third group (the distributors) and shown by a fourth group (the exhibitors). No other mass media industry is so fragmented.

Losing Money: Ticket Sales Drop   In 1946, the movies' best year, American theaters collected more than 4 billion tickets. Today, as more people watch more movies on video and DVD, the number of theater admissions has dropped to about 1 billion. Exhibitors feel that if they raise their admission prices, they'll lose more of their patrons. This is why exhibitors charge so much for refreshments, which is where they make 10 to 20 percent of their income.

Illustration 7.1
Who Goes to the Movies?

Moviemakers chase people in the under-24-year-old group and 30–39-year-olds, who form the biggest audiences for movies.

Data from the Motion Picture Association of America, 2002.

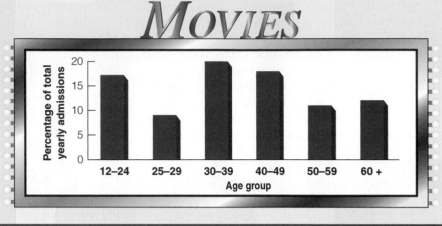

MOVIES

Percentage of total yearly admissions — Age group: 12–24, 25–29, 30–39, 40–49, 50–59, 60 +

With declining audiences and fewer successful movies, the studios complain they lose money on *most* of the pictures they underwrite. Producers say the studios make exorbitant profits on the movies they distribute, which raises the cost of making movies for producers. Today, movies, like many other media industries, are part of corporate ownership, which means that stockholder loyalty comes first. Studios tend to choose safer projects and seek proven audience-pleasing ideas rather than take many risks.

One way the movie industry collects predictable income is to make movies for television. Half the movies produced every year are made for television and are underwritten by the networks. Video and DVD sales and rentals also bring reliable revenues.

Two important factors for the future funding of the movie industry are the sale of ancillary rights and the advances of new technology.

Ancillary Rights Marketing opportunities related to a movie, in addition to direct income from the movie itself.

Making Money: Ancillary Rights for Sale
In 1950, a ticket to a movie cost about 50 cents. Today you can still see a movie for 50 cents if you rent a video or DVD for $3 and invite five friends to join you at home to watch it. The explosion of video rentals and sales since the VCR was first marketed in 1976 had a powerful effect on how the movie business operates today. The sale of movies on VHS and DVD is part of the **ancillary rights** market.

The average cost to make a theatrical movie (as opposed to a made-for-television movie) is $100 million, and only two out of ten theatrical movies make money. "Some pictures make a lot of money," says movie analyst David V. Picker, "and a lot of pictures make no money." Before a theatrical movie starts shooting, the investors want to be sure they'll make their money back. They may look to ancillary rights to secure a return on their investment. Ancillary rights can include:

- Pay television rights
- Network television rights

Movie studios today use the Internet to promote their movies. Warner Bros. created a Web site to promote the movie *The Whole Ten Yards.*

© Scott Goodwin Photography, Inc.

- Syndication rights (sales to independent TV stations)

- Airline rights for in-flight movies

- Military rights (to show films on military bases)

- College rights (to show films on college campuses)

- Song rights for soundtrack albums

- Book publishing rights (for original screenplays that can be rewritten and sold as books)

Movies also are becoming more commercialized in the sense that they are tied to products, which are another way of advertising a movie. A movie that can be exploited as a package of ancillary rights, with commercial appeal, is much more attractive to investors than a movie with limited potential.

Often the only choice for a filmmaker who wants to make a film that doesn't have substantial ancillary-rights potential is to settle for a low budget. Once the film is made, the independent filmmaker must then find a way to distribute the movie. This severely limits the number of independent films that make it to the box office.

George Lucas capitalized on ancillary rights for *Star Wars,* creating the most successful marketing campaign in movie history.

▶ Working in the Movies

Today the center of the movie industry is movie production. Most of the movies that are distributed by the major studios and exhibited at your local theater result from independent companies that produce movies under agreements with individual studios.

Although these production companies work independently, and each company is organized differently, jobs in movie production fall mainly into the following categories: screenwriters, producers, directors, actors, production, marketing and administration.

The beginning for each movie is a story idea, and these ideas come from *screenwriters*. Screenwriters work independently, marketing their story ideas through agents, who promote their clients' scripts to the studios and to independent producers.

Typically, *producers* are the people who help gather the funding to create a movie project. Financing can come from banks or from individuals who want to invest in a specific movie. Once the funding for the story is in place, a director is assigned to organize all of the tasks necessary to turn the script into a movie. The director oversees the movie's budget.

Obviously, *actors* are important to any movie project. Sometimes the producer and director approach particular stars for a project even before they seek funding, to attract interest from the investors and also to help assure the investors that the movie will have some box office appeal.

Production includes all of the people who actually create the movie—camera operators, set designers, film editors, script supervisors and costumers, for example. Once the movie is made, the *marketing* people seek publicity for the project. They also design a plan to advertise and promote the movie to the public. As in any media industry, people who work in *administration* help keep all of the records necessary to pay salaries and track the employees' expenses, as well as keep track of the paperwork involved in organizing any business.

Independent filmmakers, who usually fund their movies without support from the major studios, must find a way to exhibit their movies. The Angelika Film Center in New York is one of the nation's largest theaters to exhibit independent films.

Illustration 7.2
How the Movie Industry Makes Money

Movie industry revenue comes from three major sources: home video, movies made for television, and box office tickets.

Data from *The Veronis, Suhler Stevenson Communications Industry Forecast,* 2003–2007.

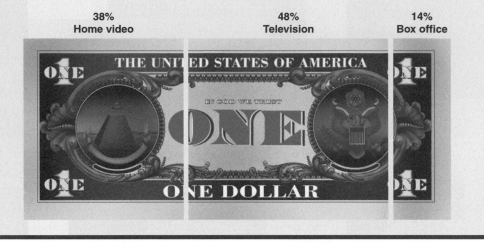

38%	48%	14%
Home video	Television	Box office

▶ Technology Transforms the Future

Technology affects three aspects of the movie business:

1. Production
2. Distribution
3. Exhibition

Production   Smaller, portable cameras mean a camera operator can move more easily through a crowd. New types of film mean that filmmakers can shoot more scenes at night and in dark places with less artificial lighting.

Directors electronically record scenes as they shoot them and immediately play back the scene to make sure they have the shot they want. Computer technology offers exciting special-effects possibilities. Filmmakers also are experimenting with the holograph, which uses lasers to make a computer-generated three-dimensional image from a flat picture.

The ability to digitize color, using computers, also means the images in movies can be intensified, adjusted and even totally transformed after the movie is shot, in a way that was impossible even ten years ago.

Distribution   Reproducing copies of films to send to theaters and guaranteeing their arrival is one of the costliest aspects of moviemaking. In the future, distribution companies plan to send their movies by satellite to satellite dishes on top of each theater and directly to consumers' homes. Live performances, such as a symphony concert or a major sports event, could be available regularly by satellite at your local theater, or even in your home.

The theater industry is poised to replace the traditional film projector, invented more than 100 years ago, with digital projectors, which can show movies

© Don Smetzer

Movies are very expensive to make because so many people are involved. The average cost to make a movie today is $100 million.

Illustration 7.3
Who's Who in Hollywood: The Big Six Movie Distributing Companies

Data from *The Veronis, Suhler Stevenson Communications Industry Forecast,* 2003–2007.

MOVIES

STUDIO	PARENT COMPANY	COUNTRY
1. SONY	SONY	JAPAN
2. BUENA VISTA (DISNEY)	DISNEY	UNITED STATES
3. NEW LINE CINEMA	NEW LINE CINEMA	UNITED STATES
4. FOX	NEWS CORP.	AUSTRALIA
5. WARNER BROS.	AOL / TIME WARNER	UNITED STATES
6. DREAMWORKS	DREAMWORKS	UNITED STATES

that are sent by satellite or recorded on optical discs. Digital movies are cheaper to distribute and can be shown on more screens, or removed quickly from distribution, depending on audience demand.

The Internet allows new moviemakers to produce movies inexpensively and transfer them to the Internet for downloading. As computer video technology gets faster and more accessible, established movie studios and independent moviemakers plan to devise a whole new distribution system, based on digital movie downloads delivered directly to consumers.

However, recordable DVDs (DVD-R) pose a new copyright hazard for the movie industry, which tried to stop their widespread use. (See Impact/Culture, "Moviemakers Shudder As Illegal Copies of Hot Films Spread on the Internet," page 146.

Exhibition   Theaters are turning to the picture-palace environment that enchanted moviegoers in the 1930s. "The movie theatre will have to become an arena; a palace to experience the full grandeur and potential of the theatrical motion picture," says futurist and electronic technology consultant Martin Polon.

In 1994, the nation's largest theater chain, United Artists, announced that it would begin to offer "motion simulation" in some of its theaters. Specially controlled seats move in conjunction with a "ridefilm" to give the feeling of space travel or other adventures. Many of the nation's theme parks, such as Dollywood, already offer ridefilms to their patrons.

"We're looking to marry the moviegoing experience to different kinds of technological experiences, thereby enhancing the attractiveness of the whole complex," said United Artists chairman Stewart Blair.

▶ International Markets and Concentrated Power

Today's movie industry is undergoing two major changes. One recent trend in the movie business is global ownership and global marketing. The second trend is the merging of the movie industry with the television industry.

Global Influence   Overseas companies own two of the major studios (Sony owns Sony Pictures Entertainment, for example, and Rupert Murdoch's News Corporation owns 20th Century Fox). This percentage of

Moviemakers Shudder As Illegal Copies of Hot Films Spread on the Internet

The same technology that allows for the spread of bootlegged music over the Internet is now threatening the movie industry. Film filchers have begun distributing copies of hot flicks like *The Matrix* using a data format similar to the so-called MP3 files that are being used to spread free music across cyberspace.

While the data files containing full-length movies are too big for the average home computer user to conveniently download, college students with high-speed hookups in their dorm rooms are doing it and the movie industry is shuddering.

"It's very nice. I get to sit here in the comfort of my own room and watch a new movie without going to the theater and spending $7.50," said a 19-year-old sophomore at the University of California, Santa Cruz, who asked that his name be withheld.

It's not very nice, said Jack Valenti, president of the Motion Picture Association of America. "The theft of copyrighted material in any format cannot be left unapprised. There is no exception in the case of Internet copyright theft. We won't condone it, and we will pursue those who steal film product and illegally transmit it via the Internet."

The movies can be found on public Web forums, including those run by America Online, and on Internet mes-

Jack Valenti, president of the Motion Picture Association of America, says "We will pursue those who steal film product and illegally transmit it via the Internet."

AP/Wide World Photos

sage boards. The movies are frequently distributed by students at colleges around the country. . . .

Internet analyst Mark Mooradian, who tracks the proliferation of music on the Web for the research firm Jupiter Communications in New York, said the large files are going to limit the widespread use of movies online until the technology improves. "It's just not going to be practical for most people," he said.

But many college students and offices have access to networks with speedy computer lines and vast memory space. With these systems, an entire movie can be downloaded in about 20 minutes.

Associated Press on America Online (AOL), April 22, 1999. Reprinted with permission.

overseas ownership at nearly 34 percent, is higher in the movie industry than in most other American media businesses.

Foreign ownership means easier access to overseas markets. American motion pictures are one of America's strongest exports, and income from foreign sales accounts for more than one-third of the movie industry's profits. "If Hollywood has learned anything the past few years," says *Business Week*, "it's that the whole world is hungry for the latest it has to offer."

Concentrating Media Power

Today, people in the television business are buying pieces of the movie business and people in the movie business want to align themselves with television companies. In 1993, the

Federal Communications Commission voted to allow the TV networks to produce and syndicate their own programs. This opens the door for TV networks to enter the movie business.

The result *could* be consolidated companies that would finance movies, make movies and show those movies in their own theaters, on their own television stations and on video. By controlling all aspects of the business, a company would have a better chance to collect a profit on the movies it makes. Sound familiar? The studios held this type of controlling interest in their movies before the courts dismantled the studio system with the 1948 consent decrees (see page 139). Today's major studios are trying to become again what they once were: a mature oligopoly in the business of dreams.

Media | Review

© Getty Images

History

▶ Eadweard Muybridge and Thomas Edison contributed the most to the creation of movies in America. Muybridge demonstrated how to photograph motion and Edison developed a projector, the kinetoscope.

▶ Edison also organized the Motion Picture Patents Company (MPPC) to control movie distribution.

▶ French filmmaker Georges Mèliés envisioned movies as a medium of fantasy.

▶ Edwin S. Porter assembled scenes to tell a story.

▶ D. W. Griffith mastered the full-length movie.

Technology

▶ Hollywood tried to lure audiences back to the movies in the 1950s with technological gimmicks and sultry starlets, but these efforts did not work very well.

▶ The biggest technological changes in moviemaking today are the result of digital technology.

▶ Independent moviemakers can use computers to create movies inexpensively and distribute them on the Internet.

▶ Digital projectors will allow theaters to receive movies by satellite and videodisc, which makes movie distribution cheaper and faster.

▶ Recordable DVDs (DVD-R) pose a serious copyright challenge for the movie industry, which is trying to stop their widespread use.

▶ In the future, distribution companies plan to send their movies by satellite to satellite dishes on top of each theater and directly to consumers' homes.

Business

▶ The practice of block booking, led by Adolph Zukor, obligated movie houses to accept several movies at once, usually without previewing them first.

▶ Biograph became the first studio to make movies using what was called the studio system. This system put the studio's stars under exclusive contract, and the contract could not be broken without an employer's permission.

▶ The formation of United Artists (UA) by Mary Pickford, Charlie Chaplin, Douglas Fairbanks and D. W. Griffith was a rebellion against the big studios.

▶ UA distributed films for independent filmmakers.

▶ As the studio system developed, the five largest Hollywood studios were able to control production, distribution and exhibition.

▶ In the 1930s, labor unions challenged studio control and won some concessions.

▶ Three factors caused Hollywood's crash in the 1950s: the House Un-American Activities Committee hearings, the U.S. Justice Department's antitrust action against the studios, and television.

▶ The median cost to make a movie today is $100 million, and only two out of ten theatrical movies make money.

▶ Today the number of moviegoers continues to decline, although video and DVD sales and rentals have added to movie industry income.

▶ Most movies are funded in part by ancillary rights sales.

▶ Most movies are sold as packages, with all their potential media outlets underwriting the movie before it goes into production. This makes independent filmmaking difficult.

▶ Foreign corporations own two out of six of the major movie studios.

▶ Overseas sales of American movies account for more than one-third of movie industry income.

▶ In 1993, the FCC voted to allow the TV networks to make and syndicate their own programs. This means that, in the future, the movie industry and the television industries may align themselves more closely. Eventually one company could control all aspects of moviemaking.

▶ DreamWorks SKG, launched in 1994 by Steven Spielberg, Jeffrey Katzenberg and David Geffen, is the first major movie studio created in the United States since United Artists was formed in 1919.

▶ The Motion Picture Producers Association (MPPA) has launched a campaign to stop widespread copying and distribution of movies on the Internet.

Culture

▶ In the 1920s, the movie industry faced two crises: scandals involving movie stars and criticism that movie content was growing too explicit.

▶ The movie industry responded to the scandals and criticism about content by forming the Motion Picture Producers and Distributors Association (MPPDA) under the direction of Will Hays.

▶ In 1930, the MPPDA adopted a production code, which created rules that governed movie content.

▶ The movies' golden age was the 1930s and 1940s, supported by the studio system and an eager audience.

▶ Today's movie ratings system began in 1966, supervised by the Motion Picture Association of America (MPAA) .

▶ Very few movies actually receive the most explicit (NC-17X) rating.

▶ American movies are a major U.S. export.

▶ Most of today's moviegoers are under 24 or over 30–39.

Impact | Interactive

The Impact/Interactive CD-ROM that accompanies this text is your gateway to many electronic resources for broadening and testing your critical understanding of the material in Chapter 7. The CD-ROM features the following interactive elements for this and every chapter in the book.

▶ A two- to three-minute timely, high-interest CNN Today video clip with critical viewing questions and a link to relevant selections available within the InfoTrac College Edition database

▶ Chapter-specific activities such as personal inventories and media projects

▶ A link to the *Media/Impact* Web site that offers helpful information and many additional electronic learning resources including:

  • An interactive chapter outline and study guide

  • Interactive glossary term flashcards and crossword puzzles, concept animations, Internet activities and practice quizzes

  • Live links for all URLs given in the chapter so you can easily access the additional information each site offers

▶ A link to InfoTrac College Edition—our online database of more than a million articles representing cutting-edge research and the latest headlines. Updated daily, this online library is available 24 hours a day, seven days a week. The InfoTrac College Edition activities provided below are designed to help you use this valuable resource.

▶ Working the Web

Live links for all of the sites listed below are provided on the *Media/Impact* book companion Web site, which can be accessed through your Impact/Interactive CD-ROM.

- ▶ **Academy of Motion Picture Arts and Sciences**
  www.oscar.org
- ▶ **DreamWorks SKG**
  www.dreamworks.com
- ▶ **DVD Entertainment Group**
  www.dvdinformation.com
- ▶ **Motion Picture Association of America**
  www.mpaa.org
- ▶ **Screenwriters Guild of America**
  www.screenwritersguild.com
- ▶ **Warner Bros.**
  www2.warnerbros.com

▶ InfoTrac College Edition Activities

Using InfoTrac College Edition's online database of full-text articles and abstracts, do the following activities as directed by your instructor. The database can be assessed through your Impact/Interactive CD-ROM.

1. Enter the keywords "movie ratings," "MPAA" or "Jack Valenti" (president of the MPAA) and read at least two articles about the Motion Picture Association of America and the issues it tackles. Consider whether movie ratings have been a success in the eyes of MPAA and Mr. Valenti, in the eyes of their critics and in the eyes of moviegoers. Why, or why not? Write a brief paper on your findings and conclusions and be prepared to discuss the issue in class.

2. Read "Impact/Culture: Moviemakers Shudder As Illegal Copies of Hot Films Spread on the Internet" in Chapter 7. Then, using InfoTrac College Edition keywords, look up "Internet movies," Web motion pictures," "motion picture piracy" or "digital movies." Read at least three articles about the problem of pirated films. Print the articles and either:

   a. write a brief paper on your findings, or

   b. bring the article to class for a small-group discussion.

3. Using InfoTrac College Edition, type in the keywords "foreign film." Read at least two articles about the subject. Look for information and points of view about the social and cultural influence of United States films seen in other countries and films from other countries shown in the United States. Look also for evidence of the success of film industries in countries outside the United States, such as India. Write a brief paper on your findings and conclusions and be prepared to discuss the issue in class.

4. Using InfoTrac College Edition, type in the keywords "movies and product placement" and consider issues associated with marketers' getting their brands placed in films. Print at least two articles about the subject, and either:

   a. write a brief paper on your findings, or

   b. bring the articles for a small-group discussion.

5. Using the InfoTrac College Edition, type in the keywords "independent film" to learn more about small budget movie projects. Read at least two articles about the subject, and consider such issues as cost versus profit potential, and the ability of independent or low-budget films to compete for theater exposure, television exposure, and movie rental exposure. Write a brief paper on your findings and conclusions and be prepared to discuss the issue in class.

CHAPTER 8

What's Ahead

> "*A new generation now has the chance to put the vision back into television, and to travel from the wasteland to the promised land.*"
>
> Newton Minow, former chairman,
> Federal Communications Commission

"Television is the pervasive American pastime," writes media observer Jeff Greenfield. "Cutting through geographic, ethnic, class and cultural diversity, it is the single binding thread of this country, the one experience that touches young and old, rich and poor, learned and illiterate. A country too big for homogeneity, filled by people from all over the globe, without any set of core values, America never had a central unifying bond. Now we do. Now it is possible to answer the question, '*What does America do?*' We watch television."

Americans, on average, watch nearly eight hours of television per household a day, according to the A. C. Nielsen Company, which monitors television usage for advertisers. Even though you may not watch TV this much, the percentage of the population that watches television a lot counterbalances the time you spend with your television set.

▶ Widespread Presence in Our Lives

It's not surprising that the effects of such a pervasive medium have attracted so much attention from parents, educators, social scientists, religious leaders, public officials and anyone else who is concerned with society's habits and

Impact | TimeFrame

Today to 1884: Television becomes the nation's major medium for news and entertainment

TODAY
Television programming is delivered on more than 200 different channels by over-the-air broadcast, cable and satellite. High definition TV is gaining acceptance.

▼

2003
TV again became a focus of nationwide attention during the live news coverage of the Iraq War.

▼

2001
Television news offered nonstop, commercial-free coverage of the terrorist plane crashes at the World Trade Center, the Pentagon and in rural Pennsylvania.

▼

1993
100 million people tune in for the final episode of *Cheers*.

▼

1987
TV broadcasts the Iran-Contra hearings.

▼

1979
Ted Turner starts Cable News Network (CNN).

▼

1973
The television networks present live broadcasts of the Watergate Hearings.

▼

1963
Network television provides nonstop coverage of the assassination and funeral of President John F. Kennedy. Public Television begins broadcasting as National Educational Television (NET).

continued on next page

values. TV has been blamed for everything from declines in literacy to rises in violent crime to the trivialization of national politics. Every once in a while it is praised, too, for giving viewers instant access to world events and uniting audiences in times of national crisis.

An industry with this much presence in American life is bound to affect the way we live. Someone who is watching television is not doing other things: playing basketball, visiting a museum or looking through a telescope at the stars, for instance. Television, however, can bring you to a museum you might never visit, or to a basketball game you cannot attend or closer to the solar system than you could see through a telescope.

Television technology, adding pictures to the sounds of radio, truly transformed Americans' living and learning patterns. The word *television*, which once meant programs delivered by antennas through over-the-air signals, now means a *television screen*, where a variety of delivery systems brings viewers a diversity of programs.

▶ Complex Program Delivery System

The programs Americans watch today are delivered by antennas, cables and satellites, but they all appear on the same television screen, and as a viewer, you can't tell how the program arrived at your television set and probably don't care. What you do know is that television gives you access to all types of programs—drama, comedy, sports, news, game shows and talk shows. You can see all kinds of people—murderers, public officials, foreign leaders, reporters, soldiers, entertainers, athletes, detectives, and doctors. The television screen is truly, as scholar Erik Barnouw observed, a "tube of plenty."

About 1,600 television stations operate in the United States. Three out of four of these are commercial stations and the others are noncommercial stations. About half the commercial stations are affiliated with a network. According to TV commentator Jeff Greenfield, "The most common misconception most people have about television concerns its product. To the viewer, the product is the programming. To the television executive, the product is the audience.

"Strictly speaking, television networks and stations do not make any money by producing a program that audiences want to watch. The money comes from selling advertisers the right to broadcast a message to that audience. The programs exist to capture the biggest possible audiences."

▶ TV Delivers an Audience to Advertisers

To understand why we get the programming we do, it is important to remember that *commercial television exists primarily as an advertising medium*. Programming surrounds the advertising, but it is the advertising that is being delivered to the audience. Commercial television, from its inception, was created to deliver audiences to advertisers.

Because television can deliver a larger audience faster than any other medium, television can charge the highest rates of any medium for its advertising—which makes TV stations rich investments. A 30-second ad during a widely watched TV program like the Super Bowl (with an estimated audience of half the U.S. population) costs about $2 million. Today, even the smallest television station is a multimillion-dollar operation. The television era began much more humbly, and with very little excitement, near the turn of the 20th century.

▶ *Visual Radio* **Becomes** *Television*

The word *television* first appeared in the June 1907 issue of *Scientific American*. Before then, experiments in image transmission had been called "visual wireless," "visual radio" and "electric vision."

Alexander Graham Bell's telephone and Samuel F. B. Morse's telegraph contributed to the idea of sending electrical impulses over long distances. The first major technological discovery to suggest that pictures also could travel was the *Nipkow disk*. Twenty-four-year-old Paul Nipkow patented his "electrical telescope" in Germany in 1884. This disk, which formed the basis for television's development through the 1920s, was about the size of a phonograph record, perforated with a spiral of tiny holes.

Also crucial in television's (and radio's) development were Guglielmo Marconi and Lee de Forest. Marconi eliminated sound's dependence on wires and put sound on airwaves. De Forest contributed the Audion tube, which amplified radio waves so that people could hear the sound clearly.

In 1927, Secretary of Commerce Herbert Hoover appeared on a 2-inch screen by wire in an experimental AT&T broadcast. On September 11, 1928, General Electric broadcast the first dramatic production, "The Queen's Messenger"—the sound came over station WGY, Schenectady, and the picture came from experimental television station W2XAD. All the pictures were close-ups, and their quality could best be described as primitive.

Two researchers, one working for a company and one working alone, brought television into the electronic age. Then the same man who was responsible for radio's original popularity, RCA's **David Sarnoff**, became television's biggest promoter.

Vladimir Zworykin was working for Westinghouse when he developed an all-electronic system to transform a visual image into an electronic signal. Zworykin's electronic signal traveled through the air. When the signal reached the television receiver, the signal was transformed again into a visual image for the viewer.

Philo T. Farnsworth, working alone in California, developed the cathode ray tube (which he called a dissector tube). Farnsworth's cathode ray tube used an electronic scanner to reproduce the electronic image much more clearly than Nipkow's earlier mechanical scanning device. In 1930, 24-year-old Farnsworth patented his electronic scanner.

Reprinted with special permission of King Features Syndicate.

▶ Impact | TimeFrame

Today to 1884: Television becomes the nation's major medium for news and entertainment

continued

▼

1962
Telstar I sends the first transatlantic satellite broadcast.

▼

1951
CBS launches *I Love Lucy*, a situation comedy, which proved to be TV's most durable type of entertainment program.

▼

1947
NBC and CBS begin broadcasting television news on the *Camel News Caravan* (NBC) and *Television News with Douglas Edwards* (CBS).

▼

1939
NBC debuts at the World's Fair in New York City with a broadcast that includes President Franklin D. Roosevelt, who becomes the first U.S. president to appear on television.

▼

1907
The word *television* first appears in the June 1907 issue of *Scientific American*.

▼

1884
Paul Nipkow patents the "electrical telescope" in Germany, which formed the basis for TV's development through the 1920s.

Illustration 8.1
Time Spent Viewing Television

Average Daily Per-Person Hours of Television Use in the United States, 1997–2003

Data from *The Veronis, Suhler Stevenson Communications Industry Forecast*, 2003-2007.

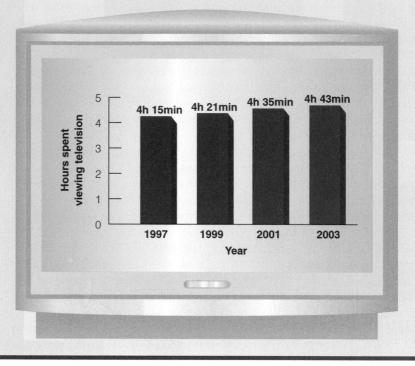

Hours spent viewing television vs. Year

- 1997: 4h 15min
- 1999: 4h 21min
- 2001: 4h 35min
- 2003: 4h 43min

Critical Question

Has the time you spend watching television changed recently? If so, how and why? If it hasn't changed, what do you think could cause it to change in the future? Explain.

NBC television's commercial debut was at the 1939 World's Fair in New York City at the Hall of Television. On April 30, 1939, President Franklin D. Roosevelt formally opened the fair and became the first president to appear on television. Sarnoff also spoke, and RCA displayed its 5-inch and 9-inch sets, priced from $199.50 to $600.

NBC and CBS were the original TV networks. A **network** is a collection of radio or television stations that offers programs, usually simultaneously, throughout the country, during designated program times. ABC, the third major network, developed in 1943 from NBC's old Blue network. ABC labored from its earliest days to equal the other two networks but didn't have as many affiliates as NBC and CBS. The two leading networks already had secured the more powerful, well-established broadcast outlets for themselves. **David Sarnoff** and **William Paley** controlled the network game.

▶ Television Takes Over Radio

By 1945, ten television stations were on the air in the United States. According to media historian Eric Barnouw, "By the late 1940s, television began its conquest of America. In 1949, the year began with radio drawing 81 percent of all broadcast audiences. By the year's end, television was grabbing 41 percent of the broadcast market. When audiences began experiencing the heady thrill of actually seeing as well as hearing events as they occurred, the superiority of television was established beyond doubt."

Black-and-white television replaced radio so quickly as the nation's major advertising medium that it would be easy to believe television erupted suddenly in a surprise move to kill radio. But remember that the two major corporate executives who developed television—Sarnoff and Paley—also held the country's largest interest in radio. They used their profits from radio to develop television, foreseeing that television eventually would expand their audience and their income.

News with Pictures

Broadcast news, pioneered by radio, adapted awkwardly at first to the new broadcast medium—television. According to **David Brinkley**, a broadcast news pioneer who began at NBC, "When television came along in about 1947–1948, the big time newsmen of that day—H. V. Kaltenborn, Lowell Thomas—did not want to do television. It was a lot of work, they weren't used to it, they were doing very well in radio, making lots of money. They didn't want to fool with it. So I was told to do it by the news manager. I was a young kid and, as I say, the older, more established people didn't want to do it. Somebody had to."

In 1947, CBS initiated *Television News with Douglas Edwards* and NBC broadcast *Camel News Caravan* (sponsored by Camel cigarettes) with John Cameron Swayze. Eventually, David Brinkley joined Swayze for NBC's 15-minute national newscast. He recalls, "The first broadcasts were extremely primitive by today's standards. It was mainly just sitting at a desk and talking. We didn't have any pictures at first. Later we began to get a little simple news film, but it wasn't much.

"In the beginning, people would call after a program and say in tones of amazement that they had seen you. 'I'm out here in Bethesda, and the picture's wonderful.' They weren't interested in anything you said. They were just interested in the fact that you had been on their screen in their house."

At first, network TV news reached only the East Coast because the necessary web of national hookups wasn't in place to deliver television across the country. By 1948, AT&T's coaxial cable linked Philadelphia with New York and Washington. The 1948 political conventions were held in Philadelphia and broadcast to the 13 Eastern states. When the 1952 conventions were broadcast, AT&T's national coaxial hookups joined 108 stations across the country.

CBS had developed a strong group of radio reporters during World War II and, by 1950, many of them had moved to the new medium. CBS News also made a practice, more than the other networks, of using the same reporters for radio and television. The major early news figure at CBS was **Edward R. Murrow**, who, along with David Brinkley at NBC, created the early standards for broadcast news (see Impact/People, p. 158).

Public affairs programs like *See It Now* continued to grow along with network news, and in 1956, NBC teamed David Brinkley with Chet Huntley to cover the political conventions. The chemistry worked, and after the convention NBC put Huntley and Brinkley together to do the evening news, *The Huntley-Brinkley Report*. Brinkley often called himself "the other side of the hyphen."

Entertainment Programming

Early television entertainment also was like late radio with pictures: It offered variety shows, situation comedies, drama, Westerns, detective stories, Hollywood movies, soap operas and quiz

Network A collection of radio or TV stations that offers programs, usually simultaneously, throughout the country, during designated program times.

AP/Wide World Photos

Among the most profitable types of TV programming today is sports. A 30-second ad during a widely watched TV program like the Super Bowl can cost more than $2 million.

Edward R. Murrow (1908—1965)

Edward R. Murrow had established a reputation for excellence as a CBS radio news broadcaster when he migrated to television news in 1951. In this profile, veteran journalist Theodore H. White outlines Murrow's broadcast career and its impact on television audiences.

It is so difficult to recapture the real Ed Murrow from the haze that now shrouds the mythical Ed Murrow of history.

Where other men may baffle friends with the infinite complexity of their natures, Ed was baffling otherwise. He was so straightforward, he would completely baffle the writers who now unravel the neuroses of today's demigods of television. When Ed was angry, he bristled; when he gave friendship, it came without withholding.

He could walk with prime ministers and movie stars, GIs and generals, as natural in rumpled GI suntans as in his diplomatic homburg. But jaunty or somber, to those of us who knew him he was just plain old Ed. In his shabby office at CBS cluttered with awards, you could loosen your necktie, put your feet up and yarn away. The dark, overhanging eyebrows would arch as

he punctured pretension with a jab, the mouth would twist quizzically as he questioned. And then there were his poker games, as Ed sat master of the table, a cigarette dangling always from his lips—he smoked 60 or 70 a day—and called the bets.

Then—I can hear him now—there was the voice. Ed's deep and rhythmic voice was compelling, not only for its range, halfway between bass and baritone, but for the words that rolled from it. He wrote for the ear—with a cadence of pauses and clipped, full sentences. His was an aural art but, in Ed, the art was natural—his inner ear composed a picture and, long before TV, the imagination of his listeners caught the sound and made with it their own picture.

We remember the voice. But there was so much more to Ed. He had not only a sense of the news but a sense of how the news fit into history. And this sense of the relation of news to history is what, in retrospect, made him the great pioneer of television journalism.

... He is very large now, for it was he who set the news system of television on its tracks, holding it, and his descendents, to the sense of history

© Bettman/CORBIS

In the 1950s, Edward R. Murrow established a very high standard for TV news.

that give it still, in the schlock-storm of today, its sense of honor. Of Ed Murrow it may be said that he made all of us who clung to him, and cling to his memory still, feel larger than we really were.

"When He Used the Power of TV, He Could Rouse Thunder," *TV Guide* 34, no. 3 (Jan. 18, 1986): 13—14. Reprinted by permission of the Julian Bach Literary Agency, Inc. © 1986 by Theodore H. White.

shows. The only type of show television offered that radio did not (besides movies, of course) was the talk show. (Ironically, today's radio has created call-in programs, its own version of the talk show.)

Quiz Shows CBS's *$64,000 Question* premiered June 7, 1955, and was sponsored by Revlon. Contestants answered questions from a glass "isolation booth." Successful contestants returned in succeeding weeks to increase their winnings, and Revlon advertised its Living Lipstick. By September, the program was drawing 85 percent of the audience, and Revlon had substituted an ad for another product; its factory supply of Living Lipstick had completely sold out.

Variety Shows The best radio stars jumped to the new medium. Three big variety-show successes were Milton Berle's *Texaco Star Theater, The Admiral Broadway Revue* (later *Your Show of Shows*) with Imogene Coca and Sid Caesar and Ed Sullivan's *Toast of the Town* (later *The Ed Sullivan Show*). These weekly shows featured comedy sketches and appearances by popular entertainers. *The Ed Sullivan Show*, for example, is where most Americans got their first glimpse of Elvis Presley and the Beatles. All of the shows were done live.

The time slot in which these programs were broadcast, 7 to 11 P.M., is known as **prime time**. Prime time simply means that more people watch television during this period than any other, so advertising during this period costs more. Berle's 8 P.M. program during prime time on Tuesday nights often gathered 85 percent of the audience. *Texaco Star Theater* became so popular that one laundromat installed a TV set and advertised, "Watch Berle while your clothes twirl."

The new program *American Idol* is a modern version of the original TV variety shows, which listeners heard first on radio.

Situation Comedies

Along with drama, the **situation comedy** (sitcom) proved to be one of TV's most durable types of programs. The situation comedy established a fixed set of characters in either a home or work situation. *I Love Lucy*, starring Lucille Ball and Desi Arnez, originated from Los Angeles because the actors wanted to live on the West Coast. In 1951, Ball began a career as a weekly performer on CBS that lasted for 23 years. *Friends*, *Frasier* and *Everybody Loves Raymond* are examples of more contemporary situation comedy successes.

Prime Time The TV time period from 7 to 11 P.M. when more people watch TV than at any other time.

Situation Comedy A TV program that establishes a fixed set of characters typically in a home or work situation.

Drama

The Loretta Young Show offered noontime drama—broadcast live—every day in the 1950s. *The Hallmark Hall of Fame* established a tradition for high-quality dramatic, live presentations. For many years, TV dramas were limited to 1- or 2-hour programs. But in the 1970s, encouraged by the success of Alex Haley's *Roots*, which dramatized Haley's search for the story of his African ancestry, television began to broadcast as many as 14 hours of a single drama over several nights. Today, the series *Six Feet Under* is an example of a popular prime-time drama.

Westerns

TV went Western in 1954, when Jack Warner of Warner Bros. signed an agreement with ABC to provide the network with a program called *Cheyenne*. The outspoken Warner had openly criticized TV's effect on the movie business, but when ABC asked Warner to produce programs for them, Warner Bros. became the first movie company to realize that the studios could profit from television.

Detective Stories

Dragnet, with Sergeant Friday, was an early TV experiment with detectives. The genre became a TV staple: *Dragnet's* successor today is a program like *Law and Order*.

Movies

The movie industry initially resisted the competition from TV, but then realized there was money to be made in selling old movies to TV. In 1957, RKO sold 740 pre-1948 movies to television for $25 million. The other studios followed. Through various distribution agreements, movie reruns and movies produced specifically for television were added to television's program lineup.

Soap Operas

Borrowed from radio serials, soap operas filled morning television programming. Today, game shows and reruns are more popular choices, but programs like *The Young and the Restless* survive. Soap operas have

I Love Lucy is an early example of one of TV's most durable types of prime-time programming—the situation comedy.

their own magazines, and some newspapers carry weekly summaries of plot development.

Talk Shows   Sylvester "Pat" Weaver (actress Sigourney Weaver's father) created and produced television's single original contribution to programming: the talk show. Weaver's *Tonight Show* (originally *Jerry Lester's Broadway Open House*) first appeared in 1954. Through a succession of hosts from Lester to Steve Allen to Jack Paar to Johnny Carson to Jay Leno, *The Tonight Show* has lasted longer than any other talk show on television. Modern-day imitators include David Letterman and Conan O'Brien.

▶ Quiz Show Scandals

As the most popular quiz show on early television, *The $64,000 Question* engendered imitation: *Treasure Hunt, Giant Step,* and *Twenty-One.* Winnings grew beyond the $64,000 limit; Charles Van Doren won $129,000 on *Twenty-One.* In the fall of 1955, CBS replaced Murrow's *See It Now* with a quiz program.

Many network quiz shows like *The $64,000 Question* were produced by sponsors for the networks, and these programs often carried the sponsor's name. In the 1958–1959 quiz show scandals, Revlon was implicated when a congressional subcommittee investigated charges that the quiz shows were rigged to enhance the ratings.

Charles Van Doren admitted before the congressional subcommittee that Twenty-One's producer had fed him the answers. Staff members from other quiz shows confirmed Van Doren's testimony.

The scandals caused the networks to reexamine the relationship between advertisers and programs. Before the scandals, advertisers and their agencies produced one-quarter to one-third of network programming. As a result of the quiz how scandals, the networks turned to other sources, such as independent producers, for their programming.

By the late 1960s, advertisers provided less than 3 percent of network programming, and soon advertisers provided no network shows. The networks programmed themselves. They also used reruns of newly acquired studio movies to replace the quiz shows, but quiz shows have resurfaced today with *Wheel of Fortune, Family Feud,* and *Jeopardy.*

Charles Van Doren, shown here, won $129,000 on the quiz show *Twenty-One.* Eventually, Van Doren admitted the show's producers had fed him the answers. He became a central figure in the 1950s quiz show scandals.

▶ Ratings Target the Audience

After the quiz show scandals, the major criticism of the networks was that they were motivated only by ratings. Ratings provide sponsors with information about the audience they're reaching with their advertising—what advertisers are getting for their money. By the late 1950s, the A. C. Nielsen Company dominated the television ratings business. The national Nielsen ratings describe the audience to advertisers; based on the Nielsens, advertisers pay for the commercial time to reach the audiences they want.

Today, Nielsen provides two sets of numbers, known as **rating** and **share.** The **rating** is a percentage of the total number of households with television sets. If there are 95 million homes with TV sets, for example, the rating shows the percentage of those sets that were tuned in to a specific program.

The **share** (an abbreviation for share-of-audience) compares the audience for one show with the audience for another. Share means the percentage of the audience with TV sets turned on that is watching each program. If TV sets

Rating   A percentage of the total number of households *with TV sets.*

Share   The percentage of the audience *with TV sets turned on* that is watching each program.

Impact | **Business**

Illustration 8.2
Measuring the Audience: What TV Ratings Mean

Suppose that at 8 P.M. on Friday, TVs are on in 50 million out of 95 million TV households and that 25 million households are tuned to program A. Program A's *rating* is 26, meaning 26 percent of the total TV households are tuned to Program A. Program A's *share* is 50, meaning 50 percent of the total number of TV households watching TV are watching Program A.

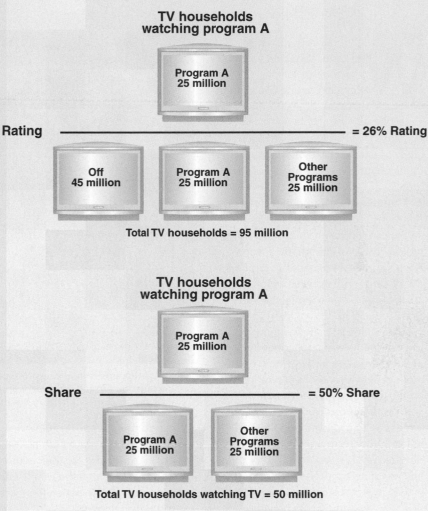

TV households watching program A

Program A
25 million

Rating ——————————————————— = 26% Rating

| Off 45 million | Program A 25 million | Other Programs 25 million |

Total TV households = 95 million

TV households watching program A

Program A
25 million

Share ——————————————————— = 50% Share

| Program A 25 million | Other Programs 25 million |

Total TV households watching TV = 50 million

in 50 million homes were turned on at 8 P.M. on Friday night, and 25 million homes were tuned to program A, that program would have a rating of 26 (25 million divided by 95 million, expressed as a percentage) and a share of 50. (See Illustration 8.2.)

The most concentrated ratings periods for local stations are "sweeps" months—February, May and November. (Ratings are taken in July, too, but the numbers are not considered accurate because so many people are on vacation.) The sweeps provide an estimate of the local TV audience, and advertisers use that information when they decide where to place their commercials.

Sweeps are the months when the ratings services gather their most important ratings, so the networks and local stations often use these important months to showcase their best programs. This is when you are most likely to see a special one-hour episode of a popular series, for example, or a very expensively produced made-for-TV movie.

Today's Nielsen ratings work essentially the same as they did in the 1950s, except that the Nielsens now deliver very specific information on **demographics**—age, occupation and income, for instance. Advertisers use this information to target their most likely consumers. Nike shoes might

Sweeps The months when TV ratings services gather their most important ratings—February, May and November.

Demographics Personal characteristics of the audience, such as age, occupation and income.

Viewers Identify with TV Characters

by Eileen Kinsella

Who cares about juicy plots and cool explosions? TV viewers want to see shows with cast members similar to themselves.

That's the conclusion of a recent study of television-viewer habits conducted by the Yale School of Management. . . .

The Yale study found that viewers' preference for characters like themselves can outweigh such show attributes as the level of comedy or action. A woman who lives with her family is 45 percent more likely to watch a show centered on a family than one that is not.

Anne Elliot, a spokeswoman for Nielsen Media Research, doesn't doubt the study's findings but argues that viewer data can be interpreted in many ways. "Every day within the television industry, networks can find information that will portray what they want," she says. She also notes that *Friends* is a favorite of hers, but she isn't single, no longer lives in the city and is past her 20s. "Do I watch *Friends* because I'm like them? No. I simply think the show is funny."

The TV program *Friends* was produced to appeal to an under-30 audience, an important age group for the networks. The Yale study says TV viewers prefer shows that feature characters like themselves.

The study's author, Ron Shachar, responds that the networks can use his findings to maximize their audiences. He argues that they should air sitcoms after 10 P.M. when there are no competing shows.

Mr. Kurlander doesn't disagree but maintains there is already such a high failure rate for such shows that a later time slot won't guarantee success. "It's difficult to pull off a hit no matter how you look at it," he says.

The Wall Street Journal, March 31, 1997, B1.
Reprinted by permission of *The Wall Street Journal,*
© 1997 Dow Jones & Co., Inc. All Rights Reserved

choose to create a new advertising campaign for the NBA playoffs, for instance, and Nielsen could tell Nike, from judging previous championships, all about the people the company will reach with its ads.

Criticism about the ratings persists. The main flaw in the ratings today, critics contend, is the way the ratings are religiously followed and used by the broadcast community to determine programming.

▶ TV Dominates the Airwaves

The 1950s were a trial period for television, as the networks and advertisers tested audience interest in various types of programming. Captured by the miracle that television offered, audiences initially seemed insatiable; they would watch almost anything that TV delivered. But in the 1960s, audiences became more discriminating and began to question how well the medium of television was serving the public.

Newton Minow Targets TV as a "Vast Wasteland"

With television established even in the smaller cities, the medium needed a public conscience. That public conscience was Newton Minow.

An unassuming soothsayer, Minow was named chairman of the FCC in 1961 by newly elected President John F. Kennedy. On May 9, 1961, speaking to the National Association of Broadcasters in his first public address since his appointment, Minow articulated what he felt were the broadcasters' responsibilities to the public. According to Newton Minow, in his book *Equal Time*, Minow told the broadcasters:

> *Your license lets you use the public's airwaves as trustees for 180 million Americans. The public is your beneficiary. If you want to stay on as trustees, you must deliver a decent return to the public—not only to your stockholders. . . .*
>
> *Your industry possesses the most powerful voice in America. It has an inescapable duty to make that voice ring with intelligence and with leadership. In a few years this exciting industry has grown from a novelty to an instrument of overwhelming impact on the American people. It should be making ready for the kind of leadership that newspapers and magazines assumed years ago, to make our people aware of their world.*
>
> *Ours has been called the jet age, the atomic age, the space age. It is also, I submit, the television age. And just as history will decide whether the leaders of today's world employed the atom to destroy the world or rebuild it for mankind's benefit, so will history decide whether today's broadcasters employed their powerful voice to enrich the people or debase them.*

Minow then asked his audience of broadcast station owners and managers to watch their own programs. He said that they would find a "vast wasteland," a phrase that resurfaces today during any critical discussion of television.

▶ Public Television Finds an Audience

The concept of educational television has been alive since the 1950s, when a few noncommercial stations succeeded in regularly presenting public service programs without advertisements. But the shows were low-budget and little national programming was done.

The educational network NET (National Educational Television) emerged in 1963 to provide some national programming (about ten hours a week), sponsored mainly by foundations, with some federal support. Then in 1967, the Ford Foundation agreed to help pay for several hours of live evening programming.

Also in 1967, the Carnegie Commission on Educational Television released its report *Public Television: A Program for Action,* which included a proposal to create the Corporation for Public Broadcasting. CPB would collect money from many sources— including the enhanced federal funds that the Carnegie report suggested—and disburse the money to the stations.

The Johnson administration and several foundations added money to CPB's budget. The Public Broadcasting Service (PBS) was created to distribute programs. The extra money underwrote the creation of programs like *Sesame Street* and *The French Chef.* PBS also began to buy successful British television programs, which were broadcast on *Masterpiece Theater.* PBS programs actually started to show up in the ratings.

Today, the Corporation for Public Broadcasting, which oversees public television, still receives funding from the federal government. Local funding

Photofest Inc.

PBS has provided many memorable programs like *Sesame Street,* yet PBS commonly attracts less than 3 percent of the national audience. In 1995, members of Congress called for the "privatization" of public television, which means it would become self-sustaining.

supplements this government underwriting, but within the past ten years, donations to public television have been declining.

This decline in funding has led public broadcasters to seek underwriting from more corporate donors. But companies accustomed to advertising on commercial networks are reluctant to advertise on a network that commonly attracts less than 3 percent of the national audience. This means that, for the first time, public television is beginning to pay attention to ratings.

This attention to an audience of consumers means the pressure is building on public television executives to make each program segment profitable. The FCC began liberalizing its rules for commercial announcements on public television in 1981. Now, corporate sponsors often make 10-second announcements, including graphics, at the beginning and the end of PBS-produced programs. These announcements often resemble advertisements on commercial television.

Critics of this commercialization of public television are calling for more government funding, but Congress seems unwilling to expand its underwriting. Today, public television is struggling to reinvent itself, and it still remains commercial television's stepchild.

▶ Satellites Bring a Technological Breakthrough

By 1965, all three networks were broadcasting in color. Television demonstrated its technological sophistication in December 1968 with its live broadcast from the *Apollo* spacecraft while the spacecraft circled the moon, and seven months later television showed Neil Armstrong stepping onto the moon.

On July 10, 1962, Telstar I sent the first transatlantic satellite broadcast. Before Telstar, copper cable linked the continents, film footage from overseas traveled only by plane, and in most homes a long-distance telephone call was a special event.

Today, Telstar's descendants orbit at a distance of more than 22,000 miles. A single modern communication satellite can carry 30,000 telephone calls and three television channels. Modern satellites made CNN and satellite-system DirecTV possible.

▶ Television Changes National Politics

Just as radio matured, first as an entertainment medium and expanded to cover important news events, television first established itself with entertainment and then developed a serious news presence. Just as Franklin D. Roosevelt had been the first president to understand and use radio, John F. Kennedy became the country's first television president. Kennedy's predecessors had appeared on television, but he instinctively knew how to *use* television.

Observers credited Kennedy's 1960 presidential victory partly because of his success in the televised debates with Richard Nixon. Kennedy also was the first president to hold live televised news conferences. In July 1962, he oversaw the launch of the first communications satellite, Telstar I. Sadly, one year later that same satellite technology was used to broadcast the news events following President Kennedy's assassination on November 22, 1963.

Television received credit for uniting the nation during TV news coverage of the Kennedy assassination, but it also was blamed for dividing it. President Lyndon Johnson, beleaguered by an unpopular war, used television to announce in 1968 that he would not run for a second term. His successor, President Richard Nixon, had always been uncomfortable with the press. Under the Nixon administration, the press was attacked for presenting per-

Television became an international window on grief in 2001 when the networks broadcast live coverage of the events following the September 11 terrorist attacks on the United States (left) and then broadcast nonstop coverage of the early days of the Iraq War in 2003.

spectives on world affairs that the Nixon administration did not like. Upset with the messages being presented, the Nixon administration battled the messenger, sparking a bitter public debate about the role of a free press (especially television) in a democratic society.

▶ Watergate and the Iran-Contra Hearings Take Viewers Inside

Ironically, television's next live marathon broadcast would chronicle an investigation of the Nixon presidency—Watergate. The Watergate scandal began when burglars broke into the offices of the Democratic party's national headquarters in the Watergate complex in Washington, D.C., on June 17, 1972. Some of the burglars had ties to President Nixon's reelection committee as well as to other questionable activities originating in the White House.

In the following months, the president and his assistants sought to squelch the resulting investigation. Although Nixon denied knowledge of the break-in and the cover-up, the U.S. Senate hearings about the scandal, televised live across the country, created a national sensation. (See also Chapter 12.) Eventually, faced with the prospect of impeachment, Nixon resigned on August 8, 1974.

In 1987, television repeated its marathon coverage of an important national investigation with the Iran-Contra hearings, a congressional investigation of the Reagan administration's role in providing weapons illegally to Nicaraguan rebels, called contras.

▶ TV News Images Share 21st Century Sadness and Grief

In 1997, TV became an international window on grief when the networks carried nonstop coverage of the events surrounding the death and funeral of Diana, Princess of Wales. In 2001, U.S. TV network news offered nonstop coverage of the terrorist events at New York's World Trade Center, the Pentagon and in rural Pennsylvania. Two years later, the TV networks brought viewers even closer to events when TV reporters and photographers sent live battlefield images and stories to viewers during the Iraq War.

Television news has matured from its early beginnings as a 15-minute newscast to today's access to 24-hour coverage of significant news events. Today, television news continues to play an important role in setting the agenda for the discussion of public issues. (For a further discussion of broadcast journalism, see Chapter 12.)

▶ Working in Television

A typical television station has eight departments: sales, programming (which includes news as well as entertainment), production, engineering, traffic, promotion, public affairs and administration.

People in the *sales* department sell the commercial slots for the programs. Advertising is divided into *national* and *local* sales. Advertising agencies, usually based on the East Coast, buy national ads for the products they handle.

Ford Motor Company, for instance, may buy time on a network for a TV ad that will run simultaneously all over the country. But the local Ford dealers, who want you to shop at their showrooms, buy their ads directly from the local station. These ads are called local (or spot) ads. For these sales, salespeople (called account executives) at each station negotiate packages of ads based on their station's rates. These rates are a direct reflection of that station's position in the ratings.

The *programming* department selects the shows that you will see and develops the station's schedule. Network-owned stations, located in big cities (KNBC in Los Angeles, for example), are called **O & Os,** which stands for owned and operated. Stations that carry network programming but that are not owned by the networks are called **affiliates** (see Chapter 1).

O & Os automatically carry network programming, but affiliates are paid by the network to carry its programming, for which the network sells most of the ads and keeps the money. The affiliate is allowed to insert into the network programming a specific number of local ads, for which the affiliate keeps the money.

Because affiliates can make money on network programming, and don't have to pay for it, many stations choose to affiliate themselves with a network. When they aren't running what the network provides, affiliates run their own programs and keep all the advertising money they collect from them.

O & Os   TV stations that are *O*wned and *O*perated by the networks.

Affiliates   Stations that carry TV network programming but are not owned by the networks.

Impact | **Business**

Illustration 8.3
Network's Share of Prime-Time Audience 1975–2002 (includes Fox beginning in 1987 and UPN and WB beginning in 1995)*

The prime-time audience for the television networks (ABC, CBS, NBC, Fox, UPN, and WB) is declining because of increased competition from satellite and cable programming.

Data from *The Veronis, Suhler Stevenson Communications Industry Forecast*, 2003–2007.

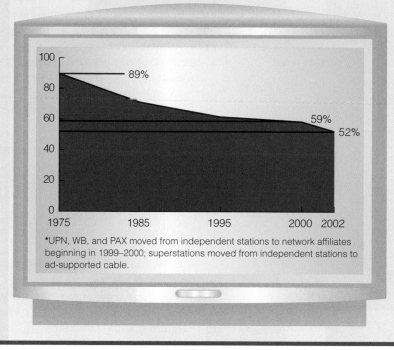

*UPN, WB, and PAX moved from independent stations to network affiliates beginning in 1999–2000; superstations moved from independent stations to ad-supported cable.

More than one-third of the nation's commercial TV stations operate as independents. Independent stations must buy and program all their own shows, but independents also can keep all money they make on advertising. They run some individually produced programs and old movies, but most of their programming consists of reruns that once ran on the networks. Independents buy these reruns from program services called **syndicators.**

Syndicators also sell independently produced programs such as *The Oprah Winfrey Show* and *Wheel of Fortune*. These programs are created and sold either by non-network stations or by independent producers. Stations pay for these first-run syndication programs individually; the price is based on the size of the station's market.

Local news usually makes up the largest percentage of a station's locally produced programming. In some large markets, such as Los Angeles, local news programming runs as long as three hours.

The *production* department manages the programs the station creates in-house. This department also produces local commercials for the station.

The *engineering* department makes sure all of the technical aspects of a broadcast operation are working: antennas, transmitters, cameras and any other broadcast equipment.

The *traffic* department integrates the advertising with the programming, making sure that all the ads that are sold are aired when they're supposed to be. Traffic also handles billing for the ads.

The *promotion* department advertises the station—on the station itself, on billboards, on radio and in the local newspaper. These people also create contests to keep the station visible in the community.

The *public affairs department* often helps organize public events, such as a fun run to raise money for the local hospital.

Administration handles the paperwork for the station—paychecks and expense accounts, for example.

Syndicators Services that sell programming to broadcast stations and cable.

▶ The Business of Television

Today's most-watched television programs are situation comedies, sports and feature movies. More than 100 million households tuned in for the final episode of the situation comedy *Cheers* in 1993, making it the highest-rated television program ever. Super Bowls generally grab nearly half of the homes in the United States.

Six developments promise to affect the television industry over the next decade: station ownership changes, the shrinking role of the networks, the accuracy of ratings, the growth of cable, the profitability of sports programming, and the availability of direct satellite broadcasts.

Station Ownership Changes and Mergers
The Telecommunications Act of 1996 (see Chapter 14) uses a station's potential audience to measure ownership limits. The Act allows one company to own TV stations that reach up to 35 percent of the nation's homes. Broadcasters also are no longer required, as they once were, to hold a station for three years before selling it. Today, stations may be sold as soon as they are purchased.

In 1999, the FCC adopted new regulations that allow media companies to own two TV stations in the market, as long as eight separately owned TV stations continue to operate in that market after the merger. The four top-rated stations in one market cannot be combined, but a station that is among the top-rated four could combine with one that is not in the top four.

About 100 of the nation's TV markets have eight or more separately owned stations. "I think [the rule change] is going to change television," said USA Networks Chairman Barry Diller, whose company owned 13 stations. "It opens up so many options . . . from buying to partnering to selling to combining."

In 2003, the FCC announced plans to relax the ownership rules even further, leaving few restrictions on network ownership. Congress is resisting the changes but, if the regulations are adopted, television ownership will become concentrated among fewer and fewer companies. Television is *concentrating* ownership, but it is also *shifting* ownership, as stations are bought and sold at an unprecedented rate. This has introduced instability and change to an industry that until 1980 witnessed very few ownership turnovers.

The Networks' Shrinking Role
Advertisers always have provided the economic support for television, so in 1986 the networks were disturbed to see the first decline in revenues in 15 years. New and continuing developments—such as cable, satellite broadcast, VCRs and DVD-players—have turned the television set into a smorgasbord of choices. Audiences—and advertisers—are deserting the networks, and network ratings are declining as a result. Because there are so many new sources of information and entertainment for the audience, advertisers are looking for new ways to capture viewers.

The network share of the *prime time audience* has gone from 90 percent in 1978 to around 50 percent today, reflecting the continued growth of independent TV stations, syndicated programming, satellite and cable systems. The networks' share of the audience for the evening news also is shrinking.

The story is familiar, paralleling the decline in radio listening in the late 1940s when it first was supplanted by television and then began competing with itself. More stations and more sources of programming mean the networks will have to redefine their audience and give the audience what it cannot get elsewhere.

How Accurate Are TV Ratings?

People meters, first used in 1987, by the A. C. Nielsen Company to record television viewing, gather data through a 4-inch by 10-inch box that sits on the television set in metered homes. People meters monitor the nation's Nielsen families (about 4,000 of them), and the results of these recorded viewing patterns (which Nielsen says reflect a cross section of American viewers) sets the basis for television advertising rates.

Nielsen family members each punch in an assigned button on top of the set when they begin to watch television. The system's central computer, linked to the home by telephone lines, correlates each viewer's number with information about that person stored in its memory. Network ratings have plunged since people meters were introduced as a ratings system, and the networks have complained that the new measuring device underestimates viewership. Still, Nielsen is the only company in the United States offering TV audience measurement.

Cable versus Broadcast

Today's cable giants, ESPN (Entertainment & Sports Programming Network) and A&E (Arts & Entertainment) are descendents of America's first cable TV system, which was established in Pennsylvania and Oregon to bring TV signals to rural areas that couldn't receive an over-the-air signal. Soon, this community-antenna television (**CATV**) system spread to remote areas all over the country where TV reception was poor.

By 1970, there were 2,500 CATV systems in the United States, and commercial broadcasters were getting nervous about what they called wired TV. Cable operators were required by the FCC to carry all local broadcast programming, and programs often were duplicated on several channels. The FCC also limited the programs that cable could carry. One FCC ruling, for example, said that movies on cable had to be at least ten years old.

Believing that cable should be able to offer its own programming, Home Box Office (then owned by Time Warner) started operating in Manhattan in 1972, offering a modest set of programs. Ted Turner's TNT first relayed programs by satellite in 1976, and in 1979 Turner started Cable News Network (CNN). Today, more than 200 different program services, ranging from ESPN to the concert sounds of VH-1 to classic 1930s and 1940s movies on American Movie Classics (AMC), are available by satellite. About 60 percent of the homes in America have basic cable.

Cable television as an alternative to the traditional networks moved to the center of the national news agenda in 1991 when CNN offered 24-hour coverage of the Gulf War in Iraq. CNN's fast response to world events underlined the new global role that CNN, and many other cable companies, will play in future television developments.

TV Changes Professional Sports

One of the most profitable types of television programming is sports. In 1964, CBS paid $28 million for television rights to the 1964–1965 National Football

Cable channels like ESPN, which offers sports programming such as WNBA Basketball, offer advertisers a very targeted audience.

CATV   Cable television.

"Hey, I'm just happy to be making an obscene amount of money."

Illustration 8.4
Household Spending on Basic Cable and Satellite Television, 1985–2005

The average monthly cost per household for basic cable and satellite television services shows that today satellite services are less expensive than cable, which may account for the increasing number of satellite subscribers.

Data from *The Veronis Suhler Stevenson Communications Industry Forecast, 2001–2005*; The Publishing & Media Group, Paul Kagan Associates.

*Projected

Average Monthly Cost per Household, 1985-2005

Year	Basic cable	Satellite
1985	$10.43	$11.83
1990	$16.79	$11.43
1995	$23.07	$21.00
2000	$29.87	$24.57
2005*	$37.05	$34.90

League (NFL) games. In 1990, the price paid for rights to broadcast NFL football totaled $3.6 billion.

Television fees fund most of the cost of organized sports. Today, televised sports have become spectacularly complex entertainment packages, turning athletes as well as sports commentators into media stars. The expansion of sports programming beyond the networks to cable channels such as ESPN means even more sports programming choices for viewers, and more money for American sports teams.

DBS Direct broadcast satellites.

Direct Broadcast Satellites
The FCC authorized **DBS** in 1982, making direct-to-home satellite broadcasts possible. In 1994, a company called DirecTV began offering services directly to the home by satellite. For a monthly fee, DirecTV provides access to more than 200 *different worldwide* channels. The monthly fee is about the same cost as, or cheaper than, a monthly cable bill. The main advantages are reliable access to worldwide programming at a reasonable cost and the elimination of the set-top box.

▶ Technology Transforms the Future

When technological developments move like a rocket, as they have in the past decade, program delivery becomes easier and less expensive. New technologies have brought more competition.

Significant Technological Developments
Several new delivery systems have been developed to bring increasingly more choices to consumers. Besides digital television, some of the most important recent technological developments are described here.

Digital Video Recorders (DVRs)
DVRs can download programming, using a device called a "set-top box" (which looks much like today's cable boxes and sits on or near the TV). DVRs use hard-drive computer storage to receive information from any program service (including the broadcast networks, satellite and cable programmers) to send viewers up-to-date information about what's on TV. DVRs transfer the information to an on-screen program guide, where viewers can decide what to watch and when, a practice called **time-shifting**. One of the biggest features of a DVR is that it allows viewers to hit the "pause" button for a show they're watching, leave the TV set on, and then start up the program again when they return, or fast-forward through the recorded portion.

Because DVRs could change viewers' control over which programming they watch (and, most importantly, which commercials), all the major TV networks have invested in the companies that are producing this technology, such as TiVo. The networks want to be able to influence what consumers can record and when, but the value of total viewer control is one of DVRs' most attractive features for consumers.

Enhanced Television
Another development using traditional broadcast television technology to give consumers online access is enhanced television, announced late in 1997. Enhanced television merges information from the World Wide Web and television programs on one screen. This technology allows someone to watch a football game as it's happening and, at the same time, follow a discussion about the game taking place in a Web-based chat session on a separate portion of the screen. To use the new technology, consumers have to buy a decoder device that attaches to the TV set.

High-Definition Television (HDTV)
A normal television picture scans 525 lines across the screen. **High-definition television (HDTV)** scans 1,125 lines. CBS first demonstrated HDTV in the United States in 1982. HDTV, which offers a wider, sharper picture and better sound requires more spectrum space than conventional television signals. HDTV is beginning to gain acceptance in the United States because sets, which originally cost $10,000, are now priced at $1,000 for a starter model.

DVR   Digital video recorders.

Time-Shifting   Recording a television program on a DVR or VCR to watch at a more convenient time.

High Definition Television (HDTV)   A type of television that provides a picture with a clearer resolution than on typical TV sets

The new digital technology available with high-definition television (HDTV) offers movie-quality pictures and CD-quality sound on a large screen. Sports programs and live events are the most widely watched HDTV broadcasts.

© Peter Da Silva

HDTV's Acceptance Picks Up Pace As Prices Drop and Networks Sign On

by Eric A. Taub

Since its rollout in 1998, HDTV has tended for most people to be the the video equivalent of a tree's falling in the forest with no one around to hear it. Digital sets have been costly and the availability of high-definition signals on cable has been skimpy. But, in fact, the technology—digital-quality television with a super-sharp picture the shape of a movie screen—has started to catch on in measurable ways.

Although HDTV still presents consumers with a confusing set of shopping issues and can be difficult to install, the sets and attendant equipment have come down in price from the ridiculous ($10,000 or more initially) to the merely expensive (now less than $1,000 at the entry level). And so, sales are beginning to expand beyond the cult of early adopters, although the number of households with HDTV sets remains only a fraction of the nation's television audience.

An estimated 4.9 million HDTV-capable sets have been sold in this country, but only about 640,000 have been purchased with a built-in tuner or add-on decoder box required for receiving an HDTV broadcast. HDTV programming, meanwhile, is steadily

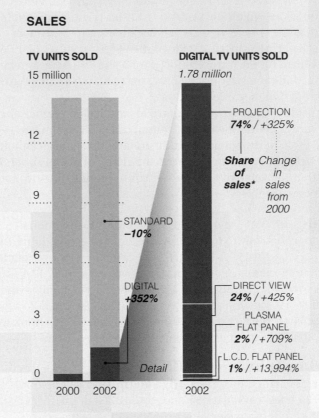

SALES

TV UNITS SOLD

15 million

12

9

STANDARD
−10%

6

DIGITAL
+352%

3

0

Detail

2000   2002

DIGITAL TV UNITS SOLD

1.78 million

PROJECTION
74% / +325%

**Share   Change
of   in
sales*   sales
from
2000**

DIRECT VIEW
24% / +425%

PLASMA
FLAT PANEL
2% / +709%

L.C.D. FLAT PANEL
1% / +13,994%

2002

moving beyond special-event status and becoming an increasingly regular part of the lineup on the leading broadcast networks, transmitted as digital simulcast feeds by the local affiliates that have the necessary equipment. . . .

"HDTV is the next great wave in technology," said ESPN's president,

George Bodenheimer. "This will give our fans the best sports television experience yet."

The New York Times, March 31, 2003, C-1. Copyright © 2003 by the New York Times Co. Reprinted with permission.

Telcos   An abbreviation for telephone companies.

Forecasting the Future: A *Telepresence?*   Forecasts for the future of television parallel the forecasts for radio—a menu board of hundreds of programs and services available to viewers at the touch of a remote-control button. In the 1990s, several regional telephone companies (called **telcos**) rushed to merge with cable TV companies to form giant telecommunications delivery systems. "Cable TV companies and telephone companies are joining forces because each has something valuable that the other wants," reports the *Los Angeles Times*.

"Telephone companies have wired virtually every household in their service area and want to deliver the wide variety of program and information services controlled by the cable companies," says the *Times*. "The cable operators, on the other hand, want to use their cable TV wires to go into the phone business, delivering voice, data and video over . . . fiber-optic lines."

The result of these mergers will be that some new financial media power-houses will have the ability to invest large sums of money in research and expansion for developing technologies with vast potential, such as fiber optics.

Fiber optics, which allows the transmission of huge amounts of data using clear glass strands as thin as a human hair, forms the basis for many of today's cable systems, and fiber optics could change television dramatically.

Imagine your television as an artificial reality machine. This machine, says *The Wall Street Journal*, would use "remarkably crisp pictures and sound to 'deliver' a viewer to a pristine tropical beach, to a big football game or to a quiet mountaintop retreat. Japanese researchers envision golfers practicing their swings in front of three-dimensional simulations of courses."

The definition of television today is expanding faster than our ability to chronicle the changes. Lanny Smoot, an executive at Bell Communications Research, calls the future of television a *telepresence*. "This," he says, "is a wave that is not possible to stop."

Media | Review

History

▶ Guglielmo Marconi put sound on airwaves. Lee de Forest invented the Audion tube. Vladimir Zworykin turned an electronic signal into a visual image. Philo T. Farnsworth added the electronic scanner.

▶ The rivalry between David Sarnoff (RCA) and William S. Paley (CBS) is central to the early history of television.

▶ The ABC network was formed when the Federal Communications Commission (FCC) ordered David Sarnoff to sell one of his two networks (Red and Blue). The Blue network became ABC.

▶ The first television news broadcasts were primitive compared to today's broadcasts. Television news, like radio news, developed its own standard of excellence, led by news pioneers Edward R. Murrow and David Brinkley.

▶ Most television entertainment programming was derived from radio. The only type of program that didn't come from radio was the talk show, which appeared on television first and then moved to radio. The situation comedy proved to be one of television's most durable types of programming.

▶ The 1950s quiz show scandals caused the networks to eliminate advertiser-produced programming.

Technology

▶ The word *television*, which once meant programs delivered by antennas through over-the-air signals, today means a *television screen*, where a variety of delivery systems brings viewers a diversity of programs.

▶ Today, traditional network audiences are shrinking, as more stations are licensed to broadcast and as rapidly changing technology competes for TV audiences.

▶ Several technological developments are changing the way programs are delivered to consumers: digital video recorders (DVRs), enhanced television, high-definition television (HDTV) and direct broadcast satellites (DBS).

▶ In the 1990s, telephone companies joined cable operators to form giant telecommunications delivery systems. The result will be some new financial powerhouses with the ability to invest large sums of money in research and expansion for developing technologies with vast potential, such as fiber optics.

▶ Digital television such as HDTV offers better pictures, clearer sound and a flatter screen than traditional TV.

▶ Digital TV makes it easier for manufacturers to combine the functions of TV and the functions of a computer in the same TV set.

▶ Today, traditional network audiences are shrinking, as more stations are licensed to broadcast and as rapidly changing technology means more companies are competing for TV audiences.

Business

▶ About 1,600 television stations operate in the United States. Three out of four of these are commercial stations and about half of U.S. stations are affiliated with a network.

▶ More than any other media industry today, commercial television exists primarily as an advertising medium.

▶ The Nielsen ratings determine the price that TV advertisers pay to air their commercials.

▶ Network ratings have plunged since people meters were introduced as a ratings system, and the networks have complained that the new measuring device underestimates network viewership.

▶ Deregulation, with relaxed ownership rules, means that instability, mergers and change have become major characteristics of the television industry.

▶ More than 200 program services now offer alternatives to network programming.

▶ Televised sports are one of the most profitable types of TV programming, and television licensing fees fund most of the cost of the nation's college and professional sports.

Culture

▶ In the 1960s, television drew criticism for the way it was perceived to influence politics and the dialogue about national issues.

▶ Many groups are concerned that, because of its pervasiveness, television influences the nation's values, habits and behavior.

▶ In the 1960s, audiences grew more discriminating and began to question how well the medium of television was serving the public. An influential person for these views was then-FCC Chairman Newton Minow, who coined the phrase "vast wasteland" to describe television.

▶ In 2001, U.S. TV network news offered nonstop coverage of the terrorist events at New York's World Trade Center, the Pentagon and in rural Pennsylvania. Two years later, the TV networks brought viewers even closer to events when TV reporters and photographers sent live battlefield images and stories to viewers during the Iraq War.

Impact | Interactive

The Impact/Interactive CD-ROM that accompanies this text is your gateway to many electronic resources for broadening and testing your critical understanding of the material in Chapter 8. The CD-ROM features the following interactive elements for this and every chapter in the book.

▶ A two- to three-minute timely, high-interest CNN Today video clip with critical viewing questions and a link to relevant selections available within the InfoTrac College Edition database

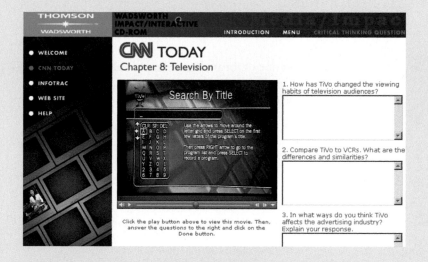

▶ Chapter-specific activities such as personal inventories and media projects

▶ A link to the *Media/Impact* Web site that offers helpful information and many additional electronic learning resources including:

  • An interactive chapter outline and study guide

  • Interactive glossary term flashcards and crossword puzzles, concept animations, Internet activities and practice quizzes

  • Live links for all URLs given in the chapter so you can easily access the additional information each site offers

▶ A link to InfoTrac College Edition—our online database of more than a million articles representing cutting-edge research and the latest headlines. Updated daily, this online library is available 24 hours a day, seven days a week. The InfoTrac College Edition activities provided below are designed to help you use this valuable resource.

▶ Working the Web

Live links for all of the sites listed below are provided on the Media/Impact book companion Web site, which can be accessed through your Impact/Interactive CD-ROM.

- ▶ **ABC Television Network**
  www.abc.com

- ▶ **HDTV Network**
  HDTV.net

- ▶ **National Association of Broadcasters**
  www.nab.org

- ▶ **Nielsen Ratings**
  nielsenmedia.com

- ▶ **Northwestern University Library Broadcast, Cable and Satellite Resources on the Net**
  www.library.northwestern.edu/media/resources/broadcast.html

- ▶ **Public Broadcasting**
  www.pbs.org

- ▶ **Television Bureau of Advertising**
  www.tvb.org

▶ InfoTrac College Edition Activities

Using InfoTrac College Edition online database of full-text articles and abstracts, do the following activities as directed by your instructor. The database can be accessed through your Impact/Interactive CD-ROM.

1. Read "HDTV's Acceptance Picks Up Pace As Prices Drop and Networks Sign On" in Chapter 8. Then using the key words "HDTV" or "digital TV," choose one sizable article from the list of citations on the InfoTrac College Edition. Write a brief summary of the article (no more than 300 words) and include some discussion of whether you think HDTV will gain popular support. Be sure to sum up the article's major points or conclusions in your overview.

2. Look up the key words "public television" using InfoTrac College Edition and find articles about PBS's ongoing struggle with issues of government funding and seeking funding from corporate donors. Then break into small groups to discuss the pros and cons of having more corporate donors, who make corporate announcements before and after programs. Does this "commercialization" dilute the quality or credibility of public television? Each group should share its conclusions with the class.

3. Using InfoTrac College Edition, look up the keywords "Newton Minow," the former FCC chairman who called television programming a "vast wasteland." Read some articles that clarify his criticisms, then and now. Print two or three of the articles, and then either:

   a. write a brief paper on your findings, or

   b. bring the articles to class for a small-group discussion.

4. Using InfoTrac College Edition, look up the keywords "ratings sweeps." Read at least three articles to learn more about issues associated with television audience measurement and the way television stations and networks use ratings to promote programs and to attract advertising. Look for information and criticism about how networks and stations juggle programming to boost ratings during sweeps periods. Consider also the effect of ratings on the life or death of certain programs, longer-term effects on the rise and fall of program genres, and the criticism of those effects. Write a brief paper on your findings and conclusions and be prepared to discuss the issue in class.

5. Using InfoTrac College Edition, look up the keywords "violence on television." Read several articles to understand several recent viewpoints about the issue. Review the list of articles to get some sense of how long the controversy has been ongoing. After your readings, decide where you stand on portrayals of violence in television and on proposals for labeling programming, electronic home screening technologies (such as V-chip) or other means of controlling viewing of violence by susceptible audiences, such as children. Do you avoid watching violent television programming? Why, or why not? What do you believe are the effects of violent television programming on society? What is the basis of your beliefs about television violence, in addition to (or in spite of) your InfoTrac College Edition readings? Write a brief paper on your findings and conclusions and be prepared to discuss the issue in class.

CHAPTER 9

Nobody ever designed the Web. There are no rules, no laws. The Web also exists without national boundaries."

Craig McKie, Department of Sociology and Anthropology, Carleton University, Ottawa, Canada, who maintains his own Web site, www.socsciresearch.com

"The Internet is the new frontier of American life, the electronic equivalent of the Wild West," writes David Shaw, media critic of the *Los Angeles Times*. "About the only point on which even the pioneers in this still primitive digital culture seem to agree is that virtually everything being done now . . . will either have to change radically or fail."

The Internet actually is a combination of thousands of computer networks sending and receiving data from all over the world—competing interests joined together by a common purpose, but no common owner. "No government or commercial entity owns the Net or directly profits from its operation," notes information designer Roger Fidler. "It has no president, chief executive officer, or central headquarters."

In its global size and absence of central control, the Internet is completely different from traditional media. Originally developed to aid communication among researchers and educators, the Internet has "evolved in a way no one planned or expected," says Fidler. "Important scientific data and scholarly thoughts have continued to account for much of the traffic [on the Internet], but it is the relationships among people that have shaped the medium. What has mattered most to Internet users is the free exchange of ideas and discussion of values."

Today to 1978: Digital media bring the world to your desktop

TODAY
The Internet is causing an expansion of digital media development, but competition is forcing many companies out of business.

▼

2003
The Recording Industry Association and the Motion Picture Association of America announce campaigns to aggressively fight online piracy.

▼

2001
Napster shuts down. The number of dot-com start-ups begins to shrink and many existing companies shut down.

▼

2000
The number of dot-com businesses explodes.

▼

1999
The Recording Industry Association sues Internet file-sharing company Napster for copyright infringement.

▼

1998
One in four U.S. households is online. Congress passes the Digital Millennium Copyright Act, which makes it illegal to share copyrighted material on the Internet.

▼

1996
Internet advertising reaches $200 million. Congress passes the Communications Decency Act, an unsuccessful attempt to control Internet content.

▼

1995
The movie *Disclosure* popularizes the concept of virtual reality.

continued on next page

(c) 2003 Tim Whyatt

whyatt.com.au

▶ What Are Digital Media?

The term **digital media** is used to describe all forms of emerging communications media. Digital media, sometimes called new media, combine text, graphics, sound and video using computer technology, to create a product that is similar to, but clearly different from, traditional media, often called old media. Old media are the seven traditional, original mass media—print (books, newspapers and magazines); audio (recordings and radio); and video (movies and television) that are discussed in Chapters 2 through 8.

The term **multimedia** is used to describe any media that combine text, graphics, sound and video. Video games, the most familiar early form of multimedia, combined text, graphics, sound and video to create games that could be played on a TV set. The latest video games, which can be played on a computer and also online, are a form of multimedia that has developed into digital media.

Digital media are based on old and new technology, with a terminology all their own. Digital media also are the fastest growing type of media and, because of their rapid growth, digital communications promises to become the biggest factor in the future development of all the mass media industries.

▶ How the New Digital Communications Network Is Different

Rather than the one-way communication of traditional media (See Chapter 1), mass communication on today's digital network makes it possible for you to receive and send information simultaneously. You can decide to produce a screenplay, put an ad for your screenplay on a bulletin board and respond to anyone who wants to see your produced screenplay. You can create a mystery roundtable with authors from different parts of the world contributing to the screenplay. Then you can produce the screenplay and distribute it on the Internet, complete with music gathered from an Internet music network.

Computer networks can "free individuals from the shackles of corporate bureaucracy and geography and allow them to collaborate and exchange ideas with the best colleague anywhere in the world," says futurist George Gilder. "Computer networks give every hacker the creative potential of a factory tycoon of the industrial [turn-of-the-century] era and the communications power of a TV magnate of the broadcasting era." In an interconnected world, the speed and convenience of the network redefines the mass media industries and erases all previous notions of how mass communication should work.

▶ Creating the New Communications Network

Digital media eventually will make all these services and many more available to every single person in the nation, even the world, at an affordable price, in the same way that telephone service today is accessible to almost everybody. In 1994, Congress named this new effort to coordinate all of the different senders, channels and receivers in the U.S. the National Information Infrastructure (**NII**). In the history of audio and video communication in the United States, the government has always played a regulatory role.

Three principles guided the creation of the new telecommunications structure:

1. Private industry, not the government, will build the digital network.

2. Programmers and information providers should be guaranteed access to the digital network to promote a diversity of consumer choices.

3. Steps should be taken to ensure universal service so that the digital network does not result in a society of information "haves" and "have-nots."

The NII is responsible for making sure all players in the telecommunications arena follow these principles.

▶ Government Regulation of the Network

The federal government regulates the new network, and the issue of government control of what is transmitted on the Internet is controversial. In 1996, Congress passed the Telecommunications Act of 1996. Part of that legislation was the Communications Decency Act (**CDA**), which outlined content that would be forbidden on the Internet. As soon as the act passed, civil liberties organizations challenged the law, and in 1997 the U.S. Supreme Court upheld the concept that the government should not control content on the Internet. (For more information about Congress and the U.S Supreme Court's view of the Internet, see Chapter 14.)

▶ Copyrights for Intellectual Property

Another reason the government supervises the development of the new network is that digitized bits, once they are widely available, can easily be stolen and reproduced for profit. Writers and other creative people who provide the content for the media industries are especially concerned about their ideas being reproduced in several different formats, with no compensation for their

---

Impact | TimeFrame

Today to 1978: Digital media bring the world to your desktop

continued

▼
1994
Marc Andreessen and his colleagues at the University of Illinois introduce Mosaic, a browser that allows people to combine pictures and text in the same online document. Congress names the new effort to coordinate all the different senders, channels and receivers in the U.S. the National Information Infrastructure (NII).

▼
1989
Tim Berners-Lee develops programming languages that allow people to share all types of information online and the first browser, which allows people to search online for the information they want.

▼
1988
Only 1 percent of U.S. households are online.

▼
1978
Nicholas Negroponte at the Massachusetts Institute of Technology first uses the term "convergence" to describe the intersection of the media industries.

Digital Media   All emerging communications media that combine text, graphics, sound and video, using computer technology.

Multimedia   Any media that combine test, graphics, sound and video.

NII   National Information Infrastructure.

CDA   Communications Decency Act.

eBay CEO Meg Whitman Talks about the Company's Policy of Self-Regulation

When eBay CEO and President Margaret C. Whitman started at the online seller in 1998, its top-selling category was Beanie Babies. Today, eBay is on track to host more than $20 billion in gross annual sales of everything from cars to industrial refrigeration units. Yet it isn't just the quality of merchandise—or the quantity of business—that distinguishes the online auction outfit. Whitman describes it as a "self-regulating marketplace" and points out that it's eBay's buyers and sellers—not management—who determine its direction.

Q. You've called eBay an economy. What do you mean?

A. It is in some ways a small economy. There are 62 million players [registered eBay members] that meet to do business every single day. The law of supply and demand absolutely works on eBay. A while back, people were saying, "Aren't you concerned that the price of collectibles on eBay is going down?" My answer was "not really." It's an economy: Categories get hot, categories get cold. It's absolutely an efficient market that runs like an economy....

Q. Empowerment seems to be a prime motivator for people to keep coming back to eBay. How do you encourage that?

A. People really pride themselves on their feedback profile. I was at Deutsche Asset Management two days ago, and we walk in and say we're with eBay, and the receptionist, who was looking a little bored, looked up and said, "My feedback is 160!" It happens to me every day....

Q. Do you still get direct feedback yourself from the community?

A. Yeah. First of all, the community has my e-mail address. It's meg@ebay.com. I read all my own e-mail—anywhere from 100 to 500 e-mails a day—many of which are from the community. So I have a pretty good pulse of what's happening out there. Also, at least a couple of times a week, I check the eBay discussion boards. I can get a real good pulse there. And I often sit in on Voice of the Customer groups [which bring in sellers and buyers and polls them on site features and plans]....

Q. Now that eBay is so large and broad, what's your main competition?

A. If we were a retailer, we'd be the 27th-largest in the world. So our sellers are competing [with retailers] for consumer dollars. If you're thinking about buying a set of golf clubs or a tennis racket or a jacket or a pair of skis, you decide whether you're going to do that at eBay, at Wal-Mart, a sporting goods store, or Macy's. I would define our competition more broadly than ever before.

Business Week Online, August 18, 2003.

AP/Wide World Photos

Meg Whitman, CEO and President of e-Bay.

Intellectual Property Ownership of ideas and content published on the Web or in any other medium.

property. This issue, the protection of what are called **intellectual property rights**, is another important part of the design of the new communications network.

It could be possible to capture video from *Everybody Loves Raymond* and join individual bits from that video with bits from an episode of *Saturday Night Live*, putting the two casts together in a newly digitized program. Once these bits are captured from a network and stored, they are available to anyone who wants to manipulate them. This is one of the dilemmas created by digitized images that can be transmitted to anyone's storage system over an international network. The creative people who contribute this content, and the people who produce and own these programs, are watching carefully that new laws and regulations are structured to protect intellectual property rights.

▶ Five Challenges for the New Communications Network

"Now comes the interesting part," says *The Wall Street Journal*. "Builders of the information highway have created a media sensation with their plans for wiring America. But to deliver on their promises they will have to meet challenges of unprecedented complexity and size. . . . Like early railroad builders who laid their tracks in different widths more than a century ago, the purveyors of the information highway are using largely incompatible technologies."

For the new communications network to operate efficiently, five technological developments must take place:

1. Improved storage

2. A coordinated delivery system

3. A "smart" set-top box

4. Usable menus

5. Secure ordering and billing systems

Improved Storage   The main technological advance that makes the new communications network possible is that today's electronic systems can now transform all text, audio and video communication into digital information. However, no current system can store all the digitized information that the new network for text, audio and video requires.

Researchers are trying to eliminate the need for so much storage. They are turning to a process called **data compression**. A copy of a major movie, such as *Finding Nemo*, contains about 100 billion bytes of data. Compression can squeeze the content down to about 4 billion bytes. But the time it takes to download a movie on a personal computer and the computer storage space movies need still make it impractical for the average consumer.

When researchers perfect data compression, it will mean that a program service, for example, will need much less storage space to keep movies available for use. This will help make the movie affordable for a program service to deliver and usable for the customer, who won't need as much data space to view the movie.

Once the data is compressed, it must be stored by the people who will deliver the service. Then researchers also must use a machine that grabs a selection from the storage area and delivers it to the customer on request. This *video transfer machine* is called a **server** because it must be able to serve hundreds of programs to thousands of subscribers, on demand, all at the same time.

A Coordinated Delivery System   Today's communication system is a mixture of old and new technologies. Before the new communications network can happen, old technology must be completely replaced with new technology throughout the system.

Many broadcasters, for example, still send pictures and sounds over airwaves using the same technology they have used since the 1930s, when broadcasting was first introduced. This technology is called **analog**.

Analog technology encodes video and audio information as continuous signals. Then these signals are broadcast through the air on specific airwave

Data-compression technology reduces the computer space necessary to store full-length movies such as *Finding Nemo*. This will soon make it possible for consumers to download first-run original movies at home.

Data Compression   The process of squeezing digital content into a smaller electronic space.

Server   The equipment that delivers programs from the program source to the program's subscribers.

Analog   In mass communications, a type of technology used in broadcasting, whereby video or audio information is sent as continuous signals through the air on specific airwave frequencies.

frequencies to your TV set, which translates them into pictures and sounds. Analog technology is a very cumbersome way to move information from one place to another because the signal takes up a lot of space on the airwaves. But because the analog signals travel through the air by transmitters, you can receive them free through an antenna. Many homes in the United States still receive only over-the-air broadcasts. They do not subscribe to cable.

Although the federal government mandated that TV stations in large cities digitize their signals by 2002, some smaller stations have not yet made the costly transition to digital.

Cable companies eliminated the need for antennas by using coaxial cable, buried underground or strung from telephone poles. Coaxial cable also uses analog technology. Cable operators capture programming, such as HBO, from satellite systems and put these together with analog broadcast signals from your local TV stations and then deliver all this programming to you, using a combination of coaxial cable, copper wire and some optical fiber.

Optical fiber is composed of microscopic strands of glass that transmit messages of digitized "bits"—zeroes and ones. Each fiber optic strand can carry 250,000 times as much information as one copper wire. It can transmit the entire contents of the *Encyclopaedia Britannica* in one second. A fiber optics communication system is very efficient because digitized information travels easily and quickly from one place to another.

Telephone companies have converted almost all their major communications delivery systems from coaxial cable and copper wire to fiber optics. The incompatibility between analog and digital technology means that all analog signals on non–fiber-optics systems would have to be converted first to digital signals to be able to travel on the information network. Conversion can be very expensive. At today's prices, it costs about $3,000 to digitize and store one feature-length movie.

The current delivery system is a combination of coaxial cable, copper wire and fiber optics. Digital technology is the most efficient method of delivery, but wiring the whole country with optical fiber is extraordinarily expensive. Satellite and cellular delivery of the digital signal directly to the consumer through a cable signal or telephone line may prove to be the most efficient method of wireless delivery.

Set-Top Box   A device that translates the various signals so the TV can display different types of digital signals.

A "Smart" Set-Top Box

Most cable subscribers need a **set-top box**, which translates the various signals so the TV set can receive the programming and also keep track of the services the subscriber uses. The set-top box sits on top of the TV. For the new national communications network to operate, the set-top box will have to become much smarter than it is now.

The set-top box will be like a switching station, connecting the delivery system coming to the television/computer with your directions for service. This will be the gateway. A set-top box also must be affordable. Some researchers have devised a $3,000 model, but no one yet has invented a successful, affordable set-top box.

Usable Menus

With all this programming and all these services awaiting, the menu will be the way someone navigates the system. Menus must be simple and capable of navigating easily through an extraordinary number of available programs and services. An easy menu system is important, because people who use the system for the first time probably won't be patient enough to figure out something complicated. Researchers say such a system will require a great deal of consumer testing.

Secure Ordering and Billing Systems   Of course, once all these nice services and programs are available, consumers must be able to buy them. That's where ordering and billing come in, and developing this process will be challenging. Telephone companies already have a fairly complex system in place that manages to match people with the phone calls they make.

But making sure that your credit card numbers and other personal information are secure from other computer users is more complicated. Software companies must develop systems that will ensure that all the records for interactive transactions are safe. An entirely new industry has evolved dedicated to the issue of Internet information security.

▶ Media Are Evolving and Interdependent

Today's media are constantly evolving. Digital media forms "do not arise spontaneously and independently from old media," says media scholar Roger Fidler. Digital media are related and connected to old media. Fidler says today's media should be examined as members of an interdependent system, with "similarities and relationships that exist among past, present and emerging forms."

The digital media that are emerging will be similar to the old media, yet different in ways that will make them distinct from their predecessors, says Fidler. Because of the interdependence of all media, this change will be more intense because changes will happen simultaneously.

▶ Are Old Media Dying?

Will the development of digital media mean the death of old media? Some observers have predicted, for example, that the medium of print is dead. "The end of the book is near!" is a headline that has appeared frequently. Yet book sales continue to be healthy and are currently at an all-time high.

Nicholas Negroponte, of the Massachusetts Institute of Technology's Media Lab, popularized the concept of convergence.

Convergence   The process by which the various media industries intersect.

The history of the evolution of media shows that the introduction of a new medium does not mean the end of an old medium. The continuing overall growth and expansion of the media industries during the last century support this conclusion.

When television was introduced, for example, radio did not disappear. Instead, radio adapted to its new place in the media mix, delivering music, news and talk. Today, radio exists very comfortably alongside television.

Movies, which also were threatened by the introduction of television, responded by delivering more spectacular and more explicit entertainment than people could see on television, and today movies still play an important role in the business of media.

"When newer forms of communication media emerge, the older forms usually do not die—they continue to evolve and adapt," says Fidler. In this way, the different media compete for the public's attention and jockey for positions of dominance, but no medium has yet disappeared. Instead, each medium contributes to the development of its successors. Together, all media that now exist will contribute to the media that are yet to be invented.

▶ Digital Media Convergence

In 1978, Nicholas Negroponte at the Massachusetts Institute of Technology began popularizing a theory called **convergence**. This theory gave a name to the process by which the work of the various media industries was beginning to intersect, and MIT was among the first places to foresee and identify this trend.

The media industries not only were combining economically, as media companies began to buy and sell each other, but the technology of the industries also was merging, according to MIT, which meant that eventually the products the media companies produced began to resemble each other.

Negroponte also said that the combination of the media industries with the computer industry would create a new type of communication. To identify what was happening, Negroponte created two models (see **Illustration 9.1**) to show the position of the media industries in 1978 and his projected vision for those industries in the year 2000. He listed three segments of the media business: (a) print and publishing, (b) broadcast and motion pictures and (c) the computer industry.

The first diagram displays the alignment of the media industries in 1978, which shows them with a small amount of integrated territory. In the second diagram, which shows Negroponte's predictions for the year 2000, the three segments of the media industries are completely overlapping. Negroponte's forecast was a very accurate prediction of exactly what happened, and it helped establish the framework for today's thinking about the Internet.

Today's economic and technological convergence in the media industries is the most important reason for the development of digital media. Each of the media industries is equally well-positioned to take advantage of new developments, and each of the media industries benefits from convergence.

Today, many media companies, because of their size, also have the money available to invest in new technologies. These companies also have a shared interest in seeing their investments succeed. So convergence is likely to continue at a very rapid pace, which means that many digital media products will become available quickly.

▶ Which Digital Media Products Will Succeed?

As digital media products flood the marketplace, some will succeed, and many will not. However, the potential reward if consumers adopt a digital

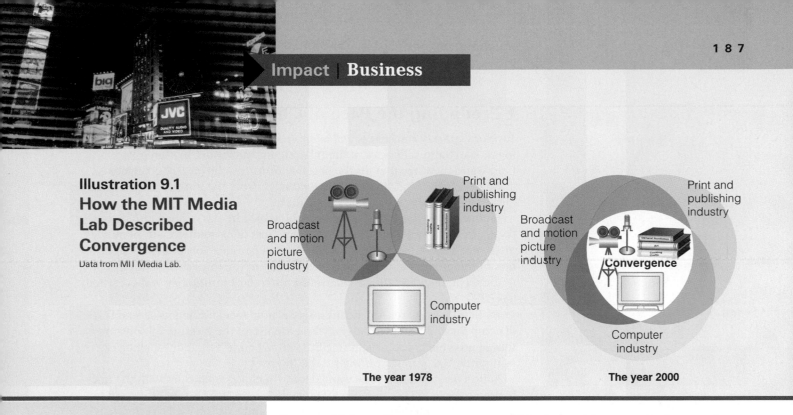

Impact | Business

**Illustration 9.1
How the MIT Media Lab Described Convergence**

Data from MIT Media Lab.

Broadcast and motion picture industry

Print and publishing industry

Computer industry

The year 1978

Broadcast and motion picture industry

Print and publishing industry

Convergence

Computer industry

The year 2000

Critical Question

Do you think media convergence would be happening on such a large scale today if media conglomerates did not exist? Why or why not?

media product is so big that all types of media companies are willing to take the risks associated with developing new products. For consumers, this means a confusing array of product choices bombarding the marketplace as each company tries to develop the one product that a large group of consumers will embrace.

There are parallels between the early history of traditional media and the emerging technologies that are being used to create a new popular product that the public craves that will eventually result in the development of a brand new medium.

▶ Digital Media Lessons from History

In the early 1900s, when movies first were introduced as flickering images on a small screen, the moving images were something consumers hadn't seen before, but many people saw the silent movies as just a passing fad. (See Chapter 7.)

The inventions that had been introduced by Thomas Edison and his colleagues at the time made the movies technologically possible, but the movies also needed creative minds like director D. W. Griffith and stars like Mary Pickford to create epic stories that people wanted to see.

When new inventions brought sound to the movies, the success of the new medium was unstoppable. This combination of technological development, creative expression and consumer demand was crucial for the movies' enduring prosperity.

The same collision of economics, technology and creativity that drove the early days of the movie industry is behind today's race to develop digital media. Today, media and computer entrepreneurs are hoping to capitalize on fast-moving developments in technology to be the first to deliver a new creative product that large numbers of people want to buy.

▶ Predicting the Pace of Change

Just how quickly consumers will adopt new technology is predictable, according to Paul Saffo, a director of the Institute for the Future in Menlo Park, Calif. Saffo theorizes that for the past five centuries the pace of change has always been 30 years, or about three decades, from the introduction of a new idea to its complete adoption by the culture.

Saffo calls his theory the **30-year rule**, which he has divided into three stages. In the first decade, he says, there is "lots of excitement, lots of puzzlement, not a lot of penetration." In the second decade, "lots of flux, penetration of the product into society is beginning." In the third decade, the reaction to the technology is, "Oh, so what? Just a standard technology and everybody has it."

By Saffo's standard, American society is probably entering its second stage of acceptance of online technology because use of the Internet by consumers started growing quickly beginning in 1988, when less than one-half of 1 percent of the U.S. population was on the Internet.

Saffo's description of the second decade of change coincides with the fluctuation seen in today's media marketplace. People face choices that seem to emerge daily: different combinations of new and existing media technology that are "guaranteed" to create the best digital world. While this technological transformation is underway, the digital media world seems very confusing.

The most confusing, yet promising, place of all is the newest digital media development, the World Wide Web.

Paul Saffo developed the 30-year rule, which says that a new idea takes about 30 years to be completely adopted within a culture.

Steve Castillo Photos

30-Year Rule   Developed by Paul Saffo, the theory that says it takes about 30 years for a new idea to be completely adopted within a culture.

E-Mail   Mail that is delivered electronically.

▶ Digital Media and the World Wide Web

The first sign of the expansion of the Internet to consumer and educational users in the early 1990s was the adoption by businesses and private users of electronic mail, or **e-mail**, technology. With a computer, a modem and a telephone line, just about anyone can learn how to communicate electronically online. Today about 64 percent of the U.S. population is online at home. (See **Illustration 9.2**.)

"The driving force for achieving large subscriber gains is the incorporation of the Internet by consumers as part of their routine," says Veronis, Suhler Stevenson, a media research company. "The Internet has become a tool that allows users to economize on what has become their scarcest resource—time. Virtually all of the leading Internet applications allow users to accomplish tasks more quickly than they can through alternative means."

Just as telephone answering machines changed voice communication by allowing people to send and receive messages on their own time schedule, e-mail allows people to communicate and receive information at their convenience. People who are online at home today are most likely to use the technology to gather news and information or to send and receive e-mail.

E-mail at school, work or home is the way most people first experience communicating in an electronic environment. E-mail is easy to use and convenient, and it is a text-based system, which means that people type in messages on a keyboard, which is a familiar tool.

Familiarity and convenience are very important in the adoption of new technologies because people's fear of something they don't understand, and misunderstandings about how new technologies work, can keep them from changing their current habits.

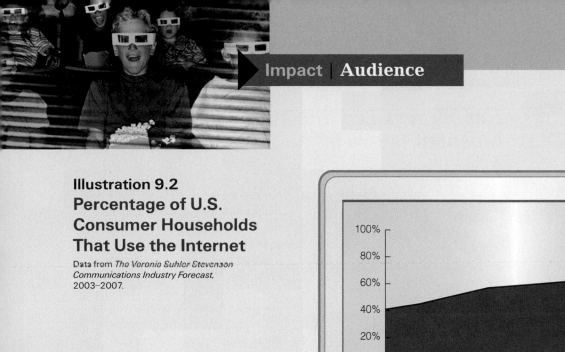

Impact | Audience

Illustration 9.2
Percentage of U.S.
Consumer Households
That Use the Internet

Data from *The Veronis Suhler Stevenson Communications Industry Forecast,* 2003–2007.

64%

*projected

▶ Understanding the Internet

Exchanging text through e-mail is a simple electronic operation, but several more developments were necessary for people to be able to share text, graphics, audio and video online. These developments made the creation of the World Wide Web possible.

The person most responsible for creating the World Wide Web is Tim Berners-Lee, a British native with an Oxford degree in physics. (See Impact/People, page 190.) Working in 1989, in Geneva, Switzerland, at the CERN physics laboratory, Berners-Lee created several new programming languages.

One of these new programming languages was **HTML (hypertext markup language)**. **HTTP (hypertext transfer protocol)** allowed people to create and send text, graphics and video information electronically and also to set up connections (called **links**) from one source of information to another. These developments were very important in the Web's early days, but today, just a few years later, people can create their own Web pages without knowing HTML and HTTP.

After he had invented the language and mechanisms that would allow people to share all kinds of information electronically, Berners-Lee gave this invention its name—the World Wide Web. "The original goal was working

HTML HyperText Markup Language.

HTTP HyperText Transfer Protocol.

Links Electronic connections from one source of information to another.

Tim Berners-Lee: The Man Who Invented the Web

by Robert Wright

You might think that someone who invented a giant electronic brain for Planet Earth would have a pretty impressive brain of his own. And Tim Berners-Lee . . . the creator of the World Wide Web, no doubt does. But his brain also has one shortcoming, and, by his own account, this neural glitch may have been the key to the Web's inception.

Berners-Lee isn't good at "random connections," he says. "I'm certainly terrible at names and faces." (No kidding. He asked me my name twice during our first two hours of conversation.) Back in 1980 he wrote some software to help keep track of such links—a memory substitute. The rest is history. . . .

Berners-Lee is the unsung—or at least undersung—hero of the information age. Even by some of the less breathless accounts, the World Wide Web could prove as important as the printing press. That would make Berners-Lee comparable to well,

Gutenberg, more or less. Yet so far, most of the wealth and fame emanating from the Web have gone to people other than him.

Marc Andreessen, co-founder of Netscape, drives a Mercedes-Benz and has graced the cover of several major magazines. Berners-Lee has graced the cover of none, and he drives a 13-year-old Volkswagen Rabbit. He has a smallish, barren office at MIT, where his nonprofit group, the World Wide Web Consortium, helps set technical standards for the Web, guarding its coherence against the potentially deranging forces of the market. . . .

Spouting acronyms while standing at a blackboard, he approaches the energy level of Robin Williams. He is British (an Oxford physics major), but to watch only his hands as he talks, you'd guess Italian. Five, six years ago, during his "evangelizing" phase, this relentless enthusiasm was what pushed the Web beyond critical mass.

The breathtaking growth of the Web has been "an incredibly good feeling," he says, and is "a lesson for all dreamers . . . that you can have a dream and it can come true."

Browser Software that allows people to search electronically among many documents to find what they want online.

Search Engine The tool used to locate information in a computer database.

together with others," says Berners-Lee. "The Web was supposed to be a creative tool, an expressive tool."

Berners-Lee also created the first **browser**, which allows people to search electronically among many documents to find what they want. Marc Andreessen and his colleagues at the University of Illinois further defined the browser, and in 1994 they introduced software called Mosaic, which allowed people to put text and pictures in the same online document. One of the successors to Mosaic is Netscape Navigator, one of the most widely used commercial browsers.

Another level of help for Web access is the **search engine**. This is a tool used to locate information in a computer database. Some familiar search engines are Lycos, Google, Ask Jeeves and Yahoo! These devices turn your typed request for information into digital bits that then go and search for what you want and return the information to you.

To encourage people to use their systems, both Berners-Lee and Andreessen placed their discoveries in the public domain, which meant that anyone with a computer and a modem could download them from the Internet and use them for free. **This culture of free information access, coupled with a creative, chaotic lack of direction, still permeates the Web today.**

The process of putting documents on the Web drew its terminology from print, the original mass medium. Placing something on the Web is called **publishing** and begins with a **home page**, which is like the front door to the site, the place that welcomes the user and explains how the site works. However, even though Web sites are similar to published documents in the way they are described, what is created on the Web has few of the legal limitations or protections placed on other published documents. (See Chapter 14.)

Reprinted with permission from Copley News Service.

▶ What's on the Web?

Once Berners-Lee had created the tools for access so that all types of text and video images could become available on the Web, it was left to anyone who could use the tools to create whatever they wanted and make it available to anyone who wanted it.

"Nobody ever designed the Web," says Canadian sociologist Craig McKie, who maintains his own Web site. "There are no rules, no laws. The Web also exists without national boundaries." Any type of information—pictures, voice, graphics and text—can travel virtually instantly to and from anyone with a computer and access to the Internet anywhere in the world.

There are Web sites devoted to every imaginable aspect of human communication. One woman, who learned that a friend had cancer, researched information about cancer treatment on the Web and then established a cancer information site to help others.

One Web site gave a digital image of the new Giants baseball park under construction in San Francisco, with video images sent every five seconds by cameras posted near the building site. The sponsoring group, Whole Earth Networks, fed the images to the Web until the park was completed in the year 2000.

One Midwest auto dealer who created a Web site to sell cars says that at least 10 percent of his buyers are Internet customers who shop their local dealership, bargain their price online and then drive up to 400 miles from the neighboring state to save money. Banking also has moved online, allowing electronic transactions that can occur anytime, not just when someone can get to an ATM or visit a bank. Several companies have created virtual banks, which are totally online, without any established offices, just online branches.

Universal access, limited only by the available technology, is what gives the Web the feeling and look of what has been called "anarchy"—a world without rules. The Web is a *new medium*, but its growth to become a true *mass medium* for a majority of people seeking information and entertainment is limited only by digital technology and economics.

▶ Commercializing the Web

When television was introduced to the public in the late 1940s, the assumption from the beginning was that it would be a commercial medium—that is, advertisers who bought the commercials surrounding the programs would

Publishing   Placing items on the Web.

Home Page   The first page of a Web site that welcomes the user.

Signs of Improvement: Video Conference Programs Expand Horizons for the Hearing-Impaired

by Benny Evangelista

For Melvin Patterson, who has been completely deaf since he was a toddler, communication is a visual experience.

In the past, conducting a conversation using traditional non-visual telecommunications tools like telephones and pagers was frustrating. Text messages or sign language conversations on jittery Web video screens were a pale substitute for a face-to-face exchange.

But that changed dramatically when Patterson tried iChat AV, new videoconferencing software, and iSight, a new Web camera, which Apple Computer Inc. introduced during the summer.

"When my girlfriend and I were able to talk to each other using iChat with iSight, I can't describe the feeling I had," the Chicago film school student said in an e-mail to the *Chronicle*. "I'm sure it is the same feeling people had long ago when the telephone was invented, being able to hear someone's voice with all their inflections from a distance."

Unlike any other technology he had seen, Patterson, 31, said the iChat AV software produced video that was clear enough to see another person's fingers and hand movements, a crucial

© Peter Thompson

Melvin Patterson (left and opposite), a hearing-impaired student, is able to talk to his friend Kent Davis online using Internet technology.

element in communicating in American Sign Language. "Now," Patterson said, "we can communicate with all the inflection and expression, as we do in person, from a distance. I have been waiting for so long for technology that improves accessibility for the deaf and hard of hearing."

San Francisco Chronicle, 10/6/03, E-1.

---

pay for the programming. This concept of advertisers underwriting the programs was a natural evolution from radio, where commercials also paid for the programming. (See **Illustration 9.3**.)

The Web, however, began as a free medium. Many people pay an **Internet service provider (ISP)** such as America Online to organize and deliver information and entertainment from many sources, including the Web, but the actual information—what's on the Web—is usually available for free.

ISP   Internet Service Provider

**Illustration 9.3
U. S. Consumer
Internet Advertising
(in billions)**

Data from *The Veronis, Suhlor Stovonoon
Communications Industry Forecast,*
2003–2007.

2000	2001	2002	2003	2004*	2005*
$8.2	$7.2	$6.0	$6.6	$7.0	$7.4

*projected

▶ Paying for Media on the Web

"Even as Internet use continues its dramatic surge, many if not most Internet ventures are losing money. . . . The standing joke on the Web is that the letters 'ISP' don't really stand for 'Internet Service Provider' but for 'I'm still profitless,'" writes media critic David Shaw. People still are unwilling to pay for most of the information that's available on the Web.

Slate, the online literary magazine published by Microsoft, planned to start charging subscribers in 1997, but then decided against it. Editor Michael Kinsley said, "It would be better to establish a brand name with wide readership first."

Nathan Myhrvold, the former director of technology operations at Microsoft, says that Internet users will not pay for access to one site when "a million free sites are just a click away. . . . There's no incentive until people are too addicted to the Net to turn off their computers, yet are bored with what's available." Myhrvold (see Impact/People in Chapter 1, page 21) says that once people exhaust what's available for free on the Web, they may be willing to pay. The situation is similar, he says, to people who previously were satisfied with network and local television, but who now pay for cable or satellite TV to get access to expanded programming.

Some explicit Web sites charge for access, and some information sites, such as *The Wall Street Journal*, charge a nominal fee (the *Journal* claims to have 160,000 subscribers for wsj.com, where subscribers pay $29.95 a year for access to the content).

Other sites, such as the sports network ESPN, give away some information and then charge for "premium" services. Internet game-makers, who offer video games on the Web, charge by the hour or use a tiered pricing structure—free, basic and premium. "Everybody's fishing right now," says Chris

Laura Noel

Electronic game players are among the small number of people who are willing to pay for Internet media. Here, game enthusiasts check out the offerings at Electronic Entertainment Expo, a video game trade show.

Sherman, director of games for Concentric Networks, "and nobody knows what they're going to catch."

▶ Buying Products on the Web

What makes the Web different from traditional media is its capacity to combine information, entertainment and commerce. People not only can retrieve information and entertainment from the Web, they can buy things. The Web is interactive, which means that people can send information back and forth. Retailers can use the Web to sell products directly, without setting up a store or spending a lot of money on expensive advertising.

One of the most resilient commercial operations on the Web is *Amazon.com*. Amazon.com began as a place where people could buy media products such as books, CDs and DVDs, but today consumers also can shop for a variety of other items—clothes and sports equipment—often at discount prices. At-home convenience, reliability and affordability seem to be sustaining the Web site as a successful commercial venture.

"The Internet has the potential to be the best sales tool—the best advertising and direct marketing vehicle—ever devised," says *Los Angeles Times* media critic David Shaw. "The Internet can turn any advertiser—any product manufacturer or service provider—into the equivalent of a direct marketer. On the Internet, consumers looking for a particular product or service can shop over the entire country—the entire world—looking at photographs and comparing prices, features and terms, and then buy what they want with a credit card and arrange to have the purchase delivered to their home."

Most Web sites now carry some form of advertising. These appear as banners across the top of the Web site or run as borders alongside the site's pages. But just like traditional media, advertising can crowd out the original message and turn away consumers. While few commercial online operations have been successful (and many have gone out of business) new Web site entrepreneurs continue to test the market to develop a pricing structure that eventually will pay the bills.

▶ Tracking Internet Buyers

Because the Web is such a targeted medium—the seller can know exactly who the buyer is—the Web holds better potential for monitoring consumers' buying habits than traditional methods of advertising. Ultimately, Web advertisers "can achieve the merchandiser's dream—targeting an audience far more precisely than it can with either newspapers or television by advertising a product only on sites that draw people likely to be interested in that product," says media critic David Shaw.

"Moreover, they will be able to get nearly instantaneous electronic feedback on whether their ads are effective: How many people saw the ad? How many 'clicked' on it and went on to a more detailed presentation? How many bought the product right then, online?"

Software already is available that offers "tracking"—information for advertisers. Many sites give advertisers information about how many "hits" the

The Digital Divide Is Growing

Net Access Use Rises, but Some Groups Lag

by Carrie Kirby

Americans of all races and incomes are going online in record numbers, but the **digital divide** still separates some racial minorities, the disabled, and low-income families from the wired world, a new government report says.

In fact, even though they are the fastest-growing groups of Internet users, Latino and African American households have fallen further behind other American families in Internet access, the Commerce Department said in a report.

Part of the reason is because white, Asian and Pacific Islander families were so far ahead to begin with that even a dramatic spurt by minorities hasn't closed the gap.

"Minority groups have made impressive gains with Internet access, but there is still a considerable gap," said Commerce Secretary Norman Y. Mineta.

The report, "Falling Through the Net: Toward Digital Inclusion," is the Commerce Department's fourth dispatch in a continuing investigation of the digital divide. The surveys are conducted by the Census Bureau.

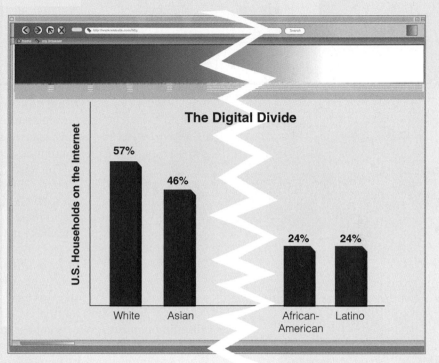

Illustration 9.4

U.S. Households on the Internet, by Race, 2000

Data from the U.S. Department of Commerce, 2000.

Since the last Commerce Department survey in December 1998, African American and Latino households increased their rate of access from about 10 percent to 25 percent, while the white households online grew from about 30 percent to nearly 50 percent.

San Francisco Chronicle, Oct. 17, 2001. © *San Francisco Chronicle.* Reprinted by permission.

sites receive—how many times people looked at the site. But this is not very reliable information because it is difficult for advertisers to track how much of the ad people read, how much time they spent at the site, or most importantly, if eventually the specific user bought a product that was advertised on the site.

One company has developed "ad robots" that allow a company to, in effect, eavesdrop on chat room conversations while the user is online. If someone mentions online that they are having a problem with their car, for example, the robot would recognize the pattern of words in the discussion and send the person an ad for car repair. But the future of direct consumer measurement on the Web is still uncertain and will become clearer only when the Web itself has further defined its direction.

Digital Divide The term used to describe the lack of access to digital technology among low-income, disabled and minority groups.

"On the Internet, nobody knows you're a dog."

DMCA   Digital Millennium
Copyright Act.

RIAA   Recording Industry
Association of America.

MPAA   Motion Picture Association
of America.

File Sharing   The distribution of
copyrighted material on the Internet
without the copyright owner's
permission.

▶ Who Owns Content on the Web?

Many different types of companies are trying to figure out how to make money from their Web sites, but the issue of ownership of already existing copyrighted material, such as recordings and movies, is particularly tricky in a medium with few controls and global access. In 1998, Congress passed the Digital Millennium Copyright Act (**DMCA**) to try to make it illegal to share copyrighted material on the Internet. (For more information about the DMCA, see Chapter 14.) Using this law and provisions of existing copyright law, industries with a big stake in content ownership have sued to stop people from sharing copyrighted content on the Internet.

The Recording Industry Association of America (**RIAA**) and the Motion Picture Association of America (**MPAA**) have been especially aggressive in seeking to prosecute people who take copyrighted content and make it available on the Web.

In 1999, RIAA sued Napster, a company that provided a music-swapping service on the Internet. In 2001, after several appeals, the courts found that Napster was liable for "vicarious copyright infringement." Napster eventually shut down and then reopened as a subscription music service that pays royalties to companies who own rights to music that's available on the site.

MP3 technology allows users to convert songs on their CDs to MP3 files, which can be circulated freely on the Internet. MP3 began as an underground movement in San Diego in 1999, among college students, and spread fiercely. The major recording companies quickly began an all-out assault on MP3, suing for copyright infringement, and in November 2000, in a series of settlements, MP3 agreed to pay more than $70 million in damages to the recording companies for the rights to license their music.

In 2001, the MPAA sued to stop publication of the code that allows someone to copy DVDs and place digital copies of the movies on the Internet. The court agreed with the MPAA, saying that even if people possess the code but don't use it, they are committing piracy. This was an important legal precedent for content sharing on the Web and has led to more corporate attempts to seek wider protections over copyrighted content.

In 2003, Apple founder Steve Jobs introduced iTunes, a music service for subscribers that allows people to download popular songs for a fee. This was in response to the various court actions designed to end **file sharing** (downloading music files placed on the Internet by another person, not by the company that produces the song). (For more information about file sharing and iTunes, see Chapter 5.) iTunes has proven popular, and imitators have sprung up to latch onto consumers who are willing to pay for music downloads.

▶ When Will the New Communications Network Happen?

The new communications network, as envisioned by industry and government leaders today, requires that everyone be able to use digitized technology. Today, broadcasters and cable operators have access to the programming and the services, but many of these companies still are using a mix of old and new technologies. Telephone companies and computer manufacturers are using digital technology, but they don't have access to the programming or the services.

No one yet has created a storage system that can keep all the programming and services digitized and ready for you to use on demand. No one yet has created a directory system that would help you find your way through the maze of services and programs that can conceivably be offered on such a system. And no one yet has devised a secure billing system that can charge everyone accurately for all of the individual services they might choose.

This new communications network, once in place, will have a profound impact on individuals, businesses and the media industries. For individuals, the new network affects many everyday activities, such as how people shop, get their news, study, manage their money, even how they socialize with friends. For businesses, national and even global information will be instantly available to more companies at once, making communication much easier, but making competition more intense.

For the media industries, the prospect of a new communications network places every element of each business in transition. Today, owners and managers at the companies that make up the media industries must decide how to invest in equipment, employees, and research and development to protect current income while ensuring the company will be able to adapt to the network's demands.

▶ Emerging Forms of Digital Media Technologies

Since the definition of digital media is so broad, the term is thrown around very easily by people hoping to get attention and financial support for new products. People who are experimenting with the process are developing new forms of media every day.

Some digital media inventions will succeed, some will be transitional products that will help develop new products and many will fail. Until the digital media landscape is clearer, however, it is important to follow emerging developments because no one can predict exactly where digital media, now in their infancy, are headed.

Some examples of currently emerging digital media technologies are:

Digital Subscriber Line (DSL)   Available now in many cities,
DSL provides Internet access that is up to 50 times faster than a dial-up modem. DSL is always on, which means subscribers don't have to dial their Internet service provider each time they want to use the Web. DSL also provides much better delivery of audio and video signals than a standard telephone line.

DSL Digital Subscriber Line.

Immersive Virtual Reality Systems   In the 1960s, computer
flight simulators began to be used to train military pilots. These simulators were predecessors of today's virtual reality systems. By the 1980s, this technology was called "artificial reality."

Today, virtual reality systems have been refined to present a remote experience that is even closer to the real thing. The 1995 movie *Disclosure* showed an example of an immersive virtual reality system, in which the lead characters in the film "walked" through a database that made them look as if they were inside the New York Public Library.

Virtual reality (VR) systems can give people the experience of being somewhere by creating the reality of that place around them, but the systems require special equipment (a helmet and/or special eyeglasses, for example). These systems, which have been popularized for their entertainment value, actually could have important future applications, allowing a doctor to examine a patient from a distance, for example, and give advice to the attending physician.

Holographic Theaters

A hologram is a three-dimensional image, created on a flat surface, but viewed without special equipment. A holographic theater would allow you to attend a live music concert at your local theater, performed by your favorite rock group at another location. What you would see at your local theater would be a holographic image of the group, projected into the theater, transmitted from the original location. The holographic image could be projected simultaneously to locations throughout the world.

Personal Channels

This technology would allow you to create your own personal set of programs and services to be delivered either on your television set, your computer or both. "By using an on-screen guide . . . viewers could select the programs they regularly watch and the movies they may want to see, then have their VCR, or digital successor, automatically record the programs as they are broadcast and sequence them to match their schedule," says Roger Fidler.

Personal channels are similar to today's practice of recording a favorite program for viewing later, but with a personal channel, you would be able to record a collection of programs whenever they were available and then view them whenever you wanted.

Intelligent Video Agents

Once you decided which programs you wanted to watch on your personal channel, an intelligent video agent would be able to track the history of the choices you made and would then be able to "learn" your interests, hunt for programs for you and hold them to watch at your leisure.

Digital Paper

Researchers at MIT are working on an entirely new type of paper. This paper would look and feel like high-quality paper, but it would be totally erasable. Digital paper pages would be bound like a book and could be turned to read like a book, but the pages would be blank.

Digital images could be "printed" on the digital paper and viewed, then the pages could be "erased," to be replaced by brand new material. MIT researchers suggest this technology could be used to create the world's first one-volume library. "A book that was *Moby Dick* one day could become *The Iliad* the next," says information designer Roger Fidler.

Portable Tablets

These palm-size devices, such as the Palm Pilot, developed by several companies, provide digital readouts of information, delivered by cellular or other technologies.

Some of today's mobile digital pagers provide a version of this technology, with running news bulletins and sports scores on the pager's small screen. Portable tablets receive and send information that is written with an electronic pen or typed on the tablet, using a small keypad about the size of today's TV remote control.

Larger, Clearer TV Screens

A common TV screen size is 32 inches to 36 inches, but some of today's new home theater systems include 125-inch TV screens. Current TV screens cannot deliver the picture quality that high-definition television (HDTV) demands.

Current broadcast TV images are created from 550 horizontal lines that run across the screen. Pictures and text that appear on screens larger than 36 inches are hard to read, but new technology called **line doublers** and

Line Doublers and Line Quadruplers　Devices that can double or quadruple the number of lines scanning the TV screen to make the picture sharper.

line quadruplers can actually double and quadruple the number of lines scanning the screen to make the picture sharper.

Doubler technology receives the 550-line broadcast image, changes it into a digital signal and doubles or quadruples the number of lines to as high as 2,200. The result is a much clearer picture. (The clarity of the picture is called **resolution**.) Doubler technology will be especially important for the development of the Internet shown on TV because people who are sitting far across the room won't be able to see the image on the screen without better picture resolution. However, the cost of such a home theater system today is prohibitive for most people.

A 125-inch projection TV with video player, laserdisc player, quadrupler, digital satellite dish and cable access runs about $250,000. The high cost will discourage widespread adoption of this technology any time soon, but as the price drops, larger screens could become the standard.

Flat Panel Video Display Screens About the same size as today's TV screens or larger, but only about 4 inches deep, flat panel video display screens hang on the wall like a picture, instead of requiring the large cabinet that houses today's TV and computer screens. Sony introduced its first flat panel video screen in 1998 with a price tag starting at $4,000, and the price of large flat panel screens has already dropped to less than $1,000. Screens like this, once they are affordable, make all video technologies much more convenient to use.

▶ The Future of Digital Media and the Web

How soon will the new communications network happen? No one can predict. One observer called this a "highway of hype," because so many people are talking about the digital highway even though progress in solving the technological problems seems to be very slow. Today, the changes are coming gradually, as each challenge to the creation of the new network is solved.

"Computers and television are coming together," says the respected international magazine *The Economist*. "Computers are continuing their relentless march toward greater power at lower cost: that is how microprocessors work. Some giant industries are betting billions on the new TV business: more deals loom. These facts alone guarantee a revolution. . . . Whether it arrives in five years or 15 is almost irrelevant. In the history of communications, 2010 is tomorrow."

The future of digital media is bound only by the needs of consumers and the imaginations of media developers, as diverse as the people who are online today and going online tomorrow. The new media universe could become a purer reflection of the real universe than any medium yet created, with unprecedented potential, like all mass media, to both reflect and direct the culture.

"The Internet is still in its infancy, and its potential is enormous," writes media critic David Shaw. "As technology continues to improve and its audience continues to grow—as users and advertisers alike become more comfortable with it and knowledgeable about it—the Internet ultimately could attract the kind of audience and generate the kind of advertising revenue that would enable it to revolutionize human communication even more dramatically than Johann Gutenberg's first printing press did more than 500 years ago."

Resolution Clarity of the picture on the screen.

"And just what was that little window you clicked off when I came in?"

© Tony Savino/The Image Works

Media | Review

History

▶ Nicholas Negroponte first created the concept of *convergence* in 1978 to describe the process by which the technologies of all the media industries are merging.

▶ Paul Saffo first defined the 30-year rule governing people's willingness to adopt new ideas.

▶ Tim Berners-Lee is the person most responsible for creating the World Wide Web.

▶ In 1994, Congress named the new effort to coordinate all the different senders, channels and receivers in the United States the National Information Infrastructure (NII).

▶ In 1996, Congress passed the Communications Decency Act (CDA), which contained provisions that attempted to control content on the Internet. So far, U.S. courts have tended to rule that the federal government cannot regulate content on the Internet, but many issues remain unresolved.

Technology

▶ The five technological challenges for the new digital network are:

  1. Improved storage

  2. A coordinated delivery system

  3. A "smart" set-top box

  4. Usable menus

  5. Secure ordering and billing systems

▶ Technological changes probably will come gradually, as each challenge to the creation of the new information network is solved.

▶ The Internet is a combination of thousands of computer networks sending and receiving data from all over the world.

▶ Some examples of currently emerging digital media technologies are immersive virtual reality systems, holographic theaters, personal channels, intelligent video agents, digital paper, portable tablets, line doublers and quadruplers for TV screens, and flat panel display screens.

▶ On the Web, any type of information—pictures, voice, graphics and text—can travel virtually instantly to and from anyone with a computer and access to the Internet anywhere in the world.

Business

▶ Because of its global size and the absence of government controls, the Internet is completely different from traditional media.

▶ Digital media are the fastest growing type of media.

▶ While a few Web sites, such as explicit sites and Internet gaming sites, charge for their services, most people remain unwilling to pay for what's on the Web.

▶ What makes the Web different from traditional media is its capacity to combine information, entertainment and commerce.

▶ Most Web sites now carry some form of advertising.

Culture

▶ The same collision of economics, technology and creativity that drove the development of traditional media is behind today's race to develop digital media.

▶ Electronic mail (e-mail) is the way most people first experience communicating in an electronic environment.

▶ Not everyone has equal access to the Internet, especially low income groups. This is called the *digital divide*.

▶ The free culture of the Web originated with its founders, who placed their discoveries in the public domain, which meant that anyone could use the services for free.

▶ Marketers have developed tracking software that can monitor consumers' online habits.

▶ The future of digital media is bound only by the needs of consumers and the imaginations of developers, as diverse as the people who are online today and going online tomorrow.

Impact | Interactive

The Impact/Interactive CD-ROM that accompanies this text is your gateway to many electronic resources for broadening and testing your critical understanding of the material in Chapter 9. The CD-ROM features the following interactive elements for this and every chapter in the book.

▶ A two- to three-minute timely, high-interest CNN Today video clip with critical viewing questions and a link to relevant selections available within the InfoTrac College Edition database

▶ Chapter-specific activities such as personal inventories and media projects

▶ A link to the *Media/Impact* Web site that offers helpful information and many additional electronic learning resources including

- An interactive chapter outline and study guide

- Interactive glossary term flashcards and crossword puzzles, concept animations, Internet activities and practice quizzes

- Live links for all URLs given in the chapter so you can easily access the additional information each site offers

▶ A link to InfoTrac College Edition—our online database of more than a million articles representing cutting-edge research and the latest headlines. Updated daily, this online library is available 24 hours a day, seven days a week. The InfoTrac College Edition activities provided below are designed to help you use this valuable resource.

▶ Working the Web

Live links for all of the sites listed below are provided on the *Media/Impact* book companion Web site, which can be accessed through your Impact/Interactive CD-ROM.

▶ **Apple Computer, Inc.**

www.apple.com

▶ **Electronic Frontier Foundation**

www.eff.org

▶ **Journal of Electronic Publishing**

www.press.umich.edu/jep

▶ **MIT Media Lab Project**

www.media.mit.edu/

▶ **Sony Corporation of America**

www.sony.com

▶ InfoTrac College Edition Activities

Using InfoTrac College Edition's online database of full-text articles and abstracts, do the following activities as directed by your instructor. The database can be accessed through your Impact/Interactive CD-ROM.

1. Using InfoTrac College Edition, type in the keywords "Internet security" or "Internet safety" using InfoTrac College Edition and read at least three articles to learn what companies or individuals are doing to protect themselves online. Print the articles and write a brief paper on how important security is to you when you use the Internet. Be prepared to discuss your point of view in class.

2. Look up three of the following keywords to get more information on the following digital media:

- Virtual reality

- Digital paper

- Flat panel video display

- Intelligent video agent

- PDAs (personal data assistants)

As you read the articles, think about how you might use some or all of those media to make your life better. Write a brief paper on how the technologies fit your lifestyle and be prepared to discuss your point of view in class.

3. Read "Impact/People: Tim Berners-Lee: The Man Who Invented the Web" in Chapter 9. Using the keywords "Tim Berners-Lee," look up three articles about Berners-Lee, and as you read them, think about why his name is not as well known as Bill Gates, founder of Microsoft, or Stephen Jobs, founder of Apple. Print at least two of the Tim Berners-Lee articles you find and either:

a. write a brief paper on your findings, or

b. bring the articles to class for a small-group discussion.

4. Using InfoTrac College Edition and the keywords "Internet regulation," read several articles published in the last two years that give you a view of different approaches to Internet regulation around the world. Read articles about regulation proposals—and proposals to limit government regulation—in the United States, in China, in Africa and in at least one European country. Then write a brief paper outlining the difference in Internet regulation among those countries and what you feel is the most practical approach to Internet regulation.

5. Using InfoTrac College Edition and the keywords "browser" and "search engine," read three articles that help you clearly understand the difference between Web browsers and search engines. Then write a brief paper outlining your understanding of the difference between them and the function of each one. Be prepared to report your findings in class.

CHAPTER 10

What's Ahead

> " The advertising industry contends that the ultimate test of any product is the marketplace, and that advertising may stimulate consumers to try a new product or a new brand, but consumers will not continue to buy an unsatisfying product."
>
> Louis C. Kaufman, author, *Essentials of Advertising*

The American Marketing Association defines *advertising* as "any paid form of nonpersonal presentation and promotion of ideas, goods or services by an identified sponsor." American consumers pay for most of their media (newspapers, magazines, radio and television) by watching, listening to and reading advertisements.

You pay directly for books, movies and recordings, although these media use advertising to sell their products. But the broadcast programs you want to hear and see and the articles you want to read are surrounded by advertisements placed by advertising people who want to sell you products.

▶ Paying for Our Pleasures: Advertising and the Media

Advertising is not a medium. Advertising carries the messages that come to you from the people who pay for the American media. Americans, however, were not the first consumers. In 1200 B.C., the Phoenicians painted messages on stones near the paths where people often walked. In the 6th century B.C., ships that came into port sent criers around town with signboards to announce their arrival.

In the 13th century A.D., the British began requiring trademarks to protect buyers and to identify faulty products. The first printed advertisement was prepared by printer William Caxton in England in 1478 to sell one of his books.

Advertising became part of the American experience even before the settlers arrived. "Never was there a more outrageous or more unscrupulous or more ill-informed advertising campaign than that by which the promoters for the American colonies brought settlers here," writes historian Daniel Boorstin. "Brochures published in England in the 17th century, some even earlier, were full of hopeful overstatements, half-truths, and downright lies, along with some facts which nowadays surely would be the basis for a restraining order from the Federal Trade Commission. Gold and silver, fountains of youth, plenty of fish, venison without limit, all these were promised, and of course some of them were found."

Advertising in Newspapers

The nation's first newspaper advertisement appeared in *The Boston News-Letter's* first issue in 1704 when the newspaper's editor included an ad for his own newspaper. The penny press of the 1800s counted on advertising to underwrite its costs. In 1833, the *New York Sun* candidly stated in its first issue: "The object of this paper is to lay before the public, at a price within the means of everyone, all the news of the day, and at the same time afford an advantageous medium for advertising."

Three years later, the *Philadelphia Public Ledger* reported that "advertising is our revenue, and in a paper involving so many expenses as a penny paper, and especially our own, the only source of revenue." Because they were so dependent on advertisers, newspapers in the 1800s accepted any ads they could get. Eventually, they got complaints from customers, especially about the patent medicines that promised cures and often delivered hangovers. (Many of these medicines were mostly alcohol.)

Products like Anti-Corpulence pills claimed they would help someone lose 15 pounds a month. "They cause no sickness, contain no poison and never fail." Dr. T. Felix Couraud's Oriental Cream guaranteed that it would "remove tan, pimples, freckles, moth patches, rash and skin diseases and every blemish on beauty."

The newspaper publishers' response to complaints was to develop an open advertising policy, which allowed the publishers to continue accepting the ads. Then publishers criticized ads on their editorial pages. The *Public Ledger's* policy was: "Our advertising columns are open to the 'public, the whole public, and nothing but the public.' We admit any advertisement of any thing or any opinion, from any persons who will pay the price, excepting what is forbidden by the laws of the land, or what, in the opinion of all, is offensive to decency and morals." But some editors did move their ads, which had been mingled with the copy, to a separate section.

Advertising historian Stephen Fox says: "Advertising was considered an embarrassment . . . the wastrel relative, the unruly servant kept backstairs and never allowed into the front parlor. . . . A firm risked its credit rating by advertising; banks might take it as a confession of financial weakness.

"Everyone deplored advertising. Nobody—advertiser, agent, or medium—took responsibility for it. The advertiser only served as an errand boy, passing the advertiser's message along to the publisher: the medium printed it, but surely would not question the right of free speech by making a judgment on the veracity of the advertiser."

Advertising in Magazines
Until the 1880s, magazines remained wary of advertising. But Cyrus H. K. Curtis, who founded *The Ladies' Home Journal* in 1887, promoted advertising as the way for magazines to succeed. Once when he was asked what made him successful, he answered, "Advertising. That's what made me whatever I am. . . . I use up my days trying to find men who can write an effective advertisement."

When Curtis hired Edward Bok as editor, Bok began a campaign against patent medicine ads and joined with *Collier's* and the American Medical Association to seek government restraints. Congress created the Federal Trade Commission (FTC) in 1914, and part of its job was to monitor deceptive advertising. The FTC continues today to be the major government watchdog over advertising (see page 219).

Advertising on Radio
WEAF in New York broadcast its first advertising in 1922, selling apartments in New Jersey. B. F. Goodrich, Palmolive and Eveready commercials followed. In September 1928, the Lucky Strike Dance Orchestra premiered on NBC, and Lucky Strike sales went up 47 percent. More cigarette companies moved to radio, and Camel cigarettes sponsored weekly, then daily, programs.

Sir Walter Raleigh cigarettes sponsored the Sir Walter Raleigh Revue. In one hour, the sponsor squeezed in 70 references to the product. According to Stephen Fox in *The Mirror Makers: A History of American Advertising and Its Creators*, "The theme song ('rally round Sir Walter Raleigh') introduced the Raleigh Revue in the Raleigh Theater with the Raleigh Orchestra and the Raleigh Rovers; then would follow the adventures of Sir Walter in Virginia and at Queen Elizabeth's court, with ample mention of his cigarettes and smoking tobacco."

"I'd like you to meet our director of scratch-and-sniff advertising."

In 1938, for the first time, radio collected more money from advertising than magazines.

Advertising on Television
Television began as an advertising medium. Never questioning how television would be financed, the TV networks assumed they would attract commercial support. They were right. In 1949, television advertisers totaled $12.3 million. In 1950, the total was $40.8 million. In 1951, advertisers spent $128 million on television.

In a practice adopted from radio, television programs usually carried **direct sponsorship**. Many shows, such as *Camel News Caravan*, carried the

Direct Sponsorship   A program that carries an advertiser's name in the program title.

sponsor's name in the title and advertised a product (Camel cigarettes, for example). Advertising agencies became television's programmers. "Given one advertiser and a show title often bearing its name, viewers associated a favorite show with its sponsor and—because of a 'gratitude factor'—would buy the products" writes Fox.

Alfred Hitchcock became legendary for leading into his show's commercials with wry remarks about the sponsor: "Oh dear, I see the actors won't be ready for another 60 seconds. However, thanks to our sponsor's remarkable foresight, we have a message that will fill in here nicely." But Hitchcock's sarcasm was the exception, and TV today welcomes advertising support without comment.

Advertising on the Internet

Advertisers flocked to major Internet sites when they first were established. They expected quick returns, as consumer use of the Internet skyrocketed. Advertisers primarily used banner advertising, which means their advertising messages scrolled across a Web site or appeared in a box on the site. Internet sites also tried **pop-up** advertisements, which means an advertisement pops up either behind a Web site screen when someone leaves the site or on top of the Web site home page when someone first visits. Advertisers quickly learned, however, that no matter how they packaged the message, advertising on an Internet site didn't necessarily bring increased sales.

What advertisers call the **click-through rate** (the rate at which someone who sees an advertising message on an Internet site actually clicks through to learn more) is less than 1 percent. This is a very disappointing return, especially when Web site advertising can be expensive. In the year 2000, online ad spending reached $8 billion, according to the Internet Advertising Bureau, but has stabilized at that amount and not grown since then.

Advertisers today are still trying to figure out just what the magic formula is to reach consumers on the Internet. Ford, BMW, Coke and Absolut Vodka created "advertainments" on their Web sites—short movies (2 to 11 minutes) featuring lots of action and familiar movie stars. Anheuser-Busch uses an image of beer pouring down the side of the CBS MarketWatch.com's Web site to promote Friday happy hour. The Web site for Steven Spielberg's movie *A.I.* featured a "chatbot" who instantly began conversations when visitors entered the site.

These new approaches all are meant to make advertisements seem less like advertisements—further blurring the line between information, entertainment and advertising.

Pop-up   An advertisement on a Web site that appears on the screen either behind a Web page when someone leaves the site or on top of the Web site home page when someone first visits.

Click-Through Rate   The rate at which someone who sees an ad on an Internet site clicks through to learn more.

▶ How Advertising Works

The word *advertise* originally meant to take note or to consider. By the 1700s, that meaning had changed. To advertise meant to persuade. "If we consider democracy not just a political system," says Daniel J. Boorstin, "but as a set of institutions which do aim to make everything available to everybody, it would not be an overstatement to describe advertising as the characteristic rhetoric of democracy."

Advertising Shares Common Characteristics

Boorstin says that advertising in America shares three characteristics: repetition, style and ubiquity.

Repetition

In 1851, When Robert Bonner bought the *New York Ledger*, he wanted to advertise his newspaper in the competing *New York Herald*, owned by James Gordon Bennett. Bennett limited all his advertisers to the

More than seventy years after this ad for luxury transportation appeared in the May 1931 issue of *Fortune* magazine (left), a 2004 issue of *Fortune* magazine still carried a similar upscale appeal (right), targeting the same audience.

same size typeface, so Bonner paid for an entire page of the *Herald*, across which he repeated the message "Bring home the *New York Ledger* tonight." This is an early example of the widespread practice of repeating a simple message for effect.

An Advertising Style

At first, advertising adopted a plain, direct style. Advertising pioneer Claude Hopkins, says Boorstin, claimed: "Brilliant writing has no place in advertising. A unique style takes attention from the subject. . . . One should be natural and simple . . . in fishing for buyers, as in fishing for bass, one should not reveal the hook."

The plain-talk tradition is a foundation of what advertisers call modern advertising. But advertising today often adopts a style of hyperbole, making large claims for products. Boorstin calls this "tall-talk."

The tall-talk ad is in the P. T. Barnum tradition of advertising. Barnum was a carnival barker and later impresario who lured customers to his circus acts with fantastic claims. You may recognize this approach in some of the furniture and car ads on television, as an announcer screams at you that you have only a few days left until all the chairs or all the cars will be gone.

Both plain talk and tall-talk combine, Boorstin says, to create advertising's new myth. "This is the world of the neither true nor false—of the statement that 60 percent of the physicians who expressed a choice said that our brand of aspirin would be more effective in curing a simple headache than any other brand. . . . It is not untrue, and yet, in its connotation it is not exactly true."

Ubiquity

In America, advertising is everywhere. Advertisers are always looking for new places to catch consumers' attention. Ads appear on shopping carts, on video screens at sports stadiums, atop parking meters. Says Daniel Boorstin, "The ubiquity of advertising is, of course, just another effect of our uninhibited efforts to use all the media to get all sorts of information to

Which of the 15 advertising appeals listed here can you identify in this current billboard ad?

everybody everywhere. Since the places to be filled are everywhere, the amount of advertising is not determined by the needs of advertising, but by the opportunities for advertising, which become unlimited."

In some cases this ubiquity works to advertising's disadvantage. Many advertisers shy away from radio and TV because the ads are grouped so closely together. In 1986, in an attempt to attract more advertisers, TV began selling the "split-30" ad, which fits two 15-second ads into a 30-second spot. Even 10-second ads are available. Wherever these shorter commercials are sold, the station runs twice or three times as many ads for different products, crowding the commercial time even more.

Grabbing Your Attention
To sell the products, advertisers must catch your eye or your ear or your heart (preferably all three). A study by the Harvard Graduate School of Business Administration reported that the average American is exposed to 500 ads a day.

With so many ads competing for your attention, the advertiser must first get you to read, to listen, or to watch one ad instead of another. "The immediate goal of advertising [is to] tug at our psychological shirt sleeves and slow us down long enough for a word or two about whatever is being sold," says Jib Fowles in *Mass Advertising as Social Forecast.*

▶ How Ads Appeal to Consumers

You make your buying decisions based on several sources of information besides advertising: friends, family and your own experience, for example. To influence your choices, the advertising message must appeal to you for some reason as you sift through the ads to make judgments and choose products. Humanities and human sciences professor Jib Fowles enumerated 15 appeals, which he calls an "inventory of human motives" that advertisers commonly use in their commercials. They are:

1. *Need for sex.* Surprisingly, Fowles found that only 2 percent of the television ads he surveyed used this appeal. It may be too blatant, he concluded, and often detracts from the product.

2. *Need for affiliation.* The largest number of ads use this approach: You are looking for friendship. Advertisers can also use this negatively, to make you worry that you'll lose friends if you don't use a certain product.

3. *Need to nurture.* Every time you see a puppy or a kitten or a child, the appeal is to your maternal or paternal instincts.

4. *Need for guidance.* A father or mother figure can appeal to your desire for someone to care for you, so you won't have to worry. Betty Crocker is a good example.

5. *Need to aggress.* We all have had a desire to get even, and some ads give you this satisfaction.

6. *Need to achieve.* The ability to accomplish something difficult and succeed identifies the product with winning. Sports figures as spokespersons project this image.

7. *Need to dominate.* The power we lack is what we can look for in a commercial: "Master the possibilities."

8. *Need for prominence.* We want to be admired and respected, to have high social status. Tasteful china and classic diamonds offer this potential.

9. *Need for attention.* We want people to notice us; we want to be looked at. Cosmetics are a natural for this approach.

10. *Need for autonomy.* Within a crowded environment, we want to be singled out, to be "a breed apart." This can also be used negatively: You may be too ordinary without a particular product.

11. *Need to escape.* Flight is very appealing; you can imagine adventures you cannot have. The idea of escape is pleasurable.

12. *Need to feel safe.* To be free from threats, to be secure is the appeal of many insurance and bank ads.

13. *Need for aesthetic sensations.* Beauty attracts us, and classic art or dance makes us feel creative, enhanced.

14. *Need to satisfy curiosity.* Facts support our belief that information is quantifiable, and numbers and diagrams make our choices seem scientific.

15. *Physiological needs.* Fowles defines sex (item no. 1) as a biological need, and so he classifies our need to sleep, eat and drink as physiological. Advertisements for juicy pizza are especially appealing late at night.

▶ Finding the Audience: Which Demographic Are You?

Advertisers target their messages to an audience according to the audience's needs. But an advertiser also seeks to determine the audience's characteristics. This analysis of observable audience characteristics is called **demographics**. Demographics are composed of data about a target audience's sex, age, income level, marital status, geographic location and occupation. These data are observable because they are available to advertising agencies through census data and other sources. Advertising agencies use demographic audience analysis to help advertisers target their messages.

A motorcycle dealer certainly wouldn't want to advertise in a baby magazine, for example; a candy manufacturer probably wouldn't profit from advertising in a diet and exercise magazine. Advertising agencies try to match a client's product to a thoroughly defined audience so each advertising dollar is well spent.

Defining the audience is very important because the goal of advertising is to market a product to people who have the desire for the product and the ability to buy the product. Audience analysis tells an advertiser whether there are enough people who can be targeted for a product to make the advertising worthwhile.

AP/Wide World Photos

A mural advertising Evian bottled water covers a wall of the Hyatt Hotel on Sunset Strip in West Hollywood. Critics of advertising claim advertising causes consumers to buy products they don't need. The advertising industry contends the ultimate test of any product is the marketplace because consumers will not continue to buy an unsatisfying product.

Demographics Data about consumers' characteristics, such as age, sex, income level, marital status, geographic location and occupation.

Someone's Watching:
How Marketers May Stalk You at Home

by Deborah Solomon

If George Orwell thought 1984 was going to be bad, he'd freak at what's coming.

Soon, what we watch, what we read, even what we keep in our refrigerators, may be accessible to someone other than ourselves.

That's because companies are working on ways to network our homes—linking every appliance together and connecting them all to the Internet. High-tech companies want to connect our TVs with our PCs, our refrigerators with the Internet and our cell phones with our ovens....

While privacy on the Internet has long been a concern, consumer advocates say the sheer number of devices that will soon be hooked to the Net and the data about consumers that will become available to companies are dangerous.

Most of the concern centers around the loss of control consumers experience once they enter cyberspace. If everything is linked to the Net, privacy advocates say, consumers won't be able to avoid leaving records of their personal information and won't be able to control how companies use that data.

San Francisco Chronicle, July 26, 1999, B1.
Reprinted by permission.

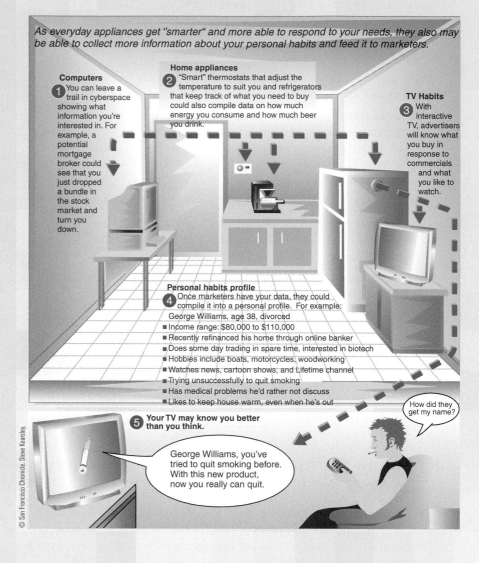

As everyday appliances get "smarter" and more able to respond to your needs, they also may be able to collect more information about your personal habits and feed it to marketers.

▶ What's Wrong with Advertising?

The study of advertising provokes three main criticisms, according to Louis C. Kaufman, author of *Essentials of Advertising*:

1. *Advertising adds to the cost of products.* Critics of advertising maintain that advertising, like everything that is part of manufacturing a product, is a cost. Ultimately, the consumer pays for the cost of advertising. But the industry argues that advertising helps make more goods and services available to the consumer, and that the resulting competition keeps prices lower.

Advertising's Big Four: It's Their World Now

College basketball is not the only American institution with a showdown among its Final Four. . . .

Besides dominating commercial speech, a $500-billion-a-year industry, these four agency companies and the men who run them . . . also hold incredible sway over the media. By deciding when and where to spend their clients' ad budgets, they can indirectly set network television schedules and starve magazines to death or help them to flourish.

"Now you have four megacompanies with revenue that are staggering, bigger than some of the companies they serve," said O. Burtch Drake, president and chief executive of the American Association of Advertising Agencies, the industry trade group.

Driving this concentration of power is an assumption that ad agencies must have a global presence, enormous size and a full range of marketing services simply to survive. That has led to decades of mergers and acquisitions, during which, for example, Omnicom bought more than 150 agencies. Interpublic grew from two American-based ad agency groups to three worldwide ad agency networks. . . .

These advertising and marketing behemoths have grown in response to fundamental changes among their clients and media companies. Clients themselves have become bigger and more global. . . . Media companies, meanwhile, have ballooned in size and range, and now package print and television with the Internet and other paths to customers. (See Illustration 10.1.)

Source: The New York Times, March 31, 2002, p. 3–1. Copyright © 2002 by the New York Times Co. Reprinted with permission.

2. *Advertising causes people to buy products they do not need.* Says media scholar Michael Schudson, "Most blame advertising for the sale of specific consumer goods, notably luxury goods (designer jeans), frivolous goods (pet rocks), dangerous goods (cigarettes), shoddy goods (some toys for children), expensive goods that do not differ at all from cheap goods (nongeneric over-the-counter drugs), marginally differentiated products that do not differ significantly from one another (laundry soaps), and wasteful goods (various unecological throw-away convenience goods)." The advertising industry contends the ultimate test of any product is the marketplace and that advertising may stimulate consumers to try a new product or a new brand, but consumers will not continue to buy an unsatisfying product.

3. *Advertising reduces competition and thereby fosters monopolies.* Critics point to the rising cost of advertising, especially television, which limits which companies can afford to launch a new product or a new campaign. The industry argues that advertising is still a very inexpensive way to let people know about new products. "The cost of launching a nationwide advertising campaign may be formidable," writes Louis C. Kaufman, "but the cost of supporting larger, nationwide sales forces for mass-marketed goods would be greater still."

Does advertising work? According to Schudson, "Apologists are wrong that advertising is simply information that makes the market work more efficiently—but so too are the critics of advertising who believe in its overwhelming power to deceive and to deflect human minds to its ends. Evaluating its impact is more difficult than these simplicities of apology and critique will acknowledge."

**Illustration 10.1
The World's Top Four
Advertising Agencies**

1. Omnicom Group, New York;
   $6.9 billion

2. Interpublic Group, New York;
   $6.9 billion

3. WPP Group, London;
   $5.8 billion

4. Publicis Groupe, Paris;
   $40 billion

▶ Working in Advertising

About 6,000 advertising agencies are in business in the United States, but most of them are small operations, earning less than $1 million a year. Advertising agencies buy time and space for the companies they represent. For this, they are usually paid a commission (commonly 15 percent). Many agencies also produce television and radio commercials and print advertising for their clients.

Depending on the size of the agency, the company may be divided into as many as six departments: marketing research, media selection, creative activity, account management, administration and public relations.

Marketing research examines the product's potential, where it will be sold and who will buy the product. Agency researchers may survey the market themselves or contract with an outside market research company to evaluate potential buyers.

Media selection suggests the best combination of buys for a client—television, newspapers, magazines, billboards.

Creative activity thinks up the ads. The "creatives" write the copy for TV, radio and print. They design the graphic art and often they produce the commercials. They also verify that the ad has run as many times as it was scheduled to run.

Account management is the liaison between the agency and the client. Account executives handle client complaints and suggestions and also manage the company team assigned to the account.

Administration pays the bills, including all the tabs for the account executives' lunches with clients.

Public relations is an extra service that some agencies offer for companies that don't have a separate public relations office.

All these departments work together on an ad campaign. An **advertising campaign** is a planned advertising effort, coordinated for a specific time period. A campaign could last anywhere from a month to a year, and the objective is a coordinated strategy to sell a product or a service.

Advertising Campaign   A planned advertising effort, coordinated for a specific time period.

If You Pitch It, They Will Eat

by David Barboza

The McDonald's Corporation wants to be everywhere that children are.

So besides operating 13,602 restaurants in the United States, it has plastered its golden arches on Barbie dolls, video games, book jackets, even theme parks.

McDonald's calls this promotion and brand extension. But, a growing number of nutritionists call it a blitzkrieg that perverts children's eating habits and sets them on a path to obesity.

Marketing fast food, snacks and beverages to children is at least as old as Ronald McDonald himself. What's new, critics say, is the scope and intensity of the assault. . . .

"What really changed over the last decade is the proliferation of electronic media," says Susan Linn, a psychologist who studies children's marketing at Harvard's Judge Baker Children's Center. "It used to just be Saturday-morning television. Now it's Nickelodeon, movies, video games, the Internet and even marketing in schools. . . ."

While the companies view these as harmless promotional pitches, lawyers

New York Times Pictures

Know how Barbie earns spending money? She works at McDonald's. That's just one way McDonald's promotes its brand to children.

are threatening a wave of obesity-related, class-action lawsuits. Legislators are pressing to lock food companies out of school cafeterias. And, some of the fiercest critics are calling for an outright ban on all food advertising aimed at children.

"The problem of obesity is so staggering, so out of control, that we have to do something," says Walter Willett, a professor of nutrition at the Harvard School of Public Health. "The vast majority of what they sell is junk," Mr. Willett says of the big food makers. "How often do you see fruits and vegetables?". . .

Food companies say their commercials don't encourage overeating, that the foods they advertise are meant to be "part of a balanced diet," and that some foods are meant to be only occasional treats.

"We talk about offering carrot sticks," says Karlin Linhardt, the director of youth marketing at McDonald's. "And we have parents come in and say, 'We offer them carrot sticks at home. When we come to McDonald's we want a treat, French fries.'"

Typically, the company assigns the account executive a team of people from the different departments to handle the account. The account executive answers to the people who control the agency, usually a board of directors. The members of the campaign team coordinate all types of advertising—print and broadcast, for example—to make sure they share consistent content. After establishing a budget based on the client's needs, the campaign team creates a slogan, recommends a strategy for the best exposure for the client, approves the design of print and broadcast commercials and then places the ads with the media outlets.

Advertising agencies tend to be clustered in big cities such as New York, Los Angeles, San Francisco and Chicago. In part, this is by tradition. The agencies may be near their clients in the city. They also have access to a larger pool of talent and facilities such as recording studios. But new technology enables greater flexibility for agency locations.

Illustration 10.2
Where U.S. Advertising Dollars Are Spent

Advertising spending in the United States is spread out among broadcast media (51%), print media (44%), and the Internet (5%).

Sources: The Veronis Suhler Stevenson Communications Industry Forecast, 2003–2007.

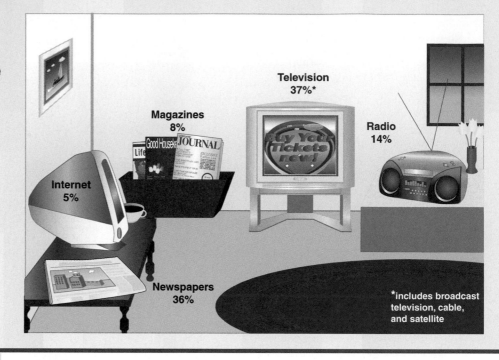

Magazines 8%

Television 37%*

Radio 14%

Internet 5%

Newspapers 36%

Buy Your Tickets now!

*includes broadcast television, cable, and satellite

Critical Question

Which medium's advertising is most likely to motivate you to actually buy something? Why do you think this medium's advertising succeeds with you?

▶ The Business of Advertising

The advertising business and the media industries are interdependent—that is, what happens in the advertising business directly affects the media industries. The advertising business is very dependent on the nation's economic health. If the national economy is expanding, the advertising business and the media industries prosper.

If the nation falls into a recession, advertisers typically reduce their ad budgets, which eventually leads to a decline in advertising revenue for the agencies and also for the media industries where the agencies place their ads. During a recession, advertisers also may change their advertising strategies—choosing radio over television because it is much less expensive, for example.

The advertising industry today, therefore, must be very sensitive to economic trends. The success of an ad agency is best measured by the results an ad campaign brings. The agency must analyze the benefits of different types of advertising and recommend the most efficient combination for their clients.

Commercials on Television
Even though the cost seems exorbitant, sponsors continue to line up to appear on network television. "Advertisers must use television on whatever terms they can get it, for television is the most potent merchandising vehicle ever devised," writes TV

producer Bob Shanks in his book *The Cool Fire: How to Make It in Television*. Shanks is talking about national advertisers who buy network time—companies whose products can be advertised to the entire country at once.

Advertising minutes within every network prime-time hour are divided into 10-, 15- and 30-second ads. If an advertiser wants to reach the broad national market, television is an expensive choice because the average price for the TV time for a 30-second commercial is $100,000. The price tag can go as high as $2 million for a widely watched program such as the Super Bowl.

National advertising on network programs like *Everybody Loves Raymond* is bought by national advertising agencies, which handle the country's biggest advertisers—Procter & Gamble and McDonald's, for example. These companies usually have in-house advertising and public relations departments, but most of the advertising strategy and production of commercials for these companies is handled by the agencies. National agencies buy advertising space based on a careful formula, calculated on a cost-per-thousand (**CPM**) basis—the cost of an ad per 1,000 people reached.

Making a TV commercial for national broadcast is more expensive per minute than making a television program, because each company wants its ads to be different from the rest. The price to create a TV commercial can run as much as $1 million a minute. That may be why, as one producer said, "the commercials are the best things on TV."

Network television commercials certainly are the most visible type of advertising, but not everyone needs the reach of network television. The goal of well-placed advertising is to deliver the best results to the client for the lowest cost, and this may mean looking to other media.

Using the Internet, Print and Radio
Different types of media deliver different types of audiences. The Internet offers a large potential audience, but consumers also can quickly click past ads on the Web, so no one is quite sure how effective Web ads are. Advertising agencies also buy less expensive time and space in local radio, newspapers and magazines to target a specific audience by demographics: age, education, gender and income (see **Illustration 10.2**). Language also can be a targeting factor. A radio station with a rock format delivers a different group from an easy-listening station. *The New York Times* delivers a different reader from the *Honolulu Advertiser*. *Sports Illustrated* targets a different group from *The Ladies' Home Journal*.

▶ Fierce Competition for Clients

The competition among different media for advertisers is heavy:

- The American Newspaper Publishers Association commissions a study that reveals that only one in five prime-time adult viewers could remember the last ad they had seen on television.

- Print advertisers claim that remote channel changers zap many TV ads, making TV commercials an unreliable way to deliver an audience.

- *Time* advertises that more airline customers read its magazine than read *Newsweek*.

PepsiCo, Inc.

Advertisers must learn to adapt their messages for new audiences as new technology, such as the Internet, creates new outlets for advertising.

CPM Stands for cost-per-thousand, the cost of an ad per 1,000 people reached. (M is the Roman Numeral for 1,000.)

- *Newsweek* advertises that it delivers more people for the money than *Time*.
- "Radio is the medium working women don't have to make time for," boasts the Radio Advertising Bureau (RAB). Whereas working women spend 15 percent of their daily media time reading a newspaper, they spend half of their media time with radio, says the RAB.
- AT&T launches a talking Web site to "express themselves better" to consumers.

Advertising agencies gather demographic information provided by Nielsen and Arbitron for broadcast and by the Audit Bureau of Circulations for print; the audience is converted into numbers. Based on these numbers, agencies advise advertisers about ways to reach buyers for their products.

Advertising Locally
Karen's Yogurt Shoppe, a small downtown business, does not need to advertise on *David Letterman* or in *The New York Times*. Karen and other local businesses need to reach only their neighbors. Businesses larger than the yogurt shop, such as a car dealer or a furniture store, may buy local television or radio time, but most of the local advertising dollar goes to newspapers.

A local advertising agency can design a campaign, produce the ad and place the ad just like the national agencies, but on a much smaller scale. Some small companies design and place their own ads directly with the local media. To attract customers, local media often help companies design their ads. Newspapers, for example, will help a small advertiser prepare an ad using ready-made art. A radio or television station may include the services of an announcer or access to a studio in the price for a series of spot ads.

Broadcast stations sometimes trade ads for services offered by the advertiser—dinner for two at the local restaurant in return for two spot ads, for example. Then the station gives the dinners away on one of its programs.

Advertising Sales Representatives
What if you manufacture sunglasses in Dubuque, Iowa, and you hire a local advertising agency to sell your product nationally? The agency tells you that they believe a good market for your product exists on the West Coast. How is the agency going to find out the most efficient way to sell your sunglasses in Los Angeles?

In this situation, many advertising agencies would contact a **rep firm**—a company of advertising sales representatives who sell advertising time and space in their market to companies outside the area. In this case, the agency in Dubuque would first decide who were the most likely customers for your sunglasses. If the agency decided that L.A.-area males age 18 to 24 are the best potential customers, the agency would budget a certain amount of money for advertising in the Los Angeles area and then call the ad reps there.

The rep firm, in return, takes a percentage (usually 15 percent) of the advertising dollars they place. Ad reps are, in effect, brokers for the media in their markets. Each rep firm handles several clients. Some ad reps sell only broadcast advertising and some specialize in print ads, but many rep firms sell all types of media.

In this case, each L.A. ad rep would enter the demographics ("demos") for your product into a computer. Based on ratings, readership and the price for the ads, each rep would come up with a CPM (cost per thousand people reached) for your product. The rep then would recommend the most efficient buy—how best to reach the people most likely to want your sunglasses.

Each rep then presents an L.A. advertising plan for your product to the agency in Dubuque. Usually the buy is based on price: The medium with the lowest CPM gets the customer. But a rep who cannot match the lowest CPM

Rep Firm   A company of advertising sales representatives who sell advertising time and space in their market to companies outside their area.

Impact | Culture

It's An Ad, Ad, Ad, Ad World

The average American sees an estimated 3,000 advertisements a day. And he's seeing them in increasingly odd places—at gas pumps, on stickers on apples and bananas, on sidewalks and rooftops, in full-color, full-sound videos at the ATM—a quick pitch for your cash before you draw it from your account. So-called ambient advertising is exploding as companies eschew traditional mass media in an attempt to get at jaded consumers where they work, shop and play. New Jersey–based Beach 'n Billboard, for example, imprints ads on sand (right). For upwards of $20,000, a company can get half a mile of ads up and down the beach every day for a month. The imprint may not last long, but it's hard not to notice an ad you have to sit on.

Time, July 9, 2001, p. 17. © 2001 Time, Inc.
Reprinted by permission.

Courtesy of Patrick Doni, President Beach 'n Billboard

Advertising company Beach 'n Billboard uses beach sand to imprint advertiser messages.

might offer incentives for you to choose his or her plan. If you agree to provide 50 pairs of sunglasses, for example, the rep's radio station will give away the glasses as prizes during a local program, each time mentioning the name of your product. So even though the ad time you buy will cost a little more, you also will get promotional announcements every time the station gives away a pair of sunglasses. Other ad reps might offer different packages.

The agency in Dubuque then would decide which package is the most attractive and would present that proposal to you. This entire process can take as little as 24 hours for a simple buy such as the one for your sunglasses account, or as long as several weeks for a complicated campaign for a big advertiser.

▶ Federal Government Regulates Advertisers

Government protection for consumers dates back to the beginning of the 20th century when Congress passed the Pure Food and Drug Act in 1906, mainly as a protection against patent medicine ads. The advertising industry itself has adopted advertising standards, and in some cases the media have established their own codes.

Advertising That Deceives the Consumer
Government oversight is the main deterrent against deceptive advertising. This responsibility is shared by several government agencies.

Although ads for beer and wine regularly appear on TV, companies that produce hard liquor had voluntarily agreed not to use television. But in 1996, some hard liquor companies challenged the ban by placing ads on local TV, and some TV networks now run hard liquor ads.

1. *The Federal Trade Commission (FTC)*, established in 1914, can "stop business practices that restrict competition or that deceive or otherwise injure consumers," according to *Essentials of Advertising*. If the FTC determines an ad is deceptive, the commission can order the advertiser to stop the campaign. The commission also can require corrective advertising to counteract the deception. In 1993, for example, the FTC launched an investigation of the nation's weight-loss clinics, charging that they were using deceptive advertising.

2. *The Food and Drug Administration (FDA)* oversees claims that appear on food labels or packaging. If the FDA finds a label is deceptive, the agency can require the advertiser to stop distributing products with that label. Orange juice that is labeled "fresh," for example, cannot be juice that has been frozen first.

3. *The Federal Communications Commission (FCC)* enforces rules that govern the broadcast media. The FCC's jurisdiction over the broadcast industry gives the commission indirect control over broadcast advertising. In the past, the FCC has ruled against demonstrations of products that were misleading and against commercials that the FCC decided were tasteless.

Advertising Liquor   Although you regularly see advertisements on television for beer and wine, the TV networks do not advertise hard liquor. For three decades, the Distilled Spirits Council of the United States, operating under a voluntary Code of Good Practice, did not run television ads. In 1996, some liquor companies decided to challenge the voluntary ban by placing ads on local television.

Seagram's, the first company to challenge the ban, advertised Royal Crown whiskey on a local TV station in Texas. "We believe distilled spirits should have the same access to electronic media, just the same way beer and wine do," said Arthur Shapiro, executive vice president in charge of marketing and strategy for Seagram's in the United States.

The Federal Trade Commission and the Bureau of Alcohol, Tobacco and Firearms regulate the spirits industry, but neither agency has the authority to ban hard liquor ads on television. Because the TV networks can gain a great deal of income from advertising hard liquor, some TV networks also decided to accept hard liquor ads.

▶ Advertising Industry Polices Itself

Other government agencies, such as the Environmental Protection Agency and the Consumer Product Safety Agency, also can question the content of advertisements. Advertising agencies have formed the National Advertising Review Board (NARB) to hear complaints against advertisers.

This effort at self-regulation parallels those of some media industries, such as the movie industry's ratings code and the recording industry's record labeling for lyrics.

▶ Technology Transforms the Future

The future of advertising will parallel changes in the media, in technology and in demographics. As more U.S. products seek international markets, advertising must be designed to reach those markets. American agencies today collect nearly half of the *world's* revenue from advertising.

International advertising campaigns are becoming more common for global products, such as Coca-Cola and McDonald's, and this has meant the creation of international advertising. Cable News Network (CNN) announced in 1991 that it would be selling advertising on CNN worldwide, so that any company in any nation with CNN's service could advertise its product to a worldwide audience. Overall, billings outside the United States are commanding an increasing share of U.S. agencies' business.

A second factor in the future of advertising is changing technology. As new media technologies create new outlets, the advertising community must adapt. Advertisers are trying to figure out how to reach consumers on their computer screens. A tennis instructional video, for example, could include advertising for tennis products. One company is using lasers to create advertising in the evening sky.

A third factor in the future of advertising is shifting demographic patterns. As the ethnicity of the nation evolves, marketing programs must adapt to reach new audiences. Future television ads may include dialogue in both English and Spanish. Some national ad campaigns already include multilingual versions of the same ad, targeted for different audiences.

The challenges for the advertising business are as great as the challenges for the media industries. The advertising industry will do what it has always done to adapt—follow the audience. The challenge for advertising will be to learn how to efficiently and effectively match the audience to the advertising messages the media deliver.

Media | Review

Jonathan Ferrey/Getty Images

History

▶ As early as 1200 B.C., the Phoenicians painted messages on stones to advertise.

▶ In 600 B.C., ship captains sent criers around to announce that their ships were in port.

▶ In the 13th century A.D., the British began requiring trademarks to protect buyers.

▶ In 1704, newspapers were the first medium to use advertising. Magazines, radio, television and the Internet followed.

Technology

▶ Today's advertising agencies use sophisticated technology to track demographics to help deliver the audience the advertiser wants.

▶ The future of advertising will parallel the development of international markets, the refinement and expansion of new media technologies (especially the Internet) and changing demographics.

▶ Advertisers flocked to major Internet sites when they first were established. They expected quick returns, as consumer use of the Internet skyrocketed. Advertisers quickly learned, however, that no matter how they packaged the message, advertising on an Internet site didn't necessarily bring increased sales.

▶ What advertisers call the *click-through rate* (the rate at which someone who sees an advertising message actually clicks through to learn more) is less than 1 percent.

▶ In the year 2000, online ad spending reached $8 billion, according to the Internet Advertising Bureau, but stabilized at $8 billion since that time and isn't going up.

▶ Advertisers today are still trying to figure out just what the magic formula is to reach consumers on the Internet. These new approaches all are meant to make advertisements seem less like advertisements— further blurring the line between information, entertainment and advertising.

Business

▶ Advertising carries the messages that come to you from the sponsors who pay for the American media.

▶ Advertising provokes three main criticisms: advertising adds to the cost of products; advertising causes people to buy products they do not need; advertising reduces competition and thereby fosters monopolies.

▶ The advertising business and the media industries are interdependent— what happens in the advertising business directly affects the media industries.

▶ The advertising business is very dependent on the nation's economic health.

▶ Advertising is divided into national and local categories.

▶ Advertising sales representatives broker local accounts to out-of-town advertisers.

▶ The media compete with each other for the advertising dollar, and some media are better than others for particular products.

▶ International advertising campaigns are becoming more common for global products, such as Coca-Cola and McDonald's, and this has meant the creation of international advertising.

Culture

▶ Daniel Boorstin says that advertising in America shares three characteristics: repetition, an advertising style and ubiquity.

▶ Advertising can catch your attention, according to Jib Fowles, in 15 ways, including playing on your need to nurture, your need for attention and your need for escape.

▶ As the ethnicity of the nation evolves, marketing programs must adapt to reach new audiences.

▶ In 1996, the distilled spirits industry challenged the industry-wide voluntary ban on hard liquor advertising on TV that had lasted for three decades. The liquor industry placed the ads on local TV stations, and some network executives indicated that they would accept the ads.

▶ Protection for consumers from misleading advertising comes from government regulation (the Federal Trade Commission, Food and Drug Administration, and Federal Communications Commission, for example); from advertising industry self-regulatory groups (National Advertising Review Board, for example); and from codes established by the media industries.

Impact | Interactive

The Impact/Interactive CD-ROM that accompanies this text is your gateway to many electronic resources for broadening and testing your critical understanding of the material in Chapter 10. The CD-ROM features the following interactive elements for this and every chapter in the book.

▶ A two- to three-minute timely, high-interest CNN Today video clip with critical viewing questions and a link to relevant selections available within the InfoTrac College Edition database

▶ Chapter-specific activities such as personal inventories and media projects

▶ A link to the *Media/Impact* Web site that offers helpful information and many additional electronic learning resources including

   • An interactive chapter outline and study guide

   • Interactive glossary term flashcards and crossword puzzles, concept animations, Internet activities and practice quizzes

   • Live links for all URLs given in the chapter so you can easily access the additional information each site offers

▶ A link to InfoTrac College Edition—our online database of more than a million articles representing cutting-edge research and the latest headlines. Updated daily, this online library is available 24 hours a day, seven days a week. The InfoTrac College Edition activities provided below are designed to help you use this valuable resource.

▶ Working the Web

Live links for all of the sites listed below are provided on the *Media/Impact* book companion Web site, which can be accessed through your Impact/Interactive CD-ROM.

- ▶ **Advertising Age**
  www.adage.com

- ▶ **Advertising Council**
  www.adcouncil.org

- ▶ **American Advertising Federation**
  www.aff.org

- ▶ **American Association of Advertising Agencies**
  www.aaaa.org

- ▶ **Federal Trade Commission**
  www.ftc.gov

▶ InfoTrac College Edition Activities

Using InfoTrac College Edition's online database of full-text articles and abstracts, do the following activities as directed by your instructor. The database can be accessed through your Impact/Interactive CD-ROM.

1. Read "Impact/Culture: Someone's Watching: How Marketers May Stalk You at Home" in Chapter 10. Using the keywords "Internet Web advertising," look up at least three articles on Web advertising and privacy issues. Then write a brief paper on your findings on one of two topics:

   a. how marketers gather information on consumers, or

   b. how advertisers are being lured to the Internet.

2. What effects do advertisements have on children? There have been many studies and expressions of opinion on this topic. Enter the keywords "advertising and children" to research viewpoints on the relationship between advertising and children, including advertising influence, advertiser responsibility and promotion of positive behaviors. Read at least three articles, form your own conclusions or questions, then either:

   a. write a brief paper on your findings, or

   b. bring the articles to class for a small-group discussion.

3. Use the keywords "alcohol advertising" to study the controversy in the last few years over advertising of beer and liquor. Read at least three articles on the subject, then draw some conclusions of your own about the controversy. In a brief paper, outline your position on alcohol advertising in various forms of media, and be prepared to discuss the issue in class.

4. Using InfoTrac College Edition and the keywords "Super Bowl advertising," find three articles in the last three years that present conflicting views on the return on investment for companies that advertise during the National Football League Super Bowl. Write a brief paper contrasting the positive and negative points of view. Have viewpoints changed from year to year? Or do you find positive and negative views on the value of Super Bowl advertising in the same year? Be prepared to discuss the issue in class.

5. How do advertisers attempt to reach minorities and specific ethnic groups? Use the keywords "advertising and minorities" to search for more information. Print at least three articles on the subject. Then bring the articles to class for a small-group discussion. Be prepared to offer your opinion on these techniques.

CHAPTER 11

What's Ahead

> *Any organization that isn't monitoring Internet traffic and Web activity could find itself in serious trouble.*"
>
> G. A. Andy Marken, *Public Relations Quarterly*

You may think the cash rebate program offered by many of today's car manufacturers is a new idea, but in 1914, Henry Ford announced that if he sold 300,000 Model Ts that year, each customer would receive a rebate. When the company reached its goal, Ford returned $50 to each buyer. This was good business. It also was good public relations. Like Henry Ford, public relations people today work to create favorable images—for corporations, public officials, products, schools, hospitals and associations.

Scholars have defined three methods to encourage people to do what you want them to do: power, patronage and persuasion. Power involves ruling by law, but it also can mean ruling by peer pressure—someone does something because his or her friends do. Patronage is a polite term for bribery—paying someone with favors or money to do what you want.

The third method—persuasion—is the approach of public relations. Like advertising, public relations is not a mass medium. Public relations is a media support industry. In the classic definition, public relations involves creating an understanding for, or goodwill toward, a company, a person or a product.

The Library of Congress

In what was the largest public relations drive of its time, the Office of War Information promoted the role of the United States in World War II.

▶ How Public Relations Grew

One of the first political leaders to realize the importance of public relations was Augustus Caesar, who commissioned statues of himself in the 1st century to be erected throughout the Roman Empire to enhance his image. Many political leaders have ordered heroic images of themselves printed on coins and stamps.

Today's public relations approach can be traced to the beginning of the 20th century. Journalists were an important reason for the eventual emergence of the public relations profession.

▶ The Press and Public Relations

Before 1900, business had felt that it could work alongside the press, or even ignore it. Many stories that appeared in the press promoted companies that bought advertising. Then the Industrial Revolution arrived, and some industrialists exploited workers and collected enormous profits. Ida Tarbell and Lincoln Steffens began to make businesspeople uncomfortable, writing stories for magazines like *McClure's* about the not so admirable characteristics of some companies. According to *This is PR: The Realities of Public Relations*: "No longer could the railroads butter up the press by giving free passes to reporters. No longer would the public buy whitewashed statements like that of coal industrialist George F. Baer, who in 1902 told labor to put their trust in 'the Christian men whom God in His infinite wisdom has given control of the property interests of the country.'"

President Theodore Roosevelt fed public sentiment against the abuses of industry when he started his antitrust campaigns. According to *Effective Public Relations*, "With the growth of mass-circulation newspapers, Roosevelt's canny ability to dominate the front pages demonstrated a new-found power for those with causes to promote. He had a keen sense of news and knew how to stage a story so that it would get maximum attention. His skill forced those he fought to develop similar means. He fully exploited the news media as a new and powerful tool of presidential leadership, and he remade the laws and the presidency in the process."

▶ Corporate and Institutional Public Relations

The first publicity firm was called The Publicity Bureau and opened in Boston in 1900 to head off the growing public criticism of the railroad companies. The best-known early practitioner of public relations was Ivy Lee, who began his PR career by opening an office in New York with George F. Parker. Lee and Parker represented coal magnate George F. Baer when coal workers went on strike.

A former newspaper reporter, Lee issued a "Declaration of Principles" that he mailed to newspaper city editors. This declaration became a manifesto for early public relations companies to follow.

Reacting to criticism that The Publicity Bureau had worked secretly to promote the railroads, in 1906, Lee wrote in *American Magazine*, "This [the firm of Lee & Parker] is not a secret press bureau. All our work is done in the open. We aim to supply news. . . . In brief, our plan is, frankly and openly, on behalf of business concerns and public institutions, to supply to the press and public of the United States prompt and accurate information concerning subjects which it is of value and interest to the public to know about."

Lee and Parker dissolved their firm in 1908, when Lee went to work as a publicity agent for the Pennsylvania Railroad. Eventually, John D. Rockefeller

▶ Impact | **Culture**

Even Critics of Iraq War Say the White House Spun It with Skill

by Elisabeth Bumiller

The second Persian Gulf war was not only a runaway victory for the United States military, but for another aggressive force that fired off round-the-clock verbal cruise missiles: the White House communications operation.

That is the assessment of the Bush administration's wartime public relations campaign by both its supporters and critics, who say the spin operation was extraordinarily successful in shaping a positive battlefield narrative at least for American audiences. They say the effort floundered in the Arab world.

Its success at home can be traced to three major factors.

First was the repeated use of phrases that critics branded propaganda, like "coalition forces" and "death squads," that became part of the accepted language of war. Second was the powerful cinema vérité journalism of reporters and photographers, whose words and pictures humanized the American soldiers they were with. Third, but not least, was the message discipline of a White House that plotted appearances by top officials on a daily "communications grid," ensuring that in the first half of the day there was a news briefing by an administration official every two hours,

Carlo Allegri/Getty Images

During the Iraq war, the Bush administration used a three-part public relations strategy to promote American involvement: 1. Repeatedly used key phrases. 2. Allowed "embedded" reporters and photographers with invading troops. 3. Created and promoted a "theme of the day." Here Brigadier General Vincent K. Brooks spoke to reporters from a $250,000 set at Central Command in Qatar.

and that everyone was saying more or less the same thing.

"As far as how you justify a war, they've pretty much done it by formula," said Robert L. Ivie, a professor of communication and culture at Indiana University who has spent his career studying the rhetoric of war. "You construct the image of the enemy as savage and barbarian. Then there are all sorts of efforts to show that the

good guys represent the forces of civilization, freedom, democracy, human rights. And of course there's the implication that we fight on the side of God."

Supporters of the administration say the narrative worked because it reflected the truth.

The New York Times, April 20, 2003, B-14. Copyright © 2003 by The New York Times Co. Reprinted with permission.

Critical Question

In what ways has your attitude about the war in Iraq changed since the government first announced its intention to take preemptive military action against the country? To what degree, if any, have changes in your attitude resulted from government public relations?

hired Lee to counteract the negative publicity that began with Tarbell's investigation of Standard Oil. (Lee worked for the Rockefellers until he died in 1934.)

The idea of in-house corporate public relations grew as Chicago Edison Company and American Telephone & Telegraph began promotional programs. The University of Pennsylvania and the University of Wisconsin opened publicity bureaus in 1904, and the YMCA of Washington, D.C. hired a full-time publicist to oversee fund-raising in 1905—the first time a publicist was hired for this job.

Doris Fleischman (top), a public relations pioneer, began her career in the 1920s. Her husband, Edward L. Bernays, pictured at bottom, wrote the first book on public relations, *Crystallizing Public Opinion*.

▶ Government Public Relations

During World War I, the government set up the Committee on Public Information, organized by former newspaper reporter George Creel, blurring the line between propaganda and publicity. Creel recruited journalists, editors, artists and teachers to raise money for Liberty Bonds and to promote the nation's participation in the war. One of the people who worked for Creel was Edward L. Bernays. Both Bernays and Ivy Lee have been called the father of public relations.

In 1923, Bernays wrote the first book on public relations, *Crystallizing Public Opinion*, and taught the first course on the subject. Bernays was interested in mass psychology—how to influence the opinions of large groups of people. Procter & Gamble, General Motors and the American Tobacco Company were among his clients. "Public relations," Bernays wrote in 1955, "is the attempt, by information, persuasion, and adjustment, to engineer public support for an activity, cause, movement or institution." In 1985, Bernays further defined public relations as "giving a client ethical advice, based on research of the public, that will win the social goals upon which the client depends for his livelihood."

To sell the New Deal in the 1930s, Franklin D. Roosevelt used every tactic he knew. Comfortable with the press and the public alike, and advised by PR expert Louis McHenry Howe, FDR "projected an image of self-confidence and happiness—just what the American public wanted to believe in. He talked to them on the radio. He smiled for the cameras. He was mentioned in popular songs. He even allowed himself to be one of the main characters in a Rodgers and Hart musical comedy (played by George M. Cohan, America's favorite Yankee Doodle Dandy)," according to *This is PR*.

To gain support for the nation's entry into World War II, the federal government mounted the largest public relations drive in its history, which centered around the Office of War Information, led by former newscaster Elmer Davis. After the war, the public relations business boomed along with the postwar economy.

▶ Women in Public Relations

Doris E. Fleischman was among the first women in public relations when she joined her husband, Edward L. Bernays, in his PR firm. Fleischman was an equal partner with Bernays in their public relations business. An early advocate of public relations as a profession for women, Fleischman wrote, in 1931, that "one finds women working side by side with men in forming the traditions and rules that will govern the profession of the future."

Two other women who were public relations pioneers were Leone Baxter and Anne Williams Wheaton. Baxter formed Baxter and Whitaker in San Francisco with her husband, Clem Whitaker—the first public relations agency to specialize in political campaigns. In 1957, President Dwight Eisenhower appointed Anne Williams Wheaton as his associate press secretary.

▶ Development of Ethics Codes

In the 1930s, the requirements for someone to work in public relations were loose, and many people who said they worked in public relations were press agents who were not above tricks to get attention for their clients. Henry Rogers, co-founder of what was then the world's largest entertainment PR firm, Rogers & Cowan (based in Beverly Hills), admitted that, in 1939, he created a "best-dressed" contest to promote little-known actress Rita Hayworth.

There had been no contest, but Rogers dubbed Hayworth the winner of this fictional event. *Look* magazine gave Hayworth a ten-page spread. "Press agents, and that's what we were, would dream up all sorts of phony stories," he said. "Journalists knew they were phony but printed them because they looked good in print."

During the 1950s, the question of ethics in public relations arose publicly when Byoir and Associates, hired by a railroad company to counteract the expansion of trucking, was charged with creating "front" organizations to speak out against the trucking industry. In court, Byoir's agency argued they were exercising free speech. In 1961, the U.S. Supreme Court upheld Byoir's right to represent a client even if the presentation was dishonest, but this left the ethical issue of honesty unresolved.

The Public Relations Society of America (PRSA) established its first code of ethics in 1954 and expanded that code in 1959 with a Declaration of Principles. That ethics code still exists today to guide the business of public relations. (Excerpts from the PRSA code are in Chapter 15.) PR professionals continue to argue among themselves about the differences between the profession's beginnings as press agentry (which often meant fabricating stories) and the concept of ethically representing a client's business, as Edward L. Bernays described.

Public relations grew throughout the 1960s and 1970s with the encouragement of television, the federal government and corporate America. In 1961, for example, the federal government had about 1,000 people working as writer-editors and public affairs specialists. Today, the total number of people working in federal government public information jobs is nearly 4,000, making the federal government the nation's largest single employer of public information people. (Public information is the name given to the job of government public relations.)

"Yes, but take away the rodent droppings and the occasional shard of glass, and you've still got a damn fine product."

▶ How Public Relations Works

Public relations is an industry of specialties. The most familiar public relations areas are financial public relations, product public relations and crisis public relations, but there are many other specialty areas.

Financial Public Relations   People in financial public relations provide information primarily to business reporters. "Business editors like a PR staff that can provide access to top management," wrote James K. Gentry in the *Washington Journalism Review*, "that knows its company well or can find needed information quickly, that demonstrates ethics and honesty and that knows and accepts the difference between news and fluff."

Gentry then listed comments gathered from editors about what makes a bad PR operation:

- "Companies that think they can hide the truth from the public or believe it's none of the public's business."

- "I despise it when a PR person intercepts our calls to a news source but then isn't capable of answering our questions."

- "When they hire an outside PR firm to handle the job."

- "The 'no-comment' attitude. When they have little or no interest in going beyond the press release."

- "People who either get in the way of you doing your job, complain too much or are no help at all."

Product Public Relations

Product PR uses public relations techniques to sell products and services. Many companies have learned that seeking publicity for a product often is less expensive than advertising the product. Public relations "is booming partly because of price," reports *The Wall Street Journal*. A PR budget of $500,000 is considered huge, whereas an ad budget that size is considered tiny.

According to *The Wall Street Journal*, "At its best, PR can work better than advertising. Coleco Industries Inc. kicked off its Cabbage Patch Kids in 1983 with press parties thrown in children's museums, to which editors and their children were invited—and at which all received dolls to 'adopt.' 'Reporters who adopted dolls felt a part of the process,' a Coleco spokeswoman says. They had 'a personal interest in. . . continuing to publicize it. . .'"

The initial publicity for the Cabbage Patch dolls snowballed, as Cartier's used the dolls to display jewelry in its windows and First Lady Nancy Reagan gave dolls to two Korean children who were in the United States for surgery. Richard Weiner, who handled the publicity, charged Coleco $500,000.

On a smaller budget, the Wieden & Kennedy agency in Seattle contracted Bigger Than Life, Inc., which makes large inflatables, to manufacture a 2½-story pair of tennis shoes. The company attached the shoes to the Westin Copley Place Hotel during the Boston Marathon and to the Westin Hotel in downtown Cincinnati during the March of Dimes walk-a-thon.

Pictures of the shoes appeared in *The New York Times*, the *Cincinnati Enquirer* and in newspapers as far away as Japan. Wieden & Kennedy estimated that buying the same advertising would have cost $7 million.

Crisis Public Relations

This aspect of public relations goes back as far as Edward Bernays responding to the charges against Standard Oil. The term *crisis public relations* has been used to describe the situation facing Johnson & Johnson after its product Tylenol was identified as the carrier of a poison that killed seven people in and near Chicago in 1982.

Johnson & Johnson and Burson-Marsteller, the company's PR agency, were credited with exceptional professionalism in handling the crisis. The Public Relations Society of America honored the companies for their performance. This is an example of responsible public relations in a crisis—when PR must counteract overwhelming negative information.

"The poisonings called for immediate action to protect the consumer," explained Johnson & Johnson's Lawrence G. Foster, who was vice president of public relations at the time, "and there wasn't the slightest hesitation about being completely open with the news media. For the same reasons, Johnson & Johnson decided to recall two batches of the product, and later to withdraw it nationally. During the crisis phase of the Tylenol tragedy, virtually every public relations decision was based on sound, socially responsible business principles, which is when public relations is most effective."

Johnson & Johnson sampled public opinion about its activities with nightly telephone surveys. Pulling the product from the shelves cost $100 million,

Wal-Mart on PR Offensive to Repair Image

by Emily Kaiser, Reuters

Chicago—Wal-Mart Stores Inc. is tired of critics who say it is a behemoth bent on destroying small town America, driving down wages, and shipping jobs to foreign sweatshops.

Wal-Mart, *Fortune* magazine's "most admired company," is also among the most sued. Dozens of cases claiming sex discrimination and wage violations have stained its image. . . . But after years of abiding unflattering views, the empire is striking back with a tough new public relations strategy.

"No one likes to hear someone say something negative about their family," said Wal-Mart spokeswoman Sarah Clark. "There are some things out there that are totally inaccurate, and we're looking to set the record straight."

Officials at the world's largest company have started firing off letters to the editor responding to critical news articles and editorials. Once-

© Jeff Mitchell/REUTERS 1999

reticent Wal-Mart executives are speaking out more, hoping to clean up the world's largest retailer's stained image.

The company has also altered its advertising campaign to showcase women managers and others who have benefited from working there. "We all want to defend our company," Clark said. . . . Despite the more aggressive approach, public relations experts say Wal-Mart's image-improvement efforts are not enough to shore up its reputation.

"For years they've been a classic example of the wrong way to do PR," said Jonathan Bernstein, president of Bernstein Crisis Management and author of *Keeping the Wolves at Bay: A Media Training Manual.*

"They're going to continue to get beat up as long as they basically have a reputation for being unfair or unreasonable to their employees," he said. "All the damage control in the world can't help them unless their policies change."

Emily Kaiser, "Wal-Mart on PR Offensive to Repair Image," Reuters, February 1, 2004, http://www.reuters.com/newsarticle.html.

---

but as soon as Tylenol was out of the stores, the company was viewed as acting responsibly. The challenge then was to rebuild the product's 37 percent share of the market.

The 2,500-member Johnson & Johnson sales force visited retailers and people in the medical community to rebuild confidence in Tylenol. Then Burson-Marsteller organized a televised 30-city satellite press conference for 600 journalists to give local media an equal chance at a nationwide story, which ensured broad coverage.

After re-launch of the product, Tylenol immediately regained a 24 percent share of the market and later regained its position as the nation's top-selling brand. The Tylenol case is often used as an example of very effective crisis public relations.

In October 1996, beverage maker Odwalla, Inc., was faced with a similar crisis when *E. coli* bacteria was traced to unpasteurized apple juice that had been sold by the natural juice company. The bacteria eventually was held responsible for the death of a 16-month-old girl in Colorado and more than 50 cases of severe illness.

Odwalla, the leading manufacturer of unpasteurized juices, had made its reputation on natural, unfiltered products. But as soon as the bacteria was detected, Odwalla announced an immediate recall of 13 products in the seven

AP/Wide World Photos

Odwalla, Inc., CEO Stephen Williamson drinks a bottle of spring water during a news conference at the company's headquarters. Odwalla's quick response to the discovery of *E. coli* bacteria in its fruit juice is cited as an example of good public relations.

western states and British Columbia. Then the company worked with the Food and Drug Administration to scour the Odwalla processing facilities, which were found to be free of the bacteria. The company continued the investigation, including the processors who supplied fruit for the juice.

At the same time, Odwalla Chief Executive Officer Stephen Williamson said the company was exploring all methods of processing the juice to kill the bacteria. Eventually, the company announced it would use a method of flash pasteurization, which the company said would keep more flavor than traditional pasteurization while maintaining better taste.

One month after the outbreak, Odwalla took out full-page ads in several newspapers, an "open letter" to its customers, thanking them for their support and offering sympathy for people diagnosed with *E. coli*–related illnesses after drinking Odwalla juices. "I think Odwalla is making all the right moves," said Pam Smith, a retail stock analyst. Smith's advice for any company facing such a crisis was, "Be brutally honest, no matter what the results. And show your customers that you care about their safety."

The Odwalla episode and the Tylenol crisis indicate how important specialization in crisis public relations can be within the public relations business.

▶ The Business of Public Relations

The estimated number of people in the country involved in public relations is 161,000, and more than 4,000 firms in the United States offer PR-related services. The largest public relations firms employ more than 1,000 people. Several major corporations have 100 to 400 public relations specialists, but most public relations firms have fewer than four employees.

Public relations people often deal with advertising agencies as part of their job, and because PR and advertising are so interrelated, several large public relations firms have joined several large advertising agencies. For example, J. Walter Thompson (advertising) bought Hill & Knowlton (public relations), and the London firm WPP Group PLC bought J. Walter Thompson Group. Combined agencies can offer both public relations and advertising services to their clients, and the trend toward advertising/public relations combinations continues today.

The difference between public relations and advertising at the nation's largest agencies can be difficult to discern. Advertising is an aspect of marketing that aims to sell products. People in advertising usually *aren't* involved in a company's policymaking. They implement the company's policies after company executives decide how to sell a product, a corporate image or an idea.

Public relations people, in comparison, usually are involved in policy. A PR person often contributes to decisions about how a company will deal with the public, the press and its own employees.

Types of Clients   Public relations people work for several types of clients, including governments, nonprofit organizations, industry and business.

Government   The federal government is the nation's largest employer of public information people. State and local governments also hire people to handle PR. Related to government are PR people who work for political candidates and for lobbying organizations. Media consultants also are involved in political PR. These people counsel candidates and officeholders about how they should present themselves to the public through the media.

Education   Universities, colleges and school districts often hire public relations people to promote these educational institutions and to handle press attention from the consequences of decisions that educators make.

Nonprofit Organizations   This includes hospitals, churches, museums and charities. PR for health and medical charities, such as the Race for the Cure run to raise money for breast cancer research, is growing especially fast as different charities compete with each other for donations.

Industry   AT&T's early use of public relations strategies was one type of industry PR. Many industries are government-regulated, so this often means that the industry PR person works with government agencies on government-related issues that affect the industry, such as utility rate increases or energy conservation programs.

Business   This is the best-known area of public relations. Large companies keep an in-house staff of public relations people, and these companies also often hire outside PR firms to help on special projects. Product publicity is one of the fastest-growing aspects of business-related public relations.

Within many large businesses are people who handle corporate PR, sometimes called financial PR. They prepare annual reports and gather financial data on the company for use by the press. They also may be assigned directly to the executives of a corporation to help establish policy about the corporation's public image. Many companies also sponsor charity events to increase their visibility in the community.

Athletic Teams and Entertainment Organizations   A professional sports team needs someone to travel with them and handle the press requests that inevitably come at each stop. Sports information people also are responsible for the coaches', the owner's and the team's relationship with the fans. College and university sports departments often hire public relations people to handle inquiries from the public and from the press.

In 1939, Henry Rogers learned how to use press agentry to gather publicity for Rita Hayworth (see page XXX). Today, entertainment public relations agencies promote movies and also handle TV personalities and well-known athletes who appear on the lecture circuit.

International   As the nation's consumer market broadens, more attention is being given to developing business in other countries. This means more opportunities in international PR. Hill & Knowlton and Burson-Marsteller, for example, are two big U.S. public relations firms that now operate in Japan.

▶ What Do Public Relations People Do?

Responsibilities of PR people include the following (for some insight on how public relations people make use of modern technology, see Impact/Culture: "Cybersmear: Negative PR Spreads Quickly on the Web," p. 237):

Writing   News releases, newsletters, correspondence, reports, speeches, booklet texts, radio and TV copy, film scripts, trade paper and magazine articles, institutional advertisements, product information and technical materials.

In Washington, D.C., with the Washington Monument in the background, participants in the 9th annual National Race for the Cure run and walk past the Museum of American History. The race, which raises funds for breast cancer research, education and treatment programs, is an example of a nonprofit event that uses public relations techniques.

AP/Wide World Photos

Editing   Special publications, employee newsletters, shareholder reports and other communications for employees and for the public.

Media Relations and Placement

Contacting news media, magazines, Sunday supplements, freelance writers and trade publications with the intent of getting them to publish or broadcast news and features about, or originated by, the organization. Responding to media requests for information or spokespersons.

Special Events   Arranging and managing press conferences, convention exhibits, open houses, anniversary celebrations, fund-raising events, special observances, contests and award programs.

Speaking   Appearing before groups and arranging platforms for others before appropriate audiences by managing a speaker's bureau.

Production   Creating art, photography and layout for brochures, booklets, reports, institutional advertisements and periodicals; recording and editing audio- and videotapes; preparing audiovisual presentations.

Research   Gathering data to help an organization plan programs; monitoring the effectiveness of public relations programs. This is a fast-growing area of public relations that includes focus groups to test message concepts; research to target specific audiences; surveys of a company's reputation for use in improving the company's image; employee and public attitude surveys; and shareholder surveys to improve relations with investors.

Programming and Counseling   Establishing a program for effective public relations within the company.

Training   Working with executives and other people within the organization to prepare them to deal with the media.

Management   Overseeing the costs of running the public relations program; paying the bills.

▶ Public Relations and the Media

Public relations work often means finding ways to attract the attention of the press. Says Seymour Topping, managing editor of *The New York Times*: "PR people do influence the news, but really more in a functional manner rather than in terms of giving new editorial direction. We get hundreds of press releases every day in each of our departments. We screen them very carefully for legitimate news, and very often there are legitimate news stories. Quite a lot of our business stories originate from press releases. It's impossible for us to cover all of these organizations ourselves."

People in public relations provide **publicity**, which creates events and presents information so the press and the public will pay attention. Publicity and advertising differ: An *advertising* message *is paid for; publicity is free*. Advertising is a *controlled* use of media, because the person or company that places

Publicity   Uncontrolled use of media by a public relations firm to create events and present information to capture press and public attention.

Cybersmear: Negative PR Spreads Quickly on the Web

by G. A. Andy Marken

In the pre-Internet days we used to say that a satisfied customer will tell one or two prospects but a dissatisfied customer will tell 10 or more. With the Internet and Web those same dissatisfied customers can tell millions of people . . . and they're doing it every day around the globe.

Don't take our word for it. Get on the Web. Go to your favorite search engine and look for Anti-Disney, Anti-McDonald's, Anti-Ford, Anti-Gun Regulation, Anti-Microsoft, Anti-AT&T, Anti-BofA, Anti-Judaism (or any race, religion or orientation), Anti-(company name) and Anti-(product name).

You'll find a range of sites from highly polished to amateurish Web pages waging a war of words against individual companies, products, services and concepts.

As if the individual Web sites weren't bad enough, there are thousands of online forums, mailing lists, chat rooms, discussion groups and Usenet groups gathering on the Internet every day.

When these virtual groups gather, people exchange positive and negative information, rumors, misinformation and even disinformation about companies, products and even individuals.

It's a tedious task but any organization that isn't monitoring Internet traffic and Web activity could find itself in serious trouble because of the slanted, malicious and downright libelous information. In short, they could suddenly have a nightmare on their hands.

Companies and agencies spend hundreds and thousands of dollars on audio, video and print clipping services to analyze how their messages are being picked up, interpreted and used by the conventional media.

They spend little or no time or effort finding out what people are saying in real-time in cyberspace about them. . . . What you don't hear can hurt you . . . and it could be fatal.

Source: *Public Relation Quarterly*, Spring 1998, 43(1), p. 31(3). Reprinted by permission.

the ad governs the message and where it will appear. *Publicity* is considered an *uncontrolled* use of the media, because the public relations person provides information to the press but has no control over how the information will appear—the press writes the story. "We know how the media work," says David Resnicow of the PR firm Ruder Finn & Rotman, "and we make judgments on that, providing access to events as it becomes necessary."

It is precisely because people in the media and people in PR know how each other work that they argue about the role of public relations in the news. The *Columbia Journalism Review* studied the relationship between corporate public relations and *The Wall Street Journal* by examining the stories in the *Journal* on a specific day and comparing the stories to press releases issued by PR people.

Specific companies were mentioned in 111 articles. Nearly half the news stories in the *Journal* that day, *CJR* reported in its analysis, were based solely on press releases. In 32 of the stories that were based on press releases, reporters paraphrased the releases almost verbatim; in the 21 remaining cases, only a small amount of additional reporting had been done.

The *Journal's* executive director, Frederick Taylor, responded to *CJR's* analysis by saying, "Ninety percent of daily coverage is started by a company making an announcement for the record. We're relaying this information to our readers."

▶ Public Relations Professionalism

Clever ways to attract attention are trademarks of today's successful public relations professional. According to Jeff and Marie Blyskal, who interviewed hundreds of PR people for their book *PR: How the Public Relations Industry Writes the News*:

> At the highest level of the profession, PR people are low-key, candid, creative, knowledgeable, warm, witty, charming, friendly, personable, self-confident. The best ones communicate as well as or better than some of the best journalists today; they are true communications technicians. We have found few hollow shells of human beings, bereft of moral conviction and marching in step with whatever "orders" their clients or employers bark out. Many were genuinely excited about their profession; some were swell-headed; only a few harkened back to their journalism days to assure us they were really "okay."
>
> Then, too, we saw no cabals or international PR conspiracies to control the public's mind—though quietly controlling minds is, in fact, what PR people attempt to do on a case-by-case basis. PR people have chosen their profession, and most seem reasonably satisfied with being effective advocates for their clients. . . . Some will even admit that what they do is manipulation, but manipulation with a noble, higher goal in mind: defending or advancing the cause of their client. There are two sides to every story, goes the argument. They are, in a sense, the equivalent of attorneys in the court of public opinion.

▶ Technology Transforms the Future

Like the future of advertising, the future of public relations is tied closely to the future of the media industries. The basic structure of the business will not change, but public relations practitioners will find themselves facing the same challenges as people in the advertising business.

Growing international markets will mean that, in the future, many U.S. public relations firms will expand overseas. Global communications will mean that public relations agencies will work internationally on some projects, and the agencies will have to adjust to the cultural differences that global exposure brings.

New technologies, especially the Internet, mean new ways to deliver public relations messages. Eventually, satellite technology will streamline all print, audio and video, giving PR agencies the same access to distributing information to news organizations that the news organizations now possess themselves.

As in the advertising industry, shifting demographic patterns mean growing potential markets for public relations services.

◀ Media | Review

Ken James/Getty Images

History

▶ Modern public relations emerged at the beginning of the 20th century as a way for business to respond to the muckrakers and to Theodore Roosevelt's antitrust campaign.

▶ The first publicity firm in the U.S., called The Publicity Bureau, opened in Boston in 1900.

▶ The best-known practitioner of early public relations was Ivy Lee, who wrote a "Declaration of Principles" to respond to the secret publicity activities of The Publicity Bureau.

▶ The Chicago Edison Company and American Telephone & Telegraph were the first companies to begin in-house promotional programs.

▶ The Committee on Public Information, headed by George Creel, promoted the war effort during World War I.

▶ The Office of War Information, headed by newscaster Elmer Davis, promoted the country's efforts during World War II.

▶ Edward L. Bernays wrote the first book on public relations, *Crystallizing Public Opinion*.

▶ Both Edward L. Bernays and Ivy Lee each have been called the father of public relations.

▶ Franklin Roosevelt, assisted by public relations expert Louis McHenry Howe, successfully used public relations to promote the New Deal.

▶ Among the pioneering women who joined the public relations business were Doris E. Fleischman, Leone Baxter and Anne Williams Wheaton.

▶ Doris Fleischman and Edward L. Bernays were equal partners in the Bernays public relations firm.

▶ Doris Fleischman was an early advocate of public relations as a career for women.

▶ The Public Relations Society established the profession's first code of ethics in 1954.

Technology

▶ New technologies, especially the Internet, mean new ways to deliver public relations messages.

▶ Electronic technology is beginning to streamline print, audio and video delivery, giving PR the same access to information distribution as news organizations.

▶ Negative PR can spread very quickly on the Web, where anyone is free to post damaging comments about a company, organization or product.

▶ Companies and agencies must be continually vigilant to monitor how their messages are being used and interpreted on the Internet.

Business

▶ Public relations expanded quickly in the 1960s and 1970s to accommodate television, the federal government and corporate America.

▶ Today, 161,000 people work in public relations nationwide. More than 4,000 firms offer PR-related services.

▶ The main difference between advertising and public relations is that advertising messages are controlled and public relations messages are uncontrolled.

▶ The trademark of today's public relations is a sophisticated approach to news.

▶ Growing international markets mean that many U.S. public relations firms have expanded overseas.

▶ Global communications mean many public relations agencies work internationally on some projects and must adjust to cultural differences that global exposure brings.

Culture

▶ Public relations people work in government, education, industry, business, nonprofit agencies, athletic teams, entertainment companies and international business.

▶ Public relations people use persuasion and publicity to attract attention for their clients.

▶ People who work in public relations have been called "attorneys in the court of public opinion."

▶ Shifting demographic patterns mean growing potential markets for public relations services.

▶ During the Iraq war, the Bush administration used a three-part public relations strategy to promote American involvement: 1. Repeatedly used key phrases. 2. Allowed "embedded" reporters and photographers with invading troops. 3. Created and promoted a "theme of the day."

Impact | Interactive

The Impact/Interactive CD-ROM that accompanies this text is your gateway to many electronic resources for broadening and testing your critical understanding of the material in Chapter 11. The CD-ROM features the following interactive elements for this and every chapter in the book.

▶ A two- to three-minute timely, high-interest CNN Today video clip with critical viewing questions and a link to relevant selections available within the InfoTrac College Edition database

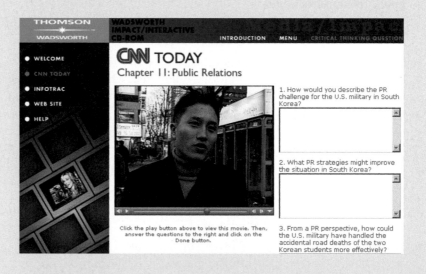

▶ Chapter-specific activities such as personal inventories and media projects

▶ A link to the *Media/Impact* Web site that offers helpful information and many additional electronic learning resources including

• An interactive chapter outline and study guide

• Interactive glossary term flashcards and crossword puzzles, concept animations, Internet activities and practice quizzes

• Live links for all URLs given in the chapter so you can easily access the additional information each site offers

▶ A link to InfoTrac College Edition—our online database of more than a million articles representing cutting-edge research and the latest headlines. Updated daily, this online library is available 24 hours a day, seven days a week. The InfoTrac College Edition activities provided below are designed to help you use this valuable resource.

▶ Working the Web

Live links for all of the sites listed below are provided on the *Media/Impact* book companion Web site, which can be accessed through your Impact/Interactive CD-ROM.

- ▶ **Institute for Public Relations (public relations research)**
  www.instituteforpr.com

- ▶ **Institute of Public Relations (association of European public relations professionals)**
  www.ipr.org.uk

- ▶ **Online Public Relations**
  www.online-pr.com

- ▶ **Public Relations Society of America**
  www.prsa.org

- ▶ **Public Relations Student Society of America**
  www.prssa.org

▶ InfoTrac College Edition Activities

Using InfoTrac College Edition's online database of full-text articles and abstracts, do the following activities as directed by your instructor. The database can be accessed through your Impact/Interactive CD-ROM.

1. Read "Impact/Business: Wal-Mart on PR Offensive to Repair Image" in Chapter 11. Then using InfoTrac College Edition with the keywords "corporate public relations products," or "Wal-Mart public relations," look up at least two articles on the subject. Then print the articles and either:

   a. write a brief paper on your findings, or

   b. bring the articles to class for a small-group discussion.

2. The moral and ethical aspects of public relations are often debated. Use the keywords "public relations ethics" to find at least three articles on the subject. Print the articles and either:

   a. write a brief paper on your findings, or

   b. bring the articles to class for a small-group discussion.

3. Using InfoTrac College Edition and the keywords "crisis public relations," find several articles on both crisis public relations and specific crisis situations. Synthesize your ideas about which public relations principles and practices are best to handle a crisis. Outline your findings in a brief paper and be prepared to discuss crisis public relations in class.

4. Consider a major U.S. corporation's public relations—"Disney public relations" or "Microsoft pubic relations" or "Procter and Gamble public relations," for example. Using InfoTrac College Edition, find at least three articles about that corporation's public image or strategies. Print the articles and either:

   a. write a brief paper on your findings, or

   b. bring the articles to class for a small-group discussion.

5. Read "Impact/Culture: Negative PR Spreads Quickly on the Web" in Chapter 11. Use the keywords "public relations Internet" or "Internet public relations," and search for other examples of three other ways the Internet is revolutionizing public relations. Print the articles and either:

   a. write a brief paper on your findings, or

   b. bring the articles to class for a small-group discussion.

CHAPTER 12

What's Ahead

> "*News is part of our communal experience . . . a public service. Surely a news operation should be the crown jewel of any corporation . . . the thing that makes a corporation feel good about itself.*"
>
> Christiane Amanpour, CNN's Chief International Correspondent

Because the First Amendment to the U.S. Constitution prescribes freedom of the press, it is important to understand the development of news reporting in this country. Today's news delivery is the result of a tug of war between audiences as they define the types of news they want and the news media who try to deliver it.

▶ A History of Independence

Publick Occurrences, the nation's first newspaper, published only one issue in 1690 before the authorities shut it down. The nation's first *consecutively issued* newspaper (published more than once) was the *Boston News-Letter,* which appeared in 1704. In the first issue, editor John Campbell reprinted the queen's latest speech, some maritime news and one advertisement telling people how to put an ad in his paper.

From 1704 until the Civil War, newspapers spread throughout New England, the South and across the frontier. The invention of the telegraph, in 1844, meant news that once took weeks to reach publication could be transmitted in minutes.

Monica Almeida/The New York Times

Today the public's appetite for news means there are more news outlets gathering more types of news than ever before.

Cooperative News Gathering
Member news organizations share the expense of getting the news.

▶ Cooperative and For-Profit News Gathering

In 1848, six newspapers in New York City decided to share the cost of gathering foreign news by telegraph from Boston. Henry J. Raymond, who owned *The New York Times*, drew up the agreement among the papers to pay $100 for 3,000 words of telegraph news.

Soon known as the New York Associated Press, this organization was the country's first **cooperative news gathering** association. This meant the member organizations shared the expense to get the news, returning any profits to the members. Today's Associated Press (AP) is the result of this early partnership, as newspapers joined together in a cooperative, with several members sharing the cost of gathering the news, domestic and foreign.

United Press, founded in 1884 to compete with AP, devised a different way of sharing information. The United Press (which eventually became United Press International (UPI) was established not as a cooperative but as a privately owned, for-profit wire service. (Today wire services are called news services.)

Using satellites and computer terminals instead of the original telegraph machines, cooperative and for-profit news gathering by news services has become virtually instantaneous. Most American newspapers and broadcast news operations subscribe to at least one news service, such as AP. Many other news services send stories and broadcasts worldwide: Agence France-Presse (France), Reuters (Great Britain), the Russian Information Telegraph Agency (RITA), Agenzia-Nationale Stampa Associate (Italy), Deutsche Presse Agentur (Germany) and Xinhua (China).

The news services especially help small newspapers and broadcast stations that can't afford overseas correspondents. Large dailies with their own correspondents around the world still rely on news services when they can't get to a story quickly.

AP today is still a cooperative, as it was when it began in New York. UPI had several owners and declined financially. Today, Associated Press serves as the nation's primary news service, constantly feeding stories to newspapers, broadcast outlets and Internet news services.

Some newspaper organizations in the United States—*The New York Times*, *The Washington Post* and *Chicago Tribune*—also run their own news services. Subscribers publish each other's news service stories. For many newspapers, news service stories provide information at a relatively low cost because the newspaper doesn't need as many staff reporters to cover the news.

▶ Accreditation and Photojournalism

In the 1860s, interest in the emotional issues of the Civil War sent many reporters to the battlefront. Hundreds of correspondents roamed freely among the soldiers, reporting for the North and the South. Two important results of Civil War reporting were the accreditation of reporters and the introduction of photographs to enhance written reports.

Government Accredits Journalists   The issue of government interests versus press freedom surfaced early in the Civil War. In 1861, Union General Winfield Scott forbade telegraph companies from transmitting military information because he was afraid some stories would help the South.

At the Battle of Bull Run in 1861, *New York Times* editor Henry J. Raymond, reporting the war from the front, mistakenly telegraphed a story that said the North had won. When he followed up with the correct story, military censors blocked the news, arguing the information should be kept secret.

New Attitudes, Tools and Techniques Change Journalism's Landscape

A sharply increased appetite for dialogue between newspapers and their readers is dramatically altering the level of interactivity between news suppliers and news consumers, an unprecedented survey of U.S. newspapers reveals.

Substantial changes in the form and substance of news, the nature of news gathering and the very mission of newspapers were reported by senior editors of 70 percent of the nation's 512 newspapers with daily circulations of 20,000 or more.

The survey reveals that nine out of ten editors believe that the future health of the newspaper industry depends on more interactions with readers—not less. Changes in the technology and the geography of journalism and in what editors perceive as topics of interest to their readers are fueling these trends.

A majority of newspaper editors report that they are covering more school districts and towns or townships than they were a decade ago. They indicate that their reporters are devoting more time to covering education and less to covering government meetings.

In looking for ways to foster greater interaction:

· Eight out of ten newspapers represented in the study provide readers with one or more options for obtaining the e-mail addresses of reporters.

· Nearly eight out of ten have established e-mail, voice-mail or Web site tip lines.

· More than seven out of ten newspapers offer readers one or more avenues other than letters to the editor for publishing their own ideas.

· More than four out of ten publish the telephone numbers of the reporters with every story, and more than one-quarter post some or all of their reporters' telephone numbers on a Web site.

· Fifty-six percent have convened conversations about a key community issue outside of the newsroom.

Nevertheless, more than seven out of ten editors feel dissatisfied with the current level of newsroom-reader interaction.

Campaign Study Group, Springfield, Va. A study conducted for Associated Press Managing Editors, Pew Center for Civic Journalism, and National Conference of Editorial Writers.

© John Neubauer/PhotoEdit

A survey of newspaper editors revealed that the future health of the industry depends on more interactions with readers.

Then General William T. Sherman ordered *New York Herald* correspondent Thomas E. Knox arrested and held as a spy for sending sensitive military information.

President Lincoln intervened to reach a compromise that would balance the needs of the press with the needs of the nation through a process called **accreditation**. This meant that the federal government certified members of the press to cover the war. Accredited journalists were required to carry press passes issued by the military. The practice of accreditation continues today as the government's method of certifying war-reporting journalists. This concept of accreditation—that a journalist was someone who could be credentialed— served to add to a sense of professionalism among journalists.

Accreditation The process by which the government certifies members of the press to cover government-related news events.

Mathew Brady's photojournalism during the Civil War created a standard for future photojournalists to follow—using images to help capture a story.

Photojournalism Using photographs to accompany text to capture a news story.

The Birth of Photojournalism   Also at the Battle of Bull Run was photographer Mathew Brady, who convinced President Lincoln that a complete photographic record of the war should be made. Until the Civil War, photography had been confined primarily to studio portraits because of the cumbersome equipment and slow chemical processing.

Brady photographed the battles of Antietam and Fredericksburg and sent photographic teams to other battles. Newspapers did not yet have a method to reproduce the photographs, but Brady's pictures were published in magazines, making Brady the nation's first news photographer. His 3,500 photographs demonstrated the practicality and effectiveness of using photographs to help report a news story, although newspaper photographs did not become widely used until the early 1900s.

The marriage of photographs and text to tell a better story than either text or photographs could tell alone formed the beginnings of today's concept of **photojournalism.** It was photojournalism that made *Life Magazine*, founded by *Time's* Henry Luce, such a success and created stars out of gifted photographers like Margaret Bourke-White. The perfect image to accompany the words—the best photojournalism—has become an essential part of any good journalistic news story.

▶ Tabloid News Takes Over

The beginning of the 20th century brought the expansion of newspapers—New York City once had more than ten daily newspapers—and intensified competition. The introduction of the penny papers meant newspapers had to grab a bigger audience to survive. And, as described in Chapter 3, the race for readers ushered in yellow journalism—featuring stories about grisly crimes and illicit sex, often married to large, startling photographs.

Substantial newspapers, covering important stories, were publishing in places all over the country, but today people still think first about tabloid journalism when they talk about newspapers.

In the 1930s, people began to turn to radio for instant news headlines and information. Newspapers still flourished but, where they once had an exclusive corner on news, now newspapers and radio shared audiences. When World War II began, both radio and newspapers were in place to bring home news of the war.

▶ Newsreels Bring Distant Events to American Movie Audiences

Beginning at the turn of the 20th century and lasting until television took over news coverage, movie newsreels showed movie audiences distant locations and newsworthy events. Produced by companies including British Pathé (from 1900 until 1970) and by Fox Movietone News (between 1919 and 1960), newsreels were shown in movie theaters to audiences hungry for the pictures that radio couldn't provide.

Newsreels usually ran no longer than ten minutes, with running commentary by a narrator, and were updated every week. Because it took time to assemble the stories and develop the film, newsreel footage usually took a week or more after the events took place to reach audiences.

Photojournalist Margaret Bourke-White photographed stories for *Fortune* and *Time* magazines, establishing a 20th-century standard for photojournalism.

Movietone News offered the most popular newsreel in the United States, produced by Fox, using more than 1,000 camera operators who roamed the globe to cover the news each day. Besides serious news stories, the photographers captured Hollywood celebrities, scoured exotic travel locations and produced sports and feature stories. Another newsreel company, All-American News, produced newsreels directed at African American audiences and was often shown before feature movies in addition to, or instead of, Movietone newsreels.

Newsreels offered an important realistic glimpse at worldwide news and information events that audiences couldn't get anywhere else.

Before TV news existed, newsreels such as Movietone News were very popular with movie audiences. Shown in movie theaters before the main feature, newsreels brought home distant locations and newsworthy events.

▶ Radio Brings Audiences the Sounds of World War II

The most honored print journalist during World War II was journalist Ernie Pyle, who worked for the Scripps Howard news organization. His reporting, which focused on the men who were fighting the war rather than battles and casualty counts, reached deep into the emotions of people who were stateside waiting for word from the front. (See Impact/People, "Ernie Pyle: The War Correspondent Who Hated War.") But radio is the news medium that began to shine during World War II because radio news broadcasts meant people could hear the action as it was happening.

Imagine the date is September 8, 1940. World War II has begun its second year in Europe. You don't have a television set. You are sitting at home in the United States, listening to your radio. CBS announces a special bulletin from journalist Edward R. Murrow, reporting the first bombing of London: 626 bombers have pounded the city, leaving more than 1,000 people dead and 2,000 people injured. You and your family listen intently in your living room as Murrow describes:

> men with white scarves around their necks instead of collars . . . dull-eyed, empty-faced women . . . Most of them carried little cheap cardboard suitcases and sometimes bulging paper shopping bags. That was all they had left. . . .
>
> A row of automobiles with stretchers racked on the roofs like skis, standing outside of bombed buildings. A man pinned under wreckage where a broken gas main sears his arms and face. . . .
>
> . . . the courage of the people, the flash and roar of the guns rolling down streets . . . the stench of air-raid shelters in the poor districts.

This was radio news reporting at its best. For 26 years, from 1921 until the advent of television news in 1947, broadcast reporters like Murrow painted pictures with words. Radio reporters described Prohibition and its repeal, the stock market crash, the Depression, the election of Franklin D. Roosevelt, the New Deal, the bombings of London and Pearl Harbor, the Normandy invasion, Roosevelt's funeral and the signing of the armistice that ended World War II.

Most radio stations maintained their own radio news departments, until the advent of format radio. Today, very few radio stations maintain full-time news departments, and radio stations with news formats tend to be concentrated in the nation's big cities. Still, the heritage of colorful, exciting radio news formed the foundation for TV news, which began to blossom in the 1950s.

▶ The Golden Age of Television News

The first network TV newscasts in the 1950s were only 15 minutes long, but by the 1960s, TV network evening news had expanded to half an hour—the

Ernie Pyle: The War Correspondent Who Hated War

Ernie Pyle worked for Scripps Howard. Dam Thomasson, the editor of Scripps Howard News Service, wrote this reflection on Pyle's work to accompany a collection of Pyle's dispatches that was published in 1986.

The other day while going through some old files in our library, I came upon a yellowed and tattered dispatch.

It made me cry.

It was about the death of a Capt. Waskow during the Italian campaign of 1944. And it probably is the most powerful treatise on war and death and the human spirit I have ever read.

I took it out and had it treated and framed and I hung it in the office in a prominent position where now and then one of the younger reporters will come by and read it and try to hide the inevitable tear.

The man who wrote it, Ernest Taylor Pyle, is but a memory as distant as the war he covered so eloquently and ultimately died in.

But unlike so many who perished beside him, Pyle's contribution to what Studs Terkel calls "the last good war" remains with us in his work—thousands of words that will forever memorialize brave men and debunk the "glory" of war.

The column that says it best perhaps is the one drafted for the end of the fighting in Europe. It was found in his pocket by the foot soldiers who had risked their lives to retrieve his body on the Japanese island of Ie Shima in 1945.

"Those who were gone would not wish themselves to be a millstone of gloom around our necks.

AP/Wide World Photos

War correspondent Ernie Pyle (1890—1945), the most honored journalist in the United States, died during the last days of World War II on the Japanese island of Ie Shima.

"But there are many of the living who have burned into their brains forever the unnatural sight of cold dead men scattered over the hillsides and in the ditches along the high rows of hedge throughout the world.

"Dead men by mass production—in one country after another—month after month and year after year. Dead men in winter and dead men in summer.

"Dead men in such familiar promiscuity that they become monotonous.

"Dead men in such infinity that you come almost to hate them."

. . . When I was a kid starting out in this business, the trade magazines were full of job-seeking ads by those who claimed they could "write like Ernie Pyle." This was 10 years after his death and he was still everyone's model.

"Why They Still Write Ernie Pyle Books," *Honolulu Advertiser*, June 20, 1986, p. A-1. Reprinted by permission of Scripps Howard News Service.

same amount of time the networks dedicate to national news today. Radio news stars like Edward R. Murrow (see Impact/People, page 158) moved from radio to television news, and eventually the TV networks created large news departments with bureaus and correspondents spread throughout the United States and overseas.

AP/Wide World Photos

What has been called the Golden Age of Television News was the decade that began in 1961, with President John F. Kennedy's inauguration. The Kennedy family was very photogenic, and they invited press coverage. Kennedy's victory as president, in fact, had been credited to his on-camera presence during the Kennedy-Nixon debates in 1960. So it was fitting that Kennedy would be the first president to play Cold War brinkmanship on television, when TV news grew to become a part of politics, not just a chronicler of political events.

TV and the Cold War   President Kennedy asked all three networks to clear him time on Monday, October 1962, at 7 P.M. Eastern time. The president had learned that missile sites were being built in Cuba with Russian help.

Kennedy used television to deliver his ultimatum to dismantle the missile bases. "Using the word 'nuclear' 11 times, Kennedy drew a panorama of devastation enveloping the whole hemisphere," according to media historian Eric Barnouw. "The moves that had made such things possible, said Kennedy, could not be accepted by the United States 'if our courage and our commitments are ever to be trusted again by either friend or foe.'"

Kennedy admonished Russian Premier Nikita Kruschev and urged him to stop the ships the Soviet Union was sending to Cuba to help build the missile sites. Faced with such a visible challenge, the Soviet Union turned its ships around in the Atlantic and sent conciliatory messages in order to reach a settlement. The Cuban missile crisis had in fact been a carefully constructed live television drama, in which Kennedy performed well.

Television news provided a sense of collective national experience covering the events that followed the assassination of President Kennedy. Here, Vice President Johnson is sworn in as president aboard *Air Force One*.

TV News As a Window on the World   In 1963, television news was forced into an unexpected role as it conveyed a sense of collective national grief following President Kennedy's assassination. For four days beginning at 1:30 P.M. Eastern time on Friday, November 22, 1963, the country witnessed the aftermath of the assassination of the president.

Vice President Lyndon Johnson was sworn in as president on television. On Saturday, TV viewers watched the world's diplomats arrive for the funeral. On Sunday, they watched the first murder ever broadcast live on television, as Jack Ruby killed assassination suspect Lee Harvey Oswald. Then, on Monday came the president's funeral.

As many as nine out of ten television sets were turned on during the marathon events surrounding the president's funeral. The networks canceled all commercials. "Some television employees had slept as little as six hours in three nights," wrote television historian Eric Barnouw. "They went on, almost welcoming the absorption in the task at hand."

The network news broadcasts during the events surrounding the Kennedy assassination were called television's finest four days. Television had become the nation's "window on the world," wrote Barnouw. "The view it offered seemed to be *the* world. They trusted its validity and completeness."

▶ Graphic War Coverage in Vietnam

The longest-running protest program in the nation's history began appearing on television news as anti–Vietnam War marchers showed up on camera daily in the late 1960s. During live coverage of the Chicago Democratic Convention in 1968, demonstrators faced police in a march toward the convention hall. Television covered the resulting violence, which caused injuries to hundreds of protesters and to 21 reporters and photographers.

Graphic TV coverage of the Vietnam War shook American viewers as no previous war coverage had. It also gave them an appetite for live news coverage—instant information about events as they were happening.

"When the war in Vietnam began to escalate in 1965," wrote TV critic Jeff Greenfield, "it was the television networks, covering the war with few official restrictions, that brought to American homes pictures of the face of war that had never been shown before: not friendly troops welcomed by the populace, but troops setting fire to villages with cigarette lighters; troops cutting off the ears of dead combat foes; allies spending American tax money for personal gain."

Candid reporting from the war itself shook viewers as previous war reporting never had, but it also gave Americans an appetite for news and for live news coverage—instant information about events as they were happening.

▶ Watergate Hearings Reveal Politics at Work

In 1973, live television news took another leap with the continuing broadcast of the U.S. Senate's Watergate hearings to investigate allegedly illegal activities of the Republican Committee to Re-elect the President (CREEP). A parade of government witnesses and political appointees fascinated viewers with descriptions of the inner workings of the Nixon presidency.

According to media scholars Christopher Sterling and John Kittross, "Running from May through August 1973, and chaired by North Carolina's crusty Sam Ervin, these hearings were a fascinating live exposition of the political process in America, and were "must" television watching as a parade of witnesses told—or evaded telling—what they knew of the broad conspiracy to assure the reelection of Nixon and then to cover up the conspiracy itself."

For more than a year the political drama continued to unfold on television's nightly news. Ultimately, the Judiciary Committee of the House of Representatives began a televised debate on whether to impeach the president. For the first time in its history, the nation faced the prospect of seeing a president brought to trial live on national television. On August 8, 1974, President Nixon brought the crisis to an end by announcing his resignation—on television.

▶ TV News Expands and Contracts

Because viewers were hungry for news, and wanted to *watch* it, local TV news operations expanded—some stations offering as much as two hours of local news plus the national news broadcasts. Throughout the 1970s and 1980s, networks and local news departments expanded. Then came broadcast deregulation in the 1980s, the networks were sold and consolidated, and local stations, many of which had been locally owned, became pieces of larger corporations.

In 1980, Ted Turner founded Cable News Network (CNN), which offered round-the-clock news on cable. CNN established overseas bureaus and the concept that all-news-all-the-time would grab an audience. Audiences responded, and CNN became an alternative to network news, often the first place audiences turned whenever there was a crucial international story that required constant updating.

In general, however, in the 1990s, the American public read fewer newspapers and watched less news on television. Network and local TV news audiences declined. News departments began to shrink. Soon, another medium

At the Watergate Hearings in 1973, viewers took a look inside the Nixon presidency as North Cartolina's Senator Sam Ervin questioned witnesses. Nixon resigned in 1974.

▶ **Impact | People**

Christiane Amanpour Criticizes TV News

Christiane Amanpour, CNN's Chief International Correspondent, has covered many international conflicts, including the War in Bosnia and the War in Afghanistan. At the annual convention of the Radio-Television News Directors in 2000, Amanpour criticized the state of TV news today. This is an excerpt from the speech she delivered.

Perhaps all of you are raking in the profits . . . but let me throw down a challenge: What's the point of having all this money if we are simply going to drive ourselves into the ground? Makes you wonder about all those mega-mergers. Yes, you are running businesses but surely there is a level beyond which profit from news is simply indecent.

We live in a society after all, not a marketplace. News is part of our com-munal experience . . . a public service. Surely a news operation should be the crown jewel of any corporation . . . the thing that makes a corporation feel good about itself. We all love *Million-aire,* make your money off that . . . make your super dollars somewhere else. Leave us alone, with only good competitive journalism as our benchmark. . . .

No matter what the hocus-pocus focus groups tell you, time has proven that all the gimmicks and cheap jour-nalism can only carry you so far. Remember the movie *Field of Dreams* when the voice said, "Build it and they will come?" Well, tell a compelling story and they will watch.

Christiane Amanpour, Chief International Correspondent, CNN, says TV news executives should remember that news is a public service and responsibility.

replaced the public's seemingly insatiable need for instant news and information—the Internet.

▶ Iraq War Produces the First "Embedded" Reporters

Since the Vietnam War, access to battlefield locations has been a battle between the press' aggressive need-to-know and the military's need-to-keep secret. (See Chapter 14, Government Attempts to Restrict Press Freedom, p. 290.) In 2003, military-press relations took a new turn when the United States declared war on Iraq.

Before the battles began, the U.S. military announced a plan to **"embed"** more than 600 reporters with American troops. Embedding offered the reporters access to the frontlines, but also kept the reporters within the military's control. Still, it was a reversal of past Pentagon policymakers, who often had sought to keep the press far from military operations.

CNN and the major television networks offered nonstop coverage in the early days of the war, and people watched. "A lot of people have been surprised at the access and cooperation we've had in the field," said Tony Maddox, Senior Vice President Europe, Middle East and Africa for CNN International. "It's produced some remarkable images."

Ted Turner founded CNN in 1980, offering round-the-clock news on cable. CNN established overseas bureaus and the concept that all-news-all-the-time would grab an audience.

My Week at Embed Boot Camp

by Andrew Jacobs

For a week in early February [2003], a flabby brigade of 57 reporters, photographers and network talking heads (9 of them women) gathered at the Quantico Marine Corps training base in Virginia, where we learned how to improve our chances of surviving a war with Iraq. As prospective embeds—journalists planted among America's fighting forces—we were given a crash course in all things military. . . .

Clearly, there is a measure of self-interest at work here: old-fashioned public relations. The Pentagon's newfound cooperative spirit was prompted, in part, by media criticism of restrictions during previous engagements, including the war in Afghanistan, when a group of correspondents were locked in a warehouse and prevented from reporting on a "friendly fire" attack that left a number of American troops wounded. Military officials have said that battlefield dis-

Spencer Platt/Getty Images

During the Iraq War the Pentagon "embedded" more than 600 reporters with American troops. Reporters prepared for Iraq duty by attending boot camp.

patches will not be censored, a departure from many past conflicts, but reporters will be expected to omit place names or troop numbers if such information compromises the secrecy of an operation. "We're pushing the envelope here," Col. Jay DeFrank, the Pentagon's director of press operations, said. . . .

In the end, many of my colleagues said that the potential glories of covering war outweighed the prospect of ending up a statistic. During a question-and-answer session with Pentagon press officials, the give and take was all about access and censorship. No one voiced concern for personal safety. Over the course of the week, many cited the vaunted writings of Ernie Pyle, the World War II correspondent whose dispatches from Normandy, Sicily, Okinawa and Tunisia have become legendary. Then there were others, like myself, who could not ignore one key fact about Pyle: he never made it back home.

New York Times Magazine, March 2, 2003, 34–36.

Embedded During the Iraq War, a term used to describe journalists who were allowed to cover the war on the frontlines with the U.S. military.

► News on the Internet

Today, the Internet is a nonstop news and information machine. Anyone with access to the Internet can choose the sources and subjects to investigate. America Online (AOL), with the nation's largest number of online subscribers, compiles headlines from television and print news outlets—photos and stories from CBS, Associated Press and *The New York Times*—as well as updated headline stories from magazines like *Time* and *Business Week*. For specialty information, and for more background, you can visit any corporate, association or nonprofit organization Web site without leaving your chair.

Not only can you choose what to look for, but also *when* you look. The Internet is available on your schedule—independent of any TV network or local broadcast time schedule. News rotates through CNN Headline News at 15-minute intervals, but you can log on to your computer and find just about anything you want to know—sports scores, the weather, international headlines—whenever you want to know it.

The Internet, unlike any other form of news and information delivery, is completely self-directed news and information—targeted to individual needs. The Internet also is the place where people can get all the news in one location that they previously had to gather from several different sources.

Impact | Audience

Illustration 12.1
Broadcast News versus Online News

Broadcast news viewership has declined sharply since 1995, while online news use has increased.

The Pew Research Center for People and the Press, 2001.

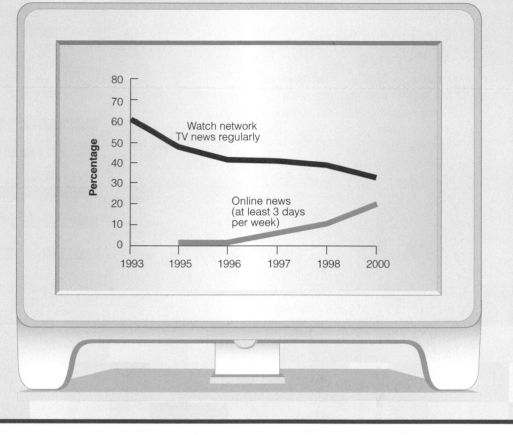

Critical Question

How much do you use the Internet to get news? Do you use news services' E-mail updates about topics that interest you? Would you rely (or have you relied) on an Internet news source whose print counterpart you'd never seen? Why or why not?

Internet Replacing Broadcast News   According to the most recent study from the Pew Research Center, Internet news is attracting large segments of the national audience. At the same time, many people are losing the news habit, according to the study. They pay attention to the news only when something important happens, and many watch broadcast news with the remote control nearby to skip uninteresting stories and move on to something they want to watch.

One in three Americans goes online for news at least once a week (compared to one in five in 1996), and 20 percent say they receive daily news reports from the Internet (compared to 6 percent in 1996). At the same time, network news viewership has dropped from 38 percent to 30 percent during the same period, and local news viewership fell from 64 percent to 56 percent. (See **Illustration 12.1**.) In general, the study also found that people who are interested in the news and go online tend to watch less network TV news.

Other important findings of the Pew study were:

- As large numbers of younger Americans turn to the Internet for news, the audience for traditional media is aging. Nearly half of those under

Illustration 12.2
Patterns of News Use by Age

Older Americans are more likely to watch TV news regularly, while people under 30 turn to the Internet for news.

The Pew Research Center.

	30 & under %	30–49 %	50 & older %	Overall average %
Goes online	74	62	33	54
Goes online at least once a week for news	46	37	20	33
Online daily for news	17	18	10	15
Watched TV news yesterday	44	51	67	55
Read newspaper yesterday	29	43	58	46

age 30 (46 percent) go online for news at least once a week, but older Americans are far more likely to say they watched TV news (67 percent) or read a paper yesterday. (See **Illustration 12.2**.)

- More than half (53 percent) of those surveyed say they would like to have more time to follow the news. Working women, in particular, say they don't have enough time to follow the news.

- Three-quarters of viewers under age 30 say they watch broadcast news with the remote control.

- Men are more likely to pursue online news about technology, while women look for news on science and health. The top news subject for both men and women, however, is the weather.

▶ A News Evolution?

This evolution in people's news habits has taken nearly a century and required several technological innovations. From print to radio to television to the Internet, as each new system of delivery emerged, the old systems still stayed in place.

This means that today there's more news available from more news sources, delivered using more types of technology, than ever before. People can select the information they want, when they want it. The news business is becoming even more competitive because consumers now have many sources—local, national and international—to research what they want and need to know.

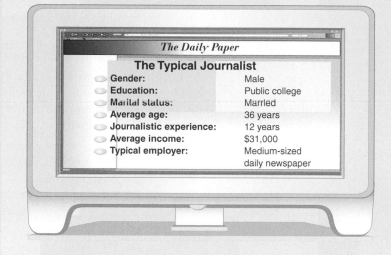

Illustration 12.3
The Typical Journalist

According to Weaver and Wilhoit's 1996 study, the typical journalist is a married 30-year-old, college-educated male.

David H. Weaver and G. Cleveland Wilhoit, *The American Journalist in the 1990s.*

The Daily Paper

The Typical Journalist

Gender:	Male
Education:	Public college
Marital status:	Married
Average age:	36 years
Journalistic experience:	12 years
Average income:	$31,000
Typical employer:	Medium-sized daily newspaper

▶ Press Performance: How Well Do Journalists Do Their Jobs?

To understand how well the press performs, you must first understand who journalists are and how they work. Then you can examine how the public feels about the way members of the press do their job.

One study of who journalists are comes from *The American Journalist in the 1990s,* by David H. Weaver and G. Cleveland Wilhoit, published in 1996. Weaver and Wilhoit surveyed 1,400 American journalists about their jobs. According to Weaver and Wilhoit, today's typical journalist "is a white Protestant male who has a bachelor's degree from a public college, is married, 36 years old, earns about $31,000 a year, has worked in journalism about 12 years, does not belong to a journalism association, and works for a medium-sized (42 journalists), group-owned daily newspaper."

Weaver and Wilhoit cautioned, however, that this typical portrait is misleading because there are:

AP/Wide World Photos

substantial numbers of women, non-Whites, non-Protestant, single, young and old, and relatively rich and poor journalists working in this country for a wide variety of small and large news media, both group and singly owned.

Many of these journalists differ from this profile of the typical journalist. For example, Black and Asian journalists are more likely to be women than men, not to be married, to have higher incomes ($37,000–$42,000) than the typical journalist, to have worked in journalism 10 or 11 years, to be members of at least one journalism association, and to work for larger (100–150 journalists) daily newspapers.

Getting the story faster and better than the competition are major factors influencing journalistic values.

Hispanic journalists are more likely to be Catholic than Protestant, and to be more similar to Blacks and Asians than to the "typical" U.S. journalist on other characteristics. Native American journalists are more likely to be of some other religion besides Protestant or Catholic, to make much less than the other groups (median income of $22,000) and to work for very small newspapers or television stations (3 or 4 journalists).

Following are some other important findings of the study:

1. **Employment growth stalls.** The substantial growth in the number of journalists working for the media that characterized the 1970s has stalled. The growth rate from 1982 to 1992 was 9 percent. Between 1971 and 1982, the growth rate was 60 percent.

2. **Minorities make some gains.** News organizations have made some progress in attracting minorities, despite the lack of growth in journalism jobs. The current minority news workforce of 8 percent is up from 4 percent in 1982–1983. . . . Recent hires are 12 percent minorities.

3. **Mixed gains for women.** In spite of more women being hired in the 1980s, they remain at the same workforce percentage as a decade ago: 34 percent. The problem may be one of retention, as well as poor job growth. Salary equity with men has improved.

4. **Abandoning ship.** A serious retention problem in journalism may be just over the horizon. More than 20 percent of those surveyed said they plan to leave the field within five years. That's twice the figure in 1982–1983. This is tied to a significant decline in job satisfaction, with complaints about pay and the need for a different challenge leading the list of major reasons for plans to leave journalism.

5. **Little shift in journalistic values.** Overall differences in ideas about journalistic roles and reporting practices are not great. . . . Two journalistic responsibilities seen as extremely important by a majority: getting information to the public quickly and investigating government claims.

6. **Some shift in political values.** More journalists now see themselves as Democrats (44.1 percent Democrat; 16.3 percent Republican; 34.4 percent Independent) than they did in 1982–1983, with Democratic Party allegiance strongest among women and minorities. However, journalists tend to regard their news organizations as more politically middle of the road than themselves.

It has not been shown in any comprehensive survey of news gathering that people with liberal or conservative values insert their personal ideology directly into their reporting or that the audience unquestioningly accepts one point of view. The belief in a causal relationship between the media and the audience's behavior is known as the **magic bullet theory**. This belief was disproved long ago.

But the assumption that journalists' personal beliefs directly influence their professional performance is common. Although the reporting by some journalists and columnists certainly can be cited to support this idea, the majority of journalists, says media scholar Herbert J. Gans, view themselves as detached observers of events.

Journalists, like everyone else, have values, [and] the two that matter most in the newsroom are getting the story and getting it better and faster than their prime competitors—both among their colleagues and at rival news media. Personal political beliefs are left at home, not only because journalists are trained to be objective and detached, but also because their credibility and their paychecks depend on their remaining detached. . . .

Magic Bullet Theory The assertion that media messages directly and measurably affect people's behavior.

The beliefs that actually make it into the news are professional values that are intrinsic to national journalism and that journalists learn on the job. However, the professional values that particularly antagonize conservatives (and liberals when they are in power) are neither liberal nor conservative but reformist, reflecting journalism's long adherence to good-government Progressivism.

"*Those are the headlines, and we'll be back in a moment to blow them out of proportion.*"

Some press critics, in fact, argue that journalists most often present establishment viewpoints and are unlikely to challenge prevailing political and social values. In addition, the pressure to come up with instant analyses of news events may lead to conformity in reporting—an unwillingness to think independently.

In mid-May 1989, for example, thousands of people gathered in China's Tiananmen Square to demonstrate against the Chinese government. Angered by the demonstrations, the government sent troops to clear the Square, and hundreds of people were killed and injured, most of them students.

In his analysis of the way the press reported on the violence, press critic David Shaw argued that journalists misread and misreported events as a pro-democracy uprising that could not be stopped. Shaw called this "**consensus journalism**"—the tendency among many journalists covering the same event to report similar conclusions about the event, rather than to report conflicting interpretations.

Consensus Journalism The tendency among many journalists covering the same event to report similar conclusions about the event.

▶ Journalists' News Values

News organizations often are criticized for presenting a consistently slanted view of the news. But as Weaver and Wilhoit observed, news values often are shaped by the way news organizations are structured and the routines they follow. The press in America, it is generally agreed, doesn't tell you what to think but does tell you what and whom to think *about*. This is called **agenda-setting**."

There are two types of agenda-setting: the flow of information from one news organization to another and the flow of information from news organizations to their audiences.

In the first type of agenda-setting, the stories that appear in the nation's widely circulated print media provide ideas to the other media. The print media, for example, often identify specific stories as important by giving them attention, so that widely circulated print media can set the news agenda on some national issues.

To analyze the second type of agenda-setting—the picture of the world that journalists give to their audiences—is to examine the social and cultural values that journalists present to the public. The most significant recent study of news values was offered by Herbert J. Gans in his book *Deciding What's News*.

Gans identified eight enduring values that emerged in his study of different types of news stories over a long period of time: **ethnocentrism** (the attitude that some cultural and social values are superior), altruistic democracy, responsible capitalism, small-town pastoralism, individualism, moderatism, order and leadership. These values, said Gans, often help define what is considered news.

Agenda-Setting The belief that journalists don't tell you *what* to think but do tell you *what to think about*.

Ethnocentrism The attitude that some cultural and social values are superior.

How the Iraq War Was Seen Overseas

by Susan Bennett

When U.S. tanks and troops rolled into Iraq and American warplanes pummeled Baghdad, readers and viewers around the world were bombarded with round-the-clock stories and images from the front lines of the world's latest war. Conflict may be the only common denominator in the storytelling.

While viewers in the U.S. were transfixed by technological gadgetry that put them atop invading tanks and alongside advancing soldiers, viewers from Germany to Indonesia to Egypt were getting decidedly different pictures of human suffering. As U.S. journalists filed tales of hardship among the American troops they were allowed to travel with, newspapers in the Middle east and Europe ran screaming headlines about the brutality of war and grisly pictures of Iraqis killed by U.S. bombs and guns.

It was the same war, but vastly divergent perspectives emerged in the media's presentation of events in Iraq, especially in countries where both populace and politicians vigorously opposed the war.

"It was presented as a different war in France and Germany," said Tom Patterson, a professor of government and press at the John F. Kennedy School of Government at Harvard. "The war coverage here was the combat war told from the American point of view, with emphasis heavily on military casualties. Over there was a lot more coverage of what it was like on the other side: how the Iraqi people were reacting, more coverage of the devastation of the bombing, and how Iraqi civilians were caught up in it."

World and I, July 2003, p. 62.

News in the United States conveys the ideas of:

Ethnocentrism. America is a nation to be valued above all others. "While the news contains many stories that are critical of domestic conditions, they are almost always treated as deviant cases, with the implication that American ideas, at least, remain viable," says Gans.

Altruistic democracy. Politics should be based on public service and the public interest. The news media expect all public officials to be scrupulously honest, efficient and public-spirited.

Responsible capitalism. Open competition will create increased prosperity for everyone. Business people should not seek unreasonable profits, and they should not exploit workers or customers.

Small-town pastoralism. Small agricultural or market towns are favored over other settlements. Suburbs are usually overlooked as a place where news happens. Big cities are viewed as places with "urban" problems.

Individualism. A heroic individual is someone who struggles against difficulties and powerful forces. Self-made people are admired.

Moderatism. Moderation is valued; excesses and extremism are not.

Order. Importance is placed on political order. Says Gans, "The values in the news derive largely from reformers and reform movements, which are themselves elites. Still, the news is not simply a compliant support of elites, or the establishment, or the ruling class; rather, it views nation and society through its own set of values and with its own conception of the good social order."

Leadership. Attention is focused on leaders. The president is seen as the nation's primary leader and protector of the national order.

These values exist throughout American society and, indeed, come from historical assumptions based in our culture. As Gans suggests, this news ideology both supports and reflects elements of the social order.

Illustration 12.4
Print Media Credibility

According to the latest study by the Pew Research Center, *The Wall Street Journal* ranked higher in credibility than other print news sources, including "your daily paper," while *People* and the *National Enquirer* rated the lowest.

Pew Research Center for The People & The Press. Used by permission.

Tuesday, April 30

| Rating (4 = most credible) | Believe | | | Cannot believe |
	4	3	2	1
Wall Street Journal	41	37	14	8
May, 1998	41	40	13	6
April, 1996	36	38	17	9
Time	29	41	22	8
May, 1998	27	47	21	5
Your Daily Paper	25	40	26	9
May, 1998	29	38	25	8
April, 1996	25	39	37	8
People	10	24	40	26
May, 1998	10	27	43	20
National Enquirer	4	4	10	82
May, 1998	3	4	13	80

12   13

▶ Blurring Distinctions: News, Reality Shows and Advertising

Today's TV reality shows, such as *Survivor*, *Real Stories of the Highway Patrol*, and *America's Most Wanted* are blurring the distinction between what is news and what is re-created drama. These shows portray events and use interviews with crime victims and reenactments of events in a documentary style that imitates news stories. These reality shows, or docudramas, can make it difficult for an audience to distinguish true news footage when they see it.

"Infomercials"—programs that pretend to give viewers information but that are really advertisements for the sponsors' products—also are making it harder to discern what is reporting and what is advertising. The line between news and entertainment on television becomes even more tricky when advertisers produce programs that look like news but are really advertisements.

"My client has been convicted by the media, but I am confident that his conviction will be overturned on appeal by the three major networks and the 'Times.'"

Illustration 12.5
Broadcast and Cable Credibility

About 30 percent of those people surveyed by the Pew Research Center gave the TV networks the top believability rating. CNN rated the highest. Local TV news rated higher than network TV news.

Pew Research Center for The People & The Press. Used by permission.

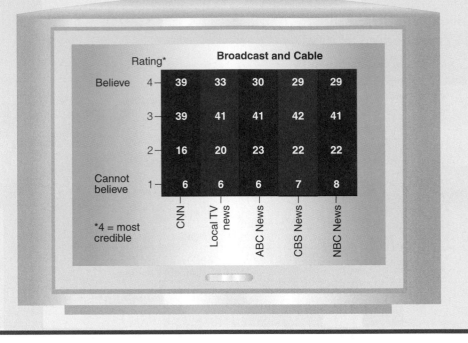

Rating*	**Broadcast and Cable**				
	CNN	Local TV news	ABC News	CBS News	NBC News
Believe 4	39	33	30	29	29
3	39	41	41	42	41
2	16	20	23	22	22
Cannot believe 1	6	6	6	7	8

*4 = most credible

This merging of entertainment and news, as well as the entertaining graphics and the lighthearted presentation style of most local TV newscasts, is making it more difficult for viewers to separate fact from fiction, reality from reenactment and news from advertising. The result could be a decline in the audience's trust in television news to deliver accurate information.

▶ The Public's Perception of the Press

Although people tend to follow the news only when something important happens, they do have strong opinions about which news outlets are most believable. According to the latest study conducted by the Pew Research Center, *The Wall Street Journal* scored the highest, among print media, with 41 percent of the respondents assigning the paper the highest rating, compared to other print news sources—*Time* magazine (29 percent) and "your daily paper" (25 percent). (See **Illustration 12.4,** page 259.) Predictably, the credibility rating for *People* magazine was much lower—10 percent—and for the *National Enquirer*, 4 percent.

People trust the broadcast networks (ABC, NBC and CBS) about equally—29 to 30 percent give these networks the highest believability rating. In the same survey, CNN was rated the most believable broadcast and cable news source, with 39 percent of the people surveyed assigning CNN the highest rating. (See **Illustration 12.5.**)

Of all the news outlets surveyed in the Pew Research Center poll, however, online sites ranked much higher than traditional sources. For example,

Impact | Audience

Illustration 12.6
Believability of Online News Sites

Overall, online news sites rate much higher than traditional sources of news.

Pew Research Center for The People & The Press. Used by permission.

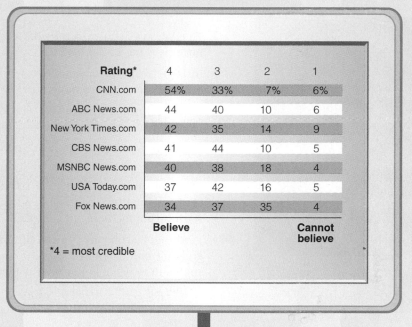

Rating*	4	3	2	1
CNN.com	54%	33%	7%	6%
ABC News.com	44	40	10	6
New York Times.com	42	35	14	9
CBS News.com	41	44	10	5
MSNBC News.com	40	38	18	4
USA Today.com	37	42	16	5
Fox News.com	34	37	35	4

Believe   **Cannot believe**

*4 = most credible

39 percent gave CNN.com high marks for believability and 44 percent gave ABCNews.com the highest rating. New York Times.com also ranked high—42 percent. (See **Illustration 12.6**.)

Overall, the believability of Internet news sources and their growing popularity may be connected. If the Internet can maintain this believability standard, even more of the audience—which was leaving the broadcast networks even before online news began—may gravitate to the Internet. This is a familiar pattern: In the nation's news history, newspaper news audiences added radio and newsreels, then moved to television. Now news audiences have moved to the Internet.

The Internet combines all the news outlets anyone could want all in one place—news and information on the news consumer's own timetable. The Pew Center calls this trend a "digital tide," and it's a tide that may be impossible to stop.

AP/Wide World Photos.

Americans tend to pay attention to the news only when something crucial happens. Here firefighters who lost ten members in the World Trade Center attacks watch a news report about Osama bin Laden.

Getty Images

Media | Review

History

▶ The nation's first consecutively issued newspaper (published more than once) was the *Boston News-Letter*, which appeared in 1704.

▶ In 1848, six newspapers in New York City formed the New York Associated Press, the first cooperative news gathering association.

▶ In 1861, during the Civil War, President Lincoln introduced the practice of accreditation for journalists.

▶ During the Civil War, Mathew Brady introduced the concept of photojournalism—using images to help capture a story.

▶ The competition for newspaper readers spawned yellow journalism—stories about grisly crimes and illicit sex, often accompanied by large, startling photographs.

▶ Produced by companies including British Pathe (from 1900 until 1970) and by Fox Movietone News (between 1919 and 1960), newsreels were shown in movie theaters to audiences hungry for the pictures that radio couldn't provide.

▶ What has been called the Golden Age of Television News was the decade that began in 1961, with President John F. Kennedy's inauguration.

▶ In 1962, President Kennedy used live television to deliver his ultimatum to Soviet leader Nikita Kruschev, urging him to stop sending ships to Cuba to help build missile sites in what was called the Cuban Missle Crisis. Faced with such an ultimatum, the Soviet Union turned its ships around.

▶ Television became a "window on the world" with its coverage of the events following the assassination of President Kennedy.

▶ Coverage of the war in Vietnam gave Americans an appetite for live television news.

▶ The Watergate hearings showed viewers the inner workings of national politics.

▶ Before the War in Iraq began, the U.S. military announced a plan to "embed" more than 600 reporters with American troops. Embedding offered the reporters access to the frontlines, but also kept the reporters within the military's control.

Technology

▶ The invention of the telegraph in 1844 meant news that once took weeks to reach publication could be transmitted in minutes.

▶ In the 1930s, people began to turn to radio for instant news headlines and information.

▶ Ted Turner founded CNN in 1980, offering round-the-clock news on cable.

▶ The Internet, unlike any other form of news and information delivery, is completely self-directed news and information—targeted to individual needs.

Business

▶ Today, most American newspapers and broadcast news operations subscribe to at least one news service, such as Associated Press (AP).

▶ Some U.S. newspaper organizations also run their own news services, which allow subscribers to publish each other's stories for a fee.

▶ In the 1930s and 1940s, most radio stations maintained their own news departments until the advent of format radio.

▶ Today, very few radio stations maintain full-time news departments, and radio stations with news formats tend to be concentrated in the nation's big cities.

▶ The 1980s brought broadcast deregulation and consolidation of the TV networks.

▶ Internet news sites rank higher in believability than either print or broadcast outlets as sources of news.

Culture

▶ Journalist Ernie Pyle gave war the human touch because he wrote stories about the soldiers' lives, not troop movements.

▶ In the 1990s, in general, the American public read fewer newspapers and watched less news on television.

▶ The Pew Research Center studies reveal that network and local news viewership has dropped substantially. People, instead, are turning to the Internet for news.

▶ *The American Journalist* study indicates that today's typical journalist is a 36-year-old Protestant white male with a bachelor's degree, is married and has children, does not belong to a journalism association and earns about $31,000 a year.

▶ *Consensus journalism* is the tendency of journalists covering the same event to report similar conclusions about the event, rather than to report conflicting interpretations.

▶ The press in America doesn't tell you what you think. It *does* tell you what and whom to think *about*. This is called *agenda-setting*.

▶ There are two types of agenda-setting: the flow of information from one news organization to another and the flow of information from news organizations to their audiences.

▶ Herbert J. Gans, in his book *Deciding What's News*, identified eight enduring news values: ethnocentrism, altruistic democracy, responsible capitalism, small-town pastoralism, individualism, moderatism, order and leadership.

▶ The view of the Iraq War from overseas was very different than the view of the war presented to the American public.

▶ Reality TV shows and "infomercials" tend to blur the line between entertainment and news.

Impact | Interactive

The Impact/Interactive CD-ROM that accompanies this text is your gateway to many electronic resources for broadening and testing your critical understanding of the material in Chapter 12. The CD-ROM features the following interactive elements for this and every chapter in the book.

▶ A two- to three-minute timely, high-interest CNN Today video clip with critical viewing questions and a link to relevant selections available within the InfoTrac College Edition database

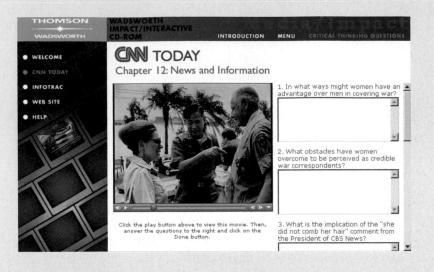

▶ Chapter-specific activities such as personal inventories and media projects

▶ A link to the *Media/Impact* Web site that offers helpful information and many additional electronic learning resources including

• An interactive chapter outline and study guide

• Interactive glossary term flashcards and crossword puzzles, concept animations, Internet activities and practice quizzes

• Live links for all URLs given in the chapter so you can easily access the additional information each site offers

▶ A link to InfoTrac College Edition—our online database of more than a million articles representing cutting-edge research and the latest headlines. Updated daily, this online library is available 24-hours a day, seven days a week. The InfoTrac College Edition activities provided below are designed to help you use this valuable resource.

▶ Working the Web

Live links for all of the sites listed below are provided on the *Media/Impact* book companion Web site, which can be accessed through your Impact/Interactive CD-ROM.

▶ **Asian-American Journalists Association**
www.aaja.org

▶ **British Pathé**
http://www.archive.org/movies/prelinger.php

▶ **Committee to Protect Journalists**
www.cpj.org

▶ **Fox Movietone News**
www.sc.edu/newsfilm

▶ **Investigative Reporters and Editors**
www.ire.org

▶ **National Association of Black Journalists**
www.nabj.org

▶ **Out There News—Frontline and First Hand Perspective on the News**
www.megastories.com

▶ **Pew Center for Civic Journalism**
www.pewcenter.org

▶ **Web Archive of Important News Events**
www.archive.org

▶ InfoTrac College Edition Activities

Using InfoTrac College Edition's online database of full-text articles and abstracts, do the following activities as directed by your instructor. The database can be accessed through your Impact/Interactive CD-ROM.

1. Using the keywords "Associated Press," look up articles in the last two years about America's best-known historic cooperative news-gathering service. Look especially for articles that report AP's adaptations and use of computer-based media technologies to improve coverage and service, or articles about other challenges AP faces today. Based on three or more articles, outline your findings in a brief paper and be prepared to discuss AP's performance and challenges in class.

2. Using InfoTrac College Edition and the keywords "media credibility," examine several viewpoints about the credibility of today's news media. After reading at least three articles and evaluating the objectivity of the sources of media credibility criticism, decide what you think about the reliability of news media and what you think the news media can do to make themselves more credible and realiable. Write your conclusions and your reasons for them in a brief article and be prepared to discuss your ideas in class.

3. Using the keywords "media bias" to examine just the first 20 articles, you'll find several accusations of liberal bias, conservative bias, international bias, bias against military, bias against medical segments—and very little evidence of fairness in journalism. Review some of the articles and decide whether you accept the arguments you read. Evaluate the credibility or fairness of the sources of the articles. Outline your conclusions in a brief article and be prepared to discuss your opinions in class.

4. The *Washington Post* news reports that precipitated the Watergate scandal and the resignation of President Richard M. Nixon were based in part on information from unnamed sources. Read two or three articles using the keywords "unnamed sources," to examine the current state of the debate on the ethics and credibility of unnamed sources in news reporting. Decide what you think about the appropriateness of using unnamed sources in news reports. What are the alternatives? Write a brief paper outlining your conclusions. Be prepared to discuss or debate the issue in class.

5. Using the keywords "embedded journalists," you'll find several articles reporting on the good and bad points of the practice of embedding journalists with coalition troops in the Iraq War. There also are articles reporting on plans or calls for journalists to be embedded in other venues, including within corporations. Read some of the articles and draw your own conclusions about whether embedding journalists is a good idea. Are there issues of media bias? Of safety? Of breach of military confidentiality? Are embedded journalists truly free to report what they learn? Outline your conclusions in a brief paper and be prepared to discuss your ideas in class.

13

tapeing
tapeng

"*No medium is excessively dangerous if its users*

understand what its dangers are."

Neil Postman, author, *Amusing Ourselves to Death*

Researchers at Southern Illinois University School of Medicine have identified a new psychiatric condition they have dubbed "celebrity worship syndrome." This affliction is an unhealthy interest in the rich and famous. (See Impact/Culture, "Are You Starstruck?" page 273). People who admire celebrities often want to be just like them, even though some celebrities set examples that aren't very positive. Celebrity worship is just one example of the effect of media on our lives.

Today, scholars understand that the media have different effects on different types of people with differing results, and generalizations about the media's effects are easy to make but difficult to prove. "We do not fully understand at present what the media system is doing to individual behavior, much less to American culture," according to William L. Rivers and Wilbur Schramm. "The media cannot simply be seen as stenciling images on a blank mind. That is too superficial a view of the communication process."

▶ Assessing the Impact: Early Media Studies

The concept that the media have different effects on different types of people is relatively new. Early media observers felt that an absolute one-to-one

Magic Bullet Theory   The assertion that media messages directly and measurably affect people's behavior.

relationship existed between what people read, heard and saw and what people did with that information. They also believed that the effects were the same for everyone.

The **magic bullet theory,** sometimes called the hypodermic needle theory, alleged that ideas from the media were in direct causal relation to behavior. The theory held that the media could inject ideas into someone the way liquids are injected through a needle. This early distrust of the media still pervades many people's thinking today, although the theory has been disproved.

Media research, like other social science research, is based on a continuum of thought, with each new study advancing slightly the knowledge from the studies that have come before. This is what has happened to the magic bullet theory. Eventually, the beliefs that audiences absorbed media messages uncritically and that all audiences reacted the same to each message were proven untrue. Research disclosed that analyzing media effects is a very complex task.

Some media research existed before television use became widespread in the mid-1950s, but TV prompted scholars to take an even closer look at media's effects. Two scholars made particularly provocative assertions about how the media influence people's lives. **David M. Potter** and **Marshall McLuhan** arrived at just the right moment—when the public and the scholarly community were anxiously trying to analyze media's effects on society.

In his book *People of Plenty*, published in 1954, Potter first articulated an important idea: that American society is a consumer society driven primarily by advertising. Potter, a historian, asserted that American advertising is rooted in American abundance. "Advertising is not badly needed in an economy of scarcity, because total demand is usually equal to or in excess of total supply, and every producer can normally sell as much as he produces. . . . It is when potential supply outstrips demand—that is, when abundance prevails—that advertising begins to fulfill a really essential economic function."

Potter then warned about the dangers of advertising. "Advertising has in its dynamics no motivation to seek the improvement of the individual or to impart qualities of social usefulness. . . . It has no social goals and no social responsibility for what it does with its influence." Potter's perspective was important in shaping the critical view of modern advertising. *People of Plenty* is still in print today.

In the 1960s, Canadian Marshall McLuhan piqued the public's interest with his phrase "The medium is the message," which he later parodied in the title of his book *The Medium Is the Massage*. One of his conclusions was that the widespread use of television was a landmark in the history of the world, "retribalizing" society and creating a "global village" of people who use media to communicate.

McLuhan suggested that electronic media messages are inherently different from print messages—to watch information on TV is different from reading the same information in a newspaper. McLuhan never offered systematic proof for his ideas, and some people criticized him as a charlatan, but his concepts still are debated widely.

Media Effects Research   An attempt to analyze how people use the information they receive from the media.

Scholars who analyze the media today look for patterns in media effects, predictable results and statistical evidence to document how the media affect us. Precisely because the media are ubiquitous, studies of their effects on American society are far from conclusive. In this chapter you will learn about some of the major studies that have examined the media's effects and some of the recent assertions about the role that the media play in our lives.

Media Content Analysis   An attempt to analyze how what the media present influences behavior.

Media research today includes **media effects research** and **media content analysis**. *Media effects research* tries to analyze how people use the information they receive from the media—whether political advertising changes people's voting behavior, for example. *Content analysis* examines what is presented by the media—how many children's programs portray violent behavior, for example. Sometimes these two types of analysis (effects research and content analysis) are combined in an attempt to evaluate what effect certain content has on an audience.

"Five thousand hours, and his vital signs are still strong."

The Payne Fund Studies

The prestigious Payne Fund sponsored the first major study of media, conducted in 1929. It contained 12 separate reports on media effects. One of these studies concentrated on the effects of movies on children. In his interviews, researcher Herbert Blumer simply asked teenagers what they remembered about the movies they had seen as children.

Using this unsystematic approach, he reported that the teenagers had been greatly influenced by the movies because they *said* they had been greatly influenced. Blumer's conclusion and other conclusions of the Payne Fund Studies about the media's direct one-to-one effect on people were accepted without question, mainly because these were the first major studies of media effects, and the results were widely reported. This became known as the magic bullet theory, the belief that media messages directly and measurably affect people's behavior.

The Payne Fund studies also contributed ammunition for the Motion Picture Producers and Distributors Association Production Code, adopted in 1930, which regulated movie content.

The Cantril Study

The Martians who landed in New Jersey on the Mercury Theater "War of the Worlds" broadcast of October 30, 1939 (see page 113) sparked the next major study of media effects, conducted by Hadley Cantril at Princeton University. The results of the Cantril study contradicted the findings of the Payne Fund studies and disputed the magic bullet theory.

The Cantril researchers wanted to find out why certain people believed the Mercury Theater broadcast and others did not. After interviewing 135 people, Cantril concluded that high critical thinking ability was the key. Better-educated people were much more likely to decide the broadcast was a fake. This might seem to be a self-evident finding today, but the importance of the Cantril study is that it differentiated among listeners: People with different personality characteristics interpreted the broadcast differently.

The Lasswell Model

In 1948, Harold D. Lasswell designed a model to describe the process of communication that is still used today. Lasswell said the communication process can be analyzed by answering five questions:

| Who? | Says what? | On which channel? | To whom? | With what effect? |

In other words, Lasswell said the process of communication can be analyzed by determining who the sender is and what the sender says. Next, you must identify which channel—meaning the method—of communication the sender used. Then you must examine the audience and define the effect on that audience. Because Lasswell described the communication process so succinctly, most communications research that followed has attempted to answer his five questions.

▶ Television and Children's Behavior

The 1950s were a time of adjustment because of the addition of the new medium of television, which was seen first as a novelty and then as a necessity. Since 1960, four of the major studies of the effects of television have focused on children.

Television in the Lives of Children
Published in 1961, by Wilbur Schramm, Jack Lyle and Edwin Parker, *Television in the Lives of Our Children* was the first major study of the effects of television on children. Researchers interviewed 6,000 children and 1,500 parents, as well as teachers and school officials.

Schramm and his associates reported that children were exposed to television more than to any other mass medium. On average, 5-year-old children watched television two hours every weekday. TV viewing time reached three hours by the time these children were 8 years old. In a finding that often was subsequently cited, Schramm said that from the ages of 3 to 16, children spent more time in front of the television set than they spent in school.

Children used television for fantasy, diversion and instruction, Schramm said. Children who had troubled relationships with their parents and children who were classified as aggressive were more likely to turn to television for fantasy, but Schramm could find no serious problems related to television viewing. Schramm also found, in support of Cantril, that different children showed different effects.

Television and Social Behavior
Television and Social Behavior, a six-volume study of the effects of television, was funded by $1 million appropriated by Congress in 1969, after the violent decade of the 1960s. The U.S. Department of Health, Education and Welfare, which sponsored the study, appointed a distinguished panel of social scientists to undertake the research.

SIGNE
PHILADELPHIA DAILY NEWS
Philadelphia
USA

Impact | Culture

Do Movies Cause Teenagers to Smoke?

by Richard Klein

Toward the end of the hit film comedy *My Best Friend's Wedding*, Julia Roberts is hunched on the floor of a hotel hallway, her back propped against the door. The man she wants to marry is in the room getting news of her betrayals. We see her extract—from her bra, it appears—a pack of Marlboros. Hesitantly, shakily, she lights a cigarette. . . .

Smoking, once again, is hot in the entertainment media. Half the movies released between 1990 and 1995 featured a major character who chose to light up on screen, a significant increase compared with 29 percent in the 1970s, according to a recent study at the University of California, San Francisco. And the trend appears to be accelerating. . . .

Children are smoking more and starting earlier. Who can doubt that they are being influenced by the new aura of cool that surrounds smoking in the media? When television isn't preaching the evils of tobacco, it's putting cigarettes in the hands of unlikable characters, the ones we love to hate. . . . Our leaders often assume that teenagers read naïvely and will imitate what they are told is good for them and avoid what is disapproved. But

Photodisc

one consequence of such assumptions is the present forms of censorship, which, however well meaning, may reinforce the behavior they seek to banish.

Young people need information, not preaching, about the harm that smoking does to their development, to their bodies and to their futures. Confronted

instead with censorship, they become skilled in, and devoted to, reading between the lines. In the end, the censor always incites aggressive curiosity about the very thing it aims to keep from view.

Richard Klein, "After the Preaching, the Lure of the Taboo," *The New York Times*, August 24, 1997, 2-1, 31. Copyright © 1997 by The New York Times Co. Reprinted by permission.

The study's major findings, published in 1971, concerned the effects of television violence on children. A content analysis of one week of prime-time programming, conducted by George Gerbner of the University of Pennsylvania, reported that eight out of ten prime-time shows contained violence. The conclusions of *Television and Social Behavior* did not make a direct connection between TV programming and violent behavior, however.

The report said there was a "tentative" indication that television viewing caused aggressive behavior. According to the study, this connection between TV violence and aggressive behavior affected only *some* children who were already classified as aggressive children and *only* in some environments.

Even though the report avoided a direct statement about violent behavior in children as a result of television viewing, the U.S. Surgeon General called for immediate action against violence on television. The television industry dismissed the results as inconclusive.

The Early Window   Several studies since 1971 have suggested that television violence causes aggression among children. In their 1988 book *The Early Window: Effects of Television on Children and Youth*, psychologists Robert M. Liebert and Joyce Sprafkin urged caution in drawing broad conclusions about the subject:

> *Studies using various methods have supported the proposition that TV violence can induce aggressive and/or antisocial behavior in children. Whether the effect will hold only for the most susceptible individuals (e.g., boys from disadvantaged homes) or whether it will hold for a wider range of youngsters obviously depends in part upon the measure being used. . . . The occurrence of serious violent or criminal acts results from several forces at once. Researchers have said that TV violence is* **a** *cause of aggressiveness, not that it is* **the** *cause of aggressiveness. There is no one, single cause of any social behavior.*

Television Advertising to Children   The effects of advertising on adults have been analyzed widely, but in 1979 the advertising of children's products became an object of serious government attention with the release of the 340-page report *Television Advertising to Children* by the Federal Trade Commission.

The report, based on a two-year study, was designed to document the dangers of advertising sugar-based products to children, but embedded in the report was some provocative information about children's advertising. Children are an especially vulnerable audience, said the FTC. The report concluded:

1. The average child sees 20,000 commercials a year, or about three hours of TV advertising a week.

2. Many children regard advertising as just another form of programming and do not distinguish between programs and ads.

3. Televised advertising for any product to children who do not understand the intent of the commercial is unfair and deceptive.

The report called for a ban on advertising to very young children, a ban on sugared products in advertising directed to children under age 12, and a requirement for counter-ads with dental and nutritional information to balance any ads for sugared products.

This report and subsequent research about children's advertising suggest that younger children pay more attention to television advertising than older children. But by sixth grade, children adopt what has been called a "global distrust" of advertising.

▶ Television and Violence

Television and Behavior: Ten Years of Scientific Progress and Implications for the Eighties, published in 1982, by the National Institute of Mental Health, compiled information from 2,500 individual studies of television. According to the National Institute of Mental Health, three findings of these 2,500 studies, taken together, were that:

1. A direct correlation exists between televised violence and aggressive behavior, yet there is no way to predict who will be affected and why.

2. Heavy television viewers are more fearful, less trusting and more apprehensive than light viewers.

3. Children who watch what the report called "pro social" programs (programs that are socially constructive, such as *Sesame Street*) are more likely to act responsibly.

Impact | Culture

Are You Starstruck?

by Keturah Gray, ABC News

"We as a society are becoming preoccupied with celebrities and the fantasy images it evokes," says James Houran, a psychologist with the Southern Illinois University School of Medicine.

After surveying more than 600 people, Houran's team of researchers from universities in the U.S. and Britain recently identified a psychiatric condition they have dubbed "celebrity worship syndrome." It's an unhealthy interest in the rich and fabulous.

According to the researchers, about a third of us have it to some degree.

To measure people's interest in celebrities, the group devised the celebrity worship scale. The three levels move from:

- **Entertainment social.** This is casual stargazing. The level of celebrity worship here is really quite mild: "My friends and I like to discuss how Ben could have moved from Gwyneth to J.Lo."
- **Intense personal.** The person seems to feel a connection with the star: "I consider Halle Berry to be my soul mate."
- **Borderline pathological.** Here, admiration has gone stalker-esque: "When he reads my love letters, Brad Pitt will leave Jennifer Aniston and live happily ever after with me."

"Celebrity worship has probably existed as long as there have been famous people," says Horan. "But it has probably only become as intense as it is given the technological advances that allow us to create societies, market them to a worldwide audience, and share information about them."

Left: Vince Bucci/Getty Images; Right: Carlos Alvarez/Getty Images

Many people become preoccupied with celebrities such as Brad Pitt and Halle Berry in a syndrome researchers have called "celebrity worship."

Most of the latest studies of the media's role have continued to reinforce the concept that different people in different environments react to the media differently.

In 1994, cable operators and network broadcasters agreed to use an independent monitor to review programming for violent content. The agreement came after Congress held hearings on the subject, in 1993, and threatened to introduce regulations to curb violence if the industry didn't police itself. The agreement also called for the development of violence ratings for TV programming and endorsed a "V" chip—V *for violence*—technology that would be built into a television set to allow parents to block programs rated as violent.

The monitoring is "qualitative" rather than "quantitative," according to the agreement. This means that the programs are examined for content, not just for incidents of violence, a system that is very controversial. The Telecommunications Act of 1996 established a ratings code for content.

1989–. © HBO/Courtesy: Everett Collection

Critics say television violence on network TV shows like HBO's *The Sopranos* affects children's behavior. TV networks responded by adopting a ratings code that warns viewers about violent content. *The Sopranos*, however, does not carry a rating because HBO does not rate its programs.

This agreement continues a tradition of media self-regulation. That is, the broadcast, recording and movie media industries have responded—often reluctantly—to congressional pressure by offering to monitor themselves rather than invite the government to intrude on the content of their programs.

▶ The Media and National Politics

The media have transformed politics in ways that could never have been imagined when President Franklin D. Roosevelt introduced what were called Fireside Chats in 1933. Roosevelt was the first president to use the media effectively to stimulate public support.

The newest technology introduced during FDR's era—radio—gave him immediate access to a national audience. Roosevelt's media skill became an essential element in promoting his economic programs. Today, politics and the media seem irreversibly dependent on each other, one of the legacies of Roosevelt's presidency.

The Fireside Chats

In March 1933, just after he was inaugurated, FDR looked for a way to avoid a financial panic after he announced that he was closing the nation's banks. For a week the country cooled off while Congress scrambled for a solution. On the Sunday night eight days after his inauguration, Roosevelt used radio to calm the nation's anxiety before the banks began to reopen on Monday. FDR went down to the basement of the White House to give his first "Fireside Chat."

There was a fireplace in the basement, but no fire was burning. The president could not find his script, so he borrowed a mimeographed copy from a reporter. In his first address to the nation as president, FDR gave a banking lesson to his audience of 60 million people: "I want to talk for a few minutes with the people of the United States about banking. . . . First of all, let me state the simple fact that when you deposit money in a bank, the bank does not put the money into a safe deposit vault. It invests your money in many different forms." When he finished, he turned to people in the room and asked, "Was I all right?" America had its first media president, an elected leader talking directly to the people through the media.

Roosevelt's chats are cited as a legendary example of media politics, yet he gave only eight fireside chats in his first term of office. His other meetings with the press also enhanced his reputation for press: In 13 years in office he held more than 900 press conferences.

The People's Choice

The first major study of the influence of media on politics was *The People's Choice*, undertaken precisely because FDR seemed to be such a good media politician. This comprehensive examination of voter behavior in the 1940 presidential election was quite systematic.

Researchers Paul Lazarsfeld, Bernard Berelson and Hazel Gaudet followed 3,000 people in rural Erie County, Ohio, from May to November 1940, to determine what influenced the way these people voted for president. The researchers tracked how people's minds changed over the six-month period and then attempted to determine why. (It is important to remember this study was undertaken before television. Radio became the prevailing medium for political advertising beginning in 1932, when the two parties spent more money for radio time than for any other item.)

What effect, the researchers wanted to know, did the media have on people's choosing one candidate over another? The results were provocative. Lazarsfeld and his colleagues found that only 8 percent of the voters in the study were actually *converted*. The majority of voters (53 percent) were *reinforced* in their beliefs by the media, and 14 percent were *activated* to vote. Mixed effects or no effects were shown by the remaining 25 percent of the people.

Lazarsfeld said opinion leaders, who got their information from the media, shared this information with their friends. The study concluded that instead of changing people's beliefs, the media primarily activate people to vote and reinforce already held opinions. *The People's Choice* also revealed that:

- Family and friends had more effect on people's decisions than the media.

- The media had different effects on different people, reinforcing Cantril's findings.

- A major source of information about candidates was other people.

This finding that opinion leaders often provide and shape information for the general population was a bonus—the researchers hadn't set out specifically to learn this. This transmission of information and ideas from mass media to opinion leaders and then to friends and acquaintances is called the **two-step flow** of communication.

The Unseeing Eye

In 1976, a second study of the media and presidential elections, called *The Unseeing Eye: The Myth of Television Power in National Elections*, revealed findings that paralleled those of *The People's Choice*. With a grant from the National Science Foundation, Thomas E. Patterson and Robert D. McClure supervised interviews with 2,707 people from early September to just before Election Day in the November 1972 race between George McGovern and Richard Nixon. The study did not discuss political media events, but it did analyze television campaign news and political advertising.

The researchers concluded that, although political advertising influenced 16 percent of the people they interviewed, only 7 percent were manipulated by political ads. The researchers defined people who were influenced as those who decided to vote for a candidate based mostly on what they knew and only slightly on what the ads told them. The 7 percent of the people in the survey who were manipulated, according to Patterson and McClure, were people who cited political advertising as a major factor in their choices.

Patterson and McClure concluded that political advertising on TV has little effect on most people. "By projecting their political biases . . . people see in candidates' commercials pretty much what they want to see. Ads sponsored by the candidate who shares their politics get a good response. They like what he has to say. And they like him. Ads sponsored by the opposing candidate are viewed negatively. They object to what he says. And they object to him."

It is important to remember, however, that in some elections a difference of a few percentage points can decide the outcome, and political advertising is designed to sway these swing voters. This is why political advertising continues to play such an important campaign role, in an effort to reach the percentage of the population that remains vulnerable.

Election Campaigns on Television

So far, no convincing systematic evidence has been presented to show that the media change the voting behavior of large groups of people. Yet, since John F. Kennedy debated Richard Nixon during the 1960 presidential campaign, a deeply felt view has persisted among many people that the media—television in particular—have changed elections and electoral politics.

Kennedy's debate with Nixon in 1960 was the first televised debate of presidential candidates in American history. Kennedy's performance in the

Two-Step Flow The transmission of information and ideas from mass media to opinion leaders and then to friends.

ABC News Uses Campaign Bus on the Road to the White House

by Julie Hinds

Detroit (January 7, 2004)—It's the hottest set of wheels around, if you're talking about the road to the White House. The ABC News Vote 2004 campaign bus is coming today to a parking space outside the Detroit auto show. At 45-feet-long, 12-feet wide and 52,000 pounds, this is no sleek concept car. But there is a concept behind it.

To perk up coverage of the presidential race, ABC News has outfitted three buses as mobile television studios.

"We think it's a great way to get out, stop in small towns and listen to what people are saying," says ABC News senior producer David Reiter.

Normally, the vehicles are home to rock stars on tour. The bus that's coming to Detroit was last used by Cher.

Now they carry a small team of news producers and engineers. "We have less peculiar demands than rock stars," jokes Reiter.

The exteriors are a star-spangled advertisement for ABC News. The inte-

© Gitika Ahuja/ABC News bus

To stimulate interest in the 2004 presidential election, ABC News chartered a bus once used by Cher to carry its newspeople around the country to cover the candidates.

riors have been equipped with editing facilities, a radio booth and interview space.

"ABC News Campaign Bus Will Stop Today at Auto Show," *Detroit Free Press* on AOL, January 7, 2004.

debates often is credited for his narrow victory in the election. In his book *Presidents and the Press*, media scholar Joseph C. Spear wrote:

> As the panel began asking questions, Nixon tended to go on the defensive, answering Kennedy point by point and ignoring his huge audience beyond the camera. Kennedy, by contrast, appeared rested, calm, informed, cocksure. Whatever the question, he aimed his answer at the millions of Americans viewing the program in their living rooms.
>
> It was an unmitigated disaster for Nixon. In the second, third, and fourth debates, he managed to recover somewhat from his initial poor performance, but it was too late. Surveys showed that an overwhelming percentage of the television audience had judged Kennedy the victor.

One legacy of Kennedy's television victory is that today, national political campaigns depend almost entirely on TV to promote presidential candidates. Television is a very efficient way to reach large numbers of people quickly, but campaigning for television also distances the candidates from direct public contact.

Television advertising also is very expensive, and the cost of national campaigns in the past 20 years has skyrocketed. According to University of

Southern California political scientist Herbert Alexander, presidential, gubernatorial and senatorial candidates devote 40 to 60 percent of their campaign budgets to advertising.

Alexander is quick to point out that not all this money goes to television. In congressional elections, according to Alexander, "fewer than half the candidates use TV. Many of them are in districts like Los Angeles, where the media markets are much larger than the political jurisdictions." Television advertising in such markets delivers a bigger audience than candidates need, so they use direct mail or print advertising. But a candidate running for Congress in Des Moines, Iowa, might use television because the entire district would be included in the local station's coverage, says Alexander.

Historian James David Barber describes the public's role in politics:

> Particularly since television has brought national politics within arm's length of nearly every American, the great majority probably have at least some experience of the quadrennial passing parade. But millions vote their old memories and habits and interests, interpreting new perceptions that strike their senses to coincide with their prejudices and impulses.
>
> At the other end of the participation spectrum are those compulsive readers of The New York Times who delve into every twitch and turn of the contest. Floating in between are large numbers of Americans who pick up on the election's major events and personalities, following with mild but open interest the dominant developments. Insofar as the campaign makes a difference, it is this great central chunk of The People who swing the choice. They respond to what they see and hear. They are interested but not obsessed. They edit out the minor blips of change and wait for the campaign to gather force around a critical concern. They reach their conclusions on the basis of a widely shared common experience. It is through that middling throng of the population that the pulse of politics beats most powerfully, synchronizing to its insistent rhythm the varied vibrations of discrete events.

John F. Kennedy's debate with Richard Nixon in 1960 was the first televised debate of presidential candidates. Kennedy's performance in the debates often is credited for his narrow victory in the election.

High profile movie star Arnold Schwarzenegger spent $1 million a day in 2003, in his successful campaign to become California's governor.

The rising cost of running for public office can exclude people without the means to raise huge sums of money. If "the People who swing the choice," described by Barber, cannot easily participate in the political process, eventually they may choose not to participate at all, eroding the number of people who run for office, vote in elections and work in political campaigns.

In the 2003 gubernatorial recall race in California, when actor Arnold Schwarzenegger became a candidate, his campaign spent unprecedented amounts of money on TV advertising in the month preceding the election, even though Schwarzenegger's high show business profile would seem to have been an advantage—demonstrating that even such a well-known candidate recognized the importance of television advertising as a central part of a political campaign.

Today, the media are essential to American politics, changing the behavior of politicians as well as the electorate, raising important questions about governance and the conduct of elections.

▶ The Mass Media Reflect Cultural Values

Because media research is a continuing process, new ideas will emerge in the next decade from today's ideas and studies. Several provocative recent studies have extended previous boundaries of media research.

Silencing Opposing Viewpoints

Elisabeth Noelle-Neumann has asserted that because journalists in all media tend to concentrate on the same major news stories, the audience is assailed on many sides by similar information. Together, the media present the consensus; journalists reflect the prevailing climate of opinion. As this consensus spreads, people with divergent views, says Noelle-Neumann, may be less likely to voice disagreement with the prevailing point of view. Thus, because of a **"spiral of silence,"** the media gain more influence because opponents of the consensus tend to remain silent. The implication for future research will be to ask whether the media neutralize dissent and create a pattern of social and cultural conformity.

Spiral of Silence The belief that people with divergent views may be reluctant to challenge the consensus of opinion offered by the media.

Losing a Sense of Place

In his book *No Sense of Place*, published in 1985, Joshua Meyrowitz provided new insight into television's possible effects on society. In the past, says Meyrowitz:

> *Parents did not know what their children knew, and children did not know what their parents knew they knew. Similarly, a person of one sex could never be certain of what a member of the other sex knew. . . . Television undermines such behavioral distinctions because it encompasses children and adults, men and women, and all other social groups in a single informational sphere or environment. Not only does it provide similar information to everyone but, even more significant, it provides it publicly and often simultaneously.*

This sharing of information, says Meyrowitz, means that subjects that rarely were discussed between men and women, for instance, and between children and adults, have become part of the public dialogue.

A second result of television viewing is the blurred distinction between childhood and adulthood, says Meyrowitz. When print dominated the society as a medium, children's access to adult information was limited. The only way

Robert Galbraith/Getty Images

to learn about "adult" concepts was to read about them, so typically a child was not exposed to adult ideas or problems, and taboo topics remained hidden from children.

In a video world, however, any topic that can be portrayed in pictures on television challenges the boundaries that print places around information. This, says Meyrowitz, causes an early loss of the naïveté of childhood.

> *Television removes barriers that once divided people of different ages and reading abilities into different social situations. The widespread use of television is equivalent to a broad social decision to allow young children to be present at wars and funerals, courtships and seductions, criminal plots and cocktail parties. . . . Television thrusts children into a complex adult world, and it provides the impetus for children to ask the meanings of actions and words they would not yet have heard or read about without television.*

Meyrowitz concedes that movies offered similar information to children before television, but he says that the pervasiveness of television today makes its effects more widespread. Television is blurring social distinctions— between children and adults, and between men and women. Complicating the current study of media effects is the increase in the variety and number of available media sources.

Linking TV to School Performance

Many studies about children and television, such as the National Institute of Mental Health report, have concentrated on the effects of the portrayals of violence. But in 1981, a California study suggested a link between television viewing and poor school performance.

The California Assessment Program (CAP), which tests academic achievement, included a new question on the achievement test: "On a typical weekday, about how many hours do you watch TV?" The students were given a choice ranging from zero to six or more hours.

An analysis of the answers to that question from more than 10,000 sixth graders was matched with the children's scores on the achievement test. The results suggested a consistent relationship between viewing time and achievement. Students who said they watched a lot of television scored lower in reading, writing and mathematics than students who didn't watch any television. The average scores for students who said they viewed six or more hours of television a day were six to eight points lower than for those children who said they watched less than a half-hour of television a day.

Because the study didn't include information about the IQ score or income levels of these students, the results cannot be considered conclusive. The study simply may show that children who watch a lot of television aren't studying. But the results are particularly interesting because of the number of children who were included in the survey.

Further research could examine whether children are poor students because they watch a lot of television or whether children who watch a lot of television are poor students for other reasons.

Stereotyping Women

Journalists often use shorthand labels to characterize ethnic and other groups. In his 1922 book *Public Opinion*, political journalist Walter Lippmann first identified the tendency of journalists to generalize about other people based on fixed ideas.

© Bill Aron/PhotoEdit

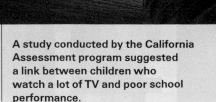

A study conducted by the California Assessment program suggested a link between children who watch a lot of TV and poor school performance.

When we speak of the mind of a group of people, of the French mind, the militarist mind, the bolshevik mind, we are liable to serious confusion unless we agree to separate the instinctive equipment from the stereotypes, the patterns, the formulae which play so decisive a part in building up the mental world to which the native character is adapted and responds. . . . Failure to make this distinction accounts for oceans of loose talk about collective minds, national souls, and race psychology.

The image of women portrayed by the media has been the subject of significant contemporary studies by many media researchers. Observers of the stereotyping of women point to past and current media portrayals showing very few women in professional roles and the lack of women shown as strong, major characters. The media's overall portrayal of women in mass culture is slowly improving, but in her book *Loving with a Vengeance: Mass-Produced Fantasies for Women*, Tania Modleski says that the portrayal in popular fiction of women in submissive roles began in 1740, with the British novel *Pamela*, which was then published in America by Benjamin Franklin in 1744.

Modleski analyzed the historical content of gothic novels, Harlequin Romances and soap operas. Her study reveals:

In Harlequin Romances, the need of women to find meaning and pleasure in activities that are not wholly male-centered such as work or artistic creation is generally scoffed at.

Soap operas also undercut, though in subtler fashion, the idea that a woman might obtain satisfaction from these activities [work or artistic creation]. . . . Indeed, patriarchal myths and institutions are. . .wholeheartedly embraced, although the anxieties and tensions they give rise to may be said to provoke the need for the texts in the first place.

The implication in Modleski's research is that women who read romance novels will believe they should act like the women in the novels they read. A stereotype that has existed since 1740 is unlikely to change quickly.

▶ Multiculturalism and the Mass Media

Beginning in the year 2000, the U.S. census allowed Americans to use more than one racial category to describe themselves, and the categories have been changed to reflect America's changing face. In the past, people were forced to choose one category from among the following: Black; White; Asian or Pacific Islander; American Indian or Alaskan Native; or "Other—specify in writing." In the 1990 census, about 10 million people checked "Other"—nearly all of Latino descent.

The new range of choices for the year 2000 census was: White; Black or African American; Asian; Hawaiian Native or Pacific Islander; American Indian or Alaska Native; and Hispanic or Latino. People who identify with more than one group also were able to check more than one description, such as African American and Asian, for example. All government forms are required to use the new categories by the year 2003.

This new method allows people to identify themselves to the government and shows the evolving social landscape of the U.S. population. Yet the American media have been very slow to acknowledge America's changing population patterns. In fact, critics charge that the media have responded reluctantly to reflect accurately America's growing multicultural mix.

During the last century, selected media outlets, such as African American and Latino newspapers and magazines, have been able to cater to specific audiences. But the mainstream media, especially daily newspapers and the TV networks, traditionally have represented the interests of the mainstream cul-

Impact | Culture

Magazine Ads Could Reflect American Culture More Accurately

by Lawrence Bowen and Jill Schmid

For most of its life as a nation, America has been referred to as the world's "melting pot." The emphasis has been on the "melt"—not what was in the pot.

. . . Mass media, in general, and advertising, in particular, were seen as important windows on the melting pot, where progress, or the lack thereof, would be readily apparent.

Television brought the window into America's living room, and a number of window gazers were quick to point out that the view was suburban, predominantly young, white, and middle class. . . .

In the past decade, we've seen the "melting pot" metaphor challenged by multiculturalists calling for separate but equal approaches of life, liberty, and the pursuit of happiness. . . .

Overall, it is encouraging to note greater use of African Americans in mainstream magazine advertising. Simple inclusion is a necessary first step, but it does not equal integration or fair representation.

Asians and Latinos are still woefully under-represented. Moreover, there are few advertisements in which minorities appear alone and, when they do appear, they are outnumbered by whites. Minorities continue to be used as "tokens" or as questionable links to some product attribute. . . .

If companies are truly trying to reach minority markets, they must do a better job of not just including minorities in their mainstream advertising, but also showing the minorities in various occupations, in meaningful roles, and in a variety of settings. Minorities read mainstream magazines and buy mainstream products. It's time they receive mainstream treatment.

Excerpted with permission from: Lawrence Bowen and Jill Schmid. "Minority Presence and Portrayal in Mainstream Magazine Advertising: An Update." *Journalism and Mass Communication Quarterly*, Spring 1997, 134–146.

Ad courtesy of AT&T. Photo by Mark Gilbert.

In "Minority Presence and Portrayal in Mainstream Magazines," researchers say minorities rarely appear alone in magazine ads.

Critical Question

To what degree, if any, do you believe you are more influenced by ads that represent people whose skin color and other physical features resemble your own? Explain.

---

ture. Scores of media studies have documented stereotypical representation, and a lack of representation, of people of color in all areas of the culture.

Media scholar Carolyn Martindale, for example, in a content analysis of *The New York Times* from 1934 to 1994, found that most nonwhite groups were visible "only in glimpses." According to Martindale, "The mainstream press in the U.S. has presented minorities as outside, rather than a part of, American Society."

After examining 374 episodes of 96 prime-time series on ABC, CBS, NBC, Fox, WB and UPN, the Center for Media and Public Affairs for the National

The Bernie Mac Show, launched in 2001, reflects an attempt by network television to present a diverse set of characters.

Council of La Raza concluded that only 2 percent of prime-time characters during the 1994–1995 season were Latinos, and most of the roles played by those characters were minor. The study, *Don't Blink: Hispanics in Television Entertainment,* also revealed that, although Latino characters were portrayed more positively than they had been in the past, they were most likely to be shown as poor or working class.

Based on a comprehensive analysis of the nation's newspapers, a 56-page *News Watch* report issued at a convention of the nation's African American, Asian, Latino and Native American journalists concluded that "The mainstream media's coverage of people of color is riddled with old stereotypes, offensive terminology, biased reporting and a myopic interpretation of American society."

To counteract stereotyping, the Center for Integration and Improvement of Journalism at San Francisco State University (which sponsored the study) offered the following Tips for Journalists:

- Apply consistent guidelines when identifying people of race. Are the terms considered offensive? Ask individual sources how they wish to be identified.

- Only refer to peoples' ethnic or racial background when it is relevant.

- When deciding whether to mention someone's race, ask yourself: Is ethnic/racial identification needed? Is it important to the context of the story?

- Consult a supervisor if you are unsure of the offensiveness or relevance of a racial or ethnic term.

- Use sensitivity when describing rites and cultural events. Avoid inappropriate comparisons. For example, Kwanzaa is not "African American Christmas."

- Be specific when using ethnic or racial identification of individuals. Referring to someone as Filipino American is preferred to calling that person Asian. The latter term is better applied to a group.

The issue of accurate reflection by the media of a complex society invites analysis as traditional media outlets struggle to reflect the evolving face of an America that is growing more diverse every day.

▶ Gender Issues and the Mass Media

In 1993, newspapers faced an editorial dilemma when cartoonist Lynn Johnston, who draws the very popular syndicated strip *For Better or Worse,* decided to reveal that Lawrence, one of the teenagers in the comic strip, is gay. Most newspapers published the strip, but 19 newspapers canceled their contracts for the comic, which is carried by Universal Press Syndicate of Kansas City. One newspaper editor who refused to carry the strip explained, "We are a conservative newspaper in a conservative town." Another editor said he "felt the sequence condoned homosexuality 'almost to the point of advocacy.'"

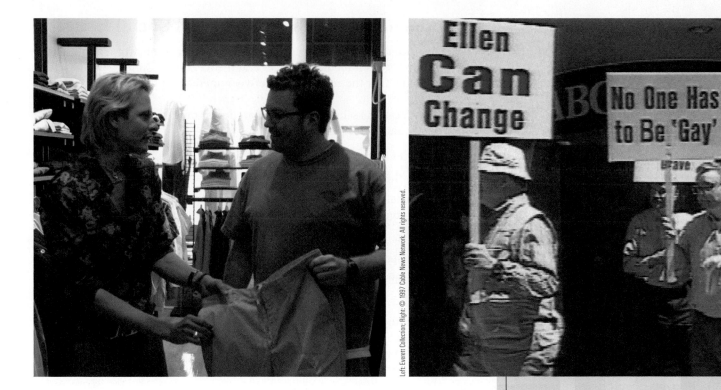

In 2003, the Bravo channel introduced an interesting twist on gay programming, with its new series *Queer Eye for the Straight Guy* (left), a program that would have been shocking to TV audiences just a few years earlier. The gender issues portrayed by the ABC program *Ellen* (right) promoted a protest outside the network's offices in 1997.

Responding to criticism that, by revealing Lawrence's sexual preference, she was advocating homosexuality, Johnston said, "You know, that's like advocating left-handedness. Gayness is simply something that exists. My strip is a reality strip, real situations, real crises, real people." One newspaper executive at a paper that carried the strip wrote, "It seems to me that what we're talking about here isn't the rightness or wrongness of homosexuality. It is about tolerance."

An understanding of the media portrayals of Americans' diverse lifestyles received extra attention in 1997, when the television program *Ellen* portrayed two women exchanging a romantic kiss. Although promoted as the nation's first female television kiss, the first romantic lesbian relationship actually had been shown on *L.A. Law* in 1991.

Gender issues remained primarily a subject for the nation's lesbian and gay newspapers and magazines, although in 1996, *The New Yorker* ran a controversial cover that portrayed two men kissing on a Manhattan sidewalk.

Bringing the issue to mainstream TV, as the *Ellen* program did, presents a dilemma for the TV networks because, when notified beforehand about the content of the program, some local TV stations refused to show the episode. The reluctance of television to portray alternative lifestyles is as much a reflection of the networks trying to protect their economic interests as it is a reflection of the nation's social values.

By 2003, society's strong reactions to the portrayals of gay people on television seemed to have subsided when Fox Television introduced its new series, *Queer Eye for the Straight Guy*. The title itself would have been shocking just a few years earlier, but audiences seemed ready for programming that featured gay men with a strong sense of fashion, home decor, cuisine and culture who advise a straight man about how to improve his lifestyle. Television adapted to changing social standards, reflecting society's ability to begin to tolerate a more diverse set of characters on television.

▶ Understanding Mass Media and Social Issues

Scholars once thought the effects of media were easy to measure, as a direct relationship between media messages and media effects. Contemporary scholars now know that the relationship between media and their audiences is complex.

Communications scholar Neil Postman poses some questions to ask about mass media and social issues:

- What are the main psychic effects of each [media] form?
- What is the main relation between information and reason?
- What redefinitions of important cultural meanings do new sources, speeds, contexts and forms of information require?
- How do different forms of information persuade?
- Is a newspaper's "public" different from television's "public?"
- How do different information forms dictate the type of content that is expressed?

These questions should be discussed, says Postman, because "no medium is excessively dangerous if its users understand what its dangers are. . . . This is an instance in which the asking of the questions is sufficient. To ask is to break the spell."

Media | Review

HECTOR MATA/AFP/Getty images

History

▶ Scholar Tania Modleski says the media's inaccurate portrayals of women is not new but began in 1740 with the publication of *Pamela*, the first novel.

▶ David Potter, in *People of Plenty*, described the United States as a consumer society driven by advertising.

▶ Canadian scholar Marshall McLuhan introduced the term *global village* to describe the way media bring people together through shared experience.

▶ The magic bullet theory, developed in the 1929 Payne Fund studies, asserted that media content had a direct causal relationship to behavior.

▶ Hadley Cantril challenged the magic bullet theory. Cantril found that better-educated people listening to "War of the Worlds" were much more likely to detect that the radio broadcast was fiction. Today, scholars believe the media have different effects on different people.

▶ Media politics began in 1933 with President Franklin Roosevelt's Fireside Chats. John F. Kennedy broadened the tradition when he and Richard Nixon appeared in the nation's first televised debate of presidential candidates in 1960.

▶ The first major study of politics and the media, *The People's Choice*, concluded that only 8 percent of the voters in the study were actually converted by media coverage of the 1940 campaign.

▶ Walter Lippmann first identified the tendency of journalists to generalize about groups of people and create stereotypes.

▶ In 1948, political scientist Harold D. Laswell described the process of communication as: "Who? Says what? On which channel? To whom? With what effect?"

▶ In 1961, Wilbur Schramm and his associates revealed that children used TV for fantasy, diversion and instruction. Aggressive children were more likely to turn to TV for fantasy, said Schramm, but he could find no serious problems related to TV viewing.

▶ The 1971 report to Congress, *Television and Social Behavior*, made a faint causal connection between TV violence and children's violent behavior, but the report said that only some children were affected, and these children already had been classified as aggressive.

▶ The 1976 study, *The Unseeing Eye*, revealed that only 7 percent of the people in the study were manipulated by TV ads. The researchers concluded that political advertising has little effect on most people.

Business

▶ The rising cost of national political campaigns is directly connected to the expense of television advertising.

Culture

▶ Media scholars look for patterns in the effects of media, rather than anecdotal evidence.

▶ Several recent studies have suggested that TV violence causes aggression among children. Researchers caution, however, that TV violence is not *the* cause of aggressiveness, but only *a* cause of aggressiveness.

▶ The Federal Trade Commission report, *Television Advertising to Children*, said that children see 20,000 commercials a year and that younger children are much more likely to pay attention to TV advertising than older ones.

▶ The summary study by the National Institute of Mental Health in 1982 asserted that a direct connection exists between televised violence and aggressive behavior, but there is no way to predict who will be affected and why.

▶ Television is a very efficient way to reach large numbers of people quickly, but campaigning for television also distances the candidates from direct public contact.

▶ Elisabeth Noelle-Newmann has asserted that, due to what she calls a "spiral of silence" supporting the consensus point of view, the media have more influence because opponents of the consensus tend to remain silent.

▶ Joshua Meyrowitz says that television viewing blurs the distinction between childhood and adulthood.

▶ A study by the California Assessment Program of children's TV viewing habits seems to support the idea that children who watch a lot of TV do not perform as well in schoolwork as children who watch less television.

▶ The year 2000 census categories for racial designations more clearly reflect the multicultural nature of the U.S. population, yet the mass media have been slow to acknowledge America's changing population patterns.

▶ The mainstream media, especially daily newspapers and the TV networks, have traditionally represented the interests of the mainstream culture.

▶ A study of *The New York Times* from 1934 to 1994 found that most non-white groups were visible "only in glimpses."

▶ A study by the National Council of La Raza concluded that only 2 percent of prime-time characters during the 1994–1995 TV season were Latinos, and most of the roles played by those characters were minor.

▶ The lesbian character on the TV program *Ellen* and the homosexual character Lawrence in the cartoon strip *For Better or Worse* focused attention on media portrayals of gender issues.

▶ By 2003, the strong reactions to the portrayals of gay people on television seemed to have subsided when Fox Television introduced its new series, *Queer Eye for the Straight Guy*.

Impact | Interactive

The Impact/Interactive CD-ROM that accompanies this text is your gateway to many electronic resources for broadening and testing your critical understanding of the material in Chapter 13. The CD-ROM features the following interactive elements for this and every chapter in the book.

▶ A two- to three-minute timely, high-interest CNN Today video clip with critical viewing questions and a link to relevant selections available within the InfoTrac College Edition database

▶ Chapter-specific activities such as personal inventories and media projects

▶ A link to the *Media/Impact* Web site that offers helpful information and many additional electronic learning resources including

- An interactive chapter outline and study guide

- Interactive glossary term flashcards and crossword puzzles, concept animations, Internet activities and practice quizzes

- Live links for all URLs given in the chapter so you can easily access the additional information each site offers

▶ A link to InfoTrac College Edition—our online database of more than a million articles representing cutting-edge research and the latest headlines. Updated daily, this online library is available 24 hours a day, seven days a week. The InfoTrac College Edition activities provided below are designed to help you use this valuable resource.

▶ Working the Web

Live links for all of the sites listed below are provided on the Media/Impact book companion Web site, which can be accessed through your Impact/Interactive CD-ROM.

- ▶ **Benton Foundation**
  www.benton.org

- ▶ **Joan Shorenstein Center on the Press, Politics and Public Policy (Harvard University)**
  http://www.ksg.harvard/edu/Shorenstein

- ▶ **Moorland-Spingarn Research Center at Howard University**
  www.howard.edu/library/moorland-spingarn

- ▶ *National Journal* **(national politics)**
  www.nationaljournal.com

- ▶ **Social Science Research Council**
  www.ssrc.org

- ▶ **University of Iowa**
  www.uiowa.edu/~commstud/resources/pol-ads.html

▶ InfoTrac College Edition Activities

Using InfoTrac College Edition's online database of full-text articles and abstracts, do the following activities as directed by your instructor. The database can be accessed through your Impact/Interactive CD-ROM.

1. A continuing controversy is the impact of television viewing on children. Look up the subject heading "children television" on InfoTrac College Edition and you'll find many articles on the subject. Choose at least three articles that discuss the effects of television on children. Summarize your findings in a brief article and be prepared to discuss the subject in class.

2. Using InfoTrac College Edition and the keywords "television and stereotypes," read several recent articles about the impact of stereotypes of various kinds on television. Then write a brief paper outlining what you think about stereotypes on television. Are there any positive uses of stereotypes in television? How serious do you think the problem is? Be prepared to discuss the issue in class.

3. Using InfoTrac College Edition and the keywords "media and diversity," read several recent articles about the state of diversity in media and advertising. Are inclusion and portrayals of members of minority groups getting better, worse or staying the same? Then write a brief paper summarizing what you've learned about diversity in media and be prepared to discuss the matter in class.

4. Celebrities continue to make good media topics. Do you think this is good or bad? Why? Using InfoTrac College Edition and the keywords "celebrities in media," read three recent articles to find several points of view on celebrities in the media. Summarize them in a brief article. Be prepared to discuss the topic in class.

5. Read "Impact/Culture: Magazine Ads Could Reflect American Culture" in Chapter 13 to learn about advertising ethics. Then using the keywords "advertising truth" look up several articles about truth in advertising. Write a brief paper in which you outline your understanding of the truth in advertising controversy and be prepared to discuss the issue in class.

CHAPTER 14

"*The republic was founded on the premise that you don't have to share your thoughts.*"

Deborah Stone, American Library Association, speaking in 2003 about the free speech restrictions imposed on library patrons by the Patriot Act.

According to the precedent-setting *New York Times* v. *Sullivan* case, which helped define press freedom, the media's role is to encourage "uninhibited, robust and wide open debate." Arguments among the public, the government and the media about the best way for the media to maintain this public trusteeship form the core of challenges and rebuttals to legal and regulatory limits on the media.

Writes *New York Times* columnist Tom Wicker, "Even though absolute press freedom may sometimes have to accommodate itself to other high constitutional values, the repeal or modification of the First Amendment seems unlikely. . . . If the true freedom of the press is to decide for itself what to publish and when to publish it, the true responsibility of the press must be to assert and defend that freedom."

The media are businesses operating to make a profit, but these businesses enjoy a special trust under the U.S. Constitution. The legal and regulatory issues faced by the media are attempts by the government to balance this special trust with (1) the interests of individuals and (2) the interests of government.

▶ U.S. Constitution Sets Free Press Precedent

All legal interpretations of the press' responsibilities attempt to determine exactly what the framers of the U.S. Constitution meant when they included the First Amendment in the Bill of Rights in 1791. The First Amendment established the concept that the press should operate freely:

> *Congress shall make no law respecting an establishment of religion, or prohibiting the free exercise thereof; or abridging the freedom of speech, or of the press; or the right of the people peaceably to assemble, and to petition the Government for a redress of grievances.*

In his book *Emergence of a Free Press*, Leonard W. Levy explained:

> *By freedom of the press the Framers meant a right to engage in rasping, corrosive, and offensive discussions on all topics of public interest. . . . The press had become the tribune of the people by sitting in judgment on the conduct of public officials. A free press meant the press as the Fourth Estate, [as]. . .an informal or extraconstitutional fourth branch that functioned as part of the intricate system of checks and balances that exposed public mismanagement and kept power fragmented, manageable, and accountable.*

A discussion of the restrictions and laws covering the press today can be divided into six categories: (1) federal government restrictions, (2) prior restraint, (3) censorship, (4) libel, (5) privacy and (6) the right of access.

▶ Government Attempts to Restrict Press Freedom

At least four times in U.S. history before 1964, the federal government felt threatened enough by press freedom to attempt to restrict that freedom. These four notable attempts to restrict the way the media operate were: the Alien and Sedition Laws of 1798, the Espionage Act of 1918, the Smith Act of 1940 and the Cold War congressional investigations of suspected Communists in the late 1940s and early 1950s. All four challenges were attempts by the government to control free speech.

*"We would like to request a change of venue to
an entirely different legal system."*

The Alien and Sedition Laws of 1798   Under the provisions of the Alien and Sedition Laws of 1798, 15 people were indicted, 11 people were tried and ten were found guilty. The Alien and Sedition Laws set a fine of up to $2,000 and a sentence of up to two years in jail for anyone who was found guilty of speaking, writing or publishing "false, scandalous and malicious writing or writings" against the government, Congress or the president. The laws expired in 1801, and when he became president that year, Thomas Jefferson pardoned everyone who had been found guilty under the laws.

The Espionage Act of 1918   Although Henry Raymond challenged censorship of Civil War reporting, journalists and the general population during that war accepted government control of information. But during World War I, Congress passed the Espionage Act of 1918. Not all Americans supported U.S. entry into the war, and to stop criticism, the Espionage Act made it a crime to say or write anything that could be viewed as helping the enemy. Under the act, 877 people were convicted. Many, but not all, of them were pardoned when the war ended.

   The most notable person cited under the Espionage Act of 1918 was Socialist party presidential candidate Eugene V. Debs, who was sentenced to two concurrent ten-year terms for giving a public speech against the war. At his trial Debs said, "I have been accused of obstructing the war. I admit it. Gentlemen, I abhor war. I would oppose the war if I stood alone." Debs was released from prison by a presidential order in 1921.

The Smith Act of 1940   During World War II, Congress passed the Smith Act of 1940, which placed some restrictions on free speech. Only a few people were cited under it, but the press was required to submit stories for government censorship. President Roosevelt created an Office of Censorship, which worked out a voluntary Code of Wartime Practices with the press.

   The code spelled out what information the press would not report about the war, such as troop and ship movements. The military retained power to censor all overseas war reporting. The Office of Censorship also issued guidelines for news broadcasts and commentaries, called the *Code of Wartime Practices for American Broadcasters*. (See Impact/Culture, p. 292.) The government exercised special influence over broadcasters because it licensed broadcast outlets.

HUAC and the Permanent Subcommittee on Investigations   The fourth major move challenging the First Amendment protection of free speech came in the late 1940s and early 1950s, culminating with the actions of the House Un-American Activities Committee (HUAC) against the Hollywood Ten and the Army-McCarthy hearings before the Permanent Subcommitee on Investigations presided over by Senator Joseph R. McCarthy.

   These congressional committees set a tone of aggressive Communist-hunting. When television broadcasts of McCarthy's investigation of Communist influence in the army and other reports eventually exposed his excesses, McCarthy's colleagues censured him by a vote of 67 to 22. But while the hearings were being held, they established a restrictive atmosphere that challenged free expression.

© Bettmann/CORBIS

Senator Joseph McCarthy explains his theory of communism during the Army-McCarthy hearings in the 1950s. Army counsel Joseph N. Welch, who was defending people who had been declared subversive by McCarthy, is seated at the table.

Excerpts from the 1943 Code of Wartime Practices for American Broadcasters

During World War II, the Office of War Information tried to control what was broadcast from the United States. Following are some of the rules radio broadcasters were expected to follow.

News Broadcasts and Commentaries

It is requested that news in any of the following classifications be kept off the air unless made available for broadcast by appropriate authority or specifically cleared by the Office of Censorship.

(a) Weather—Weather forecasts other than those officially released by the Weather Bureau.

(b) Armed forces—Types and movements of United States Army, Navy, and Marine Corps units, within or without continental United States.

Programs

(a) Request programs—No telephoned or telegraphed requests for musical selections should be accepted. No requests for musical selections made by word-of-mouth at the origin of broadcast, whether studio or remote, should be honored.

(b) Quiz programs—Any program which permits the public accessibility to an open microphone is dangerous and should be carefully supervised. Because of the nature of quiz programs, in which the public is not only permitted access to the microphone but encouraged to speak into it, the danger of usurpation by the enemy is enhanced.

Foreign Language Broadcasts

(a) Personnel—The Office of Censorship, by direction of the president, is charged with the responsibility of removing from the air all those engaged in foreign language broadcasting who, in the judgment of appointed authorities in the Office of Censorship, endanger the war effort of the United Nations by their connections, direct or indirect, with the medium.

(b) Scripts—Station managements are requested to require all persons who broadcast in a foreign language to submit to the management in advance of broadcast complete scripts or transcriptions of such material.

U.S. Government Office of Censorship, *Code of Wartime Practices for American Broadcasters*. Washington, D.C.: Government Printing Office, 1943, pp. 1–8.

▶ Prior Restraint

Prior restraint means censoring information before the information appears or is published. The framers of the Constitution clearly opposed prior restraint by law. However, in 1931, the U.S. Supreme Court established the circumstances under which prior restraint could be justified.

Near **v.** *Minnesota*   J. M. Near published the weekly *Saturday Press,* which printed the names of people who were violating the nation's Prohibition laws. Minnesota authorities obtained a court order forbidding publication of *Saturday Press,* but the U.S. Supreme Court overturned the state's action. In *Near* v. *Minnesota* in 1931, the court condemned prior restraint but acknowledged that the government could limit information about troop movements during war and could control obscenity. The court also said that "the security of community life may be protected against incitements to acts of violence and the overthrow of orderly government."

   Saturday Press had not violated any of these prohibitions, so the court order was lifted. But future attempts to stop publication were based on the *Near* v. *Minnesota* decision, making it a landmark case.

   In two important instances since *Near* (the Pentagon Papers and *United States* v. *The Progressive*), courts were asked to bar publication of information to protect national security. In two other situations (military offensive in Grenada and the Persian Gulf), the federal government took action to prevent journalists from reporting on the government's activities.

The Pentagon Papers

In June 1971, *The New York Times* published the first installment of what has become known as the Pentagon Papers, excerpts from what was properly titled *History of U.S. Decision-Making Process on Vietnam Policy*. The Pentagon Papers detailed decisions that were made about the Vietnam War during the Kennedy and Johnson administrations.

The documents were labeled top secret, but they were given to the *Times* by one of the report's authors, Daniel Ellsberg, an aide to the National Security Council. Ellsberg said he believed the papers had been improperly classified and that the public should have the information. After the first three installments were published in the *Times*, Justice Department attorneys received a restraining order against the *Times*, which stopped publication for two weeks while the *Times* appealed the case. While the case was being decided, *The Washington Post* began publishing the papers, and the *Post* was stopped, but only until the U.S. Supreme Court decided the *Times* case.

In *The New York Times Co.* v. *United States*, the court found the government had failed to prove that prior restraint was necessary. The *Times* and the *Post* then printed the papers, but publication had been delayed for two weeks. It was the first time in the nation's history that the federal government had stopped a newspaper from publishing. Legal fees cost the *Post* and the *Times* more than $270,000.

The Progressive Case

The next instance of prior restraint happened in 1979, when editors of *The Progressive* magazine announced that they planned to publish an article by Howard Morland about how to make a hydrogen bomb. The author said the article was based on information from public documents and interviews with government employees. The Department of Justice brought suit in Wisconsin, where the magazine was published, and received a restraining order to stop the information from being printed (*United States* v. *The Progressive*). *The Progressive* did not publish the article as planned.

Before the case could reach the U.S. Supreme Court, a Wisconsin newspaper published a letter from a man named Charles Hansen that contained much of the same information as the Morland article. Hansen sent eight copies of the letter to other newspapers, and the *Chicago Tribune* published it, saying that none of the information was proprietary. Six months after the original restraining order, *The Progressive* published the article.

Restricting the Press at Grenada

In an incident in 1983 that never reached the courts but that was a type of prior restraint, the Reagan administration kept reporters away from the island of Grenada, where the administration had launched a military offensive. This caused a press blackout beginning at 11 P.M. on October 24, 1983.

The administration didn't officially bar the press from covering the invasion, but the Pentagon refused to transport the press and then turned back press yachts and airplanes that attempted to enter the war zone. About a dozen print journalists and photographers were able to get in, but no television crews were allowed.

More than 400 journalists from 170 news organizations around the world who couldn't get to Grenada were left on Barbados, waiting for the news to get to them. Charles Lachman of the *New York Post* flew to Barbados, then to St. Vincent. Then he and some other reporters paid $6,000 to charter a boat to Grenada. It was five days after the invasion when they arrived and discovered that one of the casualties of the military's action had been a hospital.

News Blackouts and Press Pools

The Gulf War posed the toughest battleground yet for the rights of reporters versus the rights of the military to restrict access. On Saturday, February 23, 1991, about three weeks

Daniel Ellsberg, author of the Pentagon Papers, and his wife, Barbara, after a court hearing in Los Angeles. Ellsberg gave the papers to *The New York Times*.

J. P. Laffont/CORBIS Sygma

Pool Reporting An arrangement that places reporters in small, supervised groups to cover an event.

into the Gulf War, the Defense Department announced the first total news blackout in U.S. military history. For 24 hours, defense leaders were told to issue no statements about the actions of U.S. troops. Military officials said that instantaneous transmission of information from the battlefield meant that live TV pictures could be picked up by Iraq. Press organizations protested the ban, but the military argued that modern communications technology necessitated the blackout.

Pentagon rules for war coverage, reached in cooperation with journalists, imposed stricter limits on reporting in the Persian Gulf than in any other U.S. war. Reporters had to travel in small "pools," escorted by public affairs officers. Every story produced by the pool was subject to military censorship. This system, called **pool reporting**, had been created in response to reporters' complaints about news blackouts during the Grenada incident. An unprecedented number of journalists—1,300 in Saudi Arabia alone—posed a challenge for military press officers.

In a commentary protesting the restrictions, *The New Yorker* magazine said, "The rules, it is clear, enable the Pentagon to promote coverage of subjects and events that it wishes publicized and to prevent reporting that might cast it, or the war, in a bad light." Yet, in a *Los Angeles Times* poll of nearly 2,000 people two weeks after the fighting started, 79 percent approved of the Pentagon's restrictions and 57 percent favored even further limits. When the war ended, many members of the U.S. press in the Middle East complained bitterly about their lack of access, but the military and the public seemed satisfied with the new rules for wartime coverage.

By contrast, when the United States offered humanitarian aid to Somalia in 1992, the military offered the press unprecedented access, hoping to create a favorable impression of the military.

War in Afghanistan

During the war in Afghanistan, especially in the months immediately following the September 11, 2003, terrorist attacks in the United States, the military carefully controlled press access to information, citing security reasons. The military used press pools and also provided its own video footage of troop landings, produced by the military's combat film teams. "In World War II, accredited journalists from leading news organizations were on the front lines to give the public an independent description of what was happening," says *The New York Times*. "In the new war on terrorism, journalists have had limited access to many of the United States forces that are carrying out the war. . . . The media's access to American military operations is far more limited than in recent conflicts."

During the Iraq War in 2003, the U.S. government used a system called **embedding**, which meant that members of the press traveled with the military, but the press' movements were restricted and managed by their military units. Embedding was a reaction to the press' limited access in Afghanistan, but many journalists said they still had limited access to the real action, but the coverage left the impression with the public that the press was giving the

Gen. Richard B. Myers, chairman of the Joint Chiefs of Staff, describing to reporters images of U.S. paratroopers over Afghanistan in 2001. The scene, shot by the military's combat film team, presents an attempt by the Pentagon to carefully control its image.

whole story, when in fact the press had access to only a very limited view. (For more about embedded reporters, see Chapter 12.)

When should the government be able to prevent information from reaching the public? When should the press have access? The Supreme Court has not yet specifically answered this question, and the press and publishers remain vulnerable to military restrictions.

▶ Librarians Resist Requirements of the Patriot Act

In 2001, a few weeks after the terrorist attacks on the World Trade Center in New York City, Congress passed the Patriot Act, designed to give the U.S. government broad powers to track and detain people who were deemed a threat to the country for interrogation. Among the provisions of the Act was Section 215, which allows the Federal Bureau of Investigation to monitor public library records, including computer log-ins and the lists of books people check out of the library.

The U.S. government claims the act says the government can obtain "business records," which could include public library records, although the Act does not specifically mention libraries. Librarians say they are ready to cooperate with an investigation if they are given a search warrant, but claim the Patriot Act allows officials to seize anything they wish without a search warrant.

Some libraries have posted signs to warn patrons that federal authorities may review their records; others systematically shred patron's sign-in sheets for using library computers. The American Library Association officially has gone on record opposing unwarranted government access to library records, as specified in Section 215. The American Civil Liberties Union has sued in several different cities nationwide to keep library records private, and in 2004 a Los Angeles federal judge ruled that parts of the Patriot Act are unconstitutional violations of the First and Fifth amendments to the U.S. Constitution.

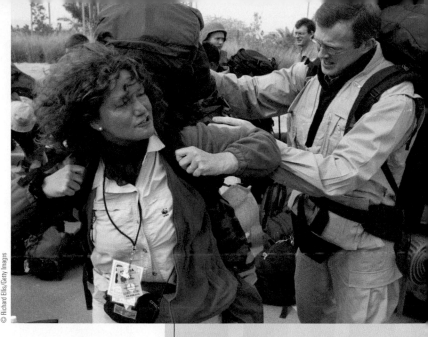

During the Iraq War in 2003, the U.S. government used a system of "embedding" reporters with the military, partly to counter criticism that reporters had been denied access to events during the 2001 war in Afghanistan (see page 294).

WARNING

Although the Santa Cruz Library makes every effort to protect your privacy, under the federal USA PATRIOT Act (Public Law 107-56), records of the books and other materials you borrow from this library may be obtained by federal agents. That federal law prohibits library workers from informing you if federal agents have obtained records about you. Questions about this policy should be directed to Attorney General John Ashcroft, Department of Justice, Washington, D.C. 20530

U.S. librarians have protested language in the Patriot Act, passed a few weeks after the terrorist attacks on the World Trade Center in New York, which librarians claim allowed federal authorities to seize public library records without a search warrant. A Santa Cruz, Calif. library posted a sign alerting patrons that federal agents can review customers' reading habits.

DON ASMUSSEN / *The Chronicle*

Don Asmussen, *San Francisco Chronicle*. Reprinted with permission.

Censorship   The practice of suppressing material that is considered morally, politically or otherwise objectionable.

▶ Free Expression versus Censorship

Different media industries historically have reacted differently to threats of **censorship**, the practice of suppressing material that is considered morally, politically or otherwise objectionable. Most threats of censorship concern matters of morality, especially obscenity.

In America, censorship is almost always an issue after the fact. Once the material is printed or displayed, it can be judged obscene and therefore censored. The motion picture and recording industries have accepted some form of self-regulation to avoid government intervention. The electronic media are governed by laws in the federal criminal code against broadcast obscenity, and the federal Cable Act of 1984 bars obscenity on cable TV.

Print media have been the most vigorous defenders of the right to publish. The print media, of course, were the earliest media to be threatened with censorship, beginning with the philosopher Plato, who suggested in 387 B.C. that Homer's *Odyssey* be expurgated for immature readers.

Local Efforts   More than 2,000 years after Homer's *Odyssey* was threatened with censorship, Boston officials banned the sale of the April 1926 issue of H. L. Mencken's magazine *The American Mercury*. The local Watch and Ward Society had denounced a fictional story in the magazine as "salacious." The title character of the story, "Hatrack," was a prostitute whose clientele included members of various religious congregations who visited her after church.

In Boston, surrounded by his supporters, Mencken sold a copy of the magazine at a prearranged time to a member of the Watch and Ward. The chief of the Boston Vice Squad arrested Mencken and marched him to jail, where he spent the night before going to court the next morning.

"Mencken passed an uneasy night," says Mencken's biographer Carl Bode, "knowing that he could be found guilty and perhaps even be imprisoned. . . . Returning to court he listened to Judge Parmenter's brief analysis of the merits of the case and then to his decision: 'I find that no offense has been committed and therefore dismiss the complaint.'" Mencken spent $20,000 defending the *Mercury*, but according to Bode, "the net gain for both the *Mercury* and Mencken was great. The *Mercury* became the salient American magazine and Mencken the international symbol of freedom of speech."

Mencken was defending his magazine against local censorship. Until 1957, censorship in America remained a local issue because the U.S. Supreme Court had not considered a censorship case. Today, censorship still is primarily a local issue, but two landmark Supreme Court cases—*Roth* v. *United States* and *Miller* v. *California*—established the major criteria for local censorship.

Roth **v.** *United States*   Two cases were involved in this 1957 decision. Samuel Roth was found guilty in New York of sending obscenity through the mail, and David S. Alberts was found guilty of selling obscene books in Beverly Hills. The case carries Roth's name because his name appeared first.

The U.S. Supreme Court upheld the guilty verdict and, according to legal scholar Ralph Holsinger, established several precedents:

- Obscenity is not protected by the First Amendment.

- Obscenity is defined as material "utterly without redeeming social importance."

- Sex and obscenity are not synonymous. Obscene material is material that appeals to "prurient [obsessively sexual] interest."

- A test of obscenity is "whether to the average person, applying contemporary community standards, the dominant theme of the material taken as a whole appeals to prurient interest." (This last description of obscenity has become known as the **Roth test**.)

Miller **v.** *California*   In the late 1960s, a California court found Marvin Miller guilty of sending obscene, unsolicited advertising material through the mail. The case reached the U.S. Supreme Court in 1973. The decision described just which materials a state could censor and also set a three-part test for obscenity.

According to the Supreme Court, states may censor material that meets this three-part local test for obscenity. The local court, according to legal scholar Ralph Holsinger, should determine:

1. Whether "the average person, applying contemporary community standards," would find that the work, taken as a whole, appeals to the prurient interest.

2. Whether the work depicts or describes, in a patently offensive way, sexual conduct specifically defined by the applicable state law.

3. Whether the work, taken as a whole, lacks serious *Literary, Artistic, Political* or *Scientific* value—often called the **LAPS test**.

The combination of the Roth and Miller cases established a standard for obscenity, leaving the decision on specific cases to local courts. The result is that there are widely differing standards in different parts of the country because local juries decide what is offensive in their communities. Books that are available to readers in some states are unavailable in other states.

School Boards as Censors
Many censorship cases begin at school and other local government boards, where parents' groups protest books, magazines and films that are available to students. For example:

- A school board in New York removed 11 books from school libraries, including the novels *Slaughterhouse-Five* by Kurt Vonnegut and *Black Boy* by Richard Wright, plus a work of popular anthropology, *The Naked Ape* by Desmond Morris.

- A School district in Little Rock, Arkansas, removed Harry Potter books from the school library because the school board claimed the tales of wizards and spells could harm schoolchildren.

- A school district in California required students to have parental permission to read *Ms.* magazine in the school library.

- A school board in Minnesota banned four books, including *Are You There, God? It's Me, Margaret* by Judy Blume, a writer well known for her young adult books.

- The state of Alabama ordered 45 textbooks pulled from the shelves after a federal judge said the books promoted "secular humanism."

Roth Test   A standard court test for obscenity, named for one of the defendants in an obscenity case.

LAPS Test   A yardstick for local obscenity judgments, which evaluates an artistic work's *Literary, Artistic, Political* or *Scientific* value.

American Library Association

The American Library Association (ALA) fiercely opposes any attempt to censor or restrict access to information. Each year, the ALA sponsors Banned Books Week to bring attention to the issue of censorship.

Familiar Titles Top the List of the American Library Association's Most Frequently Challenged Books 1990-2000

1. *Scary Stories* (Series) by Alvin Schwartz
2. *Daddy's Roommate* by Michael Willhoite
3. *I Know Why the Caged Bird Sings* by Maya Angelou
4. *The Chocolate War* by Robert Cormier
5. *The Adventures of Huckleberry Finn* by Mark Twain

6. *Of Mice and Men* by John Steinbeck
7. *Harry Potter* (Series) by J. K. Rowling
8. *Forever* by Judy Blume
9. *Bridge to Terabithia* by Katherine Paterson
10. *Alice* (Series) by Phyllis Reynolds Naylor

One-third of all censorship incidents involve attempts to censor library books and school curricula. These types of cases usually are reversed on appeal, but while the specific issues are being decided, the books, magazines and films are unavailable, and censorship efforts are increasing.

▶ National Efforts to Control Free Speech

The Meese Commission on Pornography   Censorship activities were encouraged from the federal level by the issuance, in July 1986, of the Final Report of the Attorney General's Commission on Pornography, called the Meese Commission (named for Attorney General Edwin Meese). The 1986 report reversed the conclusion of the 1970 Commission on Obscenity and Pornography, which had found that no convincing evidence existed to show pornography causes harm.

The 1986 commission concluded that pornography does cause harm and that even when sexually explicit material doesn't actually portray violence, it may be harmful to society and the family. The 1986 commission urged Congress to require convicted pornographers to give up the profits from producing and distributing offensive material, but the commission's arguments were not convincing, and no substantial legislation resulted.

The *Hazelwood* Case   In 1988, the U.S. Supreme Court for the first time gave public school officials considerable freedom to limit what appears in student publications. The case, *Hazelwood* v. *Kuhlmeier*, became known as the Hazelwood case because the issues originated at Hazelwood High School in Hazelwood, Missouri.

The high school paper, funded mostly from the school budget, was published as part of a journalism class. The principal at Hazelwood regularly reviewed the school paper before it was published, but in this case he deleted two articles the staff had written.

One of the deleted articles covered the issue of student pregnancy and included interviews with three students who had become pregnant while attending school, using pseudonyms instead of the students' names. The principal said he felt the anonymity of the students was not sufficiently protected and that the girls' discussion of their use or nonuse of birth control was inappropriate for a school publication. By a vote of 5 to 3, the U.S. Supreme Court agreed.

"Even though the legal rights of children have gained broader recognition in recent years, it remains that children are not adults and that they have no explicit or implied right to behave with the full freedom granted to adults," wrote Jonathan Yardley, a *Washington Post* columnist. "Freedom entails the responsibility to exercise it with mature judgment, and this neither young children nor adolescents possess."

The same newspaper, however, carried an editorial that opposed the decision. "Even teenagers," the *Post* editorial said, "should be allowed to publish criticism, raise uncomfortable questions and spur debate on subjects such as pregnancy, AIDS and drug abuse that are too often a very real aspect of high school culture today."

The decision is significant because it may change the way local officials monitor school publications. At Hazelwood, however, the principal's action drew the attention of the *St. Louis Post-Dispatch*, which published the censored articles, bringing them a much wider audience than the students at Hazelwood High.

▶ Libel Law

"Americans have increasingly begun to seek the refuge and vindication of litigation," writes legal scholar Rodney A. Smolla in his book *Suing the Press*. "Words published by the media no longer roll over us without penetrating; instead, they sink in through the skin and work inner damage, and a consensus appears to be emerging that this psychic damage is serious and must be paid for."

Four cases show how prominent the media are as targets of litigation:

- In 1983, actress Carol Burnett sued the *National Enquirer* for $10 million for implying in an article that she was drinking too much and acting rude in a Washington, D.C., restaurant.

- In late 1984, General William C. Westmoreland filed a $120 million suit against CBS, charging that he was defamed in a 1982 CBS documentary, *The Uncounted Enemy: A Vietnam Deception*.

- At the same time, former Israeli Defense Minister Ariel Sharon sought $50 million in a libel suit against *Time* magazine, claiming that *Time* wrongly characterized his role in a 1982 massacre of Palestinian refugees.

- In 1989, entertainer Wayne Newton was awarded $6 million in damages after he sued NBC-TV for a story that linked him to organized crime figures. NBC appealed the case, and eventually the award was overturned, but legal costs were in the millions.

These four cases involve the law of **libel**, which is only one recognized restraint on press freedom in the United States. (A libelous statement is one that unjustifiably exposes someone to ridicule or contempt.) All these cases indicate the media's legal vulnerability.

How can the country accommodate both the First Amendment concept of a free press and the right of the nation's citizens to keep their reputations from being unnecessarily damaged?

Libel   A false statement that damages a person's character or reputation by exposing that person to public ridicule or contempt.

The *Sullivan* Case Establishes a Landmark
Modern interpretation of the free speech protections of the First Amendment began in 1964 with the landmark *New York Times* v. *Sullivan* case. With this case, the U.S. Supreme Court began a process that continues today to define how the

press should operate in a free society. Many of today's arguments about the free press' role in a libel case derive from this decision.

The *Sullivan* case began in early 1960 in Alabama, where civil rights leader Dr. Martin Luther King, Jr. was arrested for perjury on his income tax form (a charge of which he was eventually acquitted). The Committee to Defend Martin Luther King bought a full-page ad in the March 29, 1960, *The New York Times,* which included statements about harassment of King by public officials and the police. The ad included a plea for money to support civil rights causes. Several notable people were listed in the ad as supporters, including singer Harry Belafonte, actor Sidney Poitier and former First Lady Eleanor Roosevelt.

L. B. Sullivan, who supervised the police and fire departments as commissioner of public affairs in Montgomery, Alabama, demanded a retraction from the *Times,* even though he had not been named in the ad. The *Times* refused, and Sullivan sued the *Times* for libel in Montgomery County, where 35 copies of the March 29, 1960, *Times* had been distributed for sale.

The trial in Montgomery County lasted three days, beginning on November 1, 1960. The jury found the *Times* guilty and awarded Sullivan $500,000. Eventually, the case reached the U.S. Supreme Court. In deciding the suit the Court said that although the *Times* might have been negligent because it did not spot some misstatements of fact that appeared in the ad, the *Times* did not deliberately lie—it did not act with what the court called *actual malice.* To prove libel, a *public official* must show that the defendant published information with *knowledge of its falsity* or out of *reckless disregard* for whether it was true or false, the court concluded. The Sullivan decision thus became the standard for subsequent libel suits: Public officials in a libel case must prove actual malice.

Redefining the *Sullivan* Decision Three important cases further defined the Sullivan decision.

Gertz v. *Robert Welch* A 1974 decision in *Gertz* v. *Robert Welch* established the concept that the expression of opinions is a necessary part of public debate, and so opinions—an editorial or a restaurant review, for example—cannot be considered libelous. The *Gertz* case also expanded the definition of public *official* to public *figure.* Today, people involved in libel suits are classified as *public figures* or *private figures.*

The criterion that distinguishes public and private figures is very important. People who are defined as private citizens by a court must show only that the libelous information was false and that the journalist or news organization acted negligently in presenting the information. *Public figures must show* not only that the libelous information was false but that the information was published with *actual malice*—that the journalist or the news organization knew that the information was untrue or that the journalist or news organization deliberately overlooked facts that would have proved the published information was untrue.

Herbert v. *Lando* A 1979 decision in *Herbert* v. *Lando* established the concept that because a public figure suing for libel must prove actual malice, the public figure can use the discovery process (the process by which potential witnesses are questioned under oath before the trial to help define the issues to be resolved at the trial) to determine a reporter's state of mind in preparing the story. Because of this decision, today reporters are sometimes asked in a libel suit to identify their sources and to give up notes and tapes of the interviews they conducted to write their stories.

Masson v. New Yorker Magazine   In 1991, the U.S. Supreme Court reinstated a $10 million libel suit brought against *The New Yorker* magazine by psychoanalyst Jeffrey M. Masson. Masson charged that author Janet Malcolm libeled him in two articles in *The New Yorker* and in a book when she deliberately misquoted him. Malcolm contended that the quotations she used were tape recorded or were written in her notes.

Malcolm wrote, for example, that Mr. Masson said, "I was like an intellectual gigolo." However, this exact phrase was not in the tape-recorded transcript of her interview. Masson contended that he never used the phrase.

Issues in the case include whether quoted material must be verbatim and whether a journalist can change grammar and syntax. When the case was heard again in 1994, the court found that Malcolm had changed Masson's words but that the changes did not libel Masson. The Masson case is the most important recent example of a continuing interest in defining the limits of libel.

Charges and Defenses for Libel   To prove libel under today's law, someone must show that:

1. The statement was communicated to a third party.
2. People who read or saw the statement would be able to identify the person, even if that person was not actually named.
3. The statement injured someone's reputation or income or caused mental anguish
4. The journalist or the print or broadcast organization is at fault.

Members of the press and press organizations that are faced with a libel suit can use three defenses: truth, privilege and fair comment.

Truth   The first and best defense against libel, of course, is that the information is true. True information, although sometimes damaging, cannot be considered libelous. Publishing true information, however, can still be an invasion of privacy, as explained later in this chapter. Furthermore, truth is a successful defense only if truth is proved to the satisfaction of a judge or jury.

Privilege   The press is free to report what is discussed during legislative and court proceedings, even though the information presented in the proceedings by witnesses and others may be untrue or damaging. This is called **qualified privilege**.

Fair Comment   The courts also have carefully protected the press' freedom to present opinions. Because opinions cannot be proved true or false, the press is free to comment on public issues and to laud a play or pan a movie, for example.

Today's Libel Laws and the Media   The four cases listed at the beginning of the Libel Law section on page 299 all involved public figures. The jury in the Carol Burnett case originally awarded her $1.6 million, but the amount was reduced to $150,000 on appeal. The William Westmoreland case was settled before it went to the jury. CBS issued a statement acknowledging that General Westmoreland had acted faithfully in performing his duties, but the combined legal costs for both parties were more than $18 million.

In the Ariel Sharon case, the jury found that *Time* had defamed former Israeli Defense Minister Sharon and reported false information but that the

Qualified Privilege   The freedom of the press to report what is discussed during legislative and court proceedings.

magazine did not act with actual malice, so no judgment was levied against *Time.* Sharon's legal costs were $1 million. The jury awarded Wayne Newton $19.2 million in 1986, but in 1990, the court threw out the award altogether, ruling there was not enough evidence to prove actual malice.

In several of these cases, members of the press were faulted for their reporting methods, even when the news organizations were not found guilty. Although *Time* magazine was exonerated in the Sharon case, for example, the jury issued a statement that said that "certain *Time* employees, particularly correspondent David Halevy, acted negligently and carelessly in reporting and verifying the information which ultimately found its way into the published paragraph of interest in this case." These cases show that the press must always be diligent.

Most successful libel judgments eventually are reversed or reduced when they are appealed. In the year 2000, there were 11 libel, privacy or related cases. The media won five cases and lost six. The median award in the lost cases was $2.5 million. In 1999, a Michigan jury returned a $25 million civil judgment for wrongful death against *The Jenny Jones Show* after a guest on the show murdered a gay man who revealed on that show that he had a crush on the show's guest, but this case also eventually was overturned on appeal. (In the meantime, *The Jenny Jones Show* was canceled.)

The major cost of a libel suit for the media is not the actual settlement but the defense lawyers' fees. Large media organizations carry libel insurance, but a small newspaper, magazine, book publisher or broadcast station may not be able to afford the insurance or the legal fees. The average libel case today costs about $150,000 in legal fees alone. These costs sometimes cause the press to be self-censoring.

"Since the Supreme Court ruled in favor of *The New York Times* in *The New York Times* v. *Sullivan* in 1964, no country in the world has offered more legal protection for those wishing to speak out frankly and fearlessly," writes eminent libel lawyer Floyd Abrams. "Yet today, American libel law manages to achieve the worst of two worlds: It does little to protect reputation. It does much to deter speech."

In the last 20 years, the dollar amounts awarded in libel cases against journalists have increased significantly. "Because no one can seriously deny that the extensive litigation of trials and subsequent appeals and high damage awards throw a chill over free speech, the ability of media to win at trial, win on appeal and keep ultimate damages low is in the longer-term interest of free speech and press in this country," said Sandra S. Baron, executive director of the Libel Defense Resource Center.

A Proposal for Libel Law Reform

Lawyer Floyd Abrams has proposed three major reforms in American libel law:

1. Publishers and broadcasters should be encouraged to print corrections quickly. When the media do offer timely corrections, no suit would be allowed.

2. Damages should be limited to amounts actually lost by those who sue. Abrams suggests that the actual amount of lost wages should be awarded and that the limit on emotional injury be $100,000.

3. The court should be able to require that the losing side pay the legal fees for the winning side.

"The libel explosion does chill the courage of the press," says legal scholar Rodney A. Smolla, "and in that chill all of us suffer, for it threatens to make the press slavishly safe, pouring out a centrist, spiceless paste of consensus thought. All of us lose if we permit the trivialization of free speech."

▶ Privacy Law

The public seems to feel that invasion of privacy is one of the media's worst faults. However, libel suits are much more common in the United States than suits about invasion of privacy. Because there is no Supreme Court decision covering privacy like *The New York Times* v. *Sullivan* covers libel, each of the states has its own privacy protections for citizens and its own restrictions on how reporters can get the news and what can be published.

Privacy is an ethical issue as well as a legal one. (See Chapter 15 for a discussion of the ethics of privacy.) Generally, the law says the media can be guilty of invasion of privacy in four ways:

1. By intruding on a person's physical or mental solitude.

2. By publishing or disclosing embarrassing personal facts.

3. By giving someone publicity that places the person in a false light.

4. By using someone's name or likeness for commercial benefit.

If they are successful, people who initiate privacy cases can be awarded monetary damages to compensate them for the wrongdoing. However, most invasion of privacy cases do not succeed.

Privacy is an ethical as well as a legal issue. In 1973, ten years after her husband President John F. Kennedy was assassinated, the court established Jacqueline Kennedy Onassis' right to privacy in *Galella* v. *Onassis.*

Physical or Mental Solitude

The courts in most states have recognized that a person has a right not to be pursued by the news media unnecessarily. A reporter can photograph or question someone on a public street or at a public event, but a person's home and office are private. For this reason, many photographers request that someone who is photographed in a private situation sign a release form, designating how the photograph can be used.

One particularly notable case establishing this right of privacy is *Galella* v. *Onassis*. Jacqueline Onassis, widow of former President John F. Kennedy, charged that Ron Galella, a freelance photographer, was pursuing her unnecessarily. He had used a telephoto lens to photograph her on private property and he had pursued her children at private schools. Galella was ordered to stay 25 feet away from her and 30 feet away from her children.

Embarrassing Personal Facts

The personal facts the media use to report a story should be newsworthy, according to the courts. If a public official is caught traveling with her boyfriend on taxpayers' money while her husband stays at home, information about the boyfriend is essential to the story. If the public official is reported to have contracted AIDS from her contact with the boyfriend, the information probably is not relevant to the story and could be covered under this provision of privacy law.

In reality, however, public officials enjoy very little legal protection from reporting about their private lives. Information available from public records, such as court proceedings, is not considered private. If the public official's husband testifies in court about his wife's disease, this information could be reported.

Bartnicki v. *Vopper*

In an important case for the press, *Bartnicki* v. *Vopper,* the U.S. Supreme Court in 2001 reaffirmed the media's right to broadcast information and to comment on that information, no matter how the information was obtained.

1992 03 30 037 DFR .HG Lights

"Lights! Camera! Justice!"

Dana Fradon

The case resulted from a cellphone conversation between Pennsylvania teachers' union negotiator Gloria Bartnicki and Anthony Kane, the union's president. The union was in the middle of negotiating a teachers' contract. During the conversation (which was intercepted and taped without Bartnicki's or Kane's knowledge), Kane is heard to say that if the school board didn't increase its offer, "We're going to have to go to their homes . . . to blow off their front porches."

A local activist gave the tape to radio station WILK-AM, and talk-show host Fred Vopper (who uses the on-air name Fred Williams) aired the tape. Bartnicki and Kane sued Vopper under the federal wiretap law, which provides civil damages and criminal prosecution for someone who disseminates information that is illegally intercepted. The case pitted the public's right to know versus the erosion of personal privacy by new technologies.

U.S. Supreme Court Justice John Paul Stevens wrote for the 6–3 majority that "a stranger's illegal conduct does not suffice to remove the First Amendment shield from speech about a matter of public concern." In this decision, the court again reaffirmed the press right to report information in the public interest.

False Light   The charge that what was implied in a story about someone was incorrect.

False Light

False Light   A writer who portrays someone in a fictional version of actual events should be especially conscious of **false light** litigation. People who believe that what a writer or photographer *implies* about them is incorrect (even if the portrayal is flattering) can bring a false-light suit.

The best-known false-light suit is the first, *Time Inc.* v. *Hill*. In 1955, *Life* magazine published a story about a Broadway play, *The Desperate Hours*, that portrayed a hostage-taking. The author of the play said he based it on several real-life incidents. One of these involved the Hill family, a husband and wife and their five children who had been taken hostage in their Philadelphia home by three escaped convicts. The Hills told police the convicts had treated them courteously, but the Hills were frightened by the events and eventually moved to Connecticut.

When *Life* decided to do the story about the play, the cast went to the Hills' old home, where *Life* photographed the actors in scenes from the play—one son being roughed up by the convicts and a daughter biting a convict's hand. None of these incidents had happened to the Hills, but *Life* published the photographs along with a review of the play.

The Hills sued Time Inc., which owned *Life* magazine, for false-light invasion of privacy and won $75,000, which eventually was reduced to $30,000. When the case went to the U.S. Supreme Court, the Court refused to uphold the decision, saying the Hills must prove actual malice. The Hills dropped the case, but *the establishment of actual malice* as a requirement in false-light cases *was important*.

In 1974, in *Cantrell* v. *Forest City Publishing Co.*, the U.S. Supreme Court held that a reporter for the Cleveland *Plain Dealer* had wrongly portrayed the widow of an Ohio man who was killed when a bridge collapsed. The story talked about the woman as if the reporter had interviewed her, although he had only interviewed her children. She was awarded $60,000 in her false-light suit, and the Supreme Court upheld the verdict. "Eight justices held that a properly instructed jury had come to the correct conclusion in finding actual malice," writes legal scholar Ralph L. Holsinger. "There was enough evidence within the story to prove that the reporter's word portrait of Mrs. Cantrell was false. The story indicated that he had seen her and perhaps had talked with her. He had done neither."

Only a few false-light cases have been successful, but the lesson for the press is that truthful portrayal of people and events avoids the problem altogether.

Right of Publicity   This facet of privacy law is especially important in the advertising and public relations industries. A portable toilet seems a strange fixture to use to establish a point of law, but a case brought by former *Tonight Show* host Johnny Carson demonstrates how the right of publicity protects someone's name from being used to make money without that person's permission.

In *Carson* v. *Here's Johnny Portable Toilets*, Carson charged, in 1983, that a Michigan manufacturer of portable toilets misappropriated Carson's name to sell the toilets. The manufacturer named his new line Here's Johnny Portable Toilets, and advertised them with the phrase "The World's Foremost Commodian." Carson said he did not want to be associated with the product and that he would be. Since he began hosting *The Tonight Show* in 1957, he said, he had been introduced by the phrase "Here's Johnny." The court agreed that "Here's Johnny" violated Carson's right of publicity.

This right can cover a person's picture on a poster or name in an advertisement. In some cases, this right is covered even after the person dies, so that the members of the immediate family of a well-known entertainer, for example, are the only people who can authorize the use of the entertainer's name or likeness.

▶ Fair Trial and Right of Access

The answers to two other questions that bear on press freedoms and individual rights remain discretionary for the courts: When does media coverage influence a jury so much that a defendant's right to a fair trial is jeopardized? How much access should the media be granted during a trial?

Fair Trial   The best-known decision affecting prejudicial press coverage of criminal cases is *Sheppard* v. *Maxwell*. In 1954, Dr. Samuel Sheppard of Cleveland was sentenced to life imprisonment for murdering his wife. His conviction followed reams of newspaper stories, many of which proclaimed his guilt before the jury had decided the case. The jurors, who went home each evening, were told by the judge not to read newspapers or pay attention to broadcast reports, but no one monitored what the jurors did.

Twelve years later, lawyer F. Lee Bailey took Sheppard's trial to the U.S. Supreme Court, where the conviction was overturned on the premise that Sheppard had been a victim of a biased jury. In writing the decision, Justice Tom C. Clark prescribed several remedies. He said that the reporters should have been limited to certain areas in the courtroom, that the news media should not have been allowed to interview the witnesses and that the court should have forbidden statements outside of the courtroom.

Courtroom Access   The outcome of the Sheppard case led to many courtroom experiments with restrictions on the press. The most widespread practices were restraining (gag) orders and closed proceedings. With a gag order, the judge limited what the press could report. Closed proceedings

Figure 14.1
**Cameras in the Court:
A State-by-State Guide**

Radio-Television News Directors Association
and Foundation

The District of Columbia is the only jurisdiction that prohibits trial and appellate coverage entirely.

TIER I: States that allow the most coverage.

TIER II: States with restrictions prohibiting coverage of important types of cases, or prohibiting coverage of all or large categories of witnesses who object to coverage of their testimony.

TIER III: States that allow appellate coverage only, or that have such restricting trial coverage rules essentially preventing coverage.

excluded the press from the courtroom. But since 1980, several court cases have overturned most of these limitations so that today the press is rarely excluded from courtroom proceedings, and the exclusion lasts only as long as it takes the news organization to appeal to a higher court for access.

Cameras in the courtroom is a sticky issue between judges, who want to avoid the disruption that cameras present, and broadcast news people, who want to photograph what is going on. In selected cases, however, cameras have been allowed to record complete trials. In 1994, for example, Court TV broadcast the entire trial of O. J. Simpson. Cameras in the courtroom is a state-by-state decision. (See Impact/Audience, above.) Some states allow cameras during civil but not criminal trials. Other states try to completely limit access. The U.S. courts and the press are not yet completely comfortable partners.

▶ Regulating Broadcast and Cable

All the American media are expected to abide by the country's laws. Regulation of the media comes from government agencies that oversee aspects of the media business. The print industry is not regulated specifically by any government agency. The largest single area of regulation comes from the Federal Communications Commission (FCC), which oversees broadcasting. Other regulating agencies, such as the Federal Trade Commission, scrutinize specific areas that relate to the media, such as advertising.

Since 1927, the concept behind broadcast regulation has been that the airwaves belong to the public and that broadcasters are trustees operating in the public interest. The history of U.S. broadcast regulation can be traced to government's early attempt to organize the airwaves. The Federal Communications Commission, based in Washington, D.C., now has five commissioners who are appointed by the president and are approved by the Senate. Each commissioner serves a five-year term and the president appoints the chairperson.

Today FCC regulation touches almost every aspect of station operations. Most important, U.S. broadcast stations must be licensed by the FCC to operate. Because the print media are unregulated by any government agency, the government exercises more direct control over the broadcast media than over the print media.

Like the print media, broadcasters must follow court rulings on issues such as libel, obscenity and the right of privacy. But broadcast stations also must follow the regulations that the FCC establishes.

▶ Telecommunications Act of 1996 Changes the Marketplace

On February 8, 1996, President Clinton signed the Telecommunications Act of 1996, the most far-reaching reform in the way the U.S. government regulates mass media in more than 60 years. The Telecommunications Act affects all aspects of the media industries, especially broadcast, cable, telephone and computer networks.

The Telecommunications Act of 1996 is transforming the nation's media industries. The last time the government intervened in a similar way to affect the development of the media business was in 1934, when Congress created the Federal Communications Commission (FCC) to regulate broadcasting in the "public interest, convenience and necessity."

The Telecommunications Act is merely an extension of the philosophy of deregulation—that free competition, with less government regulation, eventually will improve consumers' choices and encourage investment in new technologies. The theory is that free competition will lower costs for consumers and give them access to more types of media.

Critics, however, say the Act helps large media companies get bigger because only the large companies can afford to spend the money necessary to upgrade their equipment and delivery systems to take advantage of new markets. This philosophy of open competition, as established in the Telecommunications Act of 1996, will govern the media industries in the 21st century.

Goal: To Sell You "The Bundle"   "It's War!" declared *The Wall Street Journal* on September 16, 1996. The battlefield was telecommunications and the goal was "**The Bundle**." This term is being used in telecommunications to describe the combination of services the media industries will be able to offer you in the future. Following passage of the 1996 Telecommunications Act, large companies began positioning themselves to deliver the combination of telecommunications services that they think consumers will want.

"**The Bundle**"   The combination of telecommunications services that the media industries want to offer consumers in the future.

"Thanks to a combination of deregulation and new technologies, war has broken out in the communications market," says the *Journal*. "Everybody has joined the fray—long-distance telephone giants, the regional [local telephone] Bell companies and the cable-TV operators, the satellite outfits, the fledgling digital wireless phone firms and the Internet service providers. Even your old-fashioned power company.

"And they all want the same thing: to invade one another's markets and sell you one another's products and services.

"In short, they want to sell you The Bundle."

Your long-distance telephone company, such as AT&T, MCI or Sprint, would like to become your local telephone company, as well as the provider of your Internet access services.

This same long-distance company also would like to provide your TV programs, replacing the local cable system, adding these charges to your monthly telephone bill. Local telephone companies, the Regional Bell Operating Companies (**RBOCs**), sometimes called Baby Bells, want their slice of revenue, too, so in some areas of the country they are moving into the cable business. Some cable companies have announced plans to offer telephone service.

"The act so completely dismantles the existing regulatory structure that the telecommunications industry begins to look like a free-for-all," said Howard Anderson, founder and manager of Yankee Group, a Boston-based consulting firm. "Everyone is already trying to build multimedia networks to deliver everything from telephone and mobile services to Internet access and video-on-demand."

Targeting the "Power User"   This "bundling" of services would mean that you would pay one monthly bill for several types of media services to a single company, which, of course, would dramatically increase that company's portion of media revenue. "The goal for these companies is twofold," says Richard Siber, a wireless analyst for Andersen Consulting in Boston. "One is locking in a customer for life and providing one-stop shopping. And the other is revenue maximization, getting you to use their products more and more." *Business Week* magazine called this intense competition for customers a "Telescramble."

The primary target is the so-called "power-user," someone who uses a lot of media at home or in business. While the average consumer spends about $100 a month on media services, an upscale customer averages $300 a month, or $3,000 to $3,500 a year.

The Telecommunications Act of 1996 has created this battlefield for consumers' attention because the financial incentives are so huge. The economic future of every media company in the country will, in some way, be affected by this battle. That is why it is so important to understand this single piece of legislation, which is expected to have such a dramatic effect on consumers and on the future of the nation's media industries.

▶ Understanding the Telecommunications Act of 1996

The major provisions of the Telecommunications Act affect telecommunications, broadcast and cable. The Communications Decency Act, which is part of the Telecommunications Act, attempted to regulate access to cable and television programming and monitor the content of computer networks, including the Internet.

Universal Service   The Telecommunications Act of 1996 established, for the first time in federal legislation, a goal of universal service—meaning that, as a matter of public policy, everyone in the United States should have access to affordable telecommunications services. "In a time when we increasingly use information as a commodity, telecommunications are becoming increasingly important for the delivery of that commodity," according to the Benton Foundation, a public interest group. The intent of the Act is to make telecommunications available to everyone.

The FCC, of course, will define which type of access is offered in the "universal service" package. Does "universal service" mean only a telephone, or should "universal service" include access to a modem to connect a computer to the Internet? The FCC must decide what exactly constitutes "universal service" and whether access to a computer and a modem will be part of that

RBOCs   Regional Bell operating companies, or "Baby Bells."

Impact | Culture

Privacy Concerns: Can Online Public Data Be Too Public?

by Thomas E. Weber

Does the Internet know too much? Privacy advocates think so. And, increasingly, average users are inclined to agree. No wonder: Web sites have gotten downright nosy, openly demanding answers to personal questions and secretly tracking users' movements online. It is easy to get the impression that, in the age of the Internet, no secret is safe.

But it isn't that simple. Americans routinely relinquish all sorts of personal data—and they were doing so long before they ever heard of the Internet. Consumers who have applied for a credit card, earned a frequent-flier mile or signed up for a supermarket discount club have given marketers the means to look over their shoulders. And a tradition of public access to government records means that highly personal details—from divorce filings to bankruptcy judgments—have long been open to inspection by all. . . .

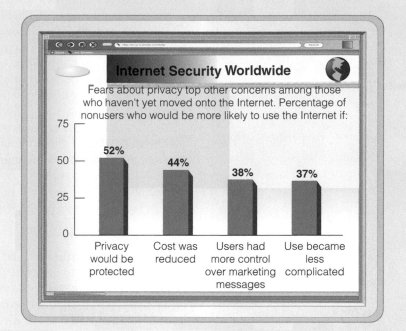

Internet Security Worldwide

Fears about privacy top other concerns among those who haven't yet moved onto the Internet. Percentage of nonusers who would be more likely to use the Internet if:

Privacy would be protected	Cost was reduced	Users had more control over marketing messages	Use became less complicated
52%	44%	38%	37%

The Federal Trade Commission grilled marketers and technologists about online privacy to determine whether the government needs to institute new safeguards or whether businesses can be trusted to regulate themselves.

Either way, consumers will ultimately have to decide where to draw the privacy line.

"Privacy Concerns Force Public to Confront Thorny Issues," *The Wall Street Journal*, June 19, 1997, B6. Reprinted by permission of *The Wall Street Journal*, © 1997 Dow Jones & Co., Inc. All Rights Reserved Worldwide.

Critical Question

What are your concerns about consumer privacy on the Internet, and what is the source of your concern(s)? Explain.

---

service, in an effort to use telecommunications to improve the economies of rural areas and central cities, as well as the rest of the nation.

Deregulation of Free Media The Telecommunications Act continues a policy of deregulation of commercial radio and television ownership that began in the 1980s. Radio and over-the-air broadcast television are viewed as "free media." Unlike cable stations, which require extra equipment and charge consumers for their services, over-the-air broadcasting is available to anyone with a radio or television—and 98 percent of U.S. households have a TV set. Over-the-air broadcasting therefore has the largest potential audience.

Relaxed Ownership and Licensing Rules Before the Act passed, broadcast companies were allowed to own only 12 television stations. The Act eliminates television station limits altogether and instead uses a station's potential audience to measure ownership limits. The Act allows one

Newsroom employees of *The Tampa Tribune*, WFLA-TV and the Tampa Bay Online Web site, all owned by Media General, work closely together in Tampa, Fla. Media deregulation allows a company like Media General to expand and buy even more broadcast properties.

Cross-Ownership   A company that owns TV and radio stations in the same broadcast market.

Telco   An abbreviation for "telephone company."

company to own television stations that reach up to 35 percent of the nation's homes. Existing television networks (such as NBC and ABC) can begin new networks, although they are not allowed to buy an existing network. NBC could not buy ABC, for example, but NBC could begin a second network of its own, such as NBC2.

Before the Act passed, radio broadcasters were allowed to own 20 AM or 20 FM radio stations nationwide. The Telecommunications Act removes the limit on the number of radio stations a company can own and in each market, the number of stations that one owner can hold depends on the size of the market. In a large market with 45 or more commercial radio stations, for example, a broadcaster may own eight stations; in a market with 14 stations, a broadcaster may own up to five stations.

The Act also allows **cross-ownership**. This means that companies can own television and radio stations in the same broadcast market. Companies also can own broadcast and cable outlets in the same market.

▶ Federal Communications Commission Proposes Further Deregulation

In 1999, the FCC further relaxed TV station ownership rules by allowing one broadcast company to own two TV stations in the same market. A company can buy a second station in the same market, says the FCC, as long as eight other stations with different owners are still operating in the market after the deal. In 2002, the FCC began considering further relaxation of the ownership rules which, among other things, would allow broadcasters also to own newspapers.

Also, the FCC licenses every broadcast station in the country, television and radio. In the past, renewal was a very complicated, rigorous process. Television stations were required to renew their licenses every five years and radio every seven. The Telecommunications Act extends the renewal period for both radio and television to every eight years.

In 2003, the FCC proposed to remove even more restrictions on broadcast ownership, making it easier for media companies to expand the number of stations they could own, including a provision that would allow a company to own TV stations that reach 45 percent of the U.S. population (up from 35 percent). FCC Commission Chair Michael Powell said the new relaxed rules were necessary to ensure competition, but Congress vowed to oppose any further easing of the ownership rules.

Local Phone Competition   Cable companies have services available to 90 percent of all homes in the Unites States, but only about 60 percent of American homes have cable. About 94 percent of all homes have a telephone. This means that, in the future, cable and telephone companies will be competing to deliver telecommunications services to home customers.

To encourage competition for delivery of video services, the Telecommunications Act allows local telephone companies to get into the video delivery business. The Act repeals the FCC's "telco-cable cross-ownership" restrictions ("**telco**" is an abbreviation for "telephone company"). Local telephone companies will be able to deliver video services either by an agreement with a cable operator or by creating their own delivery system. In turn, the cable companies are allowed to enter the business offered in the past by local telephone companies.

Large cable companies also want to deliver new types of telephone services. Cable operator TCI, for example, is developing a service with long-distance carrier Sprint to carry messages to and from wireless pocket phones.

To add to competition in the local telephone business, the Act also allows long-distance carriers to offer local telephone service to compete with the Regional Bell (local telephone) companies. Within two months of the Act's passage, the long-distance carrier AT&T filed to be allowed to offer local telephone service in all 50 states.

"If we get this right," said former FCC Chairman Reed Hundt, "you'll be buying communications services like shoes. Different styles, different vendors." Until all the rules are in place, however, the choices promise to be confusing for consumers and frustrating for people in the media industries who are trying to position themselves for a new future that isn't yet completely defined.

Unregulated Cable Rates   The rates that cable companies can charge have been regulated since 1992. In an attempt to control spiraling cable charges to consumers, Congress passed the 1992 Cable Act to regulate rates. The cable companies, facing competition from the local telephone companies, argued that Congress should remove rate regulation to allow the cable companies to compete and to help raise cable income.

The Telecommunications Act removed most rate regulation for all cable companies. All that remains is regulation to monitor the "basic tier" of cable service, often called "basic cable."

Doug Mills, *The New York Times*

FCC Chair Michael C. Powell announced new rules, in 2003, that would ease broadcast ownership restrictions even further than earlier deregulation attempts, but Congress vowed to oppose any further easing of broadcast ownership rules.

▶ Understanding the Communications Decency Act (CDA)

Along with the major provisions of the Telecommunications Act to increase competition, Congress also added three provisions to control content. These provisions in the legislation, called the Communications Decency Act, attempted to define and control the users' access to specific types of programs and content.

Program Blocking   The Telecommunications Act required cable owners to take steps within 30 days after the bill was signed to ensure that cable shows "primarily dedicated to sexually oriented programming or other programming that is indecent" did not accidentally become available to people who did not subscribe to the programs. This meant that every cable operator would have to provide a free "lock box" to every cable subscriber's home to block programs, whether or not the customer requested it.

On March 9, 1996, the day the program blocking provision of the Act was scheduled to go into effect, Playboy Enterprises successfully won a temporary restraining order, which prevented the application of the law. "Attorneys for Chicago-based Playboy argued that the provision violated constitutional protections of free speech and equal protection. Justice Department attorneys argued that the government has the right and duty to regulate the distribution of indecent material if it can be viewed or heard by children," reported *Bloomberg Business News*.

Indecent Material on the Internet   The Communications Decency Act made it a felony to send indecent material over computer networks. The Act also "prohibited using a telecommunications device to:

- Make or initiate any communication that is obscene, lewd, lascivious, filthy or indecent with intent to annoy, abuse, threaten or harass another person

Reprinted by permission of Steve Greenberg.

GREENBERG— EDITOR & PUBLISHER, 1996.

- Make or make available obscene communication
- Make or make available an indecent communication to minors
- Transmit obscene material—including material concerning abortion—or for any indecent or immoral use"

The Act relied on a very broad definition of the term "indecent," and courts have generally ruled that such speech is protected under the First Amendment. Under the Act's provisions, violators could be charged with a felony and fined up to $250,000.

More than 50 opponents of the Act's indecency provision, including the American Library Association and the American Civil Liberties Union, went to court in Philadelphia to challenge the law. On June 12, 1996, a three-judge Philadelphia panel unanimously declared that the Internet indecency provision was unconstitutional, and the judges blocked enforcement of the law. The judges issued a restraining order, which meant that the Internet indecency provisions could not be enforced and violations could not even be investigated.

The federal government had argued the Internet should be regulated like radio and television, but the judges said material on the Internet deserved the same protection as printed material. In presenting the court's opinion, Judge Stewart R. Dalzell made very strong arguments defending access to the Internet. "Just as the strength of the Internet is chaos," he wrote, "so the strength of our liberty depends upon the chaos and cacophony of the unfettered speech the First Amendment protects."

In 1997, the U.S. Supreme Court struck down the Communications Decency Act, making it much harder for Congress to limit Internet access in the future. What is interesting is that the courts are defining an electronic delivery system—the Internet—as if it were a print medium.

This is important because Congress and the president, through the FCC, have historically regulated the broadcast industries, but none of the regulations that apply to the broadcast media also apply to print. The content of the print media, by law and by practice, has historically remained unregulated because of the First Amendment's protection of free expression.

▶ Child Online Protection Act

COPA   Child Online Protection Act.

In 1998, after the Communications Decency Act was found unconstitutional, Congress passed the Child Online Protection Act (**COPA**), aimed at preventing minors from getting access to sexually explicit material, even though the material is legal for adults. Congress based the legislation on the idea that the government has a responsibility to protect children from content that is legal for adults but could be considered harmful to minors. Offenders would be fined up to $150,000 for each day they violated the law and face up to six months in prison.

Among the law's provisions was the requirement that libraries and schools that receive federal funding must install filtering software on public computers. Janet LaRue of the Family Research Council, which supported the restrictions, told *Trial* magazine, "Public libraries with unrestricted Internet access are virtual peep shows open to kids and funded by taxpayers."

Several organizations, including the American Library Association and the American Civil Liberties Union, immediately challenged the law in court on First Amendment grounds, saying the law was too restrictive. "Not one federal judge in the country has upheld these laws when applied to the Internet," ACLU attorney Chris Hansen told *Online Newsletter*. "Lawmakers should stop passing criminal laws for the Internet and focus instead on educating users to make their own choices about what content to view or avoid." In 2002, the U.S. Supreme Court agreed that Congress had no authority to limit Internet access.

▶ **U.S. Supreme Court Upholds Internet Filters for Public Libraries**

One year later, however, the U.S. Supreme Court upheld another law that said that libraries that take federal funds must equip their computers with anti-pornography filters. The case was brought to the court on behalf of 13-year-old Emalyn Rood, who logged onto the Internet in an Oregon library to research information on lesbianism, and Mark Brown, who found information about his mother's breast cancer on a Philadelphia library computer—information that might have been blocked by a commonly used Internet filter.

In a close 5–4 decision in *U.S.* v. *American Library Association,* the U.S. Supreme Court said the requirement for Internet filters is "a valid exercise of Congress' spending power." This decision means the U.S. government may now require Internet filters at libraries that receive federal funding. Librarians argued that Internet filters are a form of censorship that blocks valuable information from people who need it.

(Slip Opinion) OCTOBER TERM, 2002

Syllabus

NOTE: Where it is feasible, a syllabus (headnote) will be released, as is being done in connection with this case, at the time the opinion is issued. The syllabus constitutes no part of the opinion of the Court but has been prepared by the Reporter of Decisions for the convenience of the reader. See *United States* v. *Detroit Timber & Lumber Co.*, 200 U.S. 321, 337.

SUPREME COURT OF THE UNITED STATES

Syllabus

UNITED STATES ET AL. *v.* **AMERICAN LIBRARY ASSOCIATION, INC.**, ET AL.

APPEAL FROM THE UNITED STATES DISTRICT COURT FOR THE EASTERN DISTRICT OF PENNSYLVANIA

NO. 02–361. Argued March 5, 2003—Decided June 23, 2003

Two forms of federal assistance help public libraries provide patrons with Internet access: discounted rates under the E-rate program and grants under the Library Services and Technology Act (LSTA). Upon discovering that library patrons, including minors, regularly search the Internet for pornography and expose others to pornographic images by leaving them displayed on Internet terminals or printed at library printers, Congress enacted the Children's Internet Protection Act (CIPA), which forbids public libraries to receive federal assistance for Internet access unless they install software to block obscene or pornographic images and to prevent minors from accessing material harmful to them. Appellees, a group of libraries, patrons, Web site publishers, and related parties, sued the Government, challenging the constitutionality of CIPA's filtering provisions. Ruling that CIPA is facially unconstitutional and enjoining the Government from withholding federal assistance for failure to comply with CIPA, the District Court held, *inter alia*, that Congress had exceeded its authority under the Spending Clause because any public library that complies with CIPA's conditions will necessarily violate the First Amendment, that the CIPA filtering software constitutes a content-based restriction on access to a public forum that is subject to strict scrutiny, and that, although the Government has a compelling interest in preventing the dissemination of obscenity, child pornography, or material harmful to minors, the use of software filters is not narrowly tailored to further that interest.

Held: The judgment is reversed.

201 F. Supp. 2d 401, reversed.

The U.S. Supreme Court ruled in 2003 that schools and libraries may be required to put anti-pornography Internet filters on their computers or lose federal funding.

▶ **Violent Programming: TV Ratings and the V-Chip**

Under pressure from Congress, television executives agreed to devise a voluntary ratings system for television programs by January 1997. *Broadcasting and Cable* magazine called the imposition of the ratings system a "stunning defeat" for the television industry, which had long resisted all content regulation.

Jack Valenti, President of the Motion Picture Association of America (MPAA), led the ratings task force (Valenti also helped establish the current system of movie ratings). In January 1997, the task force announced the new ratings system, which *applies to all programming except sports, news magazines and news shows.*

The new ratings divide programming into six categories:

TVY—Appropriate for all children but specifically designed for a very young audience, including children ages two to six. Programs not expected to frighten younger children.

TV7—Designed for children age seven and above. More appropriate for children who are able to distinguish between make-believe and reality. May include mild physical or comedy violence.

TVG—Most parents would find these programs suitable for all ages. Little or no violence, no strong language and little or no sexual dialogue or situations.

TVPG—May contain some material that some parents would find unsuitable for younger children. Programs' themes may call for parental guidance. May contain infrequent coarse language, limited violence, some suggestive dialogue and situations.

TV14—May contain some material that many parents would find unsuitable for children younger than 14. These programs may contain sophisticated themes, sexual content, strong language and more intense violence.

TVMA—Specifically designed to be viewed by adults and therefore may be unsuitable for children younger than 17. May contain mature themes, profane language, graphic violence and explicit sexual content.

Unlike movies, which are rated by an independent board, the TV shows are rated by producers, networks, cable channels, syndicators and other people who originate the programs. These ratings evaluate violence and sexual content, and the results are displayed on the screen at the beginning of each program and coded into each TV program. The codes are read by a "V-chip." This microchip device is required to be included with all new television sets. The

V-chip allows parents to program the TV set to eliminate shows the parents find objectionable.

Six months after this rating system was adopted, in response to some public criticism that the first system did not address violence and sexual content, the majority of TV executives agreed to an additional ratings system that is more descriptive about program content. Using this system, a program will receive a general rating (TVY, TV7, TVG, TVPG, TV14 and TVMA) and a specific rating for violent or sexual content. The program and violent content labels are:

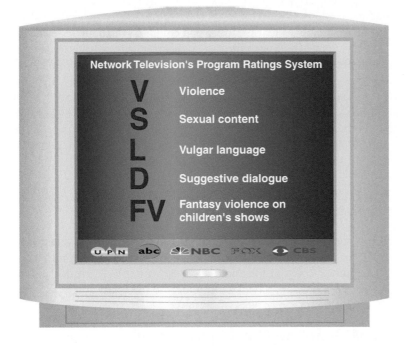

A program could receive TV14 plus an L, for example, or a TV7 and an FV. All of the broadcast networks agreed to use specific program content ratings, except NBC, which said it would offer its own advisory labels for violence and sexual content, similar to the "viewer discretion" warnings the networks traditionally had used.

▶ Government Regulation of Broadcast Indecency

In early 2004, responding to congressional pressure for more government control over the airwaves, the Federal Communications Commission proposed a $775,000 fine against Clear Channel Communications for a Florida radio broadcast of various episodes of "Bubba the Love Sponge." Clear Channel was fined $27,500 for each time the episode ran (a total of $715,000) plus $40,000 for record keeping violations at the station. Clear Channel said the programs were meant to entertain, not to offend its listeners.

FCC Chairman Michael Powell also urged Congress to increase the maximum fine for indecency to $275,000 per incident, saying the current maximum fine of $27,500 per episode isn't large enough to discourage objectionable programming.

Just a few days later, singers Janet Jackson and Justin Timberlake, performing on CBS-TV during halftime at the Super Bowl, caused another controversy when Timberlake reached over to Jackson and ripped off part of her costume, exposing her breast to an American audience estimated at 90 million people and a worldwide audience much bigger than that. Jackson

Getty

The Federal Communications Commission launched an indecency investigation of the CBS network after an incident during the 2004 Super Bowl when singer Justin Timberlake ripped off part of Janet Jackson's costume during their half-time performance.

DMCA   Digital Millennium Copyright Act.

WIPO   World Intellectual Property Organization.

apologized for the incident and so did Timberlake, but FCC Chairman Powell launched an investigation, saying, "I am outraged at what I saw. . . . Like millions of Americans, my family and I gathered around the television for a celebration. Instead, that celebration was tainted by a classless, crass and deplorable stunt. Our nation's children, parents and citizens deserve better."

Then in February 2004, Clear Channel Communications suspended radio personality Howard Stern from six of its stations—the only Clear Channel stations that carry the Howard Stern show—citing sexually explicit content aired on Stern's call-in show. Clear Channel said they would restore Stern's program when the show conformed to acceptable broadcast standards. The program continued to air on rival network Infinity Broadcasting, which syndicates the show, but by April 2004, Clear Channel had completely dropped Stern's show.

These controversies highlight the difficulties that arise when the federal government agency attempts to monitor free expression because no clear national standards of broadcast obscenity have been established. This means the definition of broadcast indecency often is based on politics and public pressure at the FCC, which shifts emphasis from one presidential administration to another. The main issue is: Should a government entity be given the power to decide what's obscene and/or indecent and then to enforce those restrictions?

▶ Congress and the U.S. Supreme Court Affirm Intellectual Property Rights

The right of ownership of creative ideas in the U.S. is legally governed by what are called intellectual property rights. Two recent developments, the Digital Millennium Copyright Act and the U.S. Supreme Court decision in *New York Times Co.* v. *Tasini,* have begun to define the issues of electronic copyright in the digital era.

Digital Millennium Copyright Act   Passed in 1998, the Digital Millennium Copyright Act (**DMCA**) is comprehensive legislation that begins to address the copyright issues provoked by the Internet. The law makes several changes in U.S. copyright law to bring it in compliance with two World Intellectual Property Organization (**WIPO**) treaties about digitally transmitted copyrighted and stored material. The WIPO is responsible for promoting the protection of intellectual property throughout the world.

The DMCA is designed to prevent illegal copying of material that is published and distributed on the Internet. The DMCA makes it illegal to circumvent technology that protects or controls access to copyrighted materials, such as the recordings shared on the Internet. The DMCA also makes it illegal to manufacture materials that will help people gain access to copyrighted materials. Congress allowed a two-year period before the Act was implemented so that Congress could study its ramifications. The DMCA became effective on October 28, 2000.

On July 16, 2001, the FBI arrested a Russian programmer, Dmitry Sklyarov, because he holds the copyright to a software program that allows people to circumvent Adobe Systems E-book format. Sklyarov's software allowed people to make backup copies of E-books that were protected with passwords. The program also made it easy to decode E-books and load them onto Palm Pilots and other portable, digital devices. Sklyarov's arrest was the first criminal lawsuit under the DMCA.

Supporters of the DMCA—which includes most of the media industries that hold the copyright on creative works, such as movies, books and recordings—say the DMCA is an important law that must be enforced to protect intellectual property. Opponents say the law goes too far by limiting

technological development. In January 2002, the U.S. Supreme Court agreed
to hear the Sklyarov case, and reversed the programmer's conviction.

The New York Times Co. **v.** *Tasini*   In 2001, a U.S. Supreme
Court decision in *New York Times Co.* v. *Tasini* affirmed that freelance writers
separately own the electronic rights to material they have written, even
though a publisher has first published their writing in printed form.

In 1993, freelance writer Jonathan Tasini, president of the National Writers' Union, discovered that an article he had written for *The New York Times*
was available on a database for Mead Data Center Corporation, which was
paying royalties for the material to the *Times*. Tasini hadn't been paid for this
use, so Tasini sued *The New York Times* and several other publishing companies
(including Newsday Inc., the Atlantic Monthly Co., and Time Inc.).

The suit claimed the publishers had violated copyright law by using writers' work on electronic databases without their permission and that this limited the rights of freelance authors to have their articles published and receive
compensation for their work. Several writers' organizations, including the
Authors' Guild, joined Tasini in the suit.

The *Times* claimed the digital versions of written works were simply "revi-
sions" of paper copies, which meant the rights belonged to the publisher so
the writers deserved no further compensation.

On June 25, 2001, by a vote of 7–2, the U.S. Supreme Court agreed with
Tasini. Writing the majority opinion, Judges Breyer and Stevens said that
upholding the freelance authors' copyright would encourage the development of new technologies and the creation of new artistic work. The court
said the *Times* must delete thousands of articles from its database for which it
had not obtained the rights. "Once again, the legal system has come down in
favor of the individual creator's rights in the digital age," Tasini told *Publishers
Weekly*. "Everywhere you look, the law supports creators."

This is a very important case—not only for freelancers, but for anyone who
creates intellectual property in the future. The court established the legal concept that the right to reproduce creative material electronically is very separate from the right to reproduce creative material in print and that writers
and other creative artists should be compensated separately for electronic
rights to their work.

Clear Channel Communications suspended and then dropped radio personality Howard Stern from 6 of its
stations in 2004, citing sexually
explicit content aired on Stern's program, another example of sensitivity
among some broadcast stations to
recent government criticism about
controversial program content.

▶ Advertising and Public Relations Law and Regulation

Advertising and public relations are governed by legal constraints and by regulation.

Legal Decisions Govern Advertisers   *New York Times* v.
Sullivan was a crucial case for advertisers as well as for journalists. Since that
decision, two other important court cases have defined the advertising and
public relations businesses—the *Central Hudson* case for advertising (which is
defined as "commercial speech" under the law) and the *Texas Gulf Sulphur*
case for public relations.

Central Hudson **Case**   In 1980, in *Central Hudson Gas & Electric Corp.*
v. *Public Service Commission*, the U.S. Supreme Court issued the most definitive
opinion yet on commercial speech. During the energy crisis atmosphere of the
1970s, the New York Public Utilities Commission had banned all advertising
by public utilities that promoted the use of electricity. Central Hudson Gas &
Electric wanted the ban lifted, so the company sued the commission.

The commission said the ban promoted energy conservation; the Supreme Court disagreed, and the decision in the case forms the basis for commercial speech protection today. "If the commercial speech does not mislead, and it concerns lawful activity," explains legal scholar Ralph Holsinger, "the government's power to regulate it is limited....The state cannot impose regulations that only indirectly advance its interests. Nor can it regulate commercial speech that poses no danger to a state interest."

The decision prescribed standards that commercial speech must meet to be protected by the First Amendment. The main provisions of the standards are that (1) the advertisement must be for a lawful product and (2) the advertisement must not be misleading. This has become known as the *Hudson test*.

To be protected, then, an advertisement must promote a legal product and must not lie. This would seem to have settled the issue, but controversy continues. Should alcohol advertising be banned? What about advertisements for condoms or birth control pills? Courts in different states have disagreed on these questions, and no Supreme Court decision on these specific issues exists, leaving many complex questions undecided. The Hudson test remains the primary criteria for determining what is protected commercial speech.

The *Texas Gulf Sulphur* Case

The most important civil suit involving the issue of public relations occurred in the 1960s in *Securities and Exchange Commission* v. *Texas Gulf Sulphur Company*. The Texas Gulf Sulphur (TGS) Company discovered ore deposits in Canada in late 1963 but did not announce the discovery publicly. TGS quietly purchased hundreds of acres surrounding the ore deposits. Although TGS officers began to accumulate more shares of the stock, the company issued a press release that said that the rumors about a discovery were "unreliable."

When TGS announced that it had made a "major strike," the Securities and Exchange Commission took the company to court. The U.S. Court of Appeals ruled that TGS officers had violated the disclosure laws of the Securities and Exchange Commission. The court also ruled that TGS had issued "a false and misleading press release." Company officers and their friends were punished for withholding the information. According to *The Practice of Public Relations*, "the case proved conclusively that a company's failure to make known material information (information likely to be considered important by reasonable investors in determining whether to buy, sell, or hold securities) may be in violation of the antifraud provision of the Securities and Exchange Acts. The *TGS* case remains today as a landmark in the history of public relations law."

The decision in the *Texas Gulf Sulphur* case means public relations people can be held legally responsible for information that they do not disclose about their companies. This case says that public relations people at publicly held corporations (businesses with stockholders) are responsible not only to their companies, but also to the public.

Government Regulates Advertisers

The main regulatory agency for advertising and public relations issues is the Federal Trade Commission (FTC), although other agencies such as the Securities and Exchange Commission and the Food and Drug Administration sometimes intervene to question advertising practices.

In 1914, the Federal Trade Commission assumed the power to oversee deceptive interstate advertising practices under the Federal Trade Commission Act. Today, the FTC's policy covering deceptive advertising says, "The Commission will find an act or practice deceptive if there is a misrepresentation, omission or other practice that misleads the consumer acting reasonably in the circumstances, to the consumer's detriment." The FTC can fine an advertiser who doesn't comply with an FTC order.

The Federal Trade Commission's five members serve seven-year terms. They are appointed by the president and confirmed by the U.S. Senate, and no more than three of the members can be from one political party. The commission acts when it receives a complaint the staff feels is worth investigating. The staff can request a *letter of compliance* from the advertiser, with the advertiser promising to change the alleged deception without admitting guilt.

Next, the advertiser can argue the case before an administrative law judge, who can write a consent agreement to outline what the advertiser must do to comply with the law. A cease-and-desist order can be issued against the advertiser, although this is rare.

Finally, because the FTC's members are presidential appointees, the commission's actions often reflect the political climate under which they operate. In the 1970s, the FTC became a very active consumer advocacy agency. This was challenged in the 1980s, when presidential policy favored easing regulations on business practices.

Under President Clinton in the 1990s, the FTC moved aggressively to cite companies for wrongdoing. For example, in 1997, the FTC conducted hearings to determine whether the government should impose safeguards on information access on the Internet to protect consumers' privacy. The George W. Bush administration has been less aggressive in monitoring advertising claims.

Legal and regulatory issues governing advertising and public relations, then, are stitched with the same conflicting values that govern all aspects of media. The courts, the FCC, the FTC and other government agencies that monitor the media industries are the major arbiters of ongoing constitutional clashes that attempt to balance the business needs of the media industries, the constitutional guarantee of freedom of speech and the government's role as a public interest representative.

Media | Review

© Mark E. Gibson/CORBIS

History

▶ Before 1964, the First Amendment faced only four notable government challenges: the Alien and Sedition Laws of 1798, the Espionage Act of 1918, the Smith Act of 1940 and the Cold War congressional investigations of suspected Communists in the late 1940s and early 1950s.

▶ In 1964, the *New York Times* v. *Sullivan* case set a precedent, establishing that to be successful in a libel suit, a public official must prove actual malice.

▶ American courts rarely have invoked prior restraint. The two most recent cases involved the publication of the Pentagon Papers by *The New York Times* and the publication of directions to build a hydrogen bomb in *The Progressive* magazine. In both cases, the information eventually was printed, but the intervention of the government delayed publication.

▶ *Gertz* v. *Robert Welch* established the concept that the expression of opinions is a necessary part of public debate.

▶ Because of the *Herbert* v. *Lando* decision, today reporters can be asked in a libel suit to identify their sources and to surrender their notes.

▶ The *Masson* v. *New Yorker Magazine* case addressed the journalist's responsibility for direct quotations.

Technology

▶ The Telecommunications Act of 1996 is the most far-reaching reform in the way the U.S. government regulates mass media in more than 60 years.

▶ Following passage of the Telecommunications Act, large companies began positioning themselves to deliver the combination of telecommunications services they think consumers want.

▶ The major provisions of the Telecommunications Act of 1996 affect telecommunications, broadcast and cable.

▶ The Communications Decency Act, which was part of the Telecommunications Act, attempted to regulate access to cable and TV programming and monitoring of computer networks, including the Internet.

▶ In 1997, the U.S. Supreme Court blocked the Internet indecency provisions of the Communications Decency Act.

▶ The right of ownership of creative ideas in the United States is legally governed by what are called intellectual property rights. Two recent developments, the Digital Millennium Copyright Act (DMCA) and the U.S. Supreme Court decision in *New York Times Co.* v. *Tasini*, have begun to define the issues of electronic copyright in the digital era.

▶ In 1998, Congress passed the Child Online Protection Act (COPA), aimed at preventing minors from getting access to sexually explicit material, even though the material is legal for adults. Several organizations, including the American Library Association and the American Civil Liberties Union, immediately challenged the law in court on First Amendment grounds. In 2002, the U.S. Supreme Court agreed that Congress has no authority to restrict Internet access.

▶ In 2003, the U.S. Supreme Court ruled that the federal government may withhold funding from schools and libraries that refuse to install Internet filters for pornography on their computers.

Business

▶ The press can use three defenses against a libel suit: truth, privilege and fair comment.

▶ The median amount awarded in a libel suit, in 2000, was $2.5 million, although most successful libel judgments eventually are reduced when they are appealed.

▶ *Sheppard* v. *Maxwell* established the legal precedent for limiting press access to courtrooms and juries.

▶ Unlike print, the broadcast media are regulated by a federal agency, the Federal Communications Commission.

▶ Under pressure from Congress, television executives devised a voluntary system of ratings for TV programming.

▶ The FCC under President Clinton moved to a policy of deregulation of station ownership and re-regulation of broadcast programming. In 2003, the FCC proposed regulations that would deregulate media ownership even further, although Congress has vowed to oppose any further easing of broadcast station ownership rules.

▶ The *Hudson* test for advertising means that to be protected by the First Amendment, an advertisement must promote a legal product and must not lie.

▶ The *Texas Gulf Sulphur* case established the concept that a publicly held company is responsible for any information it withholds from the public.

▶ The main government agency regulating advertising is the Federal Trade Commission. This agency adopted aggressive policies of protecting consumers' rights in the 1990s, but today is less forceful about policing advertisers.

Culture

▶ *Roth* v. *United States* established a three-part local test for obscenity: whether "the average person, applying contemporary community standards," would find that the work, taken as a whole, appeals to the prurient interest; whether the work depicts or describes, in a patently offensive way, sexual conduct specifically defined by the applicable state law; and whether the work, taken as a whole, lacks serious literary, artistic, political or scientific value (often called the LAPS test).

▶ The 1986 Final Report of the Attorney General's Commission on Pornography totally contradicted the findings of a similar study done in 1970. The 1986 report called for a nationwide crackdown on obscenity, linking sex crimes and other antisocial behavior to hardcore pornography. The commission's arguments were not convincing, and no substantial legislation resulted.

▶ In the 1988 *Hazelwood* case, the U.S. Supreme Court gave public school officials considerable freedom to limit what appears in student publications.

▶ Invasion-of-privacy lawsuits are much less common than libel suits. There is no U.S. Supreme Court decision that governs invasion of privacy, so each state has its own interpretation of the issue.

▶ Generally, the media can be guilty of invading someone's privacy by intruding on a person's physical or mental solitude, publishing or disclosing embarrassing personal facts, giving someone publicity that places the person in a false light or using someone's name or likeness for commercial benefit.

▶ Attempts by the Reagan administration to limit reporters' access to Grenada during the U.S. invasion in October 1983 were a subtle form of prior restraint.

▶ Pentagon rules for 1991 war coverage, reached in cooperation with journalists, imposed stricter restrictions on reporting in the Gulf War than in any previous U.S. war. In contrast, when the U.S. government delivered humanitarian aid to Somalia in 1992, the military encouraged press coverage.

▶ In 2001, the U.S. government controlled release of information to the American public about the war in Afghanistan even more than in the Gulf War.

▶ During the early months of the war in Afghanistan, the military used press pools and also provided its own video footage of troop landings, produced by the military's combat film teams.

▶ During the Iraq War in 2003, the U.S. government used a system called embedding, which meant that members of the press traveled with the military, but the press' movements were restricted and managed by their military units.

▶ In an important case for the press, *Bartnicki* v. *Vopper*, in 2001, the U.S. Supreme Court reaffirmed the media's right to broadcast information and to comment on that information, no matter how the information was obtained.

▶ Among the provisions of the Patriot Act is Section 215, which allows the Federal Bureau of Investigation to monitor library records, including computer log-ins and the lists of books people check out of public libraries. The American Library Association and the American Civil Liberties Union are challenging Section 215 in court.

Impact | Interactive

The Impact/Interactive CD-ROM that accompanies this text is your gateway to many electronic resources for broadening and testing your critical understanding of the material in Chapter 14. The CD-ROM features the following interactive elements for this and every chapter in the book.

▶ A two- to three-minute timely, high-interest CNN Today video clip with critical viewing questions and a link to relevant selections available within the InfoTrac College Edition database

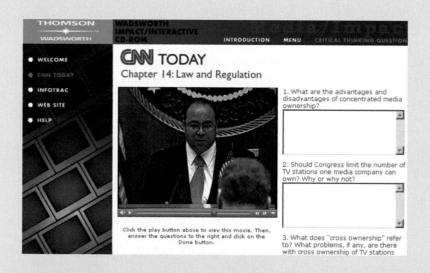

▶ Chapter-specific activities such as personal inventories and media projects

▶ A link to the *Media/Impact* Web site that offers helpful information and many additional electronic learning resources including

- An interactive chapter outline and study guide

- Interactive glossary term flashcards and crossword puzzles, concept animations, Internet activities and practice quizzes

- Live links for all URLs given in the chapter so you can easily access the additional information each site offers

▶ A link to InfoTrac College Edition—our online database of more than a million articles representing cutting-edge research and the latest headlines. Updated daily, this online library is available 24-hours a day, seven days a week. The InfoTrac College Edition activities provided below are designed to help you use this valuable resource.

▶ Working the Web

Live links for all of the sites listed below are provided on the Media/Impact book companion Web site, which can be accessed through your Impact/Interactive CD-ROM.

- ▶ **Freedom of Information Center (University of Missouri, Columbia)**
www.missouri.edu/~foiwww/index.html

- ▶ **Index on Censorship**
www.indexonline.org

- ▶ **Media Law Resource Center**
www.ldrc.com

- ▶ **Silha Center for the Study of Media Ethics and Law (University of Minnesota)**
http://silha.cla.umn.edu

- ▶ **Student Press Law Center**
www.splc.org

▶ InfoTrac College Edition Activities

Using InfoTrac College Edition's online database of full-text articles and abstracts, do the following activities as directed by your instructor. The database can be accessed through your Impact/Interactive CD-ROM.

1. Search InfoTrac College Edition using the keywords "intellectual property rights" or "DMCA." Read at least three articles on the subject, print them and either:
   a. write a brief paper on your findings, or
   b. bring the articles to class for a small-group discussion.

2. Using the keywords "newspaper libel" or "libel slander," look up at least three interesting articles in the last two years on libel. Read the articles, looking for consistency or inconsistency in the way the cases are decided, and/or interesting twists on the subject. Summarize your findings in a brief paper and be prepared to discuss this topic in class.

3. Advertising enjoys only a modified version of First Amendment protection of free speech. Using InfoTrac College Edition and the keywords "commercial free speech," read several articles that give you a view of developments in advertising's free speech protection status in the last decade. Summarize your findings in a brief article and be prepared to discuss the issue in class.

4. Controversy rages over whether cameras should be permitted in courtrooms in the United States. Court rulings vary from state to state. Using InfoTrac College Edition and the keywords "cameras in the courtroom," read several articles published in the last two years that give you a view of the many sides of the controversy. What is the legal basis of rulings and political opinions for and against cameras in the courtroom? What is your opinion about whether cameras should be present during trials and what are your reasons? Write a brief paper outlining your findings and be prepared to discuss the controversy in class.

5. Read "Impact/Culture: Privacy Concerns: Can Online Public Data Be Too Public?" in Chapter 14. Using InfoTrac College Edition, enter the keywords "online privacy" or "Internet security" and find at least three other articles on the subject. Print them and either:
   a. write a brief paper on your findings, or
   b. bring the articles to class for a small-group discussion.

Newsweek

May 26, 2003

wweek.msnbc.co

Behind the
Scandal at The
New York Times

THE
SECRET
LIFE OF
JAYSON
BLAIR

By Seth Mnookin

"Recognize that gathering and reporting information may cause harm or discomfort. Pursuit of the news is not a license for arrogance."

Society of Professional Journalists Code of Ethics

"Most of us would rather publish a story than not," explains journalist Anthony Brandt in an *Esquire* magazine article about ethics.

We're in the business of reporting, after all; most of us believe the public should know what's going on, has a right to know, has, indeed, a responsibility to know, and that this right, this responsibility, transcends the right to privacy, excuses our own pushiness, our arrogance, and therefore ought to protect us from lawsuits even when we are wrong.

But most reporters also know there are times when publishing can harm or ruin people's lives. Members of the press sometimes print gossip as truth, disregard the impact they have on people's lives, and are ready to believe the worst about people because the worst sells. . . . We in the media have much to answer for.

▶ Origin of Ethical Concepts in Journalism

Discussions about how journalists answer for what they do center on *ethics*. The word derives from the Greek word *ethos*, meaning the guiding spirit or traditions that govern a culture. Part of America's culture is the unique protection offered by the First Amendment of the U.S. Constitution, so any discussion of ethics and the American media acknowledges the cultural belief that the First Amendment privilege carries with it special obligations. Among these obligations are professional ethics.

Journalists are no more likely to exploit their positions than people in other professions, but when journalists make the wrong ethical choices, the consequences can be very damaging and very public. "It may well be that if journalism loses touch with ethical values, it will then cease to be of use to society, and cease to have any real reason for being," writes media ethics scholar John Hulteng. "But that, for the sake of all of us, must never be allowed to happen."

Journalists sometimes make poor ethical judgments because they work quickly and their actions can be haphazard; because the lust to be first with a story can override the desire to be right; because they sometimes don't know enough to question the truthfulness of what they're told; because they may win attention and professional success quickly by ignoring ethical standards; and because journalists sometimes are insensitive to the consequences of their stories for the people they cover. Consider these actual situations:

1. *Misrepresentation.* A newspaper reporter wrote in several columns that she was battling with cancer. When it was discovered that she was lying about the cancer, she said she lied because she was covering up the fact that she had AIDS, but she actually had neither disease. Her newspaper fired her after the revelations. Did her actions seriously challenge the newspaper's credibility or did the newspaper act insensitively?

2. *Insider friendships.* A nationally syndicated political columnist coached a presidential candidate before a televised debate and then praised the candidate's performance on a nationwide TV program. Did the columnist get too close to a news source, or did he simply help a friend?

3. *Reporting personal information.* A reporter verified that a well-known public figure was dying of AIDS, although the news figure would not admit his illness. Did the reporter infringe on the person's privacy, or did the readers deserve to know about the extent of this growing health hazard?

4. *Staging sensational events.* A television news magazine program showed a Chevrolet truck exploding when struck near the gas tank. But the explosion was staged, and the collision did not cause the explosion. Did the network exploit a story for its shock value, or will the public understand this type of tragedy better by viewing the staged demonstration?

WE'RE OUTSIDE THE HOME OF SOME PEOPLE WHO'VE JUST EXPERIENCED A GRAVE PERSONAL TRAGEDY TO BADGER AND HARASS THEM FOR THE SAKE OF A FEW RATINGS POINTS. LET'S WATCH.....

© Dan Piraro. Reprinted with special permission of King Features Syndicate.

▶ Defining Ethical Dilemmas

Ethical dilemmas faced by the media can be described using four categories: truthfulness, fairness, privacy and responsibility. False-hood is the issue for the journalist who embroidered characters in example 1. Bias is the question for the columnist who coached the presidential candidate in example 2. Invasion of privacy is the debate facing the reporter who published the AIDS information in example 3. The television network that staged the explosion in example 4 could be criticized for acting irresponsibly.

Some ethical debates are easier to resolve than others. These four incidents and several other examples are described here to demonstrate how vulnerable the media can be to ethical lapses.

▶ Truthfulness

Truthfulness in reporting means more than accuracy and telling the truth to get a story. Truthfulness also means not misrepresenting the people or the situations in the story to readers or viewers. Another aspect of truthfulness is the responsibility of government officials not to use the media for their own ends.

Misrepresentation   The journalist described in example 1 was Kim Stacy of the *Owensboro* (Ky.) *Messenger-Inquirer*. Stacy had written six columns for the newspaper in 1999, detailing her battle with terminal cancer. When it was discovered that she didn't have cancer, Stacy said she lied to hide the fact that she had AIDS. That claim also turned out to be a fabrication. Stacy had neither disease.

Stacy had revealed the hoax, according to *Editor & Publisher*, after friends at a newspaper where she had worked before questioned her story. After the revelations, the *Messenger-Inquirer* published a page one story about the fabrications and Stacy's firing, including an apology from the publisher.

The most celebrated recent case of a journalist misrepresenting the facts is Jayson Blair, a reporter for *The New York Times*. On May 1, 2003, the *Times* published a front page story, "Times Reporter Who Resigned Leaves Long Trail of Deception," which began: "A staff reporter for *The New York Times* committed frequent acts of journalistic fraud while covering significant news events in recent months, an investigation by *Times* journalists has found. The widespread fabrication and plagiarism represent a profound betrayal of trust and a low point in the 152-year history of the newspaper."

The *Times* said that as a reporter for the *Times*, 27-year-old Blair had:

- Written stories purported to be filed in Maryland, Texas and other states, when often he was still in New York

- Fabricated comments

- Concocted scenes

- Stolen material from other newspapers and wire services

- Selected details from photographs to create the impression he had been somewhere or seen someone, when he hadn't

The *Times* then published an exhaustive, unprecedented eight-page accounting of 73 significant falsehoods in Blair's stories the *Times* had published, detailing every traceable error, based on an internal investigation by its own reporters. In one story, for example, Blair had reported details from inside the National Naval Medical Center in Bethesda, Md., but the hospital said Blair had never visited the hospital. In another story about a stricter National Collegiate Athletic Association standard for class attendance, Blair quoted someone who said he never talked to Blair and used quotes from another newspaper as his own.

Alex S. Jones, a former *Times* reporter and co-author of *The Trust: The Private and Powerful Family Behind The New York Times*, told the *Times*, "To the best of my knowledge, there has never been anything like this at *The New York Times*. . . . There has never been a systematic effort to lie and cheat as a reporter at *The New York Times* comparable to what Jayson Blair seems to have done." Less than two months later, the *Times'* two top editors, who were responsible for hiring and supervising Blair, resigned.

AP/Wide World Photos

In May 2003, *The New York Times* admitted in a front page story that *Times* reporter Jayson Blair had fabricated comments, concocted scenes, stole material from other newspapers and news services, and selected details from photos to create an impression he had been somewhere or seen someone when he hadn't.

In another well-known case of fabrication, Janet Cooke was a reporter for the *Washington Post* in 1980 when she wrote "Jimmy's World," a story about an 8-year-old heroin addict. After she was awarded the Pulitzer Prize for the story in April 1981, reporters began to check up on her background, and the *Post* learned she had lied on her résumé. The editors then questioned her for several hours about the story. Cooke admitted "Jimmy" was a composite of several children she had interviewed. She was allowed to resign.

"'Jimmy's World' was in essence a fabrication," she wrote in her resignation letter. "I never encountered or interviewed an 8-year-old heroin addict. The September 19, 1980, article in the *Washington Post* was a serious misrepresentation which I deeply regret. I apologize to my newspaper, my profession, the Pulitzer board and all seekers of truth."

A month later, columnist Michael Daly of the New York *Daily News* resigned, admitting he had invented a British soldier in a story about Ireland. He said he had recreated the adventures of "Christopher Spell" from a description given to him by another soldier, who had witnessed the events. "The question of reconstruction and using a pseudonym—I've done it a lot," said Daly. "No one has ever said anything."

Misrepresenting the facts by creating untrue situations, as in these four cases, causes readers to question the facts in all stories: Which are actual people and which are not? Is the story fiction or fact? It also seriously affects the credibility and people's trust of the news organization where the fabrication occurs and all news organizations who strive to report the news accurately.

Disinformation   The intentional planting by government sources of false information.

Disinformation   In October 1986, the press learned that in August 1986 the Reagan administration had launched a **disinformation** campaign to scare Libyan leader Moammar Qadhafi. Selected U.S. government sources had planted stories with reporters that U.S. forces were preparing to strike Libya. The first report of the bogus preparations appeared in the August 25, 1986, issue of *The Wall Street Journal*.

On the basis of this story and a statement by White House spokesman Larry Speakes that the article was "authoritative," other newspapers, including the *Washington Post*, carried the story. This brings up the ethical question of the government's responsibility not to use the press for its own ends. State Department spokesman and former television reporter Bernard Kalb resigned when he learned about the disinformation campaign, saying, "Faith in the word of America is the pulsebeat of our democracy."

In 1988, the Drug Enforcement Administration (DEA) admitted it had used police nationwide to stage phony drug seizures and attract press attention to help DEA agents gain the confidence of major drug dealers. Law enforcement officials defended the practice as a way to outsmart criminals; the press responded that scams like these raise ethical questions similar to the planted Qadhafi story. How is the public to differentiate between true stories and those that are planted by the government?

▶ Fairness

Fairness implies impartiality—that the journalist has nothing personal to gain from a report, that there are no hidden benefits to the reporter or to the source from the story being presented. Criticism of the press for unfairness results from debates over close ties that sometimes develop between reporters and the

"Ok honesty is the best policy. Let's call that option A."

Impact | Culture

CNN Catches Fox Pirating Footage of Space Disaster

by David Bauder, Associated Press

During coverage of the space shuttle Columbia's disintegration, the folks in CNN's control room thought the picture they saw on rival Fox News Channel looked familiar.

So they tried a little experiment.

The producers superimposed a tiny CNN logo on the upper left corner of the network's screen as it showed the shuttle breaking into pieces. Blip! The same logo appeared on Fox News Channel.

Then they decided to abruptly switch cameras so a picture of correspondent Miles O'Brien appeared. For two seconds—until it was hurriedly replaced with a view of NASA's mission control—it looked like O'Brien was working for Fox, too.

The shuttle disaster provided a vivid example of how far networks sometimes go to get the most compelling pictures for a big report—and an even more vivid example of the consequences if they don't.

A Fox News Channel spokesman did not return a telephone call seeking comment. Earlier, a network representative told *Broadcasting & Cable* magazine that its request to explain the apparent piracy was "a waste of time."

As Columbia flew over Texas on the morning of February 1, Dallas station WFAA-TV followed its normal routine for fly-bys: A cameraman was assigned to capture the streak across the sky.

CNN/Getty Images

Fox News used footage of the Columbia space shuttle disaster from CNN, representing a new type of unethical misrepresentation—video piracy.

The picture appeared live on the air. But it wasn't for several minutes, until NASA said it had lost contact with the shuttle's crew, that it became clear what WFAA's pictures revealed.

Several videos of the shuttle falling apart, both amateur and professional, eventually surfaced that day. But for a certain period as the nation awoke to the unfolding tragedy—perhaps as much as an hour—WFAA's pictures were the only ones available.

WFAA has affiliation agreements with ABC and CNN. Television is a complex web of affiliations and exclusivity arrangements. Usually, they're respected. But with satellite dishes, networks can pluck virtually any pictures out of the sky, and, on a big story, it's often anything goes.

As published in the *Detroit Free Press*, www.freep.com/entertainment, 2/18/03. Reprinted with permission of The Associated Press.

people they write about—called *insider friendships;* reporters who accept personal or financial benefits from sources, sponsors, or advertisers—called *conflicts of interest;* and reporters who pay their sources for stories—called *checkbook journalism.*

Insider Friendships   The columnist in example 2 was ABC News commentator George Will; the candidate was Ronald Reagan. In 1980, Will coached Reagan before he faced President Jimmy Carter for a televised debate. On the ABC program *Nightline,* after the debate, Will compared Reagan's performance to that of a "thoroughbred." In 1983, when Will's actions were reported, Will admitted that he would not do the same thing again.

In 1987, ABC's Barbara Walters carried a private message from arms merchant Manucher Ghorbanifar to President Reagan after she conducted an exclusive interview with Ghorbanifar for an ABC story, an example of insider friendships.

ROSE M. PROUSER/AFP/Getty Images

In 1987, *The Wall Street Journal* reported that in December 1986, ABC's Barbara Walters had carried a private message from arms merchant Manucher Ghorbanifar to President Reagan after she conducted an exclusive interview with Ghorbanifar for an ABC story. Ghorbanifar was a central figure in the arrangements during 1985 and 1986 between the White House and the Iranian government to send arms to Iran in exchange for American hostages. Walters did not report on ABC that she had delivered a message to the president.

"After the interview, Mr. Ghorbanifar asked to speak with Ms. Walters again and asked that she send his views to the president," stated network spokesman Tom Goodman. "Believing that her information could be of assistance to the remaining hostages (held in Lebanon), and before informing her management, Ms. Walters did that and also gave her information to the appropriate editors" at the network.

New York Times reporter Judith Miller, who covered the Middle East for three years, criticized Walters for becoming a participant in a story she covered. "We're in the business of publishing what we know. . . . We don't deliver messages," said Miller.

Part of the job of being a reporter is learning to be friendly with many different types of people. In both the Walters and Will examples, the reporters became part of the stories they were supposed to be covering. How can the public trust a reporter who becomes more than an outside observer of events and instead takes part in the story? Insider friendships can remove a reporter's necessary detachment.

Conflicts of Interest

Reporters with conflicts of interest are divided between at least two loyalties, and the ethical question is, how will the stories the reporters write and the integrity of the organizations for which they work be affected?

In 1984, *The Wall Street Journal* fired stock tip columnist R. Foster Winans for allegedly leaking stories in advance to a group of friends who paid Winans for his help and then used the information to make profitable stock market investments. An investigation by the Securities and Exchange Commission had prompted the *Journal* to question Winans.

Winans was found guilty of 59 counts of fraud and conspiracy. "What made the conduct here a fraud was that Winans knew he was not supposed to leak the timing or contents of his articles or trade on that knowledge," wrote Judge Charles E. Stewart in his decision on the case. "Here, the fraudulent taking and misuse of confidential information stolen from *The Wall Street Journal* placed immediately in jeopardy probably its most valuable asset—its reputation for fairness and integrity." Winans was sentenced to 18 months in jail, $5,000 in fines, five years' probation, and 400 hours of community service.

A different type of conflict of interest happens when reporters accept free meals and passes to entertainment events (freebies) and free trips (junkets). In a 1986 survey of 34 newspapers, nearly half said they accepted free tickets to athletic events, and nearly two-thirds accepted free tickets to artistic events.

In another example of reporters' conflict of interest, Walt Disney World invited journalists from all over the world to attend its 15th anniversary celebration in Orlando, Florida, and more than 10,000 journalists and their guests accepted the invitation. Most of the press guests let Disney pay for the hotel, transportation and meals. *Variety* called the event "one of the biggest junkets in showbiz history," at an estimated cost of $8 million to Disney, the airlines, hotels and tourism agencies.

In an editorial about the junket, *The New York Times* said, "Accepting junkets and boondoggles does not necessarily mean that a reporter is being bought—but it inescapably creates the appearance of being bought."

Checkbook Journalism

In 1994, U.S. Olympic skater Tonya Harding reportedly received $600,000 for appearing on TV's *Inside Edition* after she was charged with participating in an attack on her opponent, Nancy Kerrigan.

When Pulitzer Prize–winning journalist Teresa Carpenter decided to write a book about a Tufts University Medical School professor who murdered a Boston prostitute, she says other writers were offering money to all of the main people involved in the case. According to *The New York Times*, even the owner of a local massage parlor, who was a minor figure in the case, left a message on Carpenter's phone machine that said, "Without compensation there will be no information."

After New York's "Son of Sam" serial killer David Berkowitz signed a lucrative film and book deal, the state passed a law to prohibit criminals from profiting from such contracts. But on December 10, 1991, the U.S. Supreme Court overturned the law as an infringement on free speech.

Besides the ethical questions about whether journalists and criminals should profit from crime, there are other hazards in any kind of checkbook journalism. One danger is that a paid interviewee will sensationalize the information to bring a higher price, so the interviewee's veracity cannot always be trusted.

A second hazard is that such interviews often become the exclusive property of the highest bidder, shutting out smaller news organizations and independent journalists from the information. In 1999, Las Vegas radio station KVBC-FM offered Monica Lewinsky $5 million for an exclusive interview about her relationship to then-President Bill Clinton. She never took the offer. ABC's Barbara Walters subsequently interviewed Lewinsky, but ABC did not pay for the interview.

A third possibility is that the person, who is paid by the news organization to comment, could possibly carry a hidden agenda, such as in an incident involving ABC News and former U.S. Secretary of State Henry Kissinger. In 1989, ABC News paid Kissinger to appear on ABC to analyze how the United States should respond to the events in Tiananmen Square. The student demonstrations in China threatened U.S. business ties there. Neither ABC nor Kissinger revealed during Kissinger's commentary that Kissinger's company had extensive investments in China at the time.

Can an influential person who is being paid for his analysis comment dispassionately about events when those events could affect his business? What responsibility did ABC have to tell its audience about Kissinger's ties to China?

AP/Wide World Photos

Walt Disney World invited more than 10,000 journalists and their guests to attend the theme park's 15th anniversary, and the journalists then reported on the park, an example of conflict of interest.

▶ Privacy

Reporting on AIDS and on rape are the most visible examples of a complex ethical dilemma: How does the press balance the goal of truthfulness and fact-finding with the need for personal privacy? Is the private grief that such a report may cause worth the public good that can result from publishing the information?

Reporting on AIDS

Because some people who contract AIDS are homosexual, announcing that a person's illness is AIDS can reflect on the person's private sexual behavior. One argument in favor of the press reporting the nature of the illness in these cases is that covering up the information means the public won't understand the widespread extent of the public health problem that AIDS represents.

"Covering up the truth, by doctors or journalists, stigmatizes other sufferers—the less widely the disease is acknowledged, the less easily they can be accepted. And it shields communities and industries from understanding the full, devastating effect of AIDS," argued *Newsweek* in a story called "AIDS and the Right to Know." The counterargument is that a person's illness and death are strictly private matters and that publishing the information is a violation of that person's privacy.

The case of the public figure with AIDS in example 3 describes two situations that occurred in the early years of the AIDS crisis. In 1986, New York lawyer Roy Cohn died of AIDS without acknowledging before his death that he suffered from the disease. Entertainer Liberace also withheld information about his illness before he died in 1987.

Roy Cohn became a public figure in the 1950s during the McCarthy hearings, as counsel for the Senate committee investigating Communist activity. As a lawyer in the 1980s, he defended many organized crime figures, and he lived a high-profile existence in New York City. A week before Cohn died, columnists Jack Anderson and Dale Van Atta published a story saying that Cohn was being treated with azidothymidine (AZT), used exclusively for AIDS patients.

Journalist William Safire criticized Anderson and Van Atta in *The New York Times*, saying, "Doctors with some sense of ethics and journalists with some regard for a core of human privacy are shamed by [this] investigative excess." After Cohn's death, *Harper's* magazine published copies of the hospital records on which Van Atta had based his column.

Liberace's illness was first revealed in the *Las Vegas Sun* about two weeks before he died. *Sun* publisher Brian Greenspun appeared on ABC's *Nightline* to defend publishing the information before the entertainer's death. Because only the *Sun* had access to the documentation, other members of the media who wrote about Liberace's illness attributed the information to the *Sun*. After Liberace died, the Riverside County coroner confirmed that Liberace suffered from a disease caused by AIDS.

A third example of a story about someone dying of AIDS represents one journalist's answer to the debate. *Honolulu Star-Bulletin* managing editor Bill Cox announced in a column published September 1, 1986, that he was going on disability leave because he had AIDS. "As a journalist," he wrote, "I have spent my career trying to shed light in dark corners. AIDS is surely one of our darkest corners. It can use some light."

Reporting on Rape　　Privacy is an important issue in reporting on rape cases. Common newsroom practice forbids the naming of rape victims in stories. In 1989, editor Geneva Overholser of *The Des Moines Register* startled the press community when she wrote an editorial arguing that newspapers contribute to the public's misunderstanding of the crime by withholding not only the woman's name, but an explicit description of what happened.

In 1990, the *Register* published a five-part series about the rape of Nancy Ziegenmeyer, with Ziegenmeyer's full cooperation. Ziegenmeyer had contacted the *Register* after Overholser's column appeared, volunteering to tell her story. The Ziegenmeyer series has provoked wide-ranging debate among editors about this aspect of privacy.

Is there more benefit to society by printing the victim's name, with the victim's permission, than by withholding it? Should the press explicitly describe sexual crimes, or is that merely sensationalism, preying on the public's salacious curiosity?

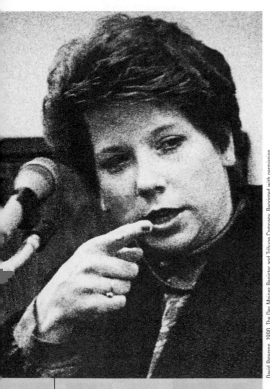

In 1990, *The Des Moines Register* published the name of rape victim Nancy Ziegenmeyer in a story about her rape, with Ziegenmeyer's cooperation. Publication of the victim's name sparked an ethical debate among news organizations about whether it is an invasion of privacy to use the victim's name in a rape story. While other adult crime victim's names are routinely used in stories, the names of rape victims commonly are not.

David Peterson, 1990, The Des Moines Register and Tribune Company. Reprinted with permission.

The Cohn, Liberace and Ziegenmeyer cases demonstrate how complex privacy issues in today's society have become. When is it in the public interest to divulge personal information about individuals? Who should decide?

▶ Responsibility

The events that journalists choose to report and the way they use the information they gather reflect on the profession's sense of public responsibility. Most reporters realize that they often change the character of an event by covering that event. The mere presence of the media magnifies the importance of what happens.

The media can be exploited by people in trouble or by people who covet the notoriety that media coverage brings. The media can exploit an event for its shock value to try to attract an audience. The following two specific examples demonstrate how differently individual media organizations and individual members of the media interpret their responsibility to the public.

A Staged Accident Demonstration

In 1992, *Dateline NBC* broadcast a story questioning the safety of General Motors trucks. To demonstrate the alleged problems with the trucks, NBC hired a company to stage an accident. In the news footage of the accident used in the broadcast, the truck's gas tank appeared to explode on impact. General Motors threatened to sue NBC, saying the footage had been edited to give the appearance of an explosion, that the company hired by NBC to stage the crash used spark igniters to cause the fire and that the staff of *Dateline NBC* knowingly aired footage that was an inaccurate portrayal of a staged event. This is example 4.

After a month-long, NBC-commissioned investigation, NBC president Robert Wright admitted that NBC News employees made "seriously flawed judgments and violated numerous [news] division guidelines in putting together a much-criticized story." The president of NBC News, who originally denied the GM charges, was forced to resign, as were three staff members directly involved with the story. The reporter on the story, who said she had argued against using the footage, was reassigned.

The NBC incident demonstrates the important responsibility that reporters share for the information they present to the public. The credibility of any news organization rests on the truthfulness of the information the reporters present, and slanting the information or portraying inaccurate information, even in just one story, ultimately can cause readers and viewers to doubt the believability of all stories presented by that organization.

A Live TV Raid

In 1993, three Cable News Network reporters accompanied Fish and Wildlife agents in Jordan, Montana, on an investigation of a ranch owned by Paul Berger, 72. Dressed in street clothes, like the Fish and Wildlife agents, the reporters spent 10 hours searching the ranch, along with the agents. The agents targeted Berger because they said they had reason to believe he was poisoning eagles who were preying on his sheep. During the aerial and ground search, agents wore recording devices that documented the raid for CNN.

"This was a case where government agents became reporters and reporters became government agents," asserted Berger's attorney, Henry Rossbacher. Eventually, a jury found that Mr. Berger was not guilty of poisoning eagles, mainly because the search of the ranch did not turn up any poisoned eagles, although Berger was found guilty of lacing two sheep carcasses

Michael Jackson's $1 Million Interview Deal

by Sharon Waxman

Los Angeles—Michael Jackson struck a deal with CBS to be paid in effect an additional $1 million for both an entertainment special . . . and his interview on *60 Minutes*. . . , part of yearlong negotiations between CBS and Mr. Jackson, a business partner of his said. . . .

A spokesman for *60 Minutes* denied that there was any payment for the interview, saying, "CBS News doesn't pay for interviews."

But Mr. Jackson's associate, who spoke on the condition of anonymity, said that the *60 Minutes* interview was part of what was originally a $5 million deal to put on an entertainment special

for CBS during a sweeps period and that CBS had already advanced the singer $1.5 million of that fee.

CBS postponed the special, which was incomplete, after the authorities issued an arrest warrant for Mr. Jackson on multiple counts of child molesting. But the Jackson associate said that in renewed negotiations, CBS agreed to pay another $1 million to the star to grant the interview so that the network could finally broadcast its entertainment special. . . .

"In essence they paid him" for the interview, the Jackson associate said of CBS, "but they didn't pay him out of the *60 Minutes* budget; they paid him from the entertainment budget, and CBS just shifts around the money internally. That way *60 Minutes* can say *60 Minutes* didn't pay for the interview. . . .

Another CBS spokesman, Chris Ender, said he had no knowledge of any payment to Mr. Jackson for an interview. "This was not a package deal," Mr. Ender said. "We licensed a special, nothing else. The only time these two projects were linked was in the wake of the charges, when we informed Mr. Jackson's people we couldn't broadcast the special if he didn't address the charges on a CBS news program."

Kevork Djansezian-Pool/Getty Images

Media critics said CBS paid singer Michael Jackson for an interview on the program *60 Minutes* as part of a package deal for a 2004 entertainment special. CBS denied it paid for the interview. The issue of paying someone for an interview is called *checkbook journalism*.

with poison, a misdemeanor. CNN aired the video of the raid in a 12-minute program called "Ring of Death," which portrayed the search as a complete success for the agents. Mr. Berger then sued CNN, claiming the network violated his Fourth Amendment rights against unreasonable search and seizure. CNN admitted no wrongdoing. "Investigative journalism is an important part of today's television market and entitled to all the safeguards of the First Amendment," the network said.

This case "raises ethical issues for the press, particularly at a time when news shows profiling law enforcement are proliferating, and reporters are increasingly eager to ride along on the execution of search warrants," reported *The Wall Street Journal*. "While a reporter's presence could work to a suspect's benefit—by keeping investigators from becoming abusive or bearing witness to a police failure to find incriminating evidence—critics worry that it more often than not inspires uncivil police theatrics. The allure of access often tempts the media into deals that give the authorities substantial power to shape both the content and timing of stories."

Are members of the media, as CNN contends, merely conduits for information? Or do they have a responsibility to protect the interests of the people they cover—in this case, the innocent as well as the guilty? And how did CNN's presence during the ranch raids change the event from a private to a public arrest? Does CNN have any responsibility for the person involved to report who actually faced charges, of which he was eventually found innocent? How are the ethics for live TV coverage different from the ethics for print coverage of the same event?

▶ Philosophical Principles of Journalistic Ethics

Scholars can prescribe only general guidelines for moral decisions because each situation presents its own special dilemmas. First it is important to understand the basic principles that underlie these philosophical discussions.

In their book *Media Ethics*, Clifford G. Christians, Kim B. Rotzoll and Mark Fackler identify five major philosophical principles underlying today's ethical decisions: (1) Aristotle's golden mean, (2) Kant's categorical imperative, (3) Mill's principle of utility, (4) Rawls' veil of ignorance and (5) the Judeo-Christian view of persons as ends in themselves.

1. *Aristotle's golden mean.* "Moral virtue is appropriate location between two extremes." This is a philosophy of moderation and compromise, often called the *golden mean*. The journalistic concept of fairness reflects this idea.

2. *Kant's categorical imperative.* "Act on that maxim which you will to become a universal law." Eighteenth-century philosopher Immanuel Kant developed this idea, an extension of Aristotle's golden mean. Kant's test—that you make decisions based on principles that you want to be universally applied—is called the *categorical imperative*. This means you would act by asking yourself the question, "What if everyone acted this way?"

3. *Mill's principle of utility.* "Seek the greatest happiness for the greatest number." In the 19th century, John Stuart Mill taught that the best decision is one with the biggest overall benefit for the most human beings.

4. *Rawls's veil of ignorance.* "Justice emerges when negotiating without social differentiations." John Rawls's 20th-century theory supports an egalitarian society that asks everyone to work from a sense of liberty and basic respect for everyone, regardless of social position.

5. *Judeo-Christian view of persons as ends in themselves.* "Love your neighbor as yourself." Under this longstanding ethic of religious heritage, people should care for one another—friends as well as enemies—equally and without favor. Trust in people and they will trust in you.

In American society, none of these five philosophies operates independently. Ethical choices in many journalistic situations are not exquisitely simple. What is predictable about journalistic ethics is their unpredictability. Therefore, journalists generally adopt a philosophy of "situational" ethics: Because each circumstance is different, individual journalists must decide what is best in each situation.

Should Parents Censor Their Children's Internet Use?

by Randy Cohen

I am the father of two early-adolescent boys, who are both active Web surfers. I'm not a prude, but I think exposure to the more extreme sexual images available online is not a good thing at their ages. I could retain a secret list of the Web sites they visit. But is that ethical? Is it equivalent to putting a hidden TV camera in their room (which I would consider a violation of their privacy), or is it an acceptable way for a parent to keep informed and be able to initiate discussion of this tricky topic?

—William S. Kessler, Seattle

Your concern for your sons' well-being necessitates neither that you cast them adrift in a sea of disturbing pornography nor that you abandon your respect for their privacy and fill your house with hidden cameras, tiny microphones and cagey men in dark glasses who would make everyone uneasy at the dinner table.

Illustration by Christoph Niemann

There's nothing wrong with being involved with what your kids see online; it is deception that is unsettling. Just as you probably wouldn't sneak a look at their diaries to learn what they're writing, you shouldn't surreptitiously tap their computer to find out what they're reading. If you intend to retain a list of the sites they visit, tell them. That way, you can discuss those sites with them, just as you might discuss a book that you saw them reading around the house.

But especially at this age, your boys may find any parental scrutiny—even of the most innocuous activities—embarrassing. The problem is balancing their right to free inquiry with your duty to shield them from truly disturbing images. And here the solution is not a technical fix but the more difficult task of teaching your kids a system of values. Part of that system reserves certain activities—drinking, driving, perusing pornography—for adults.

In any case, just as the boys can hide an ugly and upsetting magazine under the bed, they can browse online pornography with a friend's computer. But by creating a situation at home in which conversation is encouraged and privacy is respected, you have a better chance of helping them deal with the rough stuff.

The New York Times Magazine, July 25, 1999, p. 18. Reprinted by permission of the author.

Should the press adopt Rawls' idea of social equality and cover each person equally, or should public officials receive more scrutiny than others because they maintain a public trust? Is it a loving act in the Judeo-Christian tradition to allow bereaved parents the private sorrow of their child's death by drowning, or is the journalist contributing to society's greater good by warning others about the dangers of leaving a child unattended? Questions like these leave the press in a continually bubbling cauldron of ethical quandaries.

▶ How the Media Define Ethics

Ethical dilemmas might seem easier to solve with a rule book nearby, and several professional media organizations have tried to codify ethical judgments to ensure the outcomes in difficult situations. Codes of ethics can be very general ("Truth is our ultimate goal"—Society of Professional Journalists); some are very specific ("We will no longer accept any complimentary tickets, dinners, junkets, gifts or favors of any kind"—*The San Bernardino* [Calif.] *Sun*); and some are very personal ("I will try to tell people what they ought to know and avoid telling them what they want to hear, except when the two coincide, which isn't often"—former CBS commentator Andy Rooney).

Some ethical decisions carry legal consequences—for example, when a journalist reports embarrassing facts and invades someone's privacy. First Amendment protections shield the media from government enforcement of specific codes of conduct, except when ethical mistakes also are judged by the courts to be legal mistakes.

In most cases, however, a reporter or a news organization that makes an ethical mistake will not face a lawsuit. The consequences of bad ethical judgments usually involve damage to the newsmakers who are involved and to the individual journalist, damage to the reputation of the news organization where the journalist works and damage to the profession in general.

▶ Professional Ethics Codes

Professional codes of ethics set a leadership tone for a profession, an organization or an individual. Several groups have attempted to write rules governing how the media should operate. Television stations that belonged to the **National Association of Broadcasters (NAB)**, for example, once subscribed to a code of conduct developed by the National Association of Broadcasters. This code covered news reporting and entertainment programming.

NAB   National Association of Broadcasters

One provision of the NAB code said, "Violence, physical or psychological, may only be projected in responsibly handled contexts, not used exploitatively. Programs involving violence should present the consequences of it to its victims and perpetrators." Members displayed the NAB Seal of Approval before broadcasts to exhibit their compliance with the code.

In 1976, a decision by a U.S. federal judge in Los Angeles abolished the broadcast codes, claiming the provisions violated the First Amendment. Today, codes of ethics for both print and broadcast are voluntary, with no absolute penalties for people who violate the rules. These codes are meant as guidelines. Many media

organizations, such as CBS News, maintain their own detailed standards and hire people to oversee ethical conduct. Other organizations use guidelines from professional groups as a basis to develop their own philosophies. Advertising and public relations organizations also have issued ethical codes.

Three widely used codes of ethics are the guidelines adopted by the Society of Professional Journalists, the Radio-Television News Directors Association and the Public Relations Society of America.

The Society of Professional Journalists Code of Ethics

This code lists specific canons for journalists. Following are the code's major points:

Seek Truth and Report It.
Test the accuracy of information from all sources and exercise care to avoid inadvertent error. Deliberate distortion is never permissible.

- Identify sources whenever feasible. The public is entitled to as much information as possible on sources' reliability.

- Make certain that headlines, news teases and promotional material, photos, video, audio, graphics, sound bites and quotations do not misrepresent. They should not oversimplify or highlight incidents out of context.

- Never distort the content of news photos or video. Image enhancement for technical clarity is always permissible. Label montages and photo illustrations.

- Avoid misleading reenactments or staged news events.

- Never plagiarize.

- Avoid stereotyping by race, gender, age, religion, ethnicity, geography, sexual orientation, disability, physical appearance or social status.

- Distinguish between advocacy and news reporting. Analysis and commentary should be labeled and not misrepresent fact or context.

- Distinguish news from advertising and shun hybrids that blur the lines between the two.

- Recognize a special obligation to ensure that the public's business is conducted in the open and that government records are open to inspection.

Minimize Harm.
Show compassion for those who may be affected adversely by news coverage. Use special sensitivity when dealing with children and inexperienced sources or subjects.

- Be sensitive when seeking or using interviews or photographs of those affected by tragedy or grief.

- Recognize that gathering and reporting information may cause harm or discomfort. Pursuit of the news is not a license for arrogance.

- Show good taste. Avoid pandering to lurid curiosity.

- Balance a criminal suspect's fair trial rights with the public's right to be informed.

Act Independently.
Avoid conflicts of interest, real or perceived.

- Remain free of associations and activities that may compromise integrity or damage credibility.

Impact | Culture

CBS's "Voice" of Saddam was Fluent in Accents

Steve Winfield is a listed member of the Screen Actors Guild and, according to the owner of the "Fabulous Voices" Web site on which he once appeared, a translator with a particular flair for foreign accents.

Last week, for 17 million TV viewers, he was also the voice of Saddam Hussein during Dan Rather's exclusive CBS News interview of the Iraqi leader. Apparently putting on an Arabic accent, Winfield—who spoke with a seemingly everyday North American accent when he talked briefly to a reporter this week—read Saddam's answers to Rather's questions.

The translation was "100 percent accurate," CBS News said in a statement, describing Winfield as one of four translators it hired. The accent, CBS said, was meant to provide "a voice compatible with the piece.". . .

It didn't violate CBS News standards and practices, the network said, and the spokeswoman said CBS had used the technique previously.

A CNN spokeswoman said the network's standards would not allow a translator to fake an accent. Both NBC and ABC declined to comment, but

Photo by Len Irish.

Steve Winfield, who provided the voice of Saddam Hussein during a CBS interview of the Iraqi leader (shown above), used an Arabic accent to provide "a voice compatible with the piece." Critics at several other TV networks said that allowing a translator to fake an accent is not an acceptable news practice.

executives at ABC and NBC agreed that the practice is not used in their news divisions.

Elizabeth Jensen, *Los Angeles Times*, "Fake Accent for 'Voice of Hussein'?" March 5, 2003. Copyright © 2003 Tribune Media Services.

Critical Question

When no high-profile media ethics case is in the news, how often, if ever, do you think about the possibility that what you're reading, hearing, or seeing may not be true, or at least not what you understand it to be? How does this possibility affect the way you obtain or use information?

- Refuse gifts, favors, fees, free travel and special treatment, and shun secondary employment, political involvement, public office and service in community organizations if they compromise journalistic integrity.

Be Accountable. Clarify and explain news coverage and invite dialogue with the public over journalistic conduct.

- Encourage the public to voice grievances against the news media.
- Admit mistakes and correct them promptly.
- Expose unethical practices of journalists and the news media.
- Abide by the same high standards to which they hold others.

Radio-Television News Directors Association Code of Broadcast News Ethics

The RTNDA offers a seven-point program for broadcasters:

1. Strive to present the source or nature of broadcast news material in a way that is balanced, accurate and fair.

   A. They will evaluate information solely on its merits as news, rejecting sensationalism or misleading emphasis in any form.

   B. They will guard against using audio or video material in a way that deceives the audience.

   C. They will not mislead the public by presenting as spontaneous news any material which is staged or rehearsed.

   D. They will identify people by race, creed, nationality or prior status only when it is relevant.

   E. They will clearly label opinion and commentary.

   F. They will promptly acknowledge and correct errors.

2. Strive to conduct themselves in a manner that protects them from conflicts of interest, real or perceived. They will decline gifts or favors which would influence or appear to influence their judgments.

3. Respect the dignity, privacy and well-being of people with whom they deal.

4. Recognize the need to protect confidential sources. They will promise confidentiality only with the intention of keeping that promise.

5. Respect everyone's right to a fair trial.

6. Broadcast the private transmissions of other broadcasters only with permission.

7. Actively encourage observance of this Code by all journalists, whether members of the Radio-Television News Directors Association or not.

The Public Relations Society of America Standards

The Code of Professional Standards, first adopted in 1950 by the Public Relations Society of America, has been revised several times since then. Here are some excerpts:

- A member shall deal fairly with clients or employers, past, present, or potential, with fellow practitioners, and with the general public.

- A member shall adhere to truth and accuracy and to generally accepted standards of good taste.

- A member shall not intentionally communicate false or misleading information, and is obligated to use care to avoid communication of false or misleading information.

- A member shall be prepared to identify publicly the name of the client or employer on whose behalf any public communication is made.

- A member shall not guarantee the achievement of specified results beyond the member's direct control.

▶ The Media's Response to Criticism

Prescriptive codes of ethics are helpful in describing what journalists should do, and informal guidelines can supplement professional codes. Moreover, most journalists use good judgment. But what happens when they don't?

People with serious complaints against broadcasters sometimes appeal to the Federal Communications Commission, but what about complaints that must be handled more quickly? The press has offered three solutions: press councils, readers' representatives and correction boxes.

News Councils

News councils originated in Great Britain. They are composed of people who formerly worked or currently work in the news business, as well as some laypeople. The council reviews complaints from the public, and when the members determine that a mistake has been made, the council reports its findings to the offending news organization.

In 1973, the Twentieth-Century Fund established a National News Council in the United States, which eventually was funded through contributions from various news organizations. The council was composed of 18 members from the press and the public. The council was disbanded in 1984, largely because some major news organizations stopped giving money to support the idea, but also because several news managers opposed the council, arguing that the profession should police itself.

Today, only two news councils exist in the United States, the Minnesota News Council and the Honolulu Community Media Council. The Minnesota council is the oldest. Since 1970, the council's 24 members, half of them journalists and half of them public members such as lawyers and teachers, have reviewed complaints about the state's media. Half of the complaints have been ruled in favor of the journalists.

The council has no enforcement power, only the power of public scrutiny. Media ethics scholar John Hulteng writes:

> It would seem that—as with the [ethical] codes—the great impact of the press councils is likely to be on the responsible editors, publishers and broadcasters who for the most part were already attempting to behave ethically. . . . An additional value of the councils may be the mutual understanding that grows out of the exchange across the council table between the members of the public and the managers of the media. These values should not be dismissed as insignificant, of course. But neither should too much be expected of them.

Readers' Representatives

The *readers' representative* (also called an ombudsperson) is a go-between at a newspaper who responds to complaints from the public and regularly publishes answers to criticism in the newspaper. About two dozen newspapers throughout the country, including the *Washington Post*, *The Kansas City Star* and the Louisville *Courier-Journal*, have tried the idea, but most newspapers still funnel complaints directly to the editor.

Correction Boxes

The *correction box* is a device that often is handled by a readers' representative but also has been adopted by many papers without a readers' representative. The box is published in the same place, usually a prominent one, in the newspaper every day. As a permanent feature of the newspaper, the correction box leads readers to notice when the newspaper retracts or modifies a statement. It is used to counter criticism that corrections sometimes receive less attention from readers than the original stories.

Many newspapers regularly publish correction boxes in a prominent space in the newspaper to clarify and correct mistakes from previous editions.

▶ The Importance of Professional Ethics

Readers' representatives and correction boxes help newspapers to handle criticism and avert possible legal problems that some stories foster. But these solutions address only a small percentage of issues. In newsrooms every day, reporters face the same ethical decisions all people face in their daily lives—whether to be honest, how to be fair, how to be sensitive and how to be responsible.

The difference is that, unlike personal ethical dilemmas that other people can debate privately, reporters and editors publish and broadcast the results of their ethical judgments and those judgments become public knowledge—in newspapers, magazines, books and on radio, television, and the Internet. So potentially, the media's ethical decisions can broadly affect society.

A profession that accepts ethical behavior as a standard helps guarantee a future for that profession. The major commodity the press in America has to offer is information, and when the presentation of that information is weakened by untruth, bias, intrusiveness or irresponsibility, the press gains few advocates and acquires more enemies. Writes John Hulteng:

The primary objective of the press and those who work with it is to bring readers, listeners, and viewers as honest, accurate, and complete an account of the day's events as possible. . . . The need to be informed is so great that the Constitution provides the press with a First Amendment standing that is unique among business enterprises. But as with most grants of power, there is an accompanying responsibility, not constitutionally mandated but nonetheless well understood: that the power of the press must be used responsibly and compassionately.

Media | Review

History
▶ The word *ethics* derives from the Greek word *ethos*, which means the guiding spirit or traditions that govern a culture.

▶ The National Press Council, created to hear consumer complaints about the press, was created in 1973 but disbanded in 1984.

Business
▶ Staged events, such as the GM truck explosion on NBC, and live events, such as the ranch raids broadcast by CNN, offer especially perilous ethical situations.

▶ Several media professions have adopted ethical codes to guide their conduct. Three of these codes are the guidelines adopted by the Society of Professional Journalists, the Radio-Television News Directors Association and the Public Relations Society of America.

▶ The three responses of the U.S.press to press criticism have been to create news councils, to employ readers' representatives and to publish correction boxes.

▶ Today only two news councils still exist in the United States—the Minnesota News Council and the Honolulu Community Media Council.

Culture
▶ Journalists' ethical dilemmas can be discussed using four categories: truthfulness, fairness, privacy and responsibility.

▶ Truthfulness means more than telling the truth to get a story. Truthfulness also means not misrepresenting the people or the situations in the story for readers or viewers.

▶ Truthfulness means that government agencies should not knowingly provide disinformation to the press.

▶ Truthfulness means that published photographs should be accurate portrayals of events and should not intentionally distort reality.

▶ Fairness implies impartiality—that the journalist has nothing personal to gain from a report, that there are no hidden benefits to the reporter or to the source from the story being presented.

▶ Criticism of the press for unfairness results from debates over insider friendships, conflicts of interest and checkbook journalism.

▶ Two important invasion-of-privacy issues are the publication of names of AIDS victims and the publication of the names of rape victims.

▶ Responsibility means that reporters and editors must be careful about the way they use the information they gather.

▶ Five philosophical principles underlying the practical application of ethical decisions are: (1) Aristotle's golden mean, (2) Immanual Kant's categorical imperative, (3) John Stuart Mill's principle of utility, (4) John Rawls's veil of ignorance and (5) the Judeo-Christian view of persons as ends in themselves.

▶ The most celebrated recent case of a journalist misrepresenting the facts is Jayson Blair, a reporter for *The New York Times*. In May 2003, *The New York Times* admitted in a front page story that *Times* reporter Jayson Blair had fabricated comments, concocted scenes, stole material from other newspapers and news services and selected details from photos to create an impression he had been somewhere or seen someone when he hadn't.

Impact | Interactive

The Impact/Interactive CD-ROM that accompanies this text is your gateway to many electronic resources for broadening and testing your critical understanding of the material in Chapter 15. The CD-ROM features the following interactive elements for this and every chapter in the book.

▶ A two- to three-minute timely, high-interest CNN Today video clip with critical viewing questions and a link to relevant selections available within the InfoTrac College Edition database

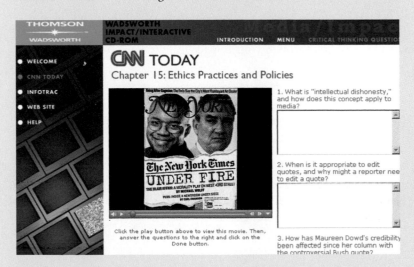

▸ Chapter-specific activities such as personal inventories and media projects

▸ A link to the *Media/Impact* Web site that offers helpful information and many additional electronic learning resources including

- An interactive chapter outline and study guide

- Interactive glossary term flashcards and crossword puzzles, concept animations, Internet activities and practice quizzes

- Live links for all URLs given in the chapter so you can easily access the additional information each site offers

▸ A link to InfoTrac College Edition—our online database of more than a million articles representing cutting-edge research and the latest headlines. Updated daily, this online library is available 24 hours a day, seven days a week. The InfoTrac College Edition activities provided below are designed to help you use this valuable resource.

▸ Working the Web

Live links for all of the sites listed below are provided on the Media/Impact book companion Web site, which can be accessed through your Impact/Interactive CD-ROM.

▸ **Columbia Journalism Review**
www.cjr.org

▸ **Freedom Forum**
www.freedomforum.org

▸ **Online Journalism Review (University of Southern California, Annenberg School)**
http://ojr.usc.edu

▸ **The Poynter Institute**
www.poynter.org

▸ **Radio-TV News Directors Association and Foundation**
www.rtnda.org

▸ **Society of Professional Journalists**
www.spj.org

▸ InfoTrac College Edition Activities

Using InfoTrac College Edition's online database of full-text articles and abstracts, do the following activities as directed by your instructor. The database can be accessed through your Impact/Interactive CD-ROM.

1. Read "Impact/Culture: Should Parents Censor Their Children's Internet Use?" in Chapter 15. Then using InfoTrac College Edition, enter the keywords "Internet children" to find articles on the subject. Print at least three articles and either:

   a. write a brief paper on your findings, or

   b. bring the articles to class for a small-group discussion.

2. Ethical issues in journalism, advertising, and public relations never quite go away no matter which code of ethics communicators follow. Search for articles on InfoTrac College Edition using the keywords "media ethics" or "public relations ethics" or "advertising ethics" or "journalism

ethics." Read three of the articles and summarize some ethics issues or points of view that have arisen in the last two years. Cite a specific case in which a journalist's (or news organization's) ethics were questioned or condemned. Consider which of the five major philosophical principles underlying ethical decisions, as listed in Chapter 15, apply to the case. Summarize your findings in a brief paper and be prepared to discuss your findings in class.

3. Read about ethics codes in Chapter 15. Search for articles on InfoTrac College Edition using keywords "RTNDA" or "PRSA" or "Society for Professional Journalists." Print out the latest ethics codes for one of these organizations. Bring the printout to class for discussion.

4. Paying news sources for interviews or access is ethically problematic and casts doubt on reliability of the source. Using InfoTrac College Edition and the keywords "checkbook journalism," read several articles that give you a view of different problems associated with checkbook journalism. Then write a brief paper outlining your findings and be prepared to discuss the issue in class.

5. Journalists are trained to be alert to a potential ethical problem called *conflict of interest.* Using InfoTrac College Edition and the keywords "journalism and conflict of interest," read several articles expressing viewpoints on conflict of interest in news reporting. Then write a brief paper summarizing your findings and be prepared to discuss the issue in class.

> *The government wants the economic benefits of the Internet without the freedom it gives. The information revolution, minus the revolution."*
>
> *Time* magazine, describing the Internet in China

I n the United States, students of the media often assume that media in most countries throughout the world operate like the U.S. media, but media industries in different countries are as varied as the countries they serve. Can you identify the countries in the following media situations?

1. Citizens of this country woke up one morning to find that, overnight, their leader had shut down several independent newspapers and broadcast stations. Heavily armed police raided the media outlets and shut them down.

2. In this country, a weekly TV game show features people eating overly spicy foods. The champion is dubbed Super Spiciness King.

3. In this country, a program called *Youth TV* broadcast racy rock videos, professional wrestling from Madison Square Garden and Oliver Stone's epic *J. F. K.* One of the sons of the government's leader ran the station. *Youth TV* ended when the government fell. The son was killed in the military conflict that followed.

4. This country's TV License Police can knock on the door of someone's house, fine the person $150 and threaten him or her with jail if the person doesn't pay the annual TV license fee.

Courtesy of BBC News

BBC News Television owners in Britain pay an annual license fee that supports the BBC. (The BBC newsroom is shown here.)

BBC British Broadcasting Corporation.

▶ Differing Standards of Practice

The armed police raid in example 1 took place in Nigeria in 1993, when the country's ruler, General Ibrahim Babangida, raided newspapers and magazines owned by his primary rival, millionaire business tycoon Moshood Abiola. One year later, the Nigerian government closed newspapers that were critical of the military government.

The TV game show with the spicy cast (example 2) is very popular in Japan, where *TV Champion* is one of several shows in which contestants vie for modest prizes and national attention by showing *gaman,* or endurance.

The manager of the Iraqian station where *Youth TV* appears (example 3) was Uday Hussein, Saddam Hussein's son. His station, Channel 2, began broadcasting the new format in 1993. Iraq's Culture Minister Hamid Youssel Hammadi told the *Los Angeles Times,* "We don't want our youth to be more or less split from what is going on outside." Uday Hussein was killed by U.S. troops who occupied Iraq in 2003 after the war.

The British are responsible for paying a yearly TV license fee (example 4). The fee is due at the post office each year, so the collectors who fine people who haven't paid the fee are actually members of the post office. The government collects more than $2 billion a year from the fees, which allows the British Broadcasting Corporation (**BBC**) to operate two TV stations without advertising.

These examples help demonstrate the complexity of defining today's international media marketplace, which clearly is a marketplace in rapid transition. This chapter examines four aspects of global media: (1) political theories and the media, (2) world media systems, (3) news and information flow and (4) global media markets.

▶ Political Theories and the Media

No institution as sizable and influential as the mass media can escape involvement with government and politics. The media are not only channels for the transmission of political information and debate, but also significant players with a direct stake in government's regulatory and economic policies, as well as government's attitude toward free speech and dissent. Remember that *the way a country's political system is organized affects the way the media within that country operate.* Media systems can be divided broadly into those systems that allow dissent and those that do not.

To categorize the political organization of media systems, scholars often begin with the 1956 book *Four Theories of the Press,* by Fred S. Siebert, Theodore Peterson and Wilbur Schramm. These four theories, which originally were used to describe the political systems under which media operated in different countries, were (1) the Soviet theory, (2) the authoritarian theory, (3) the libertarian theory and (4) the social responsibility theory. A fifth description, the more modern *developmental theory,* updates the original categories.

The Soviet Theory   Historically in the Soviet Union (which dissolved in 1991 into several independent nations and states), the government owned and operated the mass media. All media employees were government employees, expected to serve the government's interests.

Top media executives also served as leaders in the Communist party. Even when the press controls loosened in the 1980s, the mass media were part of the government's policy. Government control came *before* the media published or broadcast; people who controlled the media could exercise *prior restraint.* They could review copy and look at programs before they appeared.

This description of the Soviet press system was conceived before the events of the 1990s challenged the basic assumptions of Soviet government. Many Eastern bloc countries, such as Romania, Slovakia, and the Czech Republic that once operated under Soviet influence, based their media systems on the communist model. Today, the media systems in these countries are in transition.

The Authoritarian Theory

Media that operate under the authoritarian theory can be either publicly or privately owned. This concept of the press developed in Europe after Gutenberg. Until the 1850s, presses in Europe were privately owned, and the aristocracy (which governed the countries) wanted some sort of control over what was printed about them. The aristocracy had the financial and political power necessary to make the rules about what would be printed.

Their first idea was to license everyone who owned a press so the license could be revoked if someone published something unfavorable about the government. The British crown licensed the first colonial newspapers in America. Licensing wasn't very successful in the United States, however, because many people who owned presses didn't apply for licenses.

The next authoritarian attempt to control the press was to review material after it was published. A printer who was discovered publishing material that strongly challenged the government could be heavily fined or even put to death.

Today, many governments still maintain this type of rigid control over the media. Most monarchies, for example, operate in an authoritarian tradition, which tolerates very little dissent. Media systems that serve at the government's pleasure and with the government's approval are common.

The Libertarian Theory

The concept of a libertarian press evolved from the idea that people who are given all the information on an issue will be able to discern what is true and what is false and will make good choices. This is an idea embraced by the writers of the U.S. Constitution and by other democratic governments.

This theory assumes, of course, that the media's main goal is to convey the truth and that the media will not cave in to outside pressures, such as from advertisers or corporate owners. This theory also assumes that people with opposing viewpoints will be heard—that the media will present all points of view, in what is commonly called the free marketplace of ideas.

The First Amendment to the U.S. Constitution concisely advocates the idea of freedom of the press. Theoretically, America today operates under the libertarian theory, although this ideal has been challenged often by changes in the media industries since the Constitution was adopted.

"And, finally, after a day of record trading on Wall Street, the entire world was owned by Mickey Mouse."

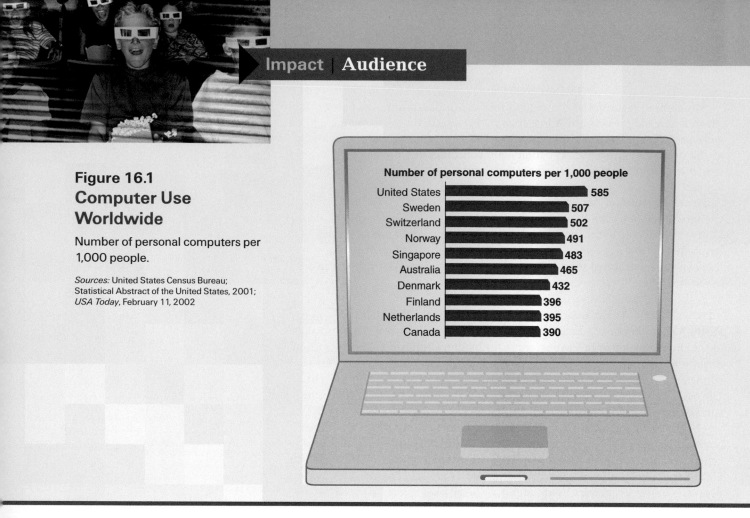

**Figure 16.1
Computer Use
Worldwide**

Number of personal computers per 1,000 people.

Sources: United States Census Bureau; Statistical Abstract of the United States, 2001; *USA Today*, February 11, 2002

Number of personal computers per 1,000 people

Country	
United States	585
Sweden	507
Switzerland	502
Norway	491
Singapore	483
Australia	465
Denmark	432
Finland	396
Netherlands	395
Canada	390

The Social Responsibility Theory This theory accepts the concept of a libertarian press but prescribes what the media should do. Someone who believes in the social responsibility theory believes that members of the press will do their jobs well only if periodically reminded about their duties.

This theory grew out of the 1947 Hutchins Commission Report on the Free and Responsible Press. The commission listed five goals for the press, including the need for truthful and complete reporting of all sides of an issue. The commission concluded that the American press' privileged position in the Constitution means that the press must always work to be responsible to society.

If the media fail to meet their responsibilities to society, the social responsibility theory holds that the government should encourage the media to comply. In this way the libertarian and the social responsibility theories differ. The libertarian theory assumes the media will work well without government interference; the social responsibility theory advocates government oversight for media that don't act in society's best interest.

The Developmental Theory A fifth description for media systems that can be added to describe today's media has been called the developmental or Third World theory. Under this system, named for the developing nations where it is most often found, the media *can* be privately owned, but usually are owned by the government.

The media are used to promote the country's social and economic goals and to direct a sense of national purpose. For example, a developmental media system might be used to promote birth control or to encourage children to attend school. The media become an outlet for some types of government propaganda, then, but in the name of economic and social progress for the country.

Although the theory that best describes the American media is the libertarian theory, throughout their history the American media have struggled with both authoritarian and social responsibility debates: Should the press be free to print secret government documents, for example? What responsibility do the networks have to provide worthwhile programming to their audiences? The media, the government and the public continually modify and adjust their interpretations of just how the media should operate.

▶ World Media Systems

It has been nearly five decades since scholars began using the four theories of the press to define the world's media systems. With today's transitional period in global history, even the recent addition of the developmental theory still leaves many media systems beyond convenient categorization.

Media systems vary throughout the world. The print media form the basis for press development in North America, Australia, Western Europe and Eastern Europe, where two-thirds of the world's newspapers are published. Many developing countries matured after broadcast media were introduced in the 1920s, and newsprint in these countries often is scarce or government-controlled, making radio their dominant communications medium. Radio receivers are inexpensive, and many people can share one radio.

Television, which relies on expensive equipment, is widely used in prosperous nations and in developing countries' urban areas. Yet most countries still have only one television service, usually run by the government. In most developing countries all broadcasting—television and radio—is owned and controlled by the government.

What follows is a description of today's media systems by region: Western Europe and Canada; Eastern Europe; the Middle East and North Africa; Africa; Asia and the Pacific; and Latin America and the Caribbean.

▶ Western Europe and Canada

Western European and Canadian media prosper under guarantees of freedom of expression similar to the First Amendment, but each nation has modified the idea to reflect differing values. For example, in Great Britain the media are prohibited from commenting on a trial until the trial is finished, and in 2003, Britain banned all tobacco advertising in newspapers, on billboards and the Internet. France and Greece, unlike the United States, give more libel protection to public figures than to private citizens.

Scandinavian journalists enjoy the widest press freedoms of all of Western Europe, including almost unlimited access to public documents. Of the Western nations, Canada is the most recent country to issue an official decree supporting the philosophy of press freedom. In 1982, Canada adopted the Canadian Charter of Rights and Freedoms. Before 1982, Canada did not have its own constitution, and instead operated under the 1867 British North America Act, sharing the British free press philosophy.

Print Media   Johannes Gutenberg's invention of movable type rooted the print media in Western Europe. Today, Western European and Canadian media companies produce many fine newspapers. *The Globe and Mail* of Toronto, *The Times* of London, *Frankfurter Allgemeine* of Germany, *Le Monde* of France and Milan's *Corriere della Sera* enjoy healthy circulations. Whereas Canadian journalists seem to have adopted the U.S. value of fairness as a journalistic ethic, Western European newspapers tend to be much more partisan than the U.S. or Canadian press, and newspapers (and journalists) are expected to reflect strong points of view.

Audio and Video Media   As in the United States, the print media in Western Europe are losing audiences to broadcast and cable. (See Illustration 16.2.) Government originally controlled most of Western Europe's broadcast stations. A board of governors, appointed by the queen, supervises the British Broadcasting Corporation (BBC), for example. To finance the government-run broadcast media, countries tax the sale of radios and TVs or charge users an annual fee. Broadcasting in Western Europe is slowly evolving to private ownership and commercial sponsorship.

In Western Europe—where the print media, including books, are more popular than broadcast—people watch half as much television as people in the United States.

Western Europeans watch less than half as much television as people in the United States—an average of three hours a day per household in Europe, compared to seven hours a day per household in the United States. One reason for the difference in viewing time may be that many Western European TV stations don't go on the air until late afternoon. In the majority of countries, commercials are shown back to back at the beginning or the end of a program.

Europe gets much of its programming from the United States. Of the 125,000 hours of TV broadcast in Western Europe each year, only 20,000 hours are produced in Europe. Most of the programming comes from the United States, with a few shows imported from Australia and Japan. U.S. imports are attractive because U.S. programs often are cheaper to buy than to produce.

The European Union (EU) constitutes a single, unified European market. The policy adopted by the EU is "Television Without Frontiers," which promotes an open marketplace for television programs among countries in the EU and between EU countries and the United States.

Some members of the EU (especially France) have proposed quotas to limit imported TV programs, charging that the U.S. imports are an example of "cultural imperialism." Countries that favor quotas fear that the importation of U.S. programs imposes a concentration of U.S. values on their viewers. The United States opposes such quotas, of course, because Western European commercial broadcasting offers a seemingly insatiable market for recycled U.S. programs.

▶ Eastern Europe

The democratization of Eastern Europe is transforming the media in these countries at an unprecedented pace. Some examples:

- In the six months after the Berlin Wall opened in 1990, circulation of East Germany's national newspapers *Neues Deutschland* and *Junge Welt* dropped 55 percent as the East German population, hungry for news from the West, embraced the flashy West German mass circulation daily *Bild*.

- In Poland, Eastern Europe's first private television station, Echo, went on the air in February 1990, with a total cash investment of $15,000. The station broadcast programs from the windowless janitor's room of a student dormitory.

Figure 16.2
Cable and Satellite Audiences in Europe

Percentage of European house-holds with cable and satellite.

Data from *The Economist*; *Wired*; Net Growth Worldwide, 1999.

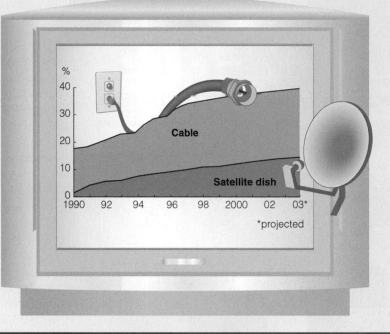

Critical Question — **What percentage of the media that you consume** do you think originate from countries other than the United States? Do you seek out global perspectives? Why or why not?

- In 2003, U.S. venture capitalist Esther Dyson announced a new technology, developed with a Russian company, that allows anyone with an Internet connection and a printer to receive exact images of participating newspapers from throughout the world. NewspaperDirect, based in New York, will sell the service throughout the world.

Everette E. Dennis, then-executive director of the Gannett Center for Media Studies, and Jon Vanden Heuvel described the Eastern European challenges in a report issued after a Gannett-sponsored fact-finding trip: "Mass communication in the several countries of the region was reinventing itself. While grassroots newspapers and magazines struggled for survival, new press laws were being debated and enacted; elements of a market economy were coming into view; the media system itself and its role in the state and society were being redefined, as was the very nature of journalism and the job description of the journalist, who was no longer a propagandist for the state."

Eastern Europe is in transition, defining a new balance between the desire for free expression and the indigenous remnants of a government-controlled system.

In many of these countries, the media played a central role in upsetting the established power structure. Often one of the first targets of the revolutionary movements was a nation's broadcast facilities. For example, in Romania in 1989, opposition leaders of the National Salvation Committee and sympathetic employees barricaded themselves in a Bucharest TV station,

New technology, developed in Russia and introduced in 2003, allows anyone with an Internet connection and a printer to receive exact images of participating newspapers from throughout the world using a New York–based service called NewspaperDirect.

rallying the audience to action. "Romania was governed from a hectic studio littered with empty bottles, cracked coffee mugs and half-eaten sandwiches, and run by people who had not slept in days," the Associated Press reported.

Audio and Video Media   Television in the Eastern bloc countries developed under Communist direction because the Communist governments were in power before TV use was widespread. Radio broadcasting also was tightly controlled, although foreign broadcasts directed across Eastern European borders, such as *Voice of America* and *Radio Free Europe,* usually evaded jamming attempts by Radio Moscow.

Print Media   Print media were strictly controlled under communism, with high-ranking party officials forming the core of media management. Because paper supplies were limited, newspapers rarely exceeded 12 pages. Revolutionary leader Vladimir Lenin, who said a newspaper should be a "collective propagandist," a "collective agitator" and a "collective organizer," founded *Pravda,* the Soviet Union's oldest newspaper, in 1912. The Eastern European nations developed their press policies following the Soviet model.

In the late 1980s, President Mikhail Gorbachev relaxed media controls as part of his policy of *glasnost.* In 1988, the first paid commercials (for Pepsi-Cola, Sony and Visa credit cards) appeared on Soviet TV, and in 1989, the Soviet daily newspaper *Izvestia* published its first Western ads (including ads for perfume and wines from the French firm Pechiney and for Dresdner, a German bank).

In 1990, the Supreme Soviet outlawed media censorship and gave every citizen the right to publish a newspaper. Within five months, more than 100 newspapers began publication. Then, showing how quickly government positions can change, in early 1991, Gorbachev asked the Supreme Soviet to suspend these press freedoms, but they refused. Less than a year later, Gorbachev's successor, President Boris Yeltsin, again began to relax government control of the press. In 1996, facing bankruptcy, *Pravda* ceased publication.

As the Eastern European governments change and realign themselves, the adjustments facing Eastern European media are unprecedented. According to Everette E. Dennis and Jon Vanden Heuvel: "Once the revolution came, among the first acts of new government was to take (they would say liberate) electronic media and open up the print press. Permitting free and eventually independent media was a vital beginning for democracy in several countries and a clear break with the past. The freeing up of the media system, speedily in some countries and incrementally in others, was the lifting of an ideological veil without saying just what would replace it."

▶ Middle East and North Africa

Press history in the Middle East and North Africa begins with the newspaper *Al-Iraq,* first published in 1817, although the first daily newspaper didn't begin publishing until 1873. With one exception, development of the press

Impact | Culture

Prague Becomes a Worldwide Center of Filmmaking

by Peter S. Green

The western edge of Uhelny Trh, a small cobbled square in Prague's historic center, was a curious sight last week. A fruit and vegetable market had sprouted in an alley better known for its doorways of ill repute, under a distinctly French street sign inscribed "rue Martin." A few passing tourists tried to buy fruit, but a gleaming new Japanese sedan and the movie camera gave away the game—another TV commercial was being filmed in Prague.

A few miles away, the Hollywood heartthrob Matt Damon was stalking a film set in a Miramax production about the fairy-tale-writing Brothers Grimm. A few weeks earlier, a nearby Prague courtyard had been transformed into the Munich beer garden where Hitler began the Beer Hall Putsch in 1923.

Since the fall of Communism in 1989, Prague has emerged as one of the world's favorite low-price, high-quality locations for filmmakers who want to shave 30 percent or more off the cost of a major production. . . .

Equipped with two of Europe's largest sound stages, and a home-grown film industry with technical crews that are among the best in the business, Prague has become a magnet for Hollywood directors and TV

Stillking Films

Prague's well-preserved architecture and thriving town squares, along with its low cost of production, have attracted U.S. filmmakers looking for a colorful European location with plenty of history.

commercial producers, and filmmaking has become a $250-million-a-year industry in the Czech Republic, the production companies say, with most of that money from abroad. . . .

Tomas Krejci built Prague Studios in 1999 and remains a partner, turning a bankrupt airplane factory in suburban Prague into a huge sound stage to

meet the demand for more places to shoot movies. . . . "Let's face it, producers are not loyal to any particular site," Mr. Krejci said. "All they want is the best for their money."

The New York Times, July 30, 2003, "Prague Is Fighting to Remain in the Picture," W-1. Copyright © 2003 by The New York Times Co. Reprinted with permission.

---

throughout this region follows the same pattern as in most developing countries: More newspapers and magazines are published in regions with high literacy rates than in regions with low literacy rates. The exception is Egypt, where less than half the people are literate. Yet Cairo is the Arab world's publishing center. *Al Ahram* and *Al Akhbar* are Egypt's leading dailies.

Print Media   The Middle Eastern press is controlled tightly by government restrictions, through ownership and licensing, and it is not uncommon for opposition newspapers to disappear and for journalists to be jailed or to leave the country following political upheaval. According to global media scholar Christine Ogan, "Following the revolution in Iran, all opposition and some moderate newspapers were closed, and according to the National Union of Iranian Journalists (now an illegal organization), more

Figure 16.3
More Europeans Downloading Music

More Europeans than Americans shared music online in October 2003, using the most popular file sharing application—Kazaa.

Nielsen//Netratings

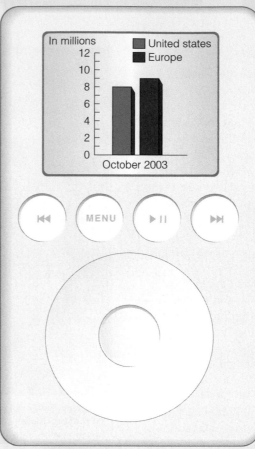

than 75 percent of all journalists left the country, were jailed, or no longer work in journalism."

The Palestinian press was subject to censorship by the Israeli government, and all Palestinian newspapers and magazines once required permission from the Israeli government to be published.

Audio and Video Media

The foreign-language press is especially strong in the Middle East because of the large number of immigrants in the area, and foreign radio is very popular. Governments within each country control radio and television almost completely, and television stations in smaller countries (Sudan and Yemen, for example) broadcast only a few hours beginning in mid-afternoon.

In the larger Arab states (Jordan, Lebanon, Saudi Arabia and Egypt) TV stations typically broadcast from early morning until midnight. Radio signals beamed from Europe have become one of the region's alternative, affordable sources of news. According to the *Los Angeles Times,* "Because of tight censorship, newspapers and television stations in the Arab world frequently reflect the biases or outright propaganda of their governments. But radio broadcasts from outside the region travel easily across borders and long distances, and many Arabs regard those stations as the most reliable sources of unbiased news." The BBC (based in London) and Radio Monte Carlo Middle East (based in Paris) are the main across-the-border program sources.

All that Jazeera: Television in the Arab World

Staff at Al Jazeera call the satellite-TV station the CNN of the Middle East. A series of scoops, notably several tapes sent in by Osama bin Laden, have made the Qatar-based station famous everywhere. It claims to be the news channel of choice for 35 million people in the Middle East.

Normally, those viewers would bring in big advertising revenues. Indeed, the station, which started with a loan of $150 million from the government of Qatar in 1996, hoped to be profitable and financially independent by 2001. That year it said it was considering an initial public offering of shares. But so far, its money-making abilities have been held back by the fact that several Gulf governments have told businessmen not to advertise on it.

Ad executives say that in Saudi Arabia, which comprises about 60 percent of the Gulf's advertising market, there is an unofficial but total ban on advertising with Al Jazeera, because of its political content. Likewise in Kuwait and Bahrain. This also scares away multinationals that would otherwise love to access Al Jazeera's large audience, according to Samar Salman at MindShare, a media buyer in Beirut. Some, such as Unilever, a consumer-goods giant, and BMW, a carmaker, have advertised on Al Jazeera. But most firms are wary of promoting shampoo or luxury cars alongside the station's famously bloody reports. . . .

Top: AP/Wide World Photos; Bottom: Getty Images

Al Jazeera, with television studios based in Qatar, has been called the CNN of the Arab world.

Thanks to its backing from Qatar, Al Jazeera still has ambitious plans. . . . Its news coverage already sells to 150,000 households in America, mostly Arab families. With an English-language service, the station hopes to win advertising revenue from American and European firms.

The Economist, June 21, 2003, p. 60.

Al Jazeera has stirred worldwide controversy by broadcasting videos of Osama bin Laden.

Also, because of careful government control of television programming, another alternative medium has emerged—the VCR. Says global media scholar Christine Ogan, "Saudi Arabia and some of the Gulf countries have the highest VCR penetration levels in the world, in spite of the high cost of the equipment. And since only Egypt, Turkey, Lebanon and Israel [of the Gulf countries] have copyright laws, pirated films from Europe, the United States, India and Egypt circulate widely in most countries. . . . The widespread availability of content that cannot be viewed on television or at the cinema (Saudi Arabia even forbids the construction of cinemas) has reduced the popularity of broadcast programming."

In the Middle East, as in other developing regions, the government-owned media are perceived as instruments of each country's social and political programs. The rapid spread of technological developments such as the VCR, however, and TV network Al Jazeera demonstrate new challenges to the insulated Middle Eastern media cocoon (see Impact/Culture, page 357).

▶ Africa

Most of the new nations of Africa were born after 1960, a remarkable year in U.S. media history that witnessed the Kennedy-Nixon debates and the maturing of U.S. television as a news medium. African history is a record of colonialism, primarily by the British, French, Dutch and Portuguese, and the early print media were created to serve the colonists, not the native population.

Print Media   The first English-language newspaper in sub-Saharan Africa, the *Capetown Gazette and African Advertiser,* appeared in 1800; a year later, the first black newspaper, the *Royal Gazette and Sierra Leone Advertiser,* appeared in Sierra Leone.

French settlement in Africa is reflected in the pages of *Fraternié-Matin,* the only major daily in French Africa. A Portuguese settler founded *Noticias,* published in Mozambique. In Kenya, three tabloid newspapers enjoy wide circulations with relative independence: the English-language *Daily Nation* and *The Standard* and the Swahili daily *Taifa Leo.*

Media scholar L. John Martin describes the African media landscape:

In Africa, radio is a much more widely used medium than television, but new technology may change that balance. Here, villagers watch a solar-powered TV in Niger.

Africans have never had an information press. Theirs has always been an opinion press. Advocacy journalism comes naturally to them. To the extent that they feel a need for hard news, that need is satisfied by the minimal coverage of the mass media, especially of radio. Soft news—human interest news or what [media scholar Wilbur] Schramm has called immediate-reward news—is equally well transmitted through the folk media, such as the "bush telegraph," or drum; the "grapevine," or word-of-mouth and gossip; town criers and drummers; traditional dances, plays, and song.

Martin points out that African culture is very diverse, with an estimated 800 to 2,000 language dialects, making it impossible to create a mass circulation newspaper that can appeal to a wide readership. The widest circulating publication is a magazine called *Drum,* published in South Africa but also distributed in West Africa and East Africa.

Today, most newspapers in South Africa, for example, are owned and edited by whites, who publish newspapers in English and in Afrikaans, a language that evolved from South Africa's 17th-century Dutch settlers. South Africa's first Afrikaans newspaper, *Di Patriot,* began in 1875.

South Africa's highest circulation newspaper is the *Star,* which belongs to the Argus Group, South Africa's largest newspaper publisher. The Argus Group also publishes the *Sowetan,* a handsome newspaper based in Johannesburg, with color graphics, an appealing design and a healthy circulation of about 120,000. Many of the Argus Group's editors spent time in jail for speaking out against apartheid. As South Africa's largest newspaper publisher, the Argus Group owns a total of nine major papers, six of them dailies, in several African states.

From 1985 to 1990, the South African government demonstrated its distaste for dissident speech when it instituted strict limits on domestic and international news coverage in the region. Because of violent demonstrations supporting the opposition African National Congress, President P. W. Botha declared a state of emergency in the country in 1985. In 1988, the government suspended the *New Nation* and four other alternative publications. The suspensions and regulations that prevented journalists from covering unrest show the power of government to limit reporting on dissent.

Audio and Video Media   Radio is a much more important medium in Africa than print or television. One reason for radio's dominance over print is that literacy rates are lower in Africa than in many other regions of the world. Radio is also very accessible and the cheapest way for people to follow the news.

Some governments charge license fees for radio sets, which are supposed to be registered, but many go unregistered. Most stations accept advertising, but the majority of funding for radio comes from government subsidies.

Less than 2 percent of the African public owns a TV set. Television in the region is concentrated in the urban areas, and TV broadcasts last only a few hours each evening. Says L. John Martin, "TV remains a medium of wealthy countries."

▶ Asia and the Pacific

The development of media in this region centers primarily in four countries: Japan, with its prosperous mix of public and private ownership; Australia, where media barons contributed their entrepreneurial fervor; India, which has seen phenomenal media growth; and the People's Republic of China, with its sustained government-controlled media monopoly.

Japan   Japan boasts more newspaper readers than any other nation in the world. Japan's three national daily newspapers are based in Tokyo—*Asahi Shimbun, Yomiuri Shimbun* and *Mainichi Shimbun.* These three papers, each of them more than 100 years old, account for almost half the nation's newspaper circulation.

Broadcast media in Japan developed as a public corporation called the Japanese Broadcasting Corporation (NHK). During World War II, NHK became a propaganda arm of the government, but after the Japanese surrender, the United States established the direction for Japanese broadcasting. Japan created a licensing board similar to the Federal Communications Commission, but an operating board similar to that of Great Britain's BBC. Japan also decided to allow private broadcast ownership.

As a result of this, Japan today has a mixed system of privately owned and publicly held broadcast media. NHK continues to prosper and, according to broadcast scholar Sydney W. Head, "NHK enjoys more autonomy than any other major public broadcasting corporation. In a rather literal sense, the general public 'owns' it by virtue of paying receiver fees. The government cannot veto any program or demand that any program be aired. It leaves the NHK free to set the level of license fees and to do its own fee collecting (which may be why it rates as the richest of the world's fee-supported broadcasting organizations)."

Private ownership is an important element in the Japanese media, and newspaper publishers own many broadcasting operations. NHK owns many more radio properties than private broadcasters; NHK shares television

Filipino Journalist Hernan dela Cruz Finds Death Threats Are Part of Job

by Carlos H. Conde

Pagadian City, the Philippines—Each time somebody entered the bar, Hernan dela Cruz watched closely, and felt for the .45-caliber semiautomatic pistol strapped to his waist. With him was another armed man, one of two soldiers assigned to protect him.

Mr. dela Cruz, 35, is not a warlord-politician in this country where politicians usually move around with armed guards. He is a journalist, one of the many in the Philippines who have armed themselves and hired bodyguards for fear of their lives.

According to the Committee to Protect Journalists, which is based in New York, the Philippines is among the most dangerous countries outside war zones for journalists, along with Algeria, Pakistan, Colombia, Cuba and Russia.

Since its founding in 1981, the committee has recorded 61 Filipino journalists killed for their work. . . . Since President Ferdinand E. Marcos was driven from office in 1986, 40 journalists have been killed, the committee said. None of the cases have been solved.

"Impunity is so standard in the Philippines, Colombia and Russia that journalists there are resigned to losing several of their colleagues each year," Ann Cooper, executive director of the committee, said in its 2002 annual report.

It is small wonder, then, that journalists like Mr. dela Cruz are arming themselves. "I cannot take chances," he said, explaining the pistol, which he keeps on his desk whenever he is in the cramped newsroom of *The Zamboanga Scribe*, the weekly he owns and edits in this city about 480 miles south of Manila, on the island of Mindanao.

Carlos H. Conde for *The New York Times*

Hernan dela Cruz, the editor of *The Zamboanga Scribe* in the Philippines, now carries a semiautomatic pistol and moves about with two armed bodyguards. The Philippines is among the most dangerous countries outside war zones for journalists.

ownership about equally with private investors. However, Japan has very few cable systems, which will hinder access to global communications networks.

Australia In Australia, acquisitions by media magnates such as Rupert Murdoch skyrocketed in the 1980s. The Murdoch empire controls an astounding 60 percent of Australia's newspaper circulation, which includes the *Daily Telegraph Mirror* in Sydney and *The Herald-Sun* in Melbourne. Murdoch, although somewhat burdened with debt because of his acquisitions binge in the 1980s, emerged in the 1990s as Australia's uncontested print media baron.

Australian Broadcasting Corporation (ABC), modeled after the BBC, dominates broadcasting in Australia. Three nationwide commercial networks operate in the country, but all three were suffering financial difficulty in the 1990s, a legacy "of the heydays of the 1980s, when aspiring buyers, backed by eager bank lenders, paid heady prices for broadcast and print assets," reported *The Wall Street Journal.*

India

Entrepreneurship is an important element in the print media of India, which gained independence from Britain in 1947. Forty years following independence, in 1987, Indian print media had multiplied 1,000 times—from 200 publications in 1947 to nearly 25,000 publications in 1987.

Broadcasting in India follows its British colonial beginnings, with radio operating under the name All India Radio (AIR) and TV as Doordarshan ("distance view"). Doordarshan uses satellite service to reach remote locations, bringing network TV to four out of five people. As in most developing countries, the network regularly broadcasts programs aimed at improving public life and about subjects such as family planning, health and hygiene.

The most prosperous industry in India today is filmmaking. The film industry, which produces 800 films a year (second in output only to Hollywood), is centered around a place called Film City near Bombay, dubbed Bollywood, where 16 film studios employ thousands of people who work at dozens of sprawling sets.

People's Republic of China

Social responsibility is a very important element of media development in the People's Republic of China, where a media monopoly gives government the power to influence change. At the center of Chinese media are the two party information sources, the newspaper *People's Daily* and Xinhua, the Chinese news agency. These two sources set the tone for the print media throughout China, where self-censorship maintains the government's direction.

Broadcasting in China, as in India, offers important potential for social change in a vast land of rural villages. China's three-tier system for radio includes a central national station; 100 regional, provincial and municipal networks; and grassroots stations that send local announcements and bulletins by wire to loudspeakers in outdoor markets and other public gathering places.

A television set is a prized possession in China, where the Chinese have bought some U.S. programs and accepted some U.S. commercials, but generally produce the programming themselves. The 1989 demonstrations in Tiananmen Square cooled official enthusiasm for relationships with the West, and Chinese media today sometimes use information and entertainment programming from the West to show the dangers of Western influence, proving the power and the reach of a government media monopoly.

In the new market economy in China, there are ten times as many newspapers and magazines today as there were in 1978. The number of newspapers has jumped from 186 in 1978 to 2,200 today. The number of magazines increased from 930 to 8,100. With the increased competition for readers, some of the print media are beginning to look like Western tabloids, running some sensationalist stories.

This sensationalism has angered Party officials, who are trying to maintain control on what is published. In 1996, the president of the popular newspaper *Beijing Youth Daily* was disciplined after the paper ran a story about a poisoning case involving a state-run business. "The leadership of the news media must be tightly held in the hands of those who are loyal to Marxism, the party and the people," said President Jiang Zemin.

© Chung Sung-Jun/Getty Images

Broadband service has grown increasingly popular in South Korea. Here, Lee Jong Gyu, a technician with Hanaro Telecom in Seoul, South Korea, installs broadband equipment.

AP/Wide World Photos

Dubbed Bollywood, India's flourishing film industry works in a place called Film City, near Bombay, where 16 film studios turn out 800 films a year, second in output only to Hollywood.

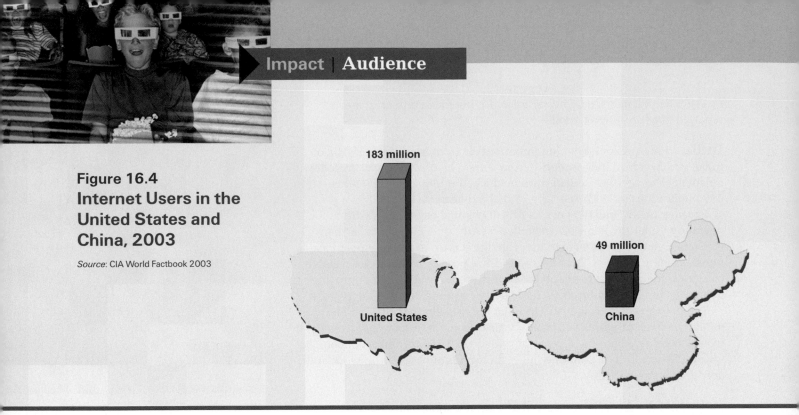

Figure 16.4
Internet Users in the United States and China, 2003

Source: CIA World Factbook 2003

183 million

49 million

United States

China

▶ Latin America and the Caribbean

In Latin America, where hectic political change is the norm, media have been as volatile as the region. Media are part of the same power structure that controls politics, business and industry; family dynasties often characterize Latin American media ownership.

Romulo O'Farrill, Jr., chairman of the board of Televisa in Mexico, owns more than 150 TV stations and eight newspapers. Mario Vásquez Raña owns more than 50 Mexican newspapers. His name became familiar in the United States in 1986 when he bought a controlling interest in United Press International, but he sold his interest a year later.

Print Media   In Santiago, Chile, the Edwards family has owned *El Mercurio* since 1880; now the *El Mercurio* newspapers total at least 14. *O Estado de São Paulo* in Brazil, owned by the Mesquita family, has represented editorial independence in the region for more than 50 years and often is mentioned as one of the country's best newspapers. Argentina's *La Prensa* refuses government subsidies and has survived great conflicts with people like former dictator Juan Peron, who shut down the newspaper from 1951 to 1955.

Home delivery for newspapers and magazines is uncommon in Latin America; the centers of print media merchandising are street-corner kiosks, where vendors offer a variety of publications. *Manchete,* published in Brazil, is one of the most widely circulated national magazines, similar in size and content to *Life* magazine.

Audio and Video Media   Broadcasting operates in a mix of government and private control, with government often owning a few key stations and regulating stations that are privately owned, but the pattern is varied.

Cuba's broadcast media are controlled totally by the government, for example. In Costa Rica and Ecuador, almost all the broadcast media are privately owned. In Brazil, private owners hold most of the radio stations and television networks, including TV Globo Network, which claims to be the world's fourth largest network (after the United States' original three TV networks).

As in many other developing regions, Latin American media often are targets for political and terrorist threats, and a journalist's life can be very hazardous. According to *Global Journalism: Survey of International Communication*, "Threats to journalists come not only from governments but from terrorist groups, drug lords, and quasi-government hit squads as well. Numerous news organizations have been bombed, ransacked, and destroyed by opponents. Dozens of Latin American journalists have been murdered for their beliefs or for writing articles that contain those beliefs."

Journalists face danger in this region because the media often represent potential opposition to the political power of a country's leadership. Perhaps more than in any other part of the world, the Latin American media are woven into the fiber of the region's revolutionary history.

▶ News and Information Flow

Countries in Latin America and in many other developing nations have criticized what they believe is a Western bias to the flow of information throughout the world. These countries charge that this practice imposes cultural imperialism, centered in Western ideology.

In fact, most of the major international news services are based in the West. The Associated Press, Reuters (Great Britain), Agence France-Presse (France), Deutsche Presse-Agentur (Germany) and Agencia Efe (Spain) supply news to the print and broadcast media. Visnews, based in Great Britain, the U.S.–based Cable News Network (CNN) and World International Network (WIN) offer international video services. Sky TV in Europe and Star TV in Asia deliver programs by satellite.

Despite Western dominance of global news organizations, many regions of the world support information services within their own countries and even within their regions. Middle East News Agency (MENA), based in Egypt, serves all the countries of the Middle East, while News Agency of Nigeria (NAN) limits services to Nigeria, for example.

Within the past 40 years, news services outside the Western orbit have been created—Russian Information Telegraph Agency (RITA); Asian-Pacific News Network in Japan; Caribbean News Agency (CANA); Pan-African News Agency (PANA); Non-Aligned News Agency (NANA), linking the non-aligned nations with the national news agencies, based in Yugoslavia; and Inter Press Service (IPS), based in Rome as an "information bridge" between Europe and Latin America.

New World Information and Communications Order

Even with the creation of these added sources of information, Western news services dominate. Critics of the present system of news and information flow have labeled this issue the New World Information and Communications Order (**NWICO**), saying that the current system is **ethnocentric,** or promoting the superiority of one ethnic group (in this case, the Western world) over another. According to Robert G. Picard in *Global Journalism: Survey of International Communication:*

> *Developing world media and newly independent governments have been highly critical of this situation, arguing that coverage from the major services contains ethnocentric occidental values that affect its content and presentation. Coverage from these media most often include political, economic, Judeo-Christian religious, and other social values that are not universal. . . . In addition, developing world media and governments have argued that Western ethnocentrism creates an unequal flow of information by providing a large stream of information about events in the developed world but only a very small flow from the developing world.*

NWICO   New World Information and Communications Order.

Ethnocentric   Promoting the superiority of one ethnic group over another.

Sally Weiner Grotta/Corbis

Digital technology has blurred the territorial boundaries between countries. Here, in a remote region of Northern Kenya, a Samburu warrior makes a cellular telephone call.

UNESCO's 1978 Declaration   The United Nations organization UNESCO adopted a declaration in 1978 supporting the principles of self-reliant communications and self-determination for countries as they establish their own communications policies. Critics of the statement, especially journalists, felt that some aspects of the declaration supported government control of the flow of information out of a country, because some news services are official government mouthpieces.

The MacBride Report   Four years later, UNESCO, which had appointed a 16-member commission headed by Irish statesman Sean MacBride, received their recommendations at the general conference of UNESCO in Belgrade, Yugoslavia. These recommendations became known as the MacBride Report. The report listed 82 ways to help achieve the New World Information and Communications Order, but after the report was issued neither critics of the current status of communications nor those who opposed the report's recommendations were satisfied. According to Sydney Head, "The West objected to the report's skepticism about a free market in communication, including its opposition to advertising, for example; many NWICO supporters objected to its downplaying of government controls (for example, its advocacy of self-imposed rather than government codes of ethics for journalists)."

The Belgrade conference passed a general resolution supporting NWICO, but in 1983, citing opposition to some of the principles outlined in the MacBride Report, the Reagan administration withdrew its $50 million in financial support for UNESCO, seriously crippling the organization because the United States had been its largest contributor.

UNESCO has since turned to other issues. The NWICO still remains a theoretical idea that scholars of global media continue to debate because of its implications for the international media community.

▶ Global Media Markets

Today's media markets are increasingly global. U.S. media companies are looking for markets overseas at the same time that overseas media companies are purchasing pieces of media industries in the United States and other countries. MTV, for example, is available 24 hours a day in St. Petersburg, Russia. Here are some more examples:

- The U.S. TV network ABC and the British Broadcasting Corporation (BBC) have formed a newsgathering partnership to share television and radio news coverage worldwide. This service will compete with CNN to deliver news by satellite.

- Rupert Murdoch expanded his Hong Kong–based satellite TV network, British Sky Network, into India. Murdoch said he planned to offer more than just TV coverage in India. "Our plan is not just to beam signals into India but also to take part in Indian films, make television programs and broadcast them."

- Jun Murai, who has been called the father of Japan's Internet, created a nonprofit network to connect all of Japan's universities to the Internet, without government approval. Ultimately, he says, he "wants to connect all the computers in this world."

- U.S./British advertising and public relations partnerships are on the rise. The British firm Shandwick is the largest agency in the United Kingdom. More than half of Shandwick's business comes from the United States.

All these companies are positioning themselves to manage the emerging global media marketplace. This media marketplace includes news and information services, print, programming, films and recordings, as well as products and the advertising to sell those products.

Fueling the move to global marketing is the decision by the European countries to eliminate all trade barriers among countries. A further sign of the times is the shrinking proportion of worldwide advertising expenditures accounted for by the United States, which has long been the world's advertising colossus. In recent years, advertising spending by companies outside the United States has overtaken the amount spent by companies in the United States.

▶ Chasing International Consumers

International communication on the Internet is just the beginning of an easy, affordable and accessible transfer of information and entertainment back and forth between other countries and the United States. Media companies in the United States also are looking longingly at the large populations in other countries that are just beginning to acquire the tools of communication, making millions of people instantly available for all types of products.

The number of TV sets in the world has jumped to more than 1 billion—a 50 percent jump in the past five years. According to the *Los Angeles Times:* "TV sets are more common in Japanese homes than flush toilets. Virtually every Mexican household has a TV, but only half have phones. Thai consumers will buy a TV before an electric fan or even a refrigerator. . . . Vans roam Bogotá streets with miniature satellite dishes on the roof and a megaphone blaring promises of hookups for $150. In New Delhi, 'dish wallahs' nail satellite receivers to crowded apartment buildings."

IHT   *International Herald Tribune*

▶ The *International Herald Tribune*

One of the largest global media presences is the *International Herald Tribune* (**IHT**), based in Paris and published in English. Called "The World's Daily Newspaper," the *International Herald Tribune* was founded in 1887, by American entrepreneur J. Gordon Bennett, Jr., and today is the world's largest English-language newspaper. Known for its independence, the newspaper was co-owned by the *Washington Post* and *The New York Times* until 2003, when *The New York Times* became the paper's sole owner.

The *IHT* is the first truly global newspaper, published at 23 sites around the world, and covering world news every day. With a global outlook and available by subscription in an electronic edition, the *IHT* counts most of the world's opinion leaders and decision makers among its subscribers. The paper has a circulation of 264,000 and an international readership in 185 countries throughout Europe, Asia, the Middle East, Africa and the Americas. Its biggest regular audience is American tourists traveling abroad.

© Scott Goodwin Photography, Inc.

The *International Herald Tribune*, published in Paris and owned by *The New York Times*, is the largest general circulation, English-language daily in the world.

Figure 16.5
International Herald Tribune Timeline

New York Times Company: International Herald Tribune Timeline, http://www.nytco.com/company-timeline-iht.html

***International Herald Tribune* Timeline**

1887

On October 4, American entrepreneur J. Gordon Bennett Jr. publishes the first issue of the *New York Herald's* European edition in Paris.

1928

The Herald becomes the first newspaper distributed by airplane, flying copies to London from Paris in time for breakfast.

1940

The occupation of Paris interrupts publishing.

1944

Publishing resumes.

1959

The *New York Herald Tribune* and its European edition are sold to John Hay Whitney, then the U.S. ambassador to Britain.

1966

The New York paper closes. The Whitney family keeps the Paris paper going through partnerships. In December the *Washington Post* becomes a joint owner.

1967

In May *The New York Times* becomes a joint owner and the newspaper becomes the *International Herald Tribune,* emphasizing its global perspective.

1974

The IHT pioneers the electronic transmission of facsimile pages across countries with the opening of a printing site near London. A second site was opened in Zurich in 1977.

1980

The IHT begins sending page images via satellite from Paris to Hong Kong, making it the first daily newspaper to be electronically sent across continents, making it simultaneously available to readers on opposite sides of the world.

1991

The *Washington Post* and *The New York Times* become sole and equal shareholders of the newspaper.

2001

IHT.TV, a fast-paced 30-minute business program, launches.

2003

The New York Times acquires full ownership of the *International Herald Tribune.*

▶ Global Access to the Internet

When communication stays within borders, it is easier for governments to control information. The Internet is a whole new story, making it possible for information and entertainment to travel effortlessly across borders.

Governments that are used to controlling information, especially in developing countries, have tried to stop the information flow by pricing Internet access out of the reach of the average consumer, charging as much as $200 a month for Internet access. Also, many countries simply don't have reliable telecommunications technology in place—telephone, broadband, cellular or satellite connections—to handle Internet access. This often means that, in

Impact | Culture

China's Internet Gold Rush: Seeds of a New Revolution

The Internet has hit the Chinese government with all the force of an electromagnetic burst. The number of Net users, now 12 million, is doubling every six months—the fastest growth in Asia. Money is pouring in from U.S venture capitalists. There are 500,000 Chinese domain names. By some calculations, China will have the second largest population of Web surfers in the world, after the United States, by 2005. Such a frenetic buildup would delight most governments. It terrifies Beijing's officials, who fear the Net will vaporize their power over the masses. . . .

China has become the cyberworld's hottest battlefield. On one side are the control freaks of the Communist Party, who believe anyone who challenges them belongs in a labor camp for 10 years. On the other side are the tech-savvy Net entrepreneurs, who expect anyone who challenges them to set up his own Web site within the next 10 minutes. . . .

Dotcoms highlight the central contradiction of China today—the drive to modernize without giving up one-party rule. The government wants the economic benefits of the Internet

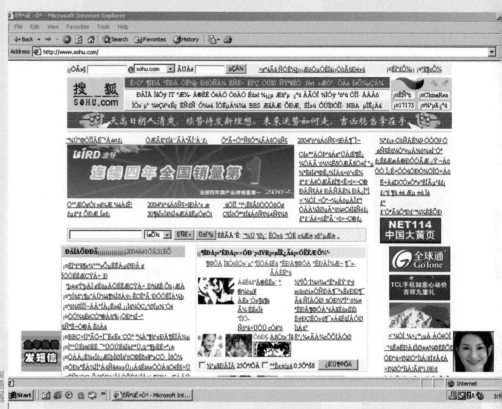

Sohu.com Inc.

Internet use in China is growing faster than in any other Asian country.

without the freedom it gives. The information revolution, minus the revolution.

"China's Internet Gold Rush: The World's Most Populous Country Prepares for a Revolution," *Time*, Feb. 28, 2000, p. 50. © 2000 Time, Inc. Reprinted by permission.

poorer countries, only the wealthy have access to the international flow of information the Internet offers.

As technology grows more affordable, however, it will be difficult for even developing countries to stop information from seeping across their borders. The Internet is as close as a laptop and an Internet connection, and is becoming an indispensable tool for business and economic growth. More than any other factor, the economic uses of the Internet guarantee its future as a global communications medium.

▶ Opening New Pathways for Ideas

Along with the transfer of information in the new global communications future, however, comes the transfer of ideas. Says the *Los Angeles Times*:

> *Historically, the empowered elite have always sought to suppress the wider distribution of ideas, wealth, rights and, most of all, knowledge.*

This is as true today as it was 536 years ago, when the German printer Gutenberg invented movable type to print the Bible. For two centuries afterward, government tightly controlled what people could read through the widespread use of "prior restraint". . . .

Just as censorship of the printed word could not continue with the emergence of democracy in 17th century Britain and 18th century America, so today suppression of the electronic media is thwarted by technology and rapidly growing economies around the world.

Governments that are accustomed to controlling the information that crosses their borders face unprecedented access within their borders to global information sources. According to media theorist Ithiel de Sola Pool, "International communications is often considered a mixed blessing by rulers. Usually they want technical progress. They want computers. They want satellites. They want efficient telephones. They want television. But at the same time they do not want the ideas that come with them."

Many governments that control the media, especially broadcast media and the Internet, are expected to continue to control the messages as long as they can supervise access to newsprint and satellites. But this is becoming increasingly difficult.

In 1994, the Chinese government passed regulations to ban satellite dishes and prohibit people from watching foreign broadcasts. Factories that own dishes were required to broadcast only approved programs. But many Chinese simply refused to abide by the edict.

Videos can travel in a suitcase across borders, and video signals can travel unseen to pirated satellite dishes, assembled without government knowledge. The airwaves are truly "borderless." Reports the *Los Angeles Times*, "Asked once what had caused the stunning collapse of communism in Eastern Europe, Polish leader Lech Walesa pointed to a nearby TV set, 'It all came from there.'"

As more and more national media boundaries open up throughout the world, news, information and entertainment will be able to move instantly from each home country to become part of the global media dialogue. In the 1990s, the media industries entered a media marketplace without boundaries, a global marketplace that is truly "transnational." According to *The Economist*, "Optimists declare that the world is headed unstoppably for an electronic Renaissance. How arrogant; how naive. The essence of a technology of freedom is that it endows its users with the freedom to fail. But pessimists are equally wrong to think that failure is inevitable. Nothing is inevitable about this technology except its advance. . . . As the universe behind the screen expands, it will be the people in front who shape the soul of the new machine."

Media | Review

ROMEO GACAD/AFP/Getty Images

History

▶ The original four theories of the press (the Soviet theory, the authoritarian theory, the libertarian theory and the social responsibility theory) plus the developmental theory, still leave many press systems beyond specific categorization.

▶ The first English-language newspaper in sub-Saharan Africa appeared in Capetown, S. Afr., in 1800; a year later, the first black newspaper appeared in Sierra Leone.

▶ Until the 1850s, presses in Europe were privately owned.

▶ Press history in the Middle East and North Africa begins with the news-paper *Al-Iraq*, first published in 1817, although the first daily newspaper didn't begin publishing until 1873.

▶ In Santiago, Chile, the Edwards family has owned *El Mercurio* since 1880.

▶ Founded in 1883 by American entrepreneur J. Gordon Bennett, Jr., the *International Herald Tribune* is the world's largest circulation, general interest English-language daily.

▶ Japan's three major newspapers are each more than 100 years old.

▶ *Pravda*, the Soviet Union's oldest newspaper, was founded in 1912.

▶ Former dictator Juan Peron shut down Argentina's independent news-paper *La Prensa* from 1951 to 1955.

▶ In 1982, Canada adopted the Canadian Charter of Rights and Freedom, becoming the most recent Western country to issue an official decree supporting the philosophy of press freedom.

Technology

▶ Radio often is the dominant medium in developing countries; television is in widespread use in prosperous nations and in urban areas of devel-oping countries. Yet most countries still have only one TV service, usu-ally run by the government.

▶ Western Europeans watch less than half as much TV as people in the United States.

▶ In Africa, radio is a much more important medium than print because it is an inexpensive way for people to follow the news.

▶ The three major Japanese national dailies account for almost half the nation's newspaper circulation.

▶ Governments that are used to controlling information, especially in developing countries, have tried to stop the information flow by pricing Internet access out of the reach of the average consumer.

▶ Many countries simply don't have reliable telecommunications technol-ogy in place—telephone, broadband, cellular or satellite connections—to handle Internet access.

Business

▶ Scandinavian journalists enjoy the widest press freedoms of all of West-ern Europe, including almost unlimited access to public documents. Canada is the most recent country to issue an official decree supporting press freedom.

▶ Western European newspapers tend to be much more partisan than either U.S. or Canadian newspapers.

▶ Most TV stations in Europe don't go on the air until late afternoon.

▶ U.S. programs are attractive to European broadcasters because buying U.S. programs is cheaper than producing their own.

▶ Some members of the European community have proposed quotas on the importation of U.S. programs.

▶ Television in the Eastern bloc countries developed under Communist direction because the Communist governments were in power before TV use was widespread; radio broadcasting also was tightly controlled.

▶ Many Eastern European nations developed their press policies following the Soviet model.

▶ In the Middle East and North Africa, more newspapers and magazines are published in regions with high literacy rates than in regions with low literacy rates; the one exception is Cairo, Egypt, which is the Arab world's publishing center.

▶ The Middle Eastern press is tightly controlled by government restrictions, through ownership and licensing.

▶ Al Jazeera is the Middle East's most-watched network, which has made its controversial reputation through comparatively independent news reporting and coverage.

▶ Radio Monte Carlo and the BBC offer alternative radio programming across Middle Eastern borders. VCRs also are very popular.

▶ Suspension of five publications in South Africa throughout the state of emergency during 1985–1990 demonstrates the power of government to limit reporting on dissent.

▶ Japan today has a mixed system of privately owned and publicly held broadcast media.

▶ Entrepreneurs, including Rupert Murdoch, control large segments of Australia's media.

▶ The Australian Broadcasting Corporation (ABC) dominates broadcasting in Australia.

▶ Since India's independence in 1947, the number of publications has increased 1,000 times.

▶ Broadcasting in India follows its British colonial beginnings.

▶ The most successful media business in India is filmmaking, based in Film City, a settlement near Bombay nicknamed Bollywood.

▶ Chinese media operate under a government monopoly, supported by a belief in the media's social responsibility.

▶ Media in Latin America are part of the power structure, and media often are owned by family dynasties.

▶ U.S. media companies are looking for markets overseas at the same time that overseas media companies are purchasing pieces of media industries in the United States and other countries.

▶ More than any other factor, the economic uses of the Internet guarantee its future as a global communications medium.

Culture

▶ The print media form the basis for press development in North America, Australia, Western Europe and Eastern Europe.

▶ Today Western European and Canadian media prosper under guarantees of freedom of expression similar to the First Amendment of the U.S. Constitution, although each nation has modified the idea to reflect differing values.

▶ Most Western European programming comes from the United States.

▶ Eastern Europe, which is in transition, is defining a new balance between the desire for free expression and the remnants of government control.

▶ In many Eastern European countries, the media play a central role in upsetting the established power structure.

▶ In the Middle East, as in other developing regions, the media are perceived as instruments of each country's social and political programs.

▶ African culture is very diverse, making it impossible to create a mass circulation newspaper that can appeal to a wide readership.

▶ Journalists in Latin America face danger because the media represent a challenge to political power.

▶ The New World Information and Communications Order (NWICO), supported by UNESCO, advocated parity for the media in all countries.

▶ Along with the transfer of information in the new global communications future comes the transfer of ideas. Governments that are accustomed to controlling the information that crosses their borders face unprecedented access within their borders to global information sources.

Impact | Interactive

The Impact/Interactive CD-ROM that accompanies this text is your gateway to many electronic resources for broadening and testing your critical understanding of the material in Chapter 16. The CD-ROM features the following interactive elements for this and every chapter in the book.

▶ A two- to three-minute timely, high-interest CNN Today video clip with critical viewing questions and a link to relevant selections available within the InfoTrac College Edition database

▶ Chapter-specific activities such as personal inventories and media projects

▶ A link to the *Media/Impact* Web site that offers helpful information and many additional electronic learning resources including

• An interactive chapter outline and study guide

• Interactive glossary term flashcards and crossword puzzles, concept animations, Internet activities and practice quizzes

• Live links for all URLs given in the chapter so you can easily access the additional information each site offers

▶ A link to InfoTrac College Edition—our online database of more than a million articles representing cutting-edge research and the latest headlines. Updated daily, this online library is available 24 hours a day, seven days a week. The InfoTrac College Edition activities provided below are designed to help you use this valuable resource.

▶ Working the Web

Live links for all of the sites listed below are provided on the Media/Impact book companion Web site, which can be accessed through your Impact/Interactive CD-ROM.

▶ **BBC News**
www.bbc.co.uk

▶ **British Pathé**
www.bbc.co.uk

▶ **Canadian Broadcasting Corporation (CBC) Newsworld**
www.cba.ca/newsworld

▶ **International Center for Journalists**
www.icfj.org

▶ *International Herald Tribune*
www.iht.com

▶ **International Journalists' Network**
www.ijnet.org

▶ **International Women's Media Foundation**
www.iwmf.org

▶ **Mediapolis (access to newspapers worldwide)**
www.mediapolis.es

▶ **World Press Review**
www.worldpress.org

▶ InfoTrac College Edition Activities

Using InfoTrac College Edition's online database of full-text articles and abstracts, do the following activities as directed by your instructor. The database can be accessed through your Impact/Interactive CD-ROM.

1. Read "Impact/Culture: All that Jazeera: Television in the Arab World" in Chapter 16. Then using keywords "Al Jazeera," look up information on the pan-Arab satellite news channel. Read and print at least two articles about the media in that country. Then either:

   a. write a brief paper on your findings, or

   b. bring the articles to class for a small-group discussion.

2. Read "Impact/Culture: China's Internet Gold Rush: Seeds of a New Revolution" in Chapter 16. Enter keywords "China Internet" to learn more about the impact of virtual world technology in China. Print at least two of the articles and either:

   a. write a brief paper on your findings, or

   b. bring the articles to class for a small-group discussion.

3. Enter the keywords "global media," "international media," or "world media" and read at least three articles about the impact of the global media revolution. Print out three articles on the topic. Then either:

   a. write a brief paper on your findings, or

   b. bring the articles to class for a small-group discussion.

4. Using InfoTrac College Edition and the keywords "media and communism," read several articles published in the last two years that give you a view of media under different political and economic systems. As you read, consider whether media freedoms and practices are changing in the communist country or countries you are reading about. Is news more reliable and less damaging to society when it's regulated by voluntary journalistic ethics or by government regulation? What is the role of censorship in communist political systems? Write a brief paper outlining your points of view on those questions and be prepared to discuss the topic in class.

5. What do you know about media in Africa or Latin America? Using InfoTrac College Edition and the keywords "media in Africa" or "media in Latin America," read several articles published in the last two years that give you a view of the media in African countries. Look for media strengths, weaknesses, developments and relationships with media-related organizations in other parts of the world. Are you able to draw comparisons and contrasts with media in the United States? Write a brief paper summarizing your findings and be prepared to discuss the topic in class.

Glossary of Media Terms

ABC   Audit Bureau of Circulations.

accreditation   the process by which the government certifies members of the press to cover government-related news events.

advance   an amount the publisher pays the author before the book is published.

advertising campaign   a planned advertising effort, coordinated for a specific time period.

affiliates   broadcast stations that use broadcast network programming but are owned by companies other than the broadcast networks.

agenda setting   the principle that members of the press do not tell people what to think but do tell people what and whom to think about.

alternative press   newspapers that become outlets for the voices of social protest; also called the dissident press.

analog   in mass communications, a type of technology used in broadcasting, whereby video or audio information is sent as continuous signals through the air on specific airwave frequencies.

ancillary rights   the revenue opportunity for a movie beyond its theater audience, including television, video, and DVD sales.

ASCAP   American Society of Composers, Authors and Publishers.

Baby Bells   see *RBOCs*.

BBC   British Broadcasting Corporation.

blanket licensing agreement   an arrangement whereby radio stations become authorized to use recorded music for broadcast by paying a fee.

blind booking   the practice of renting films to exhibitors without showing the films to the exhibitors first.

block booking   the practice of scheduling a large number of movies for a theater, combining a few good movies with many second-rate features.

blockbuster   a book or film that achieves enormous financial success.

BMI   Broadcast Music Inc., a cooperative music licensing organization.

browser   software that allows people to search electronically among many documents to find what they want online.

Bundle   the combination of services that the media industries will be able to offer consumers in the future.

CATV   cable television.

CDA   Communications Decency Act.

CDR   compact discs that can record and re-record data and music.

CD-RW   compact discs that can record as well as play music.

censorship   the practice of suppressing material that is considered morally, politically or otherwise objectionable.

channel   in mass communication, the medium that delivers the message.

click-through rate   the rate at which someone who sees an ad on an Internet site clicks to learn more.

company magazines   magazines produced by businesses for their employees, customers and stockholders.

concentration of ownership   the trend among media companies to consolidate.

conglomerates   companies that own media companies as well as businesses that are unrelated to the media business.

consensus journalism   the tendency among many journalists covering the same event to report similar conclusions about the event.

consumer magazines   all magazines sold by subscription or at newsstands, supermarkets and bookstores.

content   the multimedia term for information sources and programs that can be digitized for the new communications network.

convergence   the process by which the various media industries intersect.

cooperative news gathering   member news organizations sharing the expense of getting the news.

COPA   Child Online Protection Act.

CPM   in advertising, cost-per-thousand, which is the cost of an ad per 1,000 people reached (M is the Roman numeral for 1,000).

cross-ownership   used to describe a company that owns television and radio stations in the same broadcast market.

data compression   a process that uses software and hardware to squeeze information into a tiny electronic package.

DBS   direct broadcast satellites.

demand programming   request radio that is controlled completely by the listener.

demographics   the analysis of data used by advertising agencies to target an audience by sex, age, income level, marital status, geographic location and occupation.

deregulation   the process of ending government monitoring of an industry.

digital   a way to store and send data by reducing the information to electronic signals—digits—and then reassembling them for an exact reproduction.

digital audio broadcast (DAB)   a technology that uses computer codes to send music and information, which eliminates the static of current broadcast signals and provides more program choices.

digital audiotape (DAT)   a type of audiotape that uses computer codes to produce recordings.

digital divide   the term used to describe the lack of access to digital technology among low-income, disabled and minority groups.

digital film   the electronic manipulation of film images.

digital highway   interconnected, global communications system using broadcast, telephone, satellite, cable and computer technologies.

digital media   all emerging communications media that combine text, graphics, sound and video, using computer technology.

digital service line (DSL)   provides Internet access that is up to 50 times faster than a dial-up modem.

direct sponsorship   radio and television programming in which the advertiser sponsors an entire show, which often bears the name of the product or company in the title.

disinformation   the intentional planting by government sources of inaccurate information.

dissident press   see *alternative press*.

DMCA   Digital Millennium Copyright Act.

drive-time audience   people who listen to the radio in their cars during 6 to 9 A.M. and 4 to 7 P.M. commute hours.

DSL   Digital Subscriber Line.

duopoly   the control by one company owning two AM or two FM radio stations in the same market area. Duopoly ownership was sanctioned by a 1992 FCC ruling.

DVR   digital video recorders.

e-books   electronic books.

e-mail   electronic mail delivered over the Internet.

embedded   during the Iraq War, a term used to describe journalists who were allowed to cover the war on the front lines with the U.S. military.

ethnocentrism   the attitude that some cultural and social values are superior to others.

false light   the charge that what a writer implied in a story about someone was incorrect.

FCC   Federal Communications Commission.

feedback   in mass communication, a response sent back to the sender (source) from the receiver.

file sharing   peer-to-peer music swapping over the Internet.

freelancers   in magazine or newspaper publishing, writers who are not on the staff and are paid separately for each article published.

free media   used to describe over-the-air broadcast media.

high-definition television (HDTV)   a type of television that provides a picture with a clearer resolution than on typical television sets.

home page   the first page of a Web site that welcomes the user.

HTML   hypertext markup language, a computer programming language developed by Tim Berners-Lee that allows people to send text and pictures on the Web.

HTTP   hypertext transfer protocol, a computer programming language developed by Tim Berners-Lee that allows people to create links on the Web from one source of information to another.

information disadvantaged   used to describe people who do not have access to the Internet.

IHT   *International Herald Tribune*.

intellectual property rights   ownership of ideas and content.

interactive   able to receive as well as transmit messages.

Internet   an international web of computer networks.

ISP   Internet service provider.

jazz journalism   *see tabloid journalism*.

LAPS test   the local standard for obscenity established in *Miller* v. *California*: whether a work, taken as a whole, lacks serious Literary, Artistic, Political or Scientific value.

libel   a false statement that damages a person's character or reputation by exposing that person to public ridicule or contempt.

line doublers/line quadruplers   devices that can double and quadruple the number of lines scanning the TV screen to make the picture sharper.

links   electronic connections from one source of information to another.

LP   long-playing record.

magic bullet theory   a belief that ideas from the media create a direct causal relationship to behavior.

mass communication   communication from one person or group of persons through a transmitting device to large audiences or markets.

mass market books   books distributed through "mass" channels—newsstands, chain stores, drugstores and supermarkets.

mass media industries   the eight types of media businesses: newspapers, magazines, radio, television, movies, recordings, books and the Internet.

media   plural for *medium*.

media content analysis   an attempt to analyze how what the media present influences behavior.

medium   in mass communication, the transmitting device by which a message is carried.

message pluralism   a broad and diverse representation of opinion and culture by the media.

MPAA   Motion Picture Association of America.

muckrakers   turn-of-the-century magazine journalists who wrote articles to expose big business and corrupt government.

multimedia media that combine text, graphics, sound and video.

NAB National Association of Broadcasters.

narrowcasting in broadcasting, identifying a specific audience segment and specifically programming for that segment.

navigator a software program that allows someone to browse easily through program services.

NCTA National Cable Television Association.

network a collection of radio or television stations that offers programs, usually simultaneously, throughout the country, during designated program times.

news services originally called wire services, agencies formed to provide information to print and broadcast news operations from locations throughout the world.

NII National Information Infrastructure.

noise distortion (such as static) that interferes with clear communication.

NTIA National Telecommunications and Information Administration.

O & Os broadcast stations that are *O*wned and *O*perated by a broadcast network.

pass-along readership an audience of readers who share a magazine with its original owner.

payola a contraction of the words *pay* and *Victrola* (an early record player), used to describe the payment of a fee to a disc jockey in exchange for playing a recording on the air.

penny paper first popularized by Benjamin Day of the *New York Sun* in 1833, a newspaper produced by dropping the price of each copy to a penny and supporting the production cost through advertising.

photojournalism the use of photographs and text to tell a better story than either could tell alone.

pictograph a symbol of an object that is used to convey ideas.

point-of-purchase magazines magazines sold mainly at supermarket checkout counters.

pool reporting an arrangement that places reporters in small, supervised groups to cover an event. This approach often limits journalists' access to cover an event.

Pop-up An advertisement on a Web site that appears on the screen either behind a Web page when someone leaves the site or on top of the Web site home page when someone first visits.

prime time in broadcasting, the hours between 7 P.M. and 11 P.M., when more people watch television than during any other period.

prior restraint the power of government to stop information from being published or broadcast.

program blocking the use of a "lock-box" to block out cable channels.

publicity uncontrolled use of media by a public relations firm to create events and present information to capture press and public attention.

publishing used to denote items placed on the Web (or disseminated via print or other media).

qualified privilege the freedom of the press to report what is discussed during legislative and covert proceedings.

rating the percentage of audience for a program, based on the total number of households with receivers.

RBOCs Regional Bell Operating Companies that deliver local telephone services; sometimes called Baby Bells.

receiver the place where a message arrives.

rep firm a company of advertising sales representatives who sell advertising time and space in their market to advertisers outside their geographic area.

resolution clarity of the picture on the screen.

RIAA Recording Industry Association of America.

Roth test the local standard used to determine obscenity, established by the U.S. Supreme Court in *Roth* v. *United States*: "whether to the average person, applying contemporary community standards, the dominant theme of the material taken as a whole appeals to prurient interest."

royalty an amount the publisher pays an author, based on an established percentage of the book's price; royalties run anywhere from 6 to 15 percent.

Rpm revolutions per minute.

satellite digital radio radio transmission by satellite, with limited or no advertising.

search engine the tool used to locate information in an online computer database.

seditious language language that could incite rebellion against the government.

selective perception the concept that different people perceive different messages differently.

sender (or source) the agency that puts a message on a channel (for example, a local cable company).

server a computerized storage system used to send programs and data to consumers, using cable, phone lines or other networks.

set-top box the device that sits on top of a TV set and links viewers to cable systems (and, in the future, to the new communications network).

share an abbreviation for *share-of-audience*, which compares the audience for one show with the audience for another. *Share* means the percentage of the audience with TV sets on that is watching each program.

situation comedy a television program that establishes a fixed set of characters, typically in either a home or work situation.

small presses book publishers with fewer than 10 employees.

spiral of silence a phenomenon in which people are unlikely to voice disagreement with the prevailing climate of opinion embraced by the media.

star system a management system used by movie companies, promoting popular movie personalities to lure audiences to the movies.

studio system a movie industry system of hiring stars and production people under exclusive contracts.

subsidiary rights the rights to market a book for other uses—to make a movie or to print a character from the book on T-shirts, for example.

sweeps the months when TV ratings services gather their most important ratings—February, May and November. (See *rating*.)

syndicates agencies and news organizations that sell articles for publication to appear in many different outlets simultaneously.

syndicators services that sell programming to broadcast stations and cable.

tabloid a small-format newspaper that features large photographs and illustrations along with sensational stories.

tabloid journalism (or jazz journalism) a newspaper format style that combines large pictures and headlines to emphasize sex and violence.

telco an abbreviation for *tele*phone *co*mpany.

telco-cable cross-ownership used to describe a telephone company that owns a cable company or a cable company that owns a telephone company.

30-year rule a theory about how long people take to completely adopt a new technology; developed by futurist Paul Saffo.

time-shifting recording a television program using a DVR, VCR, or TV so that someone can watch it later.

trade magazines magazines read by people in a particular industry to learn more about their business.

two-step flow the transmittal of information and ideas from mass media to opinion leaders and then to their friends and acquaintances.

universal service the concept that everyone in the United States should have access to affordable telecommunications services.

V-chip a microchip device that allows parents to program TV sets to eliminate objectionable programs.

vertical integration the process by which one company controls several related aspects of the media business simultaneously.

WIPO World Intellectual Property Organization.

wired able to use the latest technologies.

wireless using new technologies without wires.

yellow journalism highly emotional, often exaggerated or inaccurate reporting that emphasizes crime, sex and violence.

Media Information Guide

T his directory is designed to familiarize you with some of the publications that will help you find background and current information about the media. Also included is a list of associations that can provide information about specific media businesses.

The study of media covers many areas of scholarship besides journalism and mass communication. Historians, psychologists, economists, political scientists and sociologists, for example, often contribute ideas to media studies. This directory therefore includes a variety of information sources from academic and industry publications as well as from popular periodicals.

▶ Media Sources You Should Know

The Wall Street Journal is the best daily source of information about the business of the media. Although you won't find articles specifically about the media every day, you will find regular reports on earnings, acquisitions and leaders in the media industries. *The Wall Street Journal* Index will help you find the articles you need.

The *Los Angeles Times* daily section "Calendar" follows the media business very closely, especially television and movies, because the majority of these companies are based in Los Angeles. The *Los Angeles Times* Index lists stories in the *Times*.

The New York Times and the *Washington Post* also carry media information and both are indexed.

Advertising Age publishes special issues throughout the year focusing on newspapers, magazines and broadcasting.

Columbia Journalism Review and *American Journalism Review* regularly critique developments in the print and broadcast industries. *Columbia Journalism Review* is published by New York's Columbia University Graduate School of Journalism. The University of Maryland College of Journalism publishes *American Journalism Review*.

Communication Abstracts, Communication Research, Journal of Communication and *Journalism Quarterly* offer scholarly articles and article summaries about media issues. Journals that cover specific media topics include *Journalism History, Journal of Advertising Research, Newspaper Research Journal* and *Public Relations Review*.

U.S. Industrial Outlook, published each year by the U.S. Department of Commerce, projects the expected annual earnings of American businesses, including the mass media industries.

Advertising Age publishes regular estimates of actual advertising receipts as each year progresses. McCann-Erickson in New York publishes annual projections of advertising revenue in a publication called *Insider's Report*. Included are ongoing tables on total advertising revenue for each year, as well as a breakdown of national and local advertising.

The Veronis, Suhler Stevenson Communications Industry Forecast, published annually in July, follows all the media industries. The *Forecast* offers historical media tables, tracking past performance, as well as projections for future media industry growth.

Since 1973, Paine Webber in New York has sponsored an Annual Conference on the Outlook for the Media. Conference speakers include experts on newspapers, broadcasting, cable, advertising and magazine and book publishing, as well as media investment specialists. The results are published in an annual report, *Outlook for the Media*, issued each June.

Broadcasting & Cable Yearbook is an annual compilation of material about the broadcast industry. Also listed are syndicators, brokers, advertising agencies and associations.

Editor & Publisher Yearbook, published annually, lists all U.S., and many foreign, newspapers. The yearbook also publishes newspaper statistics—the number of daily and weekly newspapers published in the United States, for example.

The Encyclopedia of American Journalism by Donald Paneth (New York: Facts on File, 1983) is a very useful alphabetical guide to events and people in the history of journalism.

Ulrich's International Periodicals Directory lists magazines alphabetically and by subject.

Standard Directory of Advertisers lists advertisers by the types of products they sell—all of the advertisers that handle automobile manufacturers, for example. *Standard Directory of Advertising Agencies* shows advertising agencies alphabetically, along with the accounts they manage.

▶ Media Web Sites

Thousands of Web sites on the Internet offer useful material. What follows is an alphabetical list of the specific sites listed at the end of each chapter. If you can't reach the Web site at the address listed, search using the site's name, listed in **bold type**.

To find a group of Web sites on a specific media topic, check Working the Web at the end of each chapter.

Academy of Motion Picture Arts and Sciences
www.oscar.org
Advertising Age
www.adage.com
Advertising Council
www.adcouncil.org
Amazon.com Online
www.amazon.com
American Advertising Federation
www.aff.org
American Association of Advertising Agencies
www.aaaa.org
American Booksellers Association
www.bookweb.org/aba
American Booksellers Foundation for Free Expression
www.abffe.org
American Society of Journalists and Authors
www.asja.org
American Society of Newspaper Editors
www.asne.org
Apple Computer, Inc.
www.apple.com

Ashland *(Ore.)* **Daily Tidings**
  www.dailytidings.com

Asian-American Journalists Association
  www.aaja.org

Association of American Publishers
  www.publishers.org

Barnes & Noble
  www.barnesandnoble.com

BBC News
  www.bbc.co.uk

Benton Foundation
  www.benton.org

The Biography Channel
  www.biography.com

Bookfinder
  www.bookfinder.com

British Pathé
  www.archiev.org/movies/prelinger.php

Canadian Broadcasting Corporation (CBC) Newsworld
  www.cbc.ca/newsworld

Canadian Broadcasting Corporation (CBC) Radio
  www.radio.cbc.ca

CD Now
  (CD sales)
  www.cdnow.com

Chicago Tribune
  www.chicagotribune.com

Columbia Journalism Review
  www.cjr.org

Committee to Protect Journalists
  www.cpj.org

Dallas Morning News
  www.morningnews.com

Denver Post
  www.denverpost.com

Dilbert
  (Scott Adams' comic)
  www.dilbert.com

DreamWorks SKG
  www.dreamworks.com

DVD Entertainment Group
  www.dvdinformation.com

Electronic Frontier Foundation
  www.eff.org

Family Genealogy
  www.genealogy.com

Federal Trade Commission
  www.ftc.gov

Folio: The Magazine for Magazine Management
  http://mediacentral.com

Fox Movietone News
  www.sc.edu/newsfilm

Freedom Forum
  www.freedomforum.org

Freedom of Information Center
  (University of Missouri, Columbia)
  www.missouri.edu~foiwww/index.html

Gannett Company, Inc.
  (owners of USA Today)
  www.gannett.com

General Electric
  (owners of NBC)
  www.ge.com/busindex.htm

HDTV Network
  www.hdtv.net

Honolulu Star-Bulletin
  http://starbulletin.com

Index on Censorship
  www.indexonline.org

Infinity Broadcasting
  www.infinityradio.com

Inside Radio
  www.insideradio.com

Institute for Public Relations
  (public relations research)
  www.institutefor pr.com

Institute of Public Relations
  (association of European public relations professionals)
  www.ipr.org.uk

International Center for Journalists
  www.icfj.org

International Herald Tribune
  www.iht.com

International Journalists' Network
  www.ijnet.org

International Women's Media Foundation
  www.iwmf.org

Interscope Records—Geffen—A & M Records
  www.geffen.com

Investigative Reporters and Editors
  www.ire.org

iTunes
  www.apple.com/itunes

Joan Shorenstein Center on the Press, Politics and Public Policy (Harvard University)
  http://ksgwwwhharvard.edu/shorenstein

Journal of Electronic Publishing
  www.press.umich.edu/jep

Kazaa
  www.kazaa.com

Libel Defense Resource Center
  www.ldrf.com

Los Angeles Times
  www.latimes.com

Media History Project on the Web
  www.mediahistory.umn.edu

Mediapolis
  (access to newspapers worldwide)
  www.mediapolis.es

Miami Herald
  www.miami.com/herald

Microsoft
  www.microsoft.com

M.I.T. Media Lab Project
  www.media.mit.edu

Moorland-Spingarn Research Center at Howard University
  www.howard.edu/library/moorland-spingarn

Motion Picture Association of America
  www.mpaa.org

MP3
www.mp3.com

Napster
www.napster.com

National Association of Black Journalists
www.nabj.org

National Association of Broadcasters
www.nab.org

National Journal
(national politics)
www.nationaljournal.com

National Public Radio
www.npr.org

Newslink to Most Major Newspapers, Network TV and Radio
www.newslink.org

Newspaper Association of America
www.naa.org

The New York Times
www.nytimes.com

Nielsen Ratings
www.nielsenmedia.com

Northwestern University Library Broadcast, Cable and Satellite Resources on the Net
www.library.northwestern.edu/media/resources/broadcast.html

O, the Oprah Magazine
www.oprah.com

Online Journalism Review
(University of Southern California, Annenberg School)
http://ojr.usc.edu

Online Public Relations
www.online-pr.com

Out There News—Frontline & First Hand Perspective on the News
www.megastories.com

Pew Center for Civic Journalism
www.pewcenter.org

Portland Oregonian
www.oregonian.com

The Poynter Institute
www.poynter.org

Public Broadcasting
www.pbs.org

Public Relations Society of America
www.prsa.org

Public Relations Student Society of America
www.prssa.org

Radio Advertising Bureau
www.rab.com

The Radio Archive
www.oldradio.com

Radio-TV News Directors Association and Foundation
www.rtnda.org

Real Networks
(audio on the Internet)
www.realnetworks.com

Recording Industry Association of America
www.riaa.com

Salon Magazine
www.salon.com

San Francisco Chronicle
www.sfgate.com

San Jose Mercury News
www.bayarea.com

Screenwriters Guild of America
www.screenwritersguild.com

Seattle Post-Intelligencer
http://seattlep-i.nwsource.com

Silha Center for the Study of Media Ethics and Law
(University of Minnesota)
http://silha.cla.umn.edu

Sirius Satellite Radio
www.siriusradio.com

Slate Magazine
www.slate.com

Social Science Research Council
www.ssrc.org

Society of Professional Journalists
www.spj.org

Sony Corporation
www.sony.com

Sports Illustrated
(shared Web site with CNN)
www.cnnsi.com

Student Press Law Center
www.splc.org

Television Bureau of Advertising
www.tvb.org

Time Warner
www.timewarner.com

University of Iowa
www.uiowa.edu/~commstud/resources/pol-ads.html

USA Today
www.usatoday.com

Viacom
(owners of CBS)
www.viacom.com

Vivendi Universal
www.vivendi.com

Walt Disney
(owners of ABC)
www.disney.com

Warner Bros.
www2.warnerbros.com

Washington Post
www.washingtonpost.com

Web Archive of Important News Events
www.archive.org

The White House
www.whitehouse.gov

World Press Review
www.worldpress.org

▶ Uncovering Media History

The Journalist's Bookshelf by Roland E. Wolseley and Isabel Wolseley (Indianapolis: R. J. Berg, 1986) is a comprehensive listing of resources about American print journalism.

The classic history of American magazines is Frank Luther Mott's *History of American Magazines* (New York: D. Appleton, 1930).

Christopher H. Sterling and John M. Kittross provide an overview of radio and television history in *Stay Tuned: A Concise History of American Broadcasting*, 2nd ed. (Belmont, Calif.: Wadsworth, 1990). The classic television history is Eric Barnouw's *Tube of Plenty* (New York: Oxford University Press, 1975).

A History of Films by John L. Fell (New York: Holt, Rinehart & Winston, 1979) and *Movie-Made America* by Robert Sklar (New York: Random House, 1975) provide a good introduction to the history of movies.

Sterling and Kittross's *Stay Tuned* (Belmont, Calif.: Wadsworth, 1990) provides some information about the recording industry. *This Business of Music* by Sidney Shemel and M. William Krasilovsky (New York: Billboard Publications, 1985) explains the way the recording industry works.

John P. Dessauer's *Book Publishing: What It Is, What It Does* (New York: R. R. Bowker, 1974) succinctly explains the book publishing business. A historical perspective and overview is available in *Books: The Culture & Commerce of Publishing* by Lewis A. Coser et al. (New York: Basic Books, 1982).

Three histories of American advertising are *The Making of Modern Advertising* by Daniel Pope (New York: Basic Books, 1983), *The Mirror Makers: A History of Twentieth Century American Advertising* by Stephen Fox (New York: Morrow, 1984), and *Advertising the American Dream* by Roland Marchand (Berkeley: University of California Press, 1985).

In 1923, Edward L. Bernays wrote the first book specifically about public relations, *The Engineering of Consent* (Norman: University of Oklahoma Press, reprinted in 1955). For an understanding of today's public relations business, you can read *This Is PR: The Realities of Public Relations* by Doug Newsom, Alan Scott, and Judy VanSlyke Turk (Belmont, Calif.: Wadsworth, 1993).

To learn more about newsreels and to view the actual films, visit the University of South Carolina Web site, www.sc.edu/newsfilm. Other major newsreel collections exist at the National Archives and Records Administration Web site at www.nara.gov and at the Library of Congress, www.loc.gov.rr/mopic. British Pathe newsreels are located at www.britishpathe.com. The All-American News collection of newsreels about African-Americans is stored at the Schomberg Center for Research Culture in New York City.

The most comprehensive academic journals specifically devoted to media history are *American Journalism*, published by the American Journalism Historians Association, and *Journalism History*, published by the History Division of the Association for Education in Journalism and Mass Communication.

For information about historical events and people in the media who often are omitted from other histories, you can refer to *Up from the Footnote: A History of Women Journalists* by Marion Marzolf (New York: Hastings House, 1977), *Great Women of the Press* by Madelon Golden Schilpp and Sharon M. Murphy (Carbondale: Southern Illinois University Press, 1983), *Minorities and Media: Diversity and the End of Mass Communication* by Clint C. Wilson and Felix Gutiérrez (Newbury Park, Calif.: Sage, 1985), *Gender, Race and Class in Media* by Gail Dines and Jean M. Humez (Newbury Park, Calif.: Sage, 1994), and *Facing Difference: Race, Gender and Mass Media* by Shirley Biagi and Marilyn Kern-Foxworth (Newbury Park, Calif.: Pine Forge Press, 1997).

Magazines for Media Research

Many magazines publish information about the mass media industries and support industries. The following is an alphabetical listing of the major magazines in each subject area.

Advertising

Advertising Age
Adweek/Adweek: National Marketing Edition
Journal of Advertising
Journal of Advertising Research

Broadcasting

Broadcasting & Cable
Cablevision
Electronic Media
Emmy, published by the Academy of Television Arts and Sciences
Federal Communications Law Journal
Journal of Broadcasting and Electronic Media, published by Broadcast Education Association
RTNDA Communicator, published by the Radio-Television News Directors Association
Television Digest
TV Guide
Video Week

Magazine and Book Publishing

AB Bookman's Weekly, collector books
Bookwoman, published by the Women's National Book Association
COSMEP Newsletter, published by the Committee of Small Magazine Editors and Publishers
Folio, the magazine for magazine management
Publishers Weekly, the journal of the book industry

Movies

American Film
Film Comment, published by the Film Society of Lincoln Center
Hollywood Reporter
Variety
Video Age International
Video Magazine
Video Week

Newspapers

Editor & Publisher: The Fourth Estate
Journalism Monographs, published by the Association for Education in Journalism and Mass Communication
Newspaper Financial Executive Journal, published by International Newspaper Financial Executives
Newspaper Research Journal, published by the Association for Education in Journalism and Mass Communication
Presstime, published by the Newspaper Association of America
Quill, published by the Society of Professional Journalists

Public Relations

Public Relations Journal
Public Relations Quarterly
Public Relations Review

Recordings

Billboard
Cash Box
Down Beat
Music Index, a separate index that covers articles on the music industry
Music Review
Rolling Stone

Digital Media and the Web

AI Magazine
Communications Daily
Computer Gaming World
High Performance Computing & Communications Weekly
Information Today
MacWorld
Networks Update
PC/Computing
PC Magazine
PC Week
Technical Communication
Telecomworldwire
Wired

Global Media

Advertising
Affiliated Advertising Agencies International, Colorado
International Journal of Advertising, England

Broadcasting
Broadcast Weekly, London
Cable and Satellite Europe, London
Eastern European & Soviet Telecon Report, Washington, D.C.

Movies
Young Cinema and Theatre/Jeune Cinéma et Théâtre, cultural magazine of the International Union of Students, Czech Republic

Newspapers
International Media Guide

Periodicals
InterMedia, London

Public Relations
Public Relations Review, England

Recordings
Musical America International Directory of the Performing Arts

Other
Media International, England
OPMA Overseas Media Guide, England
World Press Review

Media-Related Topics

Censorship News, published by the National Coalition Against Censorship
Communication Research
Communications and the Law
Entertainment Law Reporter, covers motion pictures, radio, TV and music
News Media and the Law, published by Reporters Committee for Freedom of the Press
Nieman Reports, published by the Nieman Foundation for Journalism at Harvard University

Chapter References

Chapter 1: Understanding Mass Media Today

Bagdikian, B. (1980, Spring). Conglomeration, concentration, and the media. *Journal of Communication*, 60.

Bagdikian, B. (1983). *The media monopoly*. Boston: Beacon Press.

Cerf, V. G. (2001, September). The invisible Internet. *Communications of the ACM*, 34.

Compaine, B. (1979). *Who owns the media?* White Plains, N.Y.: Knowledge Industry Publications.

DeFleur, M. L., & Dennis, E. E. (1986). *Understanding mass communication*, 2nd ed. Boston: Houghton Mifflin.

DeWitt, P. E. (1993, April 12). Electronic superhighway. *Time*, 53.

Geller, A. (2000, November 6). High tech wearables take to the catwalk, *San Francisco Chronicle*, D15.

Gilder, G. (1994, February 28). Life after television, updated. *Forbes*, 17.

Greene, J. (2003, April 28). The year of living wirelessly. *Business Week Online*.

Henry, W. A., III. (1986, September). Learning to love the chains. *Washington Journalism Review*, 16.

Higgins, J., & McClellan, S. (2001, October 8). Media executives' new boast. *Broadcasting & Cable*, 6.

Jenkins, H. (2000, March). Digital land grab. *Technology Review*, 103.

King, T. R. (1994, August 23). News Corp.'s Twentieth Century Fox forms unit to make "mainstream" films. *The Wall Street Journal*, B5.

Kirkpatrick, David D. (2003, April 14). Murdoch's first step: Make the sports fan pay. *The New York Times*, C1.

Knight-Ridder Newspapers. (1994, January 12). Launching the info revolution. *The Sacramento Bee*, G1.

Koudsi, S. (2000, February 7). Which Case brother is richer? *Fortune*, 27.

Laing, J. R. (2001, April 16). Case's colossus. *Barron's*, 23.

Landler, M. (1997, September 20). Westinghouse to acquire 98 radio stations. *The New York Times*, Y23.

Levy, S. (1997/1998, December 29–January 5). A blow to the empire. *Newsweek*, 58–60.

Liebling, A. J. (1961). *The Press*. New York: Ballantine.

Lipman, J. (1986, March 9). Ad agencies feverishly ride a merger wave. *The Wall Street Journal*, 6.

Plato (1961). *Collected works*. Princeton, N.J.: Phaedrus.

Robinson, M. J., & Olszewski, R. (1980, Spring). Books in the marketplace of ideas. *Journal of Communication*, 82.

Siebert, F., Peterson, T., & Schramm, W. (1963). *The four theories of the press*. Urbana: University of Illinois Press.

Smith, A. (1980). *Goodbye Gutenberg*. New York: Oxford University Press.

Soto, M. (2000, May 4). Microsoft executive Nathan Myhrvold resigns, *Seattle Times*.

Sutel, Seth (2003, October 9). Vivendi deal gives NBC media clout. *San Francisco Chronicle*, B1.

Thomas, S. G. (1999, November 15). Getting to know you.com. *U.S. News & World Report*, 102–104.

Weiss, P. (1987, February 2). Invasion of the Gannettoids. *The New Republic*, 18.

Ziegler, B. (1994, May 18). Building the highway: New obstacles, new solutions. *The Wall Street Journal*, B1.

Chapter 2: Books

American Library Association. (2000, November). Banned books week organizers land Harry Potter defenders. *American Libraries*, 8.

Bohlen, C. (2001, November 8). "We regret we are unable to open unsolicited mail." *The New York Times*, E4.

Carvajal, D. (1999, December 14). Two book club giants are said to be poised to join forces. *The New York Times*, C1.

Coser, L. A., Kadushin, C. & Powell, W. F. (1982). *Books: The culture and commerce of publishing*. New York: Basic Books.

Crawford, W. (2001, August). MP3 audiobooks: A new library medium? *American Libraries*, 64.

Davis, K. C. (1984). *Two-bit culture: The paperbacking of America*. Boston: Houghton Mifflin.

Dessauer, J. P. (1974). *Book publishing: What it is, what it does*. New York: R. R. Bowker.

Goldberg, B. (2001, April). Censorship watch. *American Libraries*, 25.

Goldstein, B. (2003, January 20). Some best-seller old reliables have string of unreliable sales. *The New York Times*, C-1.

Hansell, S. (2003, July 23). Amazon says rise in sales helped cut loss by half. *The New York Times*, C-4.

Hart, J. D. (1950). *The popular book*. Berkeley: University of California Press.

Jones, A. (1984, April 30). For Waldenbooks, reading is more than a pastime. *The New York Times*, C3.

Kirby, C. (2002, December 18). Russian company acquitted in Adobe eBook copyright case. *San Francisco Chronicle*, B-1.

Landro, L. (1986, February 3). Publishers' thirst for blockbusters sparks big advances and big risks. *The Wall Street Journal*, 21.

Lara, A. (2003). For superstar authors, the publicity machine runs nonstop. *San Francisco Chronicle*.

Maryles, D. (2001, September 10). Roberts scores with mass turnover. *Publishers Weekly*, 19.

Milliot, J. (2001, October 29). Children's sales up 7 percent in first half of 2001. *Publishers Weekly*, 17.

Paul, F. Digital books down but not out. Reuters on AOL, 9/15/03.

Raugust, K. (2001, October 29). Where the action is. *Publishers Weekly*, 24.

Ross, M. (2000, March 8). Simon & Schuster to release story by Stephen King on the Web only. *The Wall Street Journal*, B8.

Streitfield, D. Publisher loses ruling on e-books. *Los Angeles Times*. 7/12/07.

Veronis, Suhler & Associates. (2001, July). *Communications industry forecast: 2001–2005*, 15th ed. New York: Author.

White, E. B. (1976). *Letters of E. B. White*. New York: Harper & Row.

Whitten, R. (2001, September 27). Speaking of audio: Expose your ears to a banned book.

Zeitchik, S. (2001, April 23). ABA reaches settlement with B & N, Borders. *Publishers Weekly*, 9.

Chapter 3: Newspapers

Associated Press. (2002, April 17). Dawn of a new sun in New York. *San Francisco Chronicle*, A2.

Dertouzos, J., & Quinn, T. (1985, September). Bargaining responses to the technology revolution: The case of the newspaper industry. *Labor management cooperation brief*. Washington, D.C.: U.S. Department of Labor.

Emery, E., & Emery, M. (1988). *The press and America*, 6th ed. Englewood Cliffs, N.J.: Prentice-Hall.

Jurgenson, K. (1993, Spring). Diversity: A report from the battlefield. *Newspaper Research Journal*, 92.

Kessler, K. (1984). *The dissident press*. Beverly Hills, Calif.: Sage.

Marzolf, M. (1977). *Up from the footnote*. New York: Hastings House.

McDonald, M. (2001, May 7). A different paper chase. *U.S. News & World Report*, 35.

Reid, C. (2001, July 16). NWU, authors sue NYT again. *Publishers Weekly*, 73.

Reilly, P. (1991, May 6). Newspapers are paging young readers. *The Wall Street Journal*, B1.

Romero, S. (2003, August 4). Dallas Fort Worth papers fight it out in Spanish. *The New York Times*, C6.

Rose, A. (2001, October 30). Can newspapers hold on to postattack readers? *The Wall Street Journal*, B4.

Rutherford, L. (1963). *John Peter Zenger*. Gloucester, Mass.: Peter Smith.

Schilpp, M. G., & Murphy, S. M. (1983). *Great women of the press*. Carbondale: Southern Illinois University Press.

Singer, P. (2001, June 13). Newspaper publishes on CD. *San Francisco Chronicle*, C3.

Smith, A. (1980). *Goodbye Gutenberg*. New York: Oxford University Press.

Swanberg, W. A. (1971). *Citizen Hearst*. New York: Bantam Books.

Wells, I. B. (1970). *The crusade for justice: The autobiography of Ida B. Wells*. Chicago: University of Chicago Press.

Wenner, K. S. (2000, December). Slimming down. *American Journalism Review*, 38.

Wurman, R. S. (1989). *Information anxiety*. New York: Doubleday.

Chapter 4: Magazines

Biagi, S. (1987). *NewsTalk I*. Belmont, Calif.: Wadsworth.

Carmody, D. (1991, February 25). A guide to new magazines shows widespread vitality. *The New York Times*, C1.

Carr, D. (2003, August 4). A magazine's radical plan: Making a profit. *The New York Times*, B1.

Carr, D. (2003, August 4). Gossip goes glossy and loses its stigma. *The New York Times*, B1.

Fost, D. (2003, August 8). Bay Area still a magazine mecca. *San Francisco Chronicle*.

Hoke, H. R., III. (2001, August). Magazine land is in trouble. *Direct Marketing*, 3.

Kobak, J. B. (1985, April). 1984: A billion-dollar year for acquisitions. *Folio*, 14, 82–95.

Kuczynski, A. (2001, September 10). Variety of brash magazines upset the old stereotypes. *The New York Times*.

Lukovitz, K. (1982, September). The next 10 years: 24 predictions for the future. *Folio*, 11, 103.

Mechanic, M. (2001, March 19). Doing the bare minimum media: Magazines are rethinking the Internet. *Newsweek*, 62F.

Paneth, D. (1983). *Encyclopedia of American journalism*. New York: Facts on File.

Rose, M. (2000, November 6). Problems for magazines come into view. *The Wall Street Journal*, B18.

Schilpp, M. G., & Murphy, S. M. (1983). *Great women of the press*. Carbondale: Southern Illinois University Press.

Swanberg, W. A. (1972). *Luce and his empire*. New York: Scribner's.

Tarbell, I. (1939). *All in the day's work*. New York: MacMillan.

Chapter 5: Recordings

Barnard, B. (2000, December). Bertelsmann. *Europe*, 4.

Boucher, G. (2002, September 12). Labels, retailers face the music—cheaper CDs. *San Francisco Chronicle*, D9.

Denisoff, R. S. (1975). *Solid gold*. New Brunswick, N.J.: Transaction Books.

Deutsch, C. H. (2002, October 1). Suit settled over pricing of recordings at big chains. *The New York Times*, C1.

Epstein, R. (1990, November 22). Now it's the recording industry's turn to face the music. *Los Angeles Times*, F1.

Evangelista, B. (2000, November 15). Legal deal has MP3 singing. *San Francisco Chronicle*, C1.

Evangelista, B. (2003, April 25). Apple kicks off online music store. *San Francisco Chronicle*, B1.

Evangelista, B. (2003, April 30). New tactic by record industry. *San Francisco Chronicle*, B1.

Evangelista, B. (2003, September 3). RIAA decries drop in CD sales. *San Francisco Chronicle*, B1.

Evangelista, B. (2003, October 10). Napster back from the dead. *San Francisco Chronicle*, B3.

Gomes, L. (2001, February 13). Napster suffers a rout in appeals court. *The Wall Street Journal*, A3.

Gomes, L. (2001, March 5). Judge starts process of silencing Napster. *The Wall Street Journal*, B6.

Harless, J. D. (1985). *Mass communication: An introductory survey*. Dubuque, Iowa: Wm. C. Brown.

Holloway, L. (2003, June 26). Recording industry to sue Internet music swappers. *The New York Times*, C4.

Kopytoff, V. (2003, September 4). Music lawsuits snare 18 in Bay Area. *San Francisco Chronicle*, A1.

Leonard, D. (2001, September 3). Mr. Messier is ready for his close-up: A maverick Frenchman auditions for the part of an American media mogul. *Fortune*, 136+.

Marriott, M. (1999, August 19). New ways to play MP3 music, without plugs or speakers. *The New York Times*, D11.

Mathews, A. W. (2001, January 29). Radio firms sue to block measure on music royalties. *The Wall Street Journal*, B8.

Metz, R. (1975). *CBS: Reflections in a bloodshot eye*. Chicago: Playboy Press.

Oppelaar, J. (2000, August 28). DVD case has ripple effect on music biz. *Variety*, 6.

Pareles, J. (2003, July 20). What albums join together, everyone tears asunder. *The New York Times*, WK3.

Pauly, P. (1985, December 6). A compact sonic boom. *Newsweek*, 47.

Rendon, J. (2003, July 20). From a store with 300,000 titles, a big music lesson. *The New York Times*, BU5.

Schiesel, S. (2003, August 7). A musical theme part for 60,000. *The New York Times*, E1.

Sheinfeld, L. P. (1986, May–June). Ratings: The big chill. *Film Comment*, 10.

Smart, J. R. (1977). *A wonderful invention: A brief history of the phonograph from tinfoil to the LP*. Washington D.C.: Library of Congress.

Starrett, B. (2001, August). The end of CDR? *EMedia Magazine*, 34.

Surowiecki, J. (2001, August 20 & 27). Video kills the video star. *The New Yorker*, 59.

Tan, C. Y. (2001, August). The Internet is changing the music industry. *Communications of the ACM*, 62.

Tedeschi, B. (2003, July 23). Buy.com chief is introducing a music site. *The New York Times*, C4.

Trachtenberg, J. A. (1994, August 2). Music industry fears bandits on the information highway. *The Wall Street Journal*, B21.

Veiga, A. (2003, May 2). Students settle music suit. *San Francisco Chronicle*, B1.

Veiga, A. (2003, October 9). New version of Napster service debuts. *AOL Business News*.

Yoder, S. (1986, August 12). Digital tape is inevitable; so why the delay? *The Wall Street Journal*, 29.

Zaslow, J. (1985, May 21). New rock economics make it harder to sing your way to wealth. *The Wall Street Journal*, 1.

Chapter 6: Radio

Barnouw, E. (1978). *Tube of plenty*. New York: Oxford University Press.

Billboard. (2003, July 26). Beyond the Dixie Chicks, A8.

Bittner, J. (1982). *Broadcast law and regulation*. Englewood Cliffs, N.J.: Prentice-Hall.

Evangelista, B. (2002, October 11). FCC clears way for CD-quality FM sound. *San Francisco Chronicle*, A1.

Evangelista, B. (2001, November 19). Space-age sound. *San Francisco Chronicle*, E1.

Feder, B. J. (2002, October 11). FCC approves a digital radio technology. *The New York Times*, B1.

Fornatale, P., & Mills, J. E. (1980). *Radio in the television age.* New York: Overlook Press.

Goodman, F. (2003, February 16). Country radio: Nowhere in New York. *The New York Times*, 2-1.

MacFarland, D. R. (1979). *The development of the top 40 radio format.* New York: Arno Press.

Muto, S. (2001, February 5). The Internet offers a radio station life after death. *The Wall Street Journal*, B5.

Nugent, B. (2001, September 15). Radio active: Top 40 rules the airwaves, but there's an Internet station for every earthly genre of music. *Time*, 30+.

Pickler, N. (2001, September 26). First satellite radio service begins. *San Francisco Chronicle*, B3.

Settel, L. (1960). *A pictorial history of radio.* New York: Citadel Press.

Sperber, A. M. (1986). *Murrow: His life and times.* New York: Freundlich.

Strauss, N. (2001, September 19). After the horror, radio stations pull some songs. *The New York Times*.

Sweetland, P. (2002, January 11). Radio station ponders change, and Ole Opry's fans worry. *The New York Times*, B1.

Swett, C. (2000, October 12). New heights for car radio. *The Sacramento Bee*, D1.

Taub, E. A. (2000, October 19). Drive-time radio on 100 channels. *The New York Times*, D1.

Veronis, Suhler & Associates. (2001, July). *Communications industry forecast: 2001–2005*, 15th ed. New York: Author.

Chapter 7: Movies

Ault, S. (2001, July 9). Movies via Net still to come. *Broadcasting & Cable*, 30.

Balio, T. (1976). *The American film industry.* Madison: University of Wisconsin Press.

Cheshire, G. (2000, October 8). A moment from the past recovers its sound. *The New York Times*, AR28.

Chinnock, C. (1999, August 9). Lights! Camera! Action! It's the dawn of digital cinema. *Electronic Design*, 32F.

Cieply, M., & Barnes, P. W. (1986, August 21). Movie and TV mergers point to concentration of power to entertain. *The Wall Street Journal*, 1.

Ellis, J. C. (1985). *A history of American film*, 2nd ed. Englewood Cliffs, N.J.: Prentice-Hall.

Evanglelista, B. (2003, April 28). Heading off film piracy. *San Francisco Chronicle*, E1.

Evangelista, B. (2003, September 8). Movielink service polishes its act. *San Francisco Chronicle*, C1.

Gentile, G. (2003, May 20). Disney to test options for movie viewing. *San Francisco Chronicle*, B3.

Goldberg, B. (2001, September). DMCA nets a criminal prosecution and prompts a protest. *American Libraries*, 18.

Graser, M. (2001, July 23). Casting a wider 'Net. *Variety*, 27.

Grove, C. (2000, June 19). Digital dilemma. *Variety*, 44.

Grover, R. (2003, July 14). Hollywood heist: Will tinseltown let techies steal the show? *Business Week*, 74.

Guthman, E. (2003, January 20). Sundance grows up. *San Francisco Chronicle*, D1.

King, T. (1994, August 18). Theater chain has plans to jolt movie viewers. *The Wall Street Journal*, B1.

Lippmann, J. (2000, January 7). Movie ticket revenue rose 8 percent in '99, while number of admissions grew 4 percent. *The Wall Street Journal*, B2.

Lohr, S. (2003, June 19). Where cineastes, software and schools converge. *The New York Times*, E7.

Lyman, R. (2003, January 23). Old-style Sundance vs. starry premieres. *The New York Times*, B1.

Motion Picture Association of America. (1954). *Motion picture production code.*

Peers, M. (2001, January 29). Video on demand arrives—sort of. *The Wall Street Journal*, B1.

Sklar, R. (1975). *Movie-made America.* New York: Random House.

Smith, G. (2001, May). Fear of a digital planet. *Film Comment*, 2.

Squire, J. E. (ed.). (1983). *The movie business book.* New York: Simon & Schuster.

Stross, R. E. (2000, October 2). Chill, Hollywood, chill. *U.S. News & World Report*, 46.

Taub, E. A. (2003, July 21). DVDs meant for buying but not for keeping. *The New York Times*, C1.

Thompson, N. (2003, June 26). Nitflix's patent may reshape DVD-rental market. *The New York Times*, C4.

Trumbo, D. (1962). *Additional dialogue: Letters of Dalton Trumbo, 1942–1962.* New York: M. Evans.

Veronis, Suhler & Associates. (2001, July). *Communications industry forecast: 2001–2005*, 15th ed. New York: Author.

Chapter 8: Television

Barnouw, E. (1975). *Tube of plenty.* New York: Oxford University Press.

Biagi, S. (1987). *NewsTalk II.* Belmont, Calif.: Wadsworth.

Brown, L. (1971). *Television: The business behind the box.* New York: Harcourt Brace Jovanovich.

Carter, B. (2003, May 23). Fox mulls how to exploit the mojo of "American Idol." *The New York Times*, C1.

Chen, K., & Peers, M. (1999, August 6). FCC relaxes its rules on TV station ownership. *The Wall Street Journal*, A3.

Colker, D. (2003, April 17). Living on television's cutting edge. *Los Angeles Times*.

Evangelista, B. (2002, September 23). Thin screens, hefty prices. *San Francisco Chronicle*, E1.

Gill, J. (2000, Winter). Managing the capture of individuals viewing within a peoplemeter service. *International Journal of Market Research*, 431.

Greenfield, J. (1977). *Television: The first fifty years.* New York: Abrams.

Lippman, J. (1993, November 5). Southwestern looks to enter cable race. *Los Angeles Times*, D1.

Lopez, J. A., & Carnevale, M. (1990, July 10). Fiber optics promises a revolution of sorts, if the sharks don't bite. *The Wall Street Journal*, A1.

McClellan, S. (2001, August 20). Does TV need a nip? *Broadcasting & Cable*, 12.

Minow, N. (1964). *Equal time: The private broadcaster and the public interest.* New York: Atheneum.

Pasztor, A. (2001, July 31). DirecTV takes aim at illicit consumers. *The Wall Street Journal*, A3.

Radio Advertising Bureau. (2001, November 26). Competitive media update: High-definition television.

Ramstad, E. (2000, October 6). FCC spurs rethinking of digital-TV strategy. *The Wall Street Journal*, B6.

Schiesel, S. (2001, October 30). Now, the difficult gamble: Approval in Washington. *The New York Times*, C1.

Schiesel, S. (2003, July 31). Cable or satellite? Stay tuned. *The New York Times*, E1.

Severo, R. (2003, June 13). David Brinkley, 82, newsman model, dies. *The New York Times*, A26.

Sorkin, A. R. (2001, October 30). Trying to stack the deck so even a loss is a win. *The New York Times*, C1.

Sorkin, A. R. (2003, April 10). Murdoch adds to his empire by agreeing to buy DirectTV. *The New York Times*, C1.

Srinivasan, K. (2001, June 13). FCC chief tells cable industry not to misuse dominance. *San Francisco Chronicle*, C3.

Sterling, C., & Kittross, J. (1990). *Stay tuned: A concise history of American broadcasting*, 2nd ed. Belmont, Calif.: Wadsworth.

Tarquinio, J. A. (2003, July 20). Poised to ride the next wave in digital media equipment. *The New York Times*, BU3-7.

Taub, E. A. (2003, March 31). HDTV's acceptance picks up pace as prices drop and networks sign on. *The New York Times*, C1.

Chapter 9: Digital Communications and the Web

Angwin, J. (1997, June 20). Now you got to pay to play online. *San Francisco Chronicle*, B1.

Carter, B. (2001, September 7). Many ABC programs to be in high-definition format. *The New York Times*, C6.

Cookson, C. (2001, August 2). IBM joins push to construct next-generation Internet. *Financial Times*, 1.

Eisenberg, A. (2003, September 11). Beyond voice recognition, to a computer that reads lips. *The New York Times*, E8.

Evangelista, B. (2003, October 6). Signs of improvement. *San Francisco Chronicle*, E1.

Fidler, R. (1997). *Mediamorphosis*. Thousand Oaks, Calif.: Pine Forge Press.

Fitzgerald, M. (2001, June 25). Papers' e-content with profit. *Editor & Publisher*, 36.

Gaither, C. (2001, November 9). Microsoft explores a new territory: Fun. *The New York Times*, C1.

Glassman, M. (2003, July 31). Fortifying the in box as spammers lay siege. *The New York Times*, E8.

Hansel, S. (2003, May 25). How to unclog the information artery. *The New York Times*, 3-1.

Hildebrand, A. (2001, November 4). A computer screen for your eyes only. *The New York Times*, C2.

Kirby, C. (2003, September 4). Many more worms will wriggle into our future. *San Francisco Chronicle*, B1.

Kopytoff, V. (2000, September 25). Tracking Web traffic. *San Francisco Chronicle*, D1.

Kopytoff, V. (2001, June 18). Searching for profits. *San Francisco Chronicle*, B1.

LaSalle, M. (1998, January 13). Get a really good picture—for only $250,000. *San Francisco Chronicle*, E1.

Lewis, P. H. (1999, November 11). Picking the right data superhighway. *The New York Times*, D1.

Maher, B. (2001, February). 50+ Web surfers. *Target Marketing*, 104.

Mandel, M. J., & Hof, R. D. (2001, March 26). Rethinking the Internet. *Business Week*, 117–122.

Mann, C. C. (2001, March). Electronic paper turns the page. *Technology Review*, 44.

Mann, C. C. (2001, September). Taming the Web. *Technology Review*, 44.

McCandlish, S. (2001, November). EFF's top 12 ways to protect your online privacy.

McNichol, T. (2003, July 31). Roughing it, but not quite getting away from it all. *The New York Times*, E4.

Mossberg, W. S. (2001, October 25). Technology grows up. *The Wall Street Journal*, B1.

Petersen, A. (2000, November 6). It's not big brother invading kids' privacy, it's mom and dad. *The Wall Street Journal*, A1.

Pimentel, B. (2003, September 9). Dell says some tech firms doomed. *San Francisco Chronicle*, B1.

Richtel, M. (2003, July 6). The lure of data: Is it addictive? *The New York Times*, 3-1.

Shaw, D. (1997, June 19). Internet gold rush hasn't panned out yet for most. *Los Angeles Times*, A1.

Shaw, D. (1999, June 17). Newspapers take different paths to online publishing. *Los Angeles Times*, A1.

Simpson, G. R. (2001, March 21). The battle over Web privacy. *The New York Times*, B1.

Srinivasan, K. (1999). E-mail may be peril to privacy. *San Francisco Chronicle*, D1.

Sutel, S. (2001, November 2). Top TV networks sue over recorder. *San Francisco Chronicle*, B9.

Swett, C. (2003, September 15). Working on the railroad: Wireless technology may help riders stay connected as they ride the rails to their jobs. *The Sacramento Bee*, D1.

Swett, C. (2003, September 22). Intel pins hopes on new chips. *The Sacramento Bee*, E1.

Weber, T. E. (2001, October 22). Here's a guide to using the Internet to keep up with the latest news. *The Wall Street Journal*, B1.

Wright, R. (1997, May 19). The man who invented the Web. *Time*, 68.

Yang, D. J. (2001, April 9). New tolls on the info highway. *U.S. News & World Report*, 44.

Yi, M. (2003, July 13). Battle of wits over spam. *The New York Times*, I11.

Chapter 10: Advertising

Atwan, R. (1979). Newspapers and the foundations of modern advertising. In *The commercial connection*, ed. J. W. Wright. New York: Doubleday.

Barboza, D. (2003, April 3). If you pitch it, they will eat. *The New York Times*, 3-1.

Beatty, S. G. (1996, June 11). Seagram flouts ban on TV ads pitching liquor. *The Wall Street Journal*, B1.

Boorstin, D. J. (1986). The rhetoric of democracy. In *American mass media: Industries and issues*, 3rd ed., ed. R. Atwan, B. Orton, & W. Vesterman. New York: Random House.

Cardwell, A. (2001, February 1). The new ad game—online games are more than just a good time: They're the hottest new ad space on the Web. *Ziff Davis Smart Business for the New Economy*, 53.

Elliott, S. (2002, March 31). Advertising's big four: It's their world now. *The New York Times*, 3-1.

Flint, J., Branch, S., & O'Connell, V. (2001, December 14). Breaking longtime taboo, NBC network plans to accept liquor ads. *The Wall Street Journal*, B1.

Fowles, J. (1985). Advertising's fifteen basic appeals. In *American mass media: Industries and issues*, 3rd ed., ed. R. Atwan, B. Orton, & W. Vesterman. New York: Random House.

Fox, S. (1984). *The mirror makers: A history of American advertising and its creators*. New York: Morrow.

Ives, N. (2003, June 16). Online profiling, separating the car buff from the travel seeker, is a new tool to lure advertisers. *The New York Times*, C10.

Jones, E. R. (1979). *Those were the good old days*. New York: Simon & Schuster.

Kaufman, L. (1987). *Essentials of advertising*, 2nd ed. New York: Harcourt Brace Jovanovich.

Levere, J. L. (2001, August 6). An annual survey forecasts slow growth in communications spending for the next five years. *The Wall Street Journal*, B10.

Price, J. (1986). Now a few words about commercials, In *American mass media: Industries and issues*, 3rd ed., ed. R. Atwan, B. Orton, & W. Vesterman. New York: Random House.

Rosencrance, L. (2000, July 24). FTC warns sites to comply with children's privacy law. *Computerworld*, 10.

Schudson, M. (1984). *Advertising: The uneasy persuasion*. New York: Basic Books.

Sylvers, E. (2003, June 3). Breaking away, with a sponsor. *The New York Times*, W1.

Tedeschi, B. (2003, August 4). If you liked the Web page, try the ad. *The New York Times*, C1.

Whitaker, L. (2001, July 21). Converting Web surfers to buyers: Online promotion. *Time*, 46+.

Chapter 11: Public Relations

Ambrosio, J. (1980, March/April). It's in the Journal, but this is reporting? *Columbia Journalism Review*, 18, 35.

Bernays, E. L. (1955). *The engineering of consent*. Norman: University of Oklahoma Press.

Blyskal, B., & Blyskal, M. (1985). *PR: How the public relations industry writes the news*. New York: Morrow.

Blyskal, B., & Blyskal, M. (1985, December). Making the best of bad news. *Washington Journalism Review*, 52.

Bumiller, E. (2003, February 9). War public relations machine is put on full throttle. *The New York Times*, A1.

Bumiller, E. (2003, April 20). Even critics of war say the White House spun it with skill. *The New York Times*, B14.

Cutlip, S, Center, A., & Broom, A. (1985). *Effective public relations*, 6th ed. Englewood Cliffs, N.J.: Prentice-Hall.

Fleischman, D. E. (1931, February). Public relations—A new field for women. *Independent woman*. As quoted in S. Henry. *In her own name: Public relations pioneer Doris Fleischman Bernays*. Paper presented to the Committee on the Status of Women Research Session, Association for Education in Journalism and Mass Communication, Portland, Ore., July 1988.

Foster, L. G. (1983, March). The role of public relations in the Tylenol crisis. *Public Relations Journal*, 13.

Gentry, J. K. (1986, July). The best and worst corporate PR. *Washington Journalism Review*, 38–40.

Glover, M. (1996, March 6). Juice maker in PR mode: Odwalla's ads explain status. *The Sacramento Bee*, B6.

Goldsborough, R. (2001, June). Dealing with Internet smears. *Campaigns & Elections*, 50B6.

Lipman, J. (1986, August 26). As network TV fades, many advertisers try age-old promotions. *The Wall Street Journal*, 1.

Lustig, T. (1986, March). Great Caesar's ghost. *Public Relations Journal*, 17–19.

Marken, A. (1998, Spring). The Internet and the Web: The two-way public relations highway. *Public Relations Quarterly*, 31–34.

Morse, S. (1906, September). An awakening on Wall Street. *American Magazine*, 460.

Newsom, D., & Scott, A. (1986). *This is PR: The realities of public relations*, 3rd ed. Belmont, Calif.: Wadsworth.

Pizzi, P. (2001, July 23). Grappling with "cybersmear." *New Jersey Law Journal*, S12.

Randall, C. (1985, November). The father of public relations: Edward Bernays, 93, is still saucy. *United*, 50.

Seitel, F. P. (1984). *The practice of public relations*, 2nd ed. Columbus, Ohio: Charles E. Merrill.

U.S. Office of Personnel Management. (1989). *Occupations of federal white and blue collar workers*. Washington, D.C.: Author.

Chapter 12: News and Information

Abate, T. (2003, February 14). Technology creates a new form of activism. *San Francisco Chronicle*, A17.

Amanpour, C. (2000). Address to the Radio-Television News Directors Association.

Amanpour, C. (2001, September 25). Building worldwide alliances to combat terrorism.

Bennett, S. (2003, July 1). How the Iraq War was seen overseas. *World and I*, 62.

Benson, H. (2003, February 12). National day of poetry against the war today. *San Francisco Chronicle*, A19.

Carter, B. (2002, February 21). Networks' new life. *The New York Times*, A1.

Carter, B. (2003, April 14). Nightly news feels pinch of 24-hour news. *The New York Times*, C1.

Chepesiuk, R. (2000, June). Preserving history on film at the newsfilm library. *American Libraries*, 88.

Fisher, M. (2001, October). Meeting the challenge: How the media responded to September 11. *American Journalism Review*, 18.

Flint, J. (1999, November 11). *Washington Post*, NBC form alliance to share editorial, Internet resources. *The Wall Street Journal*, B14.

Gans, H. (1985, December). Are U.S. journalists dangerously liberal? *Columbia Journalism Review*, 32–33.

Gans, H. (1986). *The messages behind the news*. In *Readings in mass communication*, 6th ed. M. Emery & T. Smythe. Dubuque, Iowa: Wm. C. Brown.

Gordon, M. (2001, October 31). Military is putting heavier limits on reporters' access. *The New York Times*, B3.

King, N., Jr., & Cloud, D. S. (2001, December). This is all that we hoped for. *The New York Times*, B1.

Kuttab, D. (2003, April 6). The Arab TV wars. *The New York Times Magazine*, 45.

Lippmann, W. (1965). *Public opinion*. New York: Free Press.

Miller, M. C. (2002, January 7). What's wrong with this picture? *The Nation*. Pew Research Center. (2000). Internet sapping broadcast news audiences. Pew Research Center. (2000). Media credibility.

Regan, J. (2003, October 3). Newsreels of years gone by. *The Christian Science Monitor*, 25.

Robins, W. (2001, January 22). Cooperation, not competition: Newspaper of 2001 must be built around information services. *Editor & Publisher*, 32.

Rosenberg, J. (2001, September 24). A SLAPP fight over sources. *Editor & Publisher*, 4.

Rutenberg, J. (2003, April 20). Spectacular success or incomplete picture? Views of TV's war coverage are split. *The New York Times*, B15.

Rutten, T. (2003, April 5). A 24/7 war pulls viewers to cable news. *Los Angeles Times*, C1.

Salamon, J. (2003, April 6). New tools for reporters make war images instant but coverage no simpler. *The New York Times*, B13.

Schwartz, J. (2003, March 31). War puts radio giant on the defensive. *The New York Times*, C1.

Stepp, C. S. (2001, March). Signs of progress. *American Journalism Review*, special insert.

Turegano, P. (2001, October 2). Too much red, white and blue on TV news for objectivity? *The San Diego Union-Tribune*, E1.

Weaver, D. H. & Wilhoit, G. C. (1996). *The American journalist in the 1990s*. Mahwah, N.J.: Lawrence Erlbaum.

Wheeler, R. E. (1993, February-March). News for all Americans. *American Visions*, 40.

Chapter 13: Social and Political Issues

Alexander, H. E. (1983). *Financing the 1980 election*. Lexington, Mass.: D. C. Heath.

Alexander, H. E., & Haggerty, B. (1987). *Financing the 1984 election*. Lexington, Mass.: D. C. Heath.

Barber, J. D. (1986). *The pulse of politics: Electing presidents in the media age*. New York: Norton.

Bauder, D. (2001, February 3). Critics fault TV coverage of election. *San Francisco Chronicle*, A3.

Fetler, M. (1985). Television viewing and school achievement. *Mass Communication Review Yearbook*, vol. 5. Beverly Hills, Calif.: Sage.

Graham-Silverman, A. (2001, April). Campaign ad rates: Going up, up and away? *Campaigns & Elections*, 10.

Gray, K. (2003, September 23). Are you starstruck? The Daily Pulse on AOL. http://aolsvc.news.aol.com/news/article.adp 9/23/03.

Kollars, D. (1991, November 9). Callers flood AIDS hotlines; Johnson cheered on *Arsenio*. *The Sacramento Bee*, A22.

Ledbetter, J. (2000, March 27). Net out the vote. *The Industry Standard*, 116–128.

Liebert, R. M., & Sprafkin, J. (1988). *The early window*, 3rd ed. New York: Pergamon Press.

Lippmann, W. (1965). *Public opinion*. New York: Free Press.

Martindale, C. (1995, August). *Only in glimpses: Portrayal of America's largest minority groups by* The New York Times 1934–1994. Paper presented at the Association for Education in Journalism and Mass Communication Annual Convention, Washington, D.C.

Meyrowitz, J. (1985). *No sense of place*. New York: Oxford University Press.

Modleski, T. (1982). *Loving with a vengeance: Mass-produced fantasies for women*. New York: Methuen.

Nauman, A. (1993, April 11). Comics page gets serious. *The Sacramento Bee*, B1.

Patterson, T., & McClure, R. (1976). *The unseeing eye: The myth of television power in national elections*. New York: Putnam.

Postman, N. (1985). *Amusing ourselves to death*. New York: Viking Penguin.

Potter, D. M. (1954). *People of plenty*. Chicago: University of Chicago Press.

Rivers, W. L. & Schramm, W. (1986). The impact of mass communications. In *American mass media: Industries and issues*, 3rd ed., ed. R. Atwan, B. Orton, & W. Vesterman. New York: Random House.

Smith, L. (1994, June 24). Calls to L.A. domestic abuse lines jump 80 percent. *Los Angeles Times*, A1.

Spear, J. (1984). *Presidents and the press*. Cambridge, Mass.: M.I.T. Press.

Stein, M. L. (1994, August 6). Racial stereotyping and the media. *Editor & Publisher*, 6.

Tam, P. W. (2001, July 31). Crusading reporters help U.S. ethnic press thrive in tough times. *The Wall Street Journal*, A1.

Wright, J. W. (1979). *The commercial connection*. New York: Dell (Synopsis of FTC staff report on television advertising to children).

Chapter 14: Law and Regulation

Ardito, S. C. (2001, November). The case of Dmitry Sklyarov: This is the first criminal lawsuit under the Digital Millennium Copyright Act. *Information Today*, 24.

Arnst, C. (1996, April 8). Telecom's new age: The coming telescramble. *Business Week*, 33.

Associated Press. (2003, August 18). Patriot Act comes under fire. *Medford Mail-Tribune*, 1A.

Bee News Services. (1999, May 8). $25 million judgment in *Jenny Jones* case. *The Sacramento Bee*, A1.

Benton Foundation. (1996). *The Telecommunications Act of 1996 and the changing communications landscape*. Washington, D.C.: Author.

Blyskal, J., & Blyskal, M. (1985). *PR: How the public relations industry writes the news*. New York: Morrow.

Bode, C. (1969). Mencken. Carbondale: Southern Illinois University Press.

Braestrup, P. (1985). *Battle lines: Report of the Twentieth Century Fund Task Force on the Military and the Media*. New York: Priority Press.

Climan, L. (2001, September). Writers battle media companies. *Dollars & Sense*, 6.

Davis, J. (2001, April 9). Decision: A defining moment in libel law. *Editor & Publisher*, 9.

Deutsch, L. (2004, January 26). Judge rules part of Patriot Act unconstitutional. *Associated Press*.

Durbin, D. (2002, October 24). Award in gay's murder tossed. *San Francisco Chronicle*, A5.

Egelko, B. (2003, March 10). Librarians try to alter Patriot Act. *San Francisco Chronicle*, A1.

Elliott, S. (2004, February 3). The Super Bowl of Stupidity? *The New York Times*.

Fitzgerald, M. (2001, May 28). Supremely good ruling. *Editor & Publisher*, 10.

Fitzgerald, M. (2001, July 2). "Tasini" reality test. *Editor & Publisher*, 11.

Gerhardt-Powals, J. (2000, November 27). The Digital Millennium Copyright Act: A compromise in progress. *New Jersey Law Journal*, 28.

Godwin, M. (2001, October). Standards issues. *Reason*, 56.

Hellwege, J. (2001, June). Civil liberties, library groups challenge the latest law restricting Web access. *Trial*, 93.

Hill, G. C. (1996, September). It's war! The battle for the telecommunications dollar is turning into a free-for-all. *The Wall Street Journal*, B1.

Holsinger, R. (1991). *Media law*, 2nd ed. New York: McGraw-Hill.

Kitigaki, P. (2003, September 22). Librarians step up. *The Sacramento Bee*, A1.

Klein, K. E. (2001, September). The legalities of reporting the news. *The Quill*, 26.

Labaton, S. (2003, May 11). Give-and-take FCC aims to redraw media map. *The New York Times*, A1.

Labaton, S. (2003, June 5). Senators move to restore FCC limits on the media. *The New York Times*, C1.

Labaton, S. (2003, July 23). Republicans are adding weight to reversal of FCC media rule. *The New York Times*, A1.

Levy, L. (1985). *Emergence of a free press*. New York: Oxford University Press.

Lewis, P. (1996, June 13). Judges turn back law intended to regulate Internet decency. *The New York Times*, A1.

Libel Defense Resource Center. (2001, February 26). Report shows fewer media trials in 2000.

Libel Defense Resource Center. (2001, August 27). Study shows high rate of summary judgment in media case; report reviews Supreme Court media law decisions.

McGrath, P., & Stadtman, N. (1985, February 4). What the jury—and *Time* magazine—said. *Newsweek*, 58.

Milliot, J. (2000, November 6). Decision supports Web copyrights. *Publishers Weekly*, 56.

Mills, M. (1996, July 10). Burning the midnight oil on new phone rules. *Washington Post*, F6.

National Coalition Against Censorship. (1985). *Books on trial: A survey of recent cases*. New York: Author.

Peek, T. (1999, January). Taming the Internet in three acts. *Information Today*, 28.

Pike, G. H. (2001, October). Understanding and surviving *Tasini*. *Information Today*, 18.

Pope, K. (1996, December 19). ABC network loses libel suit over *20/20*. *The Wall Street Journal*, B1.

Reid, C. (2001, October 15). Writers 2, publishers 0. *Publishers Weekly*, 12.

Reuter, M., & Yen, M. (1986). Censorship rose 35 percent over previous year, study finds. *Publishers Weekly*, 8.

Rosenstiel, T. (1991, February 20). The media take a pounding. *Los Angeles Times*, A1.

Rousseau, C. (2003, April 23). *Harry Potter* back in schools. *San Francisco Chronicle*, A2.

Rubin, S. (1996, December 20). New TV ratings unveiled—to renewed criticism. *San Francisco Chronicle*, A1.

Salant, J. (2004, January 27). FCC proposes fining Clear Channel $755,000. *Associated Press*.

Seitel, F. P. (1984). *The practice of public relations*, 2nd ed. Columbus, Ohio: Charles E. Merrill.

Shields, T. (2000, December 11). Supreme consideration: Free speech vs. privacy. *Editor & Publisher*, 7.

Shrieves, L. and Owens, D. (2004, February 3). Jackson gives TV sex war wider exposure. *The Sacramento Bee*, A-1.

Smolla, R. (1986). *Suing the press*. New York: Oxford University Press.

Steinberg, J. (2003, May 26). Easier rules may not mean more newspaper-TV deals. *The New York Times*, C1.

Stern, C. (1996, February 12). The V-chip First Amendment infringement vs. empowerment tool. *Broadcasting & Cable*, 8.

Sullivan, J. (2000, August 18). Movie industry wins a round in DVD copyright case. *The New York Times*.

Sutel, S. (2004, January 14). Franken signs with liberal radio network. *Associated Press*.

Trigoboff, D. (2001, May 28). Suits, laws and audiotape. *Broadcasting & Cable*, 12.

Ungar, S. (1975). *The papers and the papers: An account of the legal and political battle over the Pentagon papers*. New York: Dutton.

Wicker, T. (1978). *On press*. New York: Viking.

Chapter 15: Ethical Practices and Policies

Alter, J., & McKillop, P. (1986, August). AIDS and the right to know. *Newsweek*, 46.

Atta, D. (1986, November). Faint light, dark print. *Harper's*, 57.

Barry, D. (2003, May 1). Times reporter who resigned leaves long trail of deception. *The New York Times,* A1.

Brandt, A. (1984, October). Truth and consequences. *Esquire,* 27.

Christians, C., Rotzoll, K., & Fackler, M. (1987). *Media ethics,* 2nd ed. New York: Longman.

Goldstein, T. (1985). *The news at any cost.* New York: Simon & Schuster.

Harwood, R. (1994, March 12). What is this thing called "news"? *Washington Post,* A12.

Helliker, K. (1997, November 25). CNN got its story about poisoned eagles, but rancher cries foul. *The Wall Street Journal,* A1.

Hulteng, J. (1985). *The messenger's motives: Ethical problems of the news media.* Englewood Cliffs, N.J.: Prentice-Hall.

Hulteng, J. (1986, Winter). Get it while it's hot. *feed/back,* 16.

Jensen, E. (1993, March 23). NBC-sponsored inquiry calls GM crash on news program a lapse in judgment. *The Wall Street Journal,* B10.

Levine, R. M. (1986, November 16). Murder, they write. *The New York Times Magazine,* 32.

Mnookin, S. (2003, May 26). The *Times* bomb. *Newsweek,* 41.

Prendergast, A. (1987, January/February). Mickey Mouse journalism. *Washington Journalism Review,* 9, 32.

Public Relations Society of America Code of Professional Standards for the Practice of Public Relations, rev. 1983.

Radio-Television News Directors Association Code of Broadcast News Ethics, January 1988.

Scott, J. (2003, June 6). A formidable run undone by scandal and discontent. *The New York Times,* A1.

Society of Professional Journalists Code of Ethics, September, 1996.

Stein, M. L. (1986, May 31). Survey on freebies. *Editor & Publisher,* 11.

Steinberg, J. (2003, June 6). *Times'* top editors resign after furor on writer's fraud. *The New York Times,* A1.

Wallace, M. (1996 December 18). The press needs a national monitor. *The Wall Street Journal,* A1.

Chapter 16: International Media

Associated Press. (1988, May 18). Ads for comrades: Soviets run U.S. commercials. *The Sacramento Bee,* E1.

Associated Press. (1991, August 27). Media chiefs fired; allegedly backed coup. *The Sacramento Bee,* A11.

Beatty, S. (2001, October 22). Obscure show helps CNN score scoops overseas. *The Wall Street Journal,* B1.

Chen, A. C., & Chaudhary, A. G. (1991). Asia and the Pacific. In *Global journalism: Survey of international communication,* 2nd ed. New York: Longman.

Conde, C. H. (2003, May 11). Filipino journalists find death threats are part of job. *The New York Times,* A10.

Cowell, A. (2003, July 31). Independent for 81 years, the BBC is facing a challenge. *The New York Times,* A3.

Damsell, K., & McFarland, J. (2000, August 1). The Hollinger selloff. *The Globe and Mail,* B1.

DeGiorgio, E. (2000, April). The African Internet revolution. *African Business,* 30.

Dennis, E., & Vanden Heuvel, J. (1990, October). Emerging voices: East European media in transition. *Gannett Center for Media Studies,* 2.

Fine, J. (2001, October 1). Arabian knight woos west. *Variety,* 34.

Fineman, M. (1993, August 3). Iraqis plugging in to youth TV. *Los Angeles Times,* H2.

Fuchs, D. (1999, October). The Americanization of the Spanish press. *The Quill,* 8. (2003, June 21). All that jazeera: Television in the Arab world. *The Economist,* 60.

Green, P. S. (2003, July 30). Prague is fighting to remain in the picture. *The New York Times,* W1.

Harden, B. (1990, March 11). "Maniacs" on TV wake up Poland. *Washington Post,* A20.

Hays, L., & Rutherford, A. (1991, January 1). Gorbachev bids to crack down on Soviet press. *The Wall Street Journal,* A8.

Head, S. W. (1985). *World broadcasting systems.* Belmont, Calif.: Wadsworth.

Heingartner, D. (2003, June 5). Roaming the globe, laptops alight on wireless hot spots. *The New York Times,* E4.

Helliker, K. (1993, September 27). Drop that remote! In Britain, watching TV can be a crime. *The Wall Street Journal,* A1.

Hindley, A. (1999, April 23). Breaking the taboos. *Middle East Economic Digest,* 6.

Hindley, A. (2000, February 11). Internet usage, the boom in access. *Middle East Economic Digest,* 27.

Jensen, E. (1993, March 26). ABC and BBC to pool their radio-TV news coverage. *The Wall Street Journal,* B1.

Josephs, R., & Josephs, J. (1994, April 1). Public relations the U.K. way. *Public Relations Journal.*

Kahn, J. (2003, January 5). Made in China, bought in China. *The New York Times,* 3-1.

Lippman, J. (1992, October 20). Tuning in the global village. *Los Angeles Times,* H2.

Lowndes, F. S. (1991). The world's media systems: An overview. In *Global journalism: Survey of international communication,* 2nd ed. New York: Longman.

Makovsky, D. (2001, May 14). A voice from the heavens. *U.S. News & World Report,* 26.

Marshall, T. (1990, July 31). East Germans dazzled by western press. *Los Angeles Times,* H8.

Martin, L. J. (1991). Africa. In *Global journalism: Survey of international communication,* 2nd ed. New York: Longman.

McDowall, A. (2001, April 20). Uncorking the bottlenecks. *Middle East Economic Digest,* 45.

Melymuka, K. (2001, July 2). Africa 1.0. *Computerworld,* 35.

Mista, N. (2003, September 15). India's film city is gobbling tribal land. *San Francisco Chronicle,* D1.

Ogan, C. (1991). Middle East and North Africa. In *Global journalism: Survey of international communication,* 2nd ed. New York: Longman.

Paraschos, M. (1991). Europe. In *Global journalism: Survey of International communication,* 2nd ed. New York: Longman.

Picard, R. G. (1991). Global communications controversies. In *Global journalism: Survey of international communication,* 2nd ed. New York: Longman.

Pollack, P. (1993, November 21). Japan's master maverick of the Internet. *The New York Times,* C3.

Porubcansky, M. (1989, January 4). Soviet paper finally prints capitalist ads. *The Sacramento Bee,* C4.

Revzin, P., & Nelson, M. (1989, October 3). European TV industry goes Hollywood. *The Wall Street Journal,* A18.

Rosenblum, M. (1989, December 1). TV takes the center stage in Romanian revolution. *The Sacramento Bee,* A11.

Salwen, M. B., Garrison, B., & Buckman, R. (1991). Latin America and the Caribbean. In *Global journalism: Survey of international communication,* 2nd ed. New York: Longman.

Scholastic, Inc. (2000, October 2). The Internet index. *New York Times Upfront,* 24.

Siebert, F., Peterson, T., & Schramm, W. (1963). *Four theories of the press.* Urbana: University of Illinois Press.

Smith, C. (2000, October 4). Tough new rules don't faze Chinese Internet start-ups. *The New York Times,* C2.

Strupp, J. (2000, March 13). More windows on the world. *Editor & Publisher,* 26.

Wallace, C. (1988, January 7). Radio: Town crier of the Arab world. *Los Angeles Times,* 1.

Weiner, T. (2001, November 20). Four foreign journalists, ambushed, are believed killed by Taliban. *The New York Times,* B1.

Williams, M. (1993, March 3). "Gaman" adds spice to Japanese life and to its TV fare. *The Wall Street Journal,* A1.

Witcher, S. K. (1990, December 11). Fairfax group to be placed in receivership. *The Wall Street Journal,* A4.

Index

Note: Page numbers followed by italicized letters *b, f, p, t,* indicate boxes, figures, photos, and tables, respectively.